The Official

Study Guide for all SAT Subject Tests™

The College Board
New York, NY

The College Board: Connecting Students to College Success

The College Board is a not-for-profit membership association whose mission is to connect students to college success and opportunity. Founded in 1900, the association is composed of more than 5,000 schools, colleges, universities, and other educational organizations. Each year, the College Board serves seven million students and their parents, 23,000 high schools, and 3,500 colleges through major programs and services in college admissions, guidance, assessment, financial aid, enrollment, and teaching and learning. Among its best-known programs are the SAT®, the PSAT/NMSQT®, and the Advanced Placement Program® (AP®). The College Board is committed to the principles of excellence and equity, and that commitment is embodied in all of its programs, services, activities, and concerns.

For further information, visit www.collegeboard.com.

Copies of this book are available from your bookseller or may be ordered from College Board Publications, P.O. Box 86900, Plano, TX 86901. 800 323-7155. The book may also be ordered online through the College Board Store at www.collegeboard.com. The price is $18.95.

Editorial inquiries concerning this book should be addressed to the College Board, SAT Program, 45 Columbus Avenue, New York, New York 10023-6992.

ISBN-13: 978-0-87447-756-6

ISBN-10: 0-87447-756-5

Library of Congress Card Catalog Number: 2006016433

Printed in the United States of America

10 9 8 7 6 5 4 3 2

Distributed by Holtzbrinck Publishers, Inc.

Writer
Elaine Israel

Contributing Writers
Elizabeth Daniel
Ed Hardin
Patty Klag
Mary Morley
Robin O'Callaghan
Judson Odell
Cynthia Woerner
Craig Wright

Project Manager
Kevin Iwano

Production Managers
John Ulicny
Barbara Locklear

Cover Design
Caitlin McClure

Interior Design
Meredith Haber, Design
Joanne Mullens, Composition

Special Thanks
Martha Bell
Michele Damiano
Jenny Fernandez
Senai Goita
Roberta Goodman
Karen Hoagland
Robin Hochman
Vanessa Marcel
Judith Morag
Kimberly Roddy
Nancy Rubino

The SAT Subject Tests™ Development Committees 2005–2006

BIOLOGY COMMITTEE

Louise A. Paquin, Chair
McDaniel College, Westminster, MD

William S. Bradshaw
Brigham Young University, Provo, UT

Nancy E. Ramos
Northside Health Careers High School, San Antonio, TX

Prue Talbot
University of California, Riverside, CA

John P. Zarnetske
Hoosick Falls Central School, Hoosick Falls, NY

CHEMISTRY COMMITTEE

Jo A. Beran, Chair
Texas A&M University, Kingsville, TX

Alexander Grushow
Rider University, Lawrenceville, NJ

George E. Miller
University of California, Irvine, CA

Melissa D Mischke,
Phillips Exeter Academy, Exeter, NH

Debra J. Reynolds
Northfield High School, Northfield, MN

CHINESE COMMITTEE

Tianwei Xie, Chair
California State University, Long Beach, CA

Baozhang He
College of the Holy Cross, Worcester, MA

Cornelius C. Kubler
Williams College, Williamstown, MA

Mindy Zhang
Indiana Academy, Muncie, IN

Yunian Zhang
West Potomac High School, Alexandria, VA

FRENCH COMMITTEE

Marie T. Noiset, Chair
University of North Carolina, Charlotte, NC

Genevieve J. Delfosse
Thomas Jefferson School for Science and Technology, Alexandria, VA

Ndinzi Masagara
Youngstown State University, Youngstown, OH

Robert F. Peloquin
Boston College High School, Dorchester, MA

Therese-Sophie Vitrant O'Connell
Jacksonville University, Jacksonville, FL

GERMAN COMMITTEE

Reinhard K. Zachau, Chair
University of the South, Sewanee, TN

Marita I. Cleaver
McKinney High School, McKinney, TX

Shadia Khalifa
Onondaga Central School, Nedrow, NY

John F. Lalande II
State University of New York at Oswego, Oswego, NY

Glenn S. Levine
University of California, Irvine, CA

ITALIAN COMMITTEE

Alessandro Vettori, Chair
Rutgers University, New Brunswick, NJ

Judith Musante Branzburg
Lowell High School, San Francisco, CA

Mariastella Cocchiara
Melrose Public Schools, Melrose, MA

Erasmo G. Gerato
Florida State University, Tallahassee, FL

Marisa S. Trubiano
Montclair State University, Montclair, NJ

JAPANESE COMMITTEE

Dan P. Dewey, Chair
University of Pittsburgh, Pittsburgh, PA

Virginia S. Marcus
Washington University, St. Louis, MO

Kazuo Tsuda
United Nations International School, New York, NY

Suwako Watanabe
Portland State University, Portland, OR

KOREAN COMMITTEE

Sungdai Cho, Chair
State University of New York, Binghamton, NY

Ah-Mi Cho
Lowell High School, San Francisco, CA

Hyo S. Lee
Indiana University, Bloomington, IN

Mee-Jeong Park
UCLA, Los Angeles, CA

Sang-suk Oh
Harvard University, Cambridge, MA

Bongsoon Yow
Flushing High School, Flushing, NY

LATIN COMMITTEE

Mary L. B. Pendergraft, Chair
Wake Forest University, Winston-Salem, NC

Margaret A. Brucia
Taft Educational Center, Watertown, CT

Jane W. Crawford
University of Virginia, Charlottesville, VA

Edward S. Ligon
The Roxbury Latin School, West Roxbury, MA

Sherwin D. Little
Indian Hill High School, Cincinnati, OH

LITERATURE COMMITTEE

Idris B. Anderson, Chair
Crystal Springs Uplands School, Hillsborough, CA

Cheng Lok Chua
California State University, Fresno, CA

Robin L. Inboden
Wittenberg University, Springfield, OH

Edward G. Schmieder
Garden City High School, Garden City, NY

Jerry W. Ward Jr.
Dillard University, New Orleans, LA

MATHEMATICS COMMITTEE

Roger Day, Chair
Illinois State University, Normal, IL

Ann Davidian
General Douglas MacArthur High School, Levittown, NY

Sam Gough
The Westminster Schools, Atlanta, GA

Phyllis P. Hillis
Oak Ridge High School, Oak Ridge, TN

Marie M. Vanisko
California State University, Turlock, CA

MODERN HEBREW

Vardit Ringvald, Chair
Brandeis University, Waltham, MA

Linda E. Alexander
Great Neck North High School, Great Neck, NY

Orit Marmel
Ida Crown Jewish Academy, Chicago, IL

Rachel Moskowitz
Hillel Community Day School, Miami, FL

Yaron Peleg
The George Washington University, Washington, DC

PHYSICS COMMITTEE

Robert Jacobsen, Chair
University of California, Berkeley, CA

Clyfe G. Beckwith
Phillips Academy, Andover, MA

John L. Kinard
Greenwood High School, Greenwood, SC

Daniel M. Smith Jr.
South Carolina State University, Orangeburg, SC

Mary R. Yeomans
Hopewell Valley Central High School, Pennington, NJ

SPANISH COMMITTEE

Carmen Silva-Corvalán, Chair
University of Southern California, Los Angeles, CA

Maria Asuncion Gomez,
Florida International University, Miami, FL

Lori Langer de Ramírez
Herricks Public Schools, New Hyde Park, NY

Lisa M. Martinez
Dublin Coffman High School, Dublin, OH

Edwin K. Padilla
University of Houston–Downtown, Houston, TX

UNITED STATES HISTORY COMMITTEE

Daniel C. Littlefield, Chair
University of South Carolina, Columbia, SC

Rosemary K. Ennis
Sycamore High School, Cincinnati, OH

Cassandra A. Osborne
Oak Ridge High School, Oak Ridge, TN

David Quigley
Boston College, Chestnut Hill, MA

Gary W. Reichard
California State University, Long Beach, CA

WORLD HISTORY COMMITTEE

David Northrup, Chair
Boston College, Chestnut Hill, MA

Alan V. Lebaron
Kennesaw State University, Kennesaw, GA

Ane J. Lintvedt
McDonogh School, Owings Mills, MD

Patricia Lopes Don
San Jose State University, San Jose, CA

Angela D. Sperotto
Bellaire High School, Bellaire, TX

Contents

The SAT Subject Tests™

Are you thinking about taking the SAT Subject Tests™? Then this book is just what you need. Here you will find guidance and information about studying for and taking the tests. You'll also find official practice tests that will help you prepare for test day.

The College Board created this book for you. We hope you will find it easy to use and helpful.

You're in Good Company

You are not alone in preparing for these tests. Every year, hundreds of thousands of college-bound students take SAT Subject Tests.

The SAT Subject Tests are part of the SAT® Program of the College Board, a not-for-profit membership association to which more than 5,000 schools, colleges, universities, and other educational associations belong. The mission of the College Board is to connect students to college success and opportunity. Every year, the College Board serves seven million students and their parents, 23,000 high schools, and 3,500 colleges through major programs and services in college admissions, guidance, assessment, financial aid, enrollment, and teaching and learning.

Who Develops the Tests?

Test development committees are appointed for the different Subject Tests. Committee members are typically teachers and college professors. The test questions are written and reviewed by each Subject Test Committee, outside experts, and external staff.

The SAT Subject Tests are not expected to change in major ways during the next few years, but minor revisions may be made in the content, types of questions, or testing schedule.

Stay Up to Date

Go online at www.collegeboard.com or pick up a copy of the *SAT Subject Tests Preparation Booklet*. This free booklet is available to every student who registers to take one or more Subject Tests. You can find copies in your high school guidance office or by calling the College Board SAT Program at 866-756-7346 within the United States or 212 713-7789 outside the United States.

Keep the Tests in Perspective

Colleges that require Subject Test scores do so because the scores are useful in making admissions or placement decisions. Even schools that don't require the tests often review them during the application process because the scores can give a fuller picture of your academic achievement. The Subject Tests are a particularly helpful tool for admissions and placement programs because the tests aren't tied to specific textbooks, grading procedures, or instruction methods. How and what students are taught and how they are graded vary from one location to another. The tests provide level ground on which colleges can compare your scores with those of students who come from schools and backgrounds that may be far different from yours.

REMEMBER

Colleges use the Subject Tests for admission, for course placement, and to advise students about course selection.

Your test scores are only one of the criteria that help colleges decide whether or not to admit you. Most college admissions officers pay more attention to high school grades than to test results. Your extracurricular activities and letters of recommendation are also taken into account.

Who Requires the SAT Subject Tests

College catalogs include information about admissions requirements, including which Subject Tests are needed or recommended. In addition, the College Board provides information about Subject Test requirements at specific colleges.

- Visit College Search at www.collegeboard.com.
- Purchase a copy of *The College Board College Handbook*.
- Visit the Web sites of the colleges and universities that interest you.

Contact college admissions officers at individual schools if you have questions or concerns about admissions policies. They are usually pleased to meet with students interested in their schools.

When to Take the Tests

Most students take the Subject Tests toward the end of their junior year or at the start of their senior year. If possible, take tests such as United States History, World History, Biology, Chemistry, and Physics right after your courses end, when the content is still fresh in your mind. For other subjects, such as languages, you would probably do better after you have studied the subject for several years.

This book suggests ways you can prepare for each Subject Test. Before taking a test in a subject you haven't studied recently, ask your teacher for advice about the best time to take the test. Then review the course material thoroughly and methodically over several weeks.

How to Register for the Tests

Here are ways to register for the SAT Reasoning Test™ and the SAT Subject Tests.

- Visit the College Board's Web site at www.collegeboard.com.
- Register by telephone (for a fee) if you have registered previously for an SAT Reasoning Test or an SAT Subject Test. Call toll free from anywhere in the U.S. 866-756-7346. From outside the U.S., dial 212-713-7789.
- Find registration forms in the *SAT Registration Booklet.* You can find the booklet in a guidance office at any high school or by writing to:

  College Board SAT Program

  P.O. Box 025505

  Miami, FL 33102

REMEMBER

You may take the test again if you don't do as well as you expected.

You will have to indicate the specific Subject Tests you plan to take on the test date you select. You may take one, two, or three tests on any given test date; your testing fee will vary accordingly. Except for the Language Tests with Listening, you may change your mind on the day of the test and instead select from any of the other Subject Tests offered that day.

You will be asked to fill out or update a Student Questionnaire when you register for the test. Although it is optional, the questionnaire can help you. Many of your responses are printed on your score report so you can compare your college plans and preferences to the characteristics of the colleges you sent scores to. Your answers will not influence your test score, and the information will be provided to colleges only with your permission.

The Listening Tests require special material, so they are only offered once a year, in November. You can only take one if you register for it by the regular deadline. Go to www.collegeboard.com or look in the current *Registration Booklet* for information.

A Handy Site

The College Board's Web site is a handy site to visit. On it, you can register for SAT tests, find information about other tests and services, try The Official SAT Question of the Day™, browse the College Board Store (where you can order *The College Board College Handbook, The Official SAT Subject Tests in Mathematics Levels 1 & 2 Study Guide*™, or *The Official SAT Subject Tests in U.S. and World History Study Guide*™), and send e-mails with your questions and concerns.

Once you create a free online account, you can print your SAT admission ticket, see your scores, and send them to schools.

Which colleges are right for you? Just go to *College Search* at www.collegeboard.com. It offers two ways to find out. The *College MatchMaker* finds colleges that meet all of your needs. If you are already familiar with a school, use the *College QuickFinder* for updates of essential information. Both methods help you to find the latest information on more than 3,600 colleges, as well as easy access to related tools.

How will you pay for college? While you're at the College Board Web site, look at the useful *Financial Aid EasyPlanner*, which can help you to work out your financial concerns. Among the questions it helps you consider: What does the school of your choice cost? How much can you save? How much can you and your family afford to pay? How much can your family afford to borrow for your education? What scholarships are available to you?

Tests You Can Take

SAT Subject Tests measure how well you know a particular subject area and your ability to apply that knowledge. SAT Subject Tests aren't connected to particular textbooks or teaching methods. The content of each test evolves to reflect the latest trends in teaching and in learning.

The tests fall into five general subject areas:

English	Languages	
Literature	Reading Only	Reading and Listening
History	French	Chinese
United States History	German	French
World History	Modern Hebrew	German
Mathematics	Italian	Japanese
Mathematics Level 1	Latin	Korean
Mathematics Level 2	Spanish	Spanish
Science		
Biology E/M		
Chemistry		
Physics		

The Language Tests with Listening include Chinese, French, German, Japanese, Korean, and Spanish. These tests have a listening section that takes about 20 minutes and a reading section that takes 40 minutes. Three languages, including Modern Hebrew, Italian, and Latin are offered as reading only tests. French, German, and Spanish are offered as reading only or reading and listening tests. The chart on page 14 lists specifics about all the Language Tests. The Language with Listening Tests are offered only in November at designated test centers.

Calculators are required for the Subject Tests in Mathematics. You cannot use a calculator for any other SAT Subject Test. The Subject Tests in Mathematics have been developed with the expectation that most students use graphing calculators.

The Biology E/M Test lets you choose questions with an ecological emphasis (Biology E) or a molecular emphasis (Biology M) in the same test. This means you can answer the questions in the area you feel best prepared. Biology E/M has 80 questions: 60 are for everyone who takes this test. The remaining 20 questions emphasize either ecology or molecular biology.

Which Tests Should You Take?

Before deciding which tests to take, make a list of all the colleges you're thinking about attending. Then review their catalogs to find out whether or not they require Subject Test scores for admission and, if so, how many and which ones.

REMEMBER

If you are strong in a particular subject, you may want to add that Subject Test score to your college portfolio.

Use your list of colleges and their admissions requirements to help plan your testing schedule. You may want to adjust your schedule to meet colleges' requirements. For example, a college to which you plan to apply may require a language Subject Test score for admission, or the college might exempt you from a freshman course requirement if you do well on a particular Subject Test.

And don't forget, you can enhance your college portfolio by taking Subject Tests in subject areas that you know very well.

Get Ready

Give yourself plenty of time to review the material in this book before test day. The rules are different for the SAT Subject Tests than for the tests you've taken in high school. You're probably used to answering questions in order, spending more time answering the hard questions, and, in the hopes of getting at least partial credit, showing all your work.

Here's the score. When you take the SAT Subject Tests, it's OK to move around within the test section and to answer questions in any order. Keep in mind that the questions go from easier to harder. You receive one point for each question answered correctly. For each question that you try, but answer incorrectly, one-quarter of a point is subtracted from the total number of correct answers. No points are added or subtracted for unanswered questions. If your final raw score includes a fraction, the score is rounded to the nearest whole number.

Avoid Surprises

Know what to expect. Become familiar with the test and test-day procedures. You'll boost your confidence and feel a lot more relaxed.

- **Know how the tests are set up.** All SAT Subject Tests are one-hour multiple-choice tests.

  The first page of each Subject Test includes a background questionnaire. You will be asked to fill it out before taking the test. The information is for statistical purposes only. It will not influence your test score. Your answers to the questionnaire will assist us in developing future versions of the test.
- **Learn the test directions.** The directions for answering the questions in this book are the same as those on the actual test. If you become familiar with the directions now, you'll leave yourself more time to answer the questions when you take the test.
- **Study the sample questions.** The more familiar you are with question formats, the more comfortable you'll feel when you see similar questions on the actual test.
- **Get to know the answer sheet.** At the back of this book, you'll find a set of sample answer sheets. The appearance of the answer sheet in this book may differ from the answer sheet you see on test day.
- **Understand how the tests are scored.** You get one point for each right answer and lose one-quarter of a point for each wrong answer. You neither gain nor lose points for omitting an answer. Hard questions count the same amount as easier questions.

A Practice Test Can Help

Find out where your strengths lie and which areas you need to work on. Do a run-through of a Subject Test under conditions that are close to what they will be on test day.

- **Set aside an hour so you can take the test without interruption.** Make sure you can complete the test in one sitting.

- **Prepare a desk or table that has no books or papers on it.** No books, including dictionaries, are allowed in the test room.
- **Read the instructions that precede the practice test.** On test day, you will be asked to do this before you answer the questions.
- **Remove and fill in an answer sheet from the back of this book.** You can use one answer sheet for up to three Subject Tests.
- **For the mathematics tests,** use the calculator that you plan to use on test day.
- **For the language with listening tests,** familiarize yourself with the CD player you will use on test day.
- **Use a clock or kitchen timer to time yourself.** This will help you to pace yourself and to get used to taking a test in 60 minutes.

How to Keep Your Nerves in Check

It's natural to be nervous. A bit of a nervous edge can keep you sharp and focused. Too much nervousness, though, can keep you from concentrating and working effectively.

Do a brief review on the day before the test. Look through the sample questions, explanations, and test directions in this book, on the College Board Web site, or in the *SAT Subject Test Preparation Booklet*. Keep the review brief; cramming the night before the tests is unlikely to help your performance and might even make you more anxious.

The night before test day, prepare everything you need to take with you. You will need:

- your admission ticket
- an acceptable photo ID (see page 9)
- Two No. 2 pencils with soft erasers. Do not bring pens or mechanical pencils.
- a watch without an audible alarm
- an acceptable calculator with fresh batteries (if you are taking the Mathematics Tests)
- a snack
- a portable CD player with fresh batteries (if you are taking a Language with Listening Test)

Know the route to the test center and any instructions for finding the entrance.

Check the time your admission ticket specifies for arrival. Arrive a little early to give yourself time to settle in.

Get a good night's sleep.

Acceptable Photo IDs

____ driver's license (with your photo)

____ state-issued ID

____ valid passport

____ school ID card

____ student ID form that has been prepared by your school on school stationery and includes your photo and the school seal (Go to www.collegeboard.com to see an example)

REMINDER **What I Need on Test Day**

Make a copy of this box and post it somewhere noticeable.

I Need	I Have
appropriate photo ID	____
admission ticket	____
Two No. 2 pencils with clean soft erasers	____
calculator with fresh batteries (for the mathematics tests only)	____
CD player with fresh batteries (for the listening tests only)	____
watch (without an audible alarm)	____
snack	____
directions to the test center	____
instructions for finding the entrance on weekends	____

I am leaving the house at ________ a.m.

****Be on time or you can't take the test.****

On Test Day

You have good reason to feel confident. You're thoroughly prepared. You're familiar with what this day will bring. You are in control.

Keep in Mind

You must be on time or you can't take the test. Leave yourself plenty of time for mishaps and emergencies.

Think positively. If you are worrying about not doing well, then your mind isn't on the test. Be as positive as possible.

Stay focused. Think only about the question in front of you. Letting your mind wander will cost you time.

Concentrate on your own test. The first thing some students do when they get stuck on a question is to look around to see how everyone else is doing. What they usually see is that others seem busy filling in their answer sheets. Instead of being concerned that you are not doing as well as everyone else, keep in mind that everyone works at a different pace. Your neighbors may not be working on the question that puzzled you. They may not even be taking the same test. Thinking about what others are doing distracts you from working on your own test.

REMEMBER

All questions are worth one point.

Making an Educated Guess

Educated guesses are helpful when it comes to taking tests with multiple-choice questions; however, random guesses are not a good idea. To correct for random guessing, one-quarter of a point is subtracted for each incorrect answer. That means random guessing—guessing with no idea of an answer that might be correct—could lower your score. The best approach is to eliminate all the choices that you know are wrong. Make an educated guess from the remaining choices. If you can't eliminate any choice, move on.

Cell phones are not allowed to be used in the test center or testing room.

10 Tips FOR TAKING THE TEST

1. **Read carefully.** Consider all the choices in each question. Avoid careless mistakes that will lose you points.
2. **Answer the easier questions first.** Work on less time-consuming questions before moving on to the more difficult ones.
3. **Eliminate choices that you know are wrong.** Cross them out in your test book so that you can clearly see which choices are left.
4. **Make educated guesses or skip the question.** If you have eliminated the choices that you know are wrong, guessing is your best strategy. If you cannot eliminate any of the answer choices, it is better to skip the question.
5. **Keep your answer sheet neat.** The answer sheet is scored by a machine, which can't tell the difference between an answer and a doodle. If the machine reads what look like two answers for one question, it will consider the question unanswered.
6. **Use your test booklet as scrap paper.** Use it to make notes or write down ideas. No one else will look at what you write.
7. **Check off questions as you work on them.** This will save time when you go back to questions you've skipped.
8. **Check your answer sheet regularly.** Make sure you are in the right place. Check the number of the question and the number on the answer sheet every few questions. This is especially important when you skip a question. Losing your place on the answer sheet will cost you time and even points.
9. **Work at an even, steady pace and keep moving.** Each question on the test takes a certain amount of time to read and answer. Good test-takers develop a sense of timing to help them complete the test. Your goal is to spend time on the questions that you are most likely to answer correctly.
10. **Keep track of time.** During the hour that each Subject Test takes, check your progress occasionally so that you know what point you are at and how much time is left. Leave a few minutes for review toward the end of the testing period.

REMEMBER

You are in control.

Come prepared.

Pace yourself.

Guess wisely.

If you erase all your answers to a Subject Test, that's the same as a request to cancel the test. All Subject Tests taken with the erased test will also be canceled.

More About Pacing

No matter how much time a test takes, the experience will be enhanced and give you an even stronger chance at success if you pace yourself.

7 Ways TO PACE YOURSELF

1. Set up a schedule. Know when you should be one-quarter of the way through and halfway through. Every now and then, check your progress against your schedule.
2. Begin to work as soon as the testing time begins. Reading the instructions and getting to know the test directions in this book ahead of time will allow you to do that.
3. Work at an even, steady pace. After you answer the questions you are sure of, move on to those for which you'll need more time.
4. Skip questions you can't answer. You might have time to return to them. Remember to mark them in your test booklet, so you'll be able to find them later.
5. As you work on a question, cross out the answers you can eliminate.
6. Go back to the questions you skipped. Guess, if you can, to eliminate some of the answer choices.
7. Leave time in the last few minutes to check your answers to avoid mistakes.

REMEMBER

Check your answer sheet. Make sure your answers are dark and completely filled in. Erase completely.

After the Tests

Most, but not all, scores will be reported online several weeks after the test date. A few days later, a full score report will be available to you online. Your score report will also be mailed to you and your high school, and to the colleges, universities, and scholarship programs that you indicated on your registration form or on the correction form attached to your admission ticket. The score report includes your scores, percentiles, and interpretive information.

What's Your Score?

Scores are available for free at www.collegeboard.com several weeks after each SAT is given. You can also get your scores—for a fee—by telephone. Call Customer Service at 866-756-7346 in the U.S. From outside the U.S., dial 212-713-7789.

Some scores may take longer to report. If your score report is not available online when expected, check back the following week. If you have not received your mailed score report by eight weeks after the test date (by five weeks for online reports), contact Customer Service by phone at 866-756-7346 or by e-mail at sat@info.collegeboard.org.

Should You Take the Tests Again?

Before you decide whether or not to retest, you need to evaluate your scores. The best way to evaluate how you really did on a Subject Test is to compare your scores to the admissions or placement requirements, or average scores, of the colleges to which you are applying. You may decide that with additional work you could do better taking the test again.

Contacting the College Board

If you have comments or questions about the tests, please write to us at The College Board SAT Program, P.O. Box 025505, Miami, FL 33102; or e-mail us at SAT@info.collegeboard.org.

SAT Subject Tests Schedule

Subject	Date					
	October	November	December	January	May	June
Literature	*	*	*	*	*	*
United States History	*	*	*	*	*	*
World History			*			*
Mathematics Level 1	*	*	*	*	*	*
Mathematics Level 2	*	*	*	*	*	*
Biology E/M	*	*	*	*	*	*
Chemistry	*	*	*	*	*	*
Physics	*	*	*	*	*	*
Languages: Reading Only						
French	*		*	*	*	*
German						*
Modern Hebrew						*
Italian			*			
Latin			*			*
Spanish	*		*	*	*	*
Languages: Reading and Listening						
Chinese		*				
French		*				
German		*				
Japanese		*				
Korean		*				
Spanish		*				

NOTES

1. You can take up to three SAT Subject Tests on a single test day.
2. You must indicate which test or tests you plan to take when you register. But, except for the Language Tests with Listening, you can change which tests you actually take.
3. You may only use a calculator for Mathematics Level 1 and Mathematics Level 2 Subject Tests. You can take these tests without a calculator, but that will put you at a disadvantage.
4. You must bring an acceptable CD player if you are taking a Language with Listening test.

Chapter 1

Literature

Purpose

The Subject Test in Literature measures how well you have learned to read literary works from different periods and cultures. There is no prescribed or suggested reading list.

Format

This one-hour test consists of approximately 60 multiple-choice questions based on six to eight reading selections. About half of the selections are poetry and half are prose. Selections include complete short poems or excerpts from various works, including longer poems, stories, novels, nonfiction writing, and drama.

You are not expected to have read or studied the particular poems or passages that appear on the test. Extensive knowledge of literary terminology is not essential, but the test does assume a good working knowledge of basic terminology.

All questions are based on selections from original works written in English from the Renaissance to the present. The date printed at the end of each passage or poem is the original publication date, or in some cases, the estimated date of composition. The set of 4 to 12 questions per selection usually covers these aspects of a text:

- meaning—overall effect and argument or theme
- form—structure and genre (how one part develops from or differs from another)
- narrative voice—the characterization of the speaker, the possible distinction between the speaker and the author, the speaker's attitude and tone
- characters represented—distinguishing traits and the techniques by which the character is presented and the traits revealed
- characteristic use of language—imagery, figures of speech, and diction
- contextual meaning—specific words, phrases, and lines within a passage or poem

Content

All of the questions are five-choice completion questions, which fall into three categories:

- Regular multiple-choice questions ask you to choose the best response
- NOT or EXCEPT questions ask you to select the inappropriate choice from among five choices
- Roman numeral questions ask you which statement or combination of statements may be the best response

Source of Questions	Approximate Percentage of Test*
English Literature	40–50
American Literature	40–50
Other Literature Written in English	0–10
Chronology	
Renaissance and 17th Century	30
18th and 19th Centuries	30
20th Century	40
Genre	
Poetry	40–50
Prose	40–50
Drama	0–10

* The distribution of passages may vary in different editions of the test. The chart above indicates typical or average content.

The Subject Test in Literature included in this book contains 61 questions based on seven selections—"A Divine Mistress" by Thomas Carew, an excerpt from *Middlemarch* by George Eliot, an excerpt from *Our Country's Good* by Timberlake Wertenbaker, an excerpt from the *Autobiography of Benjamin Franklin*, an excerpt from *Invisible Man* by Ralph Ellison, "Of English Verse" by Edmund Waller, and "Daybreak" by Gary Soto. As frequently happens when tests are composed of lengthy sets of questions based on relatively few selections, the distribution of passages in a particular test differs somewhat from the typical or average content summarized in the chart. The test in this book, for example, contains one more selection from English Literature than from American Literature.

How to Prepare

- Read widely and carefully. The best preparation is close, critical reading of literary texts in English from a variety of historical periods and genres.
- There is no suggested reading list.
- Have a working knowledge of basic literary terminology, such as speaker, tone, image, irony, alliteration, stanza, and so on.

- Familiarize yourself with the test directions in advance. The directions given in this book are identical to those that appear on the test.

Score

The total score is reported on the 200-to-800 scale.

Sample Questions

The James Merrill poem below and many of the questions that follow it are fairly easy; however, some of the other passages and questions used in the Subject Test in Literature are likely to be more difficult.

James Merrill was a twentieth-century American poet; therefore, according to the content chart on page 16, all of the questions on this poem would be classified as American Literature, Twentieth Century, Poetry.

The directions used in the test book precede the poem.

Directions: This test consists of selections from literary works and questions on their content, form, and style. After reading each passage or poem, choose the best answer to each question and fill in the corresponding circle on the answer sheet.

Note: Pay particular attention to the requirement of questions that contain the words NOT, LEAST, or EXCEPT.

Questions 1–6. Read the following poem carefully before you choose your answers.

Kite Poem

"One is reminded of a certain person,"
Continued the parson, settling back in his chair
With a glass of port, "who sought to emulate
The sport of birds (it was something of a chore)
By climbing up on a kite. They found his coat
Two counties away; the man himself was missing."

His daughters tittered: it was meant to be a lesson
To them—they had been caught kissing, or some such nonsense,
The night before, under the crescent moon.
So, finishing his pheasant, their father began
This thirty-minute discourse ending with
A story improbable from the start. He paused for breath,

Having shown but a few of the dangers. However, the wind
Blew out the candles and the moon wrought changes
Which the daughters felt along their stockings. Then,
Thus persuaded, they fled to their young men
Waiting in the sweet night by the raspberry bed,
And kissed and kissed, as though to escape on a kite.

1. The attitude of the parson (line 2) toward the "certain person" (lines 1–6) is one of
   (A) admiration
   (B) anxiety
   (C) disdain
   (D) curiosity
   (E) grief

Choice (C) is the correct answer to question 1. In order to warn his daughters of the danger of imprudent behavior, the parson uses the tale of the person who climbed up on a kite. It is unlikely, given this purpose, that he would feel either "admiration," "anxiety," "curiosity," or "grief" for the man, and nothing in the poem suggests that the parson had any of these feelings. His attitude is one of disdain for a person whose behavior he regards as foolish.

2. The descriptive detail "settling back in his chair/With a glass of port" (lines 2–3) underscores the parson's
   (A) authority
   (B) complacency
   (C) hypocrisy
   (D) gentleness
   (E) indecisiveness

Choice (B) is the correct answer to question 2. The poem suggests that the parson is a rather rigid, formal man focused on his own comforts and ignorant of his daughters' needs. It can be inferred from the context that complacency—unaware self-satisfaction—is one element of his character. There is no evidence in the poem that the parson is either hypocritical, gentle, or indecisive. Out of context, the quotation from the poem might be interpreted as behavior associated with someone in a position of authority. In context, however, the parson is more notable for his lack of authority—his daughters titter when he lectures and ignore his advice.

3. The chief reason the parson's daughters "tittered" (line 7) is that they
   (A) were embarrassed to have been caught kissing
   (B) knew where the missing man in their father's story was
   (C) wanted to flatter their father
   (D) did not take their father's lecture seriously
   (E) took cruel pleasure in the kite flyer's disaster

Choice (D) is the correct answer to question 3. It is the most plausible explanation of why the daughters "tittered"—they did not take their father's lecture seriously. This view is supported by the daughters' actions—as soon as their father paused for breath, they did what his "thirty-minute discourse" warned them not to do. There is no indication in the poem that choices (B) or (E) are true, and if the daughters had wanted to flatter their father, as choice (C) claims, they certainly would not have tittered during his serious lecture. If choice (A) were true, it is unlikely that the daughters would have "fled to their young men" so quickly the second time.

4. The speaker's tone suggests that the reader should regard the parson's "thirty-minute discourse" (line 11) as
   (A) scholarly and enlightening
   (B) serious and important
   (C) entertaining and amusing
   (D) verbose and pedantic
   (E) grisly and morbid

Choice (D) is the correct answer to question 4. The speaker's tone suggests that the reader should regard the parson's "thirty-minute discourse" as "verbose and pedantic." The parson is presented as one who speaks at length, telling "improbable" stories and taking 30 minutes to show "but a few of the dangers" he wanted to warn his daughters about. He uses lengthy phrases such as "emulate/The sport of birds" when a simple verb such as "fly" would have sufficed. The parson might well have intended his discourse to seem "scholarly and enlightening," choice (A), and "serious and important," choice (B), but neither the daughters nor the speaker suggests that the parson succeeded, and the reader has no reason to assess the effectiveness of the discourse differently from the speaker and the daughters. The reader may be entertained and amused by the speaker's account of the discourse, but that response is not the same as being amused by the discourse itself, as choice (C) states. Choice (E) is implausible.

5. The daughters are "persuaded" (line 16) by
   (A) their own fear of danger
   (B) the fate of the kite flyer
   (C) their own natural impulses
   (D) the parson's authority
   (E) respect for their father

Choice (C) is the correct answer to question 5. The daughters are "persuaded" by their own natural impulses. According to the poem, "the moon wrought changes/Which the daughters felt along their stockings" (lines 14–15). These natural impulses were, ironically, more persuasive than the long discourse delivered by their father in an attempt to dissuade them. The daughters, like the kite flyer, are attracted to the possibility of "escape on a kite" (line 18) and are not deterred by solemn and tedious warnings of danger.

6. All of the following are elements of opposition in the development of the poem EXCEPT
   (A) indoors . . outdoors
   (B) talking . . kissing
   (C) caution . . adventure
   (D) work . . play
   (E) settling back . . flying

Choice (D) is the correct answer to question 6. It is the only opposition that is not evident in the poem. Actions such as "climbing up on a kite" and "kissing…under the crescent moon" might be regarded as forms of play, but the poem really does not offer any contrasting examples of work. Choices (A), (B), (C), and (E) illustrate the contrasting actions and attitudes of the parson on the one hand and the daughters or the kite flyer, or both, on the other.

Literature Test

Practice Helps

The test that follows is an actual, recently administered SAT Subject Test in Literature. To get an idea of what it's like to take this test, practice under conditions that are much like those of an actual test administration.

- Set aside an hour when you can take the test uninterrupted. Make sure you complete the test in one sitting.
- Sit at a desk or table with no other books or papers. Dictionaries, other books, or notes are not allowed in the test room.
- Tear out an answer sheet from the back of this book and fill it in just as you would on the day of the test. One answer sheet can be used for up to three Subject Tests.
- Read the instructions that precede the practice test. During the actual administration, you will be asked to read them before answering test questions.
- Time yourself by placing a clock or kitchen timer in front of you.
- After you finish the practice test, read the sections "How to Score the SAT Subject Test in Literature" and "How Did You Do on the Subject Test in Literature?"
- The appearance of the answer sheet in this book may differ from the answer sheet you see on test day.

LITERATURE TEST

The top portion of the section of the answer sheet that you will use in taking the Literature Test must be filled in exactly as shown in the illustration below. Note carefully that you have to do all of the following on your answer sheet.

1. Print LITERATURE on the line under the words "Subject Test (print)."

2. In the shaded box labeled "Test Code" fill in four circles:

   —Fill in circle 3 in the row labeled V.
   —Fill in circle 1 in the row labeled W.
   —Fill in circle 1 in the row labeled X.
   —Fill in circle D in the row labeled Y.

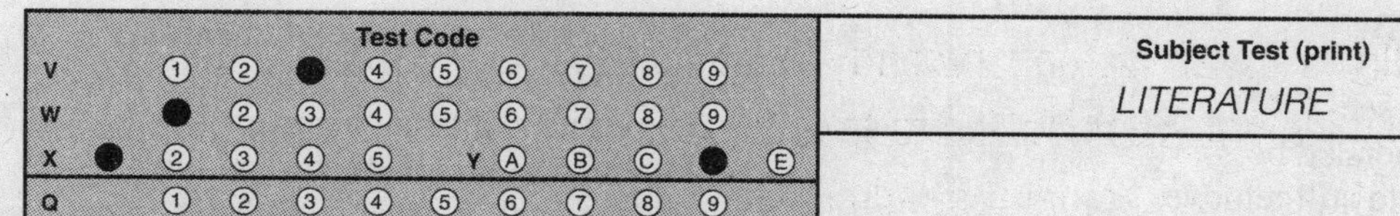

3. Please answer the two questions below by filling in the appropriate circles in the row labeled Q on the answer sheet. The information you provide is for statistical purposes only and will not affect your score on the test.

Answer both questions on the basis of the authors and works read in your English classes in grade 10 to the present.

Question I

How many semesters of English courses that were predominantly devoted to the study of literature have you taken from grade 10 to the present? (If you are studying literature in the current semester, count the current semester as a full semester.) Fill in only one circle of circles 1-3.

- One semester or less —Fill in circle 1.
- Two semesters —Fill in circle 2.
- Three semesters or more —Fill in circle 3.

Question II

Of the following, which content areas made up a significant part (at least 10 percent) of the literature you read in your English classes in grades 10-12 ? Fill in as many circles as apply.

- British and/or North American writers writing before 1800 —Fill in circle 4.
- European writers in translation —Fill in circle 5.
- African American and Black writers —Fill in circle 6.
- Ethnic American writers (Hispanic American, Asian American, American Indian, etc.) —Fill in circle 7.
- Latin American writers in translation —Fill in circle 8.
- Writers from Africa or India writing in English —Fill in circle 9.

When the supervisor gives the signal, turn the page and begin the Literature Test. There are 100 numbered circles on the answer sheet and 61 questions in the Literature Test. Therefore, use only circles 1 to 61 for recording your answers.

LITERATURE TEST

Directions: This test consists of selections from literary works and questions on their content, form, and style. After reading each passage or poem, choose the best answer to each question and fill in the corresponding circle on the answer sheet.

Note: Pay particular attention to the requirement of questions that contain the words NOT, LEAST, or EXCEPT.

Questions 1-7. Read the following poem carefully before you choose your answers.

A Divine Mistress

In Nature's pieces still I see
Some error that might mended be;
Something my wish could still remove,
Alter or add; but my fair love
Was framed by hands far more divine,
For she hath every beauteous line.
Yet I had been far happier
Had Nature, that made me, made her.
Then likeness might (that love creates)
Have made her love what now she hates;
Yet, I confess, I cannot spare
From her just shape the smallest hair;
Nor need I beg from all the store
Of heaven for her one beauty more.
She hath too much divinity for me:
You gods, teach her some more humanity.

(c. 1640)

1. Which of the following best restates the meaning of lines 1 and 2 ?

(A) The natural world contains imperfections.
(B) The natural world has only the meaning that poets give it.
(C) The natural world has been systematically destroyed by humans.
(D) The natural world was an accident of divinity.
(E) The poetic imagination can create or destroy the natural world.

2. The word "framed" in line 5 is particularly appropriate in this context because it suggests the woman's

(A) deceitfulness and evil intentions
(B) imagination and fertility
(C) virtue and benevolence
(D) fickleness and ethereal nature
(E) physical shape and aesthetic completeness

3. Which of the following could be substituted for "had been" (line 7) without changing the meaning?

(A) was
(B) will be
(C) have been
(D) would have been
(E) ought to be

4. All of the following contrasts appear in the first ten lines of the poem EXCEPT

(A) nature and divinity
(B) error and perfection
(C) similarity and difference
(D) love and hate
(E) innocence and experience

3XAC2

GO ON TO THE NEXT PAGE

5. Which of the following best states the wish of the speaker in lines 7-14 ?

(A) He wants the woman to be even more beautiful than she is.
(B) He wants the woman to ignore other men.
(C) He wants the woman to be both beautiful and accessible.
(D) He does not want the woman to love him in the same way he loves her.
(E) He does not want the woman to be so vain.

6. The speaker's tone in lines 15-16 is best described as

(A) bitter sarcasm
(B) amused indifference
(C) dignified solemnity
(D) playful exasperation
(E) cold rationality

7. The unannounced intention of the speaker in this poem is to

(A) commend a woman for her impeccable virtue
(B) praise a woman for her unequaled beauty
(C) make a woman more receptive to his passion
(D) delude a woman into thinking that he loves her
(E) flatter a woman so that she will have a better opinion of herself

GO ON TO THE NEXT PAGE

Questions 8-17. Read the following passage carefully before you choose your answers.

He had not had much foretaste of happiness in his previous life. To know intense joy without a strong bodily frame, one must have an enthusiastic soul. Mr. Casaubon had never had a strong bodily frame, and his soul was sensitive without being enthusiastic: it was too languid to thrill out of self-consciousness into passionate delight; it went on fluttering in the swampy ground where it was hatched, thinking of its wings and never flying. His experience was of that pitiable kind which shrinks from pity, and fears most of all that it should be known: it was that proud narrow sensitiveness which has not mass enough to spare for transformation into sympathy, and quivers thread-like in small currents of self-preoccupation or at best of an egoistic scrupulosity. And Mr. Casaubon had many scruples: he was capable of a severe self-restraint; he was resolute in being a man of honour according to the code; he would be unimpeachable by any recognised opinion. In conduct these ends had been attained; but the difficulty of making his *Key to all Mythologies* unimpeachable weighed like lead upon his mind; and the pamphlets—or "Parerga"[1] as he called them—by which he tested his public and deposited small monumental records of his march, were far from having been seen in all their significance. He suspected the Archdeacon of not having read them; he was in painful doubt as to what was really thought of them by the leading minds of Brasenose,[2] and bitterly convinced that his old acquaintance Carp had been the writer of that depreciatory recension which was kept locked in a small drawer of Mr. Casaubon's desk, and also in a dark closet of his verbal memory. These were heavy impressions to struggle against, and brought that melancholy embitterment which is the consequence of all excessive claim: even his religious faith wavered with his wavering trust in his own authorship, and the consolations of the Christian hope in immortality seemed to lean on the immortality of the still unwritten *Key to all Mythologies*.

(1871)

[1] Greek term for supplementary or secondary works
[2] a college at Oxford

8. The passage is best described as an example of

(A) character analysis
(B) historical commentary
(C) allegorical drama
(D) interior monologue
(E) political satire

9. By the end of the passage, Casaubon emerges as

(A) crude and inconsiderate
(B) insecure and self-centered
(C) temperamental and rebellious
(D) sensitive but self-confident
(E) ambitious but generous

10. In the context of the passage, the image of the fluttering bird "thinking of its wings and never flying" (lines 8-9) is most suggestive of

(A) Casaubon's lifelong aversion to physical activities
(B) Casaubon's control over his imagination and emotions
(C) the limiting effect of Casaubon's self-consciousness
(D) the nobility of Casaubon's physical and mental striving
(E) the liberating influence of Casaubon's scholarly intellect

11. Casaubon's struggle to make "his *Key to all Mythologies* unimpeachable" (lines 20-21) can be best viewed as an example of his

(A) dedication to an outdated code of honor
(B) enthusiasm only for intellectual pursuits
(C) unrealistic expectations of achievement
(D) rivalry with the Archdeacon
(E) tendency toward procrastination

GO ON TO THE NEXT PAGE

12. The phrase "tested his public" (line 23) means that Casaubon

    (A) tried the patience of those who were eagerly waiting for his *Key to all Mythologies*
    (B) evaluated his popularity with the general reading public
    (C) examined the public on its knowledge of mythological literature
    (D) attempted to confirm publicly the validity of his scholarly project
    (E) compared the public's reaction to his pamphlets with that of the scholarly community

13. The statement "These were . . . excessive claim" (lines 33-36) can be best interpreted as

    (A) a paraphrase of the negative responses to Casaubon's work
    (B) a generalization about human nature applicable to Casaubon's personality
    (C) an allusion to Casaubon's earlier years of unhappiness
    (D) a denunciation of harsh critics like Carp
    (E) a plea for sympathy for Casaubon

14. The repeated reference to smallness—"shrinks" (line 10), "has not mass enough" (line 12), "small currents" (line 14), "small monumental records" (line 24), and "small drawer" (lines 31-32)—has the cumulative effect of reinforcing the theme of Casaubon's

    (A) aptitude for analyzing only the small details in his life
    (B) intellectual and emotional limitations
    (C) modesty and lack of idealism
    (D) heroic struggle against the weight of public opinion
    (E) inability to live up to his reputation as an eminent scholar

15. In context, the comment "the consolations of the Christian hope in immortality seemed to lean on the immortality of the still unwritten *Key to all Mythologies*" (lines 37-40) suggests the narrator's belief that

    (A) Casaubon's scholarly work would be a contribution to the Christian community
    (B) Casaubon hoped that his work, when completed, would be as widely read as the Bible
    (C) Casaubon relied desperately on his religious faith to help him complete his manuscript
    (D) the importance Casaubon ascribed to his work was greatly inflated
    (E) the suffering and humiliation endured by Casaubon would make his work immortal

16. Which of the following references is NOT metaphorical but actually describes a physical act performed by Casaubon?

    (A) "fluttering in the swampy ground" (lines 7-8)
    (B) "quivers thread-like in small currents" (lines 13-14)
    (C) "weighed like lead" (line 21)
    (D) "deposited small monumental records of his march" (line 24)
    (E) "locked in a small drawer" (lines 31-32)

17. The narrator's attitude toward Casaubon is primarily one of

    (A) ambivalence
    (B) puzzlement
    (C) revulsion
    (D) bitter disparagement
    (E) incisive criticism

GO ON TO THE NEXT PAGE

Questions 18-27. Read the following dramatic excerpt carefully before you choose your answers.

In this scene, the somewhat inebriated officers of an eighteenth-century Australian penal colony debate the merits of Second Lieutenant Ralph Clark's proposal to stage a play—George Farquhar's "The Recruiting Officer"—using the convicts as actors.

REVEREND JOHNSON: What is the plot, Ralph?

RALPH: It's about this recruiting officer and his friend, and they are in love with these two young ladies from Shrewsbury and after some difficulties, they marry them.

REV. JOHNSON: It sanctions Holy Matrimony then?

RALPH: Yes, yes, it does.

REV. JOHNSON: That wouldn't do the convicts any harm. I'm having such trouble getting them to marry instead of this sordid cohabitation they're so used to.

ROSS: Marriage, plays, why not a ball for the convicts!

CAMPBELL: Euuh. Boxing.

ARTHUR PHILLIP: Some of these men will have finished their sentence in a few years. They will become members of society again, and help create a new society in this colony. Should we not encourage them now to think in a free and responsible manner?

TENCH: I don't see how a comedy about two lovers will do that, Arthur.

ARTHUR PHILLIP: The theatre is an expression of civilisation. We belong to a great country which has spawned great playwrights: Shakespeare, Marlowe, Jonson, and even in our own time, Sheridan. The convicts will be speaking a refined, literate language and expressing sentiments of a delicacy they are not used to. It will remind them that there is more to life than crime, punishment. And we, this colony of a few hundred will be watching this together, for a few hours we will no longer be despised prisoners and hated gaolers. We will laugh, we may be moved, we may even think a little. Can you suggest something else that will provide such an evening, Watkin?

DAWES: Mapping the stars gives me more enjoyment, personally.

TENCH: I'm not sure it's a good idea having the convicts laugh at officers, Arthur.

CAMPBELL: No. Pheeoh, insubordination, heh, ehh, no discipline.

ROSS: You want this vice-ridden vermin to enjoy themselves?

COLLINS: They would only laugh at Sergeant Kite.

RALPH: Captain Plume is a most attractive, noble fellow.

REV. JOHNSON: He's not loose, is he Ralph? I hear many of these plays are about rakes and encourage loose morals in women. They do get married? Before, that is, before. And for the right reasons.

RALPH: They marry for love and to secure wealth.

REV. JOHNSON: That's all right.

TENCH: I would simply say that if you want to build a civilisation there are more important things than a play. If you want to teach the convicts something, teach them to farm, to build houses, teach them a sense of respect for property, teach them thrift so they don't eat a week's rations in one night, but above all, teach them how to work, not how to sit around laughing at a comedy.

ARTHUR PHILLIP: The Greeks believed that it was a citizen's duty to watch a play. It was a kind of work in that it required attention, judgement, patience, all social virtues.

TENCH: And the Greeks were conquered by the more practical Romans, Arthur.

COLLINS: Indeed, the Romans built their bridges, but they also spent many centuries wishing they were Greeks. And they, after all, were conquered by barbarians, or by their own corrupt and small spirits.

TENCH: Are you saying Rome would not have fallen if the theatre had been better?

GO ON TO THE NEXT PAGE

RALPH (*very loud*): Why not? (*Everyone looks at him and he continues, fast and nervously.*) In my own small way, in just a few hours, I have seen something change. I asked some of the convict women to read me some lines, these women who behave often no better than animals. And it seemed to me, as one or two—I'm not saying all of them, not at all—but one or two, saying those well-balanced lines of Mr. Farquhar, they seemed to acquire a dignity, they seemed—they seemed to lose some of their corruption. There was one, Mary Brenham, she read so well, perhaps this play will keep her from selling herself to the first marine who offers her bread—

FADDY (*under his breath*): She'll sell herself to him, instead.

ROSS: So that's the way the wind blows—

CAMPBELL: Hooh. A tempest. Hooh.

RALPH: (*over them*): I speak about her, but in a small way this could affect all the convicts and even ourselves, we could forget our worries about the supplies, the hangings and the floggings, and think of ourselves at the theatre, in London with our wives and children, that is, we could, euh—

ARTHUR PHILLIP: Transcend—

RALPH: Transcend the darker, euh—transcend the—

JOHNSTON: Brutal—

RALPH: The brutality—remember our better nature and remember—

COLLINS: England.

RALPH: England.

(1988)

18. The positions articulated by Reverend Johnson and Arthur Phillip are alike in that both men
    - (A) believe that great art is defined by its morality
    - (B) assume the convicts will value the beliefs of the characters they observe
    - (C) see entertainment as a distraction that will pacify the convicts
    - (D) think that presenting harsh social realities will lead to moral reformation
    - (E) rely on empirical evidence for their credibility

19. Arthur Phillip's invocation of Shakespeare, Marlowe, Jonson, and Sheridan (lines 23-25) can be most aptly described as
    - (A) an irrefutable argument about the value of drama
    - (B) a pedantic display of expert learning
    - (C) an irrelevant aside
    - (D) an appeal to a tradition of national culture
    - (E) a justification of lovers' comedies

20. The arguments advanced about performing a play invoke all of the following issues EXCEPT the
    - (A) representation of immoral behavior
    - (B) desirability of reforming convicts
    - (C) values of the colonizing country
    - (D) possibility of transcending local circumstances
    - (E) merit of staging plays about convicts

21. If Tench's position in lines 52-59 is valid, then, by contrast, the views of Ralph and Arthur Phillip are
    - (A) without historical precedent
    - (B) not sufficiently pragmatic
    - (C) morally irresponsible
    - (D) philosophically questionable
    - (E) self-interested

22. The tone of Tench's question in lines 70-71 can best be described as
    - (A) sardonically contentious
    - (B) dispassionately curious
    - (C) sympathetically supportive
    - (D) personally offended
    - (E) humorously credulous

GO ON TO THE NEXT PAGE

This passage is reprinted for your use in answering the remaining questions.

In this scene, the somewhat inebriated officers of an eighteenth-century Australian penal colony debate the merits of Second Lieutenant Ralph Clark's proposal to stage a play—George Farquhar's "The Recruiting Officer"—using the convicts as actors.

REVEREND JOHNSON: What is the plot, Ralph?

RALPH: It's about this recruiting officer and his friend, and they are in love with these two young ladies from Shrewsbury and after some difficulties, they marry them.

REV. JOHNSON: It sanctions Holy Matrimony then?

RALPH: Yes, yes, it does.

REV. JOHNSON: That wouldn't do the convicts any harm. I'm having such trouble getting them to marry instead of this sordid cohabitation they're so used to.

ROSS: Marriage, plays, why not a ball for the convicts!

CAMPBELL: Euuh. Boxing.

ARTHUR PHILLIP: Some of these men will have finished their sentence in a few years. They will become members of society again, and help create a new society in this colony. Should we not encourage them now to think in a free and responsible manner?

TENCH: I don't see how a comedy about two lovers will do that, Arthur.

ARTHUR PHILLIP: The theatre is an expression of civilisation. We belong to a great country which has spawned great playwrights: Shakespeare, Marlowe, Jonson, and even in our own time, Sheridan. The convicts will be speaking a refined, literate language and expressing sentiments of a delicacy they are not used to. It will remind them that there is more to life than crime, punishment. And we, this colony of a few hundred will be watching this together, for a few hours we will no longer be despised prisoners and hated gaolers. We will laugh, we may be moved, we may even think a little. Can you suggest something else that will provide such an evening, Watkin?

DAWES: Mapping the stars gives me more enjoyment, personally.

TENCH: I'm not sure it's a good idea having the convicts laugh at officers, Arthur.

CAMPBELL: No. Pheeoh, insubordination, heh, ehh, no discipline.

ROSS: You want this vice-ridden vermin to enjoy themselves?

COLLINS: They would only laugh at Sergeant Kite.

RALPH: Captain Plume is a most attractive, noble fellow.

REV. JOHNSON: He's not loose, is he Ralph? I hear many of these plays are about rakes and encourage loose morals in women. They do get married? Before, that is, before. And for the right reasons.

RALPH: They marry for love and to secure wealth.

REV. JOHNSON: That's all right.

TENCH: I would simply say that if you want to build a civilisation there are more important things than a play. If you want to teach the convicts something, teach them to farm, to build houses, teach them a sense of respect for property, teach them thrift so they don't eat a week's rations in one night, but above all, teach them how to work, not how to sit around laughing at a comedy.

ARTHUR PHILLIP: The Greeks believed that it was a citizen's duty to watch a play. It was a kind of work in that it required attention, judgement, patience, all social virtues.

TENCH: And the Greeks were conquered by the more practical Romans, Arthur.

COLLINS: Indeed, the Romans built their bridges, but they also spent many centuries wishing they were Greeks. And they, after all, were conquered by barbarians, or by their own corrupt and small spirits.

TENCH: Are you saying Rome would not have fallen if the theatre had been better?

GO ON TO THE NEXT PAGE

RALPH (*very loud*): Why not? (*Everyone looks at him and he continues, fast and nervously.*) In my own small way, in just a few hours, I have seen something change. I asked some of the convict women to read me some lines, these women who behave often no better than animals. And it seemed to me, as one or two—I'm not saying all of them, not at all—but one or two, saying those well-balanced lines of Mr. Farquhar, they seemed to acquire a dignity, they seemed—they seemed to lose some of their corruption. There was one, Mary Brenham, she read so well, perhaps this play will keep her from selling herself to the first marine who offers her bread—

FADDY (*under his breath*): She'll sell herself to him, instead.

ROSS: So that's the way the wind blows—

CAMPBELL: Hooh. A tempest. Hooh.

RALPH: (*over them*): I speak about her, but in a small way this could affect all the convicts and even ourselves, we could forget our worries about the supplies, the hangings and the floggings, and think of ourselves at the theatre, in London with our wives and children, that is, we could, euh—

ARTHUR PHILLIP: Transcend—

RALPH: Transcend the darker, euh—transcend the—

JOHNSTON: Brutal—

RALPH: The brutality—remember our better nature and remember—

COLLINS: England.

RALPH: England.

(1988)

23. Faddy's interruption (lines 85-86) of Ralph's reflections functions as which of the following?

I. A comic aside
II. A cynical deflation of pretension
III. A reprimand for poor taste

(A) I only
(B) III only
(C) I and II only
(D) I and III only
(E) I, II, and III

24. Ross's comment in line 87 most probably refers to his

(A) appreciation of Faddy's sense of humor
(B) assessment of Mary Brenham's character
(C) perception of Ralph's underlying motives
(D) recognition of the validity of Ralph's argument
(E) indifference to the topic at hand

25. The moral effect of speaking the well-written language of the play is most persuasively argued by

(A) Reverend Johnson
(B) Tench
(C) Campbell
(D) Collins
(E) Ralph

26. The characters want to "remember . . . England" (lines 99-102) because for them England is

(A) no longer the country that Shakespeare knew
(B) the ideal civilization
(C) the home of the theatre's most skilled performers
(D) a reminder of their authority
(E) the country in which comedy serves a social purpose

27. The excerpt thematically explores the

(A) history of drama in recent centuries
(B) importance of wholesome entertainment
(C) need for reform in government
(D) nature and purpose of drama itself
(E) tendency of people everywhere to engage in acting

GO ON TO THE NEXT PAGE

Questions 28-35. Read the following passage carefully before you choose your answers.

I believe I have omitted mentioning that in my first Voyage from Boston, being becalm'd off Block Island, our People set about catching Cod and hawl'd up a great many. Hitherto I had stuck to my Resolution of not eating animal Food; and on this Occasion, I consider'd with my Master Tryon,* the taking every Fish as a kind of unprovok'd Murder, since none of them had or ever could do us any Injury that might justify the Slaughter. All this seem'd very reasonable. But I had formerly been a great Lover of Fish, and when this came hot out of the Frying Pan, it smelt admirably well. I balanc'd some time between Principle and Inclination: till I recollected, that when the Fish were opened, I saw smaller Fish taken out of their Stomachs: Then thought I, if you eat one another, I don't see why we mayn't eat you. So I din'd upon Cod very heartily and continu'd to eat with other People, returning only now and then occasionally to a vegetable Diet. So convenient a thing it is to be a *reasonable Creature*, since it enables one to find or make a Reason for every thing one has a mind to do.

(1791)

* The author of a book espousing vegetarianism

28. As it is used in line 13, "Inclination" means
    (A) leaning, bending
    (B) slant, slope
    (C) bowing, nodding
    (D) disposition, preference
    (E) decision, determination

29. Which of the following best describes the tone of the sentence "Then thought I, if you eat one another, I don't see why we mayn't eat you" (lines 15-16) ?
    (A) Witty
    (B) Inquiring
    (C) Critical
    (D) Defiant
    (E) Sincere

30. As used in lines 20-21, the phrase "find or make a Reason for" means
    (A) show enthusiasm for
    (B) understand the outcome of
    (C) think of an excuse to justify
    (D) examine the motivation behind
    (E) weigh the advantages and disadvantages of

31. In the final sentence of the passage, the speaker can be best described as
    (A) humorously self-aware
    (B) objective and matter-of-fact
    (C) slightly befuddled
    (D) selfish and immodest
    (E) thoroughly disillusioned

GO ON TO THE NEXT PAGE

32. Which statements about the speaker's vegetarianism can be inferred from the passage?

    I. It had been adopted in response to reading Tryon's book.
    II. It was based on a concern for the just treatment of animals.
    III. It was chosen because it seemed to be rational behavior.

    (A) I only
    (B) II only
    (C) I and II only
    (D) II and III only
    (E) I, II, and III

33. Which of the following shows the use of hyperbole?

    (A) "great many" (line 4)
    (B) "Murder" (line 7) and "Slaughter" (line 9)
    (C) "Injury" (line 8) and "reasonable" (line 9)
    (D) "admirably well" (line 12)
    (E) "very heartily" (line 17)

34. The tone of the final sentence is established by which of the following?

    I. The use of the word "convenient"
    II. The italicization of "*reasonable Creature*"
    III. The use of the phrase "to find or make a Reason"

    (A) II only
    (B) I and II only
    (C) I and III only
    (D) II and III only
    (E) I, II, and III

35. The speaker actually abandons vegetarianism because the speaker

    (A) cannot find a reasonable argument for continuing it
    (B) has never been convinced by the arguments for it
    (C) is convinced that the big fish deserves to be eaten
    (D) loves cod more than meat
    (E) has an appetite that outweighs abstract principles

GO ON TO THE NEXT PAGE

Questions 36-44. Read the following passage carefully before you choose your answers.

I am not ashamed of my grandparents for having been slaves. I am only ashamed of myself for having at one time been ashamed. About eighty-five years ago they were told that they were free, united with others of our country in everything pertaining to the common good, and, in everything social, separate like the fingers of the hand. And they believed it. They exulted in it. They stayed in their place, worked hard, and brought up my father to do the same. But my grandfather is the one. He was an odd old guy, my grandfather, and I am told I take after him. It was he who caused the trouble. On his deathbed he called my father to him and said, "Son, after I'm gone I want you to keep up the good fight. I never told you, but our life is a war and I have been a traitor all my born days, a spy in the enemy's country ever since I give up my gun back in the Reconstruction. Live with your head in the lion's mouth. I want you to overcome 'em with yeses, undermine 'em with grins, agree 'em to death and destruction, let 'em swoller you till they vomit or bust wide open." They thought the old man had gone out of his mind. He had been the meekest of men. The younger children were rushed from the room, the shades drawn and the flame of the lamp turned so low that it sputtered on the wick like the old man's breathing. "Learn it to the younguns," he whispered fiercely; then he died.

But my folks were more alarmed over his last words than over his dying. It was as though he had not died at all, his words caused so much anxiety. I was warned emphatically to forget what he had said and, indeed, this is the first time it has been mentioned outside the family circle. It had a tremendous effect upon me, however. I could never be sure of what he meant. Grandfather had been a quiet old man who never made any trouble, yet on his deathbed he had called himself a traitor and a spy, and he had spoken of his meekness as a dangerous activity. It became a constant puzzle which lay unanswered in the back of my mind. And whenever things went well for me I remembered my grandfather and felt guilty and uncomfortable. It was as though I was carrying out his advice in spite of myself. And to make it worse, everyone loved me for it. I was praised by the most lily-white men of the town. I was considered an example of desirable conduct—just as my grandfather had been. And what puzzled me was that the old man had defined it as *treachery*. When I was praised for my conduct I felt a guilt that in some way I was doing something that was really against the wishes of the white folks, that if they had understood they would have desired me to act just the opposite, that I should have been sulky and mean, and that that really would have been what they wanted, even though they were fooled and thought they wanted me to act as I did. It made me afraid that some day they would look upon me as a traitor and I would be lost. Still I was more afraid to act any other way because they didn't like that at all. The old man's words were like a curse. On my graduation day I delivered an oration in which I showed that humility was the secret, indeed, the very essence of progress. (Not that I believed this—how could I, remembering my grandfather?—I only believed that it worked.) It was a great success. Everyone praised me and I was invited to give the speech at a gathering of the town's leading white citizens. It was a triumph for our whole community.

(1952)

36. The narrator's central concern in the passage is

(A) curiosity about his family history
(B) uneasiness about his family's care of his dying grandfather
(C) frustration with the limitations imposed by his parents
(D) a sense of being betrayed by the leading citizens of the town
(E) uncertainty about how he should act

37. The simile of the hand (line 7) suggests

(A) acceptance of change in social worlds
(B) a rationale for a segregated social system
(C) a symbol of racial pride
(D) hard work as the basis for economic prosperity
(E) a physical basis for similarities and differences

GO ON TO THE NEXT PAGE

38. In the context of lines 1-9, the narrator is suggesting that his grandparents

(A) built an ideal life after they had been freed
(B) were proud of the efforts they made to achieve their freedom
(C) appeared to have adopted socially approved values
(D) were unusual among the former slaves of their generation
(E) lived in the past rather than the present

39. The grandfather's injunction "to overcome 'em with yeses, undermine 'em with grins" (lines 18-19) asks for

(A) optimism in the face of adversity
(B) resignation when change is impossible
(C) subtle imitation as a way to gain favor
(D) seeming acquiescence as a means of rebellion
(E) unforced graciousness toward defeated opponents

40. The fact that the narrator has never, before now, mentioned his grandfather's dying words outside the family circle suggests that he has

(A) been deliberately disrespectful to his grandfather
(B) felt that the words were entrusted to him
(C) concluded that no one would be interested in them
(D) not bothered to think about them
(E) felt profoundly anxious about them

41. The lifelong behavior and the deathbed words of his grandfather, taken together, puzzle the narrator because they

(A) imply that the grandfather was not devoted to his family
(B) require the narrator to assume a position of leadership
(C) seem to reflect contradictory impulses
(D) prove that direct confrontations are undesirable
(E) suggest that unqualified victory is attainable

42. It can be inferred from the passage that the grandfather regarded what he called treachery as

(A) an affirmative act, because the deception allows you to prevail
(B) a useless act, because those who are betrayed are too obtuse to notice
(C) an innocent act, because no one is misled by it
(D) an honorable act, because the behavior exhibited is friendly and agreeable
(E) an unintentional act, because no one would knowingly engage in such dangerous behavior

43. By "worked" (line 64), the narrator means

(A) pleased the leading citizens of the community
(B) brought about intellectual progress
(C) shocked the graduating class
(D) encouraged frank discussion of bias
(E) openly challenged racist assumptions

44. In the context of the passage, the sentence "It was a triumph for our whole community" (line 67) suggests that

(A) the triumph was not necessarily what it seemed
(B) humility and triumph are irreconcilable
(C) the grandfather's battle has temporarily been halted
(D) formal education will reduce racial discrimination
(E) the nature of language is essentially deceptive

GO ON TO THE NEXT PAGE

Questions 45-51. Read the following poem carefully before you choose your answers.

Of English Verse

Poets may boast, as safely vain,
Their works shall with the world remain;
Both, bound together, live or die,
The verses and the prophecy.

But who can hope his lines should long
Last in a daily changing tongue?
While they are new, envy prevails;
And as that dies, our language fails.

When architects have done their part,
The matter may betray their art;
Time, if we use ill-chosen stone,
Soon brings a well-built palace down.

Poets that lasting marble seek
Must carve in Latin or in Greek;
We write in sand, our language grows,
And, like the tide, our work o'erflows.

Chaucer[1] his sense can only boast,
The glory of his numbers lost!
Years have defaced his matchless strain,
And yet he did not sing in vain.

The beauties which adorned that age,
The shining subjects of his rage,[2]
Hoping they should immortal prove,
Rewarded with success his love.

This was the generous poet's scope,
And all an English pen can hope,
To make the fair approve his flame,
That can so far extend their fame.

Verse, thus designed, has no ill fate
If it arrive but at the date
Of fading beauty; if it prove
But as long-lived as present love.

(1668)

[1] Fourteenth-century poet whose works, written in Middle English, reflect features that English has lost

[2] Poetic inspiration

45. In the context of lines 5-8, "fails" presents the English language as

(A) possessing a vocabulary too narrow to express the richness of human experience
(B) reflecting the central weakness of a society consumed by jealousy of talent
(C) containing too few beauties of sound for spoken poetry to please listeners
(D) imitating the worst features of languages like Latin and Greek
(E) undergoing too many transformations to preserve all the original qualities of a poem

46. In the argument of the poem, the function of the third stanza is to show that

(A) the art of poetry is superior to the art of architecture
(B) architecture requires artistic skills as great as those of poetry
(C) worldly pomp is subject to the power of time
(D) art lasts only as long as its materials do
(E) the choice of subject may determine the usefulness of a work of art

47. In the fourth stanza, all of the following words are used metaphorically EXCEPT

(A) "Poets" (line 13)
(B) "marble" (line 13)
(C) "carve" (line 14)
(D) "sand" (line 15)
(E) "o'erflows" (line 16)

48. In line 14, the speaker refers to Latin and Greek because

(A) classical civilization is noted for its marble temples and statues
(B) they are thought of as unchanging languages
(C) the greatest poetry has been written in Latin and Greek
(D) time renders all languages obsolete
(E) the inscriptions on tombs are frequently written in Latin and Greek

GO ON TO THE NEXT PAGE

49. In lines 15-16, "grows" implies that English does which of the following?

(A) Becomes more refined in its vocabulary.
(B) Changes inevitably with the passage of time.
(C) Alters imperceptibly to reflect social transformations.
(D) Evolves away from its original purity and simplicity.
(E) Gains a new power of expression.

50. According to lines 29-32, what trait does "Verse" share with "fading beauty" and "present love" ?

(A) Sentimental appeal to nostalgic temperament
(B) Dazzling effect on the speaker
(C) Lack of recognition by fashionable society
(D) Beauty that must endure hardship before triumphing
(E) Value that can last only a limited time

51. Which of the following does the poem most frequently employ?

(A) Hyperbole
(B) Apostrophe
(C) Antithesis
(D) Euphemism
(E) Metaphor

GO ON TO THE NEXT PAGE

Questions 52-61. Read the following poem carefully before you choose your answers.

Daybreak

In this moment when the light starts up
In the east and rubs
The horizon until it catches fire,

We enter the fields to hoe,
Row after row, among the small flags of onion,
Waving off the dragonflies
That ladder the air.

And tears the onions raise
Do not begin in your eyes but in ours,
In the salt blown
From one blister into another;

They begin in knowing
You will never waken to bear
The hour timed to a heart beat,
The wind pressing us closer to the ground.

When the season ends,
And the onions are unplugged from their sleep,
We won't forget what you failed to see,
And nothing will heal
Under the rain's broken fingers.

(1977)

52. The tone of the poem is best described as one of

(A) shock
(B) anxiety
(C) rationalization
(D) bitterness and pain
(E) resignation and apathy

53. The basic opposition in the poem is between

(A) the employed and the unemployed
(B) time and timelessness
(C) worker and consumer
(D) misery and elation
(E) machines and laborers

54. In light of the poem as a whole, the figurative language of the first stanza sets a scene with an image of

(A) peace
(B) creativity
(C) affection
(D) friction
(E) chaos

55. The effect of lines 14 and 15 is to

(A) illustrate the conditions that the workers have to endure
(B) show how nature both helps and hinders those who work in the fields
(C) suggest that while nature is changeable, human will is constant
(D) imply that those who study nature will eventually realize their own shortcomings
(E) suggest that workers who have pride in what they do can withstand adversity

56. The relation between the third and fourth stanzas might best be described as a

(A) change from one explanation for the tears to another
(B) contrast between experienced and anticipated pain
(C) progression in time from the past to the present
(D) movement from the concerns of consumers to the concerns of workers
(E) shift in tone from acceptance to denial

57. In line 17, "unplugged from their sleep" means

(A) planted
(B) cultivated
(C) harvested
(D) consumed
(E) replenished

GO ON TO THE NEXT PAGE

58. Which of the following will not “heal” (line 19) ?

    I. The problems of the workers
    II. The tears of “you”
    III. The rift between “we” and “you”

    (A) I only
    (B) I and II only
    (C) I and III only
    (D) II and III only
    (E) I, II, and III

59. In context, the image of the “rain’s broken fingers” (line 20) calls attention to the

    (A) decreasing profit margin of farming
    (B) disappointment of the workers when a crop is poor
    (C) difficulty of the workers’ situation
    (D) inconveniences that adverse weather conditions produce in modern life
    (E) failure of science in predicting the weather

60. The physical labor the speaker describes is presented as

    (A) an occupation that ruthlessly exploits natural resources
    (B) a difficult but satisfying way of earning a living
    (C) an opportunity to be at one with nature
    (D) a way of life that is about to become outdated
    (E) a painful and unappreciated endeavor

61. The speaker suggests that the “you” referred to in the poem can best be characterized as

    (A) ignorant or unseeing
    (B) sentimental and foolish
    (C) greedy or wasteful
    (D) physically exhausted
    (E) emotionally unstable

STOP

IF YOU FINISH BEFORE TIME IS CALLED, YOU MAY CHECK YOUR WORK ON THIS TEST ONLY. DO NOT TURN TO ANY OTHER TEST IN THIS BOOK.

ACKNOWLEDGMENTS

From *NEW AND SELECTED POEMS* by Gary Soto © 1995. Reprinted by permission of Chronicle Books, San Francisco.

How to Score the SAT Subject Test in Literature

When you take an actual SAT Subject Test in Literature, your answer sheet will be "read" by a scanning machine that will record your responses to each question. Then a computer will compare your answers with the correct answers and produce your raw score. You get one point for each correct answer. For each wrong answer, you lose one-fourth of a point. Questions you omit (and any for which you mark more than one answer) are not counted. This raw score is converted to a scaled score that is reported to you and to the colleges you specify.

Worksheet 1. Finding Your Raw Test Score

STEP 1: Table A lists the correct answers for all the questions on the Subject Test in Literature that is reproduced in this book. It also serves as a worksheet for you to calculate your raw score.

- Compare your answers with those given in the table.
- Put a check in the column marked "Right" if your answer is correct.
- Put a check in the column marked "Wrong" if your answer is incorrect.
- Leave both columns blank if you omitted the question.

STEP 2: Count the number of right answers.

Enter the total here: ____________________

STEP 3: Count the number of wrong answers.

Enter the total here: ____________________

STEP 4: Multiply the number of wrong answers by .250.

Enter the product here: ________________

STEP 5: Subtract the result obtained in Step 4 from the total you obtained in Step 2.

Enter the result here: __________________

STEP 6: Round the number obtained in Step 5 to the nearest whole number.

Enter the result here: __________________

The number you obtained in Step 6 is your raw score.

Table A

Answers to the Subject Test in Literature, Form 3XAC2, and Percentage of Students Answering Each Question Correctly

Question Number	Correct Answer	Right	Wrong	Percentage of Students Answering the Question Correctly*	Question Number	Correct Answer	Right	Wrong	Percentage of Students Answering the Question Correctly*
1	A			94	32	E			44
2	E			75	33	B			50
3	D			75	34	E			40
4	E			81	35	E			41
5	C			44	36	E			86
6	D			32	37	B			66
7	C			55	38	C			46
8	A			84	39	D			60
9	B			69	40	E			50
10	C			68	41	C			79
11	C			57	42	A			57
12	D			20	43	A			66
13	B			33	44	A			49
14	B			49	45	E			70
15	D			34	46	D			57
16	E			59	47	A			75
17	E			41	48	B			74
18	B			62	49	B			55
19	D			52	50	E			50
20	E			57	51	E			75
21	B			52	52	D			78
22	A			38	53	C			75
23	C			55	54	D			52
24	C			33	55	A			63
25	E			75	56	A			29
26	B			70	57	C			82
27	D			70	58	C			68
28	D			72	59	C			66
29	A			54	60	E			85
30	C			82	61	A			88
31	A			69					

* These percentages are based on an analysis of the answer sheets of a representative sample of 12,064 students who took the original form of this test in December 2001, and whose mean score was 579. They may be used as an indication of the relative difficulty of a particular question. Each percentage may also be used to predict the likelihood that a typical SAT Subject Test in Literature candidate will answer that question correctly on this edition of the test.

Finding Your Scaled Score

When you take SAT Subject Tests, the scores sent to the colleges you specify are reported on the College Board scale, which ranges from 200–800. You can convert your practice test score to a scaled score by using Table B. To find your scaled score, locate your raw score in the left-hand column of Table B; the corresponding score in the right-hand column is your scaled score. For example, a raw score of 21 on this particular edition of the Subject Test in Literature corresponds to a scaled score of 500.

Raw scores are converted to scaled scores to ensure that a score earned on any one edition of a particular Subject Test is comparable to the same scaled score earned on any other edition of the same Subject Test. Because some editions of the tests may be slightly easier or more difficult than others, College Board scaled scores are adjusted so that they indicate the same level of performance regardless of the edition of the test taken and the ability of the group that takes it. Thus, for example, a score of 400 on one edition of a test taken at a particular administration indicates the same level of achievement as a score of 400 on a different edition of the test taken at a different administration.

When you take the SAT Subject Tests during a national administration, your scores are likely to differ somewhat from the scores you obtain on the tests in this book. People perform at different levels at different times for reasons unrelated to the tests themselves. The precision of any test is also limited because it represents only a sample of all the possible questions that could be asked.

Table B

Scaled Score Conversion Table Subject Test in Literature (Form 3XAC2)					
Raw Score	Scaled Score	Raw Score	Scaled Score	Raw Score	Scaled Score
61	800	32	590	3	350
60	800	31	580	2	350
59	800	30	570	1	340
58	790	29	560	0	330
57	790	28	550	-1	320
56	780	27	550	-2	320
55	770	26	540	-3	310
54	760	25	530	-4	300
53	750	24	520	-5	290
52	750	23	510	-6	280
51	740	22	510	-7	280
50	730	21	500	-8	270
49	720	20	490	-9	260
48	710	19	480	-10	250
47	710	18	470	-11	240
46	700	17	470	-12	230
45	690	16	460	-13	220
44	680	15	450	-14	210
43	680	14	440	-15	200
42	670	13	430		
41	660	12	430		
40	650	11	420		
39	640	10	410		
38	640	9	400		
37	630	8	390		
36	620	7	390		
35	610	6	380		
34	600	5	370		
33	590	4	360		

How Did You Do on the Subject Test in Literature?

After you score your test and analyze your performance, think about the following questions:

Did you run out of time before reaching the end of the test?

If so, you may need to pace yourself better. For example, maybe you spent too much time on one or two hard questions. A better approach might be to skip the ones you can't answer right away and try answering all the questions that remain on the test. Then if there's time, go back to the questions you skipped.

Did you take a long time reading the directions?

You will save time when you take the test by learning the directions to the Subject Test in Literature ahead of time. Each minute you spend reading directions during the test is a minute that you could use to answer questions.

How did you handle questions you were unsure of?

If you were able to eliminate one or more of the answer choices as wrong and guess from the remaining ones, your approach probably worked to your advantage. On the other hand, making haphazard guesses or omitting questions without trying to eliminate choices could cost you valuable points.

How difficult were the questions for you compared with other students who took the test?

Table A shows you how difficult the multiple-choice questions were for the group of students who took this test during its national administration. The right-hand column gives the percentage of students that answered each question correctly.

A question answered correctly by almost everyone in the group is obviously an easier question. For example, 84 percent of the students answered question 8 correctly. But only 20 percent answered question 12 correctly.

Keep in mind that these percentages are based on just one group of students. They would probably be different with another group of students taking the test.

If you missed several easier questions, go back and try to find out why: Did the questions cover material you haven't yet reviewed? Did you misunderstand the directions?

Chapter 2
United States History

Purpose

The emphasis of the Subject Test in United States History is on United States history from pre-Columbian times to the present as well as basic social science concepts, methods, and generalizations as they are found in the study of history. It is not tied to any single textbook or instructional approach.

Format

This is a one-hour test with 90 to 95 multiple-choice questions. The questions cover political, economic, social, intellectual, and cultural history as well as foreign policy.

Content

The questions may require you to:

- recall basic information and require you to know facts, terms, concepts, and generalizations
- analyze and interpret material such as graphs, charts, paintings, text, cartoons, photographs, and maps
- understand important aspects of U.S. history
- relate ideas to given data
- evaluate data for a given purpose, basing your judgment either on internal evidence, such as proof and logical consistency, or on external criteria, such as comparison with other works, established standards, and theories

Material Covered*	Approximate Percentage of Test
Political History	32–36
Economic History	18–20
Social History	18–22
Intellectual and Cultural History	10–12
Foreign Policy	13–17
Periods Covered	
Pre-Columbian history to 1789	20
1790 to 1898	40
1899 to the present	40

* Social science concepts, methods, and generalizations are incorporated in this material.

How to Prepare

The only essential preparation is a sound, one-year course in U.S. history at the college-preparatory level. Most of the test questions are based on material commonly taught in U.S. history courses in secondary schools, although some of the material may be covered in other social studies courses. Knowledge gained from social studies courses and from outside reading could be helpful. No one textbook or method of instruction is considered better than another. Familiarize yourself with the directions in advance. The directions in this book are identical to those that appear on the test.

Score

The total score is reported on the 200-to-800 scale.

Sample Questions

The types of questions used in the test and the abilities they measure are described below. Questions may be presented as separate items or in sets based on quotations, maps, pictures, graphs, or tables.

Directions: Each of the questions or incomplete statements below is followed by five suggested answers or completions. Select the one that is best in each case and then fill in the corresponding circle on the answer sheet.

Some questions require you to know facts, terms, concepts, and generalizations. They test your recall of basic information and your understanding of significant aspects of U.S. history and social studies. Question 1 is a sample of this type.

1. Harriet Tubman was known as the "Moses" of her people because she
   (A) helped slaves escape from the South
   (B) was instrumental in bringing about suffrage reform
   (C) advocated emigration to Africa for Black people
   (D) organized mass civil rights demonstrations
   (E) traveled as a lay minister preaching the gospel

Choice (A) is the correct answer to question 1. To answer this question you need to know that Harriet Tubman was a notable African American abolitionist. As the use of the name "Moses" may help you to remember, Tubman led many slaves to freedom in the North along the route of the Underground Railroad as referred to in choice (A). The other choices only describe activities that Tubman did not pursue.

Some questions require you to analyze and interpret materials. Question 2, based on the table below, illustrates a question that tests your ability to use these skills.

Popular Vote for Presidential Electors, Georgia, 1848 and 1852			
	Democratic Electors	**Whig Electors**	**Webster Electors**
1848	44,809	47,538	—
1852	40,516	16,660	5,324

2. Using the table above, one might conclude that the most plausible explanation for the Georgia Democrats' victory in 1852, following their defeat in 1848, was that
   (A) many new voters increased the turnout in 1852, to the advantage of the Democrats
   (B) many voters abstained from voting in 1852, to the disadvantage of the Whigs
   (C) Webster, who had not run in 1848, drew sufficient votes from the Whigs to cost them the election of 1852
   (D) the Democrats, who had run a highly unpopular candidate in 1848, ran a highly popular candidate in 1852
   (E) the Democrats cast fraudulent ballots to increase their share of the votes in 1852

Choice (B) is the correct answer to question 2. To answer this question, you must analyze the electoral data given for 1848 and 1852, noting that the voter turnout dropped dramatically in 1852 and that the Whigs suffered a much larger decline in voter turnout than did the Democrats. As a consequence, the Whigs lost their majority position. Choices (A), (C), (D), and (E) are not logically consistent with this data. For example, choice (C) is incorrect because the table shows that the Democratic Electors received more votes than the Whig and Webster Electors combined. Choice (B) is the correct answer because it is the plausible explanation for the change in the fortunes of the Georgia Democrats.

Other questions test your ability to analyze material as well as your ability to recall information related to the materials, or to make inferences and interpretations based on the material. Questions 3, 4, 5, and 6 are illustrations of questions that test a combination of interpretation and recall.

3. "What is man born for but to be a reformer, a remaker of what man has made; a renouncer of lies; a restorer of truth and good, imitating that great Nature which embosoms us all, and which sleeps no moment on an old past, but every hour repairs herself, yielding every morning a new day, and with every pulsation a new life?"

   These sentiments are most characteristic of

   (A) fundamentalism
   (B) Social Darwinism
   (C) pragmatism
   (D) neoorthodoxy
   (E) transcendentalism

Choice (E) is the correct answer to question 3. Several elements in the quotation suggest this as the correct answer. The emphasis that the quotation places on reform, on nature as a source of moral truth, and on the infinite possibilities open to people mark it as an example of the thought of the transcendentalist movement. This combination of elements is not pertinent to any of the other choices. Even if you do not know the source of the material, your understanding of the nature of transcendentalism should lead you to choice (E).

Questions 4–5 refer to the following map.

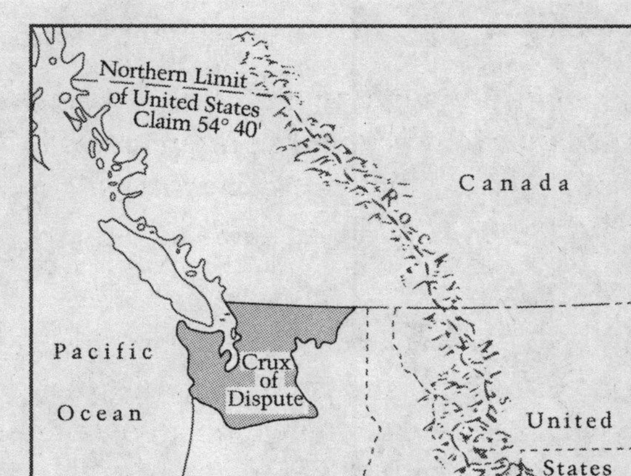

4. The controversy with Great Britain over control of the shaded section was settled during the presidency of
   (A) John Quincy Adams
   (B) James K. Polk
   (C) Franklin Pierce
   (D) James Buchanan
   (E) Andrew Johnson

Choice (B) is the correct answer to question 4. To answer this question, you must interpret the map and recognize the shaded section as part of the Oregon Territory. The Oregon dispute with Great Britain was settled during the presidency of James K. Polk.

5. To the northwest of the area shown on the map is a continental territory purchased by Secretary of State William H. Seward from
   (A) Great Britain
   (B) Canada
   (C) Russia
   (D) France
   (E) Spain

Choice (C) is the correct answer to question 5. To answer this question, you must go beyond the content of the map in order to determine that the territory referred to in the question is Alaska. If you recall that Secretary of State Seward purchased the territory from Russia in 1867, you will choose the correct answer.

Courtesy of the New-York Historical Society

6. The point of view expressed by this cartoon would probably have met with the approval of
   (A) Daniel Webster
   (B) James K. Polk
   (C) Martin Van Buren
   (D) Roger B. Taney
   (E) Stephen A. Douglas

Choice (A) is the correct answer to question 6. To answer this question, you must first note the anti-Jackson tone of the cartoon, which portrays King Andrew the First trampling the Constitution of the United States. You must then decide which of the choices given opposed Jackson's use of the veto to return important bills to Congress. Only the Whig Daniel Webster fits that description. The others were Democrats who either supported Andrew Jackson or were politically active at a later time.

Some questions require you to select or relate hypotheses, concepts, principles, or generalizations to given data. The questions may begin with concrete specifics and ask for the appropriate concept, or they may begin with a concept and apply it to particular problems or situations. Thus, you may need to use inductive and deductive reasoning. Questions 7 and 8 are examples of questions in this category.

7. From 1870 to 1930, the trend in industry was for hours to be generally reduced, while both money wages and real wages rose. What factor was primarily responsible for this trend?
   (A) A reduction in profit margins
   (B) Minimum wage laws
   (C) Restriction of the labor supply
   (D) Increased output per hour of work
   (E) Right-to-work legislation

Choice (D) is the correct answer to question 7. To arrive at this answer, you must be aware that the trend referred to in the question came about primarily because of technological advances that resulted in increased productivity. None of the other answer choices satisfactorily accounts for all the conditions described in the question.

8. Which of the following wars of the United States would fit the description of a war neither lost nor won?

    I. The War of 1812
    II. The Mexican War
    III. The Spanish-American War
    IV. The Second World War

(A) I only
(B) II only
(C) I and III only
(D) II and IV only
(E) III and IV only

Choice (A) is the correct answer to question 8. In answering this question, you must recognize that a war not won, though not necessarily lost, is one in which a country either fails to achieve clear victory on the battlefield or fails to sign a peace treaty that is definitive and fulfills its goals. Only the War of 1812 is an illustration of the kind of war defined by the question. That war was ended by The Treaty of Ghent, which provided for the *Status quo ante bellum*, or a return to things as they had been before the war.

Some questions require you to judge the value of data for a given purpose, either basing your judgment on internal evidence, such as accuracy and logical consistency, or on external criteria, such as accepted historical scholarship. Question 9 is an illustration of this kind of question.

9. Which of the following would most probably provide the widest range of information for a historian wishing to analyze the social composition of an American city in the 1880s?

(A) The minutes of the city council
(B) A debutante's diary
(C) A manuscript census tabulating the residence, ethnicity, occupation, and wealth of each city resident
(D) Precinct-level voting returns in a closely contested mayoral election held in a presidential election year
(E) A survey of slum housing conditions carried out by a Social Gospel minister in the year following several epidemics

Choice (C) is the correct answer to question 9. In answering this question, you must be able to eliminate from consideration choices that offer information about the city that is either irrelevant or less relevant than other options to understanding the social composition of the city, choices (A) and (D). You must also eliminate choices that offer relevant information but are limited to a particular section of the population of the city, choices (B) and (E). Choice (C) contains the widest range of information about the social composition of a city.

United States History Test

Practice Helps

The test that follows is an actual, recently administered SAT Subject Test in United States History. To get an idea of what it's like to take this test, practice under conditions that are much like those of an actual test administration.

- Set aside an hour when you can take the test uninterrupted. Make sure you complete the test in one sitting.
- Sit at a desk or table with no other books or papers. Dictionaries, other books, or notes are not allowed in the test room.
- Tear out an answer sheet from the back of this book and fill it in just as you would on the day of the test. One answer sheet can be used for up to three Subject Tests.
- Read the instructions that precede the practice test. During the actual administration, you will be asked to read them before answering test questions.
- Time yourself by placing a clock or kitchen timer in front of you.
- After you finish the practice test, read the sections "How to Score the SAT Subject Test in United States History" and "How Did You Do on the Subject Test in United States History?"
- The appearance of the answer sheet in this book may differ from the answer sheet you see on test day.

UNITED STATES HISTORY TEST

The top portion of the section of the answer sheet that you will use in taking the United States History Test must be filled in exactly as shown in the illustration below. Note carefully that you have to do all of the following on your answer sheet.

1. Print UNITED STATES HISTORY on the line under the words "Subject Test (print)."
2. In the shaded box labeled "Test Code" fill in four circles:
   —Fill in circle 4 in the row labeled V.
   —Fill in circle 7 in the row labeled W.
   —Fill in circle 4 in the row labeled X.
   —Fill in circle A in the row labeled Y.

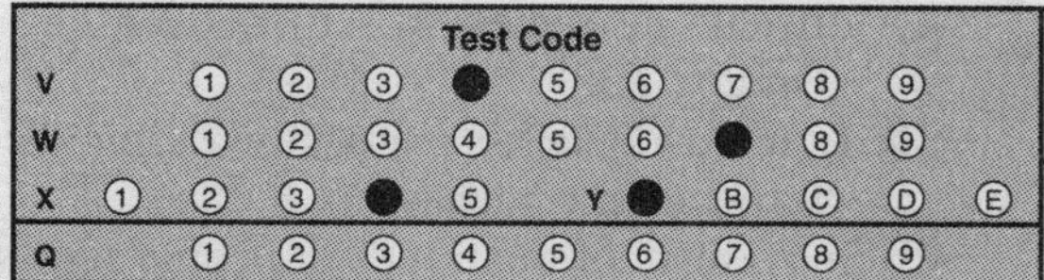

Subject Test (print)

UNITED STATES HISTORY

3. Please answer the two questions below by filling in the appropriate circles in the row labeled Q on the answer sheet. <u>The information you provide is for statistical purposes only and will not affect your score on the test.</u>

<u>Question I</u>

How many semesters of United States History have you taken from grade 9 to the present? (If you are taking United States History this semester, count it as a full semester.) Fill in only <u>one</u> circle of circles 1-4.

- One semester or less —Fill in circle 1.
- Two semesters —Fill in circle 2.
- Three semesters —Fill in circle 3.
- Four or more semesters —Fill in circle 4.

<u>Question II</u>

Which, if any, of the following social studies courses have you taken from grade 9 to the present? (Fill in ALL circles that apply.)

- One or more semesters of government —Fill in circle 5.
- One or more semesters of economics —Fill in circle 6.
- One or more semesters of geography —Fill in circle 7.
- One or more semesters of psychology —Fill in circle 8.
- One or more semesters of sociology or anthropology —Fill in circle 9.

If you have taken none of these social studies courses, leave the circles 5 through 9 blank.

When the supervisor gives the signal, turn the page and begin the United States History Test. There are 100 numbered circles on the answer sheet and 90 questions in the United States History Test. Therefore, use only circles 1 to 90 for recording your answers.

UNITED STATES HISTORY TEST

Directions: Each of the questions or incomplete statements below is followed by five suggested answers or completions. Select the one that is best in each case and then fill in the corresponding circle on the answer sheet.

1. During the seventeenth and eighteenth centuries, the English colonial system was based most explicitly on the economic and political principles of

(A) mercantilism
(B) free trade
(C) salutary neglect
(D) enlightened despotism
(E) physiocracy

2. The concept of the separation of powers, as articulated by the framers of the Constitution, refers to the

(A) right of free speech
(B) right of freedom of assembly
(C) organization of the national government in three branches
(D) separation of church and state
(E) political rights of confederated states

3. The Trail of Tears refers to the

(A) movement of slaves from eastern states into the West after the 1820's
(B) relocation of Cherokee Indians from the Southeast to settlements in what is now Oklahoma
(C) difficult movement of settlers over the Oregon Trail
(D) Lewis and Clark's expedition during the Jefferson presidency
(E) movement of thousands of people across the Great Plains during the California gold rush

4. All of the following reformers are correctly paired with the reform issue with which they were most involved EXCEPT

(A) Elizabeth Cady Stanton . . suffrage
(B) Sojourner Truth . . antislavery
(C) Harriet Beecher Stowe . . prohibition
(D) Emma Willard . . women's education
(E) Dorothea Dix . . treatment of people with mental and emotional disabilities

3WAC2

GO ON TO THE NEXT PAGE

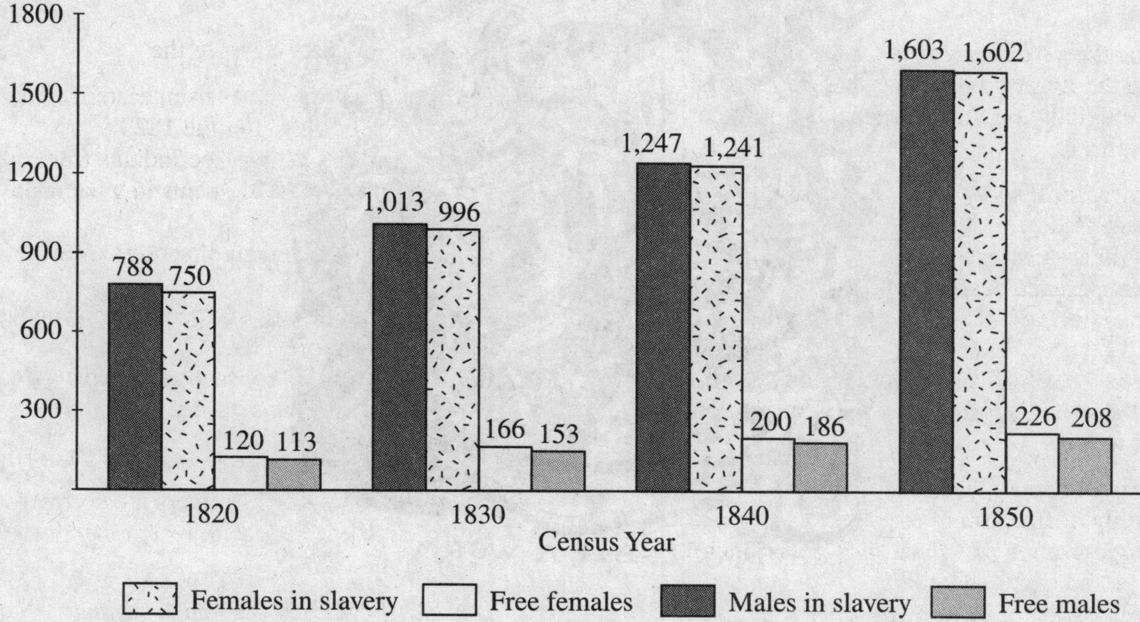

5. Which of the following statements about the period from 1820 to 1850 is supported by the diagram above?

(A) The percentage of the Black population held in slavery declined.
(B) The ratio of Black males to Black females remained fairly constant.
(C) Black males were more likely than Black females to be free.
(D) The number of Black females doubled every 20 years.
(E) The total Black population in each census exceeded two million.

GO ON TO THE NEXT PAGE

Punch Ltd.

6. The cartoon above illustrates popular reaction to publication of a theory by

   (A) Malthus
   (B) Darwin
   (C) Marx
   (D) Einstein
   (E) Freud

---

7. In the early years of the twentieth century, the majority of female workers employed outside of the home were

   (A) widowed
   (B) divorced
   (C) married with young children
   (D) married with grown children
   (E) young and unmarried

8. President Franklin D. Roosevelt attempted to "pack" the Supreme Court in 1937 for which of the following reasons?

   (A) He wanted to make sure that New Deal laws would be found constitutional.
   (B) He believed that additional conservative justices would balance the Court.
   (C) He owed favors to many political friends who were trained lawyers.
   (D) He wanted to increase minority representation on the Court.
   (E) He wanted socialists and communists to be represented on the Court.

GO ON TO THE NEXT PAGE

By Permission of Chuck Asay and Creator's Syndicate, Inc.

9. The cartoon above makes which of the following points about federal aid policies in the years following the Second World War?

(A) The federal government has always been reluctant to offer financial aid to farmers.
(B) American farmers have never needed government support to maintain self-sufficiency.
(C) Much federal aid goes to individuals in forms other than welfare payments.
(D) Congress should cease paying both welfare and price supports.
(E) Price supports paid to farmers are not a significant percentage of the federal budget.

GO ON TO THE NEXT PAGE

10. The United States supported the Bay of Pigs invasion in 1961 in an attempt to overthrow

(A) Nikita Khrushchev
(B) Gamal Abdel Nasser
(C) Fidel Castro
(D) Chiang Kai-shek
(E) Ngo Dinh Diem

11. Single women and widows in the eighteenth-century British North American colonies had the legal right to

(A) hold political office
(B) serve as Protestant ministers
(C) vote
(D) own property
(E) serve on juries

12. Which of the following was most responsible for the repeal of the Stamp Act in 1766 ?

(A) The dumping of the East India Company's tea into Boston Harbor
(B) Petitions by the First Continental Congress to Parliament
(C) The boycott of British imports
(D) Acceptance by the Massachusetts colonists of alternate taxation
(E) Pressure on Parliament by the king

13. *Marbury* v. *Madison* was a significant turning point in the interpretation of the United States Constitution because it

(A) upheld the separation of church and state
(B) validated the principle of the free press
(C) established the practice of judicial review
(D) abolished the slave trade
(E) overturned the Alien and Sedition Acts

14. After the Civil War, sharecropping was an important element in the agricultural economy of which of the following regions?

(A) The Middle Atlantic states
(B) The South
(C) The Great Plains
(D) The West Coast
(E) New England

15. "Texas has been absorbed into the Union in the inevitable fulfillment of the general law which is rolling our population westward. . . . It was disintegrated from Mexico in the natural course of events, by a process perfectly legitimate on its own part, blameless on ours. . . . [Its] incorporation into the Union was not only inevitable, but the most natural, right and proper thing in the world."

The statement above is an expression of

(A) Social Darwinism
(B) antiabolitionism
(C) federalism
(D) Manifest Destiny
(E) self-determination

GO ON TO THE NEXT PAGE

Reprinted by permission of the New York Historical Society

16. The nineteenth-century cartoon above supports which of the following conclusions about the United States economy?

(A) The emergence of strong unions resulted in loss of productivity.

(B) The emergence of big government resulted in loss of liberties.

(C) Railroad corporations wielded tremendous power in American society.

(D) Southern planters wielded tremendous power in the Senate.

(E) Rapid urbanization led to unsanitary conditions in many cities.

GO ON TO THE NEXT PAGE

17. "There was never the least attention paid to what was cut up for sausage; there would come all the way back from Europe old sausage that had been rejected, and that was moldy and white—it would be dosed with borax and glycerine, and dumped into the hoppers, and made over again for home consumption. . . . There would be meat stored in great piles in rooms; and the water from leaky roofs would drip over it, and thousands of rats would race about on it."

The passage above is most likely excerpted from

(A) John Steinbeck's *The Grapes of Wrath*
(B) Theodore Dreiser's *An American Tragedy*
(C) Jane Addams' *Twenty Years at Hull-House*
(D) Lincoln Steffens' *The Shame of the Cities*
(E) Upton Sinclair's *The Jungle*

MAJOR HOUSEHOLD EXPENDITURES, 1900 and 1928

1900	
2 Bicycles	$ 70
Wringer and washboard	$ 5
Brushes and brooms	$ 5
Sewing machine (mechanical)	$ 25
Total	$ 105
1928	
Automobile	$ 700
Radio	$ 75
Phonograph	$ 50
Washing machine	$ 150
Vacuum cleaner	$ 50
Sewing machine (electric)	$ 60
Other electrical equipment	$ 25
Telephone (year)	$ 35
Total	$1,145

18. The chart above shows the major household expenditures of a middle-class American family in 1900 and a similar family in 1928. Which of the following is an accurate statement supported by the chart?

(A) Families needed more mechanical help with housework in 1928 than they did in 1900 because they had less domestic help.
(B) Inflation caused a significant increase in the prices of most household goods by 1928.
(C) Many families moved from rural to urban areas between 1900 and 1930 in search of employment opportunities.
(D) By 1928 more consumer goods were available to families than had been available in 1900.
(E) Increased consumer spending was a major cause of the stock market crash of 1929.

GO ON TO THE NEXT PAGE

19. "Rosie the Riveter" was a nickname given during the Second World War to

    (A) American women who did industrial work in the 1940's
    (B) American women who cared for soldiers wounded in battle
    (C) a machine that increased the speed of construction work
    (D) a woman who was a popular radio talk-show host of the 1940's
    (E) a woman who broadcast Japanese propaganda to American troops

GO ON TO THE NEXT PAGE

UPI/Corbis-Bettmann

20. The picture above illustrates efforts in the 1960's to organize a boycott that focused attention on the

(A) long hours of grocery clerks and stock clerks
(B) problems of Mississippi Valley fruit growers
(C) labor shortages in produce transport companies
(D) plight of migrant farmworkers
(E) problems of West Coast wineries

GO ON TO THE NEXT PAGE

21. Which of the following statements best describes the response of Native Americans to the continued settlement of Europeans in North America during the eighteenth century?

    (A) Native Americans traded with the French and the English as a means of maintaining their autonomy.
    (B) Native Americans in the southern part of New France negotiated treaties with the French that allowed the peaceful expansion of the European timber trade.
    (C) Some Native Americans created a horse-based nomadic culture in the Northeast.
    (D) Native Americans in the Great Plains assimilated with the European settlers.
    (E) The Iroquois did not adopt European firearms and metal tools, in an effort to maintain their own traditions.

22. In the seventeenth century, the British colonies in the Chesapeake Bay region became economically viable due to the

    (A) adoption of representative government
    (B) introduction of tobacco cultivation
    (C) flourishing trade with American Indians
    (D) export of dried cod and whale tallow
    (E) cultivation of cotton

23. All of the following were aspects of the Constitution that was submitted to the states for ratification in 1787 EXCEPT

    (A) the ability to levy taxes
    (B) congressional authority to declare war
    (C) a two-term limit for Presidents
    (D) provision for impeachment of the President
    (E) provision for presidential State of the Union messages

GO ON TO THE NEXT PAGE

The St. Louis Art Museum. Gift Bank of America

24. The painting above, which shows an antebellum election site, supports which of the following statements?

    (A) Women were equal participants in the voting process.
    (B) The sale and provision of liquor was prohibited on election day.
    (C) Party workers had to remain at least 50 yards away from the polling place.
    (D) There were no property restrictions for male voters.
    (E) Elections were a welcome social event as well as a political obligation.

---

25. The introduction of canals, railroads, and new factory technology in the mid-nineteenth century affected which of the following regions LEAST?

    (A) New England
    (B) New York and Pennsylvania
    (C) New Jersey and Delaware
    (D) The South
    (E) The Midwest

GO ON TO THE NEXT PAGE

Questions 26-27 are based on the passage below.

"Unsanitary housing, poisonous sewage, contaminated water, infant mortality, the spread of contagion, adulterated food, impure milk, smoke-laden air, ill-ventilated factories . . . unwholesome crowding, prostitution and drunkenness are the enemies which the modern cities must face and overcome, would they survive. Logically their electorate should be made up of those who . . . have at least attempted to care for children, to clean houses, to prepare foods, to isolate the family from moral dangers. . . . To test the elector's fitness to deal with this situation by his ability to bear arms is absurd. . . . City housekeeping has failed partly because women, the traditional housekeepers, have not been consulted as to its multiform activities. The men have been carelessly indifferent to much of this civic housekeeping, as they have been carelessly indifferent to the details of the household."

Jane Addams, 1906.

26. Which of the following best reflects the main argument of the passage?

(A) Men should spend less time away from home and participate more fully in domestic life.
(B) Women should be able to vote in order to apply their proven housekeeping abilities to the civic sphere.
(C) Military solutions to social problems are ineffective because they ignore moral issues.
(D) Solving the problems of cities mostly depends on providing for poor children.
(E) Modern cities have been saved from ruin only by the involvement of women in civic issues.

27. The passage above suggests that Jane Addams would probably have supported all of the following EXCEPT

(A) military preparedness
(B) woman suffrage
(C) prohibition
(D) settlement houses
(E) the Pure Food and Drug Act

GO ON TO THE NEXT PAGE

McCLURE'S MAGAZINE

MAY

LINCOLN STEFFENS'S exposure of another type of municipal grafting; how Pittsburg differs from St. Louis and Minneapolis.

THE END OF THE WORLD, by Professor Newcomb. A powerful story, yet a scientific prediction; pictures by the famous French artist, Henri Lanos.

IDA M. TARBELL on the Standard tactics which brought on the famous oil crisis of 1878.

SIX SHORT STORIES

Culver Pictures, Inc.

28. The articles appearing in this 1905 issue of *McClure's Magazine* illustrate all of the following trends in the early twentieth-century United States EXCEPT:

(A) Popular magazines were beginning to turn their attention to issues of reform.
(B) Reform of municipal city governments was a growing concern.
(C) Exposure of monopolistic business practices was beginning to draw public attention.
(D) Scientific methods were increasingly called on to lend credibility to all sorts of theories.
(E) Reformers of both government and society enjoyed widespread support among leading industrialists.

GO ON TO THE NEXT PAGE

Questions 29-30 are based on the chart below.

IMMIGRATION TO THE UNITED STATES BY AREA OF ORIGIN

Year	All Countries	Europe	Asia	Americas	Africa	Australasia
1921	805,228	652,364	25,034	124,118	1,301	2,281
1922	309,556	216,385	14,263	77,448	520	915
1924	706,896	364,339	22,065	318,855	900	679
1925	294,314	148,366	3,578	141,496	412	462
1927	335,175	168,368	3,669	161,872	520	746
1928	307,255	158,513	3,380	144,281	475	606
1929	279,678	158,598	3,758	116,177	509	636

29. Which of the following areas of origin showed the greatest percentage decline in the number of immigrants to the United States between 1921 and 1929 ?

(A) Europe
(B) Asia
(C) The Americas
(D) Africa
(E) Australasia

30. Which of the following best accounts for the trend in immigration shown in the chart?

(A) Improved economic conditions in many areas of origin
(B) Warfare in several areas of the world during this period
(C) New United States immigration legislation
(D) Economic instability in the United States
(E) Increased immigration to other areas of North America

GO ON TO THE NEXT PAGE

31. In the seventeenth century, some Pueblo Indians of the desert Southwest adopted Christianity as

(A) an added dimension to their own religious culture, adding the Christian God as another deity
(B) evidence of an ancient European culture that they were willing to embrace
(C) a means of improving their agricultural practices
(D) as a means of establishing greater equality within their community
(E) a means of direct communication with the afterlife through the practice of Christian prayer

32. Of the following, who challenged the religious establishment in Puritan New England?

(A) Cotton Mather
(B) Thomas Hutchinson
(C) Anne Hutchinson
(D) John Winthrop
(E) Abigail Adams

33. Henry Clay's "American System" included which of the following?

(A) A protective tariff that would fund internal improvements
(B) Restriction on the use of federal money for national defense
(C) Restriction on immigration from Asian countries
(D) Elimination of the national bank
(E) Protection of the property rights of Native Americans

34. In 1860 a southern writer, D. R. Hundley, wrote: "Know, then, that the Poor Whites of the South constitute a separate class to themselves; the Southern Yeomen are as distinct from them as the Southern Gentleman is from the Cotton Snob."

Which of the following characterizations would Hundley probably accept as best describing the southern yeoman?

(A) A class of White plantation employees who oversaw slave labor
(B) A group of landowners who generally owned more than 100 slaves and who formed the elite of southern society
(C) A group of independent farmers who owned small plots and few, if any, slaves
(D) A small group of farmers who believed that there were few, if any, class distinctions in the South
(E) A class of people known for their poor manners and lack of education

35. The Exclusion Act of 1882 prohibited the immigration of which of the following groups?

(A) Irish
(B) Mexicans
(C) Eastern European Jews
(D) Japanese
(E) Chinese

GO ON TO THE NEXT PAGE

MONTHLY WAGES AND SEXUAL COMPOSITION OF THE WORKFORCE IN SELECTED TRADES IN NEW YORK CITY, 1850

Trade	Average Male Wage	Average Female Wage	Percent Male	Percent Female
Clothing and tailors	$ 9.75	$ 6.99	48.5	51.5
Hats and millinery	27.51	17.14	43.5	56.5
Shoes and boots	24.32	10.43	75.2	24.8
Printing	36.28	14.48	71.3	28.7

36. Which of the following statements about the trades listed above is supported by the data in the table?

(A) The majority of female workers were in the hats and millinery trade.

(B) Both men and women received wages that were inadequate to support their families.

(C) In trades where women were in the majority, the difference between men's and women's wages was less than in trades where women were in the minority.

(D) The trades in which women were most highly represented had the lowest wages in the economy.

(E) The most skilled female workers were paid less than unskilled male workers.

GO ON TO THE NEXT PAGE

37. All of the following statements about the American home front during the Second World War are correct EXCEPT:

(A) The government instituted direct price controls to halt inflation.
(B) The Supreme Court upheld the forced relocation of Japanese Americans on the West Coast.
(C) Black workers migrated in large numbers from the rural South to the industrial cities of the North and West.
(D) Unemployment continued at Depression-era levels.
(E) Business leaders served as heads of the federal war-mobilization programs.

38. Which of the following events of the civil rights movement best illustrates the concept of "nonviolent civil disobedience"?

(A) The *Brown* v. *The Board of Education of Topeka* case of 1954
(B) The lunch-counter sit-ins of the early 1960's
(C) The March on Washington, D.C., in 1963
(D) The formation of the Black Panther party in 1966
(E) The desegregation of Little Rock, Arkansas, Central High School

39. In the 1950's John Kenneth Galbraith's *The Affluent Society* and W. H. Whyte's *The Organization Man* were significant because they

(A) criticized American conformity and the belief that economic growth would solve all problems
(B) challenged the American view that the Soviet Union was responsible for the Cold War
(C) advocated the nationalization of basic industries to increase production and profits
(D) were novels describing life among the "beat generation"
(E) urged a greater role for religion in American life and acceptance of Christian ethics by business executives

The Odd Couple

Reprinted by permission of Bill Mauldin and the Watkins/Loomis Agency.

40. Which of the following policies is the subject of the cartoon above?

(A) Vietnamization
(B) Containment
(C) Détente
(D) Interventionism
(E) Isolationism

41. The Halfway Covenant adopted by many Puritan congregations in the late seventeenth century did which of the following?

(A) Strengthened the Anglican church in New England.
(B) Undermined religious toleration in New England.
(C) Promoted Christianity among American Indians in New England.
(D) Eased the requirements for church membership.
(E) Encouraged belief in the doctrine of predestination.

GO ON TO THE NEXT PAGE

42. At the time of the American Revolution, the most valuable cash crop produced in the southern states was

(A) cotton
(B) corn
(C) sugar
(D) wheat
(E) tobacco

43. The War of 1812 resulted in

(A) an upsurge of nationalism in the United States
(B) the acquisition of territories from Great Britain
(C) the strengthening of Napoleon in Europe
(D) the large-scale emigration of Europeans to the United States
(E) the elimination of United States shipping from European waters

44. Which of the following provides the best evidence of Lincoln's talents as a political leader?

(A) His success in getting his Reconstruction policies passed by Congress
(B) His skill in getting the South to acknowledge responsibility for the outbreak of the Civil War
(C) His success in securing adoption of the Fifteenth Amendment
(D) His ability to keep his party relatively united despite its internal conflicts
(E) His success in winning public support for a military draft

45. All of the following situations contributed to agrarian discontent in the late nineteenth century EXCEPT:

(A) Cotton averaged 5.8 cents a pound between 1894 and 1898, whereas it had been 15.1 cents a pound between 1870 and 1873.
(B) Short-haul railroad rates rose 60 percent in the 1890's.
(C) Farmers borrowed more heavily from banks than they had before the Civil War.
(D) European countries raised duties on agricultural products in the 1880's.
(E) The wheat harvest in Europe declined 30 percent in 1897.

46. At the beginning of the twentieth century, critics labeled individuals who exploited workers, charged high prices, and bribed public officials as

(A) robber barons
(B) free silverites
(C) knights of labor
(D) captains of industry
(E) muckrakers

GO ON TO THE NEXT PAGE

DISTRIBUTION OF TOTAL PERSONAL INCOME AMONG THE UNITED STATES POPULATION, 1950–1970

Year	Poorest Fifth	Second Poorest Fifth	Middle Fifth	Second Wealthiest Fifth	Wealthiest Fifth
1950	3.1%	10.5%	17.3%	24.1%	45.0%
1960	3.2%	10.6%	17.6%	24.7%	44.0%
1970	3.6%	10.3%	17.2%	24.7%	44.1%

47. The chart above supports which of the following statements?

(A) Federal antipoverty programs in the 1960's had little impact on the national distribution of income.
(B) Between 1950 and 1970, children tended to remain in the same socioeconomic groups as their parents.
(C) The wealthiest people earned about the same amount of money in 1970 as they earned in 1960.
(D) The increased number of women in the labor force in the 1970's had little effect on the amount of total family income.
(E) The number of people in the "poorest fifth" remained about the same from 1950 to 1970.

GO ON TO THE NEXT PAGE

48. "One who breaks an unjust law must do so openly, lovingly, and with a willingness to accept the penalty. I submit that an individual who breaks the law that conscience tells him is unjust, and who willingly accepts the penalty of imprisonment in order to arouse the conscience of the community over its injustice, is in reality expressing the highest respect for the law."

    The quotation above most clearly expresses the views of

    (A) Malcolm X
    (B) Phyllis Schlafly
    (C) Martin Luther King, Jr.
    (D) Douglas MacArthur
    (E) Barry Goldwater

49. Rachel Carson's book *Silent Spring* was a

    (A) forestry manual
    (B) description of deaf people's perception of the changing seasons
    (C) protest against noise pollution
    (D) protest against overuse of chemical insecticides
    (E) protest against the Vietnam War

50. Which of the following was a consequence of President Lyndon B. Johnson's Great Society program?

    (A) An end to the urban population decline in the East and Midwest
    (B) Full employment until the end of the 1960's
    (C) The near elimination of urban and rural poverty
    (D) A major redistribution of the income tax burden
    (E) An increase in federal spending on social services

51. "For we must consider that we shall be as a city upon a hill, the eyes of all people are upon us. So that if we shall deal falsely with our God in this work we shall have undertaken, and so cause Him to withdraw His present help from us, we shall be made a story and a by-word through the world."

    The statement above was made by

    (A) Jonathan Edwards preaching to a congregation during the Great Awakening
    (B) John Winthrop defining the purpose of the Puritan colony
    (C) Thomas Jefferson on the adoption of the Declaration of Independence
    (D) William Penn defining the purpose of the Pennsylvania colony
    (E) Benjamin Franklin gathering support for the American Revolution

52. Which of the following best characterizes the Anti-Federalists?

    (A) They wanted a strong executive branch.
    (B) They were loyal supporters of the Crown.
    (C) They drew support primarily from rural areas.
    (D) They favored universal suffrage.
    (E) They favored rapid industrial development.

53. The Missouri Compromise was, in part, an effort to maintain the balance between the number of northerners and southerners in which of the following United States institutions?

    (A) The Senate
    (B) The House of Representatives
    (C) Congress
    (D) The Supreme Court
    (E) The electoral college

GO ON TO THE NEXT PAGE

54. Which of the following is true of the Black Codes of the Reconstruction era?

(A) They promised every adult male former slave "forty acres and a mule."
(B) They were Andrew Johnson's response to criticism that he was not doing enough for former slaves.
(C) They were the result of joint actions by scalawags and carpetbaggers in the southern states.
(D) They were passed by the Radical Republicans in Congress to ensure the rights of former slaves.
(E) They were passed by Southern state legislatures to restrict the rights of former slaves.

55. Advocates of a free silver policy argued that the free coinage of silver would

(A) increase the supply of money and end economic depressions
(B) facilitate free trade between countries
(C) limit the market power of farmers
(D) stabilize the value of gold in relation to silver
(E) increase the value of the dollar in relation to currencies of foreign countries

56. Skilled male workers felt threatened by all of the following changes that occurred in the United States economy between 1890 and 1920 EXCEPT the

(A) arrival of large numbers of immigrants from southern Europe, eastern Europe, and Mexico
(B) introduction of "scientific management" to increase factory production and lower labor costs
(C) growing power of major corporations
(D) increasingly widespread distribution of inexpensive consumer goods
(E) growing presence of women workers in industry

57. Which of the following was demonstrated by the outcome of the presidential election of 1928 ?

(A) The nation had become convinced of the futility of Prohibition.
(B) "Republican prosperity" was a persuasive campaign slogan.
(C) Ethnic and religious differences among Americans exerted little influence on their voting behavior.
(D) Great numbers of ethnic minority-group voters switched from the Democratic to the Republican Party.
(E) The Ku Klux Klan was the commanding force in United States politics during the 1920's.

58. "[The American] is intensely and cocksurely moral, but his morality and his self-interest are crudely identical. He is emotional and easy to scare, but his imagination cannot grasp an abstraction. He is a violent nationalist and patriot, but he admires rogues in office and always beats the tax-collector if he can. He is violently jealous of what he conceives to be his rights, but brutally disregardful of the other fellow's."

The author of the quotation above is the noted journalist and satirist

(A) Dorothy Thompson
(B) Lillian Hellman
(C) H. L. Mencken
(D) Will Rogers
(E) Pearl Buck

GO ON TO THE NEXT PAGE

59. Which of the following contributed most to ending the post-Second World War economic boom?

(A) Women leaving the workforce
(B) Development of the computer
(C) Consolidation of agriculture
(D) A shift in population to the Sunbelt
(E) The Arab oil embargo

60. The United States of the 1970's was characterized by an increase in all of the following EXCEPT

(A) computer technology and marketing
(B) an awareness of the rights of minorities
(C) the migration of Americans from the Frostbelt to the Sunbelt
(D) the strength of political party attachments
(E) the number of multinational corporations

61. Colonists in eighteenth-century South Carolina benefited from the knowledge of Africans about the cultivation of

(A) tobacco
(B) rice
(C) sugar
(D) cotton
(E) wheat

62. In the hundred years prior to 1776, which of the following had the LEAST influence on the emergence of the movement for independence in England's North American colonies?

(A) The control of money bills by colonial legislatures
(B) The long period of conflict between England and France
(C) The models provided by the autonomous governments of other English colonies
(D) The distance between England and its colonies
(E) Constitutional developments in England

63. "To maintain the existing relations between the two races, inhabiting that section of the Union, is indispensable to the peace and happiness of both. It cannot be subverted without drenching the country in blood, and extirpating one or the other of the races."

The statement above was most likely made by which of the following?

(A) John C. Calhoun to the United States Senate
(B) Frederick Douglass to the Anti-Slavery Society
(C) Daniel Webster to the South Carolina legislature
(D) John Brown at Harpers Ferry
(E) Abraham Lincoln in Springfield, Illinois

64. "In the late nineteenth century, the federal government followed a laissez-faire policy toward the economy."

A historian could argue against this thesis using all of the following pieces of evidence EXCEPT

(A) tariff laws protecting various industries from European competition
(B) laws granting land to the transcontinental railroad corporations
(C) government policy toward the unemployed during the depression of the 1890's
(D) the Bland-Allison Act of 1878 and the Sherman Silver Purchase Act of 1890
(E) the Interstate Commerce Act of 1887

65. Booker T. Washington encouraged Black people to pursue all of the following EXCEPT

(A) accommodation to White society
(B) racial solidarity
(C) industrial education
(D) economic self-help
(E) public political agitation

GO ON TO THE NEXT PAGE

66. "What we want to consider is, first, to make our employment more secure, and, secondly, to make wages more permanent. . . . I say the labor movement is a fixed fact. It has grown out of the necessities of the people, and, although some may desire to see it fail, still the labor movement will be found to have a strong lodgment in the hearts of the people, and we will go on until success has been achieved."

    The quotation above best reflects the philosophy of which of the following organizations around 1900 ?

    (A) Industrial Workers of the World
    (B) National Labor Union
    (C) American Federation of Labor
    (D) Congress of Industrial Organizations
    (E) Knights of Labor

67. Theodore Roosevelt issued his corollary to the Monroe Doctrine primarily because

    (A) Japan's actions in Manchuria had violated the "open door"
    (B) United States protection was needed by the colonies acquired in the Spanish-American War
    (C) the Filipino people revolted against United States rule
    (D) the financial difficulties of Caribbean nations threatened to bring about European intervention
    (E) the declining toll revenue from the Panama Canal threatened Panamanian stability

68. "The problem lay buried, unspoken, for many years in the minds of American women. It was a strange stirring, a sense of dissatisfaction, a yearning that women suffered in the middle of the twentieth century in the United States. Each suburban wife struggled with it alone. As she made the beds, shopped for groceries, ate peanut butter sandwiches with her children, chauffeured Cub Scouts and Brownies, she was afraid to ask even of herself the silent question—'Is this all?'"

    The passage above supports which of the following statements about women in the middle of the twentieth century?

    (A) Women were no longer interested in political activities.
    (B) Feminism tended to be a middle-class movement.
    (C) Feminism renewed interest in religion among women.
    (D) There were very few educational opportunities for women.
    (E) Most women supported the feminist movement.

69. "Government is not the solution to our problems. Government is the problem."

    The statement above was made by

    (A) John F. Kennedy, asserting that the government did not do enough for the people
    (B) Dwight D. Eisenhower, arguing that the government interfered with the military's operations
    (C) Jimmy Carter, claiming that the government was inefficient and unfair
    (D) Gerald Ford, charging that the government was corrupt
    (E) Ronald Reagan, contending that the government had taken on functions properly belonging to the private sector

GO ON TO THE NEXT PAGE

From Herblock At Large (Pantheon, 1987)

70. Which of the following best summarizes the idea expressed in the 1987 cartoon above?

(A) In the 1980's, budget and trade deficits and scandal undermined the international standing of the United States.
(B) President Reagan expected that an international economic summit would enable the United States to solve its financial problems.
(C) In the 1980's, the United States could not look to its economic partners for help in solving its economic problems.
(D) The economic problems of the United States in the 1980's resulted from European economic policies.
(E) Had it not been for the Iran-Contra scandal, the United States could have solved its economic problems.

GO ON TO THE NEXT PAGE

71. "No man was a warmer wisher for reconciliation than myself, before the fatal nineteenth of April 1775, but the moment the event of that day was made known, I rejected the hardened, sullen tempered Pharaoh of England for ever; and disdain the wretch, that with the pretended title of FATHER OF HIS PEOPLE, can unfeelingly hear of their slaughter, and composedly sleep with their blood upon his soul."

    The passage above comes from

    (A) the Declaration of Independence
    (B) *The Federalist* papers
    (C) *Letters from a Farmer in Pennsylvania*
    (D) the Virginia Resolves against the Stamp Act
    (E) *Common Sense*

72. Alexander Hamilton's plan for stimulating economic growth in the United States included all of the following EXCEPT

    (A) acquisition of additional territory
    (B) a protective tariff
    (C) expansion of manufacturing
    (D) establishment of a national bank
    (E) federal assumption of debts incurred by states during the Revolutionary War

73. The first American party system, which developed in the 1790's, maintained party discipline at the federal level primarily by means of

    (A) caucuses
    (B) nominating conventions
    (C) rotation in office
    (D) restrictive primaries
    (E) "pork barrel" legislation

74. Which of the following was true of the Jacksonian Democrats in the 1830's?

    (A) They were the minority party in the nation.
    (B) They opposed a national bank.
    (C) They supported South Carolina's nullification of the protective tariff.
    (D) They were stronger in New England than in the West.
    (E) They generally repudiated the ideas of the Jeffersonian Republicans.

75. "We hold these truths to be self-evident: that all men and women are created equal. . . . The history of mankind is a history of repeated injuries and usurpations on the part of man toward woman, having in direct object the establishment of an absolute tyranny over her."

    The quotation above is excerpted from the

    (A) Seneca Falls Declaration of Sentiments and Resolutions
    (B) United States Declaration of Independence
    (C) United States Constitution
    (D) Declaration of Rights and Grievances
    (E) Equal Rights Amendment (ERA)

76. Which of the following is true of the Pullman strike of 1894 ?

    (A) It brought a substantial portion of American railroads to a standstill.
    (B) It started when Pullman workers were fired after the Haymarket riot.
    (C) It was caused by grievances about unsafe working conditions.
    (D) It ended when the government forced management to settle with the union.
    (E) It ended when the courts issued a blanket injunction against management.

GO ON TO THE NEXT PAGE

77. "We must be the great arsenal of democracy. For this is an emergency as serious as war itself. We must apply ourselves to our task with the same resolution, the same sense of urgency, the same spirit of patriotism, and sacrifice, as we would show were we at war."

    The emergency to which the speaker refers was

    (A) German U-boat attacks in 1917
    (B) the Spanish Civil War in 1936
    (C) German warfare against Britain in 1940
    (D) the Berlin Blockade of 1948
    (E) the Cuban missile crisis of 1962

78. The legislation passed between 1935 and 1937 dealing with the role of the United States in future wars seemed to reflect a belief that

    (A) totalitarianism directly threatened the security of the United States
    (B) the United States should quickly intervene in any future world wars
    (C) the United States had made a mistake in not joining the League of Nations
    (D) the United States should not have become involved in the First World War
    (E) the United States should take a position of leadership in world affairs

79. Civil rights organizations in the 1950's and 1960's based their court suits primarily on the

    (A) five freedoms of the First Amendment
    (B) Fourteenth Amendment
    (C) Thirteenth Amendment
    (D) "necessary and proper" clause of the Constitution
    (E) Preamble to the Constitution

80. The Nixon administration differed from previous administrations in adopting which of the following Vietnam War policies?

    I. The bombing of North Vietnam
    II. The use of American combat troops
    III. The invasion of Cambodia
    IV. The mining of North Vietnamese harbors

    (A) I only
    (B) I and III only
    (C) II and III only
    (D) II and IV only
    (E) III and IV only

81. Which of the following political ideas or philosophies inspired the American revolutionaries of the eighteenth century?

    (A) Progressivism
    (B) Populism
    (C) Manifest Destiny
    (D) Republicanism
    (E) The Social Gospel

82. The first major nineteenth-century political conflict over the issue of slavery was settled by the

    (A) Alien and Sedition Acts
    (B) Kentucky and Virginia Resolutions
    (C) Missouri Compromise
    (D) Kansas-Nebraska Act
    (E) *Dred Scott* decision

GO ON TO THE NEXT PAGE

83. During the 1850's, Kansas became a significant issue for which of the following reasons?

(A) The territory was an important way station in the Underground Railroad.
(B) Northern and southern states vied to establish the first transcontinental railway through Kansas.
(C) Kansas served as a center for the Peoples (Populist) Party's agitation against railroads and banks.
(D) John Quincy Adams invoked the gag rule to prevent the discussion of slavery in the Senate.
(E) It led to a divisive debate over the expansion of slavery into the territories.

84. Which of the following was a significant movement in American literature during the late nineteenth century?

(A) Creationism
(B) Modernism
(C) Romanticism
(D) Classicism
(E) Realism

85. Edward Bellamy's *Looking Backward*, written in the 1880's, was a utopian reaction to which of the following?

(A) The disillusionment with an increasingly competitive and industrial society
(B) The plight of farmers who were driven off their land during the Great Depression
(C) The disillusionment of the planter aristocracy in the post-Civil War era
(D) The growing number of immigrants who regretted leaving their homes in Europe
(E) Increasing concerns over the growth and power of labor unions in the railroad industry

86. The Harlem Renaissance refers to

(A) Marcus Garvey's "back to Africa" crusade
(B) the reemergence of the Ku Klux Klan as a force in American politics
(C) writers and artists in New York who expressed pride in their African American culture
(D) American expatriate writers living in Paris who wrote critically of American society
(E) the political success of the Democratic Party in northern urban neighborhoods

87. The Federal Reserve Act of 1913 established a

(A) single central bank like the Bank of England
(B) method of insuring bank deposits against loss
(C) system to guarantee the continued existence of the gold standard
(D) system of local national banks
(E) system of district banks coordinated by a central board

88. The Korean War and the Vietnam War differed in that only one involved

(A) a formal declaration of war
(B) a communist-led government
(C) troops under United Nations auspices
(D) Soviet arms support to one of the belligerents
(E) United States air and ground forces

GO ON TO THE NEXT PAGE

From Herblock On All Fronts (New American Library, 1980)

89. Which of the following best summarizes the idea expressed in the cartoon above?

(A) Most people are too dependent on computers in their daily lives.
(B) The amount of information available via computers is so overwhelming that people are no longer able to use the information effectively.
(C) Individual privacy is being threatened by the computerization of personal information.
(D) Many industries in the United States are threatened with significant layoffs as computers replace workers.
(E) People in the United States have been more reluctant to begin using computers than have people in other parts of the world.

GO ON TO THE NEXT PAGE

90. Which of the following is an accurate statement about the Equal Rights Amendment to the Constitution proposed in the 1970's?

    (A) It was opposed primarily by those who feared a loss of political power.
    (B) It guaranteed equal opportunity for women in the workplace.
    (C) It became a part of the Constitution in 1978.
    (D) It represented the first effort to enfranchise women.
    (E) It failed to gain the necessary votes for ratification within the constitutional time limit.

STOP

IF YOU FINISH BEFORE TIME IS CALLED, YOU MAY CHECK YOUR WORK ON THIS TEST ONLY.
DO NOT TURN TO ANY OTHER TEST IN THIS BOOK.

How to Score the SAT Subject Test in United States History

When you take an actual SAT Subject Test in United States History, your answer sheet will be "read" by a scanning machine that will record your responses to each question. Then a computer will compare your answers with the correct answers and produce your raw score. You get one point for each correct answer. For each wrong answer, you lose one-fourth of a point. Questions you omit (and any for which you mark more than one answer) are not counted. This raw score is converted to a scaled score that is reported to you and to the colleges you specify.

Worksheet 1. Finding Your Raw Test Score

STEP 1: Table A lists the correct answers for all the questions on the Subject Test in United States History that is reproduced in this book. It also serves as a worksheet for you to calculate your raw score.

- Compare your answers with those given in the table.
- Put a check in the column marked "Right" if your answer is correct.
- Put a check in the column marked "Wrong" if your answer is incorrect.
- Leave both columns blank if you omitted the question.

STEP 2: Count the number of right answers.

Enter the total here: ________________

STEP 3: Count the number of wrong answers.

Enter the total here: ________________

STEP 4: Multiply the number of wrong answers by .250.

Enter the product here: ______________

STEP 5: Subtract the result obtained in Step 4 from the total you obtained in Step 2.

Enter the result here: ______________

STEP 6: Round the number obtained in Step 5 to the nearest whole number.

Enter the result here: ______________

The number you obtained in Step 6 is your raw score.

Table A

Answers to the Subject Test in United States History, Form 3WAC2, and Percentage of Students Answering Each Question Correctly

Question Number	Correct Answer	Right	Wrong	Percentage of Students Answering the Question Correctly*	Question Number	Correct Answer	Right	Wrong	Percentage of Students Answering the Question Correctly*
1	A			71	33	A			43
2	C			85	34	C			38
3	B			89	35	E			42
4	C			64	36	C			46
5	B			92	37	D			64
6	B			80	38	B			64
7	E			62	39	A			32
8	A			77	40	C			29
9	C			74	41	D			37
10	C			77	42	E			54
11	D			72	43	A			52
12	C			61	44	D			37
13	C			61	45	E			33
14	B			77	46	A			57
15	D			80	47	A			32
16	C			74	48	C			48
17	E			69	49	D			30
18	D			83	50	E			57
19	A			69	51	B			39
20	D			53	52	C			47
21	A			41	53	A			28
22	B			55	54	E			63
23	C			71	55	A			49
24	E			90	56	D			39
25	D			56	57	B			32
26	B			53	58	C			19
27	A			83	59	E			27
28	E			36	60	D			29
29	B			57	61	B			15
30	C			60	62	C			23
31	A			31	63	A			18
32	C			43	64	C			25

Table A continued on next page

Table A continued from previous page

Question Number	Correct Answer	Right	Wrong	Percentage of Students Answering the Question Correctly*	Question Number	Correct Answer	Right	Wrong	Percentage of Students Answering the Question Correctly*
65	E			41	78	D			30
66	C			26	79	B			26
67	D			29	80	E			11
68	B			32	81	D			23
69	E			29	82	C			33
70	A			40	83	E			64
71	E			38	84	E			35
72	A			36	85	A			23
73	A			28	86	C			82
74	B			36	87	E			16
75	A			31	88	C			18
76	A			24	89	C			68
77	C			12	90	E			24

* These percentages are based on an analysis of the answer sheets of a representative sample of 8,509 students who took the original form of this test in December 2000, and whose mean score was 534. They may be used as an indication of the relative difficulty of a particular question. Each percentage may also be used to predict the likelihood that a typical SAT Subject Test in United States History candidate will answer that question correctly on this edition of the test.

Finding Your Scaled Score

When you take SAT Subject Tests, the scores sent to the colleges you specify are reported on the College Board scale, which ranges from 200–800. You can convert your practice test score to a scaled score by using Table B. To find your scaled score, locate your raw score in the left-hand column of Table B; the corresponding score in the right-hand column is your scaled score. For example, a raw score of 39 on this particular edition of the Subject Test in United States History corresponds to a scaled score of 560.

Raw scores are converted to scaled scores to ensure that a score earned on any one edition of a particular Subject Test is comparable to the same scaled score earned on any other edition of the same Subject Test. Because some editions of the tests may be slightly easier or more difficult than others, College Board scaled scores are adjusted so that they indicate the same level of performance regardless of the edition of the test taken and the ability of the group that takes it. Thus, for example, a score of 400 on one edition of a test taken at a particular administration indicates the same level of achievement as a score of 400 on a different edition of the test taken at a different administration.

When you take the SAT Subject Tests during a national administration, your scores are likely to differ somewhat from the scores you obtain on the tests in this book. People perform at different levels at different times for reasons unrelated to the tests themselves. The precision of any test is also limited because it represents only a sample of all the possible questions that could be asked.

Table B

Scaled Score Conversion Table Subject Test in United States History (Form 3WAC2)					
Raw Score	Scaled Score	Raw Score	Scaled Score	Raw Score	Scaled Score
90	800	52	630	14	430
89	800	51	630	13	430
88	800	50	620	12	420
87	800	49	620	11	420
86	800	48	610	10	410
85	800	47	610	9	410
84	800	46	600	8	400
83	800	45	600	7	400
82	800	44	590	6	390
81	800	43	590	5	390
80	800	42	580	4	380
79	800	41	580	3	380
78	790	40	570	2	370
77	780	39	560	1	370
76	780	38	560	0	360
75	770	37	550	-1	360
74	760	36	550	-2	350
73	750	35	540	-3	350
72	750	34	540	-4	340
71	740	33	530	-5	330
70	730	32	530	-6	330
69	730	31	520	-7	320
68	720	30	520	-8	310
67	710	29	510	-9	310
66	710	28	510	-10	300
65	700	27	500	-11	290
64	700	26	490	-12	290
63	690	25	490	-13	280
62	680	24	480	-14	270
61	680	23	480	-15	270
60	670	22	470	-16	260
59	670	21	470	-17	260
58	660	20	460	-18	250
57	660	19	460	-19	250
56	650	18	450	-20	240
55	650	17	450	-21	230
54	640	16	440	-22	230
53	640	15	440		

How Did You Do on the Subject Test in United States History?

After you score your test and analyze your performance, think about the following questions:

Did you run out of time before reaching the end of the test?

If so, you may need to pace yourself better. For example, maybe you spent too much time on one or two hard questions. A better approach might be to skip the ones you can't answer right away and try answering all the questions that remain on the test. Then if there's time, go back to the questions you skipped.

Did you take a long time reading the directions?

You will save time when you take the test by learning the directions to the Subject Test in United States History ahead of time. Each minute you spend reading directions during the test is a minute that you could use to answer questions.

How did you handle questions you were unsure of?

If you were able to eliminate one or more of the answer choices as wrong and guess from the remaining ones, your approach probably worked to your advantage. On the other hand, making haphazard guesses or omitting questions without trying to eliminate choices could cost you valuable points.

How difficult were the questions for you compared with other students who took the test?

Table A shows you how difficult the multiple-choice questions were for the group of students who took this test during its national administration. The right-hand column gives the percentage of students that answered each question correctly.

A question answered correctly by almost everyone in the group is obviously an easier question. For example, 85 percent of the students answered question 2 correctly. But only 19 percent answered question 58 correctly.

Keep in mind that these percentages are based on just one group of students. They would probably be different with another group of students taking the test.

If you missed several easier questions, go back and try to find out why: Did the questions cover material you haven't yet reviewed? Did you misunderstand the directions?

Chapter 3

World History

Purpose

The Subject Test in World History measures your understanding of the development of major world cultures and your use of historical techniques, including the application and weighing of evidence and the ability to interpret and generalize. The test covers all historical fields:

- political and diplomatic
- intellectual and cultural
- social and economic

Format

This one-hour test consists of 95 multiple-choice questions. Many of the questions are global in nature, dealing with issues and trends that have significance throughout the modern world.

Content

The questions test your:

- knowledge of important historical information
- familiarity with terms commonly used in the social sciences
- understanding of cause-and-effect relationships
- knowledge of geography necessary for understanding major historical developments
- grasp of concepts essential to historical analysis
- capacity to interpret artistic materials
- ability to assess quotations from speeches, documents, and other published materials
- ability to use historical knowledge in interpreting data based on maps, graphs, and charts

Chronological Material Covered	Approximate Percentage of Test
Prehistory and Civilizations to 500 Common Era (C.E.)*	25
500–1500 C.E.	20
1500–1900 C.E.	25
1900 C.E.–Present	20
Cross-chronological	10
Geographical Material Covered	
Global or Comparative	25
Europe	25
Africa	10
Southwest Asia	10
South and Southeast Asia	10
East Asia	10
The Americas	10

* The SAT Subject Test in World History uses the chronological designations B.C.E. (before common era) and C.E. (common era). These labels correspond to B.C. (before Christ) and A.D. (anno Domini), which are used in some world history textbooks.

How to Prepare

You can prepare academically for the test by taking a one-year comprehensive course in world or global history at the college-preparatory level and through independent reading of materials on historic topics. Because secondary school programs differ, the Subject Test in World History is not tied to any one textbook or particular course of study. Familiarize yourself with the directions in advance. The directions in this book are identical to those that appear on the test.

Score

The total score is reported on the 200-to-800 scale.

Sample Questions

All questions on the Subject Test in World History are multiple choice, requiring you to choose the BEST response from five choices. The following sample questions illustrate the types of questions on the test, their range of difficulty, and the abilities they measure. Questions may be presented as separate items or in sets based on quotations, maps, pictures, graphs, or tables.

Directions: Each of the questions or incomplete statements below is followed by five suggested answers or completions. Select the one that is best in each case and then fill in the corresponding circle on the answer sheet.

Note: The World History Test uses the chronological designation B.C.E. (before common era) and C.E. (common era). These labels correspond to B.C. (before Christ) and A.D. (anno Domini), which are used in some world history textbooks.

Some questions require you to know social science terms, factual cause-and-effect relationships, geography, and other data necessary for understanding major historical developments. Questions 1 and 2 fall into this category.

1. Which of the following was immediately responsible for precipitating the French Revolution?
   (A) The threat of national bankruptcy
   (B) An attack upon the privileges of the middle class
   (C) The desire of the nobility for a written constitution
   (D) The suffering of the peasantry
   (E) The king's attempt to restore feudalism

Choice (A) is the correct answer to question 1. To answer this question, you need to recall the circumstances that led in May 1789 to the first meeting of the French Estates-General in over a century and a half, an event that arrayed the Third Estate against the nobility and Louis XVI in the first stage of a political struggle that was to evolve into the French Revolution. With his debt-ridden government brought to a halt, the king, by mid-1788, was left with no other recourse than a promise to convene the Estates-General in the months ahead.

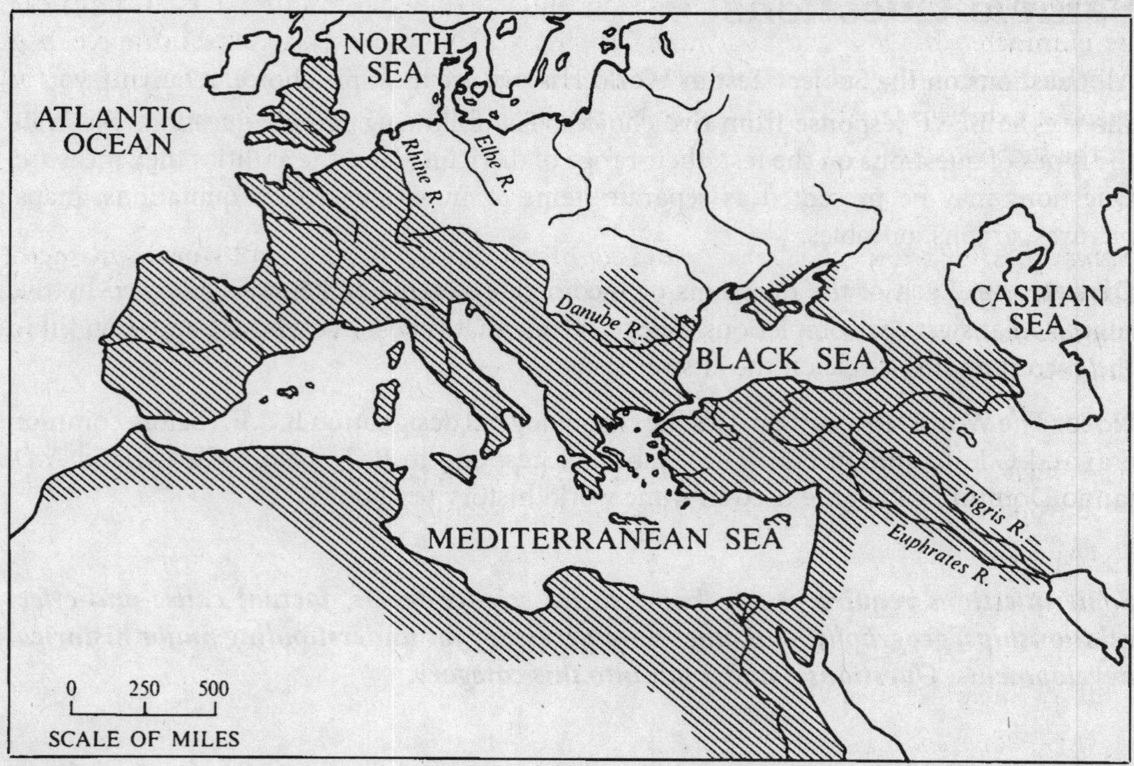

2. The shaded area in the map above shows the extent of which of the following?
   (A) Irrigation agriculture in 1000 B.C.E.
   (B) Greek colonization in 550 B.C.E.
   (C) Alexander the Great's empire in 323 B.C.E.
   (D) The Roman Empire in 117 C.E.
   (E) The Byzantine Empire in 565 C.E.

Choice (D) is the correct answer to question 2. This question tests your knowledge of both history and geography. To answer it you must know something about the extent to which irrigated farming was practiced in Africa, Europe, and Southwest Asia three thousand years ago, and you need to have a general idea of the extent of the territory controlled by four major ancient civilizations at specific points in time. Choice (A) can be eliminated because irrigation in this early period would have been confined to the regions along the major rivers of the Middle East and Southwest Asia. Choice (B) can be eliminated because Greek colonization was confined primarily to the eastern Mediterranean and did not extend as far north in Europe as shown in the shaded areas of the map. Choice (C) can be eliminated because Alexander the Great's empire did not extend into either the western Mediterranean or northwestern Europe. Choice (E) can be eliminated because the Byzantine Empire, with its capital in Constantinople, was confined primarily to the eastern Mediterranean area. Only choice (D) outlines the greatest extent of territory controlled by the Roman Empire under the Emperor Trajan in the second century C.E.

Some questions test your understanding of concepts essential to history and social science, your capacity to interpret artistic materials, and your ability to assess quotations from speeches, documents, and other published materials. Questions 3–6 fall into this category.

3. Which of the following was introduced into the diet of Europeans only after European contact with the Americas in the fifteenth century?
   (A) Tea
   (B) Rice
   (C) Cinnamon
   (D) Sugar
   (E) Potatoes

Choice (E) is the correct answer to question 3. It is correct because the potato is native to the Peruvian-Bolivian Andes and, after its "discovery" by the Europeans in the fifteenth century, became a staple of the European diet. The potato is now a major food crop worldwide. To answer this question you need to have some basic information about what has come to be known as the "Columbian Exchange," i.e., the enormous biological transfer that occurred as a result of the fifteenth- and sixteenth-century European voyages of discovery. Choice (A) can be ruled out because tea comes from China, not from the Americas, and was not widely used in Europe until the mid-seventeenth century. Choice (B) can be eliminated because the origin of rice culture has been traced to India. Rice was introduced into southern Europe in medieval times. Choice (C) can be eliminated because the cinnamon tree is native to South Asia and, like rice, has been known in Europe since medieval times. Choice (D) can be eliminated because sugarcane originated in what is now known as New Guinea, followed human migration routes from Southeast Asia through Southwest Asia to Europe and, although rare and expensive, was known to the European aristocracy in medieval times.

Giraudon/Art Resource

4. The nineteenth-century wood block print above is associated with the culture of

    (A) Japan
    (B) India
    (C) Iran
    (D) Myanmar (Burma)
    (E) Thailand

Choice (A) is the correct answer to question 4. The scene depicted in this dramatic picture is world-famous. Although the spatial arrangement and perspective are generally East Asian and the title at the upper left-hand corner is written in Chinese characters, there are a number of characteristics that identify the picture as Japanese. The dramatic subject matter, with Mount Fuji in the background, is Japanese. In addition, colorful wood-block prints depicting famous scenery, beautiful women, warriors, and well-known theater subjects were popular in Japan from the seventeenth to the nineteenth centuries because they were widely affordable. This work is by the nineteenth-century artist Hokusai.

Questions 5 and 6 refer to the following passage.

> *We have heard that in your country opium is prohibited with the utmost strictness and severity—this is a strong proof that you know full well how hurtful it is to humankind. Since then you do not permit it to injure your own country, you ought not to have the injurious drug transferred to another country, and above all others, how much less to the Middle Kingdom!*

5. The author of the diplomatic dispatch above lived in which of the following countries?
   (A) Ghana
   (B) The Netherlands
   (C) Iran
   (D) China
   (E) Germany

Choice (D) is the correct answer to question 5. The above discussion of the forced importation of opium suggests China's struggle against Great Britain, culminating in the Opium War of the mid-nineteenth century. The tone of the dispatch, expressing indignation at Great Britain's flaunting of Chinese law, is consistent with China's concern over growing opium addiction in China and with Chinese resistance to the British. From your study of China you will also remember that the Chinese used to refer to their country as the Middle Kingdom.

6. The country which went to war in the nineteenth century over the issue raised in the dispatch was
   (A) France
   (B) Egypt
   (C) Great Britain
   (D) India
   (E) Japan

Choice (C) is the correct answer to question 6. Great Britain was expanding its Asian trade and needed a product to exchange for Chinese goods. Opium from India was Great Britain's answer to this dilemma. The dispatch above was sent by a representative of the Chinese emperor to Queen Victoria shortly before the Opium War (1839–1842), in which China was defeated by the British and therefore was not able to enforce its prohibition against the importation of opium.

Questions posed in the negative, like question 7, account for at most 25 percent of the test questions. Variations of this question format employ the capitalized words NOT or LEAST, as in the following examples: "Which of the following is NOT true?" "Which of the following is LEAST likely to occur?"

7. All of the following are "Pillars of Islam" EXCEPT
   (A) giving alms for the support of society's poor
   (B) praying five times a day in the direction of Mecca
   (C) fasting for one month of the year
   (D) making a pilgrimage to Mecca at least once during a lifetime
   (E) attending mosque prayers daily

Choice (E) is the correct answer to question 7. This question asks you to identify the exception in a series of true statements. In other words, you are being asked to locate the false answer among the five options. To answer this question, you need to draw on your knowledge of Islam. Choices (A) through (D) are true because they refer to four of the five "Pillars of Islam." Choice (E) is false because Muslims are not required to attend mosque prayers daily. The fifth pillar actually is the "profession of faith."

Questions based on graphs, charts, or cartoons require you to use historical knowledge in interpreting information. Questions 8–10 fall into this category.

ANNUAL PRODUCTION OF STEEL
(in thousands of metric tons)

Year				
1865	225	13	97	41
1870	286	68	169	83
1875	723	396	370	258
1880	1,320	1,267	660	388
1885	2,020	1,739	1,202	533
1890	3,637	4,346	2,161	566
1895	3,444	6,212	3,941	899
1900	5,130	10,382	6,645	1,565
1905	5,983	20,354	10,066	2,110
1910	6,374	26,512	13,698	3,506

8. Read from left to right, the column headings for the table above should be
   (A) Great Britain, United States, Germany, and France
   (B) Italy, Great Britain, Russia, and Germany
   (C) Germany, Great Britain, Russia, and France
   (D) Great Britain, United States, France, and Germany
   (E) Germany, Russia, Great Britain, and United States

Choice (A) is the correct answer to question 8. To answer this question, you need to know in which country the Industrial Revolution began and which other countries caught up early or late. Great Britain was industrialized by 1850, the United States and Germany were next, and France, Italy, and Russia followed later in the nineteenth century.

Questions containing charts and graphs require careful study and therefore may be more time-consuming than other types of questions. Remember to budget your time accordingly.

Questions 9 and 10 are based on the August 1914 *Punch* cartoon below.

BRAVO, BELGIUM!

9. The “No Thoroughfare” sign in the cartoon is a reference to
   (A) an international treaty guaranteeing the neutrality of Belgium
   (B) the heavy defensive fortifications built by Belgium in the preceding decade
   (C) a bilateral nonaggression pact between Belgium and Germany
   (D) an alliance between Belgium and France
   (E) the treacherous, swampy terrain on the Belgian-German border

Choice (A) is the correct answer to question 9. In this question set you are asked to interpret a British political cartoon published during the tense diplomatic period before the outbreak of the First World War. Choice (A) refers to treaties signed by the Great Powers in 1839 guaranteeing the neutrality of Belgium and Luxembourg in the event of war.

10. This cartoon is a comment on Germany's attempt to
   (A) acquire valuable mineral resources in Belgium
   (B) invade France through Belgium
   (C) force Belgium to repeal tariffs on German goods
   (D) intimidate Belgium into signing a military alliance with Germany
   (E) pressure Belgium into withdrawing from the Triple Alliance

Choice (B) is the correct answer to question 10. This question focuses on Belgium's resistance to the more powerful Germany's threat of aggression if Belgium, situated between Germany and France, will not give transit to German troops.

Other types of questions rely on knowledge of historical methodology or a grasp of important issues still affecting the world today. Questions 11 and 12 fall into this category.

11. Which of the following statements would be most difficult for historians to prove true or false?
   (A) There was little organized education in Europe during the Middle Ages.
   (B) Greece contributed more to Western civilization than Rome.
   (C) The invention of the steam engine influenced the way people lived.
   (D) Russia is territorially the largest country in the world.
   (E) The tourist industry in Europe increased markedly after the Second World War.

Choice (B) is the correct answer to question 11. The assertion that Greece's contribution to Western civilization was greater than Rome's requires the most justification. In a methodology question such as the one above, you must make the distinction between statements that are verifiable by fact and statements that are based on judgments. The latter are more difficult than the former to prove true or false because they are evaluations. In this question, choice (B) is the most opinionated of the statements and therefore the one most difficult to prove or disprove.

12. The term "green revolution" refers to

(A) protests against the placement of nuclear weapons in Europe

(B) ecological changes in the ocean because of algae growth

(C) increased agricultural output resulting from development of hybrid seeds and chemical fertilizers

(D) expanded irrigation farming made possible by the construction of large dams

(E) thinning of the atmospheric ozone layer resulting in changes in the growing season

Choice (C) is the correct answer to question 12. To answer this question, you need to know about modern scientific breakthroughs in agricultural research that have allowed countries like India, formerly subject to terrible famines, to become self-sufficient in grain production.

World History Test

Practice Helps

The test that follows is an actual, recently administered SAT Subject Test in World History. To get an idea of what it's like to take this test, practice under conditions that are much like those of an actual test administration.

- Set aside an hour when you can take the test uninterrupted. Make sure you complete the test in one sitting.
- Sit at a desk or table with no other books or papers. Dictionaries, other books, or notes are not allowed in the test room.
- Tear out an answer sheet from the back of this book and fill it in just as you would on the day of the test. One answer sheet can be used for up to three Subject Tests.
- Read the instructions that precede the practice test. During the actual administration, you will be asked to read them before answering test questions.
- Time yourself by placing a clock or kitchen timer in front of you.
- After you finish the practice test, read the sections "How to Score the SAT Subject Test in World History" and "How Did You Do on the Subject Test in World History?"
- The appearance of the answer sheet in this book may differ from the answer sheet you see on test day.

WORLD HISTORY TEST

The top portion of the section of the answer sheet that you will use in taking the World History Test must be filled in exactly as shown in the illustration below. Note carefully that you have to do all of the following on your answer sheet.

1. Print WORLD HISTORY on the line under the words "Subject Test (print)."

2. In the shaded box labeled "Test Code" fill in four circles:

   —Fill in circle 1 in the row labeled V.
   —Fill in circle 7 in the row labeled W.
   —Fill in circle 3 in the row labeled X.
   —Fill in circle D in the row labeled Y.

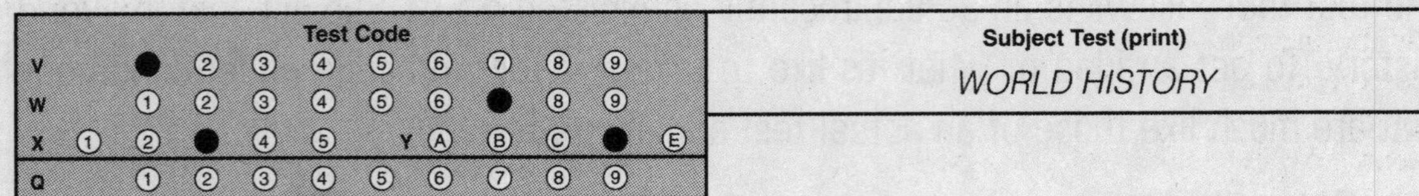

3. Please answer the three questions below by filling in the appropriate circles in the row labeled Q on the answer sheet. <u>The information you provide is for statistical purposes only and will not affect your score on the test</u>.

<u>Question I</u>

How many semesters of world history, world cultures, or European history have you taken from grade 9 to the present? (If you are taking a course this semester, count it as a full semester.) Fill in only <u>one</u> circle of circles 1-2.

- One semester or less —Fill in circle 1.
- Two semesters or more —Fill in circle 2.

<u>Question II</u>

For the courses in world history, world cultures, or European history you have taken, which of the following geographical areas did you study? Fill in <u>all</u> of the circles that apply.

- Africa —Fill in circle 3.
- Asia —Fill in circle 4.
- Europe —Fill in circle 5.
- Latin America —Fill in circle 6.
- Middle East —Fill in circle 7.

<u>Question III</u>

How recently have you studied world history, world cultures, or European history?

- I am currently enrolled in or have just completed such a course. —Fill in circle 8.
- I have not studied this subject for 6 months or more. —Fill in circle 9.

When the supervisor gives the signal, turn the page and begin the World History Test. There are 100 numbered circles on the answer sheet and 95 questions in the World History Test. Therefore, use only circles 1 to 95 for recording your answers.

WORLD HISTORY TEST

Directions: Each of the questions or incomplete statements below is followed by five suggested answers or completions. Select the one that is best in each case and then fill in the corresponding circle on the answer sheet.

Note: The World History Test uses the chronological designations B.C.E. (before common era) and C.E. (common era). These labels correspond to B.C. (before Christ) and A.D. (anno Domini), which are used in some world history textbooks.

1. Which of the following was true of both Greece and China in the period around 500 B.C.E.?

(A) Both fostered vibrant philosophical schools that debated the human condition.
(B) Both were threatened by more powerful neighboring civilizations.
(C) Both experienced economic revolutions brought on by the discovery of iron.
(D) Both underwent social revolutions that led to the seclusion of women.
(E) Both suffered from overpopulation that led to class warfare and massive emigration.

2. Which of the following is true of the epic poems the *Mahabharata*, the *Iliad*, and the *Tales of the Heike* ?

(A) All three were influenced by Chinese literary forms.
(B) All three stress the exploits of a warrior elite.
(C) All three were written down at first and later transmitted orally.
(D) All three stress humanity's independence from the influence of the gods.
(E) Historians have conclusively identified the authors of the three works.

3. Which of the following statements about the effects of Muhammad's teaching is true?

(A) Islam initially attracted many followers, but gradually became less popular.
(B) Muhammad believed that social differences needed to be preserved, which encouraged divisions in society.
(C) Islam affected every aspect of life and encouraged unity among converts with widely diverse backgrounds.
(D) Muhammad believed that wealth should be renounced; thus Islam did not attempt to expand.
(E) Muslims set up a complex priesthood that mediated the contact between Allah and individual believers.

4. The military campaigns of the Huns under Attila contributed to which of the following?

(A) The introduction of the bubonic plague to Asia
(B) The fall of the western Roman Empire
(C) The division of Charlemagne's empire
(D) The introduction of horse domestication into western Europe
(E) The defeat of the Muslims in Spain

4BAC

GO ON TO THE NEXT PAGE

5. After the fall of the Han dynasty, the nomadic peoples who invaded China did which of the following?
   (A) They attempted to restore the Han dynasty to power.
   (B) They tried unsuccessfully to convert the Chinese to Islam.
   (C) They outlawed the use of the Chinese language by governing officials.
   (D) They launched an invasion of Japan.
   (E) They adopted Chinese culture and customs.

6. Mahavira and Buddha were similar in that both
   (A) were successful military leaders who conquered most of India
   (B) resisted the spread of Islam in India
   (C) were theorists who pioneered new mathematical concepts
   (D) led religious movements that challenged the social order of Hinduism
   (E) were martyred for their beliefs

7. "Warfare in nineteenth-century southern Africa was revolutionized with the development of the short, stabbing spear, the body shield, and a tactical formation known as the ox's horns."

   The above describes innovations developed by the
   (A) Zulu
   (B) Xhosa
   (C) Sotho
   (D) Shona
   (E) Ibo

8. All of the following are central to the practice of Islam EXCEPT
   (A) Observation of Ramadan through fasting
   (B) Monotheism
   (C) Prayer five times a day facing Mecca
   (D) Making a pilgrimage to Mecca at least once
   (E) Realistic representations of people in art

9. Which of the following is a pair of neighboring countries both of which had acquired the capability of exploding nuclear weapons by the late 1990's?
   (A) Argentina and Chile
   (B) Mexico and the United States
   (C) The Czech Republic and Germany
   (D) India and Pakistan
   (E) North Korea and South Korea

10. Which of the following best describes the economic strategy of the Soviet Union under Stalin?
    (A) Development of a mixed economy
    (B) Creation of a landowning peasant class
    (C) Production for export
    (D) Centralized economic planning
    (E) Government encouragement of free enterprise

11. Historiography is
    (A) a single, accurate account of events in past time
    (B) the study of how historical accounts are produced
    (C) a chronological chart of historical events
    (D) a historical account based only on written records
    (E) the official record of past events, usually produced by a government

12. Which of the following describes the primary role of the scholar-gentry in imperial China?
    (A) The mainstay of the imperial bureaucracy
    (B) The development of political revolution
    (C) The education of China's peasantry
    (D) The dissemination of European culture in China
    (E) The advancement of engineering and agricultural science

GO ON TO THE NEXT PAGE

13. The Japanese victory in the Russo-Japanese War demonstrated to other non-Western peoples that

    (A) successful modernization was not a strictly Western phenomenon
    (B) countries that held traditional values could not defeat a European power
    (C) passive resistance could be effectively employed in the defeat of a European power
    (D) the distance between Asia and Europe would make Asian industrialization difficult
    (E) further expansion by Russia in Asia was inevitable

14. The defeat of the Umayyads by the Abbasids in 750 C.E. led to the relocation of the caliphate and of the primary center of Islamic culture from

    (A) Mecca to Medina
    (B) Jerusalem to Cairo
    (C) Damascus to Baghdad
    (D) Constantinople to Beirut
    (E) Córdoba to Alexandria

15. Which of the following is an example of an ancient megalithic structure?

    (A) Stonehenge
    (B) The Coliseum
    (C) Angkor Wat
    (D) The Acropolis
    (E) Great Zimbabwe

16. The Aztec viewed the Toltec as

    (A) barbarians who lacked culture
    (B) slaves, fit only for conquest
    (C) the givers of civilization
    (D) heretics who practiced a forbidden religion
    (E) the greatest rivals to the Aztec dominance of the valley of Mexico

17. The terms Indo-European and Bantu were created to describe

    (A) biological races
    (B) language groups
    (C) religious movements
    (D) artistic styles
    (E) ancient empires

18. According to one theory of state formation, large states first developed in river valleys because

    (A) coordination of large-scale irrigation projects created the need for more complex organizations
    (B) the healthier climates of river valleys allowed large populations to develop there
    (C) river valleys provided the best natural defensive barriers for growing states
    (D) river valleys were the only sources of drinking water large enough to support concentrated populations
    (E) river valleys were the best sources of metal ores for weapons and tools

19. In England in the late nineteenth century it was socially acceptable for young working-class women to take jobs as domestic servants because

    (A) many of their employers allowed them to do volunteer work among the urban poor on evenings and weekends
    (B) this work was believed to contribute to habits of hard work, cleanliness, and obedience, which were seen as good preparation for marriage
    (C) such jobs provided opportunities for them to meet and marry men from higher social classes
    (D) the training they received in household management provided them with skills needed for later careers in business
    (E) residence in middle- or upper-class homes contributed to their political education

20. In Chinese history, the phrase "Mandate of Heaven" refers to the

    (A) divine selection of China as the holiest place in the world
    (B) obligation of each individual to obey religious teachings
    (C) divine favor enjoyed by wise and benevolent rulers
    (D) Chinese version of the Ten Commandments
    (E) most important of the Confucian writings

GO ON TO THE NEXT PAGE

WORLD HISTORY TEST—*Continued*

21. Which of the following is the commonly accepted meaning of the term *Homo sapiens* ?

(A) The southern apes
(B) The upright-walking humans
(C) The consciously thinking humans
(D) The animal with a large brain
(E) The missing link

22. In their original form, all of the following major religions focused on humanity's relationship to a god or gods EXCEPT

(A) Buddhism
(B) Christianity
(C) Hinduism
(D) Islam
(E) Judaism

23. Social Darwinism is most closely associated with the idea that

(A) government should provide support for disadvantaged members of society
(B) competition is natural to society
(C) revolution is inevitable
(D) imperialistic expansion will increase economic pressures on citizens
(E) technological development will decrease the gap between rich and poor

24. Which of the following led Great Britain and France to declare war on Germany in 1939 ?

(A) Hitler established a fascist dictatorship in Germany.
(B) Germany occupied France.
(C) Germany annexed Austria.
(D) Germany invaded Poland.
(E) Germany passed anti-Semitic laws.

25. The pyramids in ancient Egypt were built to function primarily as

(A) temples
(B) tombs
(C) watchtowers
(D) astronomical observatories
(E) sundials

26. In the Hindu caste system, members of the Brahman caste originally served as

(A) priests
(B) farmers
(C) warriors
(D) merchants
(E) herders

27. Which of the following is attributed to Alexander the Great?

(A) Three centuries of political stability in the Middle East
(B) The establishment of the basic political forms of the Roman Empire
(C) The concept of kingship limited by elected representatives
(D) The spread of Greek cultural forms into western Asia
(E) The extension of property and inheritance rights to women

28. Prior to the Roman conquests of Gaul, Spain, and Britain, these areas were inhabited primarily by

(A) Celts
(B) Goths
(C) Greeks
(D) Mongols
(E) Scythians

29. Which of the following major ancient civilizations did NOT originate along a river valley?

(A) Chinese
(B) Indian
(C) Egyptian
(D) Mesopotamian
(E) Greek

GO ON TO THE NEXT PAGE

30. Which of the following changes best characterizes the commercial revolution that accelerated during the 1400's and continued throughout the Age of Exploration?

(A) The growth of capitalism as an economic system
(B) The shift of the center of trading from the Mediterranean Sea to the Indian Ocean
(C) The development and application of communism
(D) The decline in the production of consumer goods
(E) The loss of overseas empires by western European nations

31. The words "alchemy," "algebra," "assassin," "sugar," "zenith," and "zero" entered the English language as a result of the influence on Europe of which of the following cultures?

(A) Arabic
(B) Turkish
(C) Indian
(D) Aramaic
(E) Hebrew

32. The principal development during the Neolithic Age was the

(A) disappearance of the Neanderthals
(B) invention of writing
(C) beginning of metallurgy
(D) domestication of animals and plants
(E) appearance of craft specialization

33. Cultivation of which of the following crops most drastically changed the geographical distribution of human populations?

(A) Sugar
(B) Opium
(C) Tobacco
(D) Tea
(E) Cotton

34. Which of the following crops originated in Mesoamerica and spread to South America and the present-day United States in the pre-Columbian period?

(A) Maize
(B) Oats
(C) Peanuts
(D) Potatoes
(E) Wheat

35. The African kingdoms of Mali and Ghana acquired much of their wealth from

(A) trade across the Sahara
(B) trade with Portuguese ships along the Atlantic coast
(C) trade across the Atlantic with the Maya and Aztecs
(D) production of food for export to Europe
(E) tribute from the Islamic states north of the Sahara

GO ON TO THE NEXT PAGE

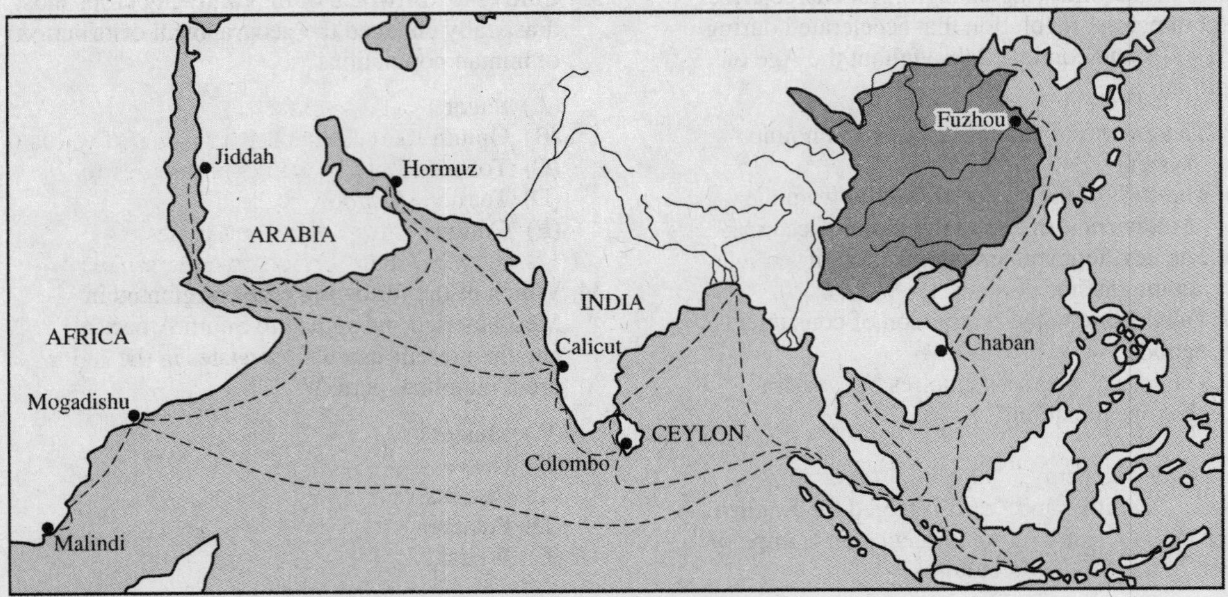

36. The map above shows the route of
    (A) Marco Polo on his travels to the court of Kublai Khan
    (B) Ibn Battutah on his travels through Dar al-Islam
    (C) Zheng He in his seafaring voyages from China
    (D) the Arab slave traders
    (E) the Buddhist pilgrim Xuanzang

GO ON TO THE NEXT PAGE

37. Which of the following was NOT a Swahili city-state?

(A) Zimbabwe
(B) Mogadishu
(C) Kilwa
(D) Mombasa
(E) Sofala

38. The large earthen mounds built in North America between the tenth and the thirteenth centuries C.E., such as those at Cahokia, are most likely evidence for

(A) the use of communal dwellings
(B) the importance of trade and commerce
(C) a large-scale commitment to road-building
(D) the importance of religious ceremonies and rituals
(E) a democratic form of government

39. Following the First World War, the governments of many of the world's industrialized nations urged women to

(A) leave the paid workforce
(B) provide food and shelter for disabled veterans
(C) take advantage of new opportunities for higher education
(D) join the army to offset war losses
(E) volunteer their services in understaffed hospitals and rehabilitation centers

40. Which of the following Southeast Asian nations has an Islamic majority?

(A) Singapore
(B) Indonesia
(C) The Philippines
(D) Vietnam
(E) Thailand

GO ON TO THE NEXT PAGE

EURASIA, 1300 C.E.

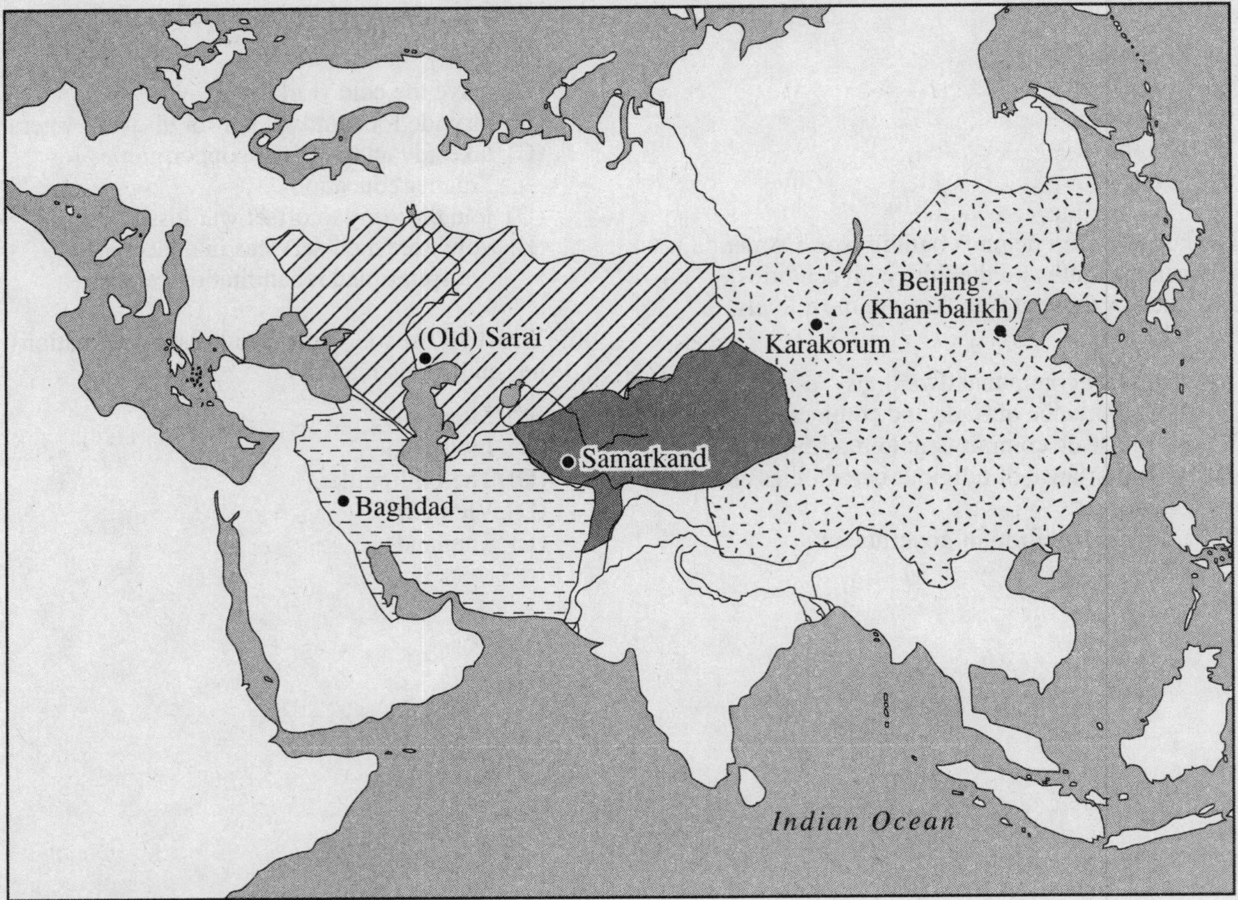

41. The four differently shaded land regions on the map above were collectively known as the

(A) Quadruple Alliance
(B) Hellenistic Kingdoms
(C) Mongol Khanates
(D) Mamluk Sultanates
(E) Tetrarchy

GO ON TO THE NEXT PAGE

42. Mayan civilization differed from Aztec civilization in that

(A) nobles governed the Aztec empire, whereas priests dominated the Mayan society
(B) the Aztecs had more peaceful relations with neighboring groups than did the Maya
(C) the Aztecs had a much longer period of predominance than did the Maya
(D) Mayan cities were generally independent, but Aztec cities were not
(E) Mayan society was much more expansionist than Aztec society

43. In the period before 1500 C.E., the two primary trading groups in the Indian Ocean were the

(A) Africans and Portuguese
(B) Arabs and Indians
(C) Arabs and Portuguese
(D) Chinese and Europeans
(E) Chinese and Indians

44. The first armed attempt to gain Mexican independence from Spain was led by

(A) Simón Bolívar
(B) Antonio López de Santa Anna
(C) Bernardo O'Higgins
(D) Father Miguel Hidalgo
(E) José de San Martín

45. The feudal periods in Japan and western Europe were similar in that both

(A) coincided with a period of growth in the money economy
(B) were characterized by frequent warfare
(C) saw the development of strong monarchies
(D) were marked by greater freedom for women than had existed previously
(E) were dominated by religious strife

46. Which of the following cities had the largest population in 1000 C.E.?

(A) Constantinople
(B) London
(C) Paris
(D) Rome
(E) Toledo

47. Which of the following is true of the legal status of Jews and Christians in early Islamic society?

(A) They were categorically forbidden from holding any public office.
(B) As "people of the book," they were exempt from taxation.
(C) They were required to serve in the army in place of Muslims.
(D) They were allowed to practice their religions with some restrictions.
(E) They were treated as equals of Muslim citizens and were accorded all the same rights and privileges as Muslims.

48. "And I say unto thee, thou art Peter and upon this rock I will build my church."

The Biblical passage cited above formed the basis in the early Catholic church for the

(A) authority of the pope
(B) emphasis on clerical celibacy
(C) seven sacraments
(D) construction of cathedrals
(E) location of the Vatican

49. What was the most significant impact of the period of the Mongol rule on Russia?

(A) The period of Mongol rule reinforced the isolation of Russia from western Europe.
(B) The Mongols aided the Russians in gaining political dominance over the peoples of the Central Asian steppes.
(C) The period of Mongol rule introduced many Muslims into the region of Russia.
(D) The Mongol domination resulted in the destruction of Eastern Orthodoxy and the rise of Nestorian Christianity.
(E) Russians' admiration of Mongol culture led them to abandon their Byzantine roots.

GO ON TO THE NEXT PAGE

50. Which of the following was an important characteristic of the Inca road system?

(A) It was well equipped for even the heaviest wheeled wagons.
(B) It was kept up by privately owned commercial companies.
(C) It required frequent repair because of the high tides and salt water of the Pacific.
(D) It facilitated transportation among the towns of the high Andes mountains.
(E) It linked independent city-states.

51. As a result of the defeats of China in the first Anglo-Chinese war (1839-1842) and in later conflicts with Westerners, the Chinese were forced to do all of the following EXCEPT

(A) allow Western missionaries to seek converts in China
(B) cede Hong Kong territory to the British
(C) open numerous port cities to foreign traders
(D) grant Westerners in China the privilege of extraterritoriality
(E) ban the import of opium into China

52. In 750 C.E., a major political difference between China and Europe was that, unlike Europe, China

(A) was a unified empire
(B) was a theocracy
(C) was controlled by rulers who came from outside its borders
(D) was under threat of invasion from all sides
(E) had a republican form of government

53. "When the personal life is cultivated, the family will be regulated; when the family is regulated, the state will be in order; and when the state is in order, there will be peace throughout the world."

The quotation above reflects a key tenet of which of the following teachings?

(A) Taoism
(B) Zen Buddhism
(C) Mahayana Buddhism
(D) Shinto
(E) Confucianism

54. Early Roman religious ritual was heavily influenced by the religious practices of the

(A) Scythians
(B) Gauls
(C) Etruscans
(D) Carthaginians
(E) Druids

55. After amassing the largest land empire ever known, most of the Mongols and Turks who invaded central and south Asia converted to

(A) Confucianism
(B) Christianity
(C) Buddhism
(D) Judaism
(E) Islam

56. In the seventeenth century, European maritime trade was dominated by the

(A) English
(B) Dutch
(C) French
(D) Swedes
(E) Spanish

57. The failure of Europe's potato crop in the late 1840's spurred mass emigration from

(A) Sweden
(B) Spain
(C) Ireland
(D) Italy
(E) Russia

58. Which of the following became important New World contributions to the world's food crops?

(A) Wheat and barley
(B) Rice and sugarcane
(C) Oats and millet
(D) Corn and potatoes
(E) Bananas and melons

GO ON TO THE NEXT PAGE

59. Alexander II emancipated the serfs and introduced government reforms following Russia's defeat in the

    (A) Balkan Wars
    (B) Crimean War
    (C) First World War
    (D) Russo-Turkish Wars
    (E) Russo-Japanese War

60. After independence, India pursued a foreign policy that led to which of the following?

    (A) Its membership in the Soviet-backed Warsaw Pact
    (B) Its membership in the Southeast Asia Treaty Organization
    (C) Its signing of a mutual defense pact with the People's Republic of China
    (D) Its emergence as a leader of the Nonaligned Movement
    (E) Its avoidance of armed conflict with its neighbors

61. Which of the following best characterizes the classical economic theory of Adam Smith?

    (A) The demands of consumers are met most cheaply by competition among individual producers.
    (B) Since land is the source of value, the whole economy will benefit if small holdings are consolidated into large estates.
    (C) An increase in wages will increase the demand for manufactured goods, making the economy as a whole grow.
    (D) Since the interests of businessmen and workers are necessarily in conflict, the interests of one can thrive only at the expense of the other.
    (E) To encourage the growth of infant national industries, government should protect them from unfair foreign competition by imposing tariffs.

62. Which of the following countries are members of the Organization of Petroleum Exporting Countries (OPEC) ?

    (A) Argentina, Mexico, and Turkey
    (B) China, Egypt, and the United States
    (C) Great Britain, Canada, and Morocco
    (D) The Soviet Union, Syria, and Kenya
    (E) Venezuela, Nigeria, and Iraq

63. The navigator James Cook was most famous for

    (A) being the first to sail around the world
    (B) charting a northwest passage
    (C) exploring the Antarctic continent
    (D) scientific observation on Caribbean islands
    (E) charting the seas around Australia and New Zealand

64. In closing Japan to Europeans, the Tokugawa shogunate was motivated primarily by a desire to limit

    (A) the influence of Westerners on Japanese government and society
    (B) a large influx of European immigrants
    (C) widespread intermarriage between Japanese and Europeans
    (D) the despoiling of Japan's pristine natural environment by Europeans
    (E) the spread of industrialization to Japan

65. Which of the following was a major consequence of the opening of large silver mines in Spanish colonies in the Americas during the 1500's?

    (A) The production of goods in Spain for export to its colonies in America was greatly stimulated.
    (B) The increased wealth circulating in Spain's colonies fueled a resurgence of Native American culture.
    (C) The European economy experienced an extended period of price inflation.
    (D) The Spanish colonies where the mines were located were successful in declaring their independence from Spain.
    (E) Other European powers succeeded in capturing the mines from Spain.

GO ON TO THE NEXT PAGE

66. Which of the following societies was the LEAST dependent on livestock?
    (A) Aztec society
    (B) Chinese society
    (C) Persian society
    (D) Tartar society
    (E) Roman society

67. Which of the following was called "the Sick Man of Europe" in the nineteenth century?
    (A) Italy
    (B) Spain
    (C) The Netherlands
    (D) The Ottoman Empire
    (E) Russia

68. The eighteenth-century philosophy of Deism was strongly denounced by
    (A) Voltaire and his followers
    (B) the Roman Catholic church
    (C) essayists in Diderot's *Encyclopèdie*
    (D) Locke and his followers
    (E) Frederick the Great of Prussia

69. Which of the following was one of the major effects of the spread of gunpowder technology in Europe in the 1400's and 1500's C.E.?
    (A) The superior firepower of European armies led to the reconquest of most lands that had been lost to the Ottoman Turks.
    (B) The widespread use of guns in hunting led to a virtual extermination of game animals and game birds in Europe.
    (C) The high cost of equipping armies with guns led to a strengthening of some centralized monarchies at the expense of feudal lords.
    (D) Fear of the new technology led to religious revivals in many areas of Europe.
    (E) Many European countries sought to avoid conflicts with each other because gunpowder made wars more destructive.

70. Which of the following factors contributed to the success of independence movements in Latin America during the early 1800's?
    (A) Military and economic aid from the United States
    (B) An increase in the production of precious metals from Latin American mines
    (C) The establishment of universities throughout Latin America
    (D) The drain on Spain's resources caused by the Napoleonic Wars
    (E) Intervention by professional revolutionaries from France

71. In the sixteenth and seventeenth centuries, the primary interest of the European powers in the East Indies was to
    (A) buy rice and other food grains
    (B) obtain wood for shipbuilding
    (C) obtain spices for trading
    (D) to seek markets for exports
    (E) exploit silver mines in the area

72. The most characteristic feature of Enlightenment thought was
    (A) opposition to slavery
    (B) antimaterialism
    (C) opposition to religious belief
    (D) an emphasis on reason
    (E) a belief in sexual equality

73. Mazzini, Cavour, and Garibaldi are most often associated with
    (A) parliamentary democracy in Italy
    (B) Italian unification
    (C) the rebuilding of Rome
    (D) Italian imperialism in Ethiopia
    (E) Italian industrialization

GO ON TO THE NEXT PAGE

74. When Siddhartha Gautama (the Buddha) embarked on his spiritual quest in the sixth century B.C.E., his primary concern was

    (A) whether there is one God or many
    (B) whether there is life after death
    (C) why humans suffer
    (D) how to convert nonbelievers
    (E) the relationship between religion and the state

75. Which of the following best explains ancient Egypt's ability to support a large population?

    (A) Its strategic location on the Mediterranean Sea
    (B) The approval its religious leaders gave to the concept of large families
    (C) The yearly flooding of the Nile River
    (D) The early introduction of technology from Mesopotamia
    (E) The use of the three-field crop rotation system

76. Which of the following best characterizes demographic change in eighteenth century England?

    (A) Destruction of the nuclear family during the Industrial Revolution caused the population to decline.
    (B) Unhealthy conditions in crowded cities caused the population to decline.
    (C) Pressures of the enclosure movement caused the population to decline.
    (D) Dramatically rising birth rates caused the population to increase.
    (E) Falling death rates caused the population to increase.

GO ON TO THE NEXT PAGE

77. The cartoon above shows President Gamal Abdel Nasser (1956-1970) encouraging Egyptians to see the advantages of

(A) maintaining equality in the workplace
(B) curbing population growth
(C) reducing consumption
(D) increasing savings
(E) legalizing unions

GO ON TO THE NEXT PAGE

78. Of the following Southeast Asian countries, which is NOT matched with the colonial power that dominated it during the colonial period?

(A) Vietnam	France
(B) Burma	Germany
(C) Indonesia	the Netherlands
(D) Malaya	Great Britain
(E) The Philippines	the United States

79. The Boxer Rebellion was a revolt of

(A) Indian soldiers against British domination
(B) Vietnamese against French domination
(C) Arabs against the Ottoman Empire
(D) Chinese against Western imperialism
(E) Koreans against Japanese rule

Mansell Collection

80. The picture above, which depicts the symbolic crowning of a twelfth-century king of Sicily by Christ, reveals the cultural influence of

(A) Russia
(B) Scandinavia
(C) Spain
(D) Islam
(E) Byzantium

GO ON TO THE NEXT PAGE

81. The political and religious center at Great Zimbabwe, which reached its height in the fifteenth century, was characterized by all of the following EXCEPT

(A) long-distance trading
(B) gold mining
(C) significant population expansion
(D) a written epic tradition
(E) copper and bronze ornament making

82. Which of the following art forms originated in the United States?

(A) Impressionism
(B) Surrealist poetry
(C) Social realism
(D) Jazz
(E) Atonal music

83. The Provisional Government failed to keep the support of the Russian people in 1917 because it

(A) executed the entire royal family
(B) collectivized agriculture and industry
(C) allowed Nicholas II to rule as a constitutional monarch
(D) suffered a humiliating defeat by the Japanese
(E) continued Russia's participation in the First World War

84. Which of the following best describes the Indian National Congress?

(A) The first national political organization in India to challenge British rule
(B) The first all-Indian legislative body formed after independence in 1947
(C) An organization formed by Hindus that primarily preached tolerance of Indian Muslims
(D) An organization formed by Hindus and Muslims that sought social reform within India
(E) A conference of Muslim religious leaders that convened to discuss Indian statehood

85. Of all the dictatorial regimes established in Europe between the First and Second World Wars, the one that held power the longest was that of

(A) Hitler
(B) Stalin
(C) Mussolini
(D) Pilsudski
(E) Franco

86. One of the principal strengths of the Byzantine empire was its

(A) constitutional monarchy
(B) sound economic base
(C) preference for decentralized government
(D) close relationship with the Roman Catholic church
(E) orderly system of succession to the throne

87. The first significant test of the ability of the League of Nations to respond when a major nation acted as an aggressor occurred when

(A) Japan invaded Manchuria
(B) the Soviet Union invaded Poland
(C) Japan declared war on China
(D) Franco's rebels attacked Spanish loyalists
(E) Hitler incorporated Austria into the Third Reich

88. In the 1980's, which of the following Muslim countries most actively promoted Islamic fundamentalism?

(A) Morocco
(B) Iran
(C) Iraq
(D) Indonesia
(E) Turkey

89. Mao Zedong revolutionized Chinese Marxist doctrine in the 1920's by advocating that the

(A) Chinese Communist Party sever its ties with the Soviet Union to preserve its independence
(B) Chinese Communist Party allow its rival, the Kuomintang, to reform a separate government on the island of Taiwan
(C) Chinese Communist Party renounce the use of violence to achieve revolution
(D) rural peasants, not the urban proletariat, lead the revolution in China
(E) landlord and capitalist classes be allowed to survive even after the communists took power

GO ON TO THE NEXT PAGE

90. The economies of China, North Korea, and North Vietnam were relatively isolated from the world economy during much of the third quarter of the twentieth century primarily because of their

(A) adherence to a planned Marxist economy
(B) inability to recover from the devastation of the Second World War
(C) subjection to a trade embargo enforced by the United Nations
(D) subjection to almost continual civil wars
(E) enduring extended droughts due to global climate change

91. The partition of Korea at the end of the Second World War in 1945 was primarily the result of

(A) rivalry between the United States and the Soviet Union
(B) Japanese dominance of important sectors of the Korean economy
(C) the emergence of China as a major world power
(D) the inability of the Koreans to agree on a form of government
(E) sharp cultural differences between northern and southern Korea

92. During the American occupation of Japan following the Second World War, authorities seeking to restructure Japanese society received the strongest support from which of the following Japanese groups?

(A) Socialist leaders
(B) Business leaders
(C) Military leaders
(D) Expatriates returning to Japan
(E) Members of the imperial court

93. Many historians believe that the end of the French Revolutionary era was the

(A) execution of King Louis XVI
(B) Reign of Terror
(C) storming of the Bastille prison
(D) defeat of Napoleon in Russia
(E) peace settlement at the Congress of Vienna

94. The nations that signed and confirmed the 1975 Helsinki Accords agreed to

(A) establish uniform prices for crude oil
(B) establish peace in the Middle East
(C) cooperate among themselves and respect human rights
(D) end the Vietnam conflict and withdraw all foreign troops
(E) end the Cold War

95. In the late twentieth century, experts began to question the value of building large dam projects in the developing world primarily because these projects tend to

(A) reduce the cost of electric power in the countries in which they are built
(B) displace people from their homes and disturb the ecology of the regions in which they are built
(C) encourage separatist movements in the areas in which they are built
(D) conflict with the development plans of the central governments of the countries in which they are built
(E) disrupt road and rail communications across the rivers on which the dams are built

STOP

If you finish before time is called, you may check your work on this test only. Do not turn to any other section in the test.

NO TEST MATERIAL ON THIS PAGE

How to Score the SAT Subject Test in World History

When you take an actual SAT Subject Test in World History, your answer sheet will be "read" by a scanning machine that will record your responses to each question. Then a computer will compare your answers with the correct answers and produce your raw score. You get one point for each correct answer. For each wrong answer, you lose one-fourth of a point. Questions you omit (and any for which you mark more than one answer) are not counted. This raw score is converted to a scaled score that is reported to you and to the colleges you specify.

Worksheet 1. Finding Your Raw Test Score

STEP 1: Table A lists the correct answers for all the questions on the World History Test that is reproduced in this book. It also serves as a worksheet for you to calculate your raw score.

- Compare your answers with those given in the table.
- Put a check in the column marked "Right" if your answer is correct.
- Put a check in the column marked "Wrong" if your answer is incorrect.
- Leave both columns blank if you omitted the question.

STEP 2: Count the number of right answers.

Enter the total here: ________________

STEP 3: Count the number of wrong answers.

Enter the total here: ________________

STEP 4: Multiply the number of wrong answers by .250.

Enter the product here: ________________

STEP 5: Subtract the result obtained in Step 4 from the total you obtained in Step 2.

Enter the result here: ________________

STEP 6: Round the number obtained in Step 5 to the nearest whole number.

Enter the result here: ________________

The number you obtained in Step 6 is your raw score.

Table A

Question Number	Correct Answer	Right	Wrong	Percentage of Students Answering the Question Correctly*	Question Number	Correct Answer	Right	Wrong	Percentage of Students Answering the Question Correctly*
Answers to the Subject Test in World History, Form 4BAC, and Percentage of Students Answering Each Question Correctly									
1	A			66	33	A			41
2	B			59	34	A			64
3	C			76	35	A			50
4	B			49	36	C			52
5	E			65	37	A			24
6	D			79	38	D			59
7	A			61	39	A			33
8	E			93	40	B			71
9	D			57	41	C			69
10	D			76	42	D			19
11	B			35	43	B			37
12	A			54	44	D			37
13	A			80	45	B			55
14	C			41	46	A			67
15	A			51	47	D			51
16	C			21	48	A			36
17	B			43	49	A			60
18	A			29	50	D			55
19	B			81	51	E			69
20	C			71	52	A			65
21	C			47	53	E			65
22	A			73	54	C			45
23	B			85	55	E			62
24	D			82	56	B			32
25	B			95	57	C			89
26	A			73	58	D			65
27	D			68	59	B			43
28	A			46	60	D			35
29	E			77	61	A			46
30	A			48	62	E			65
31	A			73	63	E			46
32	D			56	64	A			83

Table A continued on next page

Table A continued from previous page

Question Number	Correct Answer	Right	Wrong	Percentage of Students Answering the Question Correctly*	Question Number	Correct Answer	Right	Wrong	Percentage of Students Answering the Question Correctly*
65	C			53	81	D			49
66	A			27	82	D			88
67	D			63	83	E			52
68	B			50	84	A			41
69	C			36	85	E			12
70	D			52	86	B			31
71	C			71	87	A			41
72	D			82	88	B			53
73	B			60	89	D			56
74	C			77	90	A			55
75	C			65	91	A			47
76	E			20	92	B			54
77	B			80	93	E			38
78	B			39	94	C			26
79	D			74	95	B			77
80	E			67					

* These percentages are based on an analysis of the answer sheets of a representative sample of 9,745 students who took the original form of this test in June 2005, and whose mean score was 611. They may be used as an indication of the relative difficulty of a particular question. Each percentage may also be used to predict the likelihood that a typical SAT Subject Test in World History test-taker will answer that question correctly on this edition of the test.

Finding Your Scaled Score

When you take SAT Subject Tests, the scores sent to the colleges you specify are reported on the College Board scale, which ranges from 200 to 800. You can convert your practice test score to a scaled score by using Table B. To find your scaled score, locate your raw score in the left-hand column of Table B; the corresponding score in the right-hand column is your scaled score. For example, a raw score of 39 on this particular edition of the World History Test corresponds to a scaled score of 580.

Raw scores are converted to scaled scores to ensure that a score earned on any one edition of a particular Subject Test is comparable to the same scaled score earned on any other edition of the same Subject Test. Because some editions of the tests may be slightly easier or more difficult than others, College Board scaled scores are adjusted so that they indicate the same level of performance regardless of the edition of the test taken and the ability of the group that takes it. Thus, for example, a score of 400 on one edition of a test taken at a particular administration indicates the same level of achievement as a score of 400 on a different edition of the test taken at a different administration.

When you take the SAT Subject Tests during a national administration, your scores are likely to differ somewhat from the scores you obtain on the tests in this book. People perform at different levels at different times for reasons unrelated to the tests themselves. The precision of any test is also limited because it represents only a sample of all the possible questions that could be asked.

Table B

Scaled Score Conversion Table World History Test (Form 4BAC)					
Raw Score	Scaled Score	Raw Score	Scaled Score	Raw Score	Scaled Score
95	800	55	670	15	440
94	800	54	660	14	440
93	800	53	660	13	430
92	800	52	650	12	420
91	800	51	640	11	420
90	800	50	640	10	410
89	800	49	630	9	410
88	800	48	630	8	400
87	800	47	620	7	400
86	800	46	620	6	390
85	800	45	610	5	380
84	800	44	610	4	380
83	800	43	600	3	370
82	800	42	590	2	370
81	800	41	590	1	360
80	800	40	580	0	360
79	800	39	580	-1	350
78	800	38	570	-2	350
77	790	37	570	-3	340
76	790	36	560	-4	340
75	780	35	560	-5	330
74	770	34	550	-6	330
73	770	33	550	-7	330
72	760	32	540	-8	320
71	760	31	530	-9	320
70	750	30	530	-10	310
69	750	29	520	-11	310
68	740	28	520	-12	300
67	740	27	510	-13	300
66	730	26	510	-14	300
65	720	25	500	-15	290
64	720	24	490	-16	280
63	710	23	490	-17	280
62	710	22	480	-18	270
61	700	21	480	-19	260
60	690	20	470	-20	250
59	690	19	470	-21	250
58	680	18	460	-22	240
57	680	17	450	-23	230
56	670	16	450	-24	220

How Did You Do on the Subject Test in World History?

After you score your test and analyze your performance, think about the following questions:

Did you run out of time before reaching the end of the test?

If so, you may need to pace yourself better. For example, maybe you spent too much time on one or two hard questions. A better approach might be to skip the ones you can't answer right away and try answering all the questions that remain on the test. Then if there's time, go back to the questions you skipped.

Did you take a long time reading the directions?

You will save time when you take the test by learning the directions to the World History Test ahead of time. Each minute you spend reading directions during the test is a minute that you could use to answer questions.

How did you handle questions you were unsure of?

If you were able to eliminate one or more of the answer choices as wrong and guess from the remaining ones, your approach probably worked to your advantage. On the other hand, making haphazard guesses or omitting questions without trying to eliminate choices could cost you valuable points.

How difficult were the questions for you compared with other students who took the test?

Table A shows you how difficult the multiple-choice questions were for the group of students who took this test during its national administration. The right-hand column gives the percentage of students that answered each question correctly.

A question answered correctly by almost everyone in the group is obviously an easier question. For example, 82 percent of the students answered question 24 correctly. But only 19 percent answered question 42 correctly.

Keep in mind that these percentages are based on just one group of students. They would probably be different with another group of students taking the test.

If you missed several easier questions, go back and try to find out why: Did the questions cover material you haven't yet reviewed? Did you misunderstand the directions?

Chapter 4

Mathematics

Purpose

There are two, one-hour subject tests in mathematics: Mathematics Level 1 and Mathematics Level 2. The purpose of these tests is to measure your knowledge of mathematics through the first three years of college-preparatory mathematics for Level 1 and through precalculus for Level 2.

Mathematics Level 1 Subject Test

Format

Mathematics Level 1 is a one-hour broad survey test that consists of 50 multiple-choice questions. The test has questions in the following areas:

- Number and Operations
- Algebra and Functions
- Geometry and Measurement (plane Euclidean, coordinate, three-dimensional, and trigonometry)
- Data Analysis, Statistics, and Probability

How to Prepare

The Mathematics Level 1 Subject Test is intended for students who have taken three years of college-preparatory mathematics, including two years of algebra and one year of geometry. You are not expected to have studied every topic on the test. Familiarize yourself with the test directions in advance. The directions in this book are identical to those that appear on the test.

Calculator Use

It is NOT necessary to use a calculator to solve every question on the Level 1 test, but it is important to know when and how to use one. **Students who take the test without a calculator will be at a disadvantage.** For about 50 to 60 percent of the questions, there is no advantage, perhaps even a disadvantage, to using a calculator. For about 40 to 50 percent of the questions, a calculator may be useful or necessary.

A graphing calculator may provide an advantage over a scientific calculator on some questions. However, you should bring the calculator with which you are most familiar. If you are comfortable with both a scientific calculator and a graphing calculator, you should bring the graphing calculator.

Mathematics Level 2 Subject Test

Format

Mathematics Level 2 is also a one-hour test that contains 50 multiple-choice questions that cover the following areas:

- Number and Operations
- Algebra and Functions
- Geometry and Measurement (coordinate, three-dimensional, and trigonometry)
- Data Analysis, Statistics, and Probability

How to Prepare

The Mathematics Level 2 Subject Test is intended for students who have taken college-preparatory mathematics for more than three years, including two years of algebra, one year of geometry, and elementary functions (precalculus) and/or trigonometry. You are not expected to have studied every topic on the test.

If you have had preparation in trigonometry and elementary functions, have attained grades of B or better in these courses, and have skill in knowing when and how to use a scientific or a graphing calculator, you should select the Level 2 test. If you are sufficiently prepared to take Level 2, but elect to take Level 1 in hopes of receiving a higher score, you may not do as well as you expect. Familiarize yourself with the test directions in advance. The directions in this book are identical to those that appear on the test.

Calculator Use

It is NOT necessary to use a calculator to solve every question on the Level 2 test, but it is important to know when and how to use one. For about 35 to 45 percent of the questions, there is no advantage, perhaps even a disadvantage, to using a calculator. For about 55 to 65 percent of the questions, a calculator may be useful or necessary.

As with the Level 1 test, a graphing calculator may provide an advantage over a scientific calculator on some questions. However, you should bring the calculator with which you are most familiar. If you are comfortable with both a scientific calculator and a graphing calculator, you should bring the graphing calculator.

Calculator Policy: You may NOT use a calculator on any Subject Test other than the Mathematics Level 1 and Level 2 Tests.

What Calculator to Bring

- Bring a calculator that you are used to using. If you're comfortable with both a scientific calculator and a graphing calculator, bring the graphing calculator.
- Before you take the test, make sure that your calculator is in good working order. You may bring batteries and a backup calculator to the test center.
- The test center will not have substitute calculators or batteries on hand. Students may not share calculators.
- If your calculator malfunctions during one of the Mathematics Level 1 or Level 2 Tests and you do not have a backup calculator, you must tell your test supervisor when the malfunction occurs. The supervisor will then cancel the scores on that test only, if you desire to do so.

What Is NOT Permitted

- pocket organizers
- laptops and portable handheld computers
- models with typewriter keypads (e.g., T1-92 Plus, Voyage 200)
- electronic writing pads or pen-input/stylus-driven devices (e.g., Palm, PDAs, Casio ClassPad 300)
- calculators with paper tapes
- calculators that make noise or "talk"
- calculators that require an electrical outlet
- cell phone calculators

Using Your Calculator

- Only some questions on these tests require the use of a calculator. First decide how you will solve a problem, then determine if you need a calculator. For many of the questions, there's more than one way to solve the problem. **Don't pick up a calculator if you don't need to**—you might waste time.
- **The answer choices are often rounded**, so the answer you get might not match the answer in the test book. Since the choices are rounded, plugging the choices into the problem might not produce an exact answer.
- **Don't round any intermediate calculations**. For example, if you get a result from the calculator for the first step of a solution, keep the result in the calculator and use it for the second step. If you round the result from the first step, and the answer choices are close to each other, you might choose the wrong answer.
- **Read the question carefully** so that you know what you are being asked to do. Sometimes a result that you may get from your calculator is NOT the final answer. If

an answer you get is not one of the choices in the question, it may be that you didn't answer the question being asked. You should read the question again. It may also be that you rounded at an intermediate step in solving the problem, and that's why your answer doesn't match any of the choices in the question.

- **Think about how you are going to solve the question** before picking up your calculator. It may be that you only need the calculator for the final step or two and can do the rest in your test book or in your head. Don't waste time by using the calculator more than necessary.
- If you are taking the **Level 1 test, make sure your calculator is in degree mode** ahead of time so you won't have to worry about it during the test. If you're taking the Level 2 test, make sure your calculator is in the correct mode (degree or radian) for the question being asked.
- For some questions on these tests, a **graphing calculator** may provide an advantage. If you use a graphing calculator, you should know how to perform calculations (e.g., exponents, roots, trigonometric values, logarithms), graph functions and analyze the graphs, find zeros of functions, find points of intersection of graphs of functions, find minima/maxima of functions, find numerical solutions to equations, generate a table of values for a function, and perform data analysis features, including finding a regression equation.
- You may not use your calculator for sharing or exchanging, or removing part of a test book or any notes relating to the test from the test room. Such action **may be grounds for dismissal and/or cancellation of scores**. You do not have to clear your calculator's memory before or after taking the test.

Comparing the Two Tests

Although there is some overlap between Levels 1 and 2, the emphasis for Level 2 is on more advanced content. Here are the differences in the two tests.

	Approximate Percentage of Mathematics Test	
Topics Covered*	Level 1	Level 2
Number and Operations	**10–14**	**10–14**
Operations, ratio and proportion, complex numbers, counting, elementary number theory, matrices, sequences, *series, vectors*		
Algebra and Functions	**38–42**	**48–52**
Expressions, equations, inequalities, representation and modeling, properties of functions (linear, polynomial, rational, exponential, *logarithmic, trigonometric, inverse trigonometric, periodic, piecewise, recursive, parametric*)		
Geometry and Measurement	**38–42**	**28–32**
Plane Euclidean/Measurement	18–22	—
Coordinate	8–12	10–14
Lines, parabolas, circles, *ellipses, hyperbolas*, symmetry, transformations, *polar coordinates*		
Three-dimensional	4–6	4–6
Solids, surface area and volume (cylinders, cones, pyramids, spheres, prisms), *coordinates in three dimensions*		
Trigonometry	6–8	12–16
Right triangles, identities, *radian measure, law of cosines, law of sines, equations, double angle formulas*		
Data Analysis, Statistics, and Probability	**6–10**	**6–10**
Mean, median, mode, range, interquartile range, *standard deviation*, graphs and plots, least-squares regression (linear, *quadratic, exponential*), probability		

* Topics in italics are tested on the Level 2 test only. The content of Level 1 overlaps somewhat with that on Level 2, but the emphasis on Level 2 is on more advanced content. Plane Euclidean Geometry is not tested directly on Level 2.

Areas of Overlap

The content of Level 1 has some overlap with Level 2, especially in the following areas:

- elementary algebra
- three-dimensional geometry
- coordinate geometry
- statistics
- basic trigonometry

How Test Content Differs

Although some questions may be appropriate for both tests, the emphasis for Level 2 is on more advanced content. The tests differ significantly in the following areas:

Number and Operations. Level 1 measures a more basic understanding of the topics than Level 2. For example, Level 1 covers the *arithmetic of complex numbers*, but Level 2 also covers *graphical and other properties of complex numbers*. Level 2 also includes *series* and *vectors*.

Algebra and Functions. Level 1 contains mainly *algebraic* equations and functions, whereas Level 2 also contains more advanced equations and functions, such as *exponential*, *logarithmic*, and *trigonometric*.

Geometry and Measurement. A significant percentage of the questions on Level 1 is devoted to *plane Euclidean geometry and measurement*, which is not tested directly on Level 2. On Level 2, the concepts learned in plane geometry are applied in the questions on *coordinate geometry* and *three-dimensional geometry*. The trigonometry questions on Level 1 are primarily limited to *right triangle trigonometry* (*sine*, *cosine*, *tangent*) and *the fundamental relationships among the trigonometric ratios*. Level 2 includes questions about *ellipses*, *hyperbolas*, *polar coordinates*, and *coordinates in three dimensions*. The trigonometry questions on Level 2 place more emphasis on *the properties and graphs of trigonometric functions*, *the inverse trigonometric functions*, *trigonometric equations and identities*, and *the laws of sines and cosines*.

Data Analysis, Statistics, and Probability. Both Level 1 and Level 2 include *mean*, *median*, *mode*, *range*, *interquartile range*, *data interpretation*, and *probability*. Level 2 also includes *standard deviation*. Both include *least-squares linear regression*, but Level 2 also includes *quadratic and exponential regression*.

Scores

The total score for each test is reported on the 200-to-800 scale. Because the content measured by Level 1 and Level 2 differs considerably, you should not use your score on one test to predict your score on the other.

Note: Geometric Figures

Figures that accompany problems are intended to provide information useful in solving the problems. They are drawn as accurately as possible EXCEPT when it is stated in a particular problem that the figure is not drawn to scale. Even when figures are not drawn to scale, the relative positions of points and angles may be assumed to be in the order shown. Also, line segments that extend through points and appear to lie on the same line *may be assumed to be* on the same line.

When "Note: Figure not drawn to scale" appears in the text, it means that degree measures may not be accurately shown and specific lengths may not be drawn proportionately.

Mathematics Level 1

Sample Questions

All questions in the Mathematics Level 1 and Level 2 Tests are multiple-choice questions in which you must choose the BEST response from the five choices offered. The directions that follow are the same as those on the Mathematics Level 1 Test.

For each of the following problems, decide which is the BEST of the choices given. If the exact numerical value is not one of the choices, select the choice that best approximates this value. Then fill in the corresponding circle on the answer sheet.

Notes: (1) A scientific or graphing calculator will be necessary for answering some (but not all) of the questions in this test. For each question you will have to decide whether or not you should use a calculator.

(2) The only angle measure used on this test is degree measure. Make sure your calculator is in the degree mode.

(3) Figures that accompany problems in this test are intended to provide information useful in solving the problems. They are drawn as accurately as possible EXCEPT when it is stated in a specific problem that its figure is not drawn to scale. All figures lie in a plane unless otherwise indicated.

(4) Unless otherwise specified, the domain of any function f is assumed to be the set of all real numbers x for which $f(x)$ is a real number. The range of f is assumed to be the set of all real numbers $f(x)$, where x is in the domain of f.

(5) Reference information that may be useful in answering the questions in this test can be found on the page preceding Question 1.

Reference Information: The following information is for your reference in answering some of the questions in this test.

Volume of a right circular cone with radius r and height h: $V = \frac{1}{3}\pi r^2 h$

Lateral Area of a right circular cone with circumference of the base c and slant height ℓ: $S = \frac{1}{2}c\ell$

Volume of a sphere with radius r: $V = \frac{4}{3}\pi r^3$

Surface Area of a sphere with radius r: $S = 4\pi r^2$

Volume of a pyramid with base area B and height h: $V = \frac{1}{3}Bh$

Number and Operations

1. The 3rd term of an arithmetic sequence is 14 and the 17th term is 63. What is the sum of the first 10 terms of the sequence?

(A) 227.5
(B) 245
(C) 262.5
(D) 297.5
(E) 385

Choice (A) is the correct answer to question 1. In an arithmetic sequence, the difference between consecutive terms is constant. Since the 3rd term of the sequence is 14 and the 17th term is 63, the common difference is $\frac{63-14}{17-3} = 3.5$.

If the 3rd term of the sequence is 14, the 2nd term is $14 - 3.5 = 10.5$, and the 1st term is 7. Likewise, the 10th term is equal to $7 + 9(3.5) = 38.5$. The sum of the first 10 terms of the sequence is given by $S_{10} = \frac{10(7+38.5)}{2} = 227.5$.

Algebra and Functions

2. From which of the following statements must it follow that $x > y$?
   (A) $x = 2y$
   (B) $2x = y$
   (C) $x + 2 = y$
   (D) $x - 2 = y$
   (E) $2 - x = y$

Choice (D) is the correct answer to question 2. If $x > y$, then $x = y + d$ where $d > 0$. In choice (D), $x - 2 = y$, which is equivalent to $x = y + 2$ fitting the definition of "greater than."

Another way to solve this problem is to look at each of the choices to see if it implies that $x > y$ for all values of x and y.

First look at choice (A). Here x is not greater than y in the cases where both x and y are 0 or negative. For example, if $x = -2$ and $y = -1$, then $x = 2y$, but x is not greater than y.

Likewise, in choice (B) if $x = y = 0$, then $2x = y$, but x is not greater than y.

In choice (C), x is always 2 less than y, so it is not possible for $x > y$.

In choice (D), x is always 2 greater than y. Thus, the statement $x - 2 = y$ implies that $x > y$ for all values of x and y. The correct answer is choice (D).

In choice (E), when $x = y = 1$, it is true that $2 - x = y$, but x is not greater than y.

3. If $y = 2x^3 + 18x^2 - 20$ for $0 \le x \le 10$, the maximum value of y occurs when $x =$
   (A) 0
   (B) 1.13
   (C) 6
   (D) 8.87
   (E) 10

Choice (C) is the correct answer to question 3. You can use a graphing calculator to help you solve this problem. Graph the equation in an appropriate viewing window that allows you to see the maximum value of y. You can do this by setting the values of x from 0 to 10 and then selecting a zoom option that fits the y-values for the given x-values. Once you graph the equation, use the "maximum" feature of the calculator to find the maximum value of y on the interval $0 \le x \le 10$. You can see from the graph that the maximum value of y is 196, which occurs when $x = 6$. It is important to remember that the minimum or maximum values do not necessarily occur at the endpoints of the domain interval.

4. Money invested in an account paying interest at an annual percentage rate of 9 percent compounded annually doubles in value in approximately 8 years. At what annual percentage rate, compounded annually, would the same investment take 16 years to double?
   (A) 0.4%
   (B) 4.4%
   (C) 5%
   (D) 12.5%
   (E) 18%

Choice (B) is the correct answer to question 4. Let P represent the amount being invested. According to the question $P(1.09)^8$ is approximately equal to $2P$. To find the rate at which the investment will take 16 years to double, set up the equation $P(1+r)^{16} = 2P$ or $(1+r)^{16} = 2$ If you take the 16th root of both sides of the equation, you get $(1+r) = 2^{\frac{1}{16}}$ or $1 + r \approx 1.044$. Thus, the rate is 4.4%.

5. If $f(x) = x^2 + x - 6$, what are all values of a for which $f(a) = f(-a)$?
   (A) −3 and 2 only
   (B) −2 and 3 only
   (C) 0 only
   (D) 2 only
   (E) All real numbers

Choice (C) is the correct answer to question 5. If $f(a) = f(-a)$, then $a^2 + a - 6 = (-a)^2 - a - 6$. This simplifies to $a = -a$. The only value of a for which this is true is 0.

You can also use a graphing calculator to examine the graphs of $y = f(x)$ and $y = f(-x)$. The only point of intersection of the two graphs is at $x = 0$.

6. If $f(g(x)) = x$ and $f(x) = 3x + 1$, which of the following is $g(x)$?
   (A) $g(x) = \frac{1}{3}x - \frac{1}{9}$
   (B) $g(x) = \frac{1}{3}x - \frac{1}{3}$
   (C) $g(x) = \frac{1}{3}x + 1$
   (D) $g(x) = \frac{1}{3}x - 1$
   (E) $g(x) = 3x - 1$

Choice (B) is the correct answer to question 6. If $f(g(x)) = x$ and $f(x) = 3x + 1$, then $f(g(x)) = 3g(x) + 1 = x$. Solving this equation for $g(x)$ yields $x - 1 = 3g(x)$ and $g(x) = \frac{x-1}{3}$ or $\frac{1}{3}x - \frac{1}{3}$.

Geometry and Measurement: Plane Geometry

7. Square *ABCD* has sides of length 8. Square *MNOP* is formed by connecting the midpoints of the sides of *ABCD*. Square *WXYZ* is formed by connecting the midpoints of the sides of *MNOP*. What is the ratio of the area of *WXYZ* to the area of *ABCD* ?
   (A) 1 to 8
   (B) 1 to 4
   (C) 1 to 2
   (D) $\sqrt{2}$ to 4
   (E) $\sqrt{2}$ to 2

It is helpful to draw a figure.

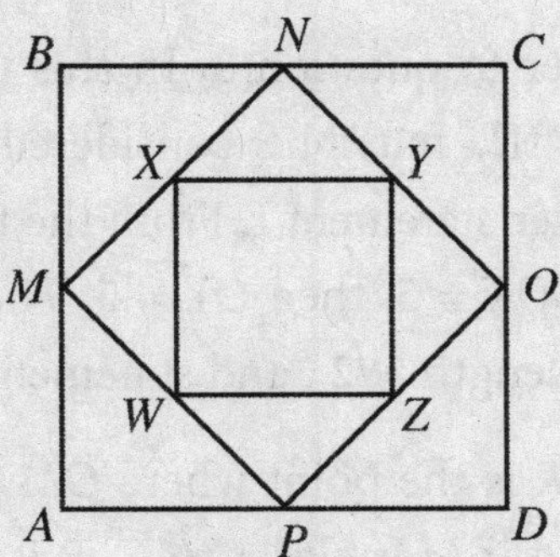

Choice (B) is the correct answer to question 7. The length of each of segments $\overline{AM}$ and $\overline{AP}$ is 4. Since $\triangle PAM$ is an isosceles right triangle, by the Pythagorean theorem, the length of segment $\overline{MP}$ is $\sqrt{4^2 + 4^2} = \sqrt{32} = 4\sqrt{2}$. Thus, the length of each of segments

$\overline{MW}$ and $\overline{MX}$ is $\frac{4\sqrt{2}}{2} = 2\sqrt{2}$. Again, by the Pythagorean theorem, the length of $\overline{WX}$ is $\sqrt{(2\sqrt{2})^2 + (2\sqrt{2})^2} = \sqrt{16} = 4$. The area of square *WXYZ* is $4^2 = 16$, and the area of square *ABCD* is $8^2 = 64$. So the ratio of the area of *WXYZ* to the area of *ABCD* is 1 to 4.

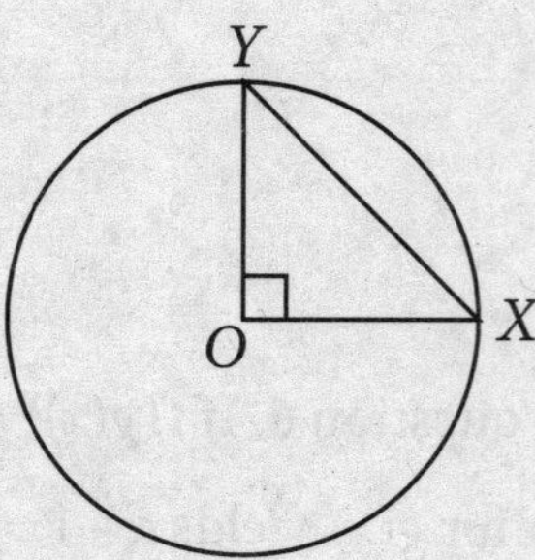

8. In the figure above, *X* and *Y* are points on the circle with center *O*. Point *M* (not shown) is a point on the minor arc $\widehat{XY}$ such that $\overline{OM}$ intersects $\overline{XY}$ at point *R* (not shown). If $OX = 5$, which of the following must be true?

   I. $XY = 5\sqrt{2}$

   II. $XR = RY$

   III. $OM = 5$

   (A) I only
   (B) II only
   (C) III only
   (D) I and II
   (E) I and III

Choice (E) is the correct answer to question 8. In this type of question, each of three statements, labeled I, II, and III, must be considered independently based on the information given. First, consider statement I. From the figure we know $\overline{OX} \perp \overline{OY}$. Since $\overline{OX}$ and $\overline{OY}$ are both radii and $OX = 5$, then $OY = 5$. Thus, $\overline{XY}$ is the hypotenuse of an isosceles right triangle and has length $5\sqrt{2}$, and statement I is true.

In statement II, we know that *R* is the point where $\overline{OM}$ intersects $\overline{XY}$. If *M* is closer to *Y*, then *R* is also closer to *Y*, and if *M* is closer to *X*, *R* is closer to *X*. Thus, it *cannot* be concluded that $XR = RY$.

In statement III, since we know the circle has radius 5 and that $\overline{OM}$ is a radius of the circle, statement III is true. Therefore, the correct answer is choice (E) because statements I and III *must* be true.

Geometry and Measurement: Coordinate Geometry

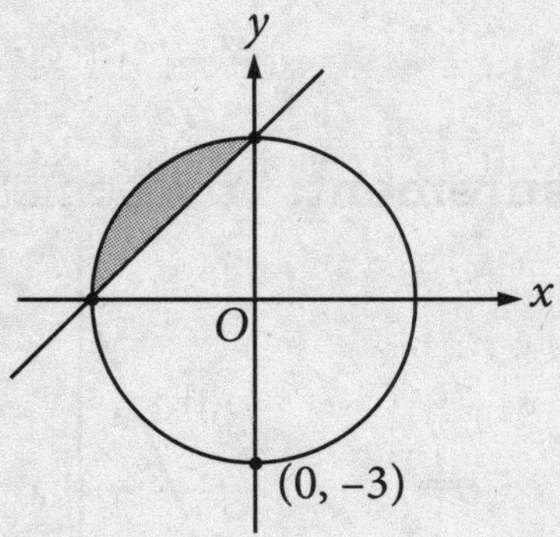

9. In the figure above, the origin O is the center of the circle. What is the area of the shaded region?
   (A) 0.21
   (B) 0.29
   (C) 2.57
   (D) 14.35
   (E) 19.27

Choice (C) is the correct answer to question 9. The figure shows a circle with radius 3. The area of the shaded region is equal to the area of a quarter circle minus the area of the right triangle shown. Thus, the area of the shaded region is $\frac{9\pi}{4} - \frac{1}{2}(3)(3)$, which is approximately equal to 2.5686.

Geometry and Measurement: Three-Dimensional Geometry

10. A cylindrical container with an inside height of 6 feet has an inside radius of 2 feet. If the container is $\frac{2}{3}$ full of water, what is the volume, in cubic feet, of the water in the container?
    (A) 25.1
    (B) 37.7
    (C) 50.3
    (D) 62.3
    (E) 75.4

Choice (C) is the correct answer to question 10. The volume V of a cylinder with radius r and height h is given by $V = \pi r^2 h$. Thus, the volume, in cubic feet, of the container is $\pi \cdot 2^2 \cdot 6 = 24\pi$. Since the container is $\frac{2}{3}$ full of water, the volume of the water in the container is $\frac{2}{3} \cdot 24\pi \approx 50.3$.

Geometry and Measurement: Trigonometry

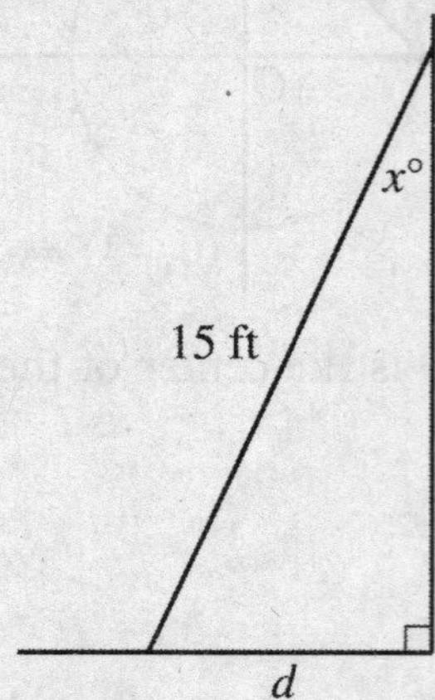

Note: Figure not drawn to scale.

11. In the figure above, a 15-foot ladder is leaning against a vertical wall so that the top of the ladder makes an angle of $x°$ with the wall. If $x = 16$, what is the ratio of the length of the ladder to d, the distance that the base of the ladder is from the base of the wall?
    (A) 0.28
    (B) 1.04
    (C) 3.48
    (D) 3.63
    (E) 4.13

Choice (D) is the correct answer to question 11. Use right triangle trigonometry to set up the equation $\sin 16° = \frac{d}{15}$. Thus, $d = 15 \sin 16°$. The ratio of the length of the ladder to d is $\frac{15}{15 \sin 16°} \approx 3.63$, since the length of the ladder is 15 feet.

You could also solve this problem by realizing that the ratio of d to 15 is equal to $\sin 16°$, so the ratio of 15 to d equals $\frac{1}{\sin 16°}$.

Data Analysis, Statistics, and Probability

12. A random number generator will randomly select an integer between 1 and 100, inclusive. What is the probability that the integer selected will be the product of two odd integers greater than 1?

(A) $\frac{25}{100}$

(B) $\frac{26}{100}$

(C) $\frac{28}{100}$

(D) $\frac{29}{100}$

(E) $\frac{30}{100}$

Choice (A) is the correct answer to question 12. An integer that satisfies the given conditions must be odd and not prime. There are 49 odd integers that are greater than 1 and less than 100. Of these, 24 are prime, which leaves 25 integers that meet the given conditions. The probability of choosing one of these integers is $\frac{25}{100}$.

Mathematics Level 1 Test

Practice Helps

The test that follows is an actual, recently administered SAT Subject Test in Mathematics Level 1. To get an idea of what it's like to take this test, practice under conditions that are much like those of an actual test administration.

- Set aside an hour when you can take the test uninterrupted. Make sure you complete the test in one sitting.
- Sit at a desk or table with no other books or papers. Dictionaries, other books, or notes are not allowed in the test room.
- Remember to have a scientific or graphing calculator with you.
- Tear out an answer sheet from the back of this book and fill it in just as you would on the day of the test. One answer sheet can be used for up to three Subject Tests.
- Read the instructions that precede the practice test. During the actual administration, you will be asked to read them before answering test questions.
- Time yourself by placing a clock or kitchen timer in front of you.
- After you finish the practice test, read the sections "How to Score the SAT Subject Test in Mathematics Level 1" and "How Did You Do on the Subject Test in Mathematics Level 1?"
- The appearance of the answer sheet in this book may differ from the answer sheet you see on test day.

MATHEMATICS LEVEL 1 TEST

The top portion of the section of the answer sheet that you will use in taking the Mathematics Level 1 Test must be filled in exactly as shown in the illustration below. Note carefully that you have to do all of the following on your answer sheet.

1. Print MATHEMATICS LEVEL 1 on the line under the words "Subject Test (print)."

2. In the shaded box labeled "Test Code" fill in four circles:

   —Fill in circle 3 in the row labeled V.
   —Fill in circle 2 in the row labeled W.
   —Fill in circle 5 in the row labeled X.
   —Fill in circle A in the row labeled Y.

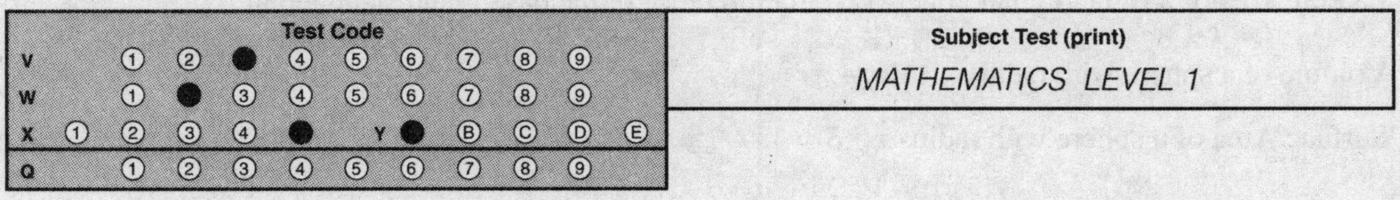

Test Code											
V		1	2	●	4	5	6	7	8	9	
W		1	●	3	4	5	6	7	8	9	
X	1	2	3	4	●	Y	●	B	C	D	E
Q		1	2	3	4	5	6	7	8	9	

Subject Test (print)
MATHEMATICS LEVEL 1

3. Please answer Part I and Part II below by filling in the specified circles in row Q that correspond to the courses you have taken or are presently taking, and the circle that corresponds to the type of calculator you are going to use to take this test. <u>The information that you provide is for statistical purposes only and will not affect your score on the test.</u>

<u>Part I.</u> Which of the following describes a mathematics course you have taken or are currently taking? (FILL IN **<u>ALL</u>** CIRCLES THAT APPLY.)

- Algebra I or Elementary Algebra **<u>OR</u>** Course I of a college preparatory mathematics sequence —Fill in circle 1.
- Geometry **<u>OR</u>** Course II of a college preparatory mathematics sequence —Fill in circle 2.
- Algebra II or Intermediate Algebra **<u>OR</u>** Course III of a college preparatory mathematics sequence —Fill in circle 3.
- Elementary Functions (Precalculus) and/or Trigonometry **<u>OR</u>** beyond Course III of a college preparatory mathematics sequence —Fill in circle 4.
- Advanced Placement Mathematics (Calculus AB or Calculus BC) —Fill in circle 5.

<u>Part II.</u> What type of calculator did you bring to use for this test? (FILL IN THE **<u>ONE</u>** CIRCLE THAT APPLIES. If you did not bring a scientific or graphing calculator, do not fill in any of circles 6-9.)

- Scientific —Fill in circle 6.
- Graphing (Fill in the circle corresponding to the model you used.)

  Casio 9700, Casio 9750, Casio 9800, Casio 9850, Casio FX 1.0, Sharp 9200, Sharp 9300, Sharp 9600, Sharp 9900, TI-82, TI-83, TI-83 Plus, TI-83 Plus Silver, TI-84 Plus, TI-84 Plus Silver, TI-85, or TI-86 —Fill in circle 7.

  Casio 9970, Casio Algebra FX 2.0, HP 38G, HP 39 series, HP 40G, HP 48 series, HP 49 series, TI-89, or TI-89 Titanium —Fill in circle 8.

  Some other graphing calculator —Fill in circle 9.

When the supervisor gives the signal, turn the page and begin the Mathematics Level 1 Test. There are 100 numbered circles on the answer sheet and 50 questions in the Mathematics Level 1 Test. Therefore, use only circles 1 to 50 for recording your answers.

MATHEMATICS LEVEL 1 TEST

REFERENCE INFORMATION

THE FOLLOWING INFORMATION IS FOR YOUR REFERENCE IN ANSWERING SOME OF THE QUESTIONS IN THIS TEST.

Volume of a right circular cone with radius r and height h: $V = \frac{1}{3}\pi r^2 h$

Lateral Area of a right circular cone with circumference of the base c and slant height ℓ: $S = \frac{1}{2}c\ell$

Volume of a sphere with radius r: $V = \frac{4}{3}\pi r^3$

Surface Area of a sphere with radius r: $S = 4\pi r^2$

Volume of a pyramid with base area B and height h: $V = \frac{1}{3}Bh$

DO NOT DETACH FROM BOOK.

GO ON TO THE NEXT PAGE

MATHEMATICS LEVEL 1 TEST

For each of the following problems, decide which is the BEST of the choices given. If the exact numerical value is not one of the choices, select the choice that best approximates this value. Then fill in the corresponding circle on the answer sheet.

Notes: (1) A scientific or graphing calculator will be necessary for answering some (but not all) of the questions in this test. For each question you will have to decide whether or not you should use a calculator.

(2) The only angle measure used on this test is degree measure. Make sure your calculator is in the degree mode.

(3) Figures that accompany problems in this test are intended to provide information useful in solving the problems. They are drawn as accurately as possible EXCEPT when it is stated in a specific problem that its figure is not drawn to scale. All figures lie in a plane unless otherwise indicated.

(4) Unless otherwise specified, the domain of any function f is assumed to be the set of all real numbers x for which $f(x)$ is a real number. The range of f is assumed to be the set of all real numbers $f(x)$, where x is in the domain of f.

(5) Reference information that may be useful in answering the questions in this test can be found on the page preceding Question 1.

USE THIS SPACE FOR SCRATCHWORK.

1. If $xy + 7y = 84$ and $x + 7 = 3$, what is the value of y?

(A) −4
(B) 4.9
(C) 8.4
(D) 12
(E) 28

3YBC

GO ON TO THE NEXT PAGE

MATHEMATICS LEVEL 1 TEST—*Continued*

USE THIS SPACE FOR SCRATCHWORK.

2. When four given numbers are multiplied together, the product is negative. Which of the following could be true about the four numbers?

(A) One is negative, two are positive, and one is zero.
(B) Two are negative, one is positive, and one is zero.
(C) Two are negative and two are positive.
(D) Three are negative and one is positive.
(E) Four are negative.

3. If $x + y = 5$ and $x - y = 3$, then $x^2 - y^2 =$

(A) 9 (B) 15 (C) 16 (D) 25 (E) 34

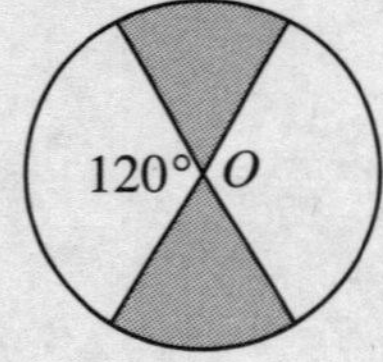

4. In the figure above, what fraction of the circular region with center O is shaded?

(A) $\frac{1}{6}$ (B) $\frac{1}{5}$ (C) $\frac{1}{4}$ (D) $\frac{1}{3}$ (E) $\frac{3}{5}$

GO ON TO THE NEXT PAGE

MATHEMATICS LEVEL 1 TEST—*Continued*

USE THIS SPACE FOR SCRATCHWORK.

5. Which of the following is the graph of a linear function with both a negative slope and a negative y-intercept?

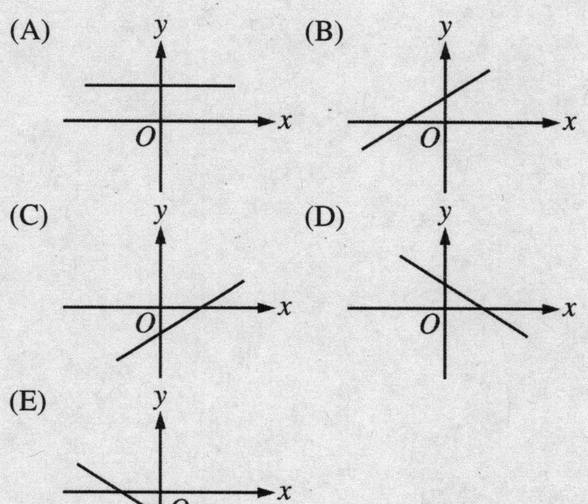

6. If $k^2 - 4 = 4 - k^2$, what are all possible values of k ?

(A) 0 only
(B) 2 only
(C) 4 only
(D) −2 and 2 only
(E) −2, 0, and 2

7. If $b^{2x+1} = b^{3x-1}$ for all values of b, what is the value of x ?

(A) 2 (B) $\frac{3}{2}$ (C) $\frac{2}{3}$ (D) −2 (E) −3

GO ON TO THE NEXT PAGE

MATHEMATICS LEVEL 1 TEST—*Continued*

USE THIS SPACE FOR SCRATCHWORK.

8. At North High School, the number of students taking French is decreasing by 20 students per year and the number of students taking Spanish is increasing by 10 students per year. This year 250 students are taking French, and 100 students are taking Spanish. Which of the following equations could be used to find the number of years n until the number of students is the same in both courses?

(A) $250 - 20n = 100 + 10n$
(B) $250 + 10n = 100 - 20n$
(C) $250 + 20n = 100 - 10n$
(D) $20n - 250 = 100 + 10n$
(E) $n(250 - 20) = n(100 + 10)$

9. If $y = x^3 - 1.5$, for what value of x is $y = 2$?

(A) 0.79
(B) 1.14
(C) 1.52
(D) 1.87
(E) 6.50

10. The length of a rectangle is four times its width. If the perimeter of the rectangle is 40 centimeters, what is its area?

(A) 4 cm^2
(B) 16 cm^2
(C) 20 cm^2
(D) 40 cm^2
(E) 64 cm^2

GO ON TO THE NEXT PAGE

MATHEMATICS LEVEL 1 TEST—*Continued*

USE THIS SPACE FOR SCRATCHWORK.

11. The function g, where $g(t) = 0.066t + 0.96$, can be used to represent the relation between grade point average $g(t)$ and the number of hours t spent studying each week. Based on this function, a student with a grade point average of 3.5 studied how many hours per week?

    (A) 0.96
    (B) 1.2
    (C) 14.5
    (D) 38.5
    (E) 67.8

12. $x^2 - 2x + 3 = x^3 + 2x + x^2$ is equivalent to

    (A) 0
    (B) $2x^2 - 4x = 0$
    (C) $-x^3 + 4x - 3 = 0$
    (D) $x^3 - 2x^2 - 3 = 0$
    (E) $x^3 + 4x - 3 = 0$

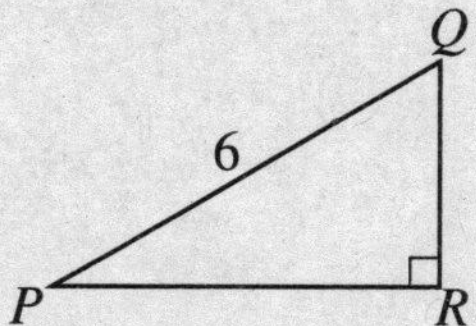

13. In right triangle PQR in the figure above, $\sin P = 0.5$. What is the length of side QR ?

    (A) 2
    (B) 3
    (C) 5
    (D) 6
    (E) 12

GO ON TO THE NEXT PAGE

MATHEMATICS LEVEL 1 TEST—*Continued*

USE THIS SPACE FOR SCRATCHWORK.

14. Which of the following numbers is a COUNTEREXAMPLE to the statement "All odd numbers greater than 2 are prime numbers" ?

(A) 2 (B) 3 (C) 5 (D) 7 (E) 9

15. If $f(x) = \frac{2x - 1}{x^2}$, what is the value of $f(-0.1)$?

(A) −120
(B) −100
(C) 100
(D) 120
(E) 220

16. On a blueprint, 0.4 inch represents 6 feet. If the actual distance between two buildings is 76 feet, what would be the distance between the corresponding buildings on the blueprint?

(A) 3.2 in
(B) 5.1 in
(C) 12.7 in
(D) 30.4 in
(E) 31.7 in

GO ON TO THE NEXT PAGE

MATHEMATICS LEVEL 1 TEST—*Continued*

USE THIS SPACE FOR SCRATCHWORK.

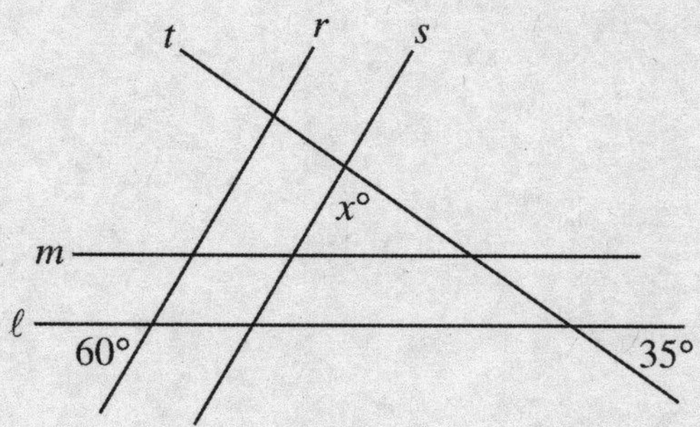

17. In the figure above, if $\ell \parallel m$ and $r \parallel s$, what is the value of x?

(A) 65
(B) 80
(C) 85
(D) 95
(E) 115

18. For what value of x is $\frac{2x}{3x-1}$ undefined?

(A) $-\frac{1}{3}$ (B) 0 (C) $\frac{1}{3}$ (D) $\frac{1}{2}$ (E) 1

19. A sales team sold an average (arithmetic mean) of 10.375 mobile phones per week during the first 8 weeks of the last quarter of the year. The members of the sales team will receive a bonus if they sell a total of 185 phones for the quarter. What must their average sales, in phones per week, be for the remaining 5 weeks of the quarter if they are to receive the bonus?

(A) 4.2
(B) 20.4
(C) 83
(D) 102
(E) 174.6

GO ON TO THE NEXT PAGE

MATHEMATICS LEVEL 1 TEST—*Continued*

USE THIS SPACE FOR SCRATCHWORK.

20. What is the y-coordinate of the point at which the line whose equation is $3x - 2y - 7 = 0$ crosses the y-axis?

(A) $-\frac{7}{2}$

(B) $-\frac{7}{3}$

(C) $\frac{7}{3}$

(D) $\frac{7}{2}$

(E) 7

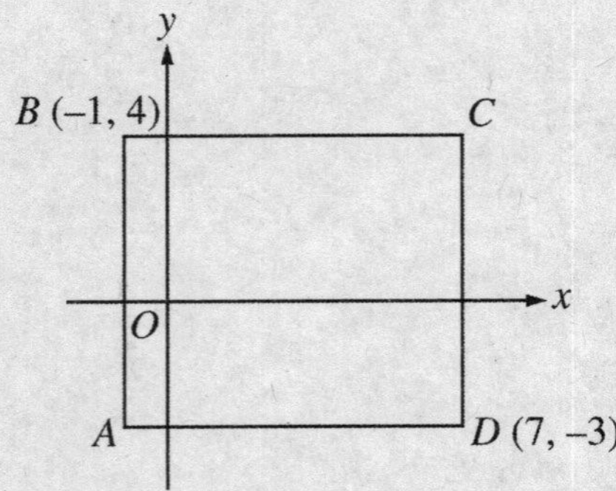

21. In the figure above, the sides of rectangle $ABCD$ are parallel to the axes. What is the distance between point A and point C?

(A) 6.07
(B) 7
(C) 10.1
(D) 10.6
(E) 15

GO ON TO THE NEXT PAGE

MATHEMATICS LEVEL 1 TEST—*Continued*

USE THIS SPACE FOR SCRATCHWORK.

22. Four signal flags — one red, one blue, one yellow, and one green — can be arranged from top to bottom on a signal pole. Every arrangement of the four flags is a different signal. How many different signals using all four flags have the red flag at the top?

(A) 3 (B) 4 (C) 6 (D) 16 (E) 24

23. Triangle FGH is similar to triangle JKL. The length of side GH is 2.1 meters, the length of corresponding side KL is 1.4 meters, and the perimeter of $\triangle JKL$ is 3.6 meters. What is the perimeter of $\triangle FGH$?

(A) 2.4 m
(B) 3.3 m
(C) 4.3 m
(D) 5.1 m
(E) 5.4 m

24. Which of the following is an equation of a line that is parallel to the line with equation $2x - y = 7$?

(A) $y = -2x - 7$

(B) $y = -2x + 7$

(C) $y = -\frac{1}{2}x - 7$

(D) $y = \frac{1}{2}x - 7$

(E) $y = 2x + 7$

GO ON TO THE NEXT PAGE

MATHEMATICS LEVEL 1 TEST—*Continued*

USE THIS SPACE FOR SCRATCHWORK.

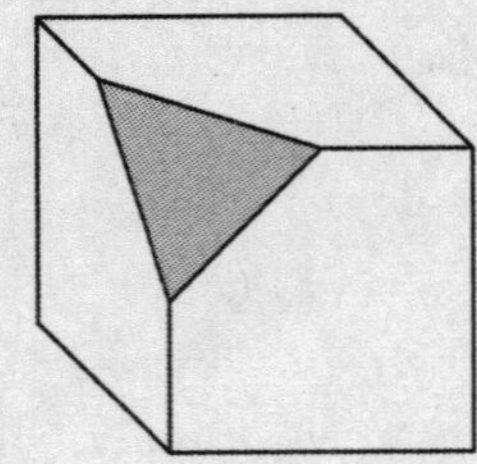

25. A tetrahedron was cut from the corner of the cube shown above, with three of its vertices at the midpoints of three edges of the cube. If tetrahedrons of the same size are cut from the remaining seven corners of the cube, how many faces will the resulting solid have?

(A) 6 (B) 8 (C) 12 (D) 14 (E) 16

26. The consecutive vertices of a certain parallelogram are A, B, C, and D. Which of the following are NOT necessarily congruent?

(A) $\angle A$ and $\angle C$
(B) $\angle B$ and $\angle D$
(C) $\overline{AC}$ and $\overline{BD}$
(D) $\overline{AB}$ and $\overline{CD}$
(E) $\overline{AD}$ and $\overline{BC}$

GO ON TO THE NEXT PAGE

MATHEMATICS LEVEL 1 TEST—*Continued*

USE THIS SPACE FOR SCRATCHWORK.

27. A car traveled 200 miles at an average speed of 45 miles per hour. Of the following, which is the closest approximation to the amount of time that could be saved on this 200-mile trip if the average speed had increased 20 percent?

(A) 1 hour

(B) $\frac{3}{4}$ hour

(C) $\frac{1}{2}$ hour

(D) $\frac{1}{4}$ hour

(E) $\frac{1}{5}$ hour

28. If c is a negative integer, for which of the following values of d is $|c - d|$ greatest?

(A) -10 (B) -4 (C) 0 (D) 4 (E) 10

29. In $\triangle PQR$, $\angle Q$ is a right angle. Which of the following is equal to $\cos P$?

(A) $\frac{PQ}{PR}$

(B) $\frac{PR}{PQ}$

(C) $\frac{PR}{QR}$

(D) $\frac{QR}{PQ}$

(E) $\frac{QR}{PR}$

GO ON TO THE NEXT PAGE

MATHEMATICS LEVEL 1 TEST—*Continued*

USE THIS SPACE FOR SCRATCHWORK.

30. The junior class is sponsoring a drama production to raise funds and plans to charge the same price for all admission tickets. The class has \$700 in expenses for this production. If 300 tickets are sold, the class will make a profit of \$1,100. What will be the profit for the class if 500 tickets are sold?

(A) \$1,133
(B) \$1,833
(C) \$2,300
(D) \$3,000
(E) \$3,700

31. In the xy-plane, the point (6, 3) is the midpoint of the line segment with endpoints $(x, 5)$ and $(9, y)$. What is the value of $x + y$?

(A) 4 (B) 9 (C) 14 (D) 18 (E) 32

32. If $\frac{1}{2}$ is $\frac{3}{4}$ of $\frac{4}{5}$ of a certain number, what is that number?

(A) $\frac{3}{10}$
(B) $\frac{5}{6}$
(C) $\frac{11}{10}$
(D) $\frac{6}{5}$
(E) $\frac{10}{3}$

GO ON TO THE NEXT PAGE

MATHEMATICS LEVEL 1 TEST—*Continued*

USE THIS SPACE FOR SCRATCHWORK.

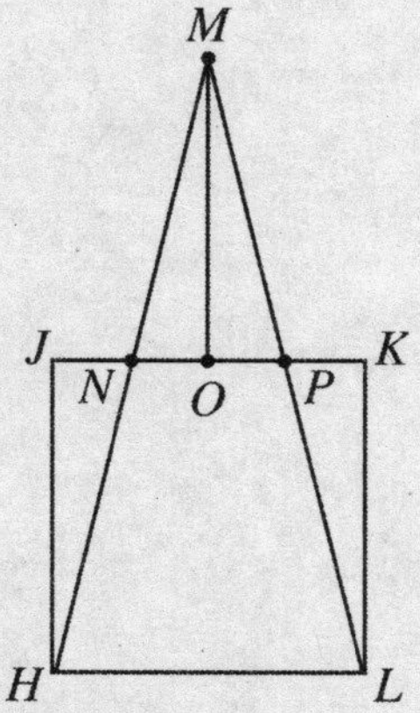

33. In the figure above, $HJKL$ is a square and $JN = NO = OP = PK$. What is the ratio of the area of $\triangle MNP$ to the area of square $HJKL$?

(A) $\frac{1}{8}$ (B) $\frac{1}{4}$ (C) $\frac{1}{3}$ (D) $\frac{3}{8}$ (E) $\frac{1}{2}$

34. Which of the following numbers is NOT contained in the domain of the function f if $f(x) = \frac{x+2}{x+3} - \frac{1}{x}$?

(A) -3 (B) -2 (C) 1 (D) $\sqrt{3}$ (E) 3

35. Which of the following is the graph of all values of x for which $1 \leq x^2 \leq 4$?

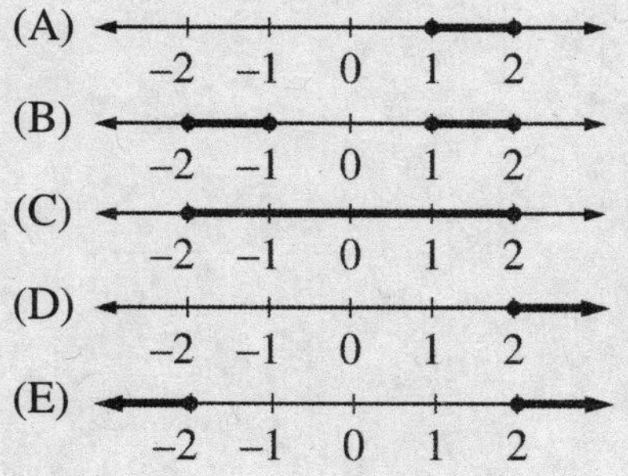

GO ON TO THE NEXT PAGE

MATHEMATICS LEVEL 1 TEST—*Continued*

USE THIS SPACE FOR SCRATCHWORK.

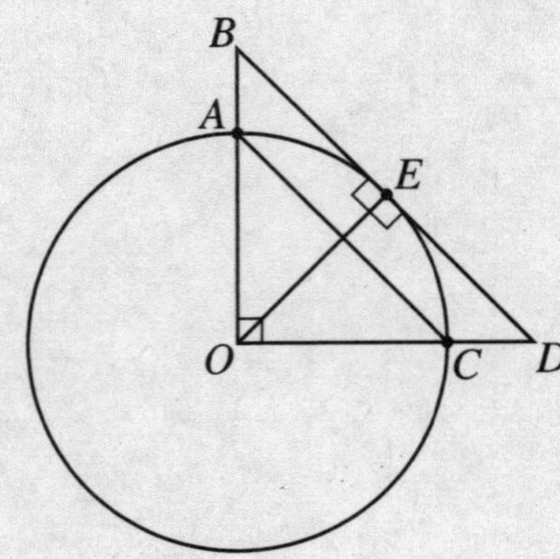

36. The circle in the figure above has center O and radius r. If $OB = OD$, how many of the line segments shown (with labeled endpoints) have length r?

(A) Two
(B) Three
(C) Four
(D) Five
(E) Six

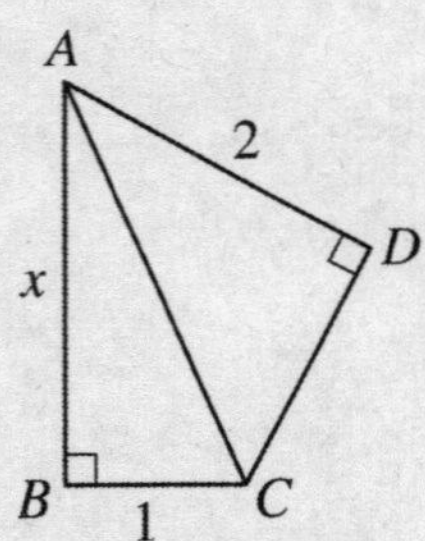

37. In the figure above, if $\triangle ABC$ and $\triangle ADC$ are right triangles, then $CD =$

(A) $\sqrt{x^2 - 3}$

(B) $\sqrt{x^2 + 1}$

(C) $\sqrt{x^2 + 1} + 2$

(D) $\sqrt{x^2 + 3}$

(E) $x^2 + 5$

GO ON TO THE NEXT PAGE

MATHEMATICS LEVEL 1 TEST—*Continued*

USE THIS SPACE FOR SCRATCHWORK.

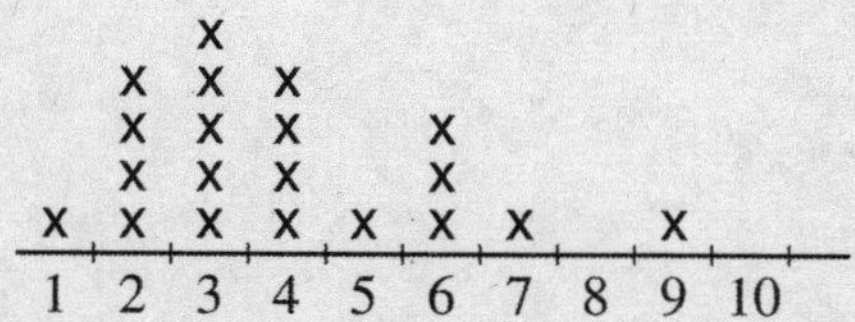

38. Each of 20 students in a class took a sample of 10 candies from a large bag and counted the number of red candies in the sample. The distribution of red candies in their samples is shown above. If one of the students were chosen at random, what is the probability that the student's sample would have at least 5 red candies?

(A) $\frac{3}{5}$

(B) $\frac{3}{10}$

(C) $\frac{1}{4}$

(D) $\frac{3}{20}$

(E) $\frac{1}{20}$

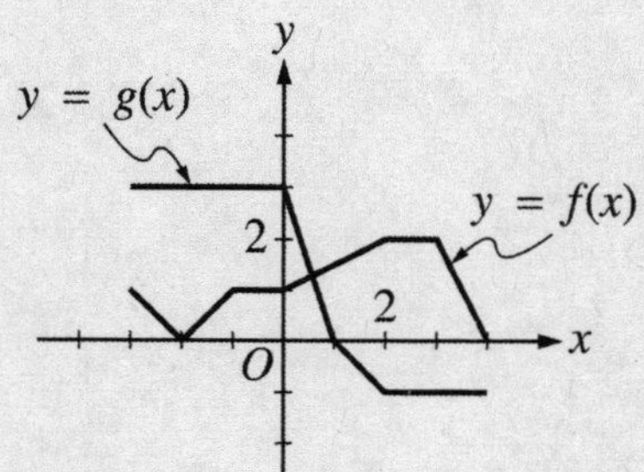

39. The figure above shows the graphs of functions f and g. What is the value of $f(g(3))$?

(A) −2 (B) −1 (C) 0 (D) 1 (E) 2

GO ON TO THE NEXT PAGE

MATHEMATICS LEVEL 1 TEST—*Continued*

USE THIS SPACE FOR SCRATCHWORK.

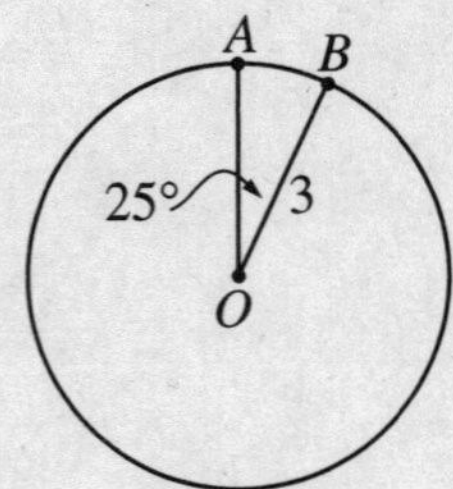

40. If O is the center of the circle in the figure above, what is the length of minor arc AB ?

(A) 0.65
(B) 1.27
(C) 1.31
(D) 1.40
(E) 1.96

41. In the xy-plane, which of the following are the points of intersection of the circles whose equations are $x^2 + y^2 = 4$ and $(x - 2)^2 + y^2 = 4$?

(A) $(-1, \sqrt{3}), (-1, -\sqrt{3})$
(B) $(1, \sqrt{3}), (1, -\sqrt{3})$
(C) $(1, \sqrt{3}), (-1, \sqrt{3})$
(D) $(1, 1), (-1, 1)$
(E) $(1, 1), (1, -2)$

GO ON TO THE NEXT PAGE

MATHEMATICS LEVEL 1 TEST—*Continued*

USE THIS SPACE FOR SCRATCHWORK.

42. The area of one face of a cube is x square meters. Which of the following gives an expression for the volume of this cube, in cubic meters?

(A) $x\sqrt{x}$

(B) $3\sqrt{x}$

(C) $x^2\sqrt{x}$

(D) x^3

(E) $3x^3$

43. For which of the following equations is it true that the sum of the roots equals the product of the roots?

(A) $x^2 - 4 = 0$
(B) $x^2 - 2x + 1 = 0$
(C) $x^2 - 4x + 4 = 0$
(D) $x^2 - 5x + 6 = 0$
(E) $x^2 + 4x + 4 = 0$

44. If the positive integers, starting with 1, are written consecutively, what will be the 90th digit written?

(A) 0 (B) 1 (C) 5 (D) 8 (E) 9

GO ON TO THE NEXT PAGE

MATHEMATICS LEVEL 1 TEST—*Continued*

USE THIS SPACE FOR SCRATCHWORK.

45. The function f is defined by
$f(x) = x^4 - 4x^2 + x + 1$ for $-5 \le x \le 5$.
In which of the following intervals does the minimum value of f occur?

(A) $-5 < x < -3$
(B) $-3 < x < -1$
(C) $-1 < x < 1$
(D) $1 < x < 3$
(E) $3 < x < 5$

46. In convex polygon P, the sum of the measures of the interior angles is 1,800°. How many sides does P have?

(A) 8 (B) 10 (C) 12 (D) 14 (E) 18

47. What is the least integer value of k such that $x^2(3k + 1) - 6x + 2 = 0$ has no real roots?

(A) 5 (B) 2 (C) 1 (D) -1 (E) -2

48. If $\angle A$ is an acute angle and $\dfrac{\sin^2 A}{\cos^2 A} = 2.468$, what is the value of $\tan A$?

(A) 1.234
(B) 1.571
(C) 2.468
(D) 4.936
(E) 6.091

GO ON TO THE NEXT PAGE

MATHEMATICS LEVEL 1 TEST—*Continued*

USE THIS SPACE FOR SCRATCHWORK.

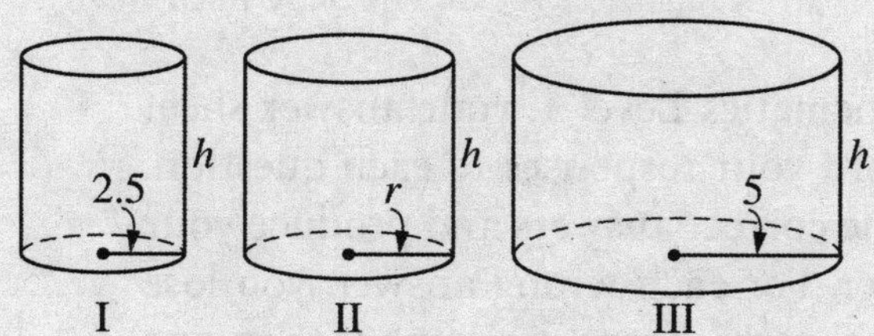

49. In the figure above, all of the right circular cylinders have height h. Cylinders I and III have a base radius of 2.5 and 5, respectively. If the volume of cylinder II is the mean of the volumes of cylinders I and III, what is the radius r of cylinder II?

(A) 1.98
(B) 3.75
(C) 3.95
(D) 4.00
(E) 15.63

50. If f and g are functions, where $f(x) = x^3 - 10x^2 + 27x - 18$ and $g(x) = x^3 - x^2 - 6x$, which of the following gives a relationship between f and g?

(A) $g(x) = 3f(x)$
(B) $g(x) = f(x) - 3$
(C) $g(x) = f(x) + 3$
(D) $g(x) = f(x - 3)$
(E) $g(x) = f(x + 3)$

STOP

IF YOU FINISH BEFORE TIME IS CALLED, YOU MAY CHECK YOUR WORK ON THIS TEST ONLY. DO NOT TURN TO ANY OTHER TEST IN THIS BOOK.

How to Score the SAT Subject Test in Mathematics Level 1

When you take an actual SAT Subject Test in Mathematics Level 1, your answer sheet will be "read" by a scanning machine that will record your responses to each question. Then a computer will compare your answers with the correct answers and produce your raw score. You get one point for each correct answer. For each wrong answer, you lose one-fourth of a point. Questions you omit (and any for which you mark more than one answer) are not counted. This raw score is converted to a scaled score that is reported to you and to the colleges you specify.

Worksheet 1. Finding Your Raw Test Score

STEP 1: Table A lists the correct answers for all the questions on the Subject Test in Mathematics Level 1 that is reproduced in this book. It also serves as a worksheet for you to calculate your raw score.

- Compare your answers with those given in the table.
- Put a check in the column marked "Right" if your answer is correct.
- Put a check in the column marked "Wrong" if your answer is incorrect.
- Leave both columns blank if you omitted the question.

STEP 2: Count the number of right answers.

Enter the total here: ____________________

STEP 3: Count the number of wrong answers.

Enter the total here: ____________________

STEP 4: Multiply the number of wrong answers by .250.

Enter the product here: ________________

STEP 5: Subtract the result obtained in Step 4 from the total you obtained in Step 2.

Enter the result here: __________________

STEP 6: Round the number obtained in Step 5 to the nearest whole number.

Enter the result here: __________________

The number you obtained in Step 6 is your raw score.

Table A

Answers to the Subject Test in Mathematics Level 1, Form 3YBC, and Percentage of Students Answering Each Question Correctly									
Question Number	Correct Answer	Right	Wrong	Percentage of Students Answering the Question Correctly*	Question Number	Correct Answer	Right	Wrong	Percentage of Students Answering the Question Correctly*
1	E			92	26	C			64
2	D			95	27	B			68
3	B			83	28	E			59
4	D			91	29	A			71
5	E			91	30	C			53
6	D			83	31	A			59
7	A			90	32	B			56
8	A			83	33	B			53
9	C			88	34	A			66
10	E			85	35	B			45
11	D			84	36	D			49
12	E			84	37	A			41
13	B			81	38	B			49
14	E			89	39	D			41
15	A			70	40	C			42
16	B			87	41	B			36
17	C			89	42	A			33
18	C			81	43	C			29
19	B			78	44	C			29
20	A			75	45	B			30
21	D			77	46	C			28
22	C			63	47	B			18
23	E			75	48	B			46
24	E			78	49	C			37
25	D			70	50	E			41

* These percentages are based on an analysis of the answer sheets of a representative sample of 21,848 students who took the original form of this test in October 2002, and whose mean score was 605. They may be used as an indication of the relative difficulty of a particular question. Each percentage may also be used to predict the likelihood that a typical SAT Subject Test in Mathematics Level 1 candidate will answer that question correctly on this edition of the test.

Finding Your Scaled Score

When you take SAT Subject Tests, the scores sent to the colleges you specify are reported on the College Board scale, which ranges from 200–800. You can convert your practice test score to a scaled score by using Table B. To find your scaled score, locate your raw score in the left-hand column of Table B; the corresponding score in the right-hand column is your scaled score. For example, a raw score of 28 on this particular edition of the Subject Test in Mathematics Level 1 corresponds to a scaled score of 600.

Raw scores are converted to scaled scores to ensure that a score earned on any one edition of a particular Subject Test is comparable to the same scaled score earned on any other edition of the same Subject Test. Because some editions of the tests may be slightly easier or more difficult than others, College Board scaled scores are adjusted so that they indicate the same level of performance regardless of the edition of the test taken and the ability of the group that takes it. Thus, for example, a score of 400 on one edition of a test taken at a particular administration indicates the same level of achievement as a score of 400 on a different edition of the test taken at a different administration.

When you take the SAT Subject Tests during a national administration, your scores are likely to differ somewhat from the scores you obtain on the tests in this book. People perform at different levels at different times for reasons unrelated to the tests themselves. The precision of any test is also limited because it represents only a sample of all the possible questions that could be asked.

Table B

Scaled Score Conversion Table Subject Test in Mathematics Level 1 (Form 3YBC)					
Raw Score	Scaled Score	Raw Score	Scaled Score	Raw Score	Scaled Score
50	800	28	600	6	390
49	800	27	580	5	390
48	790	26	570	4	380
47	780	25	560	3	370
46	770	24	550	2	360
45	760	23	540	1	360
44	750	22	530	0	350
43	740	21	520	-1	340
42	730	20	510	-2	330
41	720	19	500	-3	330
40	720	18	490	-4	320
39	710	17	490	-5	310
38	700	16	480	-6	300
37	690	15	470	-7	290
36	680	14	460	-8	280
35	670	13	450	-9	270
34	660	12	440	-10	260
33	650	11	440	-11	260
32	640	10	430	-12	250
31	630	9	420		
30	620	8	410		
29	610	7	400		

How Did You Do on the Subject Test in Mathematics Level 1?

After you score your test and analyze your performance, think about the following questions:

Did you run out of time before reaching the end of the test?

If so, you may need to pace yourself better. For example, maybe you spent too much time on one or two hard questions. A better approach might be to skip the ones you can't answer right away and try answering all the questions that remain on the test. Then if there's time, go back to the questions you skipped.

Did you take a long time reading the directions?

You will save time when you take the test by learning the directions to the Subject Test in Mathematics Level 1 ahead of time. Each minute you spend reading directions during the test is a minute that you could use to answer questions.

How did you handle questions you were unsure of?

If you were able to eliminate one or more of the answer choices as wrong and guess from the remaining ones, your approach probably worked to your advantage. On the other hand, making haphazard guesses or omitting questions without trying to eliminate choices could cost you valuable points.

How difficult were the questions for you compared with other students who took the test?

Table A shows you how difficult the multiple-choice questions were for the group of students who took this test during its national administration. The right-hand column gives the percentage of students that answered each question correctly.

A question answered correctly by almost everyone in the group is obviously an easier question. For example, 89 percent of the students answered question 14 correctly. But only 29 percent answered question 43 correctly.

Keep in mind that these percentages are based on just one group of students. They would probably be different with another group of students taking the test.

If you missed several easier questions, go back and try to find out why: Did the questions cover material you haven't yet reviewed? Did you misunderstand the directions?

Mathematics Level 2

Sample Questions

All questions in the Mathematics Level 2 Test are multiple-choice questions in which you must choose the BEST response from the five choices offered. The directions that follow are the same as those that are in the Mathematics Level 2 test.

For each of the following problems, decide which is the BEST of the choices given. If the exact numerical value is not one of the choices, select the choice that best approximates this value. Then fill in the corresponding circle on the answer sheet.

Notes: (1) A scientific or graphing calculator will be necessary for answering some (but not all) of the questions in this test. For each question you will have to decide whether or not you should use a calculator.

(2) For some questions in this test you may have to decide whether your calculator should be in the radian mode or the degree mode.

(3) Figures that accompany problems in this test are intended to provide information useful in solving the problems. They are drawn as accurately as possible EXCEPT when it is stated in a specific problem that its figure is not drawn to scale. All figures lie in a plane unless otherwise indicated.

(4) Unless otherwise specified, the domain of any function f is assumed to be the set of all real numbers x for which $f(x)$ is a real number. The range of f is assumed to be the set of all real numbers $f(x)$, where x is in the domain of f.

(5) Reference information that may be useful in answering the questions in this test can be found on the page preceding Question 1.

Reference Information: The following information is for your reference in answering some of the questions in this test.

Volume of a right circular cone with radius r and height h: $V = \frac{1}{3}\pi r^2 h$

Lateral Area of a right circular cone with circumference of the base c and slant height ℓ: $S = \frac{1}{2}c\ell$

Volume of a sphere with radius r: $V = \frac{4}{3}\pi r^3$

Surface Area of a sphere with radius r: $S = 4\pi r^2$

Volume of a pyramid with base area B and height h: $V = \frac{1}{3}Bh$

Number and Operations

1. From a group of 6 juniors and 8 seniors on the student council, 2 juniors and 4 seniors will be chosen to make up a 6-person committee. How many different 6-person committees are possible?

(A) 84
(B) 85
(C) 1,050
(D) 1,710
(E) 1,890

Choice (C) is the correct answer to question 1. The 2 juniors on the committee can be chosen from the 6 juniors in $\binom{6}{2} = 15$ ways. The 4 seniors on the committee can be chosen from the 8 seniors in $\binom{8}{4} = 70$ ways. Therefore, there are $(15)(70) = 1{,}050$ possibilities for the 6-person committee.

Algebra and Functions

2. If $2^x = 3$, what does 3^x equal?

(A) 5.7
(B) 5.2
(C) 2.0
(D) 1.8
(E) 1.6

A calculator is useful for this problem. To solve for x, you can take the natural log of both sides of the equation.

$$\ln 2^x = \ln 3$$
$$x \ln 2 = \ln 3$$
$$x = \frac{\ln 3}{\ln 2} = \frac{1.0986}{0.6931} \approx 1.5850$$
$$3^x \approx 5.7045$$

Choice (A) is the correct answer to question 2. Since the directions to this test state, "If the exact numerical value is not one of the choices, select the choice that best approximates this value," the correct answer is choice (A).

You can also solve this problem by graphing $Y1 = 2^x$ and $Y2 = 3$ and finding the point of intersection of the two graphs in the standard viewing window. The two graphs intersect at the point with x-coordinate $\approx$ 1.5850. You can store this x-value and then evaluate 3^x, which gives 5.7045. Many graphing calculators retain the last calculation from the graph screen in memory. If you return to the home screen immediately after finding the point of intersection, you can use the x-coordinate (called "X" or "xc," depending on the calculator) to evaluate 3^x.

$$ax^5 + bx^4 + cx^3 + dx^2 + e = 0$$

3. Let a, b, c, d, and e represent nonzero real numbers in the equation above. If the equation has $2i$ as a root, which of the following statements must be true?
   (A) The only other nonreal root of the equation is $-2i$.
   (B) The equation has an odd number of nonreal roots.
   (C) The equation has exactly one real root.
   (D) The equation has an odd number of real roots.
   (E) All real roots of the equation are positive.

Choice (D) is the correct answer to question 3. Since $ax^5 + bx^4 + cx^3 + dx^2 + e = 0$ is a 5th-degree polynomial equation with real coefficients, the equation has exactly 5 roots in the complex number system. Because $2i$ is a root of the equation, $-2i$ is also a root. Complex roots always occur in conjugate pairs $a \pm bi$, where a and b are real numbers and $b \neq 0$.

There are two possibilities for the other 3 roots of the equation.
(1) 1 real root, 2 complex (nonreal) roots
(2) 3 real roots

Since the equation could have 4 nonreal roots, choice (A) does not have to be true. Since nonreal roots always occur in pairs, choice (B) cannot be true. Since the equation could have 3 real roots, choice (C) does not have to be true. We do not have enough information about the polynomial equation to determine the sign of the real roots. Therefore, choice

(E) does not have to be true. Since the equation could have 1 or 3 real roots, choice (D) must be true.

4. Two environmentalists have proposed two different function models for the survival rate of a particular endangered species.

$$f(t) = 100(0.7)^t$$

$$g(t) = 100(0.999993)^{t^5}$$

For the functions f and g above, $f(t)$ and $g(t)$ represent the percentage of the species that survive t years from a starting point $t = 0$. Which of the following statements about the models are true?

I. Both models give the same prediction at approximately $t = 15$ years.

II. Model g predicts that the population size will decrease most rapidly from $t = 0$ to $t = 5$ years.

III. The greatest difference in the two model predictions occurs at approximately $t = 6$ years.

(A) I only
(B) I and II only
(C) I and III only
(D) II and III only
(E) I, II, and III

Choice (C) is the correct answer to question 4 since statements I and III are true. You can use a graphing calculator to help you solve this problem. Enter functions f and g in the calculator as $Y1$ and $Y2$, respectively.

By examining the graphs of the two functions or a table of values for the two functions, you can determine that $f(t) = g(t)$ for a value between $t = 15$ and $t = 16$. Both models give the same prediction at approximately $t = 15.024$. Thus, statement I is true.

By examining the graph of g or a table of values for g on the interval from $t = 0$ to $t = 5$, you can see that the $g(t)$ values are fairly constant and show little decrease. The function values start to decrease after $t = 5$ years. Thus, statement II is not true.

You can look at the graph of $Y1 - Y2$ or a table of values for $Y1 - Y2$ to determine where the greatest difference between the two model predictions occurs. The greatest difference occurs at approximately $t = 5.976$. Thus, statement III is true.

5. If $f(x) = \frac{1-x}{x-1}$ for all $x \neq 1$, which of the following statements must be true?

   I. $f(3) = f(2)$

   II. $f(0) = f(2)$

   III. $f(0) = f(4)$

(A) None
(B) I only
(C) II only
(D) II and III only
(E) I, II, and III

Choice (E) is the correct answer to question 5. Realizing that $\frac{1-x}{x-1} = -1$ for all $x \neq 1$ greatly simplifies this problem. Since $f(0)$, $f(2)$, $f(3)$, and $f(4)$ are all equal to –1, statements I, II, and III are all true. If you do not realize $f(x) = -1$, you can easily substitute the numbers in f. Using a calculator may actually be a disadvantage to you if you spend time substituting the numbers into an expression of this kind to find the answer. However, using a graphing calculator, you can graph $y = \frac{1-x}{x-1}$ and see that the graph is a horizontal line crossing the y-axis at –1. Therefore, $f(x) = -1$ for all values of x except 1.

6. Let h be the function defined by $h(t) = |5\cos\left(\frac{2}{3}t\right) - 2|$. What is the period of h ?

(A) $\frac{2}{3}$
(B) 3
(C) 5
(D) 2π
(E) 3π

Choice (E) is the correct answer to question 6. The period of h corresponds to the length of one cycle of the graph of h. The smallest positive real number k such that $h(x+k) = h(x)$ for every value of x in the domain of h is the period. By examining the graph of h on your graphing calculator, you can see that the values of $h(x)$ repeat every 3π units.

Alternately, note that the graph of h is obtained from the graph of $y = \cos t$ by applying several transformations. The vertical "stretch" by a factor of 5 units and the shift down 2 units do not affect the period of the function. The absolute value, in this case, also does not affect the period of the function. The horizontal "stretch" is a result of the $\frac{2}{3}$.

This affects the period. Since the period of $\cos t$ is 2π, the period of h can be found by $\dfrac{2\pi}{\left|\frac{2}{3}\right|} = 3\pi$.

7. If $f(x) = \dfrac{1}{x-5}$ and $g(x) = \sqrt{x+4}$, what is the domain of $f-g$?

   (A) All x such that $x \neq 5$ and $x \leq 4$

   (B) All x such that $x \neq -5$ and $x \leq 4$

   (C) All x such that $x \neq 5$ and $x \geq -4$

   (D) All x such that $x \neq -4$ and $x \geq -5$

   (E) All real numbers x

Choice (C) is the correct answer to question 7. The function $f-g$ will be defined at exactly those points where f and g are both defined. In other words, the domain of $f-g$ is the intersection of the domain of f and the domain of g. Since $f(x) = \dfrac{1}{x-5}$ is defined for all $x \neq 5$, and $g(x) = \sqrt{x+4}$ is defined for all $x \geq -4$, the domain of $f-g$ is all x such that $x \neq 5$ and $x \geq -4$.

You can also examine the graph of $f-g$. The graph is defined for all real numbers $x \geq -4$ except for $x = 5$, where the graph has a vertical asymptote.

Geometry and Measurement: Coordinate Geometry

8. A translation in the xy-plane moves the point with coordinates (x, y) to the point with coordinates $(x-4, y+7)$. If point A' is the image of point A under this translation, what is the distance between points A and A'?

   (A) 3.0

   (B) 5.7

   (C) 7.9

   (D) 8.1

   (E) 11.0

Choice (D) is the correct answer to question 8. Point A' is 4 units to the left and 7 units above point A in the xy-plane. Point A can be represented by coordinates (x, y) and point A' can be represented by coordinates $(x-4, y+7)$. You can use the distance formula to find the distance between the two points.

$$\begin{aligned}\text{distance} &= \sqrt{((x-4)-x)^2 + ((y+7)-y)^2}\\ &= \sqrt{16+49} = \sqrt{65} \approx 8.1\end{aligned}$$

Geometry and Measurement: Three-Dimensional Geometry

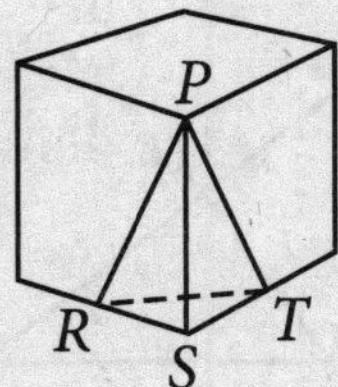

9. In the figure above, R and T are the midpoints of two adjacent edges of the cube. If the length of each edge of the cube is h, what is the volume of pyramid $PRST$?

(A) $\frac{h^3}{24}$

(B) $\frac{h^3}{12}$

(C) $\frac{h^3}{8}$

(D) $\frac{h^3}{6}$

(E) $\frac{h^3}{4}$

The formula for the volume of the pyramid and several other formulae are given in the reference information at the beginning of the test. The volume of a pyramid is $\frac{1}{3}Bh$, where B is the area of the base of the pyramid and h is its height. It may be helpful to mark the figure to indicate those parts whose lengths are given or that can be deduced.

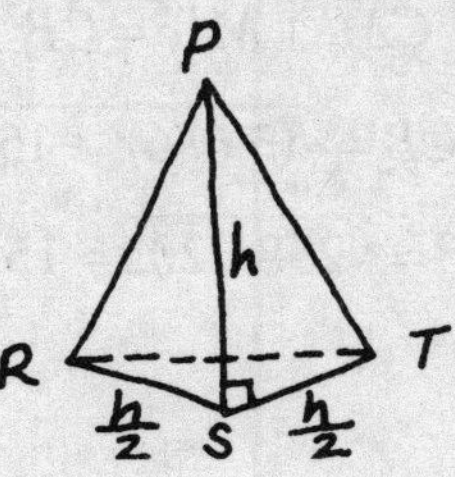

Choice (A) is the correct answer to question 9. Since $\overline{PS}$ is perpendicular to the triangular base RST, its length h is the height of the pyramid $PRST$. R and T are the midpoints of the two adjacent edges of the cube; therefore, $RS = ST = \frac{h}{2}$. Since $\triangle RST$ is a right triangle, its area is $\left(\frac{1}{2}\right)\left(\frac{h}{2}\right)\left(\frac{h}{2}\right) = \frac{h^2}{8}$. Thus, the volume of $PRST$ is $\left(\frac{1}{3}\right)\left(\frac{h^2}{8}\right)(h) = \frac{h^3}{24}$.

Geometry and Measurement: Trigonometry

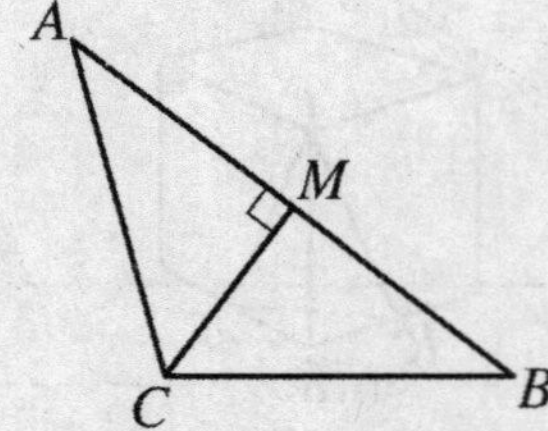

Note: Figure not drawn to scale.

10. In $\triangle ABC$ above, $\overline{CM} \perp \overline{AB}$. If $AM = 9$, $MB = 15$, and the measure of $\angle BAC$ is 22°, what is the length of $\overline{CB}$?

(A) 3.64

(B) 9.71

(C) 15.43

(D) 17.16

(E) 17.49

Choice (C) is the correct answer to question 10. You can use right triangle ACM to find the length of $\overline{CM}$.

$$\tan 22° = \frac{CM}{9}; \text{ thus, } CM \approx 3.636.$$

Now you can use the Pythagorean theorem on right triangle CMB to find the length of $\overline{CB}$.

$$CM^2 + MB^2 = CB^2$$

$$CB = \sqrt{(3.636)^2 + 15^2}$$

$$CB \approx \sqrt{238.2205} \approx 15.43$$

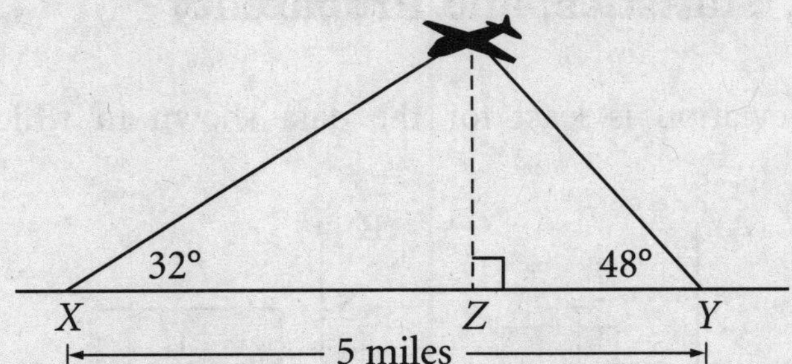

11. The airplane in the figure above is flying directly over point Z on a straight, level road. The angles of elevation for points X and Y are 32° and 48°, respectively. If points X and Y are 5 miles apart, what is the distance, in miles, from the airplane to point X?
    (A) 1.60
    (B) 2.40
    (C) 2.69
    (D) 3.77
    (E) 7.01

Choice (D) is the correct answer to question 11. Label the location of the airplane as point W. Then in $\triangle XYW$, the measure of $\angle X$ is 32°, the measure of $\angle Y$ is 48°, and the measure of $\angle W$ is 100°. Let x, y, and w denote the lengths, in miles, of the sides of $\triangle XYW$ opposite $\angle X$, $\angle Y$, and $\angle W$, respectively. By the law of sines, $\frac{x}{\sin X} = \frac{y}{\sin Y} = \frac{w}{\sin W}$. Since $w = 5$ and the distance from the plane to point X is y, it follows that $\frac{5}{\sin 100°} = \frac{y}{\sin 48°}$. This gives $y \approx 3.77$ for the distance, in miles, from the plane to point X.

Data Analysis, Statistics, and Probability

12. The standard deviation is least for the data shown in which of the following histograms?

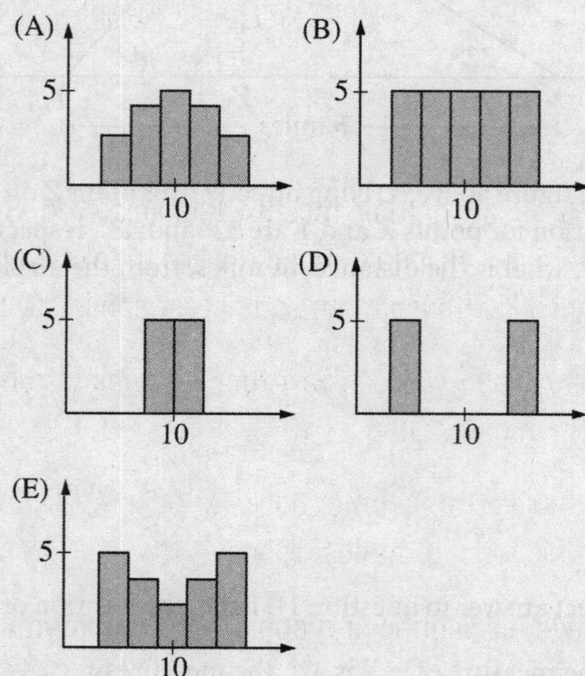

Choice (C) is the correct answer to question 12. The standard deviation is a measure of spread—how far the observations in a set of data are from their mean.

The data is closest to 10 in the histogram in choice (C), and thus has the least standard deviation. In each of the other choices, the data is further spread from 10.

Mathematics Level 2 Test

Practice Helps

The test that follows is an actual, recently administered SAT Subject Test in Mathematics Level 2. To get an idea of what it's like to take this test, practice under conditions that are much like those of an actual test administration.

- Set aside an hour when you can take the test uninterrupted. Make sure you complete the test in one sitting.
- Sit at a desk or table with no other books or papers. Dictionaries, other books, or notes are not allowed in the test room.
- Remember to have a scientific or graphing calculator with you.
- Tear out an answer sheet from the back of this book and fill it in just as you would on the day of the test. One answer sheet can be used for up to three Subject Tests.
- Read the instructions that precede the practice test. During the actual administration, you will be asked to read them before answering test questions.
- Time yourself by placing a clock or kitchen timer in front of you.
- After you finish the practice test, read the sections "How to Score the SAT Subject Test in Mathematics Level 2" and "How Did You Do on the Subject Test in Mathematics Level 2?"
- The appearance of the answer sheet in this book may differ from the answer sheet you see on test day.

MATHEMATICS LEVEL 2 TEST

The top portion of the section of the answer sheet that you will use in taking the Mathematics Level 2 Test must be filled in exactly as shown in the illustration below. Note carefully that you have to do all of the following on your answer sheet.

1. Print MATHEMATICS LEVEL 2 on the line under the words "Subject Test (print)."

2. In the shaded box labeled "Test Code" fill in four circles:

   —Fill in circle 5 in the row labeled V.
   —Fill in circle 3 in the row labeled W.
   —Fill in circle 5 in the row labeled X.
   —Fill in circle E in the row labeled Y.

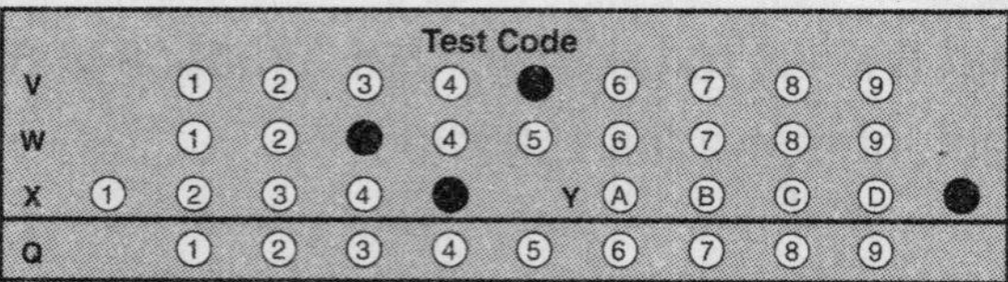

3. Please answer Part I and Part II below by filling in the specified circles in row Q that correspond to the courses you have taken or are presently taking, and the circle that corresponds to the type of calculator you are going to use to take this test. <u>The information that you provide is for statistical purposes only and will not affect your score on the test.</u>

<u>Part I.</u> Which of the following describes a mathematics course you have taken or are currently taking? (FILL IN **<u>ALL</u>** CIRCLES THAT APPLY.)

- Algebra I or Elementary Algebra **<u>OR</u>** Course I of a college preparatory mathematics sequence —Fill in circle 1.
- Geometry **<u>OR</u>** Course II of a college preparatory mathematics sequence —Fill in circle 2.
- Algebra II or Intermediate Algebra **<u>OR</u>** Course III of a college preparatory mathematics sequence —Fill in circle 3.
- Elementary Functions (Precalculus) and/or Trigonometry **<u>OR</u>** beyond Course III of a college preparatory mathematics sequence —Fill in circle 4.
- Advanced Placement Mathematics (Calculus AB or Calculus BC) —Fill in circle 5.

<u>Part II.</u> What type of calculator did you bring to use for this test? (FILL IN THE **<u>ONE</u>** CIRCLE THAT APPLIES. If you did not bring a scientific or graphing calculator, do not fill in any of circles 6-9.)

- Scientific —Fill in circle 6.
- Graphing (Fill in the circle corresponding to the model you used.)

  Casio 9700, Casio 9750, Casio 9800, Casio 9850, Casio FX 1.0, Sharp 9200, Sharp 9300, Sharp 9600, Sharp 9900, TI-82, TI-83, TI-83 Plus, TI-83 Plus Silver, TI-84 Plus, TI-84 Plus Silver, TI-85, or TI-86 —Fill in circle 7.

  Casio 9970, Casio Algebra FX 2.0, HP 38G, HP 39 series, HP 40G, HP 48 series, HP 49 series, TI-89, or TI-89 Titanium —Fill in circle 8.

  Some other graphing calculator —Fill in circle 9.

When the supervisor gives the signal, turn the page and begin the Mathematics Level 2 Test. There are 100 numbered circles on the answer sheet and 50 questions in the Mathematics Level 2 Test. Therefore, use only circles 1 to 50 for recording your answers.

MATHEMATICS LEVEL 2 TEST

REFERENCE INFORMATION

THE FOLLOWING INFORMATION IS FOR YOUR REFERENCE IN ANSWERING SOME OF THE QUESTIONS IN THIS TEST.

Volume of a right circular cone with radius r and height h: $V = \frac{1}{3}\pi r^2 h$

Lateral Area of a right circular cone with circumference of the base c and slant height ℓ: $S = \frac{1}{2}c\ell$

Volume of a sphere with radius r: $V = \frac{4}{3}\pi r^3$

Surface Area of a sphere with radius r: $S = 4\pi r^2$

Volume of a pyramid with base area B and height h: $V = \frac{1}{3}Bh$

DO NOT DETACH FROM BOOK.

GO ON TO THE NEXT PAGE

MATHEMATICS LEVEL 2 TEST

For each of the following problems, decide which is the BEST of the choices given. If the exact numerical value is not one of the choices, select the choice that best approximates this value. Then fill in the corresponding circle on the answer sheet.

Notes: (1) A scientific or graphing calculator will be necessary for answering some (but not all) of the questions in this test. For each question you will have to decide whether or not you should use a calculator.

(2) For some questions in this test you may have to decide whether your calculator should be in the radian mode or the degree mode.

(3) Figures that accompany problems in this test are intended to provide information useful in solving the problems. They are drawn as accurately as possible EXCEPT when it is stated in a specific problem that its figure is not drawn to scale. All figures lie in a plane unless otherwise indicated.

(4) Unless otherwise specified, the domain of any function f is assumed to be the set of all real numbers x for which $f(x)$ is a real number. The range of f is assumed to be the set of all real numbers $f(x)$, where x is in the domain of f.

(5) Reference information that may be useful in answering the questions in this test can be found on the page preceding Question 1.

USE THIS SPACE FOR SCRATCHWORK.

1. If $3x + 6 = \frac{k}{4}(x + 2)$ for all x, then $k =$

(A) $\frac{1}{4}$ (B) 3 (C) 4 (D) 12 (E) 24

3YBC

GO ON TO THE NEXT PAGE

MATHEMATICS LEVEL 2 TEST—*Continued*

USE THIS SPACE FOR SCRATCHWORK.

2. The relationship between a reading C on the Celsius temperature scale and a reading F on the Fahrenheit temperature scale is $C = \frac{5}{9}(F - 32)$, and the relationship between a reading on the Celsius temperature scale and a reading K on the Kelvin temperature scale is $K = C + 273$. Which of the following expresses the relationship between readings on the Kelvin and Fahrenheit temperature scales?

   (A) $K = \frac{5}{9}(F - 241)$

   (B) $K = \frac{5}{9}(F + 305)$

   (C) $K = \frac{5}{9}(F - 32) + 273$

   (D) $K = \frac{5}{9}(F - 32) - 273$

   (E) $K = \frac{5}{9}(F + 32) + 273$

3. What is the slope of the line containing the points $(3, 11)$ and $(-2, 5)$?

   (A) 0.17
   (B) 0.83
   (C) 1.14
   (D) 1.20
   (E) 6

4. If $x + y = 2$, $y + z = 5$, and $x + y + z = 10$, then $y =$

   (A) -3

   (B) $\frac{3}{17}$

   (C) 1

   (D) 3

   (E) $\frac{17}{3}$

GO ON TO THE NEXT PAGE

MATHEMATICS LEVEL 2 TEST—*Continued*

USE THIS SPACE FOR SCRATCHWORK.

5. If $f(x) = 3\ln(x) - 1$ and $g(x) = e^x$, then $f(g(5)) =$

(A) 6.83
(B) 12
(C) 14
(D) 45.98
(E) 568.17

6. The intersection of a cube with a plane could be which of the following?

I. A square
II. A parallelogram
III. A triangle

(A) I only
(B) II only
(C) III only
(D) I and III only
(E) I, II, and III

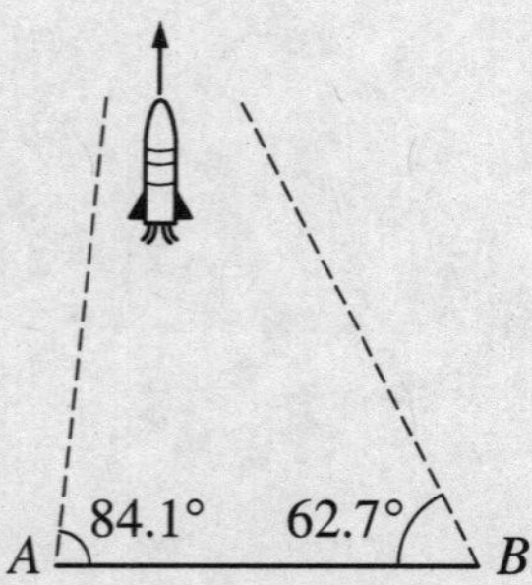

7. The figure above shows a rocket taking off vertically. When the rocket reaches a height of 12 kilometers, the angles of elevation from points A and B on level ground are 84.1° and 62.7°, respectively. What is the distance between points A and B?

(A) 0.97 km
(B) 6.36 km
(C) 7.43 km
(D) 22.60 km
(E) 139.37 km

GO ON TO THE NEXT PAGE

MATHEMATICS LEVEL 2 TEST—*Continued*

USE THIS SPACE FOR SCRATCHWORK.

8. What is the value of x^2 if $x = \sqrt{15^2 - 12^2}$?

(A) $\sqrt{3}$ (B) 3 (C) 9 (D) 81 (E) 81^2

9. The points in the rectangular coordinate plane are transformed in such a way that each point $P(x, y)$ is moved to the point $P'(2x, 2y)$. If the distance between a point P and the origin is d, then the distance between the point P' and the origin is

(A) $\frac{1}{d}$

(B) $\frac{d}{2}$

(C) d

(D) $2d$

(E) d^2

10. If $f(g(x)) = \dfrac{2\sqrt{x^2+1} - 1}{\sqrt{x^2+1} + 1}$ and $f(x) = \dfrac{2x-1}{x+1}$,

then $g(x) =$

(A) $\sqrt{x}$

(B) $\sqrt{x^2+1}$

(C) x

(D) x^2

(E) $x^2 + 1$

GO ON TO THE NEXT PAGE

MATHEMATICS LEVEL 2 TEST—*Continued*

USE THIS SPACE FOR SCRATCHWORK.

11. If A is the degree measure of an acute angle and $\sin A = 0.8$, then $\cos(90° - A) =$

(A) 0.2
(B) 0.4
(C) 0.5
(D) 0.6
(E) 0.8

12. The set of points (x, y, z) such that $x^2 + y^2 + z^2 = 1$ is

(A) empty
(B) a point
(C) a sphere
(D) a circle
(E) a plane

13. The graph of the rational function f, where $f(x) = \dfrac{5}{x^2 - 8x + 16}$, has a vertical asymptote at $x =$

(A) 0 only
(B) 4 only
(C) 5 only
(D) 0 and 4 only
(E) 0, 4, and 5

GO ON TO THE NEXT PAGE

MATHEMATICS LEVEL 2 TEST—*Continued*

USE THIS SPACE FOR SCRATCHWORK.

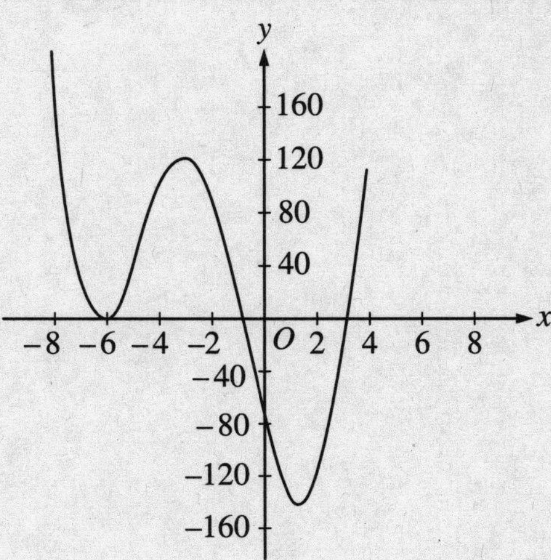

14. The graph of $y = x^4 + 10x^3 + 10x^2 - 96x + c$ is shown above. Which of the following could be the value of c ?

    (A) 3,240
    (B) 1,080
    (C) 72
    (D) −72
    (E) −3,240

15. If $\cos x = 0.4697$, then $\sec x =$

    (A) 2.1290
    (B) 2.0452
    (C) 1.0818
    (D) 0.9243
    (E) 0.4890

GO ON TO THE NEXT PAGE

MATHEMATICS LEVEL 2 TEST—*Continued*

USE THIS SPACE FOR SCRATCHWORK.

16. A club is planning a trip to a museum that has an admission price of \$7 per person. The club members going on the trip must share the \$200 cost of a bus and the admission price for 2 chaperones who will accompany them on the trip. Which of the following correctly expresses the cost, in dollars, for each club member as a function of n, the number of club members going on the trip?

(A) $c(n) = \dfrac{200 + 7n}{n}$

(B) $c(n) = \dfrac{214 + 7n}{n}$

(C) $c(n) = \dfrac{200 + 7n}{n + 2}$

(D) $c(n) = \dfrac{200 + 7n}{n - 2}$

(E) $c(n) = \dfrac{214 + 7n}{n - 2}$

17. Which of the following is an equation whose graph is the set of points equidistant from the points (0, 0) and (0, 4) ?

(A) $x = 2$
(B) $y = 2$
(C) $x = 2y$
(D) $y = 2x$
(E) $y = x + 2$

18. What is the sum of the infinite geometric series

$\frac{1}{4} + \frac{1}{8} + \frac{1}{16} + \frac{1}{32} + \ldots$?

(A) $\frac{1}{2}$ (B) 1 (C) $\frac{3}{2}$ (D) 2 (E) $\frac{5}{2}$

GO ON TO THE NEXT PAGE

MATHEMATICS LEVEL 2 TEST—*Continued*

USE THIS SPACE FOR SCRATCHWORK.

19. Which of the following is equivalent to $p + s > p - s$?

(A) $p > s$
(B) $p > 0$
(C) $s > p$
(D) $s > 0$
(E) $s < 0$

20. If a and b are in the domain of a function f and $f(a) < f(b)$, which of the following must be true?

(A) $a = 0$ or $b = 0$
(B) $a < b$
(C) $a > b$
(D) $a \neq b$
(E) $a = b$

21. In a recent survey, it was reported that 75 percent of the population of a certain state lived within ten miles of its largest city and that 40 percent of those who lived within ten miles of the largest city lived in single-family houses. If a resident of this state is selected at random, what is the probability that the person lives in a single-family house within ten miles of the largest city?

(A) 0.10
(B) 0.15
(C) 0.30
(D) 0.35
(E) 0.53

22. To the nearest degree, what is the measure of the smallest angle in a right triangle with sides of lengths 3, 4, and 5 ?

(A) 27°
(B) 30°
(C) 37°
(D) 45°
(E) 53°

GO ON TO THE NEXT PAGE

MATHEMATICS LEVEL 2 TEST—*Continued*

USE THIS SPACE FOR SCRATCHWORK.

23. Which of the following is an equation of a line perpendicular to $y = -2x + 3$?

(A) $y = 3x - 2$

(B) $y = 2x - 3$

(C) $y = \frac{1}{2}x + 4$

(D) $y = -\frac{1}{2}x + 3$

(E) $y = \frac{1}{-2x + 3}$

24. What is the range of the function f, where $f(x) = -4 + 3\sin(2x + 5\pi)$?

(A) $-7 \leq f(x) \leq 3$
(B) $-7 \leq f(x) \leq -1$
(C) $-3 \leq f(x) \leq 3$
(D) $-3 \leq f(x) \leq -1$
(E) $-1 \leq f(x) \leq 1$

25. Of the following lists of numbers, which has the smallest standard deviation?

(A) 1, 5, 9
(B) 3, 5, 8
(C) 4, 5, 8
(D) 7, 8, 9
(E) 8, 8, 8

GO ON TO THE NEXT PAGE

MATHEMATICS LEVEL 2 TEST—*Continued*

USE THIS SPACE FOR SCRATCHWORK.

26. The formula $A = Pe^{0.08t}$ gives the amount A that a savings account will be worth after an initial investment P is compounded continuously at an annual rate of 8 percent for t years. Under these conditions, how many years will it take an initial investment of \$1,000 to be worth approximately \$5,000 ?

(A) 4.1
(B) 5.0
(C) 8.7
(D) 20.1
(E) 23.0

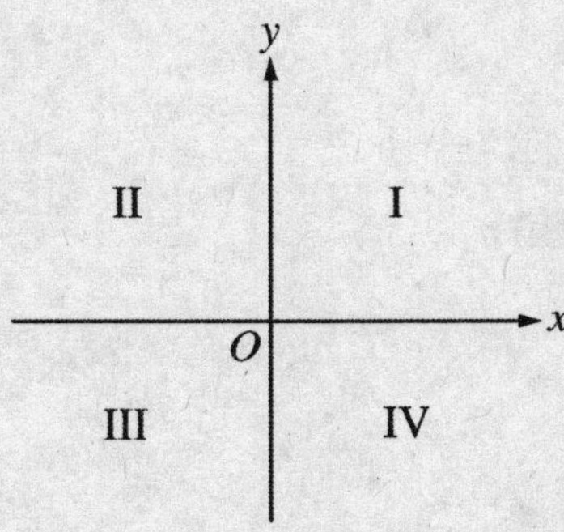

27. If $\sin \theta > 0$ and $\sin \theta \cos \theta < 0$, then θ must be in which quadrant in the figure above?

(A) I
(B) II
(C) III
(D) IV
(E) There is no quadrant in which both conditions are true.

GO ON TO THE NEXT PAGE

MATHEMATICS LEVEL 2 TEST—*Continued*

USE THIS SPACE FOR SCRATCHWORK.

28. If $f(-x) = f(x)$ for all real numbers x and if (3, 8) is a point on the graph of f, which of the following points must also be on the graph of f?

(A) (−8, −3)
(B) (−3, −8)
(C) (−3, 8)
(D) (3, −8)
(E) (8, 3)

If $x = y$, then $x^2 = y^2$.

29. If x and y are real numbers, which of the following CANNOT be inferred from the statement above?

(A) In order for x^2 to be equal to y^2, it is sufficient that x be equal to y.
(B) A necessary condition for x to be equal to y is that x^2 be equal to y^2.
(C) x is equal to y implies that x^2 is equal to y^2.
(D) If x^2 is not equal to y^2, then x is not equal to y.
(E) If x^2 is equal to y^2, then x is equal to y.

30. In how many different orders can 9 students arrange themselves in a straight line?

(A) 9
(B) 81
(C) 181,440
(D) 362,880
(E) 387,420,489

GO ON TO THE NEXT PAGE

MATHEMATICS LEVEL 2 TEST—*Continued*

USE THIS SPACE FOR SCRATCHWORK.

31. What value does $\frac{\ln x}{x-1}$ approach as x approaches 1 ?

(A) 0
(B) 0.43
(C) 1
(D) 2
(E) It does not approach a unique value.

32. If $f(x) = |5 - 3x|$, then $f(2) =$

(A) $f(-2)$
(B) $f(-1)$
(C) $f(1)$
(D) $f\left(\frac{4}{3}\right)$
(E) $f\left(\frac{7}{3}\right)$

33. What is the period of the graph of $y = 2\tan(3\pi x + 4)$?

(A) $\frac{2\pi}{3}$
(B) $\frac{2}{3}$
(C) 2
(D) $\frac{1}{3}$
(E) $\frac{\pi}{3}$

GO ON TO THE NEXT PAGE

MATHEMATICS LEVEL 2 TEST—*Continued*

USE THIS SPACE FOR SCRATCHWORK.

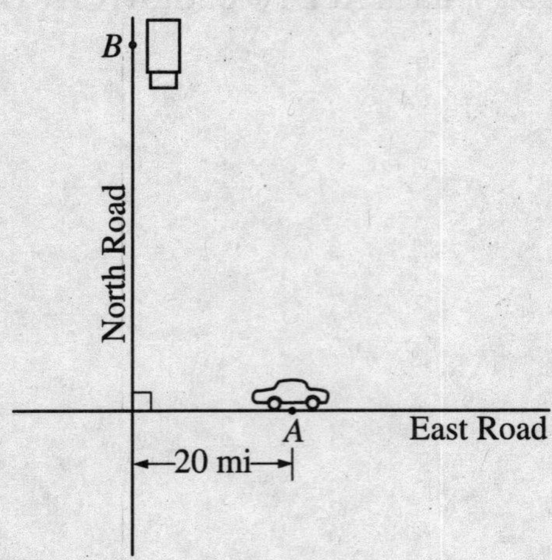

34. The figure above shows a car that has broken down on East Road. A tow truck leaves a garage on North Road at point B. The straight-line distance between points A and B is 50 miles. If the tow truck travels at an average speed of 45 miles per hour along North and East Roads, how long will it take the tow truck to get to the car?

(A) 27 minutes
(B) 1 hour and 7 minutes
(C) 1 hour and 28 minutes
(D) 1 hour and 33 minutes
(E) 1 hour and 46 minutes

GO ON TO THE NEXT PAGE

MATHEMATICS LEVEL 2 TEST—*Continued*

USE THIS SPACE FOR SCRATCHWORK.

x	$f(x)$
−1	0
0	1
1	−1
2	0

35. If f is a polynomial of degree 3, four of whose values are shown in the table above, then $f(x)$ could equal

(A) $\left(x+\frac{1}{2}\right)(x+1)(x+2)$

(B) $(x+1)(x-2)\left(x-\frac{1}{2}\right)$

(C) $(x+1)(x-2)(x-1)$

(D) $(x+2)\left(x-\frac{1}{2}\right)(x-1)$

(E) $(x+2)(x+1)(x-2)$

36. The only prime factors of a number n are 2, 5, 7, and 17. Which of the following could NOT be a factor of n ?

(A) 10 (B) 20 (C) 25 (D) 30 (E) 34

37. If $0 \leq x \leq \frac{\pi}{2}$ and $\sin x = 3\cos x$, what is the value of x ?

(A) 0.322
(B) 0.333
(C) 0.340
(D) 1.231
(E) 1.249

GO ON TO THE NEXT PAGE

MATHEMATICS LEVEL 2 TEST—*Continued*

USE THIS SPACE FOR SCRATCHWORK.

38. If $f(x) = 5\sqrt{2x}$, what is the value of $f^{-1}(10)$?

(A) 0.04
(B) 0.89
(C) 2.00
(D) 2.23
(E) 22.36

39. The Fibonacci sequence can be defined recursively as

$a_1 = 1$

$a_2 = 1$

$a_n = a_{n-1} + a_{n-2}$ for $n \geq 3$.

What is the 10th term of this sequence?

(A) 21
(B) 34
(C) 55
(D) 89
(E) 144

40. If $f(x) = x^3 - 4x^2 - 3x + 2$, which of the following statements are true?

I. The function f is increasing for $x \geq 3$.
II. The equation $f(x) = 0$ has two nonreal solutions.
III. $f(x) \geq -16$ for all $x \geq 0$.

(A) I only
(B) II only
(C) I and II
(D) I and III
(E) II and III

GO ON TO THE NEXT PAGE

MATHEMATICS LEVEL 2 TEST—*Continued*

USE THIS SPACE FOR SCRATCHWORK.

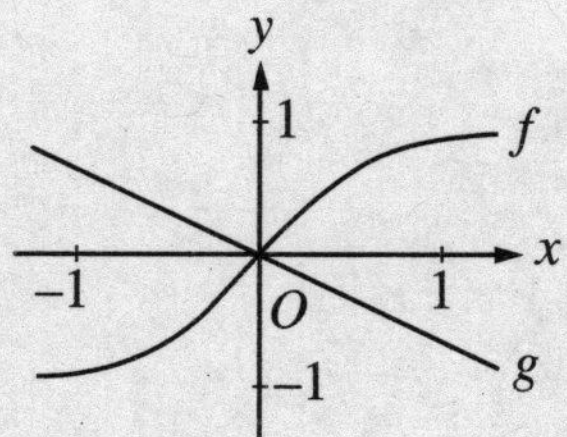

41. Portions of the graphs of f and g are shown above. Which of the following could be a portion of the graph of fg ?

(A)

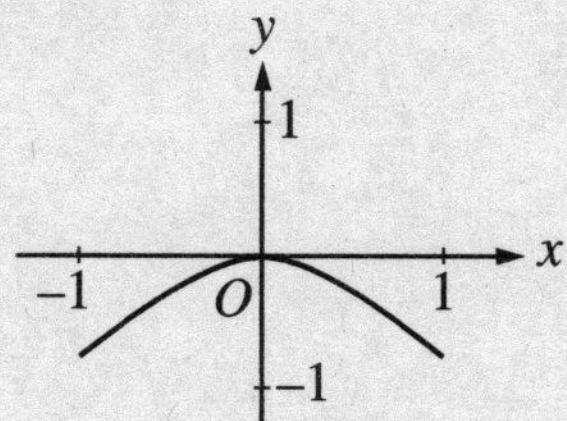

(B)

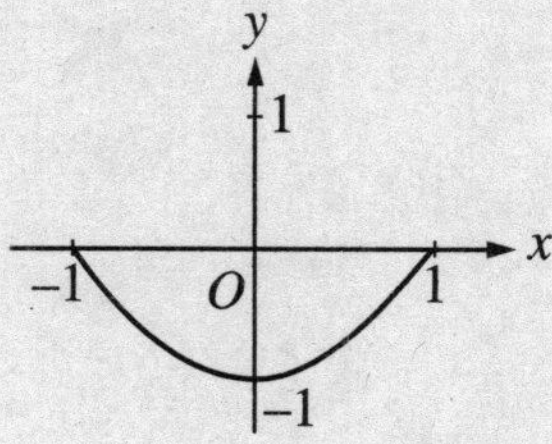

(C)

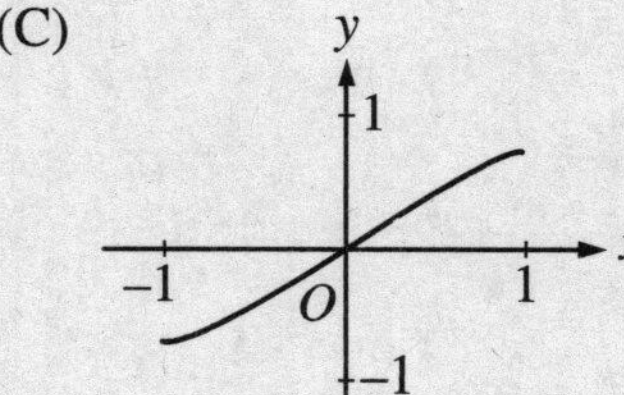

(D)

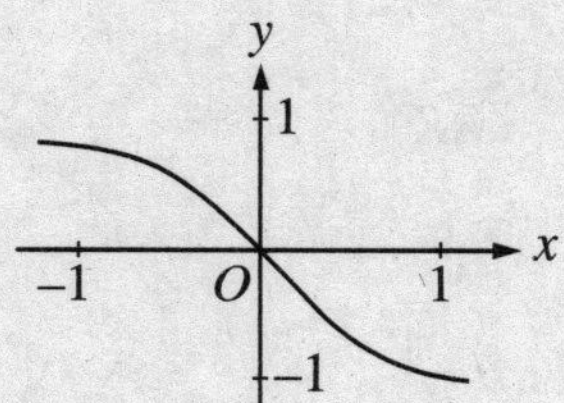

(E)

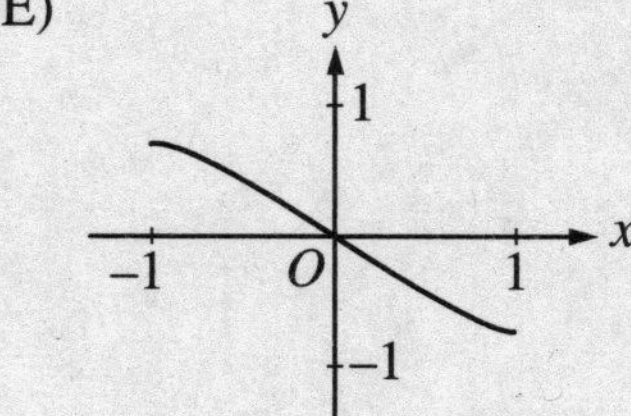

GO ON TO THE NEXT PAGE

MATHEMATICS LEVEL 2 TEST—*Continued*

USE THIS SPACE FOR SCRATCHWORK.

42. The set of all real numbers x such that $\sqrt{x^2} = -x$ consists of

(A) zero only
(B) nonpositive real numbers only
(C) positive real numbers only
(D) all real numbers
(E) no real numbers

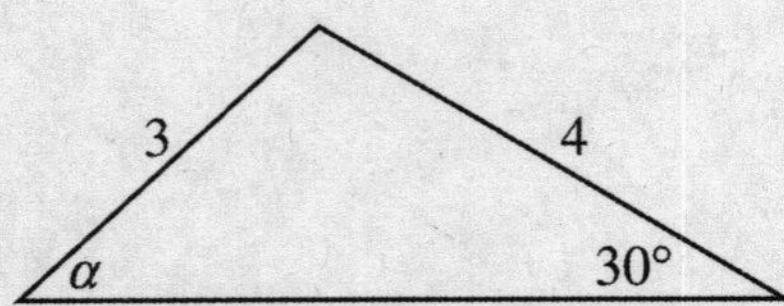

43. In the triangle shown above, $\sin \alpha =$

(A) $\frac{3}{8}$

(B) $\frac{1}{2}$

(C) $\frac{2}{3}$

(D) $\frac{3}{4}$

(E) $\frac{4}{5}$

44. The length, width, and height of a rectangular solid are 8, 4, and 1, respectively. What is the length of the longest line segment whose end points are two vertices of this solid?

(A) $4\sqrt{5}$
(B) 9
(C) $3\sqrt{10}$
(D) 10
(E) 12

GO ON TO THE NEXT PAGE

MATHEMATICS LEVEL 2 TEST—*Continued*

USE THIS SPACE FOR SCRATCHWORK.

45. If $\log_a 3 = x$ and $\log_a 5 = y$, then $\log_a 45 =$

(A) $2x + y$
(B) $x^2 + y$
(C) x^2y
(D) $x + y$
(E) $9x + y$

46. If $\sin \theta = t$, then, for all θ in the interval $0 < \theta < \dfrac{\pi}{2}$, $\tan \theta =$

(A) $\dfrac{1}{\sqrt{1 - t^2}}$
(B) $\dfrac{t}{\sqrt{1 - t^2}}$
(C) $\dfrac{1}{1 - t^2}$
(D) $\dfrac{t}{1 - t^2}$
(E) 1

47. Which of the following shifts of the graph of $y = x^2$ would result in the graph of $y = x^2 - 2x + k$, where k is a constant greater than 2 ?

(A) Left 2 units and up k units
(B) Left 1 unit and up $k + 1$ units
(C) Right 1 unit and up $k + 1$ units
(D) Left 1 unit and up $k - 1$ units
(E) Right 1 unit and up $k - 1$ units

GO ON TO THE NEXT PAGE

USE THIS SPACE FOR SCRATCHWORK.

48. If the height of a right circular cone is decreased by 8 percent, by what percent must the radius of the base be decreased so that the volume of the cone is decreased by 15 percent?

(A) 4%
(B) 7%
(C) 8%
(D) 30%
(E) 45%

49. If matrix A has dimensions $m \times n$ and matrix B has dimensions $n \times p$, where m, n, and p are distinct positive integers, which of the following statements must be true?

I. The product BA does not exist.
II. The product AB exists and has dimensions $m \times p$.
III. The product AB exists and has dimensions $n \times n$.

(A) I only
(B) II only
(C) III only
(D) I and II
(E) I and III

GO ON TO THE NEXT PAGE

MATHEMATICS LEVEL 2 TEST—*Continued*

USE THIS SPACE FOR SCRATCHWORK.

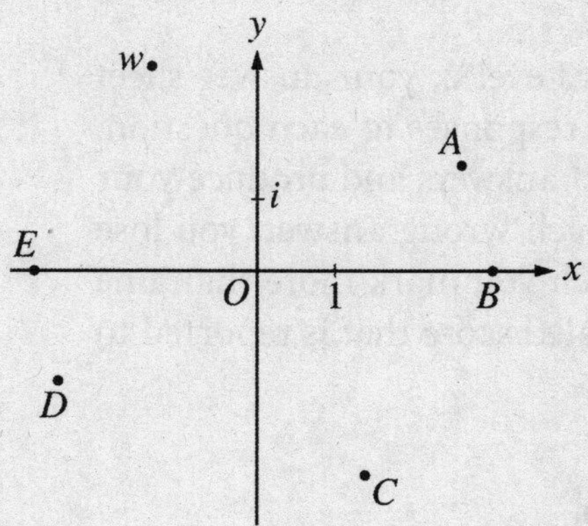

50. If w is the complex number shown in the figure above, which of the following points could be $-iw$?

(A) A (B) B (C) C (D) D (E) E

STOP

IF YOU FINISH BEFORE TIME IS CALLED, YOU MAY CHECK YOUR WORK ON THIS TEST ONLY. DO NOT TURN TO ANY OTHER TEST IN THIS BOOK.

How to Score the SAT Subject Test in Mathematics Level 2

When you take an actual SAT Subject Test in Mathematics Level 2, your answer sheet will be "read" by a scanning machine that will record your responses to each question. Then a computer will compare your answers with the correct answers and produce your raw score. You get one point for each correct answer. For each wrong answer, you lose one-fourth of a point. Questions you omit (and any for which you mark more than one answer) are not counted. This raw score is converted to a scaled score that is reported to you and to the colleges you specify.

Worksheet 1. Finding Your Raw Test Score

STEP 1: Table A lists the correct answers for all the questions on the Subject Test in Mathematics Level 2 that is reproduced in this book. It also serves as a worksheet for you to calculate your raw score.

- Compare your answers with those given in the table.
- Put a check in the column marked "Right" if your answer is correct.
- Put a check in the column marked "Wrong" if your answer is incorrect.
- Leave both columns blank if you omitted the question.

STEP 2: Count the number of right answers.

Enter the total here: ____________________

STEP 3: Count the number of wrong answers.

Enter the total here: ____________________

STEP 4: Multiply the number of wrong answers by .250.

Enter the product here: ________________

STEP 5: Subtract the result obtained in Step 4 from the total you obtained in Step 2.

Enter the result here: __________________

STEP 6: Round the number obtained in Step 5 to the nearest whole number.

Enter the result here: __________________

The number you obtained in Step 6 is your raw score.

Table A

Answers to the Subject Test in Mathematics Level 2, Form 3YBC, and Percentage of Students Answering Each Question Correctly									
Question Number	Correct Answer	Right	Wrong	Percentage of Students Answering the Question Correctly*	Question Number	Correct Answer	Right	Wrong	Percentage of Students Answering the Question Correctly*
1	D			88	26	D			85
2	C			91	27	B			70
3	D			90	28	C			65
4	A			87	29	E			47
5	C			90	30	D			73
6	E			54	31	C			54
7	C			62	32	D			72
8	D			93	33	D			23
9	D			85	34	C			62
10	B			89	35	B			57
11	E			84	36	D			51
12	C			54	37	E			63
13	B			87	38	C			52
14	D			75	39	C			52
15	A			88	40	D			48
16	B			67	41	A			42
17	B			62	42	B			33
18	A			70	43	C			63
19	D			76	44	B			54
20	D			72	45	A			46
21	C			82	46	B			46
22	C			67	47	E			44
23	C			70	48	A			35
24	B			66	49	D			25
25	E			60	50	A			26

* These percentages are based on an analysis of the answer sheets of a representative sample of 15,855 students who took the original form of this test in May 2002, and whose mean score was 652. They may be used as an indication of the relative difficulty of a particular question. Each percentage may also be used to predict the likelihood that a typical SAT Subject Test in Mathematics Level 2 candidate will answer that question correctly on this edition of the test.

Finding Your Scaled Score

When you take SAT Subject Tests, the scores sent to the colleges you specify are reported on the College Board scale, which ranges from 200–800. You can convert your practice test score to a scaled score by using Table B. To find your scaled score, locate your raw score in the left-hand column of Table B; the corresponding score in the right-hand column is your scaled score. For example, a raw score of 26 on this particular edition of the Subject Test in Mathematics Level 2 corresponds to a scaled score of 620.

Raw scores are converted to scaled scores to ensure that a score earned on any one edition of a particular Subject Test is comparable to the same scaled score earned on any other edition of the same Subject Test. Because some editions of the tests may be slightly easier or more difficult than others, College Board scaled scores are adjusted so that they indicate the same level of performance regardless of the edition of the test taken and the ability of the group that takes it. Thus, for example, a score of 400 on one edition of a test taken at a particular administration indicates the same level of achievement as a score of 400 on a different edition of the test taken at a different administration.

When you take the SAT Subject Tests during a national administration, your scores are likely to differ somewhat from the scores you obtain on the tests in this book. People perform at different levels at different times for reasons unrelated to the tests themselves. The precision of any test is also limited because it represents only a sample of all the possible questions that could be asked.

Table B

Scaled Score Conversion Table Subject Test in Mathematics Level 2 (Form 3YBC)					
Raw Score	Scaled Score	Raw Score	Scaled Score	Raw Score	Scaled Score
50	800	28	630	6	470
49	800	27	630	5	460
48	800	26	620	4	450
47	800	25	610	3	440
46	800	24	600	2	430
45	800	23	600	1	420
44	800	22	590	0	410
43	790	21	580	-1	400
42	780	20	580	-2	390
41	770	19	570	-3	370
40	760	18	560	-4	360
39	750	17	560	-5	350
38	740	16	550	-6	340
37	730	15	540	-7	340
36	710	14	530	-8	330
35	700	13	530	-9	330
34	690	12	520	-10	320
33	680	11	510	-11	310
32	670	10	500	-12	300
31	660	9	490		
30	650	8	480		
29	640	7	480		

How Did You Do on the Subject Test in Mathematics Level 2?

After you score your test and analyze your performance, think about the following questions:

Did you run out of time before reaching the end of the test?

If so, you may need to pace yourself better. For example, maybe you spent too much time on one or two hard questions. A better approach might be to skip the ones you can't answer right away and try answering all the questions that remain on the test. Then if there's time, go back to the questions you skipped.

Did you take a long time reading the directions?

You will save time when you take the test by learning the directions to the Subject Test in Mathematics Level 2 ahead of time. Each minute you spend reading directions during the test is a minute that you could use to answer questions.

How did you handle questions you were unsure of?

If you were able to eliminate one or more of the answer choices as wrong and guess from the remaining ones, your approach probably worked to your advantage. On the other hand, making haphazard guesses or omitting questions without trying to eliminate choices could cost you valuable points.

How difficult were the questions for you compared with other students who took the test?

Table A shows you how difficult the multiple-choice questions were for the group of students who took this test during its national administration. The right-hand column gives the percentage of students that answered each question correctly.

A question answered correctly by almost everyone in the group is obviously an easier question. For example, 93 percent of the students answered question 8 correctly. But only 23 percent answered question 33 correctly.

Keep in mind that these percentages are based on just one group of students. They would probably be different with another group of students taking the test.

If you missed several easier questions, go back and try to find out why: Did the questions cover material you haven't yet reviewed? Did you misunderstand the directions?

Chapter 5

Biology E/M

Purpose

The Subject Test in Biology E/M measures the knowledge students would be expected to have after successfully completing a college-preparatory course in high school. The test is designed to be independent of whichever textbook you used or the instructional approach of the biology course you have taken. The Biology E/M Test is for students taking a biology course that has placed particular emphasis on either ecological or molecular biology, with the understanding that evolution is inherent in both. The test lets you choose the area in biology for which you feel best prepared. If you are unsure of the emphasis in your biology course, consult your teacher.

Format

The Subject Test in Biology E/M with either ecological (Biology-E) or molecular (Biology-M) emphasis has a common core of 60 questions, followed by 20 questions in each specialized section (Biology-E or Biology-M). Each test-taker answers 80 questions.

Content

The content covered in the Subject Test in Biology E/M and descriptions of the topics are shown in the chart on page 214.

Biology E/M Test Topics Covered in Common Core	Approximate Percentage of E Test	Approximate Percentage of M Test
Cellular and Molecular Biology	15	27
Cell structure and organization, mitosis, photosynthesis, cellular respiration, enzymes, biosynthesis, biological chemistry		
Ecology	23	13
Energy flow, nutrient cycles, populations, communities, ecosystems, biomes, conservation biology, biodiversity, effects of human intervention		
Genetics	15	20
Meiosis, Mendelian genetics, inheritance patterns, molecular genetics, population genetics		
Organismal Biology	25	25
Structure, function, and development of organisms (with emphasis on plants and animals), animal behavior		
Evolution and Diversity	22	15
Origin of life, evidence of evolution, natural selection, speciation, patterns of evolution, classification and diversity of organisms		

How to Prepare

Before you take the Biology E/M Test, you should have completed a one-year course not only in biology but also in algebra so that you can understand simple algebraic concepts (including ratios and direct and inverse proportions) and apply such concepts to solving word problems. Success in high school biology courses typically requires good reasoning and mathematical skills. Your preparation in biology should have enabled you to develop these and other skills that are important to the study of biology. Familiarize yourself with directions in advance. The directions in this book are identical to those that appear on the test.

Biology-E and Biology-M Skills Specifications	Approximate Percentage of Test
Knowledge of Fundamental Concepts:	30
remembering specific facts; demonstrating straightforward knowledge of information and familiarity with terminology	
Application:	35
understanding concepts and reformulating information into other equivalent forms; applying knowledge to unfamiliar and/or practical situations; solving problems using mathematical relationships	
Interpretation:	35
inferring and deducing from qualitative and quantitative data and integrating information to form conclusions; recognizing unstated assumptions	

You should be able to recall and understand the major concepts of biology and to apply the principles you have learned to solve specific problems in biology. You should also be able to organize and interpret results obtained by observation and experimentation and to draw conclusions or make inferences from experimental data, including data presented in graphic and/or tabular form. Laboratory experience is a significant factor in developing reasoning and problem-solving skills. Although testing of laboratory skills in a multiple-choice test is necessarily limited, reasonable experience in the laboratory will help you prepare for the test.

Notes: (1) You will not be allowed to use a calculator during the Biology E/M Test.

(2) Numerical calculations are limited to simple arithmetic.

(3) The metric system is used in these tests.

How to Choose Biology-E or Biology-M

- Take Biology-E if you feel more comfortable answering questions pertaining to biological communities, populations, and energy flow.
- Take Biology-M if you feel more comfortable answering questions pertaining to biochemistry, cellular structure and processes, such as respiration and photosynthesis.
- Indicate choice of Biology-E or Biology-M on your answer sheet on test day.

You can decide whether you want to take Biology-E or Biology-M on the test day by gridding the appropriate code for the test you have chosen on your answer sheet. *Only questions pertaining to the test code that is gridded on your answer sheet will be scored.*

Note: Because there is a common core of questions, you are not allowed to take Biology-E and Biology-M on the same test date. You can take them on two different test dates.

Score

The total score for each test is reported on the 200-to-800 scale.

Sample Questions

Classification Questions

Each set of classification questions has five lettered choices in the heading that are used in answering all of the questions in the set. The choices may be statements that refer to concepts, principles, organisms, substances, or observable phenomena; or they may be graphs, pictures, equations, formulas, or experimental settings or situations.

Because the same five choices are applicable to several questions, classification questions usually require less reading than other types of multiple-choice questions. Answering a question correctly depends largely on the sophistication of the set of questions. One set may test recall; another may ask you to apply your knowledge to a specific situation or to translate information from one form to another (descriptive, graphical, mathematical). The directions for this type of question specifically state that you should not eliminate a choice simply because it is the correct answer to a previous question.

The following are directions for and an example of a classification set.

Core Section of Biology E/M

Directions: Each set of lettered choices below refers to the numbered statements immediately following it. Select the one lettered choice that best fits each statement and then fill in the corresponding circle on the answer sheet. A choice may be used once, more than once, or not at all in each set.

Questions 1–3 refer to the following pairs of organisms.

(A) Prokaryotes and eukaryotes
(B) Angiosperms and gymnosperms
(C) Algae and fungi
(D) Ferns and mosses
(E) Monocots and dicots

1. Distinguished from each other by the presence or absence of a nuclear envelope

2. Distinguished from each other by the presence or absence of flowers

3. Distinguished from each other by the presence or absence of vascular tissue

The questions in this group are based on biological diversity and refer, in particular, to identification of distinguishing characteristics among certain groups of organisms that have arisen during evolutionary history.

Choice (A) is the correct answer to question 1. This question asks you to recognize that the absence of a nuclear envelope in cells separates prokaryotic cells from all other cells that do have a nuclear envelope, namely the eukaryotes. This characteristic is significant enough to place prokaryotes (including bacteria) in a separate taxonomic group.

Choice (B) is the correct answer to question 2. This question asks you to recognize that the presence or absence of flowers depends on whether seed plants produce seeds that are not enclosed in specialized structures or whether they are contained in specialized complex reproductive structures called ovaries. The former are called gymnosperms and appeared about 200 million years before the emergence of the flowering plants or angiosperms.

Choice (D) is the correct answer to question 3. This question is based on the recognition that the development of vascular tissue (phloem and xylem) was a major adaptation in the long evolution of photosynthetic organisms. Mosses were among the first autotrophs to display evolutionary adaptations to land existence, but they are usually less than 20 centimeters tall because they lack the woody tissue required to support tall plants on land. The evolutionary development of vascular tissue made possible the transporting of water and minerals and food between leaves and roots. Ferns are examples of vascular plants.

Five-Choice Completion Questions

The five-choice question is written either as an incomplete statement or as a question. It is used when: (1) the problem presented is clearly delineated by the wording of the question so that you are asked to choose not a universal solution but the best of the solutions offered; (2) the problem is such that you are required to evaluate the relevance of five plausible, or even scientifically accurate, options and to select the one most pertinent; (3) the problem has several pertinent solutions and you are required to select the one inappropriate solution that is presented. Such questions normally contain a word in capital letters such as NOT, LEAST, or EXCEPT.

A special type of five-choice question is used in some tests, including the SAT Subject Test in Biology E/M, to allow for the possibility of multiple correct answers. For these questions, you must evaluate each response independently of the others in order to select the most appropriate combination. In questions of this type several (usually three or four) statements labeled by Roman numerals are given with the question. One or more of these statements may correctly answer the question. You must select from among the five lettered choices that follow the one combination of statements that best answers the question. In the test, questions of this type are mixed in with the more standard five-choice questions. (Question 5 is an example of this type of question.)

In five-choice questions, you may be asked to convert the information given in a word problem into graphical form or to select and apply the mathematical relationship necessary to solve the scientific problem. Alternatively, you may be asked to interpret experimental data, graphical stimulus, or mathematical expressions.

When the experimental data or other scientific problems to be analyzed are comparatively extensive, it is often convenient to organize several five-choice questions into sets, that is, to direct each question in a set to the same material. This practice allows you to answer several questions based on the same material. In no case, however, is the answer to one question necessary for answering a subsequent question correctly. Each question in a set is independent of the others but refers to the same material given for the entire set.

The following are directions for and examples of five-choice questions.

Directions: Each of the questions or incomplete statements below is followed by five suggested answers or completions. Some questions pertain to a set that refers to a laboratory or experimental situation. For each question, select the one choice that is the best answer to the question and then fill in the corresponding circle on the answer sheet.

4. All of the following are population characteristics EXCEPT

   (A) number of individuals
   (B) phenotype
   (C) sex ratio
   (D) age distribution
   (E) death rate

Choice (B) is the correct answer to question 4. This is a question on population ecology and asks you to consider what constitutes a population. An investigator necessarily has to define the limits of the population, but once those parameters are set, it is possible to study the variations in the time and space in the size and density of the population thus defined. A population can be characterized by the number of individuals present, the age distribution, the death rate within the population, and the sex ratio among the individuals. However, the phenotype is a characteristic of an organism and is observed at the level of the individual rather than at the level of a population.

5. ATP is produced during which of the following processes?

I. Photosynthesis

II. Aerobic respiration

III. Fermentation

(A) I only
(B) II only
(C) I and III only
(D) II and III only
(E) I, II, and III

Choice (E) is the correct answer to question 5. This is a question on cellular and molecular biology that asks you to consider whether ATP is produced by more than one metabolic pathway. Each of the processes designated by a Roman numeral must be evaluated independently. In photosynthesis, solar energy captured by chlorophyll-containing plants creates a flow of electrons that results in the synthesis of ATP. Thus I is correct. Aerobic respiration, the process by which glucose is broken down to CO_2 and H_2O in the presence of O_2, is the most efficient mechanism by which cells produce the ATP they need to carry on their other metabolic activities. Thus II is also correct. Fermentation also involves the breakdown of glucose but without O_2. Under these conditions, substances such as lactic acid or ethyl alcohol and CO_2 are produced, together with limited quantities of ATP. Although the carbon-containing end products of fermentation still have much of the energy contained in the original glucose, fermentation permits a cell to produce some ATP under anaerobic conditions.

Questions 6–8

In a breeding experiment using gray and white mice of unknown genotypes, the following results were obtained.

	Parents			Offspring	
Cross	Female		Male	Gray	White
I	Gray	X	White	82	78
II	Gray	X	Gray	118	39
III	White	X	White	0	50
IV	Gray	X	White	74	0

6. Heterozygous gray female parents occur in

(A) cross I only
(B) cross II only
(C) cross IV only
(D) crosses I and II only
(E) crosses II and IV only

7. If two gray progeny of cross IV mate with each other, what is the probability that any individual offspring will be gray?
   (A) 100%
   (B) 75%
   (C) 50%
   (D) 25%
   (E) 0%

8. If the gray female from cross IV were mated with the gray male from cross II, then which of the following would most likely be true?
   (A) All of the offspring would be gray.
   (B) All of the offspring would be white.
   (C) Half of the offspring would be gray.
   (D) One-quarter of the offspring would be gray.
   (E) One-quarter of the offspring would be white.

Questions 6–8 are on heredity. They refer to the experiment described in the introductory material. You are asked to draw conclusions from the results of the experiment and to predict the results of further experimentation on the basis of the information obtained.

Choice (D) is the correct answer to question 6. This question asks you to determine which gray female parents were heterozygous. First you must realize from the ratio of offspring obtained in all the crosses that gray coat color is dominant over white in these mice. Next, you should note that no white offspring were obtained in cross IV. Thus, the gray female in this cross was homozygous gray. In cross I, approximately 50 percent of the offspring were gray. Therefore, the gray female, mated with a white male, must have been heterozygous. In cross II, a gray female was mated with a gray male, and a 3:1 ratio of gray to white offspring was obtained. Therefore, both gray female and gray male parents were heterozygous. Thus heterozygous females occurred only in crosses I and II.

Choice (B) is the correct answer to question 7. This question proposes a hypothetical mating between two gray progeny of cross IV. Since these progeny resulted from a cross between a gray female and a white male and no white offspring were produced, you can conclude that the female parent was homozygous gray and that all the offspring are heterozygous gray. Therefore, the mating of the gray progeny of cross IV will produce offspring in the ratio of 3 gray to 1 white. The probability, therefore, of an offspring of this cross being gray is 75 percent.

Choice (A) is the correct answer to question 8. This question asks you to predict the results of a cross between the gray female from cross IV and the gray male from cross II. From the data given, you can determine that the gray female in cross IV is homozygous, and the male in cross II is heterozygous. Thus you could expect that all of the offspring from such a mating would be gray.

Questions 9–11

Three students added equal volumes of pond water to each of four beakers (I–IV) and placed each in a different constant-temperature bath.

The baths were maintained at 5°C, 15°C, 25°C, and 35°C, respectively. The students then added 6 water fleas, *Daphnia pulex*, to each of the four beakers. After 1 hour, the students removed 3 *Daphnia pulex* from each beaker and each student immediately observed one *Daphnia pulex* under low-power magnification of a light microscope. (The transparent body of the *Daphnia pulex* can be seen easily under a light microscope.) Heart rates were recorded as beats per minute. The results of the experiment are summarized below.

Beaker	Temperature	Time Daphnia Added	Time Daphnia Removed	Heartbeats per Minute (average of 3 Daphnia)
I	5°C	2:00 p.m.	3:00 p.m.	41
II	15°C	2:10 p.m.	3:10 p.m.	119
III	25°C	2:20 p.m.	3:20 p.m.	202
IV	35°C	2:30 p.m.	3:30 p.m.	281

9. The independent variable in this experiment is the
   - (A) amount of light
   - (B) number of water fleas
   - (C) pH of the water
   - (D) temperature of the water
   - (E) average heart rate

10. If a graph is constructed using the data given in the table, it will most closely resemble which of the following?

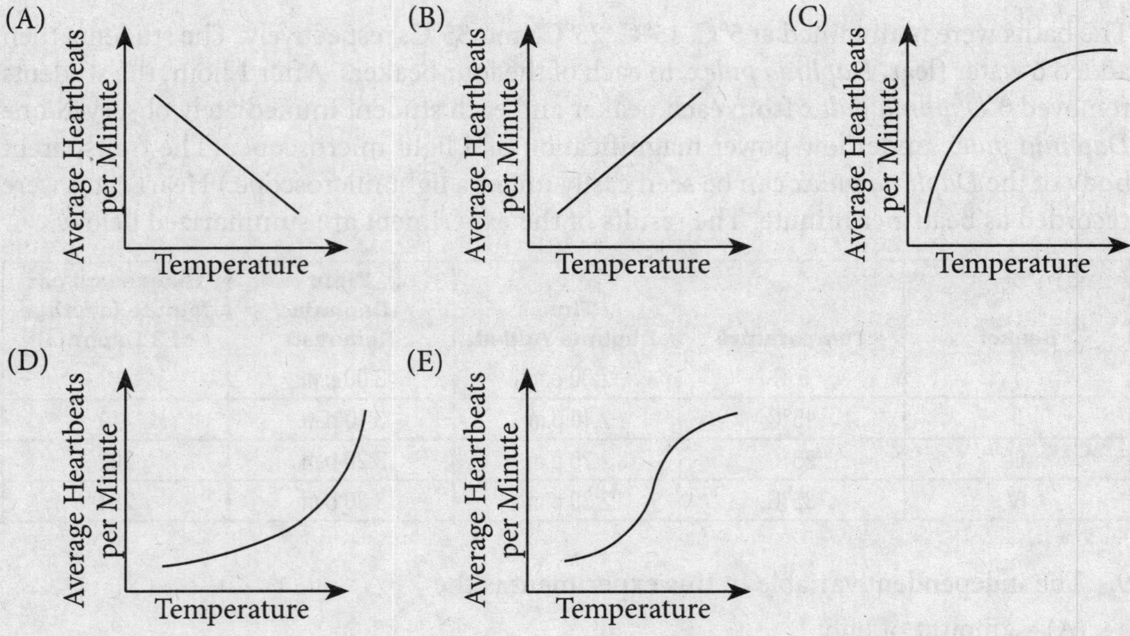

11. The data obtained in this experiment lend support to which of the following hypotheses?
    (A) At 45°C the heart rate of Daphnia would be 320 beats/minute.
    (B) Daphnia swim more slowly at high temperature.
    (C) Metabolic rate in Daphnia is directly proportional to water temperature.
    (D) Heart rate in Daphnia is inversely proportional to water temperature.
    (E) Between 0°C and 5°C, the heart rate of Daphnia would remain constant.

Questions 9–11 describe an experiment that seeks to determine how the metabolism of water fleas is affected by temperature. The experimental setup states that equal volumes of pond water were added to each of four beakers and the same number of fleas were added to each beaker.

Choice (D) is the correct answer to question 9. In this question, choices (B) and (C) are incorrect because both remained constant. Choice (A) is irrelevant in the case of water fleas, and choice (E) is the result the experiment seeks to measure, which is the dependent variable. The only variable that the students manipulated that changed during the course of the experiment was the temperature.

Choice (B) is the correct answer to question 10. This question requires examination of the data in the table. The results show that the average heartbeat per minute of these water fleas increased by about 80 heartbeats per every 10°C increase in temperature.

This represents a linear increase of heartbeat with temperature, and only one of the five graphs given shows this.

Choice (C) is the correct answer to question 11. This question asks students to evaluate which of the five choices given is a hypothesis that is supported by the data. Choice (A) is incorrect because, although there are no data for the heart rate of the fleas at 45°C, a reasonable inference would be that the heart rate should increase about 80 heartbeats above that at 35°C, to about 360. Choice (B) is not a reasonable hypothesis since the water fleas are likely to move more rapidly at high temperatures when the heart rate is higher. Choice (D) is incorrect because it directly contradicts the data, and choice (E) is also incorrect because there is no reason to infer from the data, that the heart rate would remain constant at lower temperatures. However, since heart rate increases linearly with temperature, data support the hypothesis that metabolic rate is also directly proportional to heart rate.

Biology-E Section

12. Which of the following individuals is most fit in evolutionary terms?
    - (A) A child who does not become infected with any of the usual childhood diseases, such as measles or chicken pox
    - (B) A woman of 40 with seven adult offspring
    - (C) A woman of 80 who has one adult offspring
    - (D) A 100-year-old man with no offspring
    - (E) A childless man who can run a mile in less than five minutes

Choice (B) is the correct answer to question 12. For this question you must know the premises upon which Darwin based his explanation of evolutionary change in terms of natural selection. To be fit in evolutionary terms means not only that organisms possessing favorable variations will be able to survive better than those with less favorable variations, but also that the most fit organism will have a higher ability to leave more viable offspring in the next generation. Thus a child who is resistant to certain diseases has not yet demonstrated fitness. Therefore, choice (A) is not the answer to this question. Similarly a person with no offspring has not demonstrated fitness, whether or not she or he is actively exercising. Thus, choices (D) and (E) are incorrect. Finally a woman with numerous surviving offspring is more fit in the evolutionary sense than a woman with one surviving offspring, regardless of the life span of the woman. Thus choice (B) is a better answer than choice (C).

Questions 13–15

Known numbers of seeds from two species (*X* and *Y*) of annual plants are mixed together in different proportions and planted in five small plots of soil in the spring. The plants grow, flower, and produce seeds. It is found that the percentage of seeds of species *X* and species *Y* in the harvest is usually different from the proportion that was planted, although the total number of seeds produced is the same as the number of seeds planted. The data are plotted on the graph below.

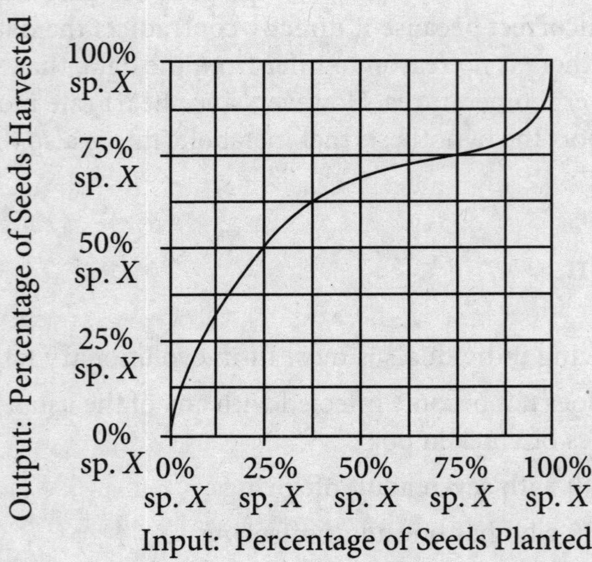

13. What mixture of seeds was harvested in the plot that was planted with 25 percent species *X* and 75 percent species *Y*?

	X	*Y*
(A)	25%	75%
(B)	40%	60%
(C)	50%	50%
(D)	60%	40%
(E)	75%	25%

14. What do the data indicate about the ecological relationship between species *X* and species *Y*?
    - (A) They are mutualistic for low percentages of *X* seeds.
    - (B) They are mutualistic for high percentages of *X* seeds.
    - (C) *X* and *Y* compete when both *X* and *Y* seeds are present.
    - (D) *Y* competes successfully against *X* at all percentages of *X* and *Y* seeds.
    - (E) *X* is a parasite of *Y* when *Y* is rare.

15. If you started out with 25 percent species *X* seeds and 75 percent species *Y* seeds and replanted a plot year after year with the seeds produced each autumn, what pattern would you expect to see in the mixture of the two species over the years of the experiment?

 (A) Species *X* would increase to 100% while species *Y* would decrease to 0%.
 (B) Species *Y* would increase to 100% while species *X* would decrease to 0%.
 (C) One of the species would increase to 100% but which one depends on the initial mixture used to start the experiment.
 (D) The mixture of seeds would eventually stabilize at 75% *X* and 25% *Y*.
 (E) None of the patterns above is consistent with the data.

Questions 13–15 test the ecological concept of competition among species. The graph presented with the introductory material shows that the survival of either of two species depends on the relative abundance of each species at the time of seed planting.

Choice (C) is the correct answer to question 13. This question is a straightforward graph-reading question: when 25% of the seeds planted were species *X* and therefore 75% were species *Y*, the graph shows that 50% of the seeds harvested were species *X* and thus 50% were species *Y*.

Choice (C) is the correct answer to question 14. This question asks you to draw a conclusion about the ecological relationship described in this experiment. In a mutualistic relationship, both species benefit but the data do not show that this is true at either low or high percentages of species *X*. Thus choices (A) and (B) can be eliminated. There is no evidence for parasitism so choice (E) can be eliminated. Competition is occurring but not in a manner such that one species is successful over the other no matter what the percentage of seeds of each species planted. Thus choice (D) is incorrect.

Choice (D) is the correct answer to question 15. In this question, you are asked to predict the results of a proposed experiment. If you started by planting 25% species *X* seeds and 75% species *Y* seeds, you would recover 50% species *X* seeds and 50% species *Y* seeds at harvest time. If these seeds were replanted the following year, the graph shows about 70% species *X* and 30% species *Y* seeds would be harvested. Replanting these results year after year would increase the percentage of species *X* seeds harvested to 75% but there will be no further change in percentage of seeds planted and harvested. The percentage of seeds of each species would stabilize when 75% species *X* and 25% species *Y* are planted. Neither species would reach either 100% or 0% given the percentage of seeds from each species originally planted. Thus choices (A), (B), and (C) can be eliminated. Choice (E) can be eliminated because the pattern in choice (D) is consistent with the data.

Biology-M Section

16. Which of the following most accurately reveals common ancestry among many different species of organisms?
    (A) The amino acid sequence of their cytochrome C
    (B) Their ability to synthesize hemoglobin
    (C) The percentage of their body weight that is fat
    (D) The percentage of their body surface that is used in gas exchange
    (E) The mechanism of their mode of locomotion

Choice (A) is the correct answer to question 16. To assess common ancestry, or evolutionary relationship, among organisms, it is necessary to examine the similarities and differences among species for one or more structures that are homologous. For homologous structures—whether complex structures such as limbs or less complex structure such as a single gene product—the differences arise through the accumulation of mutations over time. Great similarity reflects a shorter time of divergence from a common ancestor. By this reasoning, only choice (A), examination of an enzyme of identical function in various organisms, represents a comparison of a homologous structure. Choice (B) can be ruled out because organisms either possess or lack the ability to synthesize hemoglobin; thus, this character allows one to sort organisms only into two groups, without providing information on relationships within those groups. Choice (C) can be ruled out because the amount of body fat is controlled physiologically, and varies within a single species. Choice (D) can be ruled out because gas exchange does not occur through the surface of some organisms that are only distantly related (e.g., mammals vs. insects) or occurs through the entire surface of many organisms that vary tremendously in relationship (e.g., all unicellular organisms). Choice (E) can be ruled out because many unrelated organisms do not move at all (e.g., plants vs. fungi), or derived their mode of locomotion independently (e.g., bats vs. birds vs. flying insects).

Questions 17–19

Thymine is used by animal cells primarily for the synthesis of DNA. A group of sea urchin eggs was fertilized in sea water containing radioactive thymine. Following fertilization samples of embryos were removed at regular intervals and the radioactivity in the embryos' nucleic acid was measured in counts per minute. The results obtained are shown in the figure below.

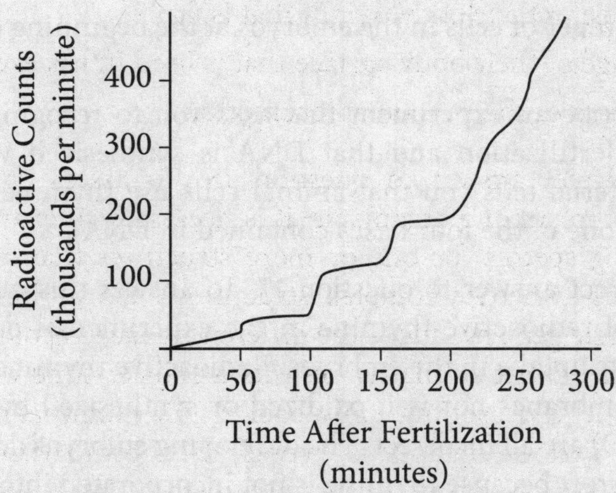

17. The increase in radioactivity of the embryos with time probably results from
    (A) synthesis of new proteins by the developing embryos
    (B) synthesis of radioactive thymine by the developing embryos
    (C) oxidation of radioactive thymine
    (D) incorporation of radioactive thymine in new cell membranes
    (E) incorporation of radioactive thymine in new DNA during replication

18. The time required for a complete cell division cycle in the sea urchin embryos studied in the experiment is approximately
    (A) 25 minutes
    (B) 50 minutes
    (C) 75 minutes
    (D) 100 minutes
    (E) 200 minutes

19. An appropriate control to show that this experiment measures DNA synthesis and not RNA synthesis would be to perform the same procedures but
    (A) not fertilize the eggs
    (B) sample the embryos at longer time intervals
    (C) add radioactive uracil instead of radioactive thymine
    (D) fertilize the eggs in sea water that does not contain radioactive thymine
    (E) count the number of cells in the embryos at the beginning and at the end of the experiment

Questions 17–19 describe an experiment that asks you to recognize that cell division occurs rapidly after fertilization and that DNA is synthesized when cells replicate. The introductory material tells you that animal cells use thymine primarily for DNA synthesis (thymine is one of the four bases contained in DNA).

Choice (E) is the correct answer to question 17. To answer this question, you need to realize that the use of radioactive thymine in the experimental design is needed as a means of measuring its uptake in the embryos. Radioactive thymine is not incorporated in embryonic cell membranes nor is it oxidized or synthesized by the embryos. Thus choices (B), (C), and (D) are all incorrect. The developing embryos do synthesize proteins but choice (A) is incorrect because thymine is not incorporated into proteins.

Choice (B) is the correct answer to question 18. To answer this question, you need to know that DNA is synthesized most rapidly during replication so that the largest increase in uptake of radioactive thymine would occur at that time. The graph indicates that the steepest jumps in radioactivity occur every 50 minutes so that would represent a complete cell division cycle.

Choice (C) is the correct answer to question 19. To answer this question, you need to know that uracil is contained in RNA but thymine is not. Thus using radioactive thymine measures DNA synthesis and not RNA synthesis. Use of radioactive uracil would yield data that measures RNA synthesis. Without the use of radioactive thymine in the sea water, the experimenter would have no mechanism for measuring any DNA synthesis at all, so choice (D) would not be an appropriate control. Collecting samples either at longer time intervals or only at the start and end of the experiment would provide less data and could not provide any appropriate control. Thus choices (B) and (E) are incorrect. Not fertilizing the eggs would provide no cell division whatsoever and so would provide no supporting evidence to show that the experiment measures DNA synthesis and not RNA synthesis. Thus choice (A) is also incorrect.

Biology E/M Test

Practice Helps

The test that follows is an actual, recently administered SAT Subject Test in Biology E/M. To get an idea of what it's like to take this test, practice under conditions that are much like those of an actual test administration.

- Set aside an hour when you can take the test uninterrupted. Make sure you complete the test in one sitting.
- Sit at a desk or table with no other books or papers. Dictionaries, other books, or notes are not allowed in the test room.
- Tear out an answer sheet from the back of this book and fill it in just as you would on the day of the test. One answer sheet can be used for up to three Subject Tests.
- Read the instructions that precede the practice test. During the actual administration, you will be asked to read them before answering test questions.
- Time yourself by placing a clock or kitchen timer in front of you.
- After you finish the practice test, read the sections "How to Score the SAT Subject Test in Ecological Biology" or "How to Score the SAT Subject Test in Molecular Biology" and "How Did You Do on the Subject Test in Ecological Biology?" or "How Did You Do on the Subject Test in Molecular Biology?"
- The appearance of the answer sheet in this book may differ from the answer sheet you see on test day.

BIOLOGY–E TEST or BIOLOGY–M TEST

You MUST decide now whether you want to take a Biology Test with Ecological Emphasis (BIOLOGY-E) or Molecular Emphasis (BIOLOGY-M). The top portion of the section of the answer sheet that you will use in taking the Biology Test you have selected must be filled in exactly as shown in one of the illustrations below. Note carefully that you have to do all of the following on your answer sheet.

1. Print BIOLOGY-E or BIOLOGY-M on the line under the words "Subject Test (print)."

2. In the shaded box labeled "Test Code" fill in four circles as follows:

   For BIOLOGY-E

   — Fill in circle 1 in the row labeled V.
   — Fill in circle 9 in the row labeled W.
   — Fill in circle 4 in the row labeled X.
   — Fill in circle B in the row labeled Y.

   For BIOLOGY-M

   — Fill in circle 5 in the row labeled V.
   — Fill in circle 7 in the row labeled W.
   — Fill in circle 5 in the row labeled X.
   — Fill in circle C in the row labeled Y.

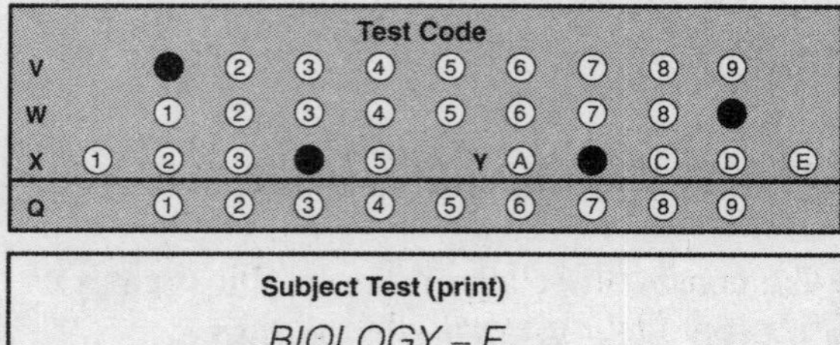

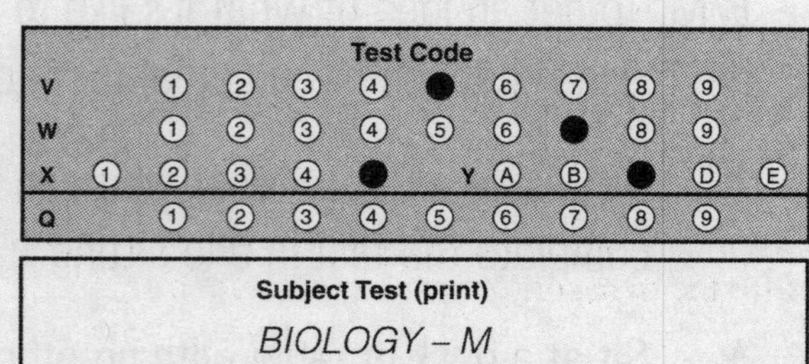

3. Please answer the questions below by filling in the appropriate circles in the row labeled Q on the answer sheet. <u>The information you provide is for statistical purposes only and will not affect your score on the test</u>.

<u>Question I</u> How many semesters of biology have you taken in high school? (If you are taking biology this semester, count it as a full semester.) Fill in only <u>one</u> circle of circles 1-3.

- One semester or less — Fill in circle 1.
- Two semesters — Fill in circle 2.
- Three semesters or more — Fill in circle 3.

<u>Question II</u> Which of the following best describes your biology course? Fill in only <u>one</u> circle of circles 4-6.

- General Biology — Fill in circle 4.
- Biology with emphasis on ecology — Fill in circle 5.
- Biology with emphasis on molecular biology — Fill in circle 6.

<u>Question III</u> Which of the following best describes your background in algebra? (If you are taking an algebra course this semester, count it as a full semester.) Fill in only <u>one</u> circle of circles 7-8.

- One semester or less — Fill in circle 7.
- Two semesters or more — Fill in circle 8.

<u>Question IV</u> Are you currently taking Advanced Placement Biology? If you are, fill in circle 9.

When the supervisor gives the signal, turn the page and begin the Biology Test. There are 100 numbered circles on the answer sheet. There are 60 questions in the core Biology Test, 20 questions in the Biology-E section, and 20 questions in the Biology-M section. Therefore use ONLY circles 1-80 (for Biology-E) OR circles 1-60 <u>plus</u> 81-100 (for Biology-M) for recording your answers.

BIOLOGY E/M TEST

FOR BOTH BIOLOGY-E AND BIOLOGY-M, ANSWER QUESTIONS 1-60

Directions: Each set of lettered choices below refers to the numbered questions or statements immediately following it. Select the one lettered choice that best answers each question or best fits each statement and then fill in the corresponding circle on the answer sheet. A choice may be used once, more than once, or not at all in each set.

Questions 1-4 refer to the following plant cell types.

(A) Tracheids and vessel elements
(B) Guard cells
(C) Parenchyma cells
(D) Sieve tube members and companion cells
(E) Sclerenchyma cells

1. Chains of these nonliving cells form continuous tubes for the transport of water in vascular plants.

2. These cells take up potassium ions and water when sunlight and low concentrations of carbon dioxide are present, which causes them to become rigid.

3. These versatile cells serve as storage sites for sugars and starches in stems and roots.

4. These cells form a living tissue which transports sugar from one part of a vascular plant to another.

Questions 5-6 refer to the following.

(A) 2
(B) 4
(C) 16
(D) 25
(E) 50

5. The expected percentage of offspring with the recessive phenotype from a cross between two individuals heterozygous for a particular trait

6. The number of different phenotypes possible for the progeny of the cross $AaBb \times AaBb$, where A and B exhibit simple dominance

Questions 7-10

(A) Monera
(B) Protista
(C) Fungi
(D) Plantae
(E) Animalia

7. Contains all the protozoa and most of the algae

8. Contains multicellular heterotrophic organisms that reproduce asexually by spores

9. Contains organisms without membrane-bound organelles such as nuclei

10. Contains autotrophic organisms with cells that are organized into tissues and organs

3YAC

GO ON TO THE NEXT PAGE

Questions 11-14 refer to the following illustration of protein synthesis in a mammalian cell.

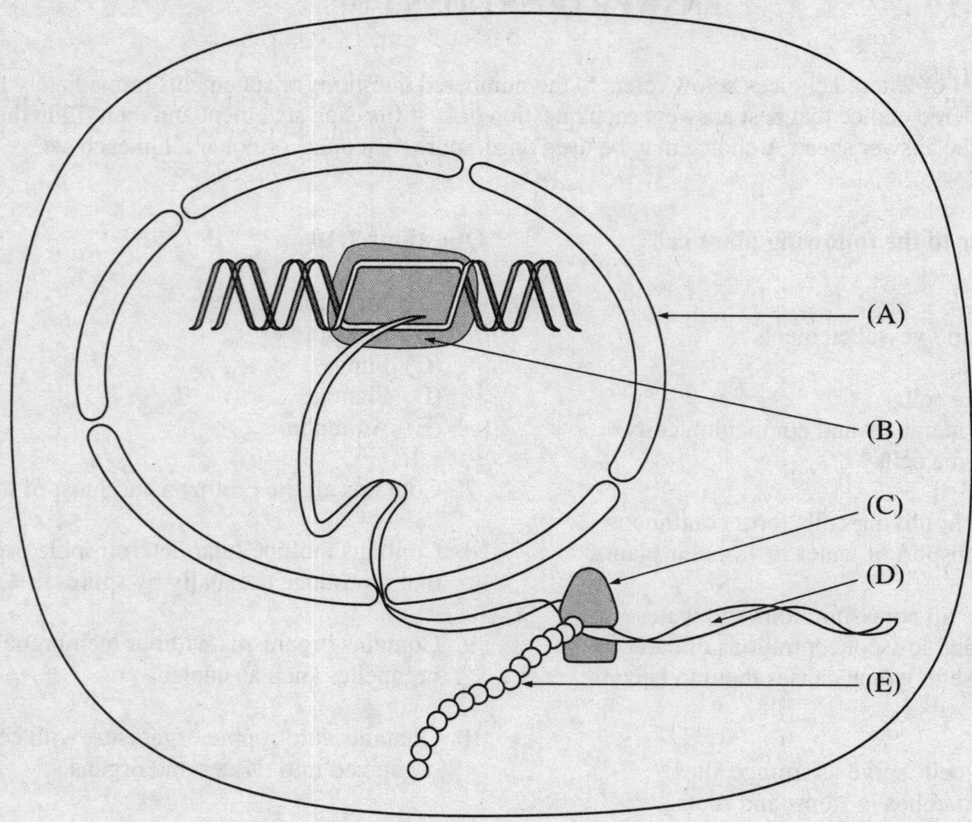

11. A strand of mRNA being translated

12. A polypeptide being synthesized

13. A barrier to diffusion of large proteins from nucleus to cytoplasm

14. A structure that contains a lipid bilayer

GO ON TO THE NEXT PAGE

Questions 15-17

(A) Insulin
(B) Growth hormone
(C) Progesterone
(D) Thyroxin
(E) Secretin

15. It is secreted by the pituitary gland.

16. It directly controls metabolic rate.

17. Its concentration in the blood rises when the corpus luteum develops.

GO ON TO THE NEXT PAGE

Directions: Each of the questions or incomplete statements below is followed by five suggested answers or completions. Some questions pertain to a set that refers to a laboratory or experimental situation. For each question, select the one choice that is the best answer to the question and then fill in the corresponding circle on the answer sheet.

18. The ribosomes of a cell are of primary importance for

(A) DNA replication
(B) transcription
(C) translation
(D) translocation
(E) repression

19. If a couple has two boys and one girl, what is the probability that the next child born to this couple will be a girl?

(A) $\frac{1}{4}$

(B) $\frac{1}{3}$

(C) $\frac{1}{2}$

(D) $\frac{2}{3}$

(E) $\frac{3}{4}$

20. Eggs fertilized by two sperm instead of one sometimes form a mitotic spindle with three poles. After mitosis the daughter cells will probably

(A) be indistinguishable from normal cells
(B) eliminate the chromosomes contributed by the second sperm
(C) eliminate the chromosomes contributed by the egg
(D) display an abnormal number of chromosomes
(E) stop protein synthesis immediately

21. In higher plant cells, a pigment important in the manufacture of carbohydrates from CO_2 and H_2O is contained in the

(A) nucleus
(B) vacuole
(C) cytoplasm
(D) chloroplast
(E) centrosome

GO ON TO THE NEXT PAGE

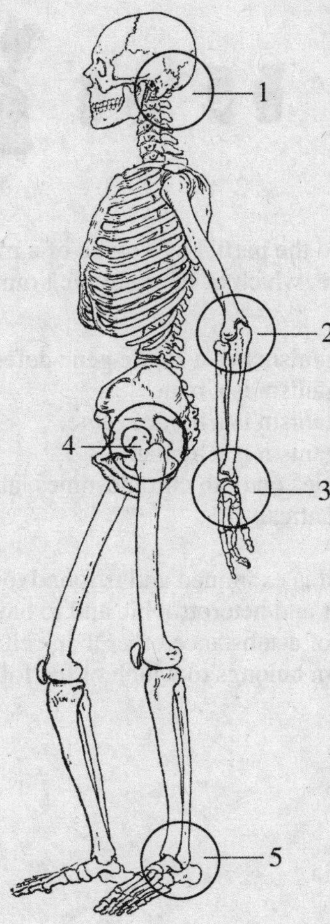

22. In the diagram of the human skeleton above, which of the following is a ball-and-socket joint?

    (A) 1
    (B) 2
    (C) 3
    (D) 4
    (E) 5

23. Which of the following statements is true for red blood cells that have been added to a flask of saturated NaCl solution?

    (A) The cells will undergo mitosis.
    (B) The cells will increase in volume.
    (C) The cells will lose water.
    (D) The cells are hypertonic relative to the surrounding medium.
    (E) The concentration of NaCl is lower outside the cells than inside.

24. Today's worldwide human population can best be described as

    (A) oscillating
    (B) declining
    (C) fluctuating near equilibrium
    (D) growing arithmetically
    (E) growing exponentially

25. The base of the food web of the open ocean is provided by

    (A) phytoplankton
    (B) zooplankton
    (C) kelp
    (D) fish
    (E) whales

26. Nitrogen fixation is the conversion of atmospheric nitrogen into

    (A) ammonia
    (B) protein
    (C) urea
    (D) carbon dioxide
    (E) DNA

GO ON TO THE NEXT PAGE

27. In the fruit fly, the allele for normal wings (*W*) is dominant over the allele for vestigial wings (*w*). A cross of two normal-winged flies produced 76 normal-winged and 23 vestigial-winged offspring. It can be concluded that the genotypes of the two parent flies were which of the following?

(A) *WW* and *ww*
(B) *WW* and *Ww*
(C) *Ww* and *ww*
(D) *Ww* and *Ww*
(E) *WW* and *WW*

28. Factors that have been known to result in the elimination of a species in a particular area include which of the following?

I. Use of insecticides
II. Hunting of the species' prey
III. Habitat destruction

(A) I only
(B) II only
(C) I and III only
(D) II and III only
(E) I, II, and III

1 2 3 *X* *Y*

29. According to the partial karyotype of a mammal shown above, which of the following must be true?

(A) The organism has a single gene defect.
(B) The organism is a male.
(C) The organism is a homozygote.
(D) The organism is a human.
(E) The alleles on both chromosomes labeled 3 are identical.

30. An organism is examined and is found to be multicellular and heterotrophic and to have cell walls made of a substance other than cellulose. The organism belongs to which of the following kingdoms?

(A) Monera
(B) Protista
(C) Fungi
(D) Plantae
(E) Animalia

GO ON TO THE NEXT PAGE

31. Which of the following statements is correct?

    (A) Heritable variation allows for evolution.
    (B) Adaptive radiation allows for mutation.
    (C) Crossing-over allows for mitosis.
    (D) Translocation allows for DNA replication.
    (E) Cellular differentiation allows for meiosis.

32. Behavior that remains unaffected by environmental changes is most likely

    (A) territorial
    (B) learned
    (C) innate
    (D) stereotyped
    (E) conditioned

33. A man who has hemophilia and a woman who does not have hemophilia have a daughter who has hemophilia. Hemophilia is a recessive condition, and the gene is located on the X chromosome. Which of the following can be concluded?

    (A) The mother is a carrier for hemophilia.
    (B) Hemophilia is not a sex-linked trait.
    (C) Crossing-over has occurred.
    (D) All subsequent daughters of this couple will have hemophilia.
    (E) All sons of this couple will have hemophilia.

34. All of the following are measures useful in describing a given population's growth rate EXCEPT

    (A) fertility
    (B) mortality
    (C) survivorship
    (D) age structure
    (E) habitat

35. Which of the following is LEAST consistent with the fossil record?

    (A) Bony fish evolved from amphibians.
    (B) Mammals evolved from reptiles.
    (C) Birds evolved from reptiles.
    (D) Reptiles evolved from amphibians.
    (E) Cartilaginous fish evolved from jawless fish.

36. Which of the following is NOT true of enzymes?

    (A) Enzyme activity is affected by changes in temperature.
    (B) Enzymes change the rate at which biochemical reactions proceed.
    (C) Enzyme activity is affected by large shifts in pH.
    (D) Enzymes often require the presence of cofactors or coenzymes to become active.
    (E) Enzymes are assembled from vitamin subunits.

37. The gene for a particular trait that is passed only from fathers to sons is most likely

    (A) autosomal recessive
    (B) autosomal dominant
    (C) codominant
    (D) *Y*-linked
    (E) *X*-linked

GO ON TO THE NEXT PAGE

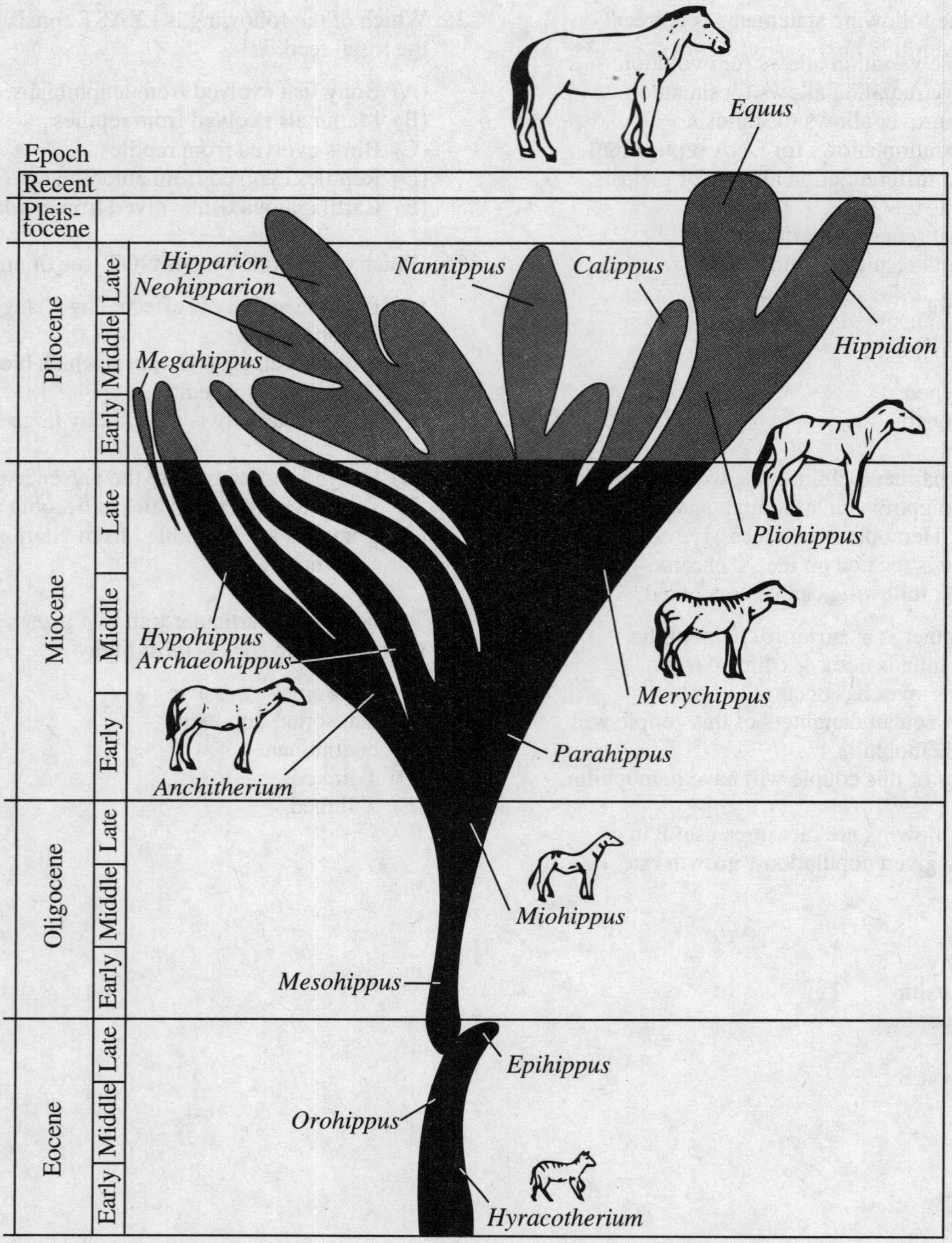

Equus
Epoch
Recent
Pleistocene
Pliocene: Late, Middle, Early
Miocene: Late, Middle, Early
Oligocene: Late, Middle, Early
Eocene: Late, Middle, Early
Hipparion
Neohipparion
Nannippus
Calippus
Hippidion
Megahippus
Pliohippus
Hypohippus
Archaeohippus
Merychippus
Anchitherium
Parahippus
Miohippus
Mesohippus
Epihippus
Orohippus
Hyracotherium

38. The diagram above illustrates a proposed phylogeny for horses. Which of the following genera is currently represented by live animals?

(A) *Epihippus*
(B) *Equus*
(C) *Hippidion*
(D) *Hyracotherium*
(E) *Nannippus*

GO ON TO THE NEXT PAGE

39. Which of the following organelles in human sperm provides the energy needed by the sperm?

(A) Flagellum
(B) Mitochondrion
(C) Y chromosome
(D) Centriole
(E) Nucleus

40. Which of the following organs secretes the hormone responsible for the “fight-or-flight” reaction in mammals?

(A) Liver
(B) Kidney
(C) Pancreas
(D) Cowper’s gland
(E) Adrenal gland

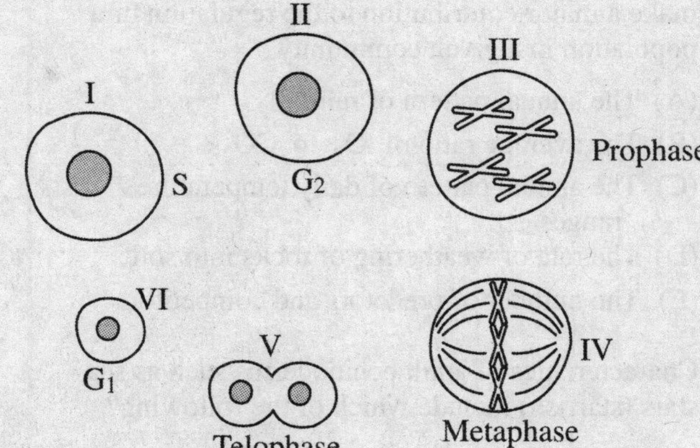

41. Most replication of DNA takes place during which of the following stages of the cell cycle?

(A) I
(B) II and III
(C) IV only
(D) IV and V
(E) VI

GO ON TO THE NEXT PAGE

42. Which of the following is a biotic factor that can make a major contribution to the regulation of a population in a given community?

    (A) The annual pattern of rainfall
    (B) The average ratio of O_2 to CO_2
    (C) The annual pattern of daily temperature ranges
    (D) The rate of weathering of rocks into soil
    (E) The number of predators and competitors

43. Characteristics of adult echinoderms such as sea stars (starfish) include which of the following?

    I. Tube feet
    II. Bilateral symmetry
    III. Water vascular system

    (A) I only
    (B) II only
    (C) I and III only
    (D) II and III only
    (E) I, II, and III

44. If in an adult organism the genes *A* and *B* occur on one chromosome and their alleles *a* and *b* occur on its homologue, which of the following explains a combination of *Ab* or *aB* occurring in the gametes?

    (A) Sex-linkage
    (B) Lack of dominance
    (C) Nondisjunction
    (D) Crossing-over
    (E) Blending

45. Which of the following is NOT a major function of the mammalian kidney?

    (A) Elimination of urea and other nitrogenous wastes
    (B) Maintenance of water balance
    (C) Manufacture of antibodies
    (D) Regulation of salt excretion
    (E) Formation of urine from glomerular filtrate

46. An ecologically sound reason for conserving tropical rain forests is that they

    (A) supply most of the oxygen that humans breathe
    (B) occupy four-fifths of Earth's surface
    (C) are the major producers of atmospheric nitrogen
    (D) are crucial to migratory ungulates like bison and wildebeest
    (E) are an important reservoir of biodiversity

GO ON TO THE NEXT PAGE

Questions 47-48

A population study of plants was done in an abandoned field. Each year for 3 years the vegetation was sampled. The chart below indicates the results of the study.

Year	Number of Plants per Acre				
	Sandspur	Ragweed	Timothy Grass	Goldenrod	Wire Grass
1	3,800	4,900	600	0	412
2	1,500	2,209	1,185	75	796
3	752	180	2,234	790	1,643

47. According to the data, which of the following are initially most successful in the succession taking place in the field described above?

(A) Sandspur and ragweed
(B) Sandspur and timothy grass
(C) Ragweed and timothy grass
(D) Ragweed and wire grass
(E) Sandspur and goldenrod

48. The data above suggest that

(A) fires cause the changes in the populations
(B) floods cause the changes in the populations
(C) the plants in the population have similar life spans
(D) plant populations are replacing one another
(E) the reproductive capacity of plants changes with time

GO ON TO THE NEXT PAGE

Questions 49-51

The figure below represents the increase in prevalence of both keratoses (thickened pigmented patches on the skin) and skin cancers in males of Irish descent in several geographic areas.

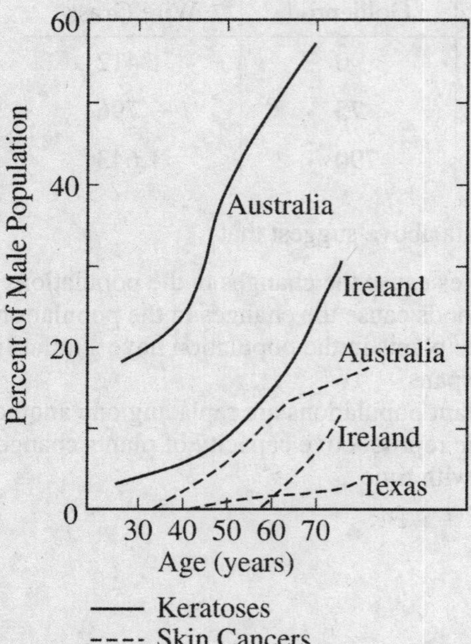

49. For which of the following groups can 20 percent of the male population be expected to have the indicated condition?

(A) Skin cancers in Australia at age 50
(B) Keratoses in Australia at age 30
(C) Keratoses in Australia at age 70
(D) Keratoses in Ireland at age 40
(E) Keratoses in Ireland at age 80

50. Which of the following can be inferred from these data?

(A) Skin cancers develop from keratoses.
(B) Keratoses develop from skin cancers.
(C) The majority of males with keratoses also have skin cancer.
(D) The environment in Australia is more likely to cause keratoses than is the environment in Ireland.
(E) The intensity of sunlight is the primary factor causing the development of skin cancers.

51. If the study were conducted as a function of the age of the female population in the same geographic areas, which of the following results would be most likely?

(A) The data would show a higher percentage of females with the diseases at all ages.
(B) The data would show a lower incidence of the diseases, because females have higher levels of estrogen.
(C) The data would be the same as for males in Australia and Ireland, but no predictions can be made for Texas.
(D) The data would be the same as for males with regard to keratoses but not for skin cancers.
(E) No accurate predictions can be made from the data because the sample populations would be different.

GO ON TO THE NEXT PAGE

NO TEST MATERIAL ON THIS PAGE

Questions 52-55

Charles Darwin and his son Francis performed a series of experiments on phototropism (growth toward light) of the coleoptile (the cap that covers the first leaves of new seedlings of grass). The treatments they used are described below.

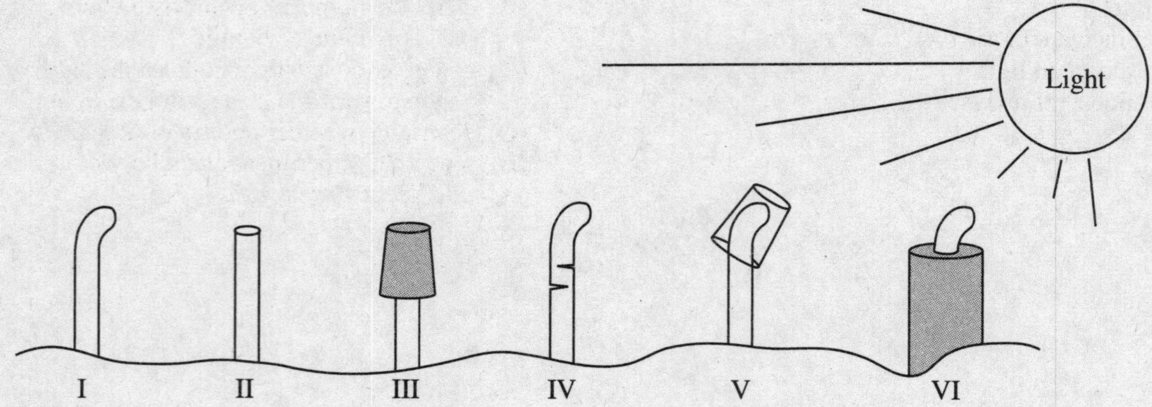

	Treatment	Growth Toward Light
I	Coleoptile untreated.	Allowed
II	Tip of coleoptile cut off.	Prevented
III	Opaque cap placed over coleoptile tip.	Prevented
IV	Coleoptile cut halfway through.	Allowed
V	Transparent cap placed over coleoptile tip.	Allowed
VI	Opaque sleeve placed over base of coleoptile.	Allowed

52. Comparison of treatments I and II shows which of the following?

(A) Growth is promoted by cutting off the tip.
(B) The tip is the site of sensing light.
(C) The tip is the site of auxin synthesis.
(D) The tip is necessary for the response to light.
(E) There is a range of response to a single treatment.

53. The fact that the effect of cutting off the tip (treatment II) is not simply due to wounding of the plant is demonstrated by comparison of which of the following treatments?

(A) IV and V
(B) I, II, and III
(C) I, II, and IV
(D) II, III, and IV
(E) IV, V, and VI

GO ON TO THE NEXT PAGE

54. Comparison of treatments III, V, and VI shows that

    (A) the tip plays a role in sensing the light
    (B) the base plays a role in sensing the light
    (C) confinement of the tip inhibits the response to light
    (D) confinement of the base facilitates the response to light
    (E) confinement reverses the response to light

55. To test the hypothesis that the response to light involves differential cell elongation, an experimenter could

    (A) measure the distance between marks made on the seedling after it has bent
    (B) count the number of cells visible in a cross section of the coleoptile
    (C) compare the length of cells on the sides of the stem toward and away from the light
    (D) determine whether mitosis is affected by light
    (E) repeat the experiment using light of a different wavelength

GO ON TO THE NEXT PAGE

Questions 56-60

During normal development of the sea urchin, the egg divides once to give two cells. Each of these cells divides again. The cells continue to divide and, eventually, a sea-urchin larva is formed. It is possible to separate the cells of a young sea-urchin embryo and allow them to develop independently. The results of several such experiments are shown below.

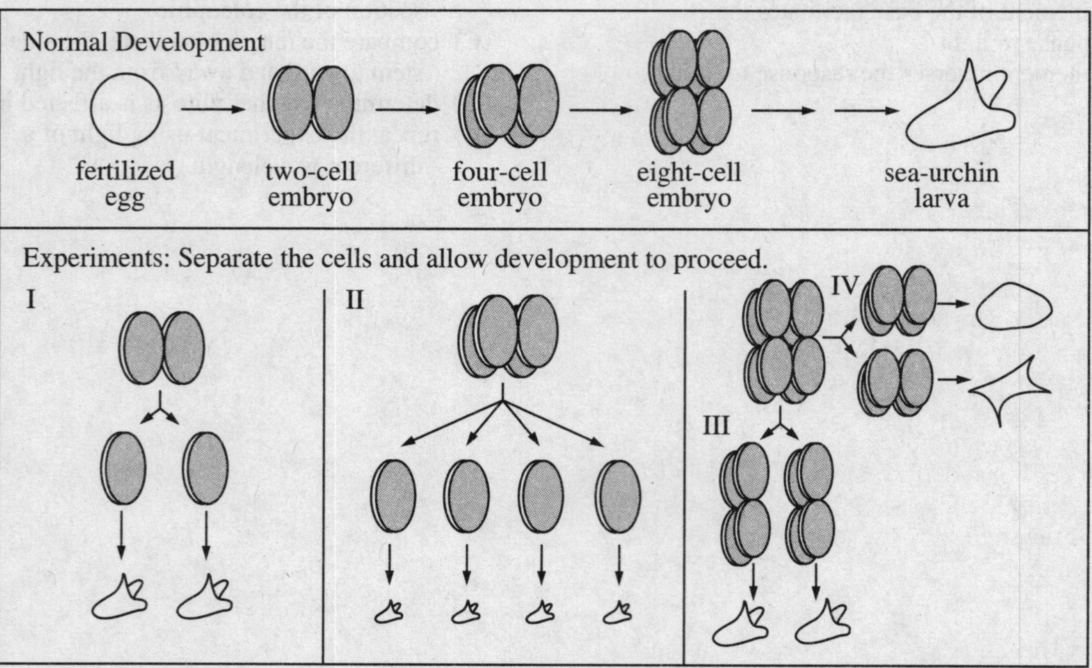

56. Experiment I suggests that

    (A) sea urchins would be better adapted if they had smaller eggs
    (B) embryo cells are committed to different developmental fates
    (C) different cells of an embryo can have equal potential for development
    (D) a particular cell of an embryo always develops into the same structure
    (E) cell division ensures that both cells will develop identically

57. Experiments I and II suggest that

    (A) sea-urchin embryos often grow to full-size adults
    (B) larva size is determined by the amount of material in the embryo
    (C) development must always occur the same way in every embryo
    (D) embryo cells do not interact with each other
    (E) natural selection favors the formation of small larvae

GO ON TO THE NEXT PAGE

58. Experiments III and IV together suggest that
    (A) there is a difference between separating cells along the vertical axis and the horizontal axis of an eight-cell embryo
    (B) embryo cells cannot be separated without damaging development
    (C) material at the top of the embryo is the same as material at the bottom
    (D) cells divide correctly only when they are vertical
    (E) embryo cells do not differ until gastrulation

59. The different results in experiments III and IV probably are caused by
    (A) failure of mitosis to occur normally at the third cell division
    (B) loss of chromosomes by the top four cells
    (C) fertilization of the top and bottom of the egg by two different sperm
    (D) different genes being expressed in the top four cells than in the bottom four cells
    (E) some genes in the left half of the embryo that are different from those in the right half of the embryo

60. Which of the following questions is NOT addressed by this series of experiments?
    (A) When do the cells of an embryo become different from each other?
    (B) Can cells of an embryo survive when separated from each other?
    (C) Can smaller larvae be produced by experimental manipulation?
    (D) When are components in the fertilized egg activated?
    (E) Can the cells of an embryo be made to develop abnormally?

If you are taking the Biology-E test, continue with questions 61-80.
If you are taking the Biology-M test, go to question 81 now.

GO ON TO THE NEXT PAGE

BIOLOGY-E TEST

Directions: Each of the questions or incomplete statements below is followed by five suggested answers or completions. Some questions pertain to a set that refers to a laboratory or experimental situation. For each question, select the one choice that is the best answer to the question and then fill in the corresponding circle on the answer sheet.

61. Stream and river ecosystems differ from other aquatic ecosystems because streams and rivers

(A) move continuously in one direction and have a nutrient content that is dependent on location
(B) support a greater diversity of aquatic plants
(C) have highly variable salinity
(D) include the greatest biodiversity of all ecosystems because of the fluctuating water levels
(E) support the largest stationary plankton communities

62. A trophic level within an ecosystem is best characterized by the

(A) size of food eaten at that level
(B) nutrient source of the organisms in each level
(C) stages in ecological succession
(D) habitats of the organisms within that level
(E) elevation above sea level

63. According to most scientific theories of the origin of life, the first organisms were

(A) eukaryotic
(B) parasitic
(C) symbiotic
(D) anaerobic
(E) pathogenic

64. The global cycles of nitrogen and phosphorus differ in that

(A) nitrogen is recycled whereas phosphorus is not
(B) animals get most of their nitrogen from the water they drink whereas they get their phosphorus from the food they eat
(C) nitrogen occurs primarily in deep sediments whereas phosphorus occurs primarily in the atmosphere
(D) nitrogen is lost to the oceans whereas phosphorus is not
(E) nitrogen has a gaseous phase whereas phosphorus does not

GO ON TO THE NEXT PAGE

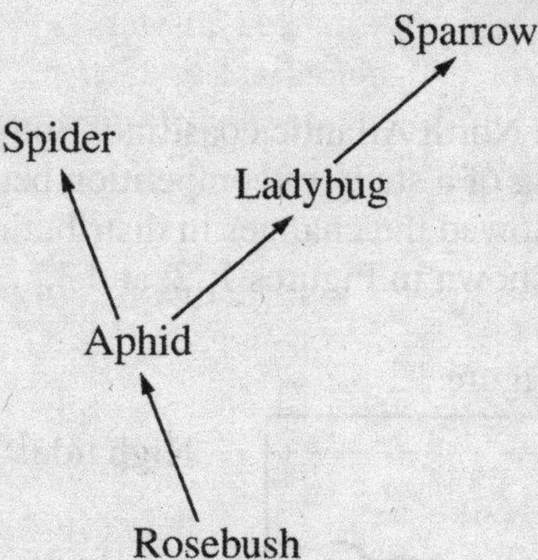

65. In the food web shown above, in which the arrows indicate the direction of energy flow, the ladybug is considered to be a

    (A) herbivore
    (B) primary consumer
    (C) decomposer
    (D) producer
    (E) carnivore

66. A stream is free of pollutants within a few miles downstream of a point at which a small amount of sewage is being dumped into it. This is most likely the result of

    (A) succession
    (B) biological magnification
    (C) evaporation
    (D) photosynthesis
    (E) decomposition

67. The term "adaptive radiation" refers to the

    (A) ability of one species to adapt to only one niche
    (B) ability of a species to adapt itself to rapidly changing conditions
    (C) evolution from a single ancestral species into several species adapted to various environments
    (D) ability of a species to adjust its temperature by radiating heat
    (E) advantages of radial symmetry to a stationary species

68. Which of the following does NOT refer primarily to a relationship between members of different species?

    (A) Mutualism
    (B) Hibernation
    (C) Parasitism
    (D) Commensalism
    (E) Predation

69. Plant seeds can be dispersed by which of the following?

    I. Wind
    II. Water
    III. Birds

    (A) I only
    (B) III only
    (C) I and II only
    (D) I and III only
    (E) I, II, and III

GO ON TO THE NEXT PAGE

Questions 70-72

Two types of barnacles, *Chthamalus* and *Balanus*, grow on rocks along the North Atlantic coastline. Both grow on rock surfaces exposed at low tide and covered at high tide. At the beginning of a study of competition between these barnacles, a researcher removed selected *Balanus* from a region and followed the changes in distribution of both species for 12 months. The distribution of *Chthamalus* and *Balanus* are shown in Figures 1, 2, and 3.

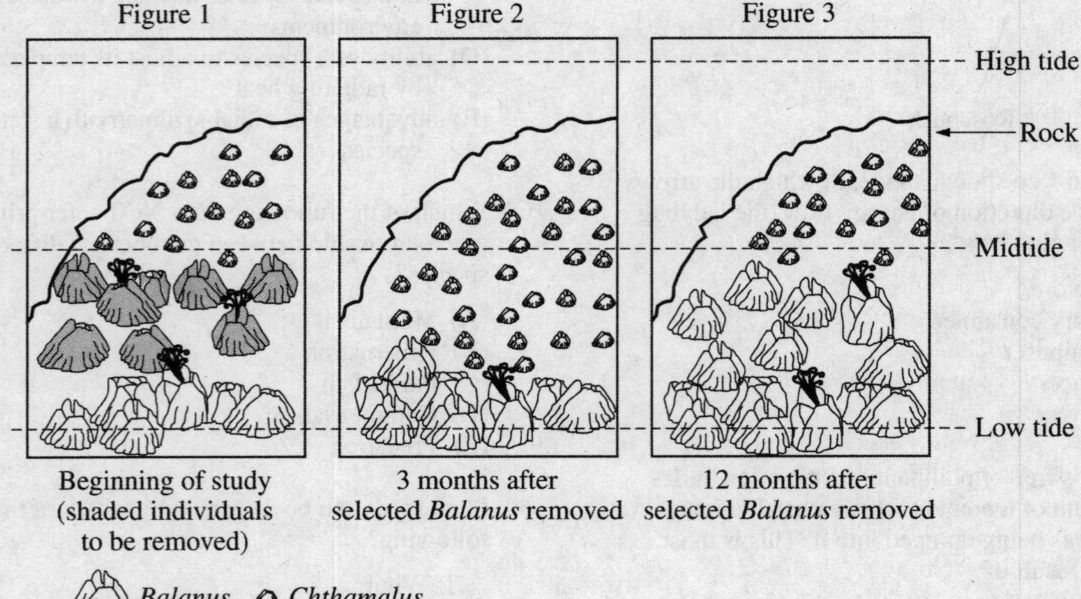

GO ON TO THE NEXT PAGE

70. Since both species of barnacles have free-swimming larvae that settle on hard surfaces, the change in the distribution of *Chthamalus* observed 3 months after removal of the larger *Balanus* individuals could best be explained by which of the following?

(A) *Balanus* feeds on *Chthamalus* larvae.
(B) *Balanus* does not reproduce as quickly as *Chthamalus*.
(C) *Balanus* has less tolerance for wet conditions.
(D) *Balanus* adults are mobile.
(E) *Balanus* is less susceptible to predators.

71. The distribution of the two species at 3 and 12 months suggests all of the following EXCEPT:

(A) *Balanus* sometimes dominates over the smaller *Chthamalus*.
(B) *Chthamalus* can tolerate more drying than *Balanus*.
(C) *Balanus* adults are swept away more often than *Chthamalus*.
(D) *Balanus* and *Chthamalus* larvae can settle in the same area.
(E) *Balanus* is larger and thus needs more feeding time in the water.

72. Based on this study, on rocks with tops below the midtide line, it can be predicted that

(A) more of the rock surface would be covered by *Chthamalus*
(B) the two barnacle populations would be equal
(C) there would be few, if any, *Balanus*
(D) there would be few, if any, *Chthamalus*
(E) *Balanus* individuals would become smaller

GO ON TO THE NEXT PAGE

Questions 73-75 refer to the following experiment in which an agar petri dish was prepared as shown below. Using aseptic techniques, an experimenter spread *E. coli* bacteria on the agar uniformly throughout the dish. The dish was then incubated at 37°C for 24 hours.

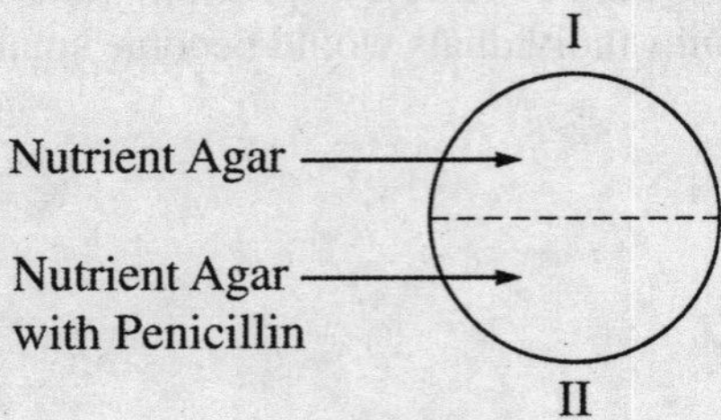

73. Which of the following distributions of bacterial colonies is most likely to be observed on completion of the experiment? (Dots represent bacterial colonies.)

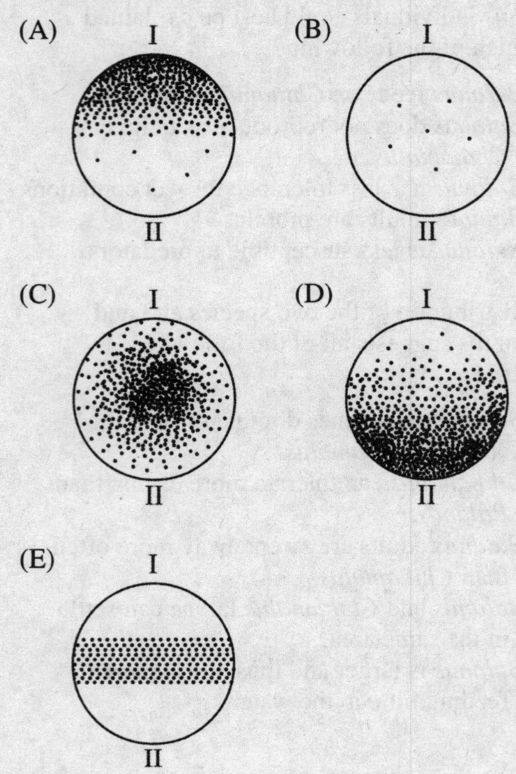

GO ON TO THE NEXT PAGE

74. The cells that survived exposure to penicillin were most likely able to do so because they

    (A) mutated as a result of the exposure
    (B) had a more rapid metabolism than the other cells
    (C) lacked cell walls
    (D) already possessed penicillin resistance
    (E) formed spores

75. In the experiment, penicillin causes a stress that, in an ecosystem, would promote

    (A) natural selection
    (B) Lamarckian evolution
    (C) competition
    (D) mutation
    (E) parasitism

GO ON TO THE NEXT PAGE

Questions 76-80

A scientist studied a field that had been burned in a brushfire ten years before. She identified seven different species and produced the table below.

Scientific Name	Gross Form	Microscopic Form	Stem Form	Color	Reproduction
Platismartia glauca	sheetlike	eukaryotic and prokaryotic filaments	not applicable	green on top white below	none evident
Funaria americana	cushionlike	eukaryotic multicellular	not applicable	green throughout	spore-producing structures on stalks
Dryopteris spinulosa	roots, under-ground stems, compound leaves	eukaryotic multicellular	fleshy	green leaves, white stem and roots	spores on underside of leaves
Picea rubens	roots, stems, needlelike leaves	eukaryotic multicellular	erect, woody	green leaves, brown stem and roots	cones
Smilax herbacea	roots, vine, broad leaves	eukaryotic multicellular	erect, herbaceous	green leaves and stem, white roots	flowers
Smilax rotundifolia	roots, woody vine, broad leaves	eukaryotic multicellular	erect	green leaves, brown stem and roots	none evident
Monotropa uniflora	roots, stems, broad leaves	eukaryotic multicellular	erect	white throughout	fruits

76. The organism that evolutionarily is most closely related to *Smilax herbacea* is

(A) *Platismatia glauca*
(B) *Dryopteris spinulosa*
(C) *Picea rubens*
(D) *Smilax rotundifolia*
(E) *Monotropa uniflora*

77. Symbiosis is best illustrated by which of the following organisms?

(A) *Platismatia glauca*
(B) *Dryopteris spinulosa*
(C) *Picea rubens*
(D) *Smilax herbacea*
(E) *Smilax rotundifolia*

GO ON TO THE NEXT PAGE

78. Which of the following shows the simplest level of physical organization?

    (A) *Funaria americana*
    (B) *Monotropa uniflora*
    (C) *Dryopteris spinulosa*
    (D) *Picea rubens*
    (E) *Smilax rotundifolia*

79. Which of the following is most likely a flowering plant?

    (A) *Platismatia glauca*
    (B) *Funaria americana*
    (C) *Dryopteris spinulosa*
    (D) *Picea rubens*
    (E) *Monotropa uniflora*

80. The appearance of these plants in the burned area is an example of what biological process?

    (A) Evolution by natural selection
    (B) Succession
    (C) Mutation
    (D) Eutrophication
    (E) Recombination

STOP

IF YOU FINISH BEFORE TIME IS CALLED, YOU MAY CHECK YOUR WORK ON THE ENTIRE BIOLOGY-E TEST.

BIOLOGY-M SECTION

If you are taking the Biology-M test, continue with questions 81-100.
Be sure to start this section of the test by filling in circle 81 on your answer sheet.

Directions: Each of the questions or incomplete statements below is followed by five suggested answers or completions. Some questions pertain to a set that refers to a laboratory or experimental situation. For each question, select the one choice that is the best answer to the question and then fill in the corresponding circle on the answer sheet.

I

II

81. Which of the following is correct about the phospholipid shown above?

(A) Only I would be found in the middle of the lipid bilayer.
(B) Only II would be found in the middle of the lipid bilayer.
(C) Both I and II would be found in the middle of the lipid bilayer.
(D) II is hydrophilic.
(E) I and II are hydrophobic.

GO ON TO THE NEXT PAGE

82. Products of the light reactions of photosynthesis that later participate in the dark reactions of photosynthesis include which of the following?

    I. Reduced NADP (NADPH)
    II. ATP
    III. O_2

    (A) I only
    (B) II only
    (C) III only
    (D) I and II only
    (E) I, II, and III

83. The way in which an enzyme and its specific substrate interact is best described by the

    (A) fluid-mosaic model
    (B) induced-fit model
    (C) Oparin hypothesis
    (D) Lyon hypothesis
    (E) competitive-exclusion principle

84. If a somatic cell in a diploid organism contains ten pairs of chromosomes, what is the total number of <u>chromatids</u> that are present in the cell after the DNA has replicated but before mitosis has taken place?

    (A) 10
    (B) 20
    (C) 30
    (D) 40
    (E) 80

85. Which of the following atmospheric gases shows a net release during photosynthesis in plants?

    (A) Carbon dioxide
    (B) Oxygen
    (C) Methane
    (D) Hydrogen
    (E) Nitrogen

86. Which of the following are the final products of fermentation?

    (A) Carbon and oxygen
    (B) Glucose and alcohol
    (C) Carbon dioxide and oxygen
    (D) Carbon dioxide and alcohol
    (E) Oxygen and water

87. A function of transfer RNA is to

    (A) receive the genetic information from nuclear DNA
    (B) store the genetic information in the nucleus
    (C) store RNA in the ribosomes
    (D) transfer the genetic information from the nucleus to the cytoplasm
    (E) position amino acids for protein synthesis by pairing with codons in messenger RNA

GO ON TO THE NEXT PAGE

88. Which of the following statements most accurately describes a basic difference between mitosis and meiosis?

(A) Homologous chromosomes form tetrads in mitosis but not in meiosis.
(B) Homologous chromosomes form tetrads in meiosis but not in mitosis.
(C) The nuclear membrane disappears in mitosis but not in meiosis.
(D) A spindle forms in mitosis but not in meiosis.
(E) A spindle forms in meiosis but not in mitosis.

89. The *Bt* protein produced in the bacterium, *Bacillus thuringiensis*, kills corn earworms that ingest the *Bacillus*. If the *Bt* gene were transferred to corn so that corn could express the *Bt* protein, which of the following would be expected to occur when corn earworms eat the corn?

I. Corn earworms that eat the *Bt* corn would be killed.
II. *Bacillus* bacteria that infect the *Bt* corn would be killed.
III. The corn earworms would incorporate the *Bt* gene into their chromosomes.

(A) I only
(B) II only
(C) III only
(D) I and III only
(E) II and III only

90. The wavelengths of light absorbed by chlorophyll are similar to the wavelengths of light that are associated with the greatest amount of oxygen release by plants. Based on these observations which of the following is a reasonable hypothesis about the function of chlorophyll?

(A) It plays a role in cell respiration.
(B) It plays a role in the light reactions of photosynthesis.
(C) It takes part in H_2O release.
(D) It takes part in CO_2 fixation.
(E) It generates energy.

91. Cellular respiration shares which of the following characteristics with the light-dependent reactions of photosynthesis?

(A) Production of ATP
(B) Production of AMP
(C) Production of GTP
(D) Production of oxygen
(E) Use of carbon dioxide in synthetic reactions

92. The position of a mutation in a gene and the location of an altered amino acid sequence in the corresponding protein are

(A) not related
(B) inversely related
(C) related in bacteria but not in mammals
(D) species-dependent
(E) in the same relative position

93. In order for an animal that was cloned from its mother to grow and develop normally, it must have received

(A) half of its mother's DNA sequences
(B) half of its father's RNA sequences
(C) all of its mother's RNA sequences
(D) all of its father's DNA sequences
(E) all of its mother's DNA sequences

GO ON TO THE NEXT PAGE

Questions 94-97

Bowls 1 and 7 — water only
Bowls 2 and 8 — water + 20 water plants
Bowls 3 and 9 — water + 40 water plants
Bowls 4 and 10 — water + 2 goldfish
Bowls 5 and 11 — water + 4 goldfish
Bowls 6 and 12 — water + 20 water plants + 2 goldfish

A biologist set up 12 bowls as described above. She exposed bowls 1 to 6 to light for 24 hours and placed bowls 7 to 12 in the dark for 24 hours. She determined the CO_2 content of the water in micromoles per liter for each bowl at the end of the 24 hours. The results are indicated below.

Experimental Results

Light		Dark	
Bowl #	$[CO_2]$	Bowl #	$[CO_2]$
1	10.0	7	10.2
2	4.3	8	13.7
3	2.1	9	16.9
4	14.9	10	14.1
5	18.3	11	17.9
6	10.2	12	19.2

94. The process responsible for the relatively low concentrations of CO_2 in bowls 2 and 3 is

(A) respiration
(B) fermentation
(C) photosynthesis
(D) photoperiodism
(E) transpiration

95. The main controls for bowl 4 are

(A) 1 and 3
(B) 1 and 6
(C) 1 and 10
(D) 2 and 5
(E) 2 and 8

96. The difference in CO_2 concentrations for bowls 2 and 6 can best be explained by

(A) photosynthesis carried out by water plants
(B) respiration carried out by water plants
(C) respiration carried out by goldfish
(D) competition between water plants and goldfish
(E) experimental error

97. Which of the following is the best explanation for the fact that the CO_2 concentration of bowl 4 is almost the same as that of bowl 10 and the CO_2 concentration of bowl 5 is almost the same as that of bowl 11 ?

(A) Photosynthesis does not occur in the light.
(B) Photosynthesis does not occur in the dark.
(C) Respiration and photosynthesis occur at the same rate in the light.
(D) Respiration is not affected by either light or dark.
(E) Goldfish are more active in the absence than in the presence of plants.

GO ON TO THE NEXT PAGE

Questions 98-100 refer to the following experimental procedure.

A protein is purified from a frog embryo. The protein sample is divided into five fractions. One fraction is not treated. The other fractions are partially digested by using enzymes that act on specific amino acid sequences. In every case, the digestions are carried out at the appropriate temperature and pH. The samples are then separated by electrophoresis as shown below.

Unaltered Protein	Protein Digested by Enzyme X	Protein Digested by Enzyme Y	Protein Digested by Enzyme Z

GO ON TO THE NEXT PAGE

98. In the electrophoresis experiment described, the distance moved by a fragment within the electric field is influenced by which of the following?

 I. The number of amino acids in the fragment
 II. The amount of electric current used in the apparatus
 III. The porosity of the gel matrix

(A) I only
(B) II only
(C) I and II only
(D) II and III only
(E) I, II, and III

99. Which of the following techniques could have been used as an alternative to electrophoresis to separate the products of digestion with enzyme Z ?

 I. Translation
 II. Chromatography
 III. Serial dilution

(A) I only
(B) II only
(C) III only
(D) II and III only
(E) I, II, and III

100. Of the two fragments resulting from the digestion of the protein with enzyme Z, one is larger and the other is smaller than either of the fragments resulting from the digestion with enzyme Y. The most logical explanation for this is that

(A) the protein fragments produced by enzyme Y have the same molecular weights as those produced by enzyme Z
(B) proteins are produced by ribosomes
(C) enzymes Y and Z have different amino acid sequences
(D) electric current is divided into discrete units
(E) the protein is cut at different amino acid sequences by enzymes Y and Z

STOP

IF YOU FINISH BEFORE TIME IS CALLED, YOU MAY CHECK YOUR WORK ON THE ENTIRE BIOLOGY-M TEST.

How to Score the SAT Subject Test in Ecological Biology

When you take an actual SAT Subject Test in Ecological Biology, your answer sheet will be "read" by a scanning machine that will record your responses to each question. Then a computer will compare your answers with the correct answers and produce your raw score. You get one point for each correct answer. For each wrong answer, you lose one-fourth of a point. Questions you omit (and any for which you mark more than one answer) are not counted. This raw score is converted to a scaled score that is reported to you and to the colleges you specify.

Worksheet 1. Finding Your Raw Test Score

STEP 1: Table A lists the correct answers for all the questions on the Subject Test in Ecological Biology that is reproduced in this book. It also serves as a worksheet for you to calculate your raw score.

- Compare your answers with those given in the table.
- Put a check in the column marked "Right" if your answer is correct.
- Put a check in the column marked "Wrong" if your answer is incorrect.
- Leave both columns blank if you omitted the question.

STEP 2: Count the number of right answers.

Enter the total here: ________________

STEP 3: Count the number of wrong answers.

Enter the total here: ________________

STEP 4: Multiply the number of wrong answers by .250.

Enter the product here: ________________

STEP 5: Subtract the result obtained in Step 4 from the total you obtained in Step 2.

Enter the result here: ________________

STEP 6: Round the number obtained in Step 5 to the nearest whole number.

Enter the result here: ________________

The number you obtained in Step 6 is your raw score.

Table A

Answers to the Subject Test in Ecological Biology, Form 3YAC, and Percentage of Students Answering Each Question Correctly

Question Number	Correct Answer	Right	Wrong	Percentage of Students Answering the Question Correctly*	Question Number	Correct Answer	Right	Wrong	Percentage of Students Answering the Question Correctly*
1	A			45	33	A			75
2	B			48	34	E			53
3	C			32	35	A			47
4	D			37	36	E			65
5	D			79	37	D			78
6	B			45	38	B			89
7	B			68	39	B			64
8	C			72	40	E			80
9	A			68	41	A			37
10	D			55	42	E			80
11	D			64	43	C			34
12	E			74	44	D			69
13	A			78	45	C			80
14	A			57	46	E			54
15	B			54	47	A			78
16	D			44	48	D			69
17	C			49	49	B			83
18	C			47	50	D			77
19	C			76	51	E			78
20	D			54	52	D			59
21	D			85	53	C			32
22	D			78	54	A			77
23	C			60	55	C			60
24	E			70	56	C			47
25	A			76	57	B			58
26	A			60	58	A			72
27	D			76	59	D			55
28	E			73	60	D			59
29	B			71	61	A			85
30	C			44	62	B			57
31	A			55	63	D			63
32	C			64	64	E			46

Table A continued on next page

Table A continued from previous page

Question Number	Correct Answer	Right	Wrong	Percentage of Students Answering the Question Correctly*	Question Number	Correct Answer	Right	Wrong	Percentage of Students Answering the Question Correctly*
65	E			61	73	A			83
66	E			67	74	D			71
67	C			47	75	A			56
68	B			83	76	D			73
69	E			77	77	A			32
70	B			65	78	A			75
71	C			44	79	E			80
72	D			67	80	B			68

* These percentages are based on an analysis of the answer sheets of a representative sample of 3,130 students who took the original form of this test in May 2002, and whose mean score was 601. They may be used as an indication of the relative difficulty of a particular question. Each percentage may also be used to predict the likelihood that a typical SAT Subject Test in Ecological Biology candidate will answer that question correctly on this edition of the test.

Finding Your Scaled Score

When you take SAT Subject Tests, the scores sent to the colleges you specify are reported on the College Board scale, which ranges from 200–800. You can convert your practice test score to a scaled score by using Table B. To find your scaled score, locate your raw score in the left-hand column of Table B; the corresponding score in the right-hand column is your scaled score. For example, a raw score of 21 on this particular edition of the Subject Test in Ecological Biology corresponds to a scaled score of 450.

Raw scores are converted to scaled scores to ensure that a score earned on any one edition of a particular Subject Test is comparable to the same scaled score earned on any other edition of the same Subject Test. Because some editions of the tests may be slightly easier or more difficult than others, College Board scaled scores are adjusted so that they indicate the same level of performance regardless of the edition of the test taken and the ability of the group that takes it. Thus, for example, a score of 400 on one edition of a test taken at a particular administration indicates the same level of achievement as a score of 400 on a different edition of the test taken at a different administration.

When you take the SAT Subject Tests during a national administration, your scores are likely to differ somewhat from the scores you obtain on the tests in this book. People perform at different levels at different times for reasons unrelated to the tests themselves. The precision of any test is also limited because it represents only a sample of all the possible questions that could be asked.

Table B

Scaled Score Conversion Table Subject Test in Ecological Biology (Form 3YAC)					
Raw Score	Scaled Score	Raw Score	Scaled Score	Raw Score	Scaled Score
80	800	46	610	12	390
79	800	45	610	11	380
78	800	44	600	10	370
77	800	43	600	9	370
76	790	42	590	8	360
75	780	41	590	7	350
74	780	40	580	6	350
73	770	39	570	5	340
72	770	38	570	4	340
71	760	37	560	3	330
70	750	36	560	2	330
69	750	35	550	1	320
68	740	34	540	0	320
67	730	33	540	-1	310
66	730	32	530	-2	310
65	720	31	520	-3	300
64	720	30	520	-4	300
63	710	29	510	-5	290
62	710	28	500	-6	290
61	700	27	500	-7	280
60	690	26	490	-8	280
59	690	25	480	-9	270
58	680	24	480	-10	270
57	680	23	470	-11	270
56	670	22	460	-12	260
55	670	21	450	-13	260
54	660	20	450	-14	260
53	650	19	440	-15	250
52	650	18	430	-16	250
51	640	17	420	-17	240
50	640	16	420	-18	240
49	630	15	410	-19	230
48	630	14	400	-20	220
47	620	13	400		

How Did You Do on the Subject Test in Ecological Biology?

After you score your test and analyze your performance, think about the following questions:

Did you run out of time before reaching the end of the test?

If so, you may need to pace yourself better. For example, maybe you spent too much time on one or two hard questions. A better approach might be to skip the ones you can't answer right away and try answering all the questions that remain on the test. Then if there's time, go back to the questions you skipped.

Did you take a long time reading the directions?

You will save time when you take the test by learning the directions to the Subject Test in Ecological Biology ahead of time. Each minute you spend reading directions during the test is a minute that you could use to answer questions.

How did you handle questions you were unsure of?

If you were able to eliminate one or more of the answer choices as wrong and guess from the remaining ones, your approach probably worked to your advantage. On the other hand, making haphazard guesses or omitting questions without trying to eliminate choices could cost you valuable points.

How difficult were the questions for you compared with other students who took the test?

Table A shows you how difficult the multiple-choice questions were for the group of students who took this test during its national administration. The right-hand column gives the percentage of students that answered each question correctly.

A question answered correctly by almost everyone in the group is obviously an easier question. For example, 85 percent of the students answered question 21 correctly. But only 32 percent answered question 77 correctly.

Keep in mind that these percentages are based on just one group of students. They would probably be different with another group of students taking the test.

If you missed several easier questions, go back and try to find out why: Did the questions cover material you haven't yet reviewed? Did you misunderstand the directions?

How to Score the SAT Subject Test in Molecular Biology

When you take an actual SAT Subject Test in Molecular Biology, your answer sheet will be "read" by a scanning machine that will record your responses to each question. Then a computer will compare your answers with the correct answers and produce your raw score. You get one point for each correct answer. For each wrong answer, you lose one-fourth of a point. Questions you omit (and any for which you mark more than one answer) are not counted. This raw score is converted to a scaled score that is reported to you and to the colleges you specify.

Worksheet 1. Finding Your Raw Test Score

STEP 1: Table A lists the correct answers for all the questions on the Subject Test in Molecular Biology that is reproduced in this book. It also serves as a worksheet for you to calculate your raw score.

- Compare your answers with those given in the table.
- Put a check in the column marked "Right" if your answer is correct.
- Put a check in the column marked "Wrong" if your answer is incorrect.
- Leave both columns blank if you omitted the question.

STEP 2: Count the number of right answers.

Enter the total here: ________________

STEP 3: Count the number of wrong answers.

Enter the total here: ________________

STEP 4: Multiply the number of wrong answers by .250.

Enter the product here: ________________

STEP 5: Subtract the result obtained in Step 4 from the total you obtained in Step 2.

Enter the result here: ________________

STEP 6: Round the number obtained in Step 5 to the nearest whole number.

Enter the result here: ________________

The number you obtained in Step 6 is your raw score.

Table A

Answers to the Subject Test in Molecular Biology, Form 3YAC, and Percentage of Students Answering Each Question Correctly

Question Number	Correct Answer	Right	Wrong	Percentage of Students Answering the Question Correctly*	Question Number	Correct Answer	Right	Wrong	Percentage of Students Answering the Question Correctly*
1	A			51	33	A			84
2	B			55	34	E			57
3	C			37	35	A			54
4	D			47	36	E			80
5	D			87	37	D			84
6	B			54	38	B			91
7	B			75	39	B			73
8	C			76	40	E			85
9	A			74	41	A			55
10	D			63	42	E			81
11	D			73	43	C			39
12	E			84	44	D			80
13	A			84	45	C			87
14	A			73	46	E			57
15	B			62	47	A			82
16	D			49	48	D			72
17	C			58	49	B			86
18	C			66	50	D			78
19	C			85	51	E			81
20	D			61	52	D			64
21	D			92	53	C			35
22	D			78	54	A			79
23	C			68	55	C			68
24	E			71	56	C			54
25	A			78	57	B			62
26	A			67	58	A			78
27	D			85	59	D			62
28	E			73	60	D			62
29	B			81	81	B			53
30	C			52	82	D			52
31	A			64	83	B			77
32	C			71	84	D			48

Table A continued on next page

Table A continued from previous page

Question Number	Correct Answer	Right	Wrong	Percentage of Students Answering the Question Correctly*	Question Number	Correct Answer	Right	Wrong	Percentage of Students Answering the Question Correctly*
85	B			86	93	E			79
86	D			65	94	C			82
87	E			69	95	C			64
88	B			67	96	C			79
89	A			67	97	D			86
90	B			77	98	E			43
91	A			77	99	B			35
92	E			60	100	E			76

* These percentages are based on an analysis of the answer sheets of a representative sample of 3,964 students who took the original form of this test in May 2002, and whose mean score was 640. They may be used as an indication of the relative difficulty of a particular question. Each percentage may also be used to predict the likelihood that a typical SAT Subject Test in Molecular Biology Subject candidate will answer that question correctly on this edition of the test.

Finding Your Scaled Score

When you take SAT Subject Tests, the scores sent to the colleges you specify are reported on the College Board scale, which ranges from 200–800. You can convert your practice test score to a scaled score by using Table B. To find your scaled score, locate your raw score in the left-hand column of Table B; the corresponding score in the right-hand column is your scaled score. For example, a raw score of 21 on this particular edition of the Subject Test in Molecular Biology corresponds to a scaled score of 470.

Raw scores are converted to scaled scores to ensure that a score earned on any one edition of a particular Subject Test is comparable to the same scaled score earned on any other edition of the same Subject Test. Because some editions of the tests may be slightly easier or more difficult than others, College Board scaled scores are adjusted so that they indicate the same level of performance regardless of the edition of the test taken and the ability of the group that takes it. Thus, for example, a score of 400 on one edition of a test taken at a particular administration indicates the same level of achievement as a score of 400 on a different edition of the test taken at a different administration.

When you take the SAT Subject Tests during a national administration, your scores are likely to differ somewhat from the scores you obtain on the tests in this book. People perform at different levels at different times for reasons unrelated to the tests themselves. The precision of any test is also limited because it represents only a sample of all the possible questions that could be asked.

Table B

Scaled Score Conversion Table
Subject Test in Molecular Biology (Form 3YAC)

Raw Score	Scaled Score	Raw Score	Scaled Score	Raw Score	Scaled Score
80	800	46	620	12	400
79	800	45	620	11	390
78	800	44	610	10	390
77	800	43	610	9	380
76	790	42	600	8	370
75	790	41	590	7	370
74	780	40	590	6	360
73	780	39	580	5	350
72	770	38	580	4	350
71	760	37	570	3	340
70	760	36	560	2	340
69	750	35	560	1	330
68	750	34	550	0	330
67	740	33	550	-1	320
66	730	32	540	-2	320
65	730	31	530	-3	310
64	720	30	530	-4	310
63	720	29	520	-5	300
62	710	28	510	-6	300
61	710	27	510	-7	290
60	700	26	500	-8	290
59	690	25	490	-9	280
58	690	24	490	-10	280
57	680	23	480	-11	280
56	680	22	470	-12	270
55	670	21	470	-13	270
54	670	20	460	-14	270
53	660	19	450	-15	260
52	650	18	440	-16	260
51	650	17	440	-17	250
50	640	16	430	-18	250
49	640	15	420	-19	240
48	630	14	420	-20	240
47	630	13	410		

How Did You Do on the Subject Test in Molecular Biology?

After you score your test and analyze your performance, think about the following questions:

Did you run out of time before reaching the end of the test?

If so, you may need to pace yourself better. For example, maybe you spent too much time on one or two hard questions. A better approach might be to skip the ones you can't answer right away and try answering all the questions that remain on the test. Then if there's time, go back to the questions you skipped.

Did you take a long time reading the directions?

You will save time when you take the test by learning the directions to the Subject Test in Molecular Biology ahead of time. Each minute you spend reading directions during the test is a minute that you could use to answer questions.

How did you handle questions you were unsure of?

If you were able to eliminate one or more of the answer choices as wrong and guess from the remaining ones, your approach probably worked to your advantage. On the other hand, making haphazard guesses or omitting questions without trying to eliminate choices could cost you valuable points.

How difficult were the questions for you compared with other students who took the test?

Table A shows you how difficult the multiple-choice questions were for the group of students who took this test during its national administration. The right-hand column gives the percentage of students that answered each question correctly.

A question answered correctly by almost everyone in the group is obviously an easier question. For example, 87 percent of the students answered question 5 correctly. But only 35 percent answered question 53 correctly.

Keep in mind that these percentages are based on just one group of students. They would probably be different with another group of students taking the test.

If you missed several easier questions, go back and try to find out why: Did the questions cover material you haven't yet reviewed? Did you misunderstand the directions?

Chapter 6

Chemistry

Purpose

The Subject Test in Chemistry measures the understanding of chemistry you would be expected to have after successfully completing a college-preparatory course in high school and is designed to be independent of the particular textbook or instructional approach used.

Format

This is a one-hour test with 85 multiple-choice questions.

Content

The test covers the topics listed in the chart on the next page. Different aspects of these topics are stressed from year to year. However, because high school courses differ, both in the amount of time devoted to each major topic and in the specific subtopics covered, it is likely that most students will encounter some questions on topics with which they are not familiar. Every edition of the test contains approximately five questions on equation balancing and/or predicting products of chemical reactions; these are distributed among the various content categories.

Topics Covered	Approximate Percentage of Test
I. Structure of Matter	25
Atomic Structure, including experimental evidence of atomic structure, quantum numbers and energy levels (orbitals), electron configurations, periodic trends **Molecular Structure**, including Lewis structures, three-dimensional molecular shapes, polarity **Bonding**, including ionic, covalent, and metallic bonds; relationships of bonding to properties and struc-tures; intermolecular forces such as hydrogen bonding, dipole-dipole forces, dispersion (London) forces	
II. States of Matter	16
Gases, including the kinetic molecular theory, gas law relationships, molar volumes, density, stoichiometry **Liquids and Solids**, including intermolecular forces in liquids and solids, types of solids, phase changes and phase diagrams **Solutions**, including molarity and percent by mass concentrations; solution preparation and stoichiometry; factors affecting solubility of solids, liquids, and gases; qualitative aspects of colligative properties	
III. Reaction Types	14
Acids and Bases, including Brønsted-Lowry theory, strong and weak acids and bases, pH, titrations, indicators **Oxidation-Reduction**, including recognition of oxidation-reduction reactions, combustion, oxidation numbers, use of acitvity series **Precipitation**, including basic solubility rules	
IV. Stoichiometry	14
Mole Concept, including molar mass, Avogadro's number, empirical and molecular formulas **Chemical Equations**, including the balancing of equations, stoichiometric calculations, percent yield, limiting reactants	
V. Equilibrium and Reaction Rates	5
Equilibrium Systems, including factors affecting position of equilibrium (LeChâtelier's principle) in gaseous and aqueous systems, equilibrium constants, equilibrium expressions **Rates of Reactions**, including factors affecting reaction rates, potential energy diagrams, activation energies	
VI. Thermochemistry	6
Including conservation of energy, calorimetry and specific heats, enthalpy (heat) changes associated with phase changes and chemical reactions, heating and cooling curves, randomness (entropy)	
VII. Descriptive Chemistry	12
Including common elements, nomenclature of ions and compounds, periodic trends in chemical and physical properties of the elements, reactivity of elements and prediction of products of chemical reactions, examples of simple organic compounds and compounds of environmental concern	
VIII. Laboratory	8
Including knowledge of laboratory equipment, measurements, procedures, observations, safety, calculations, data analysis, interpretation of graphical data, drawing conclusions from observations and data	

Skills Specifications	Approximate Percentage of Test
Recall of Knowledge	20
Remembering fundamental concepts and specific information; demonstrating familiarity with terminology	
Application of Knowledge	45
Applying a single principle to unfamiliar and/or practical situations; to obtain a qualitative result or solve a quantitative problem	
Synthesis of Knowledge	35
Inferring and deducing from qualitative data and/or quantitative data; integrating two or more relationships to draw conclusions or solve problems	

How to Prepare

- Take a one-year introductory chemistry course at the college-preparatory level.
- Laboratory experience is a significant factor in developing reasoning and problem-solving skills and should help in test preparation even though laboratory skills can be tested only in a limited way in a multiple-choice test.
- Mathematics preparation that enables handling simple algebraic relationships and applying these to solving word problems will help.
- Familiarize yourself with the concepts of ratio and direct and inverse proportions, exponents, and scientific notation.
- Familiarize yourself with directions in advance. The directions in this book are identical to those that appear on the test.

You should have the ability to

- recall and understand the major concepts of chemistry and to apply the principles to solve specific problems in chemistry.
- organize and interpret results obtained by observation and experimentation and to draw conclusions or make inferences from experimental data, including data presented in graphic and/or tabular form.

Notes: (1) A periodic table indicating the atomic numbers and masses of elements is provided for all test administrations.

(2) Calculators aren't allowed to be used during the test.

(3) Problem solving requires simple numerical calculations.

(4) The metric system of units is used.

Score

The total score is reported on the 200-to-800 scale.

Sample Questions

Three types of questions are used in the Chemistry Subject Test: classification questions, relationship analysis questions, and five-choice completion questions.

Note: For all questions involving solutions, assume that the solvent is water unless otherwise noted.

Classification Questions

Each set of classification questions has, in the heading, five lettered choices that you will use to answer all of the questions in the set. The choices may be statements that refer to concepts, principles, substances, or observable phenomena; or they may be graphs, pictures, equations, numbers, or experimental settings or situations.

Because the same five choices are applicable to several questions, the classification questions usually require less reading than other types of multiple-choice questions. Answering a question correctly depends on the sophistication of the set of questions. One set may test your ability to recall information; another set may ask you to apply information to a specific situation or to translate information from one form to another (descriptive, graphical, mathematical). The directions for this type of question specifically state that you should not eliminate a choice simply because it is the correct answer to a previous question.

Following are the directions for and an example of a classification set.

Directions: Each set of lettered choices below refers to the numbered statements immediately following it. Select the one lettered choice that best fits each statement or answers each question and then fill in the corresponding circle on the answer sheet. A choice may be used once, more than once, or not at all in each set.

Questions 1–3 refer to the following aqueous solutions:

(A) 0.1 M HCl
(B) 0.1 M NaCl
(C) 0.1 M $HC_2H_3O_2$
(D) 0.1 M CH_3OH
(E) 0.1 M KOH

1. Is weakly acidic

2. Has the highest pH

3. Reacts with an equal volume of 0.05 M $Ba(OH)_2$ to form a solution with pH = 7

These three questions belong to the topic category of acids and bases and require you to apply knowledge in this area to the particular solutions specified in the five choices.

Choice (C) is the correct answer to question 1. To answer the first question, you must recognize which of the choices above are acidic solutions. Only choices (A) and (C) satisfy this requirement. Choice (B) refers to a neutral salt solution, choice (D) is a solution of an alcohol, and choice (E) is a basic solution. Both choices (A) and (C) are acidic solutions, but choice (A) is a strong acid that is completely ionized in aqueous solution, while choice (C) is only partially ionized in aqueous solution. Since the concentrations of all the solutions are the same, you do not need to consider this factor. The hydrogen ion concentration of a 0.1-molar acetic acid solution is considerably smaller than 0.1-molar. The hydrogen ion concentration in choice (A) is equal to 0.1-molar. Thus, choice (C) is a weakly acidic solution and is the correct answer.

Choice (E) is the correct answer to question 2. To answer the second question, you need to understand the pH scale, which is a measure of the hydrogen ion concentration in solution and is defined as pH = – log [H^+]. The higher the pH, the lower the hydrogen ion concentration and the more basic the solution. Among the choices given above, choice (E) is the most basic solution.

Choice (A) is the correct answer to question 3. To answer the third question, you need to know that acids react with bases to form salts and water. Since the question refers to equal volumes of each solution, assume 1 liter of each solution is available. Barium hydroxide solution is a strong base, i.e., is completely ionized in water, and 1 liter of 0.05 *M* $Ba(OH)_2$ provides 0.1 mole of OH^- ions in solution. When 1 liter of this solution is added to 1 liter of either 0.1 *M* NaCl, 0.1 *M* CH_3OH, or 0.1 *M* KOH no reactions occur and the resulting solutions remain basic, i.e., the pH will be greater than 7 in each case. When 0.1 mole OH^- ions reacts with 0.1 mole of acetic acid, the resulting solution will also be basic and have a pH greater than 7 because acetic acid is a weak acid, i.e., is incompletely ionized in water. The acetic acid reacts with the OH^- ions as follows:

$$HC_2H_3O_2 + OH^- \rightleftarrows C_2H_3O_2^- + H_2O$$

The acetate salt formed hydrolyzes in water yielding a solution containing more OH^- ions than H^+ ions. When 1 liter of 0.05 *M* $Ba(OH)_2$ reacts with 1 liter of 0.1 *M* HCl, there is a reaction between 0.1 mole OH^- ions and 0.1 mole H^+ to form 0.1 mole H_2O. The resulting solution contains Ba^{2+} ions and Cl^- ions and equal concentrations of OH^- and H^+ ions. The solution formed is neutral and the pH is 7.

Relationship Analysis Questions

This type of question consists of a specific statement or assertion (Statement I) followed by an explanation of the assertion (Statement II). The question is answered by determining if the assertion and the explanation are each true statements and, if so, whether the explanation (or reason) provided does in fact properly explain the statement given in the assertion.

This type of question tests your ability to identify proper cause-and-effect relationships. It probes whether you can assess the correctness of the original assertion and then evaluate the truth of the "reason" proposed to justify it. The analysis required by this type of question provides you with an opportunity to demonstrate developed reasoning skills and the scope of your understanding of a particular topic.

On the actual Chemistry Test, the following type of question must be answered on a special section (labeled "Chemistry") at the lower left-hand corner of your answer sheet. These questions will be numbered beginning with 101 and must be answered according to the following directions.

SAMPLE ANSWER GRID

	I		II		CE*
101	(T)	(F)	(T)	(F)	◯

Directions: Each question below consists of two statements, I in the left-hand column and II in the right-hand column. For each question, determine whether statement I is true or false and whether statement II is true or false and fill in the corresponding T or F circles on your answer sheet. Fill in circle CE only if statement II is a correct explanation of the true statement I.

EXAMPLES:		
I		II
EX 1. H_2SO_4 is a strong acid	BECAUSE	H_2SO_4 contains sulfur.
EX 2. An atom of oxygen is electrically neutral	BECAUSE	an oxygen atom contains an equal number of protons and electrons.

SAMPLE ANSWERS

	I		II		CE
EX 1	●	Ⓕ	●	Ⓕ	○
EX 2	●	Ⓕ	●	Ⓕ	●

	I		II
4.	The electrolysis of a concentrated solution of sodium chloride produces chlorine	BECAUSE	sodium chloride is a covalent compound.

The above question has several components. Statement I, the assertion, has to do with an oxidation-reduction reaction, more specifically, an electrochemical reaction. This statement is true because the electrolysis of a concentrated sodium chloride solution yields chlorine gas at the anode (oxidation) and hydrogen gas at the cathode (reduction). The electrolytic solution gradually becomes alkaline with the accumulation of hydroxide ions (i.e., OH^- ions) as the reaction proceeds.

Statement II, the reason, is false because the type of chemical bonding in sodium chloride is ionic. According to the directions for answering this question type, you should fill in the corresponding T and F circles on your answer sheet.

	I		II
5.	Atoms of different elements can have the same mass number	BECAUSE	atoms of each element have a characteristic number of protons in the nucleus.

This is a question on atomic structure. The sum of the number of protons plus the number of neutrons contained in the nucleus of an atom is the mass number. However, atoms of the same element may have different numbers of neutrons in their nuclei and thus have different masses. Such atoms, which have the same number of protons but different numbers of neutrons, are called isotopes of an element ($^{12}_{6}C$ and $^{14}_{6}C$, for example). The existence of isotopes makes it possible for atoms of different elements, that is, with different numbers of protons, to have the same total mass or mass number ($^{14}_{6}C$ and $^{14}_{7}N$, for example). Thus Statement I is true. Statement II is also true because the number of protons in the nucleus of an atom is a characteristic feature that identifies each element. But it is not the reason that explains the existence of isotopes and so does not properly explain Statement I. Thus, to answer this question, you should fill in both T circles for this question, but not the CE circle.

	I		II
6.	When the system $CO(g)$ + $Cl_2(g) \rightleftarrows COCl_2(g)$ is at equilibrium and the pressure on the system is increased by decreasing the volume at constant temperature, more $COCl_2(g)$ will be produced	BECAUSE	an increase of pressure on a system will be relieved when the system shifts to a smaller total number of moles of gas.

Statement I is true because whenever stress is applied to a system at equilibrium the system will tend to shift to relieve the stress (Le Chatelier's principle). In the system described, the stress is caused by an increase in pressure resulting from a decrease in the volume and will be relieved by the reaction of some CO and Cl_2 to form more $COCl_2$. The new equilibrium that will be established will contain a smaller total number of moles of gas, thereby reducing the pressure stress. This is the explanation given in Statement II, which is not only true but also correctly explains the phenomenon described in Statement I. Thus, to answer this question correctly you should fill in both T circles as well as the CE circle.

Five-Choice Completion Questions

The five-choice question is written either as an incomplete statement or as a question. It is used when: (1) the problem presented is clearly delineated by the wording of the question so that you are asked to choose not a universal solution but the best of the solutions offered; (2) the problem is such that you are required to evaluate the relevance of five plausible, or even scientifically accurate, options and to select the one most pertinent; (3) the problem has several pertinent solutions and you are required to select the one inappropriate solution that is presented. These questions normally contain a word in capital letters such as NOT, LEAST, or EXCEPT.

A special type of five-choice question is used in some tests, including the SAT Subject Test in Chemistry, to allow for the possibility of multiple correct answers. For these questions, you must evaluate each response independently of the others in order to select the most appropriate combination. In questions of this type, several (usually three or four) statements labeled by Roman numerals are given with the question. One or more of these statements may correctly answer the question. You must select, from among the five lettered choices that follow, the one combination of statements that best answers the question. In the test, questions of this type are intermixed among the more standard five-choice questions. (Question 8 is an example of this type of question.)

In five-choice completion questions, you may be asked to convert the information given in a word problem into graphical form or to select and apply the mathematical relationship necessary to solve the scientific problem. Alternatively, you may be asked to interpret experimental data, graphical stimuli, or mathematical expressions.

When the experimental data or other scientific problems to be analyzed are comparatively extensive, it is often convenient to organize several five-choice completion questions into sets, that is, direct each question in a set to the same material. This practice allows you to answer several questions based on the same material. In no case, however, is the answer to one question necessary for answering a subsequent question correctly. Each question in a set is independent of the others and refers only to the material given for the entire set.

Directions: Each of the questions or incomplete statements below is followed by five suggested answers or completions. Select the one that is best in each case and then fill in the corresponding circle on the answer sheet.

7. The hydrogen ion concentration of a solution prepared by diluting 50 milliliters of 0.100-molar HNO_3 with water to 500 milliliters of solution is

(A) 0.0010 *M*
(B) 0.0050 *M*
(C) 0.010 *M*
(D) 0.050 *M*
(E) 1.0 *M*

Choice (C) is the correct answer to question 7. This is a question that concerns solution concentrations. One way to solve the problem is through the use of ratios. In this question, a solution of nitric acid is diluted 10-fold; therefore, the concentration of the solution will decrease by a factor of 10, that is, from 0.100-molar to 0.010-molar. Alternatively, you could calculate the number of moles of H^+ ions present and divide this value by 0.50 liter: $(0.100 \times 0.050)/0.5 = M$ of the diluted solution.

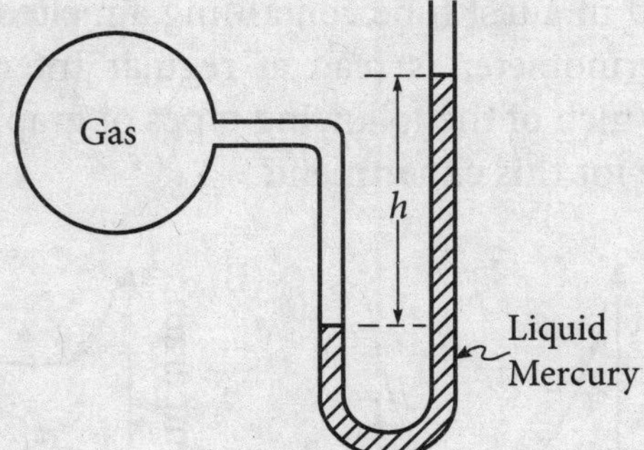

8. The bulb of the open-end manometer shown above contains a gas. True statements about this system include which of the following?

I. Only atmospheric pressure is exerted on the exposed mercury surface in the right side of the tube.

II. The gas pressure is greater than atmospheric pressure.

III. The difference in the height, *h*, of mercury levels is equal to the pressure of the gas.

(A) II only
(B) III only
(C) I and II only
(D) I and III only
(E) I, II, and III

Choice (C) is the correct answer to question 8. This is a laboratory-oriented question pertaining to the measurement of gas pressures. It demands higher-level analytical skills that involve drawing conclusions from results obtained in an experiment. To answer this question correctly, you must first understand that, in an open type of manometer, the air exerts pressure on the column of liquid in the open side of the U-tube and the gas being studied exerts pressure on the other side of the U-tube. It is clear then that Statement I is true since the data given show that the manometer is open-ended and its right side is exposed to the atmosphere. Statement II is also a true statement because the level of liquid mercury is higher in the right side, which is exposed to the atmosphere, than in the left side, which is exposed to the gas. Thus the gas pressure is greater than atmospheric pressure. Statement III is not a correct statement because the pressure of the gas in the bulb, expressed in millimeters of mercury, is equal to the difference in height, *h*, of the two mercury levels, plus the atmospheric pressure. Thus only Statements I and II are correct.

9. A thermometer is placed in a test tube containing a melted pure substance. As slow cooling occurs, the thermometer is read at regular intervals until well after the sample has solidified. Which of the following types of graphs is obtained by plotting temperature versus time for this experiment?

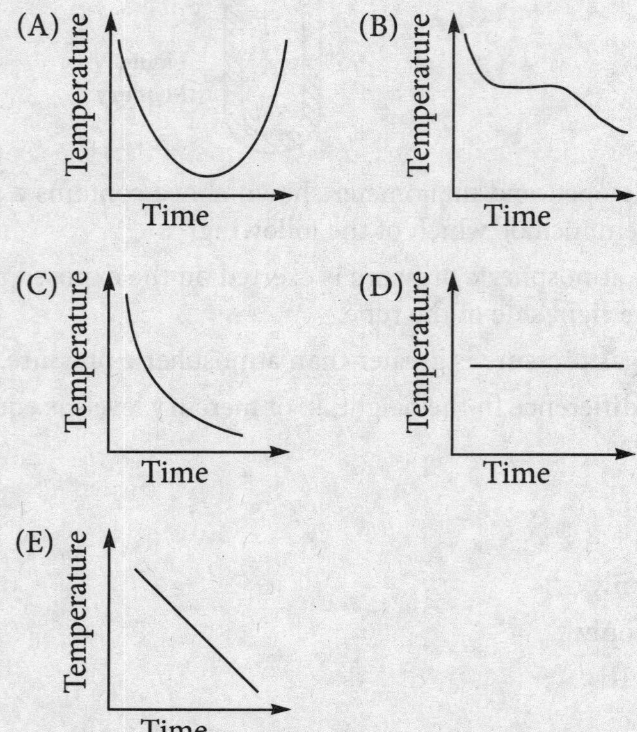

Choice (B) is the correct answer to question 9. This is a question on states of matter. You must convert the description of the physical phenomenon given in the question to graphical form. When a liquid is cooled slowly, its temperature will decrease with time. Thus the first portion of a graph depicting this phenomenon must show a decrease when temperature is plotted against time. When a pure liquid substance reaches its fusion (melting) point, continued cooling will release heat with time as the substance solidifies. During this period there is no drop in temperature. After the substance has completely solidified, further cooling will cause an additional drop in temperature. The only graph shown that accurately depicts the events described is (B), which is the answer.

$$\ldots Cu^{2+}(aq) + \ldots I^{-}(aq) \rightarrow \ldots CuI(s) + \ldots I_2(s)$$

10. When the equation above is balanced and all coefficients are reduced to lowest whole-number terms, the coefficient for I^- *(aq)* is

(A) 1

(B) 2

(C) 3

(D) 4

(E) 5

Choice (D) is the correct answer to question 10. This question pertains to the balancing of chemical equations. In order to answer this question correctly, you need to recognize that both mass and charge must be conserved in any chemical equation. With this in mind, the chemical equation is correctly written as

$$2\ Cu^{2+}(aq) + 4\ I^{-}(aq) \rightarrow 2\ CuI(s) + I_2(s)$$

The coefficient for $I^{-}(aq)$ is 4.

11. From their electron configurations, one can predict that the geometric configuration for which of the following molecules is NOT correct?
   (A) PF_3 trigonal planar
   (B) CF_4 tetrahedral
   (C) $CHCl_3$ irregular tetrahedron
   (D) OF_2 bent (v-shaped)
   (E) HF linear

Choice (A) is the correct answer to question 11. This is a question on chemical bonding and requires you to apply the principles of molecular bonding. Each of the molecules given is correctly paired with the term describing its molecular geometry except choice (A). The geometry of PF_3 is not trigonal planar, but trigonal pyramidal, because this geometry corresponds to a maximum possible separation of the electron pairs around the central atom, phosphorus, and therefore yields the most stable configuration; the central atom of the molecule is surrounded by three single bonds and one unshared electron pair. Thus, the correct answer is choice (A). Note that this is the type of question that asks you to identify the *one* solution to the problem that is *inappropriate.*

$$\ldots SO_2(g) + \ldots O_2(g) \rightarrow .\overset{?}{.}.$$

12. According to the reaction above, how many moles of $SO_2(g)$ are required to react completely with 1 mole of $O_2(g)$?
   (A) 0.5 mole
   (B) 1 mole
   (C) 2 moles
   (D) 3 moles
   (E) 4 moles

Choice (C) is the correct answer to question 12. This is a question on descriptive chemistry that also tests your ability to balance chemical equations. The correct answer to this question depends first on your knowing that the combustion of sulfur dioxide, $SO_2(g)$, produces sulfur trioxide, $SO_3(g)$. The stoichiometry of the correctly balanced equation indicates that 2 moles of $SO_2(g)$ are needed to react completely with 1 mole of $O_2(g)$ to form 2 moles of $SO_3(g)$.

13. Analysis by mass of a certain compound shows that it contains 14.4 percent hydrogen and 85.6 percent carbon. Which of the following is the most informative statement that can properly be made about the compound on the basis of these data?

    (A) It is a hydrocarbon.

    (B) Its empirical formula is CH_2.

    (C) Its molecular formula is C_2H_4.

    (D) Its molar mass is 28 grams.

    (E) It contains a triple bond.

Choice (B) is the correct answer to question 13. This is a question on stoichiometry that tests the important skill of scientific reasoning based on experimental evidence. The question states that 100 percent of the composition of the compound analyzed can be accounted for with the elements hydrogen and carbon. Thus, this compound is a hydrocarbon and choice (A) is a correct statement. It is not the correct answer to the question, however, because you can deduce more specific conclusions about this compound from the information given. The relative percentage composition provides evidence that the atomic ratio of carbon to hydrogen in the compound must be 85.6/12.0 : 14.4/1.0 or 1:2. Therefore, you can conclude that the empirical formula for the compound is CH_2, a hydrocarbon. Thus choice (B) is a better answer than choice (A). Since you do not know the total number of moles of the compound used for analysis, you cannot calculate the molar mass or derive the molecular formula for this compound. Thus choices (C) and (D) cannot be determined from the information given and so they are not correct answers to the question. It is known, however, that a substance with an empirical formula of CH_2 cannot have a triple bond. Therefore, choice (E) is incorrect.

Chemistry Test

Practice Helps

The test that follows is an actual, recently administered SAT Subject Test in Chemistry. To get an idea of what it's like to take this test, practice under conditions that are much like those of an actual test administration.

- Set aside an hour when you can take the test uninterrupted. Make sure you complete the test in one sitting.
- Sit at a desk or table with no other books or papers. Dictionaries, other books, or notes are not allowed in the test room.
- Tear out an answer sheet from the back of this book and fill it in just as you would on the day of the test. One answer sheet can be used for up to three Subject Tests.
- Read the instructions that precede the practice test. During the actual administration, you will be asked to read them before answering test questions.
- Time yourself by placing a clock or kitchen timer in front of you.
- After you finish the practice test, read the sections "How to Score the SAT Subject Test in Chemistry" and "How Did You Do on the Subject Test in Chemistry?"
- The appearance of the answer sheet in this book may differ from the answer sheet you see on test day.

CHEMISTRY TEST

The top portion of the section of the answer sheet that you will use in taking the Chemistry Test must be filled in exactly as shown in the illustration below. Note carefully that you have to do all of the following on your answer sheet.

1. Print CHEMISTRY on the line under the words "Subject Test (print)."

2. In the shaded box labeled "Test Code" fill in four circles:

   —Fill in circle 2 in the row labeled V.
   —Fill in circle 2 in the row labeled W.
   —Fill in circle 4 in the row labeled X.
   —Fill in circle D in the row labeled Y.

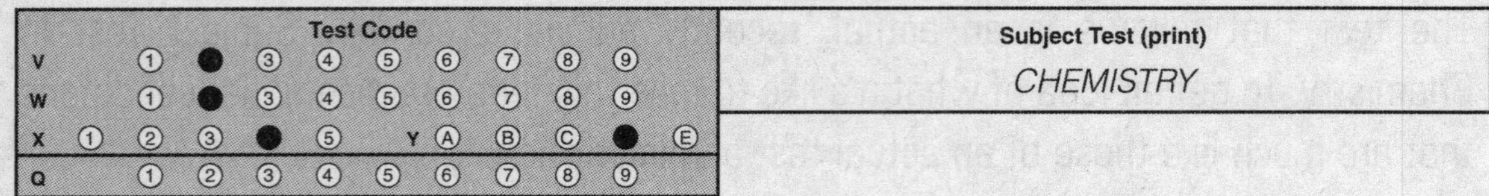

3. Please answer the questions below by filling in the appropriate circles in the row labeled Q on the answer sheet. The information you provide is for statistical purposes only and will not affect your score on the test.

Question I

How many semesters of chemistry have you taken in high school? (If you are taking chemistry this semester, count it as a full semester.) Fill in only one circle of circles 1-3.

- One semester or less —Fill in circle 1.
- Two semesters —Fill in circle 2.
- Three semesters or more —Fill in circle 3.

Question II

How recently have you studied chemistry?

- I am currently enrolled in or have just completed a chemistry course. —Fill in circle 4.
- I have not studied chemistry for 6 months or more. —Fill in circle 5.

Question III

Which of the following best describes your preparation in algebra? (If you are taking an algebra course this semester, count it as a full semester.) Fill in only one circle of circles 6-8.

- One semester or less —Fill in circle 6.
- Two semesters —Fill in circle 7.
- Three semesters or more —Fill in circle 8.

Question IV

Are you currently taking Advanced Placement Chemistry? If you are, fill in circle 9.

When the supervisor gives the signal, turn the page and begin the Chemistry Test. There is a total of 85 questions in the Chemistry Test (1-70 plus questions 101-115 that must be answered on the special section at the lower left-hand corner of the answer sheet).

CHEMISTRY TEST

MATERIAL IN THE FOLLOWING TABLE MAY BE USEFUL IN ANSWERING THE QUESTIONS IN THIS EXAMINATION.

DO NOT DETACH FROM BOOK.

PERIODIC TABLE OF THE ELEMENTS

1 **H** 1.0079																	2 **He** 4.0026
3 **Li** 6.941	4 **Be** 9.012											5 **B** 10.811	6 **C** 12.011	7 **N** 14.007	8 **O** 16.00	9 **F** 19.00	10 **Ne** 20.179
11 **Na** 22.99	12 **Mg** 24.30											13 **Al** 26.98	14 **Si** 28.09	15 **P** 30.974	16 **S** 32.06	17 **Cl** 35.453	18 **Ar** 39.948
19 **K** 39.10	20 **Ca** 40.08	21 **Sc** 44.96	22 **Ti** 47.90	23 **V** 50.94	24 **Cr** 52.00	25 **Mn** 54.938	26 **Fe** 55.85	27 **Co** 58.93	28 **Ni** 58.69	29 **Cu** 63.55	30 **Zn** 65.39	31 **Ga** 69.72	32 **Ge** 72.59	33 **As** 74.92	34 **Se** 78.96	35 **Br** 79.90	36 **Kr** 83.80
37 **Rb** 85.47	38 **Sr** 87.62	39 **Y** 88.91	40 **Zr** 91.22	41 **Nb** 92.91	42 **Mo** 95.94	43 **Tc** (98)	44 **Ru** 101.1	45 **Rh** 102.91	46 **Pd** 106.42	47 **Ag** 107.87	48 **Cd** 112.41	49 **In** 114.82	50 **Sn** 118.71	51 **Sb** 121.75	52 **Te** 127.60	53 **I** 126.91	54 **Xe** 131.29
55 **Cs** 132.91	56 **Ba** 137.33	57 ***La** 138.91	72 **Hf** 178.49	73 **Ta** 180.95	74 **W** 183.85	75 **Re** 186.21	76 **Os** 190.2	77 **Ir** 192.2	78 **Pt** 195.08	79 **Au** 196.97	80 **Hg** 200.59	81 **Tl** 204.38	82 **Pb** 207.2	83 **Bi** 208.98	84 **Po** (209)	85 **At** (210)	86 **Rn** (222)
87 **Fr** (223)	88 **Ra** 226.02	89 **†Ac** 227.03	104 **Rf** (261)	105 **Db** (262)	106 **Sg** (263)	107 **Bh** (262)	108 **Hs** (265)	109 **Mt** (266)	110 § (269)	111 § (272)	112 § (277)	§Not yet named					

*Lanthanide Series	58 **Ce** 140.12	59 **Pr** 140.91	60 **Nd** 144.24	61 **Pm** (145)	62 **Sm** 150.4	63 **Eu** 151.97	64 **Gd** 157.25	65 **Tb** 158.93	66 **Dy** 162.50	67 **Ho** 164.93	68 **Er** 167.26	69 **Tm** 168.93	70 **Yb** 173.04	71 **Lu** 174.97
†Actinide Series	90 **Th** 232.04	91 **Pa** 231.04	92 **U** 238.03	93 **Np** 237.05	94 **Pu** (244)	95 **Am** (243)	96 **Cm** (247)	97 **Bk** (247)	98 **Cf** (251)	99 **Es** (252)	100 **Fm** (257)	101 **Md** (258)	102 **No** (259)	103 **Lr** (260)

CHEMISTRY TEST

Note: For all questions involving solutions, assume that the solvent is water unless otherwise stated.

Throughout the test the following symbols have the definitions specified unless otherwise noted.

H	= enthalpy	atm	= atmosphere(s)
M	= molar	g	= gram(s)
n	= number of moles	J	= joule(s)
P	= pressure	kJ	= kilojoule(s)
R	= molar gas constant	L	= liter(s)
S	= entropy	mL	= milliliter(s)
T	= temperature	mm	= millimeter(s)
V	= volume	mol	= mole(s)
		V	= volt(s)

Part A

Directions: Each set of lettered choices below refers to the numbered statements or questions immediately following it. Select the one lettered choice that best fits each statement or answers each question and then fill in the corresponding circle on the answer sheet. A choice may be used once, more than once, or not at all in each set.

Questions 1-3 refer to the following pieces of laboratory equipment.

(A) Condenser
(B) Funnel
(C) Pipet
(D) Balance
(E) Barometer

1. Commonly used to transfer an exact volume of liquid from one container to another

2. Commonly used in a distillation setup

3. Commonly used in a filtration setup

Questions 4-6 refer to the following information.

Na_2CrO_4, a soluble yellow solid
$PbCrO_4$, an insoluble yellow solid
$NaNO_3$, a soluble white solid
$Pb(NO_3)_2$, a soluble white solid

(A) Yellow solid and colorless solution
(B) Yellow solid and yellow solution
(C) White solid and colorless solution
(D) No solid and yellow solution
(E) No solid and colorless solution

4. Observed when 1.0 mol of Na_2CrO_4 and 2.0 mol of $Pb(NO_3)_2$ are mixed with 1 L of water

5. Observed when 3.0 mol of Na_2CrO_4 and 1.0 mol of $Pb(NO_3)_2$ are mixed with 1 L of water

6. Observed when 1.0 mol of $NaNO_3$ and 1.0 mol of $Pb(NO_3)_2$ are mixed with 1 L of water

3YAC2

GO ON TO THE NEXT PAGE

Questions 7-9 refer to the following.

(A) Reduction potential
(B) Ionization energy (ionization potential)
(C) Electronegativity
(D) Heat of formation
(E) Activation energy

7. Is the energy change accompanying the synthesis of a compound from its elements in their standard states

8. Is the energy needed to remove an electron from a gaseous atom in its ground state

9. Is the minimum energy needed for molecules to react and form products

Questions 10-13 refer to the following pairs of substances.

(A) NH_3 and N_2H_4
(B) ^{16}O and ^{17}O
(C) NH_4Cl and NH_4NO_3
(D) CH_3OCH_3 and CH_3CH_2OH
(E) O_2 and O_3

10. Are isotopes

11. Have both ionic and covalent bonds

12. Are allotropes

13. Are strong electrolytes in aqueous solution

Questions 14-17 refer to the following subshells.

(A) 1*s*
(B) 2*s*
(C) 3*s*
(D) 3*p*
(E) 3*d*

14. Contains up to ten electrons

15. Contains one pair of electrons in the ground-state electron configuration of the lithium atom

16. Is exactly one-half filled in the ground-state electron configuration of the phosphorus atom

17. Contains the valence electrons in the ground-state electron configuration of the magnesium atom

Questions 18-20 refer to the following gases.

(A) O_3
(B) O_2
(C) CO
(D) Cl_2
(E) SO_2

18. Contributes to acid rain

19. In the stratosphere, screens out a large fraction of ultraviolet rays from the Sun

20. Is a product of the incomplete combustion of hydrocarbons

GO ON TO THE NEXT PAGE

Questions 21-24 refer to the lettered solutions in the laboratory schemes represented below.

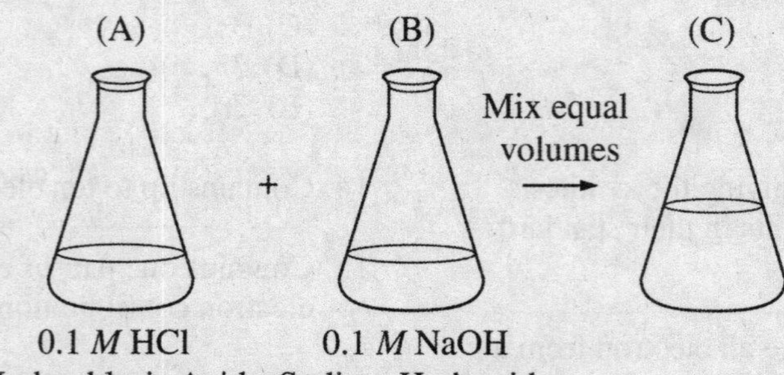

0.1 *M* HCl Hydrochloric Acid — 0.1 *M* NaOH Sodium Hydroxide

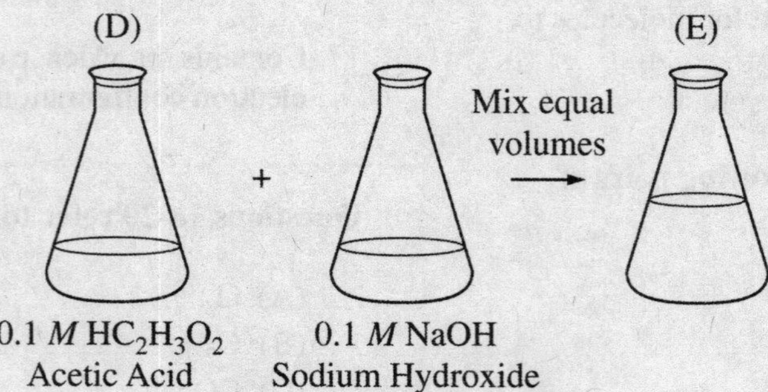

0.1 *M* $HC_2H_3O_2$ Acetic Acid — 0.1 *M* NaOH Sodium Hydroxide

21. Has a hydroxide ion concentration of 10^{-7} *M* at 298 K

22. Has the highest pH at 298 K

23. Has a pH greater than 7, but less than 13 at 298 K

24. Has a pH greater than 2, but less than 7 at 298 K

GO ON TO THE NEXT PAGE

PLEASE GO TO THE SPECIAL SECTION LABELED CHEMISTRY AT THE LOWER LEFT-HAND CORNER OF THE PAGE OF THE ANSWER SHEET YOU ARE WORKING ON AND ANSWER QUESTIONS 101-115 ACCORDING TO THE FOLLOWING DIRECTIONS.

Part B

Directions: Each question below consists of two statements, I in the left-hand column and II in the right-hand column. For each question, determine whether statement I is true or false and whether statement II is true or false and fill in the corresponding T or F circles on your answer sheet. Fill in circle CE only if statement II is a correct explanation of the true statement I.

EXAMPLES:

	I		II
EX 1.	**H_2SO_4 is a strong acid**	**BECAUSE**	**H_2SO_4 contains sulfur.**
EX 2.	**An atom of oxygen is electrically neutral**	**BECAUSE**	**an oxygen atom contains an equal number of protons and electrons.**

SAMPLE ANSWERS

	I		II		CE*
EX1	●	Ⓕ	●	Ⓕ	○
EX2	●	Ⓕ	●	Ⓕ	●

	I		II
101.	C_2H_2 and C_6H_6 have the same chemical and physical properties	BECAUSE	C_2H_2 and C_6H_6 have the same percentages by mass of hydrogen.
102.	The melting of ice is an exothermic process	BECAUSE	water has a relatively high specific heat capacity.
103.	A 2 g sample of nitrogen and a 2 g sample of oxygen contain the same number of molecules	BECAUSE	equal masses of gaseous substances contain the same number of molecules.
104.	When an atom absorbs a photon of visible light, one of its electrons is promoted to a higher energy state	BECAUSE	an electron has a negative charge.
105.	The alkali metals are very good reducing agents	BECAUSE	the alkali metals are easily oxidized.
106.	A 1.0 g sample of calcium citrate, $Ca_3(C_6H_5O_7)_2$ (molar mass 498 g/mol), contains more Ca than a 1.0 g sample of calcium carbonate, $CaCO_3$ (molar mass 100 g/mol),	BECAUSE	there are more Ca atoms in 1.0 mol of calcium carbonate than in 1.0 mol of calcium citrate.
107.	The water molecule is polar	BECAUSE	the radius of an oxygen atom is greater than that of a hydrogen atom.

GO ON TO THE NEXT PAGE

	I		II
108.	All indicators are colorless in neutral solution	BECAUSE	indicators develop color only in the presence of a strong acid or a strong base.
109.	A 1 *M* sucrose solution and a 1 *M* NaCl solution have the same freezing point	BECAUSE	a 1 *M* sucrose solution and a 1 *M* NaCl solution contain the same number of solute particles per liter of solution.
110.	The average kinetic energy of gas molecules increases as the temperature increases	BECAUSE	the average speed of gas molecules decreases as the temperature increases.
111.	When a concentrated acid is diluted, the acid should be added slowly to the water	BECAUSE	if water is added to a concentrated acid, violent splattering might occur.
112.	Methane, CH_4, is very soluble in water	BECAUSE	water molecules form hydrogen bonds with methane molecules.
113.	A 1 mol sample of electrons is required to reduce 0.5 mol of chlorine gas to chloride ions	BECAUSE	chlorine molecules are diatomic and the charge on the chloride ion is −1.
114.	In 0.1 *M* acetic acid, $[H^+]$ is smaller than $[H^+]$ is in 0.1 *M* hydrochloric acid	BECAUSE	a molecule of acetic acid contains more atoms than does a molecule of hydrogen chloride.
115.	A fluoride ion, F^-, and an oxide ion, O^{2-}, have the same diameter	BECAUSE	the fluoride ion, F^-, and the oxide ion, O^{2-}, have the same number of electrons.

RETURN TO THE SECTION OF YOUR ANSWER SHEET YOU STARTED FOR **CHEMISTRY** AND ANSWER QUESTIONS 25-70.

GO ON TO THE NEXT PAGE

Part C

Directions: Each of the questions or incomplete statements below is followed by five suggested answers or completions. Select the one that is best in each case and then fill in the corresponding circle on the answer sheet.

$\ldots H_2S(g) + \ldots O_2(g) \rightarrow \ldots H_2O(g) + \ldots SO_2(g)$

25. When 2 mol of $H_2S(g)$ react with an excess of oxygen according to the equation above, how much $H_2O(g)$ is produced? (Equation is not balanced.)

(A) 1 mol
(B) 2 mol
(C) 3 mol
(D) 4 mol
(E) 6 mol

26. Increasing the temperature of a gas in a rigid closed container increases which of the following?

I. The pressure of the gas
II. The average speed of the gas molecules
III. The mass of the gas

(A) I only
(B) II only
(C) I and II only
(D) II and III only
(E) I, II, and III

27. The number of electrons in ${}^{118}_{50}Sn^{2+}$ is

(A) 2
(B) 48
(C) 50
(D) 52
(E) 68

28. When two colorless liquid reagents are mixed, which of the following observations would suggest that a chemical reaction has occurred?

I. Formation of a precipitate
II. A color change
III. Appearance of gas bubbles

(A) I only
(B) III only
(C) I and II only
(D) II and III only
(E) I, II, and III

29. Which of the following is the correct and complete Lewis electron-dot diagram for PF_3 ?

(A)
```
    ..
F : P : F
    ..
    F
```

(B)
```
 ..       ..
:F : P : F:
 ..  ..   ..
    :F:
     ..
```

(C)
```
 ..       ..
:F : P : F:
 ..  ::   ..
    :F:
     ..
```

(D)
```
 ..  ..   ..
:F : P : F:
 ..  ::   ..
    :F:
```

(E)
```
 ..  ..   ..
:F : P : F:
 ..  ..   ..
    :F:
     ..
```


GO ON TO THE NEXT PAGE

30. Which of the following is a transition element?

(A) Iron
(B) Carbon
(C) Potassium
(D) Tin
(E) Radium

31. When 50. mL of 1.5 *M* NaCl(*aq*) is diluted with pure water to a final volume of 150. mL, what is the molarity of the resulting solution?

(A) 0.10 *M*
(B) 0.50 *M*
(C) 1.5 *M*
(D) 4.5 *M*
(E) 5.0 *M*

32. A 40.0 g sample of a hydrated salt was heated until all the water was driven off. The mass of the solid remaining was 32.0 g. What was the percent of water by mass in the original sample?

(A) 13.0%
(B) 20.0%
(C) 25.0%
(D) 75.0%
(E) 80.0%

33. A solution that has pH of 6.0 is

(A) strongly basic
(B) slightly basic
(C) neutral
(D) slightly acidic
(E) strongly acidic

34. Which of the following molecules is a saturated hydrocarbon?

(A) C_3H_8
(B) C_2H_4
(C) CH_3Cl
(D) CCl_4
(E) CO_2

$$\ldots Fe_2O_3(s) + \ldots CO(g) \rightarrow \ldots Fe(s) + \ldots CO_2(g)$$

35. When the equation above is balanced and all the coefficients are reduced to lowest whole-number terms, what is the coefficient for $Fe_2O_3(s)$?

(A) 1
(B) 2
(C) 3
(D) 4
(E) 5

36. In which of the following compounds does nitrogen have an oxidation number of +5 ?

(A) HNO_3
(B) N_2
(C) NO_2
(D) N_2O
(E) NH_2OH

37. If both NaOH and KOH were the same price per kilogram, it would be cheaper to use NaOH to neutralize a quantity of acid because NaOH

(A) weighs less per mole than KOH
(B) weighs more per mole than KOH
(C) neutralizes more acid per mole than KOH
(D) neutralizes less acid per mole than KOH
(E) is less dense than KOH

38. When a given amount of $Ca(OH)_2$ is completely neutralized with H_2SO_4, which of the following is the mole ratio of $Ca(OH)_2$ to H_2SO_4 in this reaction?

(A) 1 : 4
(B) 1 : 2
(C) 1 : 1
(D) 2 : 1
(E) 4 : 1

GO ON TO THE NEXT PAGE

39. Factors that influence whether or not two colliding molecules will react include which of the following?

    I. The energy of the collision
    II. The orientation of the molecules
    III. The size difference between the reactant and product molecules

    (A) I only
    (B) III only
    (C) I and II only
    (D) I and III only
    (E) I, II, and III

$$2\,SO_2(g) + O_2(g) \rightleftarrows 2\,SO_3(g)$$

40. What is the expression for the equilibrium constant, K_{eq}, for the reaction represented above?

    (A) $K_{eq} = \dfrac{[SO_3]}{[SO_2][O_2]}$

    (B) $K_{eq} = \dfrac{[SO_3]^2}{[SO_2]^2[O_2]}$

    (C) $K_{eq} = \dfrac{[SO_2] + [O_2]}{[SO_3]}$

    (D) $K_{eq} = \dfrac{[SO_2]^2 + [O_2]}{[SO_3]^2}$

    (E) $K_{eq} = \dfrac{[SO_3]}{[SO_2] + [O_2]}$

41. A solution contains 1.00 mol of glucose, $C_6H_{12}O_6$, and 2.00 mol of urea, $(NH_2)_2CO$, in 7.00 mol of water. What is the mole fraction of glucose in the solution?

    (A) 0.100
    (B) 0.143
    (C) 0.200
    (D) 0.333
    (E) 0.500

Temperature (°C)	Vapor Pressure of Ethyl Alcohol (mm Hg)
60	350
70	538
80	813
90	1,182
100	1,698

42. The barometric pressure on Pikes Peak (14,109 feet) in Colorado averages 455 mm Hg. From the table above, one can conclude that the boiling point of ethyl alcohol at this altitude would be

    (A) 100°C
    (B) between 90°C and 100°C
    (C) between 80°C and 90°C
    (D) between 70°C and 80°C
    (E) between 60°C and 70°C

$$\ldots Zn(s) + \ldots H^+(aq) \rightarrow$$

43. When the equation for the reaction represented above is completed and balanced and all coefficients are reduced to lowest whole-number terms, the coefficient for $H^+(aq)$ is

    (A) 2
    (B) 3
    (C) 4
    (D) 5
    (E) 6

44. Which of the following statements is true concerning a saturated solution of a salt at a constant temperature?

    (A) The concentrations of salt and solvent are usually equal.
    (B) The amount of dissolved salt is constant.
    (C) Addition of solid salt shifts the equilibrium, which results in an increase in the amount of dissolved salt.
    (D) The solution is unstable and sudden crystallization could occur.
    (E) At the same temperature, a saturated solution of any other salt has the same concentration.

GO ON TO THE NEXT PAGE

$$2\,CO(g) + O_2(g) \rightarrow 2\,CO_2(g)$$

45. According to the reaction represented above, 1.00 mol of $CO(g)$ reacts at 0°C and 1 atm to consume how much $O_2(g)$?

(A) 32.0 g
(B) 11.2 L
(C) 22.4 L
(D) 1.00 mol
(E) 2.00 mol

46. Species that in water can either accept or donate protons include which of the following?

I. CH_4
II. HCO_3^-
III. HPO_4^{2-}

(A) I only
(B) II only
(C) III only
(D) II and III only
(E) I, II, and III

47. The ionization energies of Li and H are 520 kJ/mol and 1,312 kJ/mol, respectively. The ionization energy of He is

(A) 496 kJ/mol
(B) 656 kJ/mol
(C) 899 kJ/mol
(D) 1,086 kJ/mol
(E) 2,372 kJ/mol

48. An active ingredient in common household bleach solutions is most likely to be which of the following?

(A) NaCl
(B) NaClO
(C) $NaHCO_3$
(D) Na_2SO_4
(E) $HC_2H_3O_2$

$${}^{2}_{1}H + {}^{3}_{1}H \rightarrow {}^{1}_{0}n + \_\_\_\_$$

49. The missing product in the nuclear reaction represented above is

(A) ${}^{1}_{1}H$
(B) ${}^{3}_{2}He$
(C) ${}^{4}_{2}He$
(D) ${}^{4}_{3}Li$
(E) ${}^{5}_{3}Li$

$$HCl(g) + H_2O(l) \rightarrow H_3O^+(aq) + Cl^-(aq)$$

50. All of the following statements are correct for the reaction represented by the equation above EXCEPT:

(A) H_3O^+ is the conjugate acid of H_2O.
(B) Cl^- is the conjugate base of HCl.
(C) H_2O is behaving as a Brønsted-Lowry base.
(D) HCl is a weaker Brønsted-Lowry acid than H_2O.
(E) The reaction proceeds essentially to completion.

GO ON TO THE NEXT PAGE

P (atm)	2	1	0.5	0.4
V (L)	100	200	400	500
T (K)	200	200	200	200

51. The data given in the table above describe the behavior of a sample of gas. Which of the following empirical laws does the data illustrate? (k is a constant.)

(A) $P = kT$ at constant V

(B) $P_T = P_1 + P_2 + P_3 + \ldots$ at constant V and T

(C) $P = \frac{k}{V}$ at constant T

(D) $V = kT$ at constant P

(E) $P = kn$ (number of moles) at constant V and T

52. Of the following, which is an example of an oxidation-reduction reaction?

(A) $Fe(s) + Sn^{2+}(aq) \rightarrow Sn(s) + Fe^{2+}(aq)$
(B) $HCO_3^-(aq) + OH^-(aq) \rightarrow CO_3^{2-}(aq) + H_2O(l)$
(C) $Pb^{2+}(aq) + 2\,I^-(aq) \rightarrow PbI_2(s)$
(D) $HCl(g) + NH_3(g) \rightarrow NH_4Cl(s)$
(E) $Ba^{2+}(aq) + MnO_4^{2-}(aq) \rightarrow BaMnO_4(s)$

$$N_2(g) + 3\,H_2(g) \rightleftarrows 2\,NH_3(g) + \text{heat}$$

53. Which of the following statements about the reaction represented above is true?

(A) The forward reaction is endothermic.
(B) A 28 g sample of $N_2(g)$ reacts completely with a 3 g sample of $H_2(g)$.
(C) $NH_3(g)$ will dissociate into equal masses of $N_2(g)$ and $H_2(g)$.
(D) The reactants occupy a smaller volume than the products when measured at the same temperature and pressure.
(E) The equilibrium concentration of ammonia is affected by a change in temperature.

GO ON TO THE NEXT PAGE

54. The element carbon is the chief constituent of all of the following EXCEPT

(A) coal
(B) glass
(C) diamond
(D) charcoal
(E) graphite

55. At 0°C and 1.0 atm, the density of C_2H_4 gas is approximately

(A) 0.80 g/L
(B) 1.0 g/L
(C) 1.3 g/L
(D) 2.5 g/L
(E) 28 g/L

56. Which of the following contains a weak organic acid?

(A) Vinegar
(B) Hydrogen peroxide
(C) Baking soda
(D) Freon gas
(E) Ammonia

$$\ldots P_4O_{10}(s) + \ldots H_2O(l) \rightarrow \ldots H_3PO_4(aq)$$

57. When 1 mol of $P_4O_{10}(s)$ reacts completely with water to produce $H_3PO_4(aq)$ according to the reaction represented by the unbalanced equation above, the number of moles of $H_2O(l)$ consumed is

(A) 1 mol
(B) 3 mol
(C) 4 mol
(D) 6 mol
(E) 12 mol

58. Increased randomness results under which of the following conditions?

I. A 1 L sample of He(g) and a 1 L sample of Ne(g) are mixed in a 2 L flask.
II. Ice melts.
III. CaO(s) reacts with $CO_2(g)$ to form $CaCO_3(s)$.

(A) I only
(B) II only
(C) I and II only
(D) II and III only
(E) I, II, and III

$$C_5H_{12}(l) + 8\,O_2(g) \rightarrow 5\,CO_2(g) + 6\,H_2O(l)$$

59. According to the balanced equation above, when 4 mol of $O_2(g)$ react completely with $C_5H_{12}(l)$, which of the following is true?

(A) 1 mol of $C_5H_{12}(l)$ must react.
(B) 2 mol of $C_5H_{12}(l)$ must react.
(C) 3 mol of $H_2O(l)$ must be formed.
(D) 12 mol of $H_2O(l)$ must be formed.
(E) 5 mol of $CO_2(g)$ must be formed.

60. True statements about transition metals include which of the following?

I. Most can exhibit more than one stable oxidation state.
II. Their compounds are often colored.
III. Their ions have partially filled *p*-orbitals.

(A) I only
(B) III only
(C) I and II only
(D) II and III only
(E) I, II, and III

61. The molarity of solution X is to be determined by a titration procedure. To carry out this procedure, all of the following must be known EXCEPT the

(A) equation for the chemical reaction that occurs during the titration
(B) volume of solution X that is used
(C) mass of solution X that is used
(D) volume of the solution that reacts with X
(E) molarity of the solution that reacts with X

62. The primary intermolecular attraction that makes it possible to liquefy hydrogen gas is called

(A) London dispersion forces
(B) dipole-dipole attraction
(C) covalent bonding
(D) ionic bonding
(E) hydrogen bonding

GO ON TO THE NEXT PAGE

Questions 63-65

$$Mg(s) + 2H^+ \rightarrow Mg^{2+} + H_2(g)$$

A student performed an experiment to determine the amount of hydrogen gas released in a reaction. The student produced the hydrogen gas by reacting hydrochloric acid and a strip of magnesium metal according to the equation above. All of the magnesium metal was consumed and the hydrogen gas was collected by displacement of water in an inverted bottle. The student's data contain the following information.

Mass of Mg .... 0.024 g
Volume of gas collected over water......25.2 mL
Water temperature............................. 22.0°C
Room temperature.............................. 22.0°C
Atmospheric pressure........................749.8 mm Hg
Vapor pressure of water at 22°C......... 19.8 mm Hg

63. What number of moles of magnesium was used?

(A) 5.8×10^{-1} mol
(B) 3.0×10^{-2} mol
(C) 2.4×10^{-2} mol
(D) 1.4×10^{-3} mol
(E) 1.0×10^{-3} mol

64. Why is it essential to know the water temperature in this experiment?

I. To find the vapor pressure of the water
II. To control the rate of reaction
III. To make sure that the reaction goes to completion

(A) I only
(B) II only
(C) I and III only
(D) II and III only
(E) I, II, and III

65. The volume of the dry hydrogen gas at 1 atm and room temperature would be

(A) $\frac{(25.2)(749.8 + 19.8)}{760}$ mL

(B) $\frac{(25.2)(760 - 19.8)}{749.8}$ mL

(C) $\frac{(25.2)(749.8 - 19.8)}{760}$ mL

(D) $\frac{(749.8 - 19.8)}{(760)(25.2)}$ mL

(E) $\frac{(760 - 19.8)}{(749.8)(25.2)}$ mL

GO ON TO THE NEXT PAGE

$H_2(g) + F_2(g) \rightarrow 2\,HF(g) + 537.6\text{ kJ}$

66. If 0.10 mol of $HF(g)$ is formed according to the reaction represented above, approximately how much heat is evolved?

(A) 13 kJ
(B) 27 kJ
(C) 54 kJ
(D) 110 kJ
(E) 220 kJ

67. A chemical reaction is used to separate a mixture into separate substances in which of the following situations?

(A) Pure water is obtained from ocean water by evaporating the water and condensing it.
(B) Iron filings are separated from sand by the use of a magnet.
(C) Iron metal is produced from ore containing iron(III) oxide.
(D) Plant pigments in a solution are separated by the use of paper chromatography.
(E) Sand is obtained from a sand-sugar mixture by adding water to dissolve the sugar.

68. If a compound has an empirical formula of CH_2 and a molar mass of 70 g/mol, which of the following is most likely to be its molecular formula?

(A) C_3H_6
(B) C_4H_4
(C) C_4H_8
(D) C_5H_5
(E) C_5H_{10}

$PCl_5(g) + \text{energy} \rightleftarrows PCl_3(g) + Cl_2(g)$

69. The system above is at equilibrium in a closed container. Which of the following would increase the amount of PCl_3 in the system?

(A) Decreasing the pressure of the system at constant temperature
(B) Lowering the temperature at constant pressure
(C) Adding a catalyst
(D) Adding some $Cl_2(g)$ to the reaction vessel
(E) Removing some $PCl_5(g)$ from the reaction vessel

70. Which of the following terms gives a qualitative rather than a quantitative description of the concentration of a solution?

(A) Molality
(B) Mass percentage
(C) Dilute
(D) Mole fraction
(E) Molarity

STOP

IF YOU FINISH BEFORE TIME IS CALLED, YOU MAY CHECK YOUR WORK ON THIS TEST ONLY. DO NOT TURN TO ANY OTHER TEST IN THIS BOOK.

How to Score the SAT Subject Test in Chemistry

When you take an actual SAT Subject Test in Chemistry, your answer sheet will be "read" by a scanning machine that will record your responses to each question. Then a computer will compare your answers with the correct answers and produce your raw score. You get one point for each correct answer. For each wrong answer, you lose one-fourth of a point. Questions you omit (and any for which you mark more than one answer) are not counted. This raw score is converted to a scaled score that is reported to you and to the colleges you specify.

Worksheet 1. Finding Your Raw Test Score

STEP 1: Table A lists the correct answers for all the questions on the Subject Test in Chemistry that is reproduced in this book. It also serves as a worksheet for you to calculate your raw score.

- Compare your answers with those given in the table.
- Put a check in the column marked "Right" if your answer is correct.
- Put a check in the column marked "Wrong" if your answer is incorrect.
- Leave both columns blank if you omitted the question.

STEP 2: Count the number of right answers.

Enter the total here: ________________

STEP 3: Count the number of wrong answers.

Enter the total here: ________________

STEP 4: Multiply the number of wrong answers by .250.

Enter the product here: ______________

STEP 5: Subtract the result obtained in Step 4 from the total you obtained in Step 2.

Enter the result here: ________________

STEP 6: Round the number obtained in Step 5 to the nearest whole number.

Enter the result here: ________________

The number you obtained in Step 6 is your raw score.

Table A

Answers to the Subject Test in Chemistry, Form 3YAC2, and Percentage of Students Answering Each Question Correctly

Question Number	Correct Answer	Right	Wrong	Percentage of Students Answering the Question Correctly*	Question Number	Correct Answer	Right	Wrong	Percentage of Students Answering the Question Correctly*
1	C			77	33	D			80
2	A			71	34	A			58
3	B			75	35	A			60
4	A			35	36	A			61
5	B			31	37	A			54
6	E			59	38	C			63
7	D			60	39	C			55
8	B			69	40	B			66
9	E			77	41	A			60
10	B			79	42	E			73
11	C			52	43	A			56
12	E			39	44	B			44
13	C			48	45	B			50
14	E			68	46	D			55
15	A			51	47	E			42
16	D			71	48	B			33
17	C			69	49	C			66
18	E			66	50	D			53
19	A			73	51	C			74
20	C			78	52	A			53
21	C			48	53	E			48
22	B			48	54	B			71
23	E			40	55	C			32
24	D			51	56	A			63
25	B			85	57	D			70
26	C			84	58	C			24
27	B			71	59	C			76
28	E			78	60	C			41
29	E			66	61	C			45
30	A			66	62	A			25
31	B			64	63	E			52
32	B			78	64	A			37

Table A continued on next page

Table A continued from previous page

Question Number	Correct Answer	Right	Wrong	Percentage of Students Answering the Question Correctly*	Question Number	Correct Answer	Right	Wrong	Percentage of Students Answering the Question Correctly*
65	C			23	106	F,F			22
66	B			54	107	T,T			51
67	C			51	108	F,F			38
68	E			70	109	F,F			37
69	A			37	110	T,F			81
70	C			67	111	T,T,CE			62
101	F,T			40	112	F,F			43
102	F,T			47	113	T,T,CE			45
103	F,F			68	114	T,T			26
104	T,T			58	115	F,T			36
105	T,T,CE			67					

* These percentages are based on an analysis of the answer sheets of a representative sample of 5,571 students who took the original form of this test in November 2002, and whose mean score was 593. They may be used as an indication of the relative difficulty of a particular question. Each percentage may also be used to predict the likelihood that a typical SAT Subject Test in Chemistry candidate will answer that question correctly on this edition of the test.

Finding Your Scaled Score

When you take SAT Subject Tests, the scores sent to the colleges you specify are reported on the College Board scale, which ranges from 200–800. You can convert your practice test score to a scaled score by using Table B. To find your scaled score, locate your raw score in the left-hand column of Table B; the corresponding score in the right-hand column is your scaled score. For example, a raw score of 39 on this particular edition of the Subject Test in Chemistry corresponds to a scaled score of 590.

Raw scores are converted to scaled scores to ensure that a score earned on any one edition of a particular Subject Test is comparable to the same scaled score earned on any other edition of the same Subject Test. Because some editions of the tests may be slightly easier or more difficult than others, College Board scaled scores are adjusted so that they indicate the same level of performance regardless of the edition of the test taken and the ability of the group that takes it. Thus, for example, a score of 400 on one edition of a test taken at a particular administration indicates the same level of achievement as a score of 400 on a different edition of the test taken at a different administration.

When you take the SAT Subject Tests during a national administration, your scores are likely to differ somewhat from the scores you obtain on the tests in this book. People perform at different levels at different times for reasons unrelated to the tests themselves. The precision of any test is also limited because it represents only a sample of all the possible questions that could be asked.

Table B

Scaled Score Conversion Table Subject Test in Chemistry (Form 3YAC2)					
Raw Score	Scaled Score	Raw Score	Scaled Score	Raw Score	Scaled Score
85	800	49	640	13	450
84	800	48	630	12	440
83	800	47	630	11	440
82	800	46	620	10	430
81	790	45	620	9	420
80	790	44	610	8	420
79	780	43	610	7	410
78	780	42	600	6	400
77	770	41	600	5	400
76	770	40	590	4	390
75	760	39	590	3	390
74	760	38	580	2	380
73	750	37	580	1	370
72	750	36	570	0	370
71	740	35	570	-1	360
70	740	34	560	-2	350
69	730	33	560	-3	350
68	730	32	550	-4	340
67	720	31	550	-5	340
66	720	30	540	-6	330
65	710	29	540	-7	320
64	710	28	530	-8	320
63	710	27	530	-9	310
62	700	26	520	-10	310
61	700	25	520	-11	300
60	690	24	510	-12	300
59	690	23	500	-13	300
58	680	22	500	-14	290
57	680	21	490	-15	290
56	670	20	490	-16	290
55	670	19	480	-17	280
54	660	18	480	-18	280
53	660	17	470	-19	280
52	650	16	470	-20	270
51	650	15	460	-21	270
50	640	14	450		

How Did You Do on the Subject Test in Chemistry?

After you score your test and analyze your performance, think about the following questions:

Did you run out of time before reaching the end of the test?

If so, you may need to pace yourself better. For example, maybe you spent too much time on one or two hard questions. A better approach might be to skip the ones you can't answer right away and try answering all the questions that remain on the test. Then if there's time, go back to the questions you skipped.

Did you take a long time reading the directions?

You will save time when you take the test by learning the directions to the Subject Test in Chemistry ahead of time. Each minute you spend reading directions during the test is a minute that you could use to answer questions.

How did you handle questions you were unsure of?

If you were able to eliminate one or more of the answer choices as wrong and guess from the remaining ones, your approach probably worked to your advantage. On the other hand, making haphazard guesses or omitting questions without trying to eliminate choices could cost you valuable points.

How difficult were the questions for you compared with other students who took the test?

Table A shows you how difficult the multiple-choice questions were for the group of students who took this test during its national administration. The right-hand column gives the percentage of students that answered each question correctly.

A question answered correctly by almost everyone in the group is obviously an easier question. For example, 79 percent of the students answered question 10 correctly. But only 40 percent answered question 23 correctly.

Keep in mind that these percentages are based on just one group of students. They would probably be different with another group of students taking the test.

If you missed several easier questions, go back and try to find out why: Did the questions cover material you haven't yet reviewed? Did you misunderstand the directions?

Chapter 7

Physics

Purpose

The Subject Test in Physics measures the knowledge you would be expected to have after successfully completing a college-preparatory course in high school. The test is not based on any one textbook or instructional approach, but concentrates on the common core of material found in most texts.

Format

This one-hour test consists of 75 multiple-choice questions. Topics that are covered in most high school courses are emphasized. Because high school courses differ, both in percentage of time devoted to each major topic and in the specific subtopics covered, most students will find that there are some questions on topics with which they are not familiar.

Content

This test covers topics listed in the chart on the next page.

Topics Covered	Approximate Percentage of Test
I. Mechanics	36–42
Kinematics, such as velocity, acceleration, motion in one dimension, motion of projectiles **Dynamics**, such as force, Newton's laws, statics **Energy and Momentum**, such as potential and kinetic energy, work, power, impulse, conservation laws **Circular Motion**, such as uniform circular motion and centripetal force **Simple Harmonic Motion**, such as mass on a spring, and the pendulum **Gravity**, such as the law of gravitation, orbits, Kepler's Laws	
II. Electricity and Magnetism	18–24
Electric Fields, Forces, and Potentials, such as Coulomb's law, induced charge, field and potential of groups of point charges, charged particles in electric fields **Capacitance**, such as parallel-plate capacitors and transients **Circuit Elements and DC Circuits**, such as resistors, lightbulbs, series and parallel networks, Ohm's law, Joule's law **Magnetism**, such as permanent magnets, fields caused by currents, particles in magnetic fields, Faraday's law, Lenz's law	
III. Waves and Optics	15–19
General Wave Properties, such as wave speed, frequency, wavelength, superposition, standing waves, Doppler effect **Reflection and Refraction**, such as Snell's law, changes in wavelength and speed **Ray Optics**, such as image formation using pinholes, mirrors, and lenses **Physical Optics**, such as single-slit diffraction, double-slit interference, polarization, color	
IV. Heat and Thermodynamics	6–11
Thermal Properties, such as temperature, heat transfer, specific and latent heats, thermal expansion **Laws of Thermodynamics**, such as first and second laws, internal energy, entropy, heat engine efficiency	
V. Modern Physics	6–11
Quantum Phenomena, such as photons, photoelectric effect **Atomic**, such as the Rutherford and Bohr models, atomic energy levels, atomic spectra **Nuclear and Particle Physics**, such as radioactivity, nuclear reactions, fundamental particles **Relativity**, such as time dilation, length contraction, mass-energy equivalence	
VI. Miscellaneous	4–9
General, such as history of physics and general questions that overlap several major topics **Analytical Skills**, such as graphical analysis, measurement, and math skills **Contemporary Physics**, such as astrophysics, superconductivity, and chaos theory	

How to Prepare

The test is intended for students who have completed a one-year introductory physics course at the college-preparatory level. You should be able to:

- recall and understand the major concepts of physics and to apply these physical principles you have learned to solve specific problems
- understand simple algebraic, trigonometric, and graphical relationships, and the concepts of ratio and proportion and apply these to physics problems

Laboratory experience is a significant factor in developing reasoning and problem-solving skills. This multiple-choice test can measure laboratory skills only in a limited way, such as data analysis. Familiarize yourself with directions in advance. The directions in this book are identical to those that appear on the test.

Skills Specification	Approximate Percentage of Test
Recall	20–33
Generally involves remembering and understanding concepts or information	
Single-Concept Problem	40–53
Recall and use of a single physical relationship	
Multiple-Concept Problem	20–33
Recall and integration of two or more physical relationships	
Laboratory Skills	
In each of the six major content topics, some questions may deal with laboratory skills in context	

Notes: (1) This test assumes that the direction of any current is the direction of flow of positive charge (conventional current).

(2) Calculator use is not allowed during the test.

(3) Numerical calculations are not emphasized and are limited to simple arithmetic.

(4) This test predominantly uses the metric system.

Score

The total score for each test is reported on the 200-to-800 scale.

Sample Questions

Two types of questions are used in the Subject Test in Physics and are shown in the following samples. All questions in the test are multiple-choice questions in which you must choose the BEST response from the five choices offered.

Classification Questions

Each set of classification questions includes five lettered choices that you will use to answer all of the questions in the set (see sample questions 1–4). These choices appear before the questions in the set. In addition, there may be descriptive material that is relevant in answering the questions in the set. The choices may take various forms, such as words, phrases, sentences, graphs, pictures, equations, or data. The numbered questions themselves may also take such forms, or they may be given in the question format directly. To answer each question, select the lettered choice that provides the most appropriate response. You should consider all of the lettered choices before answering a question. The directions for this type of question state specifically that a choice cannot be eliminated just because it is the correct answer to a previous question.

Because the same five choices are applicable to several questions, the classification questions usually require less reading than other types of multiple-choice questions. Therefore, classification questions provide a quick means, in terms of testing time, of determining how well you have mastered the topics represented. The set of questions may ask you to recall appropriate information, or the set may ask you to apply information to a specific situation or to translate information between different forms (descriptive, graphical, mathematical). Thus, different types of abilities can be tested by this type of question.

Directions: Each set of lettered choices below refers to the numbered questions immediately following it. Select the one lettered choice that best answers each question and then fill in the corresponding circle on the answer sheet. A choice may be used once, more than once, or not at all in each set.

Questions 1–2

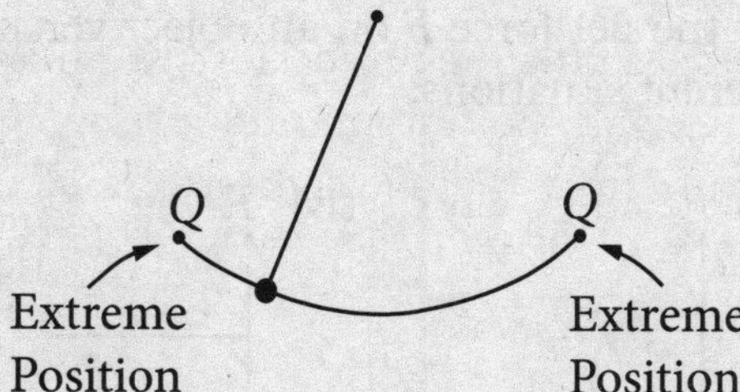

A small sphere attached to the end of a string swings as a simple pendulum. The sphere moves along the arc shown above. Consider the following properties of the sphere.

(A) Acceleration
(B) Kinetic energy
(C) Mass
(D) Potential energy
(E) Velocity

1. Which property remains constant throughout the motion of the sphere?

2. Which property goes to zero and changes direction at each extreme position Q?

Choice (C) is the correct answer to question 1. To answer this question, you may know that in classical mechanics mass is a fundamental property of an object that does not depend on the position or velocity of the object. Alternately, you may realize that, since a pendulum during its motion repeatedly speeds up, slows down, and changes direction, the sphere's velocity, kinetic energy, and acceleration must also change. Also, since the height of the sphere varies, so must its potential energy. Thus you can also obtain the answer by the process of elimination.

Choice (E) is the correct answer to question 2. To answer this question, you must know some specific details about the motion of the pendulum. At each extreme position Q, the velocity and the kinetic energy (which is proportional to the square of the speed) are both zero, but kinetic energy has magnitude only and thus no direction to change. Velocity does have direction, and in this case the velocity of the sphere is directed away from the center, or equilibrium position, just before the sphere reaches Q, but directed toward the center just after leaving Q. The velocity changes direction at each point Q. The only other choice that has direction is acceleration, but acceleration has its maximum magnitude at each point Q and is directed toward the center, both shortly before and shortly after the sphere is at Q.

Questions 3–4

The following graphs show the net force F on an object versus time t, for the object in straight-line motion in different situations.

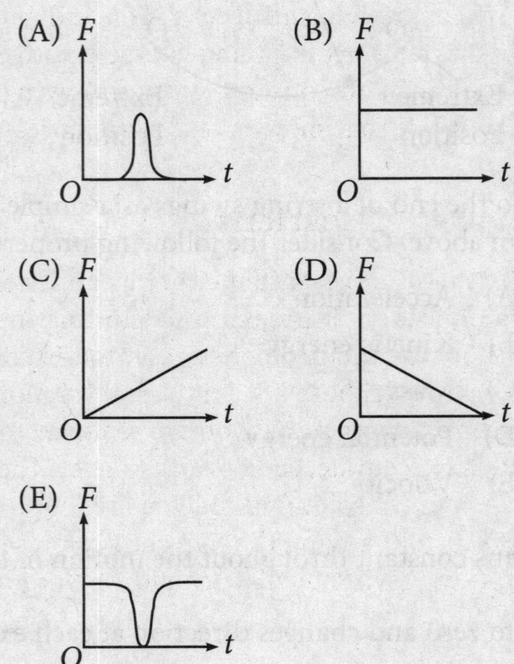

For each of the following speed v versus time t graphs for the object, choose the graph above with which it is consistent.

3. 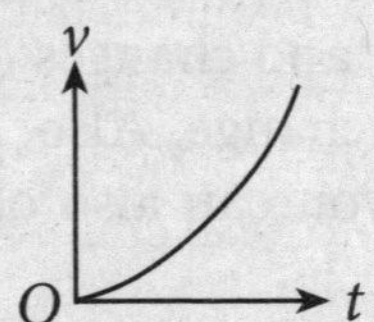

4. 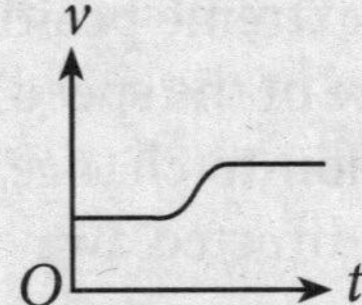

Questions 3 and 4 test the application of physical principles to information presented in graphical form. In each of these questions two concepts are involved. From Newton's second law we know that the net force on an object is equal to the object's acceleration multiplied by the object's mass, a constant. Thus graphs of acceleration versus time must have the same shape as the graphs of force versus time that are given in the options. We must also know that at a particular time the acceleration of an object in its direction of motion is equal to the rate of change of its speed, as determined by the slope of the speed v versus time t graph at that particular time.

Choice (C) is the answer to question 3. The slope of the graph continually increases with increasing *t*; therefore, the object's acceleration and consequently the net force on the object must also increase continually. The only graph that shows this relationship is graph (C). Choice (A) is the correct answer to question 4. In this question, the graph initially shows a constant speed, implying an acceleration and net force of zero. Then the curve sharply increases for a brief time, implying a large positive acceleration and large net force. Finally the curve returns to constant speed, implying a return to a zero net force. Graph (A) is the only choice that shows a force that varies in this manner.

Five-Choice Completion Questions

The five-choice completion question is written either as an incomplete statement or as a question. In its simplest application, it poses a problem that intrinsically has a unique solution. It is also used when: (1) the problem presented is clearly delineated by the wording of the question so that you choose not a universal solution but the best of the five offered solutions; (2) the problem is such that you are required to evaluate the relevance of five plausible, or scientifically accurate, choices and to select the one most pertinent; or (3) the problem has several pertinent solutions and you are required to select the one that is *inappropriate* or *not correct* from among the five choices presented. Questions of this latter type (see sample question 6) will normally contain a word in capital letters such as NOT, EXCEPT, or LEAST.

A special type of five-choice completion question is used in some tests to allow for the possibility of more than one correct answer. Unlike many quantitative problems that must by their nature have one unique solution, situations do arise in which there may be more than one correct answer. In such situations, you should evaluate each answer independently of the others in order to select the most appropriate combination (see sample question 7). In questions of this type, several (usually three) statements labeled by Roman numerals are given with the question. One or more of these statements may correctly answer the question. The statements are followed by five lettered choices, with each choice consisting of some combination of the Roman numerals that label the statements. You must select from among the five lettered choices the one that gives the combination of statements that best answers the question. In the test, questions of this type are intermixed among the more standard five-choice completion questions.

The five-choice completion question also tests problem-solving skills. With this type of question, you may be asked to convert the information given in a word problem into graphical forms or to select and apply the mathematical relationship necessary to solve the scientific problem. Alternatively, you may be asked to interpret experimental data, graphs, or mathematical expressions. Thus, the five-choice completion question can be adapted to test several kinds of abilities.

When the experimental data or other scientific problems to be analyzed are comparatively long, it is often convenient to organize several five-choice completion questions into sets, with each question in the set relating to the same common material that precedes the set (see sample questions 8–9). This practice allows you to answer several questions based on information that may otherwise take considerable testing time to read and comprehend. Such sets also test how thorough your understanding is of a particular situation. Although the questions in a set may be related, you do not have to know the answer to one question in a set to answer a subsequent question correctly. Each question in a set can be answered directly from the common material given for the entire set.

Directions: Each of the questions or incomplete statements below is followed by five suggested answers or completions. Select the one that is best in each case and then fill in the corresponding circle on the answer sheet.

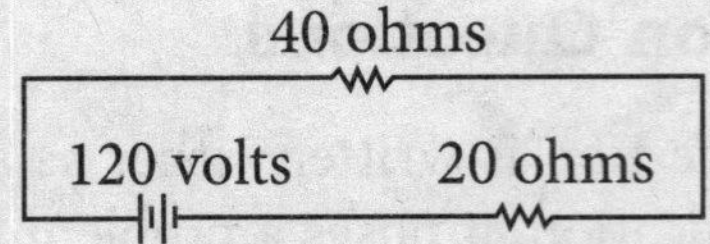

5. If the internal resistance of the 120-volt battery in the circuit shown above is negligible, the current in the wire is
   (A) 0 A
   (B) 2 A
   (C) 3 A
   (D) 6 A
   (E) 9 A

Choice (B) is the correct answer to question 5. In this question, you must apply two concepts to solve the problem. First, you must recognize that the two resistors are connected in series and thus are equivalent to a single resistor whose resistance is 60 ohms, the sum of the two component resistances. Next, applying Ohm's law, you will find that the current is given by the potential difference divided by this equivalent resistance. Thus, the answer is $\frac{120 \text{ volts}}{60 \text{ ohms}}$, which equals 2 amperes.

6. All of the following are vector quantities EXCEPT
   (A) force
   (B) velocity
   (C) acceleration
   (D) power
   (E) momentum

Choice (D) is the correct answer to question 6. This question is a straightforward question that tests your knowledge of vector and scalar quantities. A vector quantity is one that has both magnitude and direction. All five quantities have a magnitude associated with them, but only quantities (A), (B), (C), and (E) also have a direction. Power, a rate of change of energy, is not a vector quantity, so the correct answer is choice (D).

7. A ball is thrown upward. Air resistance is negligible. After leaving the hand, the acceleration of the ball is downward under which of the following conditions?

   I. On the way up
   II. On the way down
   III. At the top of its rise

   (A) I only
   (B) III only
   (C) I and II only
   (D) II and III only
   (E) I, II, and III

Choice (E) is the correct answer to question 7. In this question, one or several of the phrases represented by the Roman numerals may be correct answers to the question. One must evaluate each in turn. When the ball is on the way up, its speed is decreasing so the acceleration of the ball must be directed in the direction opposite to the ball's velocity. Since the velocity is upward, the acceleration must be downward, making I correct. When the ball is on the way down, its speed is increasing, so its acceleration must be directed in the same direction as its velocity, which is downward. So II is also correct. Finally, at the top of the rise, the ball has an instantaneous speed of zero, but its velocity is changing from upward to downward, implying a downward acceleration and making III correct also. A simpler analysis would be to realize that in all three cases, the ball is acted on by the downward force of gravity and no other forces. By Newton's second law, the acceleration must be in the direction of the net force, so it must be downward in all three cases. Since the phrases in I, II, and III are each correct answers to the question, the correct answer is choice (E).

Questions 8–9

In the following graph, the speed of a small object as it moves along a horizontal straight line is plotted against time.

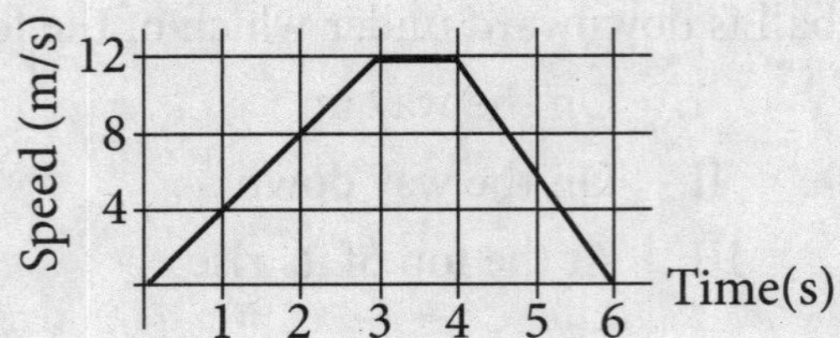

8. The magnitude of the acceleration of the object during the first 3 seconds is
   - (A) 3 m/s^2
   - (B) 4 m/s^2
   - (C) 6 m/s^2
   - (D) 12 m/s^2
   - (E) 36 m/s^2

9. The average speed of the object during the first 4 seconds is
   - (A) 1.9 m/s
   - (B) 3.0 m/s
   - (C) 4.0 m/s
   - (D) 6.0 m/s
   - (E) 7.5 m/s

Questions 8 and 9 are a set of questions, both based on the graph provided.

Choice (B) is the correct answer to question 8. To answer this question, you need to know that the magnitude of the acceleration is equal to the magnitude of the slope of a graph of speed versus time. In this situation, from time = 0 to time = 3 seconds, the graph has a constant slope of $\frac{12\text{ m/s}}{3\text{ s}} = 4\text{ m/s}^2$, which is the magnitude of the acceleration. So the correct answer is choice (B).

Choice (E) is the correct answer to question 9. The average speed of an object during a certain time is equal to the total distance traveled by the object during that time divided by the time. In question 9, the total distance traveled by the object during the first 4 seconds is equal to the area under the graph from time = 0 to time = 4 seconds. This area is $\frac{1}{2}(3\text{ s})(12\text{ m/s}) + (1\text{ s})(12\text{ m/s}) = 18\text{ m} + 12\text{ m} = 30\text{m}$. The average speed is therefore $\frac{30\text{ m}}{4\text{ s}} = 7.5\text{ m/s}$.

Physics Test

Practice Helps

The test that follows is an actual, recently administered SAT Subject Test in Physics. To get an idea of what it's like to take this test, practice under conditions that are much like those of an actual test administration.

- Set aside an hour when you can take the test uninterrupted. Make sure you complete the test in one sitting.
- Sit at a desk or table with no other books or papers. Dictionaries, other books, or notes are not allowed in the test room.
- Do not use a calculator. Calculators are not allowed for the Subject Test in Physics.
- Tear out an answer sheet from the back of this book and fill it in just as you would on the day of the test. One answer sheet can be used for up to three Subject Tests.
- Read the instructions that precede the practice test. During the actual administration, you will be asked to read them before answering test questions.
- Time yourself by placing a clock or kitchen timer in front of you.
- After you finish the practice test, read the sections "How to Score the SAT Subject Test in Physics" and "How Did You Do on the Subject Test in Physics?"
- The appearance of the answer sheet in this book may differ from the answer sheet you see on test day.

PHYSICS TEST

The top portion of the section of the answer sheet that you will use in taking the Physics Test must be filled in exactly as shown in the illustration below. Note carefully that you have to do all of the following on your answer sheet.

1. Print PHYSICS on the line under the words "Subject Test (print)."
2. In the shaded box labeled "Test Code" fill in four circles:

   —Fill in circle 2 in the row labeled V.

   —Fill in circle 3 in the row labeled W.

   —Fill in circle 3 in the row labeled X.

   —Fill in circle C in the row labeled Y.

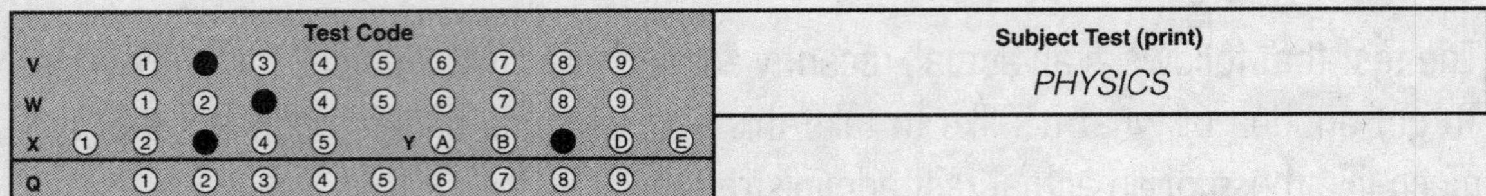

3. Please answer the three questions below by filling in the appropriate circles in the row labeled Q on the answer sheet. The information you provide is for statistical purposes only and will not affect your score on the test.

Question 1

How many semesters of physics have you taken in high school, including any semester in which you are currently enrolled? (Count as two semesters any case in which a full year's course is taught in a one-semester [half-year] compressed schedule.) Fill in only one circle of circles 1-3.

- One semester or less —Fill in circle 1.
- Two semesters —Fill in circle 2.
- Three semesters or more —Fill in circle 3.

Question 2

About how often did you do lab work in your first physics course? (Include any times when you may have watched a film or a demonstration by your teacher and then discussed or analyzed data.) Fill in only one circle of circles 4-7.

- Less than once a week —Fill in circle 4.
- About once a week —Fill in circle 5.
- A few times a week —Fill in circle 6.
- Almost every day —Fill in circle 7.

Question 3

If you have taken or are currently taking an Advanced Placement (AP) Physics course, which of the following describes the course? Fill in both circles if applicable. (If you have never had AP Physics, leave circles 8 and 9 blank.)

- A course that uses algebra and trigonometry but NOT calculus (Physics B) —Fill in circle 8.
- A course that uses calculus (Physics C) —Fill in circle 9.

When the supervisor gives the signal, turn the page and begin the Physics Test. There are 100 numbered circles on the answer sheet and 75 questions in the Physics Test. Therefore, use only circles 1 to 75 for recording your answers.

PHYSICS TEST

Note: To simplify calculations, you may use $g = 10\ m/s^2$ in all problems.

Part A

Directions: Each set of lettered choices below refers to the numbered questions immediately following it. Select the one lettered choice that best answers each question, and then fill in the corresponding circle on the answer sheet. A choice may be used once, more than once, or not at all in each set.

Questions 1-3

(A) Coefficient of linear expansion
(B) Latent heat of fusion
(C) Latent heat of vaporization
(D) Specific heat
(E) Coefficient of thermal conductivity

Select the quantity above that should be used in the calculation of each of the following.

1. The amount of heat required to change 100 grams of ice at 0° C into water at 0° C

2. The temperature at which a 0.5-centimeter gap between 1.0-meter concrete slabs in a sidewalk will close up completely

3. The time required for 100 joules of heat to pass through a copper rod of length 2 meters and cross-sectional area 0.5 square meter that connects two objects at different temperatures

Questions 4-5 relate to the following particles.

(A) Electron
(B) Neutron
(C) Proton
(D) Neutrino
(E) Photon

4. Which particle constitutes the nucleus of an ordinary hydrogen atom?

5. Which charged particle in the list is the least massive?

Questions 6-7

An automobile starts from rest and moves along a straight road. In the graph below, the distance x of the automobile from its starting point is given as a function of time t.

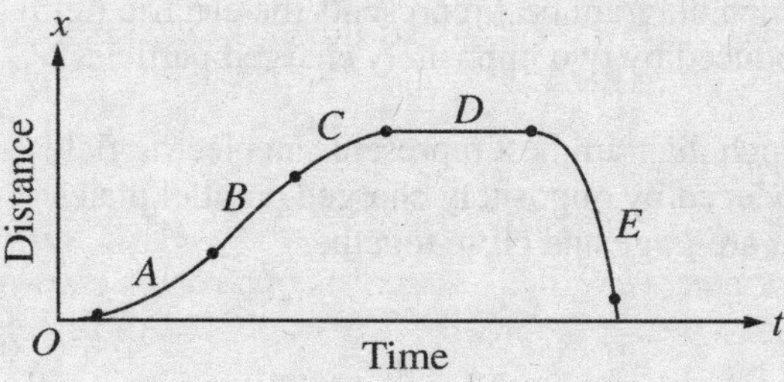

(A) Interval A
(B) Interval B
(C) Interval C
(D) Interval D
(E) Interval E

6. During which interval is the automobile stationary and farthest from its starting position?

7. During which interval does the speed of the automobile have its maximum value?

K-3XAC

GO ON TO THE NEXT PAGE

Questions 8-9 relate to the field lines that are shown in the following diagrams.

(A) 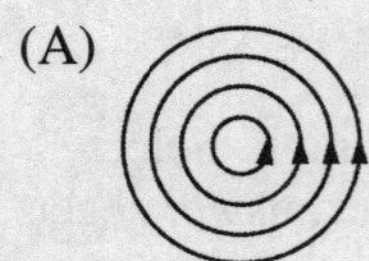
(B) 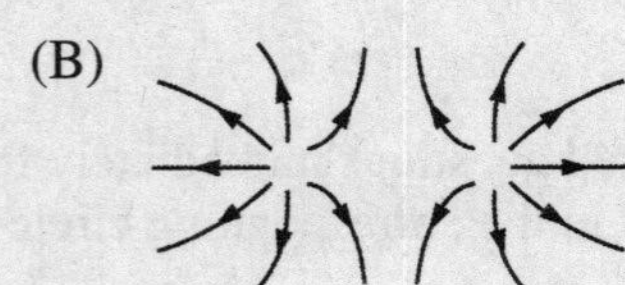

(C) 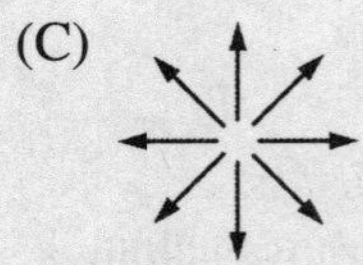
(D) 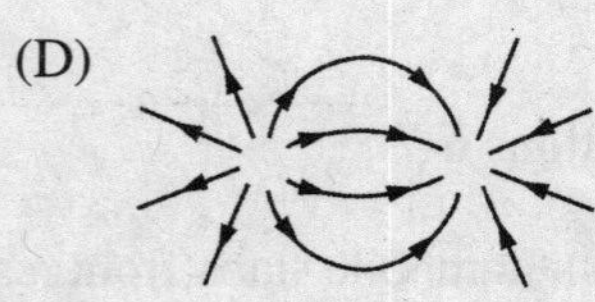

(E) 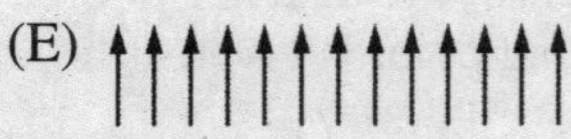

8. Which diagram best represents the electric field produced by two oppositely charged particles?

9. Which diagram best represents an electric field produced by oppositely charged parallel plates that are large and close together?

Questions 10-12 relate to calculations or explanations based on the following principles.

(A) Conservation of energy alone
(B) Conservation of momentum alone
(C) Conservation of both energy and momentum
(D) Conservation of charge
(E) Mechanical equivalence of heat

10. Used to calculate the velocity of two moving freight cars, after they couple and move together, given the initial masses and velocities of the freight cars

11. Used to calculate the speed of a lump of clay that hits and sticks to a block of wood suspended as a pendulum, given the height to which the block swings and the masses of the block and the clay

12. Used to calculate the speed of a pendulum bob at the bottom of its swing given the height from which the bob is released from rest

GO ON TO THE NEXT PAGE

Part B

Directions: Each of the questions or incomplete statements below is followed by five suggested answers or completions. Select the one that is best in each case and then fill in the corresponding circle on the answer sheet.

13. A skydiver has been in the air long enough to be falling at a constant terminal speed of 50 meters per second. How much farther will the skydiver fall in the next 2.00 seconds?

(A) 19.6 m
(B) 50 m
(C) 98 m
(D) 100 m
(E) 120 m

14. It takes about 1.0 second for an object to fall 5 meters vertically. If this same object is thrown horizontally with a speed of 30 meters per second from a roof-top 5 meters above ground, about how many meters from the base of the building will the object land?

(A) 30 m
(B) $30\sqrt{2}$ m
(C) $30\sqrt{3}$ m
(D) 60 m
(E) 90 m

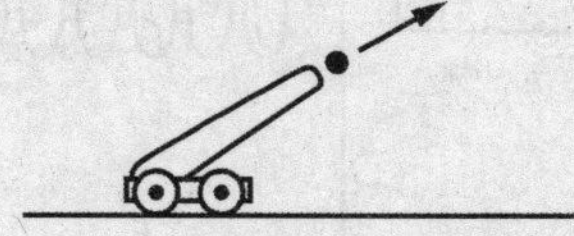

15. Assume that every projectile fired by the toy cannon shown above experiences a constant net force F along the entire length of the barrel. If a projectile of mass m leaves the barrel of the cannon with a speed v, at what speed will a projectile of mass $2m$ leave the barrel?

(A) $\dfrac{v}{2}$

(B) $\dfrac{v}{\sqrt{2}}$

(C) v

(D) $2v$

(E) $4v$

GO ON TO THE NEXT PAGE

Questions 16-17

The following diagram shows a permanent magnet and a coil of copper wire that is part of a closed circuit.

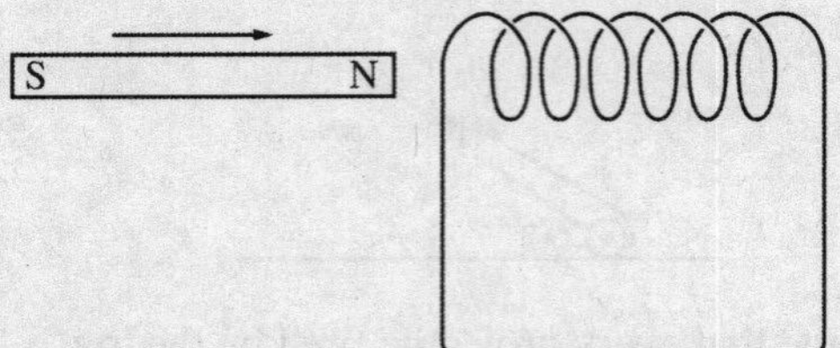

16. What happens as the north pole of the magnet is moved at constant speed into the coil?

    (A) The magnet gains potential energy.
    (B) The magnet attracts the coil.
    (C) The coil attracts the magnet.
    (D) A current flows in the coil, producing a magnetic field.
    (E) The magnet loses kinetic energy.

17. Which of the following would be different if the magnet were turned around so the south pole moved into the coil at the same speed as before?

    (A) The direction of the forces on the magnet
    (B) The direction of the energy transfer
    (C) The direction of the current in the coil
    (D) The magnitude of the current in the coil
    (E) The sign of the charges moving in the coil

18. An electric current in a copper wire is the result of the motion of which of the following?

    (A) Copper atoms
    (B) Copper oxide molecules
    (C) Protons
    (D) Electrons
    (E) Neutrons

19. Eyeglasses, magnifying glasses, and optical microscopes depend for their operation primarily on the phenomenon of

    (A) reflection
    (B) refraction
    (C) interference
    (D) dispersion
    (E) diffraction

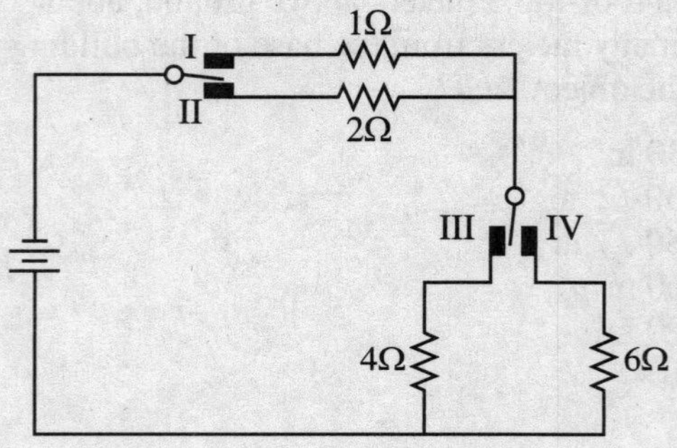

20. In the circuit shown above, the current through the battery will be greatest when the switches are in which of the following positions?

    (A) I and III
    (B) I and IV
    (C) II and III
    (D) II and IV
    (E) The current will be the same regardless of how the switches are positioned.

GO ON TO THE NEXT PAGE

Questions 21-23

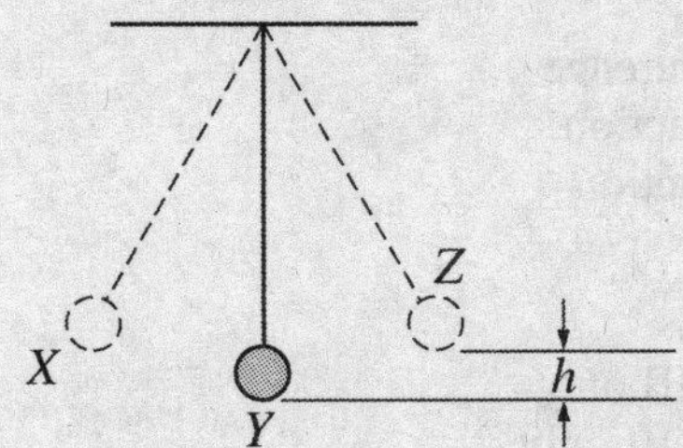

The diagram above shows a pendulum that swings to a maximum height h above its lowest point Y. The mass of the pendulum bob is 0.05 kilogram. At point Y, the bob has a speed of 3.0 meters per second.

21. The momentum of the pendulum bob as it passes through point Y is most nearly

    (A) 0.05 kg·m/s
    (B) 0.15 kg·m/s
    (C) 0.23 kg·m/s
    (D) 0.45 kg·m/s
    (E) 0.50 kg·m/s

22. The height h is most nearly

    (A) 0.15 m
    (B) 0.30 m
    (C) 0.45 m
    (D) 0.60 m
    (E) 0.90 m

23. If the potential energy of the pendulum bob is zero at point Y, the total energy (kinetic plus potential) of the pendulum bob is most nearly

    (A) 0.05 J
    (B) 0.15 J
    (C) 0.23 J
    (D) 0.45 J
    (E) 0.50 J

Questions 24-25

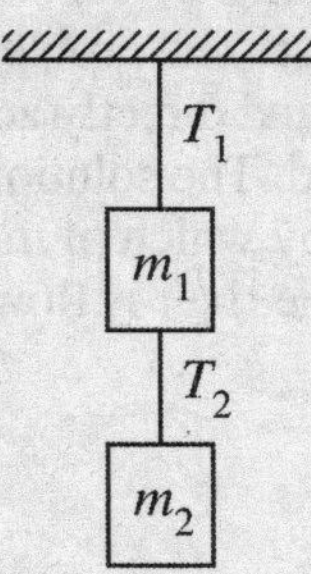

Two masses m_1 and m_2 are hung from the ceiling by two ropes as shown above. The tension in the upper rope is T_1 and the tension in the lower rope is T_2.

24. Which of the following is correct?

    (A) T_1 is always greater than T_2.
    (B) T_1 is always less than T_2.
    (C) T_1 is always equal to T_2.
    (D) T_1 is greater than T_2 only if m_1 is greater than m_2.
    (E) T_1 is greater than T_2 only if m_2 is greater than m_1.

25. Which of the following best represents the forces acting on m_2 ?

    (A)

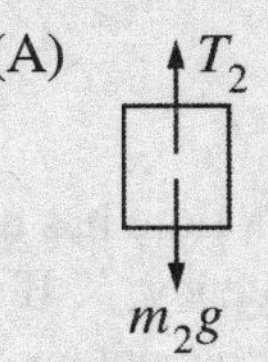

(B)

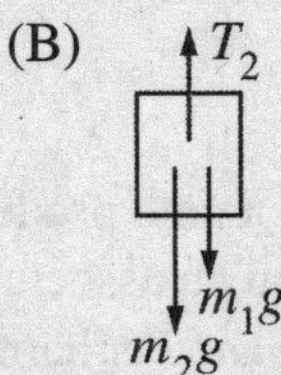

(C)

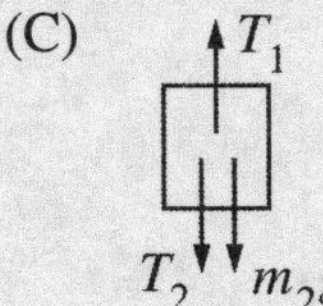

(D)

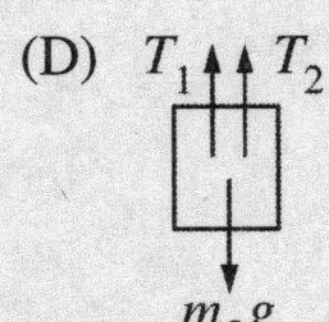

(E)

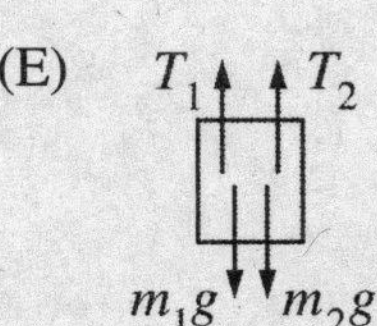

GO ON TO THE NEXT PAGE

26. A boat that can move at 5 kilometers per hour in still water is crossing a river whose current is 2 kilometers per hour. The problem is to steer the boat so that it will land directly across the river from where it started. The solution to the problem is best represented by which of the following sketches in which the river is flowing to the right?

(A) 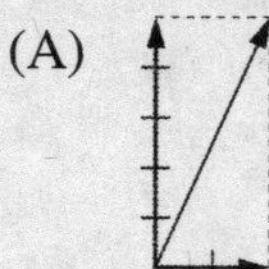

(B) 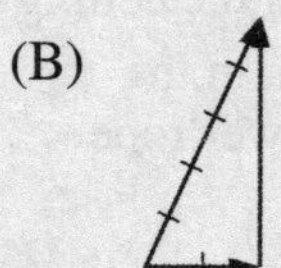

(C) 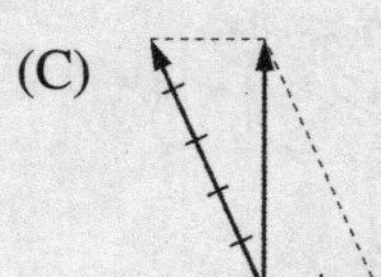

(D) 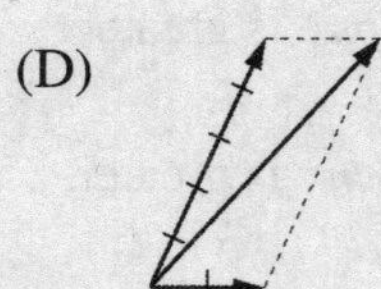

(E) 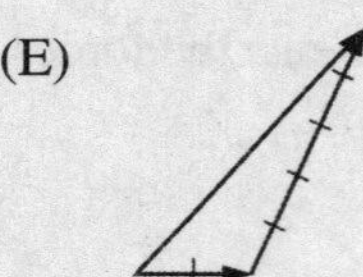

27. One harmonic of a note produced by a flute has a wavelength λ and an associated frequency f. If the wavelength of another harmonic of this note is 2λ, what is its associated frequency?

(A) $\frac{1}{4}f$

(B) $\frac{1}{2}f$

(C) f

(D) $2f$

(E) $4f$

28. Sound waves can exhibit which of the following wave properties?

I. Interference
II. Diffraction
III. Refraction

(A) I only
(B) II only
(C) I and III only
(D) II and III only
(E) I, II, and III

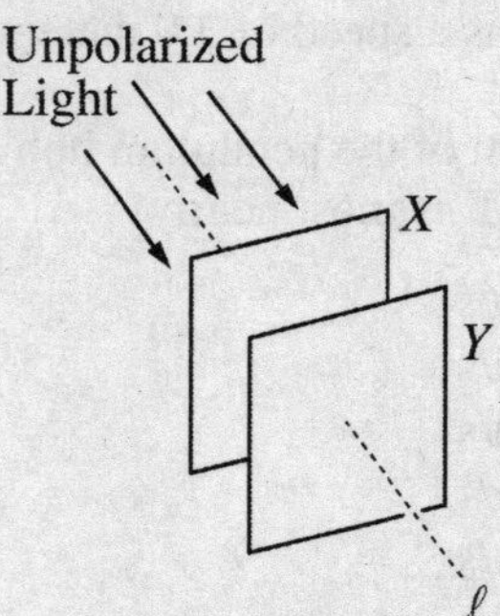

29. Polarizing sheets X and Y shown above are oriented so that none of the unpolarized light shining on X is transmitted through Y. Axis ℓ is perpendicular to both sheets. Which of the following will result in the transmission of light through Y?

(A) Rotation of Y by 90° about axis ℓ
(B) Rotation of Y by 180° about axis ℓ
(C) Rotation of Y by 360° about axis ℓ
(D) Placement of a third polarizer between X and Y, with its polarizing axis oriented the same way as X
(E) Placement of a third polarizer between X and Y, with its polarizing axis oriented the same way as Y

GO ON TO THE NEXT PAGE

Questions 30-32

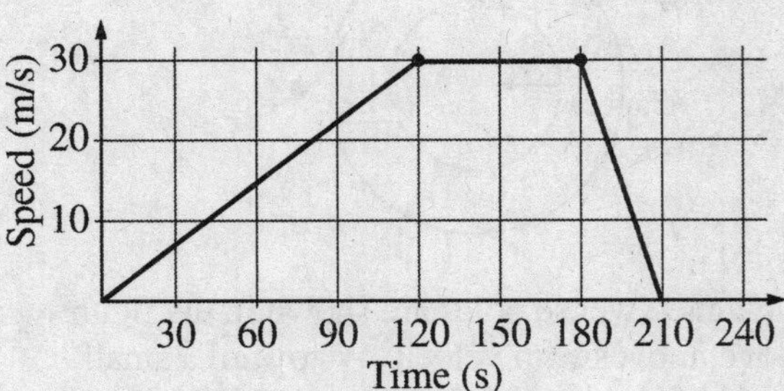

An automobile with a mass of 1.5×10^3 kilograms is traveling on a flat, level road. The above graph shows the automobile's speed as a function of time.

30. The automobile's acceleration at the end of 60 seconds is

(A) $0.25\ m/s^2$
(B) $2.5\ m/s^2$
(C) $4\ m/s^2$
(D) $15\ m/s^2$
(E) $60\ m/s^2$

31. The constant braking force applied to stop the car is

(A) 1.7 N
(B) 50 N
(C) 1.5×10^3 N
(D) 4.5×10^4 N
(E) 1.4×10^5 N

32. The speed of the automobile 10 seconds after the brakes are applied is

(A) 1 m/s
(B) 10 m/s
(C) 15 m/s
(D) 20 m/s
(E) 30 m/s

33. An object of mass m is attached to a vertically mounted spring that has spring constant k. The object is displaced from its equilibrium position and allowed to oscillate. Assume that air resistance and friction are negligible. To increase the frequency of the motion, one could

(A) increase the amplitude of the motion
(B) change to a spring with a greater spring constant
(C) mount the spring horizontally
(D) attach an object of greater mass
(E) attach an object of the same mass but greater density

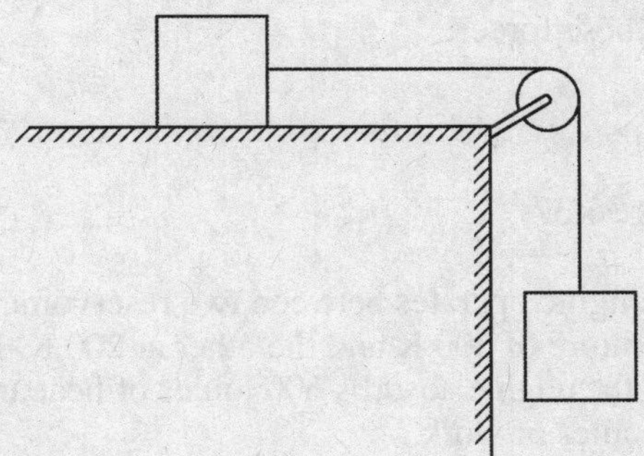

34. Two blocks of identical mass are connected by a light string as shown above. The surface is frictionless and the pulley is massless and frictionless. The acceleration of the two-block system is most nearly

(A) $20\ m/s^2$
(B) $15\ m/s^2$
(C) $10\ m/s^2$
(D) $5\ m/s^2$
(E) $2.5\ m/s^2$

GO ON TO THE NEXT PAGE

35. Consider the following four forces involving an object at rest on a tabletop.

    I. The gravitational force on the object due to the Earth
    II. The gravitational force on the Earth due to the object
    III. The force on the tabletop due to the object
    IV. The force on the object due to the tabletop

    Which, if any, of these forces are action-reaction pairs in accordance with Newton's third law?

    (A) Pair I and II only
    (B) Pair I and IV only
    (C) Pair I and II, and pair III and IV
    (D) Pair I and IV, and pair II and III
    (E) There are no action-reaction pairs among these forces.

Questions 36-37

A heat engine operates between two reservoirs, one at a temperature of 300 K and the other at 200 K. In one cycle, the engine absorbs 600 joules of heat and does 150 joules of work.

36. How much heat is exhausted by the engine in one cycle?

    (A) 150 J
    (B) 450 J
    (C) 550 J
    (D) 600 J
    (E) 750 J

37. The actual efficiency of the engine is most nearly

    (A) 75%
    (B) 67%
    (C) 50%
    (D) 33%
    (E) 25%

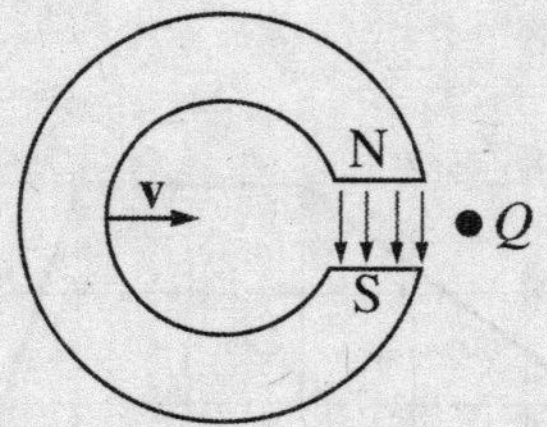

38. A magnet, whose poles are shown in the figure above, moves with velocity **v** toward a small object of charge Q initially at rest. Which of the following is a correct statement about the force on the object due to the magnet as the object initially encounters the field?

    (A) It is zero.
    (B) It is perpendicular to the page.
    (C) It is directed parallel to the magnetic field.
    (D) It is in the same direction as **v**.
    (E) It is in the direction opposite to **v**.

GO ON TO THE NEXT PAGE

5 m

3 m

4 m

$B = 6$ teslas

39. A loop of wire shaped into a triangle, shown above, carries a current of 2 amperes in a clockwise direction. A magnetic field of 6 teslas is directed into the paper. What are the magnitude and direction of the force applied by the magnetic field to the 5-meter edge of the triangle?

	Magnitude	Direction
(A)	60 N	↖
(B)	60 N	↑
(C)	48 N	↖
(D)	48 N	↘
(E)	36 N	↘

40. If two electrically charged particles repel each other with forces of equal magnitude, then the charges must

(A) have different magnitudes
(B) have the same magnitude
(C) have different signs
(D) have the same sign
(E) be separated by unit distance

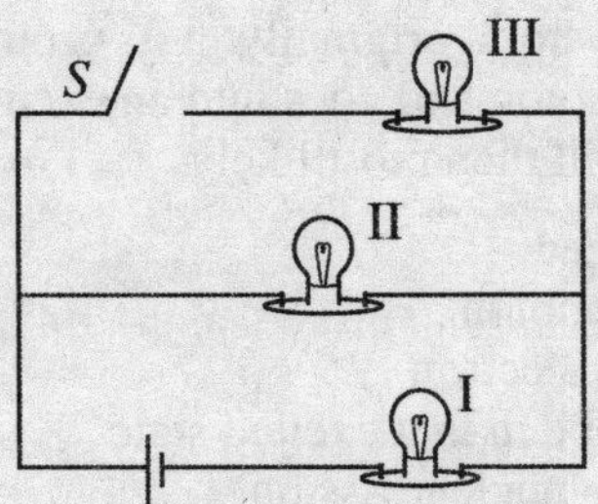

41. A battery and three identical lightbulbs are connected as shown in the figure above. With the switch S closed, the brightness of each lightbulb is noted. When switch S is opened, the brightness of which of the lightbulbs will change?

(A) I only
(B) III only
(C) I and II only
(D) II and III only
(E) I, II, and III

42. All of the following scientists made significant contributions to the field of nuclear physics EXCEPT

(A) Galileo
(B) Rutherford
(C) Becquerel
(D) Curie
(E) Fermi

43. Which of the following distinguishes an atom of one isotope of an element from an atom of a different isotope of the same element?

(A) The addition or loss of a beta particle
(B) The addition or loss of an alpha particle
(C) The amount of nuclear charge
(D) The number of orbital electrons
(E) The amount of nuclear mass

GO ON TO THE NEXT PAGE

44. A hydrogen atom, originally in its ground state, absorbs a photon and goes into an excited state. The atom will then most likely

(A) be ionized
(B) emit a photon
(C) emit an electron
(D) always be in that excited state
(E) undergo nuclear fission

45. A worker hits a metal pipe with a hammer. The ratio of the intensity of loudness as heard by people standing 100 meters away from the worker to the intensity as heard by people standing 200 meters away from the worker is

(A) 4:1
(B) 2:1
(C) 1:1
(D) 1:2
(E) 1:4

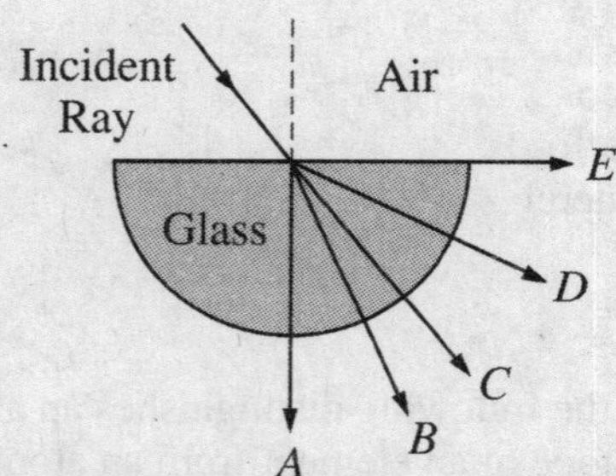

46. A light ray is incident from air upon a semicircular piece of glass as shown above. Which of the labeled rays best represents the subsequent path of the light?

(A) *A*
(B) *B*
(C) *C*
(D) *D*
(E) *E*

47. Huygens' principle states that every point on a wave front is the source of a new wave front. To which of the following types of waves does Huygens' principle apply?

I. Water waves
II. Sound waves
III. Electromagnetic waves

(A) I only
(B) II only
(C) III only
(D) II and III only
(E) I, II, and III

48. When coal burns, it produces heat in the amount of 2.5×10^4 joules per gram. About 4,000 joules of heat is required to raise the temperature of one kilogram of water by one degree. The amount of coal required to heat 5 kilograms of water from 10°C to 60°C is most nearly

(A) 10 grams
(B) 40 grams
(C) 100 grams
(D) 400 grams
(E) 1,600 grams

49. When a person touches the metal part of a bicycle handlebar on a cold day, the metal seems much colder than the plastic handgrip, even though both are at the same temperature. This phenomenon is due primarily to which of the following?

(A) The thermal conductivity of the metal is greater than that of the plastic.
(B) The thermal conductivity of the metal is less than that of the plastic.
(C) The density of the metal is greater than that of the plastic.
(D) The density of the metal is less than that of the plastic.
(E) The latent heat of fusion of the metal is greater than that of the plastic.

GO ON TO THE NEXT PAGE

50. An object of mass m rests on a horizontal frictionless surface. A force F making an angle θ with the horizontal is then applied to the object to move it along the surface. The acceleration of the object is

(A) $\frac{F}{m}$

(B) $\frac{F}{2m}$

(C) $\frac{F\cos\theta}{m}$

(D) $\frac{F\sin\theta}{m}$

(E) $\frac{F\tan\theta}{m}$

Questions 51-52

A person is standing on a scale that is located on a platform at the surface of Earth. The platform is supported by a machine that can move the platform up and down at various accelerations while keeping it level.

51. At what acceleration of the platform does the machine have to exert the LEAST force on the platform?

(A) Zero
(B) $4.9\ m/s^2$ down
(C) $9.8\ m/s^2$ up
(D) $9.8\ m/s^2$ down
(E) $19.6\ m/s^2$ up

52. If the person's weight has apparently doubled according to the reading on the scale, what is the acceleration of the platform?

(A) About $9.8\ m/s^2$ up
(B) About $9.8\ m/s^2$ down
(C) About $19.6\ m/s^2$ up
(D) About $19.6\ m/s^2$ down
(E) It cannot be determined without knowing the mass of the person.

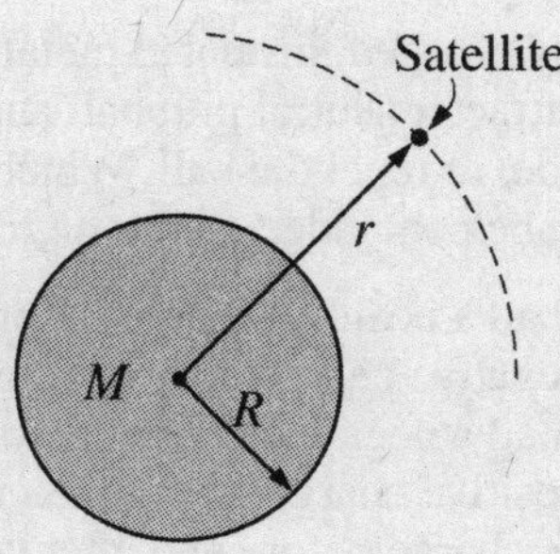

53. A satellite moves in a circular orbit of radius r around a planet of mass M and radius R, as shown above. The speed of the satellite would be greater if M and r were changed in which of the following ways?

	$\underline{M}$	$\underline{r}$
(A)	Decreased	No change
(B)	Decreased	Increased
(C)	No change	No change
(D)	No change	Increased
(E)	Increased	No change

54. A circuit consists of a battery of voltage V and a resistor of resistance R. The current through the circuit is I. If the battery is changed to one of voltage $2V$ and the resistor to one with resistance $4R$, the current through the circuit is

(A) $4I$

(B) $2I$

(C) I

(D) $\frac{I}{2}$

(E) $\frac{I}{4}$

GO ON TO THE NEXT PAGE

55. An electrically charged, insulated metal rod is observed to attract a neutral pith ball and, after contact is made, to repel the ball. Which of the following can be concluded about the rod?

(A) The rod had a positive charge before contact and a negative charge after contact.
(B) The rod had a negative charge before contact and a positive charge after contact.
(C) The rod's charge before and after contact had the same sign.
(D) The rod had a charge before contact, but no charge after contact.
(E) The rod had less charge before contact than after contact.

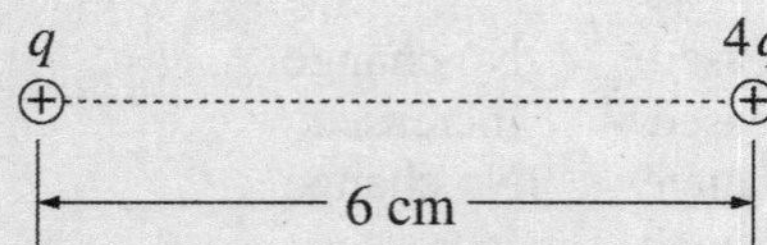

56. Two positive charges of magnitudes q and $4q$ are 6 centimeters apart, as shown above. If the electric field is zero at a point P (not shown) located on the line segment joining the charges, what is the distance of point P from the charge of magnitude q?

(A) 1 cm
(B) 2 cm
(C) 3 cm
(D) 4 cm
(E) 5 cm

57. A beam of light traveling through the air strikes the surface of a material in which the speed of light is different from what it is in the air. Which of the following is true of the light as it passes into the new medium?

(A) The frequency changes but the wavelength stays the same.
(B) The wavelength changes but the frequency stays the same.
(C) Neither the frequency nor the wavelength change.
(D) Both the frequency and the wavelength change.
(E) Since the speed of light is a universal constant, the speed in the new material is the same as it was in air.

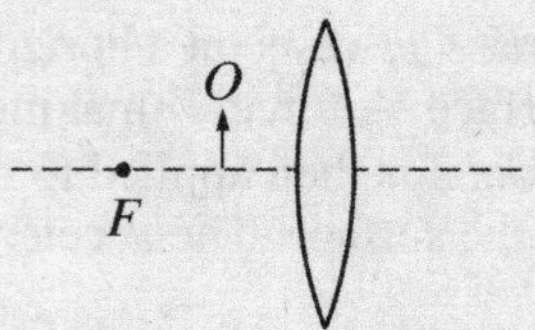

58. A convex lens is used as a magnifier when a real object O is placed inside the focus F, as shown above. The image produced is

(A) real and inverted
(B) real and upright
(C) virtual and inverted
(D) virtual and upright
(E) none of the above

59. The separation of white light into colors by a glass prism is a result of

(A) interference
(B) diffraction
(C) total internal reflection
(D) variation of absorption with wavelength
(E) variation of index of refraction with frequency

60. An object with a mass of 5 kilograms is placed at rest on an imaginary planet where the gravitational field is 4 newtons per kilogram. One can be certain that the object on this planet, as compared to the object when it is on Earth, will

(A) require a greater force to accelerate it on a horizontal surface at $1\ \text{m/s}^2$
(B) have less weight
(C) have less mass
(D) have greater mass
(E) have greater acceleration during free fall

GO ON TO THE NEXT PAGE

61. A car travels around a circular track that has a radius of 1 kilometer. If the car completes 3 trips around the track in 5 minutes, which of the following expressions gives the average speed of the car in kilometers per hour?

(A) $\frac{(3)(2\pi)(1)}{5(1/60)}$

(B) $\frac{(5)(60)(2\pi)(1)}{3}$

(C) $\frac{(3)(2\pi)(1)}{5(60)}$

(D) $\frac{(5)(2\pi)(1)}{(3)(60)}$

(E) $\frac{(3\pi)(1)}{5(1/60)}$

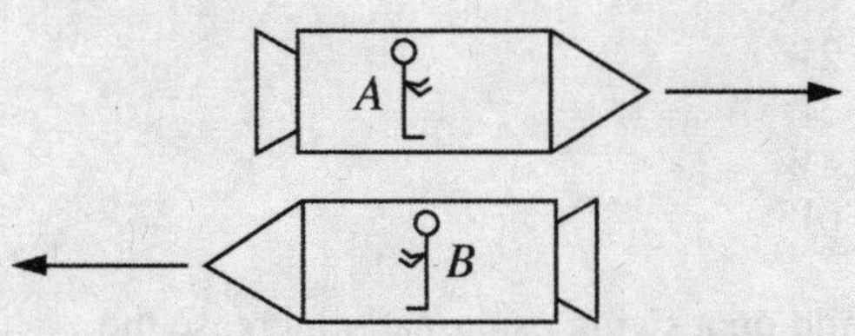

62. Two identical, human-looking robots are standing and facing forward in separate spaceships. Both ships are moving at $0.8c$ but are traveling in opposite directions, as shown above. If a person on the spaceship with robot *A* could make measurements on both robots, which of the following would the person observe to be different?

(A) The robots' heights
(B) The length of the robots' feet from toe to heel
(C) The width of the robots' faces
(D) The length of the robots' legs
(E) The width of the robots' shoulders

63. The experimental study of the photoelectric effect and its analysis by Einstein confirmed the assumption of the

(A) photon aspect of light
(B) crystal structure of materials
(C) discrete charge on the electron
(D) energy-mass relationship of special relativity
(E) uncertainty principle of position and momentum

64. The radius of the first Bohr orbit of an electron in a hydrogen atom is about 10^{-11} meter. The radius of the nucleus is about 10^{-15} meter. If a model of the hydrogen atom were built with the diameter of the electron orbit equal to the width of a classroom (about 10 meters), which of the following would most closely represent the size of the nucleus?

(A) The chair you are sitting in
(B) Your head
(C) The eraser on the end of a new pencil
(D) The point of a ball point pen
(E) A red blood cell

65. Which of the following is true of any material in a superconducting state that carries a current?

(A) It has a large internal magnetic field.
(B) It has no external magnetic field.
(C) It has no resistance.
(D) It has a temperature of absolute zero.
(E) It has a very high temperature.

GO ON TO THE NEXT PAGE

66. The graphs below represent velocity as a function of time t for five different particles, each moving along a straight line. Which particle experiences the greatest displacement between $t = 0$ and $t = 1$ second?

(A) Velocity (m/s)

1, O, -1, t(s), 1

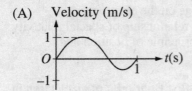

(B) Velocity (m/s)

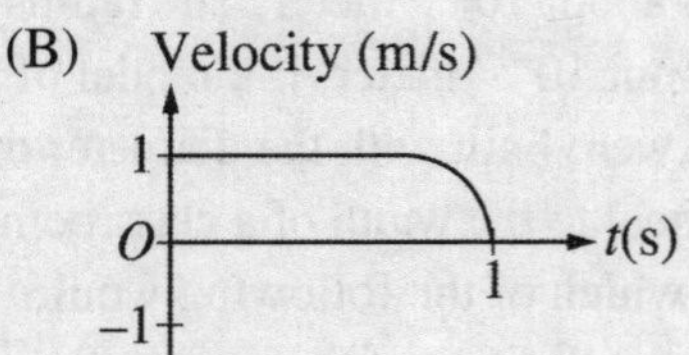

(C) Velocity (m/s)

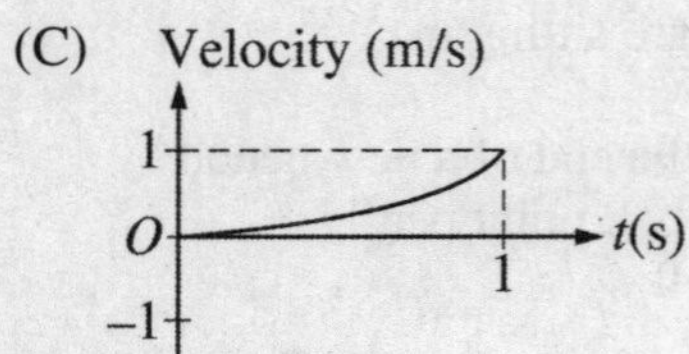

(D) Velocity (m/s)

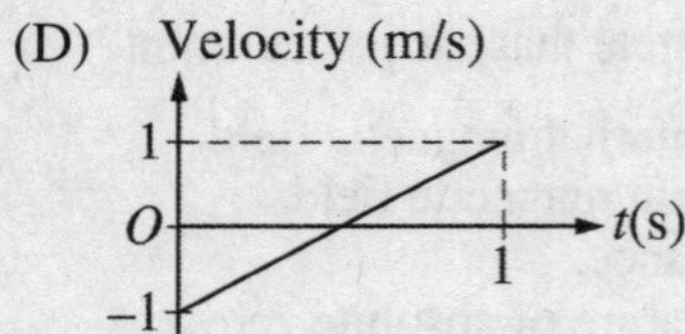

(E) Velocity (m/s)

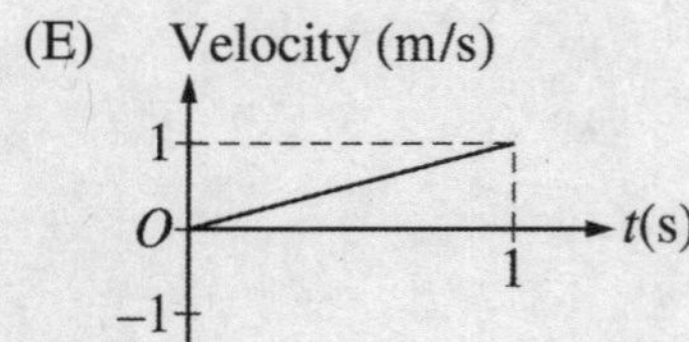

67. The density of a certain material is 3 grams per cubic centimeter. What is the density of the material expressed in kilograms per cubic meter?

(A) 0.3 kg/m^3
(B) 3 kg/m^3
(C) 30 kg/m^3
(D) 300 kg/m^3
(E) 3,000 kg/m^3

68. A system consists of two pucks moving without friction on a horizontal surface. If the pucks collide elastically, properties of the system that are the same before and after the collision include which of the following?

I. Momentum
II. Kinetic energy
III. Total energy

(A) I only
(B) III only
(C) I and II only
(D) II and III only
(E) I, II, and III

69. It takes an amount of work W to stretch a spring a distance x beyond its natural length. If the spring obeys Hooke's law, how much work is required to stretch the spring a distance $2x$ beyond its natural length?

(A) W
(B) $2W$
(C) $3W$
(D) $4W$
(E) $6W$

70. A child on a swing can greatly increase the amplitude of the swing's motion by "pumping" at the natural frequency of the swing. This is an example of which of the following?

(A) Conservation of momentum
(B) Newton's first law of motion
(C) Newton's third law of motion
(D) Resonance
(E) Interference

GO ON TO THE NEXT PAGE

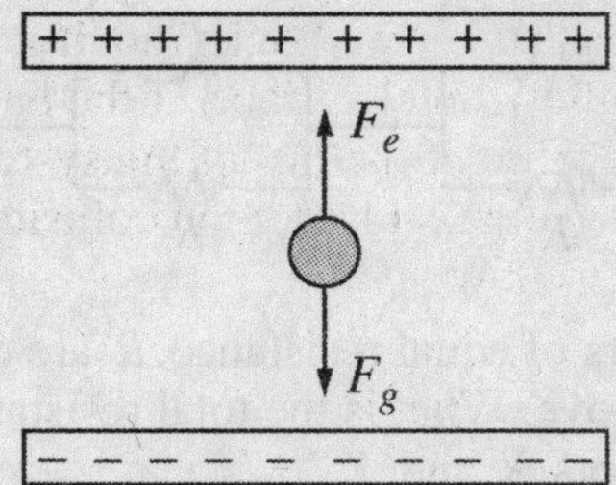

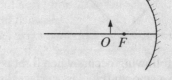

71. A negatively charged oil drop is maintained at rest between charged parallel plates, as shown above, by balancing the downward gravitational force F_g on the drop with an upward electric force F_e. If the mass of the oil drop is 1×10^{-6} kilogram and the electric field strength between the plates is 10 newtons per coulomb, then the charge on the oil drop is most nearly

(A) 1×10^{-3} C
(B) 1×10^{-4} C
(C) 1×10^{-5} C
(D) 1×10^{-6} C
(E) 1×10^{-19} C

72. An object O is just outside the focal point F of a concave mirror, as shown in the diagram above. As the object is moved away from the mirror, the image will do which of the following?

(A) Decrease in size and move closer to the mirror.
(B) Decrease in size and move farther from the mirror.
(C) Increase in size and move closer to the mirror.
(D) Increase in size and move farther from the mirror.
(E) It cannot be determined without knowing the exact focal length.

GO ON TO THE NEXT PAGE

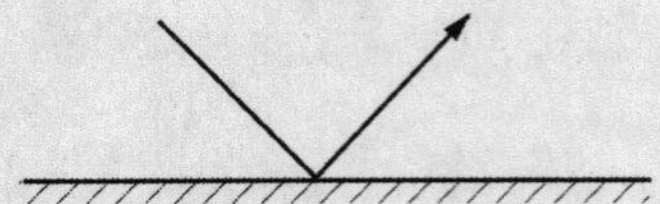

73. Which of the following occurs when light is reflected from a smooth flat glass surface, as shown above?

    (A) The light is somewhat intensified.
    (B) The light is somewhat polarized.
    (C) The light is focused.
    (D) The velocity of the light is reduced.
    (E) The color of the light is shifted toward the blue end of the spectrum.

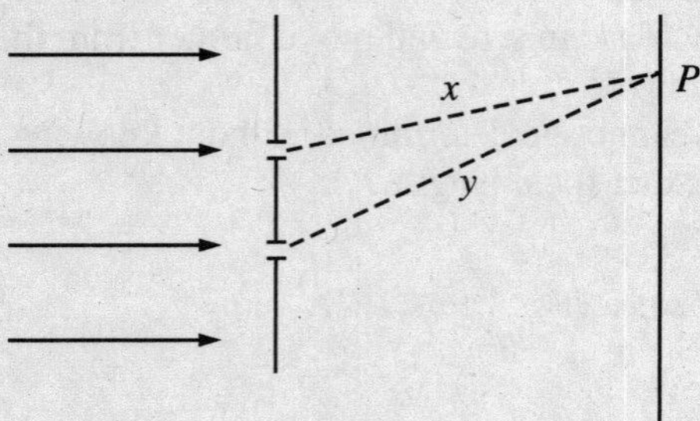

74. Light of wavelength λ is incident from the left on a pair of narrow slits, as shown above. If point P is a bright spot (maximum intensity) on a distant screen, one can be certain that the difference between distances x and y is

    (A) zero

    (B) $\lambda/2$

    (C) $n\lambda$, where n is an integer

    (D) $\left(n + \frac{1}{2}\right)\lambda$, where n is an integer

    (E) $\left(n - \frac{1}{2}\right)\lambda$, where n is an integer

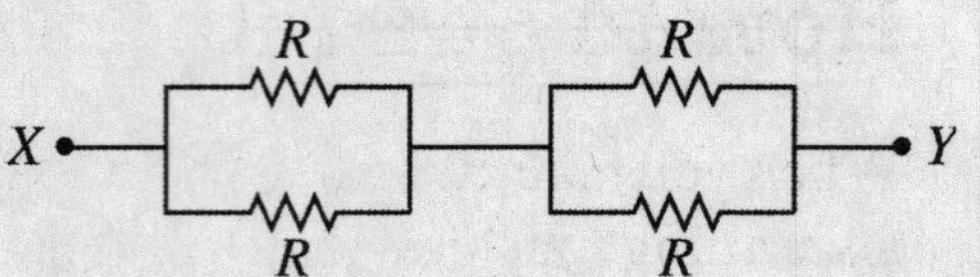

75. Four resistors of equal resistance R are connected as shown above. What is the total resistance between points X and Y?

    (A) $\frac{R}{4}$

    (B) $\frac{R}{2}$

    (C) R

    (D) $2R$

    (E) $4R$

STOP

If you finish before time is called, you may check your work on this test only. Do not turn to any other test in this book.

How to Score the SAT Subject Test in Physics

When you take an actual SAT Subject Test in Physics, your answer sheet will be "read" by a scanning machine that will record your responses to each question. Then a computer will compare your answers with the correct answers and produce your raw score. You get one point for each correct answer. For each wrong answer, you lose one-fourth of a point. Questions you omit (and any for which you mark more than one answer) are not counted. This raw score is converted to a scaled score that is reported to you and to the colleges you specify.

Worksheet 1. Finding Your Raw Test Score

STEP 1: Table A lists the correct answers for all the questions on the Subject Test in Physics that is reproduced in this book. It also serves as a worksheet for you to calculate your raw score.

- Compare your answers with those given in the table.
- Put a check in the column marked "Right" if your answer is correct.
- Put a check in the column marked "Wrong" if your answer is incorrect.
- Leave both columns blank if you omitted the question.

STEP 2: Count the number of right answers.

Enter the total here: ____________________

STEP 3: Count the number of wrong answers.

Enter the total here: ____________________

STEP 4: Multiply the number of wrong answers by .250.

Enter the product here: ________________

STEP 5: Subtract the result obtained in Step 4 from the total you obtained in Step 2.

Enter the result here: ___________________

STEP 6: Round the number obtained in Step 5 to the nearest whole number.

Enter the result here: ___________________

The number you obtained in Step 6 is your raw score.

Table A

Answers to the Subject Test in Physics, Form K-3XAC, and Percentage of Students Answering Each Question Correctly

Question Number	Correct Answer	Right	Wrong	Percentage of Students Answering the Question Correctly*	Question Number	Correct Answer	Right	Wrong	Percentage of Students Answering the Question Correctly*
1	B			54	33	B			57
2	A			76	34	D			28
3	E			80	35	C			66
4	C			72	36	B			59
5	A			63	37	E			61
6	D			89	38	B			38
7	E			55	39	A			30
8	D			76	40	D			65
9	E			60	41	E			40
10	B			70	42	A			64
11	C			65	43	E			56
12	A			69	44	B			33
13	D			83	45	A			40
14	A			67	46	B			58
15	B			14	47	E			38
16	D			80	48	B			49
17	C			69	49	A			77
18	D			87	50	C			71
19	B			71	51	D			65
20	A			61	52	A			46
21	B			87	53	E			57
22	C			49	54	D			69
23	C			58	55	C			35
24	A			76	56	B			39
25	A			61	57	B			37
26	C			60	58	D			37
27	B			62	59	E			32
28	E			44	60	B			65
29	A			42	61	A			48
30	A			78	62	B			34
31	C			66	63	A			41
32	D			74	64	D			29

Table A continued on next page

Table A continued from previous page

Question Number	Correct Answer	Right	Wrong	Percentage of Students Answering the Question Correctly*	Question Number	Correct Answer	Right	Wrong	Percentage of Students Answering the Question Correctly*
65	C			40	71	D			30
66	B			51	72	A			24
67	E			42	73	B			28
68	E			56	74	C			33
69	D			43	75	C			51
70	D			43					

* These percentages are based on an analysis of the answer sheets of a representative sample of 2,410 students who took this test in January 2003, and whose mean score was 628. They may be used as an indication of the relative difficulty of a particular question. Each percentage may also be used to predict the likelihood that a typical SAT Subject Test in Physics candidate will answer that question correctly on this edition of the test.

Finding Your Scaled Score

When you take SAT Subject Tests, the scores sent to the colleges you specify are reported on the College Board scale, which ranges from 200–800. You can convert your practice test score to a scaled score by using Table B. To find your scaled score, locate your raw score in the left-hand column of Table B; the corresponding score in the right-hand column is your scaled score. For example, a raw score of 41 on this particular edition of the Subject Test in Physics corresponds to a scaled score of 670.

Raw scores are converted to scaled scores to ensure that a score earned on any one edition of a particular Subject Test is comparable to the same scaled score earned on any other edition of the same Subject Test. Because some editions of the tests may be slightly easier or more difficult than others, College Board scaled scores are adjusted so that they indicate the same level of performance regardless of the edition of the test taken and the ability of the group that takes it. Thus, for example, a score of 400 on one edition of a test taken at a particular administration indicates the same level of achievement as a score of 400 on a different edition of the test taken at a different administration.

When you take the SAT Subject Tests during a national administration, your scores are likely to differ somewhat from the scores you obtain on the tests in this book. People perform at different levels at different times for reasons unrelated to the tests themselves. The precision of any test is also limited because it represents only a sample of all the possible questions that could be asked.

Table B

Scaled Score Conversion Table
Subject Test in Physics (Form K-3XAC)

Raw Score	Scaled Score	Raw Score	Scaled Score	Raw Score	Scaled Score
75	800	39	660	3	410
74	800	38	650	2	400
73	800	37	640	1	400
72	800	36	640	0	390
71	800	35	630	-1	380
70	800	34	620	-2	380
69	800	33	620	-3	370
68	800	32	610	-4	360
67	800	31	600	-5	360
66	800	30	600	-6	350
65	800	29	590	-7	340
64	800	28	580	-8	330
63	800	27	580	-9	330
62	800	26	570	-10	320
61	800	25	560	-11	310
60	800	24	560	-12	310
59	800	23	550	-13	300
58	790	22	540	-14	290
57	780	21	530	-15	290
56	780	20	530	-16	280
55	770	19	520	-17	280
54	760	18	510	-18	270
53	750	17	510	-19	270
52	750	16	500		
51	740	15	490		
50	730	14	490		
49	730	13	480		
48	720	12	470		
47	710	11	470		
46	710	10	460		
45	700	9	450		
44	690	8	450		
43	690	7	440		
42	680	6	430		
41	670	5	420		
40	670	4	420		

How Did You Do on the Subject Test in Physics?

After you score your test and analyze your performance, think about the following questions:

Did you run out of time before reaching the end of the test?

If so, you may need to pace yourself better. For example, maybe you spent too much time on one or two hard questions. A better approach might be to skip the ones you can't answer right away and try answering all the questions that remain on the test. Then if there's time, go back to the questions you skipped.

Did you take a long time reading the directions?

You will save time when you take the test by learning the directions to the Subject Test in Physics ahead of time. Each minute you spend reading directions during the test is a minute that you could use to answer questions.

How did you handle questions you were unsure of?

If you were able to eliminate one or more of the answer choices as wrong and guess from the remaining ones, your approach probably worked to your advantage. On the other hand, making haphazard guesses or omitting questions without trying to eliminate choices could cost you valuable points.

How difficult were the questions for you compared with other students who took the test?

Table A shows you how difficult the multiple-choice questions were for the group of students who took this test during its national administration. The right-hand column gives the percentage of students that answered each question correctly.

A question answered correctly by almost everyone in the group is obviously an easier question. For example, 89 percent of the students answered question 6 correctly. But only 14 percent answered question 15 correctly.

Keep in mind that these percentages are based on just one group of students. They would probably be different with another group of students taking the test.

If you missed several easier questions, go back and try to find out why: Did the questions cover material you haven't yet reviewed? Did you misunderstand the directions?

Chapter 8

Chinese with Listening

Purpose

The Subject Test in Chinese with Listening measures your understanding of Mandarin Chinese in the context of contemporary Chinese culture. The questions on the test are written to reflect general trends in high school curricula and are independent of particular textbooks or methods of instruction.

Format

This is a one-hour test with about 20 minutes of listening comprehension and 40 minutes of usage and reading comprehension. There are 85 multiple-choice questions in three sections.

Content

Listening Comprehension questions test the ability to understand the spoken language and are based on short, spoken dialogues and narratives primarily about everyday topics. There are two different kinds of listening comprehension questions: (A) a spoken statement, question, or exchange, followed by a choice of three possible responses (also spoken); (B) a spoken dialogue or monologue with a printed question or questions (in English) about what was said.

Usage questions ask you to select the answer that best completes a Chinese sentence in a way that is structurally and logically correct. Questions are written to reflect instructional practices of the curriculum. This section of the test is therefore presented in four columns across two pages of the test book to allow each question and its answer choices to be shown in four different ways of representing Chinese: traditional and simplified Chinese characters on the left page, and phonetic transcriptions in Pinyin romanization and the Chinese phonetic alphabet (Bopomofo) on the right page. You should choose the writing form you are most familiar with and read only from that column.

Reading Comprehension questions test your understanding of such points as main and supporting ideas, themes, and the setting of passages. Some of the passages are based on real-life materials such as timetables, forms, advertisements, notes, letters, diaries, and newspaper articles. All passages are printed in both traditional and simplified Chinese characters. While most questions deal with understanding of literal meaning, some inference questions may also be included. All reading comprehension questions are in English.

Chinese with Listening	
Skills Measured	Approximate Percentage of Test
Listening Comprehension	33
Usage	33
Reading Comprehension	33

CD Players

Using CD Players for Language Tests with Listening

Take an acceptable CD player to the test center. Your CD player must be in good working order, so insert fresh batteries on the day before the test. You may bring additional batteries and a backup player to the test center.

Test center staff won't have batteries, CD players, or earphones for your use, so your CD player must be:

- equipped with earphones
- portable (hand-held)
- battery operated
- for your use only. CD players cannot be shared with other test-takers.

Note

If the volume on your CD player disturbs other test-takers, the test center supervisor may ask you to move to another seat.

What to do if your CD player malfunctions:

- Raise your hand and tell the test supervisor.
- Switch to backup equipment if you have it and continue the test. If you don't have backup equipment, your score on the Chinese with Listening Test will be canceled. But scores on other Subject Tests you take that day will still be counted.

What if you receive a defective CD on test day? Raise your hand and ask the supervisor for a replacement.

How to Prepare

The best preparation is gradual development of competence in Chinese over a period of years. The test is appropriate for students who have studied Mandarin Chinese as a second or foreign language for two to four years in high school, or the equivalent. A practice CD with different sample questions can be obtained, along with a copy of the *SAT Subject Tests Preparation Booklet* from your school counselor, or you can access the listening files at www.collegeboard.com. You should also take the practice test included with this book. Familiarize yourself with the test directions in advance. The directions in this book are identical to those that appear on the test.

Note

The SAT Subject Test in Chinese with Listening is offered once a year only at designated test centers. To take the test, you MUST bring an acceptable CD player with earphones to the test center.

Scores

The total score is reported on the 200-to-800 scale. Listening, usage, and reading subscores are reported on the 20-to-80 scale.

Sample Questions

Following are some samples for each section of the SAT Subject Test in Chinese with Listening. All questions are multiple choice. You must choose the best response from the three or four choices offered for each question.

In an actual test administration, all spoken Chinese will be presented as recorded audio. Text that appears in this section in brackets ([ ]) will be recorded in an actual test and it will not be printed in your test book. Spoken text appears in printed form here because a recorded version is not available.

Sample Listening Questions

Please note that the CD does not start here. Begin using the CD when you start the actual practice test on page 355.

Part A

Directions: In this part of the test, you will hear short questions, statements, or commands in Mandarin Chinese followed by three responses in Mandarin Chinese designated (A), (B), and (C). You will hear the questions or statements, as well as the responses, just one time, and they are not printed in your test book. Therefore, you must listen very carefully. Select the best choice and fill in the corresponding circle on your answer sheet.

Question 1

(Narrator) [Number 1

(Woman) 請問圖書館在哪兒?

(Man) (A) 圖書館九點開門。

(B) 圖書館裏書很多。

(C) 圖書館就在前面。] (5 seconds)

Choice (C) is the correct answer because it responds to the question "where is the library?" Choice (A) is incorrect because it tells when the library opens, and choice (B) is incorrect because it tells what's inside the library.

Question 2

(Narrator) [Number 2

(Man) 這本書貴不貴?

(Woman) 不貴，也不便宜。

(Man) (A) 多久了?

(B) 多少錢?

(C) 多不多?] (5 seconds)

Choice (B) is the correct answer because it asks how much the book costs. The conversation concerns the price of a book. The man asks if the book is expensive, and the woman replies that it is neither expensive nor cheap. Choice (A) is incorrect because it asks about length of time. Choice (C) is incorrect because it asks if there are many.

Part B

Directions: You will now hear a series of short selections. You will hear them only once, and they are not printed in your test book. After each selection, you will be asked to answer one or more questions about what you have just heard. These questions, each with four possible answers, are printed in your test book. Select the best answer to each question from among the four choices printed and fill in the corresponding circle on your answer sheet. You will have fifteen seconds to answer each question.

Questions 3–4

(Narrator) [Questions 3 and 4. Listen to find out what the woman will do next summer.

(Woman) 你去過香港嗎?

(Man) 沒去過，可是我明年夏天從日本到中國去的時候會經過香港。

(Woman) 明年夏天我得留在美國上暑期班，哪兒都不能去。

(Narrator) Now answer questions 3 and 4.] (30 seconds)

3. Where will the woman spend the summer next year?
   (A) In China
   (B) In Japan
   (C) In Hong Kong
   (D) In the United States

Choice (D) is the correct answer because the woman states in the conversation that she will stay in the United States next summer. Choices (A), (B), and (C) are the places where the man will go next summer.

4. What will the woman do?
   (A) Visit friends
   (B) Go to school
   (C) Look for a job
   (D) Travel abroad

Choice (B) is the correct answer because the woman states in the conversation that she will go to summer school. None of the other answer choices are mentioned by the woman in the conversation.

Sample Usage Questions

Directions: This section consists of a number of incomplete sentences, each of which has four possible completions. Select the word or phrase that best completes the sentence structurally and logically and fill in the corresponding circle on your answer sheet.

This section of the test is presented in four columns to allow each question to be shown in four different ways of representing Chinese: traditional characters, simplified characters, Pinyin romanization, and the Chinese phonetic alphabet (Bopomofo). TO SAVE TIME, IT IS RECOMMENDED THAT YOU CHOOSE THE WRITING FORM WITH WHICH YOU ARE MOST FAMILIAR AND **READ ONLY FROM THAT COLUMN** AS YOU WORK THROUGH THIS SECTION OF THE TEST.

Question 5

5. 我很喜歡這部電影。
你 ____ ?

(A) 阿
(B) 嗎
(C) 吧
(D) 呢

5. 我很喜欢这部电影。
你 ____ ?

(A) 阿
(B) 吗
(C) 吧
(D) 呢

5. Wǒ hěn xǐhuan zhèi bù diànyǐng.
Nǐ ____ ?

(A) a
(B) ma
(C) ba
(D) ne

5. ㄨㄛˇ ㄏㄣˇ ㄒㄧˇ ㄏㄨㄢ ㄓㄟˋ ㄅㄨˋ ㄉㄧㄢˋ ㄧㄥˇ。
ㄋㄧˇ ____ ?

(A) ˙ㄚ
(B) ˙ㄇㄚ
(C) ˙ㄅㄚ
(D) ˙ㄋㄜ

This question tests the use of sentence-final particles.

Choice (D) is the correct answer to question 5. Of the four answer choices, only choice (D) *ne* following the second-person singular pronoun *ni* conveys the intended meaning “How about you?” as a question appended to the preceding statement, “I really like this movie.”

Question 6

6. 他____生氣____臉紅。

(A) 連 ..... 都
(B) 一 ..... 就
(C) 不跟 ..... 一樣
(D) 雖然 ..... 可是

6. 他____生气____脸红。

(A) 连 ..... 都
(B) 一 ..... 就
(C) 不跟 ..... 一样
(D) 虽然 ..... 可是

6. Tā ____ shēngqì ____ liǎnhóng.

(A) lián ..... dōu
(B) yì ..... jiù
(C) bù gēn ..... yíyàng
(D) suīrán ..... kěshì

6. ㄊㄚ ____ ㄕㄥ ㄑㄧˋ ____ ㄌㄧㄢˇ ㄏㄨㄥˊ。

(A) ㄌㄧㄢˊ ..... ㄉㄡ
(B) ㄧˋ ..... ㄐㄧㄡˋ
(C) ㄅㄨˋ ㄍㄣ ..... ㄧˊ ㄧㄤˋ
(D) ㄙㄨㄟ ㄖㄢˊ ..... ㄎㄜˇ ㄕˋ

This question tests the use of sentence-linking constructions.

Choice (B) is the correct answer to question 6 because the nonmovable forwarding-linking adverb *yi* is paired with *jiu* to convey the meaning "as soon as … then." None of the other answer choices are structurally or logically correct in this context.

Sample Reading Questions

Directions: Read the following texts carefully for comprehension. Each is followed by one or more questions or incomplete statements. Select the answer or completion that is best according to the text and fill in the corresponding circle on the answer sheet.

This section of the test is presented in two writing systems: traditional characters and simplified characters. IT IS RECOMMENDED THAT YOU CHOOSE THE WRITING SYSTEM WITH WHICH YOU ARE MORE FAMILIAR AND **READ ONLY THAT VERSION** AS YOU WORK THROUGH THIS SECTION OF THE TEST.

Questions 7–8

國立台灣師範大學音樂系

張 鳴 欣
教授　作曲家

國立台灣師範大學
台北市和平東路一段162號

電話: 公(02)321-8400

国立台湾师范大学音乐系

张 鸣 欣
教授　作曲家

国立台湾师范大学
台北市和平东路一段162号

电话: 公(02)321-8400

7. What is this?
   (A) A business card
   (B) A thank-you note
   (C) A return envelope
   (D) A concert ticket

Choice (A) is the correct answer to question 7. The text contains a person's name, workplace, profession, office address, and telephone number, all arranged in the standard format for an individual's business card.

8. The person named is a
   (A) professor
   (B) singer
   (C) conductor
   (D) journalist

Choice (A) is the correct answer to question 8. The text of the business card shows that the person works in the music department of a university and gives the person's professional title as "professor and composer."

Chinese with Listening Test

Practice Helps

The test that follows is an actual, recently administered SAT Subject Test in Chinese with Listening. To get an idea of what it's like to take this test, practice under conditions that are much like those of an actual test administration.

- Set aside an hour when you can take the test uninterrupted. Make sure you complete the test in one sitting.
- Sit at a desk or table with no other books or papers. Dictionaries, other books, or notes are not allowed in the test room.
- Tear out an answer sheet from the back of this book and fill it in just as you would on the day of the test. One answer sheet can be used for up to three Subject Tests.
- Read the instructions that precede the practice test. During the actual administration, you will be asked to read them before answering test questions.
- Time yourself by placing a clock or kitchen timer in front of you.
- After you finish the practice test, read the sections "How to Score the SAT Subject Test in Chinese with Listening" and "How Did You Do on the Subject Test in Chinese with Listening?"
- The appearance of the answer sheet in this book may differ from the answer sheet you see on test day.

NO TEST MATERIAL ON THIS PAGE

CHINESE TEST WITH LISTENING

The top portion of the section of the answer sheet that you will use in taking the Chinese Test with Listening must be filled in exactly as shown in the illustration below. Note carefully that you have to do all of the following on your answer sheet.

1. Print CHINESE WITH LISTENING on the line under the words "Subject Test (print)."

2. In the shaded box labeled "Test Code" fill in four circles:

—Fill in circle 3 in the row labeled V.
—Fill in circle 5 in the row labeled W.
—Fill in circle 4 in the row labeled X.
—Fill in circle D in the row labeled Y.

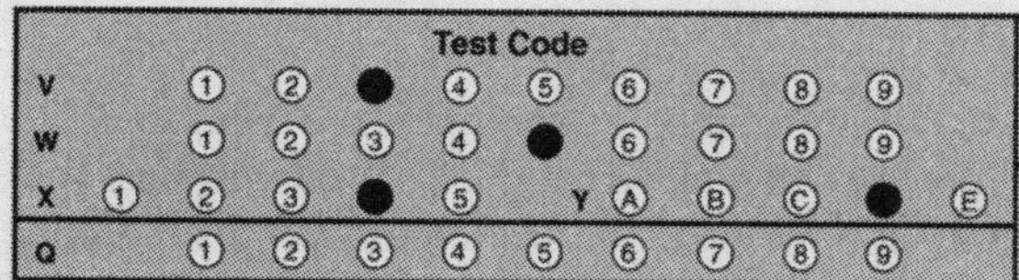

Please answer Part I and Part II below by filling in the appropriate circles in the row labeled Q on your answer sheet. Select the answers that correspond to your Chinese language experience and to the Chinese language classes you have taken or are taking at present. The information that you provide is for statistical purposes only and will not affect your score on the test.

PART I Which of the following is the primary source of your knowledge of the Chinese language? (Choose only one.)

—**Circle 1** — Living in a place and/or a home in which Mandarin Chinese is used

—**Circle 2** — Living in a place and/or a home in which Chinese other than Mandarin is used

—**Circle 3** — Studying Chinese in an extracurricular (after-school, weekend, summer, and/or study-abroad) program (e.g., Chinese language school)

—**Circle 4** — Studying Chinese in classes at your regular elementary and/or middle school (grades K through 8)

—**Circle 5** — Studying Chinese in classes at your regular high school (grades 9 through 12)

PART II How long have you studied Chinese in your regular high school (grades 9 through 12)? (Choose only one.)

—**Circle 6** — 0 (zero) to 2 years

—**Circle 7** — 2 to 2½ years

—**Circle 8** — 3 to 3½ years

—**Circle 9** — 4 years

When the supervisor tells you to do so, turn the page and begin the Chinese Test with Listening. There are 100 numbered circles on your answer sheet. Use only circles 1 to 85 to record your answers to the 85 questions in the Chinese Test with Listening.

CHINESE TEST WITH LISTENING

PLEASE NOTE THAT YOUR ANSWER SHEET HAS FIVE ANSWER POSITIONS, MARKED A, B, C, D, AND E, WHILE THE QUESTIONS THROUGHOUT THIS TEST CONTAIN EITHER THREE OR FOUR ANSWER CHOICES. BE SURE NOT TO MAKE ANY MARKS IN COLUMN E, AND DO NOT MAKE ANY MARKS IN COLUMN D IF THERE ARE ONLY THREE CHOICES GIVEN.

SECTION I
LISTENING

Approximate time—20 minutes

Questions 1-30

Part A

Directions: In this part of the test, you will hear short questions, statements, or commands in Mandarin Chinese, followed by three responses in Mandarin Chinese, designated (A), (B), and (C). You will hear the questions or statements, as well as the responses, just one time, and they are not printed in your test booklet. Therefore, you must listen very carefully. Select the best response and fill in the corresponding circle on your answer sheet. Now listen to the following example, but do not mark the answer on your answer sheet.

You will hear:

You will also hear:

The answer that most logically responds to the question is (C). Therefore, you should choose answer (C).

Now listen to the first exchange.

1. Mark your answer on your answer sheet.
2. Mark your answer on your answer sheet.
3. Mark your answer on your answer sheet.
4. Mark your answer on your answer sheet.
5. Mark your answer on your answer sheet.
6. Mark your answer on your answer sheet.
7. Mark your answer on your answer sheet.
8. Mark your answer on your answer sheet.
9. Mark your answer on your answer sheet.
10. Mark your answer on your answer sheet.
11. Mark your answer on your answer sheet.
12. Mark your answer on your answer sheet.
13. Mark your answer on your answer sheet.
14. Mark your answer on your answer sheet.
15. Mark your answer on your answer sheet.
16. Mark your answer on your answer sheet.
17. Mark your answer on your answer sheet.
18. Mark your answer on your answer sheet.
19. Mark your answer on your answer sheet.

3ZLC

END OF PART A.
GO ON TO PART B.

GO ON TO THE NEXT PAGE

Part B

Directions: You will now hear a series of short selections. You will hear them only once, and they are not printed in your test booklet. After each selection, you will be asked to answer one or more questions about what you have just heard. These questions, each with four possible answers, are printed in your test booklet. Select the best answer to each question from among the four choices printed and fill in the corresponding circle on your answer sheet. You will have fifteen seconds to answer each question.

Now listen to the following example, but do not mark the answer on your answer sheet.

You will hear:

You will see:

What are the two people talking about?

(A) Food
(B) Homework
(C) History
(D) Language

The best answer to the question is (D), "Language." Therefore, you should choose answer (D).

Now listen to the first selection.

Questions 20-21

20. What is the man's native language?

(A) French
(B) Chinese
(C) English
(D) German

21. How did the man's son learn German?

(A) His father taught him.
(B) He took lessons from the woman.
(C) He studied it in college.
(D) He grew up in Germany.

Question 22

22. What is the speaker's problem?

(A) He spent too long debating an issue.
(B) He got up too late for work.
(C) His sleeping pills are all gone.
(D) He has a headache and can't concentrate.

Question 23

23. Which of the following activities is NOT mentioned by the speaker?

(A) Watching television
(B) Singing songs
(C) Riding bicycles
(D) Playing tennis

Question 24

24. What happened to the man?

(A) He forgot to return all the books.
(B) He missed the train.
(C) He lost his football tickets.
(D) He took the wrong bus.

GO ON TO THE NEXT PAGE

Questions 25-26

25. What color shoes did Xiaohua originally want?

(A) White
(B) Yellow
(C) Brown
(D) Black

26. What does Xiaohua dislike about the pair of brown shoes?

(A) The price
(B) The size
(C) The style
(D) The quality

Question 27

27. What information is provided in the announcement?

(A) A change of location
(B) Additional show times
(C) A revision to the program
(D) The deadline for purchasing tickets

Questions 28-29

28. On which day of the week is the event being held?

(A) Monday
(B) Wednesday
(C) Saturday
(D) Sunday

29. Which of the following statements about the male speaker is true?

(A) He is living in a dormitory.
(B) He is the woman's classmate.
(C) He is a Chinese history major.
(D) He is the organizer of the event.

Question 30

30. Which of the following items is the man NOT required to bring?

(A) Photos
(B) Transcript
(C) Medical report
(D) ID card

END OF SECTION I.
DO NOT GO ON TO SECTION II UNTIL YOU ARE TOLD TO DO SO.

CHINESE TEST WITH LISTENING—*Continued*

TIME FOR SECTIONS II AND III - 40 minutes

SECTION II
USAGE
Suggested time—15 minutes
Questions 31-55

Directions: This section consists of a number of incomplete statements, each of which has four possible completions. Select the word or phrase that best completes the sentence structurally and logically and fill in the corresponding circle on your answer sheet.

This section of the test is presented in four columns across two pages to allow each question to be shown in four different ways of representing Chinese: traditional characters, simplified characters, Pinyin romanization, and the Chinese phonetic alphabet (Bopomofo). TO SAVE TIME, IT IS RECOMMENDED THAT YOU CHOOSE THE WRITING FORM WITH WHICH YOU ARE MOST FAMILIAR AND **READ ONLY FROM THAT COLUMN** AS YOU WORK THROUGH THIS SECTION OF THE TEST.

Example:

他____有空____喜歡看書。	他____有空____喜欢看书。	Tā____ yǒu kòng ____ xǐhuan kànshū.	ㄊㄚ____ㄧㄡˇ ㄎㄨㄥˋ____ㄒㄧˇ ㄏㄨㄢ ㄎㄢˋ ㄕㄨ。
(A) 連 ..... 都	(A) 连 ..... 都	(A) lián ..... dōu	(A) ㄌㄧㄢˊ ..... ㄉㄡ
(B) 一 ..... 就	(B) 一 ..... 就	(B) yī ..... jiù	(B) ㄧ ..... ㄐㄧㄡˋ
(C) 從 ..... 到	(C) 从 ..... 到	(C) cóng ..... dào	(C) ㄘㄨㄥˊ ..... ㄉㄠˋ
(D) 是 ..... 的	(D) 是 ..... 的	(D) shì ..... de	(D) ㄕˋ ..... ˙ㄉㄜ

The best completion is answer (B). Therefore, you should choose answer (B) and fill in the corresponding circle on your answer sheet. **Remember to work with one column only** and start by filling in one of the circles next to number 31 on your answer sheet.

GO ON TO THE NEXT PAGE

31. 校長説的話，你
都 _____ 嗎？
(A) 看得到
(B) 拿不出
(C) 聽懂了
(D) 放下去

32. 今天上午他 _____ 。
(A) 很得晚起來
(B) 起來得很晚
(C) 來得晚起很
(D) 晚得起很來

33. 做了一天的事， _____ 。
(A) 大家了都累也
(B) 也累了都大家
(C) 累了大家也都
(D) 大家也都累了

34. 他的車子壞了， _____
要我去接他。
(A) 所以
(B) 以外
(C) 不論
(D) 如此

35. 她唱歌唱得比我 _____ 好。
(A) 再
(B) 就
(C) 更
(D) 並

31. 校长说的话，你
都 _____ 吗？
(A) 看得到
(B) 拿不出
(C) 听懂了
(D) 放下去

32. 今天上午他 _____ 。
(A) 很得晚起来
(B) 起来得很晚
(C) 来得晚起很
(D) 晚得起很来

33. 做了一天的事， _____ 。
(A) 大家了都累也
(B) 也累了都大家
(C) 累了大家也都
(D) 大家也都累了

34. 他的车子坏了， _____
要我去接他。
(A) 所以
(B) 以外
(C) 不论
(D) 如此

35. 她唱歌唱得比我 _____ 好。
(A) 再
(B) 就
(C) 更
(D) 并

GO ON TO THE NEXT PAGE

31. Xiàozhǎng shuō de huà, nǐ dōu _____ ma?

    (A) kàn de dào

    (B) ná bu chū

    (C) tīngdǒngle

    (D) fàng xiaqu

32. Jīntiān shàngwǔ tā _____ .

    (A) hěn de wǎn qǐlai

    (B) qǐlai de hěn wǎn

    (C) lái de wǎn qǐ hěn

    (D) wǎn de qǐ hěn lái

33. Zuòle yì tiān de shì, _____ .

    (A) dàjiā le dōu lèi yě

    (B) yě lèile dōu dàjiā

    (C) lèile dàjiā yě dōu

    (D) dàjiā yě dōu lèi le

34. Tā de chēzi huài le, _____ yào wǒ qù jiē tā.

    (A) suǒyǐ

    (B) yǐwài

    (C) búlùn

    (D) rúcǐ

35. Tā chànggē chàng de bǐ wǒ _____ hǎo.

    (A) zài

    (B) jiù

    (C) gèng

    (D) bìng

31. ㄒㄧㄠˋ ㄓㄤˇ ㄕㄨㄛ ˙ㄉㄜ ㄏㄨㄚˋ, ㄋㄧˇ ㄉㄡ _____ ˙ㄇㄚ?

    (A) ㄎㄢˋ ˙ㄉㄜ ㄉㄠˋ

    (B) ㄋㄚˊ ˙ㄅㄨ ㄔㄨ

    (C) ㄊㄧㄥ ㄉㄨㄥˇ ˙ㄌㄜ

    (D) ㄈㄤˋ ㄒㄧㄚˋ ㄑㄩ

32. ㄐㄧㄣ ㄊㄧㄢ ㄕㄤˋ ㄨˇ ㄊㄚ _____ 。

    (A) ㄏㄣˇ ˙ㄉㄜ ㄨㄢˇ ㄑㄧˇ ˙ㄌㄞ

    (B) ㄑㄧˇ ˙ㄌㄞ ˙ㄉㄜ ㄏㄣˇ ㄨㄢˇ

    (C) ㄌㄞˊ ˙ㄉㄜ ㄨㄢˇ ㄑㄧˇ ㄏㄣˇ

    (D) ㄨㄢˇ ˙ㄉㄜ ㄑㄧˇ ㄏㄣˇ ㄌㄞˊ

33. ㄗㄨㄛˋ ˙ㄌㄜ ㄧˋ ㄊㄧㄢ ˙ㄉㄜ ㄕˋ, _____ 。

    (A) ㄉㄚˋ ㄐㄧㄚ ˙ㄌㄜ ㄉㄡ ㄌㄟˋ ㄧㄝˇ

    (B) ㄧㄝˇ ㄌㄟˋ ˙ㄌㄜ ㄉㄡ ㄉㄚˋ ㄐㄧㄚ

    (C) ㄌㄟˋ ˙ㄌㄜ ㄉㄚˋ ㄐㄧㄚ ㄧㄝˇ ㄉㄡ

    (D) ㄉㄚˋ ㄐㄧㄚ ㄧㄝˇ ㄉㄡ ㄌㄟˋ ˙ㄌㄜ

34. ㄊㄚ ˙ㄉㄜ ㄔㄜ ˙ㄗ ㄏㄨㄞˋ ˙ㄌㄜ, _____ ㄧㄠˋ ㄨㄛˇ ㄑㄩˋ ㄐㄧㄝ ㄊㄚ。

    (A) ㄙㄨㄛˇ ㄧˇ

    (B) ㄧˇ ㄨㄞˋ

    (C) ㄅㄨˊ ㄌㄨㄣˋ

    (D) ㄖㄨˊ ㄘˇ

35. ㄊㄚ ㄔㄤˋ ㄍㄜ ㄔㄤˋ ˙ㄉㄜ ㄅㄧˇ ㄨㄛˇ _____ ㄏㄠˇ。

    (A) ㄗㄞˋ

    (B) ㄐㄧㄡˋ

    (C) ㄍㄥˋ

    (D) ㄅㄧㄥˋ

GO ON TO THE NEXT PAGE

36. 我們可不可以 _____ 休息一會兒？
    (A) 唱起來
    (B) 坐下來
    (C) 聽出來
    (D) 看上來

37. 他 _____ 去了。
    (A) 到公園孩子帶已經
    (B) 孩子帶公園已經到
    (C) 公園已經帶到孩子
    (D) 已經帶孩子到公園

38. 我上班的地方 _____ 。
    (A) 不遠太離我家
    (B) 太不遠我家離
    (C) 我家離不遠太
    (D) 離我家不太遠

39. 雖然他在英國住過，_____ 他不太會說英文。
    (A) 然後
    (B) 但是
    (C) 而且
    (D) 於是

40. 我去他家的時候，他 ____ 睡覺。
    (A) 正在
    (B) 剛才
    (C) 從來
    (D) 然後

36. 我们可不可以 _____ 休息一会儿？
    (A) 唱起来
    (B) 坐下来
    (C) 听出来
    (D) 看上来

37. 他 _____ 去了。
    (A) 到公园孩子带已经
    (B) 孩子带公园已经到
    (C) 公园已经带到孩子
    (D) 已经带孩子到公园

38. 我上班的地方 _____ 。
    (A) 不远太离我家
    (B) 太不远我家离
    (C) 我家离不远太
    (D) 离我家不太远

39. 虽然他在英国住过，_____ 他不太会说英文。
    (A) 然后
    (B) 但是
    (C) 而且
    (D) 于是

40. 我去他家的时候，他 ____ 睡觉。
    (A) 正在
    (B) 刚才
    (C) 从来
    (D) 然后

GO ON TO THE NEXT PAGE

36. Wǒmen kě bù kěyǐ _____ xiūxi yíhuìr?
    (A) chàng qilai
    (B) zuò xialai
    (C) tīng chulai
    (D) kàn shanglai

37. Tā _____ qù le.
    (A) dào gōngyuán háizi dài yǐjīng
    (B) háizi dài gōngyuán yǐjīng dào
    (C) gōngyuán yǐjīng dài dào háizi
    (D) yǐjīng dài háizi dào gōngyuán

38. Wǒ shàngbān de dìfang _____ .
    (A) bù yuǎn tài lí wǒ jiā
    (B) tài bù yuǎn wǒ jiā lí
    (C) wǒ jiā lí bù yuǎn tài
    (D) lí wǒ jiā bú tài yuǎn

39. Suīrán tā zài Yīngguó zhùguo, _____ tā bú tài huì shuō Yīngwén.
    (A) ránhòu
    (B) dànshì
    (C) érqiě
    (D) yúshì

40. Wǒ qù tā jiā de shíhou, tā _____ shuìjiào.
    (A) zhèngzài
    (B) gāngcái
    (C) cónglái
    (D) ránhòu

36. ㄨㄛˇ ˙ㄇㄣ ㄎㄜˇ ㄅㄨˋ ㄎㄜˇ ㄧˇ _____ ㄒㄧㄡ ㄒㄧˊ ㄧˋ ㄏㄨㄟˇ ˙ㄦ?
    (A) ㄔㄤˋ ㄑㄧˇ ˙ㄌㄞ
    (B) ㄗㄨㄛˋ ㄒㄧㄚˋ ˙ㄌㄞ
    (C) ㄊㄧㄥ ㄔㄨ ˙ㄌㄞ
    (D) ㄎㄢˋ ㄕㄤˋ ˙ㄌㄞ

37. ㄊㄚ _____ ㄑㄩˋ ˙ㄌㄜ。
    (A) ㄉㄠˋ ㄍㄨㄥ ㄩㄢˊ ㄏㄞˊ ˙ㄗ ㄉㄞˋ ㄧˇ ㄐㄧㄥ
    (B) ㄏㄞˊ ˙ㄗ ㄉㄞˋ ㄍㄨㄥ ㄩㄢˊ ㄧˇ ㄐㄧㄥ ㄉㄠˋ
    (C) ㄍㄨㄥ ㄩㄢˊ ㄧˇ ㄐㄧㄥ ㄉㄞˋ ㄉㄠˋ ㄏㄞˊ ˙ㄗ
    (D) ㄧˇ ㄐㄧㄥ ㄉㄞˋ ㄏㄞˊ ˙ㄗ ㄉㄠˋ ㄍㄨㄥ ㄩㄢˊ

38. ㄨㄛˇ ㄕㄤˋ ㄅㄢ ˙ㄉㄜ ㄉㄧˋ ㄈㄤ _____ 。
    (A) ㄅㄨˋ ㄩㄢˇ ㄊㄞˋ ㄌㄧˊ ㄨㄛˇ ㄐㄧㄚ
    (B) ㄊㄞˋ ㄅㄨˋ ㄩㄢˇ ㄨㄛˇ ㄐㄧㄚ ㄌㄧˊ
    (C) ㄨㄛˇ ㄐㄧㄚ ㄌㄧˊ ㄅㄨˋ ㄩㄢˇ ㄊㄞˋ
    (D) ㄌㄧˊ ㄨㄛˇ ㄐㄧㄚ ㄅㄨˊ ㄊㄞˋ ㄩㄢˇ

39. ㄙㄨㄟ ㄖㄢˊ ㄊㄚ ㄗㄞˋ ㄧㄥ ㄍㄨㄛˊ ㄓㄨˋ ˙ㄍㄨㄛ， _____ ㄊㄚ ㄅㄨˊ ㄊㄞˋ ㄏㄨㄟˋ ㄕㄨㄛ ㄧㄥ ㄨㄣˊ。
    (A) ㄖㄢˊ ㄏㄡˋ
    (B) ㄉㄢˋ ㄕˋ
    (C) ㄦˊ ㄑㄧㄝˇ
    (D) ㄩˊ ㄕˋ

40. ㄨㄛˇ ㄑㄩˋ ㄊㄚ ㄐㄧㄚ ˙ㄉㄜ ㄕˊ ˙ㄏㄡ，ㄊㄚ _____ ㄕㄨㄟˋ ㄐㄧㄠˋ。
    (A) ㄓㄥˋ ㄗㄞˋ
    (B) ㄍㄤ ㄘㄞˊ
    (C) ㄘㄨㄥˊ ㄌㄞˊ
    (D) ㄖㄢˊ ㄏㄡˋ

GO ON TO THE NEXT PAGE

41. _____ 火車站走路 _____ 宿舍要多久？
(A) 向 ..... 在
(B) 從 ..... 到
(C) 往 ..... 同
(D) 由 ..... 沿

41. _____ 火车站走路 _____ 宿舍要多久？
(A) 向 ..... 在
(B) 从 ..... 到
(C) 往 ..... 同
(D) 由 ..... 沿

42. 晚上我們 _____ 去看個朋友。
(A) 向
(B) 從
(C) 更
(D) 得

42. 晚上我们 _____ 去看个朋友。
(A) 向
(B) 从
(C) 更
(D) 得

43. 去年他 _____ 寫了三封信給我。
(A) 曾
(B) 沒
(C) 送
(D) 會

43. 去年他 _____ 写了三封信给我。
(A) 曾
(B) 没
(C) 送
(D) 会

44. 這間房間是 _____ 為你預備的。
(A) 特別
(B) 比較
(C) 相當
(D) 非常

44. 这间房间是 _____ 为你预备的。
(A) 特别
(B) 比较
(C) 相当
(D) 非常

45. 那份報告 _____ 去了。
(A) 給叫借同事
(B) 叫同事給借
(C) 借同事叫給
(D) 同事借給叫

45. 那份报告 _____ 去了。
(A) 给叫借同事
(B) 叫同事给借
(C) 借同事叫给
(D) 同事借给叫

GO ON TO THE NEXT PAGE

41. _____ huǒchēzhàn zǒulù _____ sùshè yào duō jiǔ?

(A) Xiàng ..... zài

(B) Cóng ..... dào

(C) Wàng ..... tóng

(D) Yóu ..... yán

41. ______ ㄏㄨㄛˇ ㄔㄜ ㄓㄢˋ ㄗㄡˇ ㄌㄨˋ ______ ㄙㄨˋ ㄕㄜˋ ㄧㄠˋ ㄉㄨㄛ ㄐㄧㄡˇ ?

(A) ㄒㄧㄤˋ ..... ㄗㄞˋ

(B) ㄘㄨㄥˊ ..... ㄉㄠˋ

(C) ㄨㄤˋ ..... ㄊㄨㄥˊ

(D) ㄧㄡˊ ..... ㄧㄢˊ

42. Wǎnshang wǒmen _____ qù kàn ge péngyǒu.

(A) xiàng

(B) cóng

(C) gèng

(D) děi

42. ㄨㄢˇ ˙ㄕㄤ ㄨㄛˇ ˙ㄇㄣ _____ ㄑㄩˋ ㄎㄢˋ ˙ㄍㄜ ㄆㄥˊ ㄧㄡˇ。

(A) ㄒㄧㄤˋ

(B) ㄘㄨㄥˊ

(C) ㄍㄥˋ

(D) ㄉㄟˇ

43. Qùnián tā _____ xiěle sān fēng xìn gěi wǒ.

(A) céng

(B) méi

(C) sòng

(D) huì

43. ㄑㄩˋ ㄋㄧㄢˊ ㄊㄚ ______ ㄒㄧㄝˇ ˙ㄌㄜ ㄙㄢ ㄈㄥ ㄒㄧㄣˋ ㄍㄟˇ ㄨㄛˇ。

(A) ㄘㄥˊ

(B) ㄇㄟˊ

(C) ㄙㄨㄥˋ

(D) ㄏㄨㄟˋ

44. Zhèi jiān fángjiān shì _____ wèi nǐ yùbèi de.

(A) tèbié

(B) bǐjiào

(C) xiāngdāng

(D) fēicháng

44. ㄓㄟˋ ㄐㄧㄢ ㄈㄤˊ ㄐㄧㄢ ㄕˋ ______ ㄨㄟˋ ㄋㄧˇ ㄩˋ ㄅㄟˋ ˙ㄉㄜ。

(A) ㄊㄜˋ ㄅㄧㄝˊ

(B) ㄅㄧˇ ㄐㄧㄠˇ

(C) ㄒㄧㄤ ㄉㄤ

(D) ㄈㄟ ㄔㄤˊ

45. Nèi fèn bàogào _____ qù le.

(A) gěi jiào jiè tóngshì

(B) jiào tóngshì gěi jiè

(C) jiè tóngshì jiào gěi

(D) tóngshì jiè gěi jiào

45. ㄋㄟˋ ㄈㄣˋ ㄅㄠˋ ㄍㄠˋ ______ ㄑㄩˋ ˙ㄌㄜ。

(A) ㄍㄟˇ ㄐㄧㄠˋ ㄐㄧㄝˋ ㄊㄨㄥˊ ㄕˋ

(B) ㄐㄧㄠˋ ㄊㄨㄥˊ ㄕˋ ㄍㄟˇ ㄐㄧㄝˋ

(C) ㄐㄧㄝˋ ㄊㄨㄥˊ ㄕˋ ㄐㄧㄠˋ ㄍㄟˇ

(D) ㄊㄨㄥˊ ㄕˋ ㄐㄧㄝˋ ㄍㄟˇ ㄐㄧㄠˋ

46. 學費大概要三千塊錢，可是吃跟住並不包括 _____ 。
(A) 另外
(B) 在內
(C) 以上
(D) 其中

47. 他最喜歡 _____ 別人的毛病。
(A) 拿
(B) 放
(C) 做
(D) 挑

48. 雖然你不想去，可是 _____ 得去。
(A) 已
(B) 剛
(C) 也
(D) 連

49. 他想讀幾本 _____ 中國歷史的書。
(A) 對於
(B) 關於
(C) 由於
(D) 至於

50. 前天他剛從英國回美國來，明天 _____ 要去英國了。
(A) 還
(B) 再
(C) 才
(D) 又

46. 学费大概要三千块钱，可是吃跟住并不包括 _____ 。
(A) 另外
(B) 在内
(C) 以上
(D) 其中

47. 他最喜欢 _____ 别人的毛病。
(A) 拿
(B) 放
(C) 做
(D) 挑

48. 虽然你不想去，可是 _____ 得去。
(A) 已
(B) 刚
(C) 也
(D) 连

49. 他想读几本 _____ 中国历史的书。
(A) 对于
(B) 关于
(C) 由于
(D) 至于

50. 前天他刚从英国回美国来，明天 _____ 要去英国了。
(A) 还
(B) 再
(C) 才
(D) 又

GO ON TO THE NEXT PAGE

46. Xuéfèi dàgài yào sānqiān kuài qián, kěshì chī gēn zhù bìng bù bāokuò _____ .
    (A) lìngwài
    (B) zài nèi
    (C) yǐshàng
    (D) qízhōng

46. ㄒㄩㄝˊ ㄈㄟˋ ㄉㄚˋ ㄍㄞˋ ㄧㄠˋ ㄙㄢ ㄑㄧㄢ ㄎㄨㄞˋ ㄑㄧㄢˊ，ㄎㄜˇ ㄕˋ ㄔ ㄍㄣ ㄓㄨˋ ㄅㄧㄥˋ ㄅㄨˋ ㄅㄠ ㄎㄨㄛˋ _____ 。
    (A) ㄌㄧㄥˋ ㄨㄞˋ
    (B) ㄗㄞˋ ㄋㄟˋ
    (C) ㄧˇ ㄕㄤˋ
    (D) ㄑㄧˊ ㄓㄨㄥ

47. Tā zuì xǐhuan _____ biéren de máobing.
    (A) ná
    (B) fàng
    (C) zuò
    (D) tiāo

47. ㄊㄚ ㄗㄨㄟˋ ㄒㄧˇ ㄏㄨㄢ _____ ㄅㄧㄝˊ ㄖㄣˊ ˙ㄉㄜ ㄇㄠˊ ˙ㄅㄧㄥ。
    (A) ㄋㄚˊ
    (B) ㄈㄤˋ
    (C) ㄗㄨㄛˋ
    (D) ㄊㄧㄠ

48. Suīrán nǐ bù xiǎng qù, kěshì _____ děi qù.
    (A) yǐ
    (B) gāng
    (C) yě
    (D) lián

48. ㄙㄨㄟ ㄖㄢˊ ㄋㄧˇ ㄅㄨˋ ㄒㄧㄤˇ ㄑㄩˋ，ㄎㄜˇ ㄕˋ _____ ㄉㄟˇ ㄑㄩˋ。
    (A) ㄧˇ
    (B) ㄍㄤ
    (C) ㄧㄝˇ
    (D) ㄌㄧㄢˊ

49. Tā xiǎng dú jǐ běn _____ Zhōngguó lìshǐ de shū.
    (A) duìyú
    (B) guānyú
    (C) yóuyú
    (D) zhìyú

49. ㄊㄚ ㄒㄧㄤˇ ㄉㄨˊ ㄐㄧˇ ㄅㄣˇ _____ ㄓㄨㄥ ㄍㄨㄛˊ ㄌㄧˋ ㄕˇ ˙ㄉㄜ ㄕㄨ。
    (A) ㄉㄨㄟˋ ㄩˊ
    (B) ㄍㄨㄢ ㄩˊ
    (C) ㄧㄡˊ ㄩˊ
    (D) ㄓˋ ㄩˊ

50. Qiántiān tā gāng cóng Yīngguó huí Měiguó lái, míngtiān _____ yào qù Yīngguó le.
    (A) hái
    (B) zài
    (C) cái
    (D) yòu

50. ㄑㄧㄢˊ ㄊㄧㄢ ㄊㄚ ㄍㄤ ㄘㄨㄥˊ ㄧㄥ ㄍㄨㄛˊ ㄏㄨㄟˊ ㄇㄟˇ ㄍㄨㄛˊ ㄌㄞˊ，ㄇㄧㄥˊ ㄊㄧㄢ _____ ㄧㄠˋ ㄑㄩˋ ㄧㄥ ㄍㄨㄛˊ ˙ㄌㄜ。
    (A) ㄏㄞˊ
    (B) ㄗㄞˋ
    (C) ㄘㄞˊ
    (D) ㄧㄡˋ

GO ON TO THE NEXT PAGE

CHINESE TEST WITH LISTENING—*Continued*

51. 報紙 _____ 風 _____ 吹到地上去了。
(A) 讓 ..... 給
(B) 為 ..... 都
(C) 把 ..... 也
(D) 連 ..... 還

52. 林老師 _____ 放春假的機會，帶學生去了趟中國。
(A) 藉著
(B) 靠著
(C) 按著
(D) 顧著

53. 今天你過生日，我們應該 _____ 吃一頓！
(A) 好
(B) 大
(C) 更
(D) 很

54. 你是不是去年到英國去 _____ ？
(A) 嗎
(B) 吧
(C) 的
(D) 著

55. 你 _____ 給他寫信，不如給他打電話。
(A) 關於
(B) 因而
(C) 與其
(D) 無論

51. 报纸 _____ 风 _____ 吹到地上去了。
(A) 让 ..... 给
(B) 为 ..... 都
(C) 把 ..... 也
(D) 连 ..... 还

52. 林老师 _____ 放春假的机会，带学生去了趟中国。
(A) 借着
(B) 靠着
(C) 按着
(D) 顾着

53. 今天你过生日，我们应该 _____ 吃一顿！
(A) 好
(B) 大
(C) 更
(D) 很

54. 你是不是去年到英国去 _____ ？
(A) 吗
(B) 吧
(C) 的
(D) 着

55. 你 _____ 给他写信，不如给他打电话。
(A) 关于
(B) 因而
(C) 与其
(D) 无论

GO ON TO THE NEXT PAGE

51. Bàozhǐ _____ fēng _____ chuī dào dìshang qù le.
    (A) ràng ..... gěi
    (B) wèi ..... dōu
    (C) bǎ ..... yě
    (D) lián ..... hái

51. ㄅㄠˋ ㄓˇ _____ ㄈㄥ _____ ㄔㄨㄟ ㄉㄠˋ ㄉㄧˋ ㄕㄤ˙ ㄑㄩˋ ㄌㄜ˙。
    (A) ㄖㄤˋ ..... ㄍㄟˇ
    (B) ㄨㄟˋ ..... ㄉㄡ
    (C) ㄅㄚˇ ..... ㄧㄝˇ
    (D) ㄌㄧㄢˊ ..... ㄏㄞˊ

52. Lín lǎoshī _____ fàng chūnjià de jīhuì, dài xuésheng qù le tàng Zhōngguó.
    (A) jièzhe
    (B) kàozhe
    (C) ànzhe
    (D) gùzhe

52. ㄌㄧㄣˊ ㄌㄠˇ ㄕ _____ ㄈㄤˋ ㄔㄨㄣ ㄐㄧㄚˋ ㄉㄜ˙ ㄐㄧ ㄏㄨㄟˋ，ㄉㄞˋ ㄒㄩㄝˊ ㄕㄥ˙ ㄑㄩˋ ㄌㄜ˙ ㄊㄤˋ ㄓㄨㄥ ㄍㄨㄛˊ。
    (A) ㄐㄧㄝˋ ㄓㄜ˙
    (B) ㄎㄠˋ ㄓㄜ˙
    (C) ㄢˋ ㄓㄜ˙
    (D) ㄍㄨˋ ㄓㄜ˙

53. Jīntiān nǐ guò shēngri, wǒmen yīnggāi _____ chī yí dùn!
    (A) hǎo
    (B) dà
    (C) gèng
    (D) hěn

53. ㄐㄧㄣ ㄊㄧㄢ ㄋㄧˇ ㄍㄨㄛˋ ㄕㄥ ㄖˋ，ㄨㄛˇ ㄇㄣ˙ ㄧㄥ ㄍㄞ _____ ㄔ ㄧˊ ㄉㄨㄣˋ！
    (A) ㄏㄠˇ
    (B) ㄉㄚˋ
    (C) ㄍㄥˋ
    (D) ㄏㄣˇ

54. Nǐ shì bú shì qùnián dào Yīngguó qù _____ ?
    (A) ma
    (B) ba
    (C) de
    (D) zhe

54. ㄋㄧˇ ㄕˋ ㄅㄨˊ ㄕˋ ㄑㄩˋ ㄋㄧㄢˊ ㄉㄠˋ ㄧㄥ ㄍㄨㄛˊ ㄑㄩˋ _____ ?
    (A) ㄇㄚ˙
    (B) ㄅㄚ˙
    (C) ㄉㄜ˙
    (D) ㄓㄜ˙

55. Nǐ _____ gěi tā xiě xìn, bùrú gěi tā dǎ diànhuà.
    (A) guānyú
    (B) yīn'ér
    (C) yǔqí
    (D) wúlùn

55. ㄋㄧˇ _____ ㄍㄟˇ ㄊㄚ ㄒㄧㄝˇ ㄒㄧㄣˋ，ㄅㄨˋ ㄖㄨˊ ㄍㄟˇ ㄊㄚ ㄉㄚˇ ㄉㄧㄢˋ ㄏㄨㄚˋ。
    (A) ㄍㄨㄢ ㄩˊ
    (B) ㄧㄣ ㄦˊ
    (C) ㄩˇ ㄑㄧˊ
    (D) ㄨˊ ㄌㄨㄣˋ

END OF SECTION II.
GO ON TO SECTION III.

SECTION III
READING COMPREHENSION

Suggested time—25 minutes
Questions 56-85

WHEN YOU BEGIN THIS SECTION, BE SURE THAT YOU MARK YOUR ANSWER TO THE FIRST QUESTION BY FILLING IN ONE OF THE CIRCLES NEXT TO NUMBER 56 ON YOUR ANSWER SHEET.

Directions: Read the following texts carefully for comprehension. Each is followed by one or more questions or incomplete statements. Select the answer or completion that is best according to the text and fill in the corresponding circle on your answer sheet. There is no example for this section.

This section of the test is presented in two writing systems: traditional characters and simplified characters. IT IS RECOMMENDED THAT YOU CHOOSE THE WRITING SYSTEM WITH WHICH YOU ARE MORE FAMILIAR AND **READ ONLY THAT VERSION** AS YOU WORK THROUGH THIS SECTION OF THE TEST.

Question 56

大華電影院　購票須知

十二歲以下兒童，
必須由家長陪同入場。
凡超過二十人以上的團體，
必須以電話預訂門票。

大华电影院　购票须知

十二岁以下儿童，
必须由家长陪同入场。
凡超过二十人以上的团体，
必须以电话预订门票。

56. What information is given?

(A) Title of the movie being shown
(B) Date and time of the show
(C) Procedure for requesting a refund
(D) Procedure for purchasing group tickets

GO ON TO THE NEXT PAGE

Question 57

食品 八折優待 星期一、二、三、四	食品 八折优待 星期一、二、三、四

57. On what day can the coupon be used?

(A) Tuesday
(B) Friday
(C) Saturday
(D) Sunday

Questions 58-59

愛用者請注意 (一) 本品藥效可維持十二小時，一天只須服用兩次，每次三粒。 (二) 只有六粒盒裝，盒上印有康明400感冒藥，才是眞品。	爱用者请注意 (一) 本品药效可维持十二小时，一天只须服用两次，每次三粒。 (二) 只有六粒盒装，盒上印有康明400感冒药，才是真品。

58. Where would this message most likely be found?

(A) On a bulletin board
(B) On a medicine label
(C) In an appliance manual
(D) In a cookbook

59. How often should this product be used?

(A) Twice each month
(B) Every three weeks
(C) Once a day
(D) Every twelve hours

GO ON TO THE NEXT PAGE

Questions 60-61

黄教授喜歡自己一個人住在山上。他寫信告訴我他住的地方不但風景好而且空氣新鮮。家裏有電話也有電視，只是交通不太方便。每天早上他坐六點半的公共汽車到山脚下的學校去上班。下午下班以後，再走四十分鐘的路回家。因爲山上沒有河也沒有湖，所以喝的水都得從山下運上去，因此他每個月最大的開支就是水費。

黄教授喜欢自己一个人住在山上。他写信告诉我他住的地方不但风景好而且空气新鲜。家里有电话也有电视，只是交通不太方便。每天早上他坐六点半的公共汽车到山脚下的学校去上班。下午下班以后，再走四十分钟的路回家。因为山上没有河也没有湖，所以喝的水都得从山下运上去，因此他每个月最大的开支就是水费。

60. What does Professor Huang like about the place where he lives?

(A) Fresh air
(B) Convenient location
(C) Lake-front view
(D) Friendly neighbors

61. According to the passage, which of the following is true about Professor Huang?

(A) He lives with his family.
(B) He takes the bus to work every day.
(C) He likes to go swimming in the lake.
(D) He walks to school in the morning.

Question 62

【本報專訊】 今年感恩節前後出入機場的旅客特別多，停車位更是難找。市政府特別提醒市民，不要開車去機場。最好的方式是坐地鐵到體育館，然後在體育館前面乘公共汽車前往。

【本报专讯】 今年感恩节前后出入机场的旅客特别多，停车位更是难找。市政府特别提醒市民，不要开车去机场。最好的方式是坐地铁到体育馆，然后在体育馆前面乘公共汽车前往。

62. The passage recommends boarding a bus in front of the

(A) sports arena
(B) city hall
(C) hotel parking lot
(D) airport

GO ON TO THE NEXT PAGE

Question 63

金　園	金　园
新張營業	新张营业
菜式任點，附湯、水果	菜式任点，附汤、水果

63. What is this advertisement about?

(A) A grand opening
(B) A special rate
(C) A new location
(D) An end-of-season sale

Questions 64-66

盛暑之下，天氣炎熱，不宜大魚大肉。在此介紹一道簡易涼拌黃瓜。這道小菜不但味美，而且消暑。

材料：　小黃瓜四條，切薄片加鹽。約半小時後倒去所出汁水。

調味料：加入白沙糖和醋，拌勻即成。

盛暑之下，天气炎热，不宜大鱼大肉。在此介绍一道简易凉拌黄瓜。这道小菜不但味美，而且消暑。

材料：　小黄瓜四条，切薄片加盐。约半小时后倒去所出汁水。

调味料：加入白沙糖和醋，拌匀即成。

64. This excerpt is most likely from a

(A) fast-food advertisement
(B) restaurant review
(C) newspaper food column
(D) room-service menu

65. The featured item is a

(A) beverage
(B) vegetable dish
(C) main course
(D) dessert

66. Which of the following is true of the item described in the excerpt?

(A) It contains various herbs and spices.
(B) It is quite expensive.
(C) It tastes best when served hot.
(D) It is a simple, easily prepared dish.

GO ON TO THE NEXT PAGE

Question 67

一律八折　　　　一律八折

67. What information is given in the sign?

(A) An exchange rate
(B) A dosage
(C) A discount
(D) A time period

Question 68

北京新街口外大街二十五號 王鐵群先生收 上海南京路六十三號　李寄	北京新街口外大街二十五号 王铁群先生收 上海南京路六十三号　李寄

68. Who sent this letter?

(A) A student
(B) A manager
(C) A resident of Shanghai
(D) A resident of Beijing

GO ON TO THE NEXT PAGE

Questions 69-71

紅紅是我的小學同學也是鄰居。她的父親開了一家照相館，離我父親的理髮店不遠。小時候我們常常去找她父親給我們照相。紅紅有個當老師的哥哥，他喜歡到處拍風景照，可是技術不太好。照出來的照片，不是距離不對，就是光線太暗。紅紅常說她哥哥沒有她跟她父親那麼有藝術眼光。

红红是我的小学同学也是邻居。她的父亲开了一家照相馆，离我父亲的理发店不远。小时候我们常常去找她父亲给我们照相。红红有个当老师的哥哥，他喜欢到处拍风景照，可是技术不太好。照出来的照片，不是距离不对，就是光线太暗。红红常说她哥哥没有她跟她父亲那么有艺术眼光。

69. What does Honghong's brother like to do?
   (A) Take pictures of scenery
   (B) Design new hairstyles
   (C) Teach Honghong to read
   (D) Repair neighbors' appliances

70. What is the occupation of Honghong's father?
   (A) Hairdresser
   (B) Photographer
   (C) Technician
   (D) Teacher

71. What can be concluded about Honghong?
   (A) She very much enjoys nature photography.
   (B) She wants to become a hair designer.
   (C) She does not consider her brother an artist.
   (D) She does not like to have her picture taken.

Question 72

文化學院留學生聯誼會，為歡迎一九九五年春季漢語進修班的外國學生，特訂於一月三十日晚上六時在廣信大樓七號大廳舉行招待會。

邀請本學院各系教職員工，

踴躍出席。

文化学院留学生联谊会，为欢迎一九九五年春季汉语进修班的外国学生，特订于一月三十日晚上六时在广信大楼七号大厅举行招待会。

邀请本学院各系教职员工，

踊跃出席。

72. This is an invitation to a
   (A) spring festival
   (B) welcoming reception
   (C) class reunion
   (D) student orientation

GO ON TO THE NEXT PAGE

Question 73

自然博物馆
開放時間： 星期二至星期日 上午九點至下午七點 午飯時間照常開放
短片放映時間：週六下午三點至四點

自然博物馆
开放时间： 星期二至星期日 上午九点至下午七点 午饭时间照常开放
短片放映时间：周六下午三点至四点

73. When is this place closed?

(A) Saturday afternoon
(B) Every Monday
(C) During lunchtime
(D) From 3 P.M. to 4 P.M.

Questions 74-75

《黄河大合唱》是許多中國人所喜愛的一首歌曲。一九三八年十一月，有一位姓張的詩人，搭船經過黃河。他看到黃河的滾滾流水和船夫們跟黃河急流的搏鬥，得到了啓發。後來他和一位作曲家談起黃河的壯觀景象，作曲家也非常感動。兩個人用了五、六天的時間，合作寫出了《黄河大合唱》這首歌。

《黄河大合唱》是许多中国人所喜爱的一首歌曲。一九三八年十一月，有一位姓张的诗人，搭船经过黄河。他看到黄河的滚滚流水和船夫们跟黄河急流的搏斗，得到了启发。后来他和一位作曲家谈起黄河的壮观景象，作曲家也非常感动。两个人用了五、六天的时间，合作写出了《黄河大合唱》这首歌。

74. What inspired Mr. Zhang?

(A) Watching a traditional Chinese dance
(B) Hearing a famous singer
(C) Seeing the view from a boat
(D) Reading a work by a young poet

75. How long did the two people take to complete their work?

(A) Three to four hours
(B) Five to six days
(C) Two to three weeks
(D) One to two months

GO ON TO THE NEXT PAGE

Questions 76-77

日本餐馆
本州中部請有經驗營業經理
週六日有休假並提供宿舍
有意者請電 555-7729

日本餐馆
本州中部请有经验营业经理
周六日有休假并提供宿舍
有意者请电 555-7729

76. What position is being advertised?
    (A) Salesperson
    (B) Research librarian
    (C) Restaurant manager
    (D) Dietitian

77. Which of the following is required of the applicant?
    (A) Be a college graduate
    (B) Be experienced
    (C) Be willing to work long hours
    (D) Be fluent in Japanese

Questions 78-79

劉立最喜歡他的爺爺。因爲小時候爸爸媽媽白天去上班，只有爺爺在家照顧他。每天早上爺爺都在後院打太極拳。劉立以爲爺爺在跳舞，所以就一邊唱歌，一邊跟爺爺學。可是爺爺打拳的時候，總是不理他，也不跟他說話。劉立長大以後才明白，原來打太極拳的時候，非得集中精神不可。劉立還記得爺爺下午午睡起來以後，一定先喝杯熱茶，然後看報紙。有時候晚上爺爺也跟劉立一起看電視上的體育節目。

刘立最喜欢他的爷爷。因为小时候爸爸妈妈白天去上班，只有爷爷在家照顾他。每天早上爷爷都在后院打太极拳。刘立以为爷爷在跳舞，所以就一边唱歌，一边跟爷爷学。可是爷爷打拳的时候，总是不理他，也不跟他说话。刘立长大以后才明白，原来打太极拳的时候，非得集中精神不可。刘立还记得爷爷下午午睡起来以后，一定先喝杯热茶，然后看报纸。有时候晚上爷爷也跟刘立一起看电视上的体育节目。

78. Why is Liu Li especially fond of his grandfather?
    (A) He taught Liu Li how to read.
    (B) He was a kung fu master.
    (C) He knew many folk songs.
    (D) He took care of Liu Li as a child.

79. What did Liu Li's grandfather usually do in the afternoon?
    (A) Watch television
    (B) Read the newspaper
    (C) Do stretching exercises
    (D) Go for a walk

GO ON TO THE NEXT PAGE

Question 80

有人說可以根據以下情況來預測天氣：	有人说可以根据以下情况来预测天气：
一．冬天吹東風時會下雨，吹西風時是好天。	一．冬天吹东风时会下雨，吹西风时是好天。
二．下雪的第二天會是好天。	二．下雪的第二天会是好天。
三．山看起來很近的時候，第二天會下雨。	三．山看起来很近的时候，第二天会下雨。
四．煙一直往上飄時，會是好天。	四．烟一直往上飘时，会是好天。

80. According to the passage, which of the following is supposed to predict fair weather?

(A) A west wind blowing in the summer
(B) Smoke rising straight up into the sky
(C) Snow melting when it touches the ground
(D) Mountains appearing to be closer than they really are

Questions 81-82

實用中級英語會話	实用中级英语会话
□ 全套九卷錄音帶包括：發音練習專輯、生字詞匯表和會話朗讀。	□ 全套九卷录音带包括：发音练习专辑、生字词汇表和会话朗读。
□ 介紹口語語法及基本句型。	□ 介绍口语语法及基本句型。
□ 中級會話十課包括：家庭、職業、天氣、打電話、上餐館、去銀行、買東西、看醫生、邀請朋友和找工作。	□ 中级会话十课包括：家庭、职业、天气、打电话、上餐馆、去银行、买东西、看医生、邀请朋友和找工作。

81. What does this flyer advertise?

(A) A class in business English
(B) A new method for teaching conversational English
(C) A video for beginning English learners
(D) An audiocassette series for learning English

82. Which of the following is NOT included?

(A) Pronunciation drills
(B) Sentence patterns
(C) Writing exercises
(D) A vocabulary list

GO ON TO THE NEXT PAGE

Questions 83-85

人人書局與您共渡中秋節	人人书局与您共渡中秋节
電腦書籍、禮品八折優待 文具半價	电脑书籍、礼品八折优待 文具半价
優待時間：本月十九日至二十一日	优待时间：本月十九日至二十一日

83. For which of the following is the largest discount offered?

(A) Books
(B) Gift items
(C) Computers
(D) Stationery

84. What is the occasion for the sale?

(A) A grand opening
(B) An anniversary
(C) A holiday
(D) A closeout

85. How long does the sale last?

(A) One day
(B) Three days
(C) A week
(D) A month

END OF SECTION III.

STOP

IF YOU FINISH BEFORE TIME IS CALLED, YOU MAY CHECK YOUR WORK ON SECTIONS II AND III. DO NOT TURN TO ANY OTHER TEST IN THIS BOOK.

How to Score the SAT Subject Test in Chinese with Listening

When you take an actual SAT Subject Test in Chinese with Listening, you receive an overall composite score as well as three subscores: one for the listening section, one for the reading section, and one for the usage section.

The listening, reading, and usage scores are reported on the College Board's 20–80 scale. However the composite score, which is the most significant of the scores reported to the colleges you specify, is in the form of the College Board's 200–800 scale.

Worksheet 1. Finding Your Raw Listening Subscore

STEP 1: Table A lists the correct answers for all the questions on the Subject Test in Chinese with Listening that is reproduced in this book. It also serves as a worksheet for you to calculate your raw Listening subscore.

- Compare your answers with those given in the table.
- Put a check in the column marked "Right" if your answer is correct.
- Put a check in the column marked "Wrong" if your answer is incorrect.
- Leave both columns blank if you omitted the question.

STEP 2: Count the number of right answers for questions 1–19.

Enter the total here: ________________

STEP 3: Count the number of wrong answers for questions 1–19.

Enter the total here: ________________

STEP 4: Multiply the number of wrong answers from Step 3 by .500.

Enter the product here: ________________

STEP 5: Subtract the result obtained in Step 4 from the total you obtained in Step 2.

Enter the result here: ________________

STEP 6: Count the number of right answers for questions 20–30.

Enter the total here: ________________

STEP 7: Count the number of wrong answers for questions 20–30.

Enter the total here: ________________

STEP 8: Multiply the number of wrong answers from Step 7 by .333.

Enter the product here: ________________

STEP 9: Subtract the result obtained in Step 8 from the total you obtained in Step 6.

Enter the result here: ________________

STEP 10: Add the result obtained in Step 5 to the result obtained in Step 9.

Enter the sum here: ____________________

STEP 11: Round the number obtained in Step 10 to the nearest whole number.

Enter the result here: ____________________

The number you obtained in Step 11 is your raw Listening subscore.

Worksheet 2. Finding Your Raw Reading Subscore

STEP 1: Table A lists the correct answers for all the questions on the Subject Test in Chinese with Listening that is reproduced in this book. It also serves as a worksheet for you to calculate your raw Reading subscore.

STEP 2: Count the number of right answers for questions 56–85.

Enter the total here: ________________

STEP 3: Count the number of wrong answers for questions 56–85.

Enter the total here: ________________

STEP 4: Multiply the number of wrong answers by .333.

Enter the product here: ______________

STEP 5: Subtract the result obtained in Step 4 from the total you obtained in Step 2.

Enter the result here: _______________

STEP 6: Round the number obtained in Step 5 to the nearest whole number.

Enter the result here: _______________

The number you obtained in Step 6 is your raw Reading subscore.

Worksheet 3. Finding Your Raw Usage Subscore

STEP 1: Table A lists the correct answers for all the questions on the Subject Test in Chinese with Listening that is reproduced in this book. It also serves as a worksheet for you to calculate your raw Usage subscore.

STEP 2: Count the number of right answers for questions 31–55.

Enter the total here: ____________________

STEP 3: Count the number of wrong answers for questions 31–55.

Enter the total here: ____________________

STEP 4: Multiply the number of wrong answers by .333.

Enter the product here: ________________

STEP 5: Subtract the result obtained in Step 4 from the total you obtained in Step 2.

Enter the result here: __________________

STEP 6: Round the number obtained in Step 5 to the nearest whole number.

Enter the result here: __________________

The number you obtained in Step 6 is your raw Usage subscore.

Worksheet 4. Finding Your Raw Composite Score

STEP 1: Enter your unrounded raw Listening subscore from Step 10 of Worksheet 1.

Enter the result here: ____________________

STEP 2: Enter your unrounded raw Reading subscore from Step 5 of Worksheet 2.

Enter the result here: ____________________

STEP 3: Enter your unrounded raw Usage subscore from Step 5 of Worksheet 3.

Enter the result here: ____________________

STEP 4: Add the results obtained in Steps 1, 2, and 3.

Enter the sum here: ____________________

STEP 5: Round the number obtained in Step 4 to the nearest whole number.

Enter the result here: ____________________

The number you obtained in Step 5 is your raw composite score.

Table A

Answers to the Subject Test in Chinese with Listening, Form 3ZLC, and Percentage of Students Answering Each Question Correctly									
Question Number	Correct Answer	Right	Wrong	Percentage of Students Answering the Question Correctly*	Question Number	Correct Answer	Right	Wrong	Percentage of Students Answering the Question Correctly*
1	B			99	33	D			98
2	C			98	34	A			98
3	C			99	35	C			96
4	C			98	36	B			97
5	A			98	37	D			98
6	C			93	38	D			97
7	A			85	39	B			94
8	C			90	40	A			91
9	C			94	41	B			95
10	C			98	42	D			79
11	A			98	43	A			69
12	B			99	44	A			82
13	A			98	45	B			60
14	C			97	46	B			69
15	C			94	47	D			70
16	A			98	48	C			78
17	B			96	49	B			78
18	A			67	50	D			79
19	A			93	51	A			72
20	B			82	52	A			42
21	D			95	53	B			70
22	D			97	54	C			65
23	C			99	55	C			37
24	D			98	56	D			92
25	A			98	57	A			97
26	C			97	58	B			92
27	B			69	59	D			91
28	C			69	60	A			91
29	A			64	61	B			94
30	D			79	62	A			67
31	C			98	63	A			80
32	B			96	64	C			67

Table A continued on next page

Table A continued from previous page

Question Number	Correct Answer	Right	Wrong	Percentage of Students Answering the Question Correctly*	Question Number	Correct Answer	Right	Wrong	Percentage of Students Answering the Question Correctly*
65	B			75	76	C			79
66	D			71	77	B			71
67	C			70	78	D			83
68	C			64	79	B			79
69	A			92	80	B			70
70	B			82	81	D			55
71	C			68	82	C			68
72	B			45	83	D			59
73	B			70	84	C			83
74	C			78	85	B			94
75	B			90					

* These percentages are based on an analysis of the answer sheets of a representative sample of 1,363 students who took the original form of this test in November 2003, and whose mean composite score was 723. They may be used as an indication of the relative difficulty of a particular question. Each percentage may also be used to predict the likelihood that a typical SAT Subject Test in Chinese with Listening candidate will answer that question correctly on this edition of the test.

Finding Your Scaled Score

When you take SAT Subject Tests, the scores sent to the colleges you specify are reported on the College Board scale, which ranges from 200–800. Subscores are reported on a scale which ranges from 20–80. You can convert your practice test scores to scaled scores by using Tables B, C, D and E. To find your scaled score, locate your raw score in the left-hand column of the table; the corresponding score in the right-hand column is your scaled score. For example, a raw score of 59 on this particular edition of the Subject Test in Chinese with Listening corresponds to a scaled composite score of 690.

Raw scores are converted to scaled scores to ensure that a score earned on any one edition of a particular Subject Test is comparable to the same scaled score earned on any other edition of the same Subject Test. Because some editions of the tests may be slightly easier or more difficult than others, College Board scaled scores are adjusted so that they indicate the same level of performance regardless of the edition of the test taken and the ability of the group that takes it. Thus, for example, a score of 400 on one edition of a test taken at a particular administration indicates the same level of achievement as a score of 400 on a different edition of the test taken at a different administration.

When you take the SAT Subject Tests during a national administration, your scores are likely to differ somewhat from the scores you obtain on the tests in this book. People perform at different levels at different times for reasons unrelated to the tests themselves. The precision of any test is also limited because it represents only a sample of all the possible questions that could be asked.

Your scaled composite score from Table B is ____________________.

Your scaled listening score from Table C is ____________________.

Your scaled reading score from Table D is ____________________.

Your scaled usage score from Table E is ____________________.

Table B

Scaled Score Conversion Table Subject Test in Chinese with Listening Composite Score (Form 3ZLC)					
Raw Score	Scaled Score	Raw Score	Scaled Score	Raw Score	Scaled Score
85	800	47	630	9	430
84	800	46	620	8	420
83	800	45	620	7	420
82	800	44	610	6	410
81	800	43	610	5	410
80	800	42	600	4	400
79	790	41	590	3	400
78	790	40	590	2	390
77	780	39	580	1	390
76	780	38	580	0	380
75	770	37	570	-1	380
74	770	36	570	-2	370
73	760	35	560	-3	370
72	750	34	560	-4	360
71	750	33	550	-5	360
70	740	32	550	-6	350
69	740	31	540	-7	350
68	730	30	540	-8	340
67	730	29	530	-9	340
66	720	28	530	-10	330
65	720	27	520	-11	330
64	710	26	520	-12	320
63	710	25	510	-13	320
62	700	24	510	-14	310
61	700	23	500	-15	310
60	690	22	500	-16	300
59	690	21	490	-17	290
58	680	20	490	-18	290
57	680	19	480	-19	280
56	670	18	480	-20	280
55	670	17	470	-21	270
54	660	16	470	-22	270
53	660	15	460	-23	260
52	650	14	460	-24	260
51	650	13	450	-25	250
50	640	12	440	-26	250
49	640	11	440	-27	240
48	630	10	430	-28	240
				-29	230
				-30	230
				-31	220

Table C

Scaled Score Conversion Table Subject Test in Chinese with Listening Listening Subscore (Form 3ZLC)					
Raw Score	Scaled Score	Raw Score	Scaled Score	Raw Score	Scaled Score
30	80	15	54	0	42
29	78	14	53	-1	41
28	74	13	53	-2	40
27	71	12	52	-3	39
26	69	11	51	-4	38
25	66	10	51	-5	37
24	64	9	50	-6	35
23	63	8	49	-7	34
22	61	7	49	-8	33
21	60	6	48	-9	32
20	59	5	47	-10	31
19	58	4	46	-11	30
18	57	3	45	-12	29
17	56	2	44	-13	28
16	55	1	43		

Table D

Scaled Score Conversion Table Subject Test in Chinese with Listening Reading Subscore (Form 3ZLC)					
Raw Score	Scaled Score	Raw Score	Scaled Score	Raw Score	Scaled Score
30	80	16	68	2	50
29	80	15	68	1	47
28	79	14	67	0	45
27	78	13	66	-1	44
26	77	12	65	-2	42
25	76	11	64	-3	41
24	75	10	63	-4	41
23	75	9	62	-5	40
22	74	8	61	-6	40
21	73	7	59	-7	40
20	72	6	58	-8	39
19	71	5	56	-9	39
18	70	4	54	-10	38
17	69	3	52		

Table E

Scaled Score Conversion Table Subject Test in Chinese with Listening Usage Subscore (Form 3ZLC)					
Raw Score	Scaled Score	Raw Score	Scaled Score	Raw Score	Scaled Score
25	80	14	65	3	49
24	80	13	64	2	47
23	79	12	62	1	46
22	77	11	61	0	44
21	76	10	59	-1	43
20	74	9	58	-2	41
19	73	8	56	-3	40
18	71	7	55	-4	38
17	70	6	53	-5	37
16	68	5	52	-6	35
15	67	4	50	-7	34
				-8	32

How Did You Do on the Subject Test in Chinese with Listening?

After you score your test and analyze your performance, think about the following questions:

Did you run out of time before reaching the end of the test?

If so, you may need to pace yourself better. For example, maybe you spent too much time on one or two hard questions. A better approach might be to skip the ones you can't answer right away and try answering all the questions that remain on the test. Then if there's time, go back to the questions you skipped.

Did you take a long time reading the directions?

You will save time when you take the test by learning the directions to the Subject Test in Chinese with Listening ahead of time. Each minute you spend reading directions during the test is a minute that you could use to answer questions.

How did you handle questions you were unsure of?

If you were able to eliminate one or more of the answer choices as wrong and guess from the remaining ones, your approach probably worked to your advantage. On the other hand, making haphazard guesses or omitting questions without trying to eliminate choices could cost you valuable points.

How difficult were the questions for you compared with other students who took the test?

Table A shows you how difficult the multiple-choice questions were for the group of students who took this test during its national administration. The right-hand column gives the percentage of students that answered each question correctly.

A question answered correctly by almost everyone in the group is obviously an easier question. For example, 98 percent of the students answered question 4 correctly. But only 37 percent answered question 55 correctly.

Keep in mind that these percentages are based on just one group of students. They would probably be different with another group of students taking the test.

If you missed several easier questions, go back and try to find out why: Did the questions cover material you haven't yet reviewed? Did you misunderstand the directions?

Chapter 9

French

Purpose

There are two Subject Tests in French: French and French with Listening. Both tests evaluate your reading skills through precision of vocabulary, structure use, and comprehension of a variety of texts. The Subject Test in French with Listening measures your ability to understand spoken as well as written French.

Format

- The Subject Test in French takes one hour and includes 85 multiple-choice questions.
- The Subject Test in French with Listening also takes one hour, with about 20 minutes for listening questions and 40 minutes for reading questions. There are 85 to 90 multiple-choice listening and reading questions.

Content

Both tests evaluate your reading ability in three areas through a variety of questions requiring a wide-ranging knowledge of French:

Precision of Vocabulary questions test knowledge of words representing different parts of speech and some basic idioms within culturally authentic contexts.

Structure questions measure your ability to select an appropriate word or expression that is grammatically correct within a sentence. One part of the test contains vocabulary and structure questions embedded in longer paragraphs.

Reading comprehension questions test your understanding of such points as main and supporting ideas, themes, and setting of a passage. Selections are drawn from fiction, essays, historical works, newspaper and magazine articles, or everyday materials such as advertisements, timetables, forms, and tickets.

French	
Skills Measured	Approximate Percentage of Test
Vocabulary in Context	30
Structure	30–40
Reading Comprehension	30–40

In addition to these reading questions, the Subject Test in French with Listening also measures your ability to understand the spoken language with three types of *listening questions*:

Type One asks you to identify the sentence that most accurately describes what is presented in a picture or a photograph or what someone in the picture or photograph might say.

Type Two tests your ability to answer general content questions based on short dialogues or monologues.

Type Three requires you to answer more specific questions based on longer dialogues or monologues.

French with Listening		
Types of Questions		Approximate Percentage of Test
Listening Section	(20 Minutes)	35
Pictures:	8–12 questions	
Short dialogues:	6–12 questions	
Long dialogues:	10–15 questions	
Reading Section	(40 minutes)	65
Vocabulary:	16–20 questions	
Structure:	16–20 questions	
Reading Comprehension:	20–25 questions	

How to Prepare

Both tests are written to reflect general trends in high school curricula and are independent of particular textbooks or methods of instruction. The French Tests are appropriate for you if you have studied the language for three or four years in high school, or the equivalent; however, if you have two years of strong preparation in French, you are also encouraged to take the tests. Your best preparation for the tests is a gradual development of competence in French over a period of years. Familiarize yourself with the directions in advance. The directions in this book are identical to those that appear on the test.

French with Listening

A practice audio CD is included with this book. A practice CD with different sample questions can be obtained, along with a copy of the *SAT Subject Tests Preparation Booklet,* from your school counselor, or you can access the listening files at www.collegeboard.com. You should also take the practice test included with this book

CD Players

Using CD Players for Language Tests with Listening

Take an acceptable CD player to the test center. Your CD player must be in good working order, so insert fresh batteries on the day before the test. You may bring additional batteries and a backup player to the test center.

Test center staff won't have batteries, CD players, or earphones for your use, so your CD player must be:

- equipped with earphones
- portable (hand-held)
- battery operated
- for your use only. CD players cannot be shared with other test-takers

Note

If the volume on your CD player disturbs other test-takers, the test center supervisor may ask you to move to another seat.

What to do if your CD player malfunctions:

- Raise your hand and tell the test supervisor.
- Switch to backup equipment if you have it and continue the test. If you don't have backup equipment, your score on the Subject Test in French with Listening will be canceled. But scores on other Subject Tests you take that day will still be counted.

What if you receive a defective CD on test day? Raise your hand and ask the supervisor for a replacement.

Scores

For both tests, the total score is reported on the 200-to-800 scale. For the listening test, listening and reading subscores are reported on the 20-to-80 scale.

Sample Reading Questions

Four types of reading questions are used in the French Tests. All questions in the tests are multiple-choice questions in which you must choose the BEST response from the four choices offered.

Your answer sheet has five answer positions marked A, B, C, D, and E, while the questions throughout this test contain only four choices. Be sure NOT to make any marks in column E.

Part A

Directions: This part consists of a number of incomplete statements, each having four suggested completions. Select the most appropriate completion and fill in the corresponding circle on the answer sheet.

1. J'ai perdu mon argent parce qu'il y avait un trou dans la … de mon pantalon.

   (A) manche
   (B) jambe
   (C) poche
   (D) ceinture

Choice (C) is the correct answer because pants have pockets in which people keep money. This question tests vocabulary. You are asked to choose the appropriate noun from the four answer choices. Choices (A) and (D) are not normally used to carry money, and choice (B) refers to a part of the body.

2. Charles avait tant mangé qu'il ne pouvait plus … une bouchée.

   (A) soutenir
   (B) emporter
   (C) avaler
   (D) évaluer

Choice (C) is the correct answer to question 2. In this question, you are asked to find the appropriate verb from the four answer choices. The verb *avaler* is the only option that can be used correctly in connection with *une bouchée*. Choices (A), (B), and (D) are incorrect.

Part B

Directions: Each of the following sentences contains a blank. From the four choices given, select the one that can be inserted in the blank to form a grammatically correct sentence and fill in the corresponding circle on the answer sheet. Choice (A) may consist of dashes that indicate that no insertion is required to form a grammatically correct sentence.

3. Dans sa cuisine, il fallait toujours que tout_____impeccable et reluisant.
   (A) est
   (B) soit
   (C) était
   (D) serait

Choice (B) is the correct answer to question 3 because from the four answer choices *soit* is the correct form of the verb *être*. You need to know that *il fallait que* in the sentence is the past tense of *il faut que*, an impersonal expression that is followed by a verb in the subjunctive. Choices (A), (C), and (D) are forms of *être* in the indicative and are therefore incorrect.

4. _____ est le meilleur joueur de cette équipe?
   (A) Qu'
   (B) Quelle
   (C) Qu'est-ce qu'
   (D) Qui

Choice (D) is the correct answer to question 4. In this question you are asked to choose the appropriate pronoun from the four answer choices. The question mark tells you that the missing pronoun is interrogative and the verb *est* tells you that it is the subject of the sentence. *Qui* is an interrogative pronoun and the subject. Choices (A), (B), and (C) are incorrect because choice (A) cannot be used as a subject, choice (B) is an interrogative adjective, and choice (C) is an interrogative pronoun used as a direct object.

Part C

Directions: The paragraphs below contain blank spaces indicating omissions in the text. For some blanks it is necessary to choose the completion that is most appropriate to the meaning of the passage; for other blanks, to choose the one completion that forms a grammatically correct sentence. In some instances, choice (A) may consist of dashes that indicate that no insertion is required to form a grammatically correct sentence. In each case, indicate your answer by filling in the corresponding circle on the answer sheet. Be sure to read the paragraph completely before answering the questions related to it.

Dès que vous __5__ le temps de prendre contact avec elle, donnez- __6__ un coup de téléphone. Il faut l'avertir que tout soit arrangé et que j'arriverai __7__ vingt.

5. (A) auriez
   (B) ayez
   (C) aurez
   (D) aviez

6. (A) lui
   (B) elle
   (C) vous
   (D) la

7. (A) le
   (B) au
   (C) sur le
   (D) dans le

5. Choice (C) is the correct answer to question 5; *aurez* is the future tense of the verb *avoir.* Expressions such as *quand* and *dès que* are followed by the future in French when the verb in the main clause is in the present tense, as it is here with the present imperative *donnez*. Choice (A) *auriez* is the conditional, choice (B) *ayez* is the present subjunctive, and choice (D) *aviez* is the imperfect.

6. Choice (A) is the correct answer to question 6. What is missing in this part of the sentence is an indirect object pronoun that refers back to *elle* (in *avec elle*). The indirect object indicates the person to whom the *coup de téléphone* should be given. The correct pronoun form in question 6 is *lui*. Choice (B) *elle* is not correct because it is used for the subject of a sentence or after a preposition, choice (C) *vous* is incorrect because something should be given to the woman designated by *elle*, not the person spoken to, and choice (D) *la* is incorrect because it is the direct object pronoun, not the indirect object pronoun.

7. Choice (A) is the correct answer to question 7. When giving arrival and departure dates in French (the sentence here provides an arrival date), the date is preceded by *le* without a preposition. The other suggested answers contain prepositions and are therefore incorrect.

Part D

Directions: Read the following selections carefully for comprehension. Each selection is followed by a number of questions or incomplete statements. Select the completion or answer that is BEST according to the selection and fill in the corresponding circle on the answer sheet.

«Image Center» est l'histoire d'une passion. Hésitant entre l'art et la science, Sylvie Magnus, 24 ans, passe deux ans à l'Ecole des Beaux Arts et complète sa formation à Londres, où elle apprend les applications de l'informatique sur l'image. Et c'est le déclic, peindre avec la lumière, créer des décors magiques pour des défilés de mode, ou des effets spéciaux pour le cinéma, tout la fascine. Une étude de marché lui apprend qu'il n'existe pas d'agence spécialisée dans la conception de ces images. Sylvie décide donc de combler l'espace: elle crée, grâce à un prêt de famille et à des subventions, la première agence européenne conseil en image de synthèse: «Image Center».

8. Qu'est-ce que Sylvie Magnus a étudié après ses deux ans à l'Ecole des Beaux Arts?
   (A) Les arts décoratifs
   (B) La cinématographie
   (C) Les nouvelles technologies
   (D) La médicine

Choice (C) is the correct answer to question 8. The text tells you that Sylvie Magnus studied computer graphics after finishing her fine arts education *(Sylvie Magnus passe deux ans à l'Ecole des Beaux Arts et complète sa formation à Londres, où elle apprend les applications de l'informatique sur l'image*, lines 2–5). The other choices are incorrect.

9. A la ligne 10, «combler l'espace» veut dire
   (A) répondre à un besoin
   (B) louer un bureau
   (C) faire des recherches scientifiques
   (D) faire des subventions

Choice (A) is the correct answer to question 9. The text states that Sylvie Magnus has learned that there was no agency that specialized in computer graphics and decided to create one. The expression does not mean that she rented an office (B), did scientific research (C), or subsidized anything (D). On the contrary, she received a subsidy (line 11).

10. Comment est-ce que Sylvie Magnus a trouvé l'argent pour lancer «Image Center»?
    (A) Elle a travaillé dans un hôpital.
    (B) Elle en a gagné pendant la révolution.
    (C) Elle a organisé des défilés de mode.
    (D) Elle en a emprunté à ses parents.

Choice (D) is the correct answer to question 10. The text tells you that *grâce à un prêt de famille* (lines 10–11) Sylvie Magnus was able to create her agency. She did not obtain the money by working in a hospital (A), earning it during a revolution (B), or organizing fashion shows (C).

Sondage

Vous, amateurs de télé—

Question 1

Utilisez-vous personnellement une télécommande?

Question 2

Vous-même, quand vous utilisez cette télécommande, vous vous en servez pour: couper le son et faire autre chose? changer de chaîne dès que le programme ne vous plaît pas? suivre plusieurs émissions en même temps? chercher une émission particulière? éviter la publicité? rechercher la publicité?

Résultats:	en %
Proportion des Français âgés de 15 ans et plus	
Question 1: qui utilisent personnellement une télécommande	**46**
Question 2: qui s'en servent pour	
—couper le son pour faire autre chose	26
—changer de chaîne dès que le programme ne leur plaît pas	43
—suivre plusieurs émissions en même temps	12
—chercher une émission particulière	31
—éviter la publicité	23
—rechercher la publicité	2

11. Qu'est-ce qu'une télécommande?
    (A) Une sorte de téléviseur
    (B) Une émission de télévision
    (C) Une sorte de publicité
    (D) Un appareil électronique

Choice (D) is the correct answer to question 11. What a *télécommande* is must be inferred because it is not stated directly in the survey. The text tells you that, among other things, a *télécommande* can be used to change television channels and to cut the sound of a program. It is a remote control. It is not a kind of television set (A), nor a television program (B), nor publicity (C).

12. Selon ce sondage, on se sert le plus souvent d'une télécommande pour
    (A) acheter quelque chose
    (B) trouver une émission plus intéressante
    (C) pouvoir regarder deux émissions à la fois
    (D) vérifier le bon fonctionnement de son téléviseur

Choice (B) is the correct answer to question 12. This question asks you what the remote control is most frequently used for, according to the survey results. You must select the use in the chart that was selected by the most respondents and has the highest percentage. This use is *changer de chaîne dès que le programme ne leur plaît pas*, or "change the channel as soon as they no longer like the program." The other choices were selected by a lower percentage of respondents.

French Test

Practice Helps

The test that follows is an actual, recently administered SAT Subject Test in French. To get an idea of what it's like to take this test, practice under conditions that are much like those of an actual test administration.

- Set aside an hour when you can take the test uninterrupted. Make sure you complete the test in one sitting.
- Sit at a desk or table with no other books or papers. Dictionaries, other books, or notes are not allowed in the test room.
- Tear out an answer sheet from the back of this book and fill it in just as you would on the day of the test. One answer sheet can be used for up to three Subject Tests.
- Read the instructions that precede the practice test. During the actual administration, you will be asked to read them before answering test questions.
- Time yourself by placing a clock or kitchen timer in front of you.
- After you finish the practice test, read the sections "How to Score the SAT Subject Test in French" and "How Did You Do on the Subject Test in French?"
- The appearance of the answer sheet in this book may differ from the answer sheet you see on test day.

FRENCH TEST

The top portion of the section of the answer sheet that you will use in taking the French Test must be filled in exactly as shown in the illustration below. Note carefully that you have to do all of the following on your answer sheet.

1. Print FRENCH on the line under the words "Subject Test (print)."

2. In the shaded box labeled "Test Code" fill in four circles:

—Fill in circle 3 in the row labeled V.
—Fill in circle 3 in the row labeled W.
—Fill in circle 1 in the row labeled X.
—Fill in circle B in the row labeled Y.

Test Code		Subject Test (print)
V	① ② ● ④ ⑤ ⑥ ⑦ ⑧ ⑨	FRENCH
W	① ② ● ④ ⑤ ⑥ ⑦ ⑧ ⑨	
X	● ② ③ ④ ⑤ Y Ⓐ ● Ⓒ Ⓓ Ⓔ	
Q	① ② ③ ④ ⑤ ⑥ ⑦ ⑧ ⑨	

Please answer either Part I or Part II by filling in the specific circle in row Q. You are to fill in ONE and ONLY ONE circle, as described below, to indicate how you obtained your knowledge of French. <u>The information you provide is for statistical purposes only and will not influence your score on the test.</u>

Part I If your knowledge of French <u>does not</u> come primarily from courses taken in grades 9 through 12, fill in <u>circle 9</u> and leave the remaining circles blank, regardless of how long you studied the subject in school. For example, you are to fill in circle 9 if your knowledge of French comes primarily from any of the following sources: study prior to the ninth grade, courses taken at a college, or special study, living in a home in which French is the principal language spoken, or extensive residence abroad that includes significant experience in the French language.

Part II If your knowledge of French <u>does</u> come primarily from courses taken in secondary school, fill in the circle that indicates the level of the French course in which you are currently enrolled. If you are not now enrolled in a French course, fill in the circle that indicates the level of the most advanced course in French that you have completed.

• First year:	first or second half	—Fill in circle 1.
• Second year:	first half	—Fill in circle 2.
	second half	—Fill in circle 3.
• Third year:	first half	—Fill in circle 4.
	second half	—Fill in circle 5.
• Fourth year:	first half	—Fill in circle 6.
	second half	—Fill in circle 7.
• Advanced Placement course or a course at a level higher than fourth year, second half or high school course work plus a minimum of four weeks of study abroad		—Fill in circle 8.

When the supervisor gives the signal, turn the page and begin the French Test. There are 100 numbered circles on the answer sheet and 85 questions in the French Test. Therefore, use only circles 1 to 85 for recording your answers.

FRENCH TEST

PLEASE NOTE THAT YOUR ANSWER SHEET HAS FIVE ANSWER POSITIONS MARKED A, B, C, D, and E, WHILE THE QUESTIONS THROUGHOUT THIS TEST CONTAIN ONLY FOUR CHOICES. BE SURE NOT TO MAKE ANY MARKS IN COLUMN E.

Part A

Directions: This part consists of a number of incomplete statements, each having four suggested completions. Select the most appropriate completion and fill in the corresponding circle on the answer sheet.

1. Elle ne peut pas se le payer. C'est beaucoup trop ------- pour elle.

(A) cher
(B) fort
(C) gentil
(D) plein

2. Ce matin je n'ai pas eu le temps de lire le -------.

(A) paquet
(B) nouveau
(C) journal
(D) magasin

3. Le chef du personnel a ordonné que toutes les portes des bureaux soient ------- à cinq heures.

(A) serrées
(B) fumées
(C) levées
(D) fermées

4. Tu as vraiment mauvaise mémoire; tu ------- toujours mon anniversaire!

(A) oublies
(B) obliges
(C) perds
(D) poses

5. Attendez! Je ne peux pas vous comprendre si vous parlez tous -------.

(A) à la fois
(B) à l'heure
(C) à l'occasion
(D) à la prochaine

6. Nous sommes en retard. Il faut nous -------.

(A) endormir
(B) dépêcher
(C) promener
(D) moucher

7. Suzanne est punie parce qu'elle a ------- une gifle à sa soeur.

(A) pris
(B) donné
(C) prêté
(D) volé

8. Il pourra quitter l'hôpital dès qu'il n'aura plus de -------.

(A) coffre
(B) fièvre
(C) drogue
(D) confort

9. Claudette s'est servie d'une ------- pour s'essuyer les mains.

(A) assiette
(B) fourchette
(C) allumette
(D) serviette

10. Denise a été ------- affectée par le vol de sa voiture.

(A) brillamment
(B) cordialement
(C) sagement
(D) fortement

3XAC

GO ON TO THE NEXT PAGE

11. Quel temps magnifique! Il n'y a pas un seul -------.

(A) nuage
(B) champ
(C) ciel
(D) moment

12. Dans cet immeuble il y a un ------- qui s'arrête au quinzième étage.

(A) ascenseur
(B) éleveur
(C) trottoir
(D) aspirateur

13. Je voudrais recoudre un bouton à ce veston. As-tu -------?

(A) une épingle
(B) une aiguille
(C) un clou
(D) une boutonnière

14. L'herbe était toute ------- parce qu'il n'avait pas plu depuis des semaines.

(A) molle
(B) forte
(C) vide
(D) sèche

15. Pour faire du bateau à -------, il faut du vent.

(A) voiles
(B) vapeur
(C) rames
(D) réaction

16. Mon chien m'adore et il me suit comme mon -------.

(A) idole
(B) souffle
(C) idéal
(D) ombre

17. Plus de télé ce soir! L'électricité est -------.

(A) en désordre
(B) en haut
(C) en vente
(D) en panne

18. Qu'on est bien près du feu à écouter les ------- crépiter dans la cheminée!

(A) bûches
(B) coupures
(C) bâtons
(D) allumettes

19. Elle a planté toute une variété d'arbres fruitiers dans son -------.

(A) fermier
(B) berger
(C) prunier
(D) verger

20. Vous n'aurez pas de peine à la faire parler. Elle est très -------.

(A) économe
(B) réservée
(C) bavarde
(D) généreuse

21. Il faut se faire ------- pour voter aux élections présidentielles.

(A) raccorder
(B) afficher
(C) écrire
(D) inscrire

22. Le Père Noël a ------- le fond de son sac pour trouver encore des cadeaux.

(A) aperçu
(B) gardé
(C) surveillé
(D) fouillé

GO ON TO THE NEXT PAGE

Part B

Directions: Each of the following sentences contains a blank. From the four choices given, select the one that can be inserted in the blank to form a grammatically correct sentence and fill in the corresponding circle on the answer sheet. Choice (A) may consist of dashes that indicate that no insertion is required to form a grammatically correct sentence.

23. On me demande toujours ------- je vais faire de ma vie. Je n'en sais rien!

(A) ce dont
(B) quoi
(C) ce que
(D) qu'est-ce qui

24. Je vois que vous aimez les livres. Vous ------- avez beaucoup dans votre bibliothèque.

(A) lui
(B) leur
(C) en
(D) y

25. David et Daniel sont sortis de la maison en -------.

(A) courant
(B) ayant couru
(C) courir
(D) avoir couru

26. Il est important de ------- soigner, Madame. Prenez un cachet d'aspirine et téléphonez au médecin.

(A) vous
(B) toi
(C) lui
(D) te

27. Je ------- qu'il devait me téléphoner.

(A) regrette
(B) pense
(C) doutais
(D) craignais

28. Après l'accident, on a transporté Sandrine au ------- hôpital de la ville.

(A) nouvel
(B) neuf
(C) beau
(D) moderne

29. Les agents ont suggéré que tu t'addresses à ------- pour te renseigner.

(A) leur
(B) eux
(C) soi
(D) ceux

30. Je préfère cette voiture à la -------.

(A) sienne
(B) autre
(C) leurs
(D) bleu

31. Il me semble que la Tour d'Argent est un des ------- restaurants de France; la cuisine y est excellente.

(A) meilleurs
(B) mieux
(C) supérieurs
(D) bien

32. J'ai rendu visite à Philippe en -------.

(A) juillet
(B) Paris
(C) printemps
(D) dimanche

GO ON TO THE NEXT PAGE

33. Heureusement, le roman n'était pas ------- ennuyeux que le film.

    (A) assez
    (B) tant
    (C) peu
    (D) aussi

34. Nous invitons ------- amis.

    (A) plusieurs
    (B) beaucoup
    (C) un peu
    (D) un peu d'

35. Même si tu n'as pas beaucoup de temps pour visiter la ville, va ------- voir le musée.

    (A) moins
    (B) moins de
    (C) le moindre
    (D) au moins

36. D'un seul geste, elles ont toutes ------- la main.

    (A) levé
    (B) levés
    (C) levée
    (D) levées

37. Quelle peinture préférez-vous, cette peinture-ci ou ------- qui est là-bas?

    (A) laquelle
    (B) l'une
    (C) cette
    (D) celle

38. A ma grande surprise, ce film ------- a beaucoup plu.

    (A) lui
    (B) l'
    (C) en
    (D) les

39. Cette année, les cerises coûtent douze francs ------- kilo.

    (A) par
    (B) un
    (C) le
    (D) pour

GO ON TO THE NEXT PAGE

Part C

Directions: The paragraphs below contain blank spaces indicating omissions in the text. For some blanks, it is necessary to choose the completion that is most appropriate to the meaning of the passage; for other blanks, to choose the one completion that forms a grammatically correct sentence. In some instances, choice (A) may consist of dashes that indicate that no insertion is required to form a grammatically correct sentence. In each case, indicate your answer by filling in the corresponding circle on the answer sheet. Be sure to read the paragraph completely before answering the questions related to it.

C'était en général __(40)__ la fin de l'après-midi que __(41)__ à la porte de l'immeuble. Je montais vite jusqu'à l'appartement. Jacques m'accueillait avec un sourire empressé. «Je ne __(42)__ dérange pas?» «Tu ne me déranges __(43)__ .» «Comment ça va?» «Ça va toujours très bien __(44)__ je te vois.» Sa gentillesse me touchait et me __(45)__ le coeur.

40. (A) vers
    (B) par
    (C) autour de
    (D) à travers

41. (A) je sonnais
    (B) j'ouvrais
    (C) je sortais
    (D) je quittais

42. (A) lui
    (B) les
    (C) me
    (D) te

43. (A) jamais
    (B) rien
    (C) aucun
    (D) personne

44. (A) quand
    (B) mais
    (C) donc
    (D) pourtant

45. (A) réchauffait
    (B) battait
    (C) lançait
    (D) rendait

GO ON TO THE NEXT PAGE

Le juge d'instruction pensait au début qu'il __(46)__ arriver à une décision la semaine suivante. Pourtant, __(47)__ entendu __(48)__ disaient les témoins, il a changé __(49)__.

46. (A) a pu
(B) pourrait
(C) pourra
(D) puisse

47. (A) après
(B) bien
(C) ayant
(D) sans

48. (A) ce qui
(B) ce que
(C) quoi
(D) à quoi

49. (A) d'avis
(B) l'opinion
(C) sa mémoire
(D) de l'esprit

GO ON TO THE NEXT PAGE

Sophie et Michel pensent déjà __(50)__ leurs vacances de l'été __(51)__. Ils ont l'intention de traverser __(52)__ Europe à bicyclette et en train avec des amis __(53)__ ont déjà fait ce voyage. Chacun n'emportera __(54)__ un sac à dos pour __(55)__ les excédents de bagage. Leur itinéraire sera établi d'avance et le club sportif qui organise __(56)__ a prévu de nombreuses __(57)__ afin que les cyclistes se reposent et fassent un peu de tourisme.

50. (A) de
(B) pour
(C) à
(D) sur

51. (A) passé
(B) prochain
(C) futur
(D) présent

52. (A) ---
(B) en
(C) l'
(D) dans

53. (A) quels
(B) qui
(C) qu'
(D) dont

54. (A) d'
(B) qu'
(C) ni
(D) pas

55. (A) payer
(B) créer
(C) éviter
(D) traîner

56. (A) ce match
(B) ce chemin
(C) cette course
(D) cette randonnée

57. (A) averses
(B) escalades
(C) démarches
(D) étapes

GO ON TO THE NEXT PAGE

Part D

Directions: Read the following texts carefully for comprehension. Each is followed by a number of questions or incomplete statements. Select the answer or completion that is best according to the text and fill in the corresponding circle on the answer sheet.

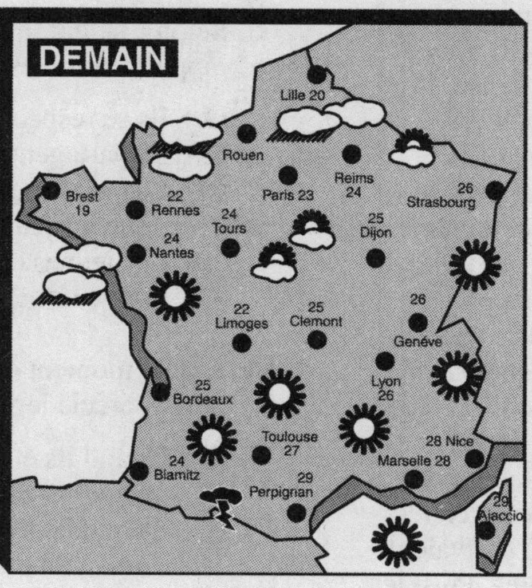

Orages en fuite, chaleur à la baisse, vents d'ouest et nuages arrivent.

58. Demain il y aura moins de

(A) chaleur
(B) vent
(C) nuages
(D) fraîcheur

59. Quel temps fera-t-il demain à Lyon?

(A) Il pleuvra.
(B) Il fera beau.
(C) Il neigera.
(D) Il y aura des orages.

GO ON TO THE NEXT PAGE

Peter Schulz avait soixante-quinze ans. Il était de santé délicate, et l'âge ne l'avait pas épargné. Sa vie avait été pauvre en événements. Il était seul depuis des années. Sa femme était morte. Il en conservait un souvenir attendri. Il y avait vingt-cinq ans qu'il l'avait perdue: et, pas un soir depuis, il ne s'était endormi, sans un petit entretien mental, triste et tendre, avec elle; il l'associait à chacune de ses journées. Il n'avait pas eu d'enfants: c'était le grand regret de sa vie. Il avait reporté son besoin d'affection sur ses élèves, auxquels il était attaché, comme un père à ses fils. Il avait trouvé peu de retour. Un vieux coeur peut se sentir très près d'un jeune coeur, et presque du même âge: il sait combien sont brèves les années qui l'en séparent. Mais le jeune homme ne s'en doute point: le vieillard est pour lui un homme d'une autre époque.

Le vieux Schulz avait rencontré parfois quelque reconnaissance chez des élèves, touchés par l'intérêt vif et frais qu'il prenait à tout ce qui leur arrivait d'heureux ou de malheureux: ils venaient le voir de temps en temps; ils lui écrivaient, pour le remercier, quand ils quittaient l'université; certains lui écrivaient encore, une ou deux fois, les années suivantes. Puis, le vieux Schulz n'entendait plus parler d'eux, sinon par les journaux, qui lui faisaient connaître l'avancement de tel ou tel: et il se réjouissait de leurs succès, comme si c'étaient les siens. Il ne leur en voulait pas de leur silence: il y trouvait mille excuses; il ne doutait point de leur affection, et prêtait aux plus égoïstes les sentiments qu'il avait pour eux.

60. Le grand regret de la vie de Schulz était

(A) d'avoir perdu sa femme
(B) d'avoir des élèves ingrats
(C) d'être sans enfants
(D) de ne pas avoir une bonne santé

61. Qu'est-ce qui décrit le mieux l'attitude de Schulz envers ses anciens élèves?

(A) Il s'intéresse beaucoup à leurs vies.
(B) Il les trouve égoïstes.
(C) Il est jaloux de leur succès.
(D) Il ne les trouve pas du tout reconnaissants.

62. Quelle a été la profession de Peter Schulz?

(A) Médecin
(B) Professeur
(C) Journaliste
(D) Psychologue

63. Selon l'auteur, qu'est-ce qui décrit le mieux les rapports entre les jeunes et les vieux?

(A) Ils se respectent mutuellement.
(B) Ils partagent les mêmes idées.
(C) Les vieux se sentent plus proches des jeunes que les jeunes des vieux.
(D) Les jeunes estiment plus les vieux quand ils ont eux-mêmes vieilli.

64. A quel moment de leur vie les jeunes ont-ils le plus apprécié le vieillard?

(A) Quand ils étaient enfants
(B) Quand ils étaient heureux
(C) Quand ils avaient fini leurs études universitaires
(D) Quand ils avaient trouvé du travail

65. Comment Schulz apprend-il les nouvelles de ses anciens élèves?

(A) Ses anciens élèves lui écrivent souvent.
(B) Il leur écrit pour demander des nouvelles.
(C) Il lit les journaux.
(D) L'université lui envoie des nouvelles.

66. Selon l'auteur, Peter Schulz a eu une vie

(A) très malheureuse
(B) active et mouvementée
(C) bien appréciée et respectée
(D) consacrée au succès des autres

GO ON TO THE NEXT PAGE

Cela devient malheureusement une banalité que de constater le déclin de la natalité dans notre pays et, plus particulièrement, dans les grandes villes.

Pour des parents, avoir des enfants et les élever représente, en milieu urbain, des contraintes beaucoup plus fortes qu'ailleurs, notamment lorsque le père et la mère travaillent.

Une contrainte se situe souvent au niveau du logement. Il est cher et, dans les logements neufs, les dimensions des pièces sont souvent réduites au minimum, les plans sont mal conçus pour des familles nombreuses. La venue d'un enfant supplémentaire conduit bien souvent à un changement d'appartement, ce qui pose des problèmes financiers difficiles.

67. Le sujet principal que traite l'auteur est

(A) la population des grandes villes
(B) le manque de logements en milieu urbain
(C) le nombre croissant de familles nombreuses
(D) la baisse du nombre de naissances

68. L'auteur exprime son point de vue sur les faits qu'il présente surtout par le mot

(A) malheureusement (ligne 1)
(B) notamment (ligne 6)
(C) logement (ligne 9)
(D) minimum (ligne 11)

69. Le "changement d'appartement" (ligne 13) est causé par

(A) l'arrivée d'un nouveau-né
(B) une femme qui travaille
(C) des problèmes financiers
(D) la peur des grandes villes

GO ON TO THE NEXT PAGE

Bonjour, voisin.

Dans la grande communauté humaine, nous sommes tous voisins. Et être un bon voisin, c'est aussi apprendre à s'intégrer dans la texture locale de la communauté.

Chez Komatsu, nous produisons des machines industrielles et des engins de construction tels que: excavateurs, robots, lasers et machines-outils. C'est-à-dire des instruments permettant d'obtenir une meilleure qualité de vie. De même, nous nous efforçons d'oeuvrer pour le bien de la communauté, en développant la collaboration locale dans le monde des affaires, des entreprises alliées, des échanges commerciaux et des services. En un mot, à coopérer pour un monde meilleur.

70. Cette publicité a pour titre "Bonjour, voisin" pour suggérer qu'on
    - (A) doit dire "bonjour" aux voisins
    - (B) veut vendre des tentures aux voisins
    - (C) habite tous la terre
    - (D) veut tous se rencontrer

71. Komatsu est une compagnie qui fabrique des machines pour
    - (A) l'industrie d'équipements
    - (B) les petits commerces
    - (C) les besoins ménagers
    - (D) l'aérospatiale

72. Selon cette publicité, la philosophie de Komatsu est
    - (A) de construire des machines moins chères
    - (B) de créer un monde plus harmonieux
    - (C) d'encourager l'artisanat
    - (D) de prévoir le monde à venir

GO ON TO THE NEXT PAGE

La rue était maintenant déserte et silencieuse. Les lampadaires s'étaient allumés depuis un instant seulement. Le ciel demeurait rougeâtre à l'horizon. Un imperceptible souffle de vent passa. Un chat noir aussi.

Le mendiant, assis dos au mur d'un immeuble sombre et vétuste, s'étira et bâilla. D'un regard circulaire, il embrassa la rue étroite et maintenant calme du marché. Il tira à lui la petite cuvette de bois et compta les pièces de monnaie qui s'y trouvaient; puis il fourra sa main dans une poche de son boubou qui avait dû être blanc, et en sortit d'autres pièces de monnaie qu'il compta aussi avant de tout mettre dans un minuscule sac de toile. Il resta ainsi un moment, pensif. Il sortit d'une autre poche une pièce de monnaie et la contempla un long moment; c'était une pièce que lui avait donnée la dame au foulard. Elle lui en donnait tous les matins en ressortant du marché, et c'était son seul bon moment de la journée. Quand il la voyait surgir d'entre deux rangées d'étalages puis traverser la ruelle et s'avancer vers lui, il était heureux. Il la regardait s'avancer de sa démarche calme et régulière, quelque peu nonchalante, avec son éternel foulard blanc noué autour du cou. Arrivée devant lui, elle s'arrêtait et le regardait; lui aussi la regardait. Puis elle lui tendait une pièce; il la prenait et elle s'en allait. Tous les matins, il guettait sa venue. Tous les matins, sauf le dimanche. Elle ne venait jamais le dimanche; c'est pour cela que le mendiant n'aimait pas le dimanche, même si les gens lui donnaient beaucoup plus d'argent ce jour-là.

Et justement demain c'est dimanche.

Il remit la pièce dans la poche d'où il l'avait prise.

Demain dimanche.

Il inclina tristement la tête.

73. D'après le début du texte, à quel moment de la journée la scène se passe-t-elle?

(A) A l'aube
(B) Dans l'après-midi
(C) Au crépuscule
(D) En pleine nuit

74. Le mendiant met la pièce que la dame au foulard lui donne dans une autre poche parce que cette pièce

(A) a une grande valeur monétaire
(B) a une grande valeur affective
(C) est une pièce de collection
(D) est contrefaite

75. Quand la dame au foulard s'avançait vers le mendiant, comment marchait-elle?

(A) Avec hésitation
(B) A pas rapides
(C) Sans regarder où elle allait
(D) Sans se presser

76. La dame au foulard rend le mendiant heureux parce qu'elle

(A) jette une pièce dans sa cuvette
(B) le guette tous les matins
(C) communique silencieusement avec lui
(D) contemple la pièce

77. A la fin de l'histoire le mendiant est triste parce que, le dimanche, la dame au foulard

(A) lui manque
(B) le chasse
(C) lui donne peu d'argent
(D) lui remet une vieille pièce

GO ON TO THE NEXT PAGE

Les Routes ROI RENÉ

Les Routes Roi René, qui furent aussi celles des **Plantagenêts,** regroupent, notamment, l'essentiel des châteaux de l'Anjou ouverts au public; pour la plupart habités par leurs propriétaires, ils offrent une image vivante du patrimoine historique et architectural angevin.
Elles permettent également de découvrir de nombreux sites et monuments et de comprendre l'âme du "pays": l'Art de vivre en Anjou se perpétue et fait du Maine–et–Loire d'aujourd'hui une terre privilégiée de la Vallée de la Loire.
Le Roi René, cousin du Roi de France, fut l'instigateur de la vie artistique et littéraire de l'Anjou. Quel plus bel emblème pour ces itinéraires?
Les Routes Roi René font partie des **Routes de Beauté.**

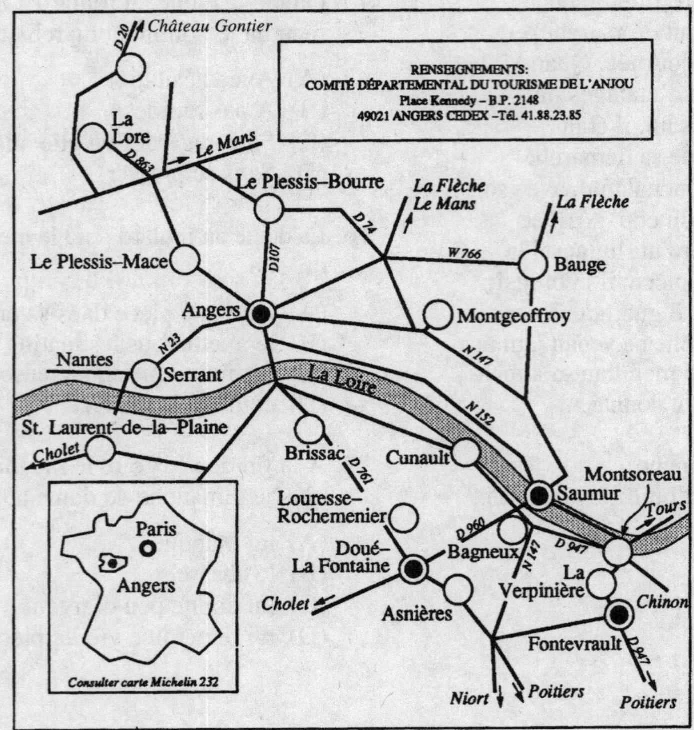

78. Le Comité du Tourisme a choisi ces châteaux parce qu'ils

    (A) intéressent les spécialistes
    (B) appartiennent tous à l'Etat
    (C) sont ouverts au public de temps en temps
    (D) sont un bel exemple de l'architecture angevine

79. Parmi les "Routes de Beauté", on a nommé ce segment les "Routes Roi René" parce

    (A) qu'il parcourt une région où le déplacement est pratique
    (B) qu'on y trouve des monuments de toute époque
    (C) qu'il honore un protecteur des lettres et des arts
    (D) qu'il est l'emblème des Rois de France

GO ON TO THE NEXT PAGE

C'était dans l'hiver de 1792. La disette régnait à Strasbourg. La maison de Dietrich, le maire, était pauvre, la table frugale, mais hospitalière pour Rouget de Lisle.

Accablé d'une inspiration sublime, le jeune officier s'endormit la tête sur son clavecin et ne s'éveilla qu'au jour. Les chants de la nuit, impressions d'un rêve, lui remontèrent avec peine dans la mémoire. Il les écrivit, les nota, et courut chez Dietrich. La femme et les filles du vieux patriote n'étaient pas encore levées. Dietrich les éveilla, il appela quelques amis, tous passionnés comme lui pour la musique.

Sa fille ainée accompagna, Rouget chanta. A la première strophe les visages pâlirent; à la seconde, les larmes coulèrent; aux dernières, le délire de l'enthousiasme éclata. L'hymne de la patrie était trouvé!

Le nouveau chant, exécuté quelques jours après à Strasbourg, vola de ville en ville sur tous les orchestres populaires. Marseille l'adopta pour être chanté au commencement et à la fin des séances de ses clubs. Les Marseillais le répandirent en France, en le chantant sur leur route. De là lui vint le nom de "Marseillaise".

80. Où est-ce que la "Marseillaise" a été composée?

(A) A Marseille
(B) A Strasbourg
(C) A Lille
(D) Sur la route

81. L'inspiration pour la musique est née

(A) d'un rêve
(B) d'un poème
(C) d'un repas
(D) d'une bataille

82. Quelle profession Rouget de Lisle exerçait-il à ce moment-là?

(A) Troubadour
(B) Maire
(C) Chef d'orchestre
(D) Soldat

83. Qui a interprété la "Marseillaise" pour la première fois?

(A) Le maire et sa femme
(B) Rouget de Lisle et la femme du maire
(C) Rouget de Lisle et la fille du maire
(D) Le maire et sa fille

84. D'après le texte, quel a été le destin du nouveau chant?

(A) On ne l'a plus joué.
(B) Les autres villes l'ont volé.
(C) On l'a beaucoup modifié.
(D) On l'a chanté un peu partout.

85. Pourquoi l'hymne national français s'appelle-t-il la "Marseillaise"?

(A) Un Marseillais l'a composé.
(B) Les Marseillais l'ont rendu populaire.
(C) Les Marseillais étaient les plus patriotiques.
(D) Les Marseillais étaient les meilleurs chanteurs.

STOP

IF YOU FINISH BEFORE TIME IS CALLED, YOU MAY CHECK YOUR WORK ON THIS TEST ONLY. DO NOT TURN TO ANY OTHER TEST IN THIS BOOK.

How to Score the SAT Subject Test in French

When you take an actual SAT Subject Test in French, your answer sheet will be "read" by a scanning machine that will record your responses to each question. Then a computer will compare your answers with the correct answers and produce your raw score. You get one point for each correct answer. For each wrong answer, you lose one-third of a point. Questions you omit (and any for which you mark more than one answer) are not counted. This raw score is converted to a scaled score that is reported to you and to the colleges you specify.

Worksheet 1. Finding Your Raw Test Score

STEP 1: Table A lists the correct answers for all the questions on the Subject Test in French that is reproduced in this book. It also serves as a worksheet for you to calculate your raw score.

- Compare your answers with those given in the table.
- Put a check in the column marked "Right" if your answer is correct.
- Put a check in the column marked "Wrong" if your answer is incorrect.
- Leave both columns blank if you omitted the question.

STEP 2: Count the number of right answers.

Enter the total here: ____________________

STEP 3: Count the number of wrong answers.

Enter the total here: ____________________

STEP 4: Multiply the number of wrong answers by .333.

Enter the product here: ________________

STEP 5: Subtract the result obtained in Step 4 from the total you obtained in Step 2.

Enter the result here: __________________

STEP 6: Round the number obtained in Step 5 to the nearest whole number.

Enter the result here: __________________

The number you obtained in Step 6 is your raw score.

Table A

Answers to the Subject Test in French, Form 3XAC, and Percentage of Students Answering Each Question Correctly									
Question Number	Correct Answer	Right	Wrong	Percentage of Students Answering the Question Correctly*	Question Number	Correct Answer	Right	Wrong	Percentage of Students Answering the Question Correctly*
1	A			92	33	D			45
2	C			92	34	A			51
3	D			88	35	D			58
4	A			95	36	A			51
5	A			74	37	D			49
6	B			85	38	A			25
7	B			70	39	C			23
8	B			81	40	A			57
9	D			78	41	A			31
10	D			74	42	D			86
11	A			83	43	A			79
12	A			66	44	A			92
13	B			36	45	A			39
14	D			75	46	B			53
15	A			83	47	C			35
16	D			54	48	B			39
17	D			43	49	A			49
18	A			22	50	C			47
19	D			22	51	B			84
20	C			52	52	C			49
21	D			35	53	B			77
22	D			21	54	B			48
23	C			67	55	C			66
24	C			75	56	D			16
25	A			74	57	D			13
26	A			88	58	A			39
27	B			60	59	B			89
28	A			71	60	C			93
29	B			68	61	A			79
30	A			66	62	B			88
31	A			70	63	C			53
32	A			61	64	C			61

Table A continued on next page

Table A continued from previous page

Question Number	Correct Answer	Right	Wrong	Percentage of Students Answering the Question Correctly*	Question Number	Correct Answer	Right	Wrong	Percentage of Students Answering the Question Correctly*
65	C			56	76	C			44
66	D			45	77	A			61
67	D			34	78	D			76
68	A			69	79	C			49
69	A			63	80	B			83
70	C			30	81	A			81
71	A			83	82	D			65
72	B			85	83	C			60
73	C			38	84	D			39
74	B			61	85	B			70
75	D			57					

* These percentages are based on an analysis of the answer sheets of a representative sample of 3,607 students who took the original form of this test in June 2001, and whose mean score was 600. They may be used as an indication of the relative difficulty of a particular question. Each percentage may also be used to predict the likelihood that a typical SAT Subject Test in French candidate will answer that question correctly on this edition of the test.

Finding Your Scaled Score

When you take SAT Subject Tests, the scores sent to the colleges you specify are reported on the College Board scale, which ranges from 200–800. You can convert your practice test score to a scaled score by using Table B. To find your scaled score, locate your raw score in the left-hand column of Table B; the corresponding score in the right-hand column is your scaled score. For example, a raw score of 37 on this particular edition of the Subject Test in French corresponds to a scaled score of 570.

Raw scores are converted to scaled scores to ensure that a score earned on any one edition of a particular Subject Test is comparable to the same scaled score earned on any other edition of the same Subject Test. Because some editions of the tests may be slightly easier or more difficult than others, College Board scaled scores are adjusted so that they indicate the same level of performance regardless of the edition of the test taken and the ability of the group that takes it. Thus, for example, a score of 400 on one edition of a test taken at a particular administration indicates the same level of achievement as a score of 400 on a different edition of the test taken at a different administration.

When you take the SAT Subject Tests during a national administration, your scores are likely to differ somewhat from the scores you obtain on the tests in this book. People perform at different levels at different times for reasons unrelated to the tests themselves. The precision of any test is also limited because it represents only a sample of all the possible questions that could be asked.

Table B

Scaled Score Conversion Table
Subject Test in French (Form 3XAC)

Raw Score	Scaled Score	Raw Score	Scaled Score	Raw Score	Scaled Score
85	800	47	630	9	420
84	800	46	620	8	420
83	800	45	610	7	410
82	800	44	610	6	410
81	800	43	600	5	400
80	800	42	600	4	400
79	800	41	590	3	390
78	800	40	590	2	390
77	800	39	580	1	380
76	800	38	580	0	380
75	800	37	570	-1	370
74	790	36	570	-2	370
73	790	35	560	-3	370
72	780	34	560	-4	360
71	770	33	550	-5	360
70	770	32	550	-6	350
69	760	31	540	-7	350
68	750	30	530	-8	350
67	750	29	530	-9	340
66	740	28	520	-10	340
65	730	27	520	-11	330
64	730	26	510	-12	330
63	720	25	510	-13	330
62	710	24	500	-14	320
61	710	23	500	-15	320
60	700	22	490	-16	310
59	700	21	490	-17	310
58	690	20	480	-18	300
57	680	19	470	-19	300
56	680	18	470	-20	290
55	670	17	460	-21	290
54	660	16	460	-22	280
53	660	15	450	-23	280
52	650	14	450	-24	270
51	650	13	440	-25	260
50	640	12	440	-26	250
49	640	11	430	-27	240
48	630	10	430	-28	230

How Did You Do on the Subject Test in French?

After you score your test and analyze your performance, think about the following questions:

Did you run out of time before reaching the end of the test?

If so, you may need to pace yourself better. For example, maybe you spent too much time on one or two hard questions. A better approach might be to skip the ones you can't answer right away and try answering all the questions that remain on the test. Then if there's time, go back to the questions you skipped.

Did you take a long time reading the directions?

You will save time when you take the test by learning the directions to the Subject Test in French ahead of time. Each minute you spend reading directions during the test is a minute that you could use to answer questions.

How did you handle questions you were unsure of?

If you were able to eliminate one or more of the answer choices as wrong and guess from the remaining ones, your approach probably worked to your advantage. On the other hand, making haphazard guesses or omitting questions without trying to eliminate choices could cost you valuable points.

How difficult were the questions for you compared with other students who took the test?

Table A shows you how difficult the multiple-choice questions were for the group of students who took this test during its national administration. The right-hand column gives the percentage of students that answered each question correctly.

A question answered correctly by almost everyone in the group is obviously an easier question. For example, 95 percent of the students answered question 4 correctly. But only 22 percent answered question 19 correctly.

Keep in mind that these percentages are based on just one group of students. They would probably be different with another group of students taking the test.

If you missed several easier questions, go back and try to find out why: Did the questions cover material you haven't yet reviewed? Did you misunderstand the directions?

French with Listening

The Subject Test in French with Listening is offered once a year only at designated test centers. To take the test you MUST bring an acceptable CD player with earphones to the test center.

Sample Listening Questions

The following three types of questions appear on the Subject Test in French with Listening. All questions in this section of the test are multiple-choice questions in which you must choose the BEST response from three or four choices offered. Text in brackets [ ] is recorded on the CD only; it will not appear in your test book. Please note that the CD does not start here. Begin using the CD when you start the actual practice test on page 432.

Part A

Your answer sheet has five answer positions marked A, B, C, D, and E, while the questions throughout this part contain only four choices. Be sure NOT to make any marks in column E.

Directions: For each item in this part, you will hear four sentences designated (A), (B), (C), and (D). They will not be printed in your test book. As you listen, look at the picture in your test book and select the choice that best reflects what you see in the picture or what someone in the picture might say. Then fill in the corresponding circle on the answer sheet. You will hear the choices only once. Now look at the following example.

You see:

You hear:

[(A) Quelle joie d'être seul!
(B) Que c'est agréable de faire du vélo!
(C) Le moteur fait trop de bruit!
(D) Nous adorons la course à pied.]

Choice (B) is the correct answer. Statement (B), "Que c'est agréable de faire du vélo!" best reflects what you see in the picture or what someone in the picture might say.

1. You see:

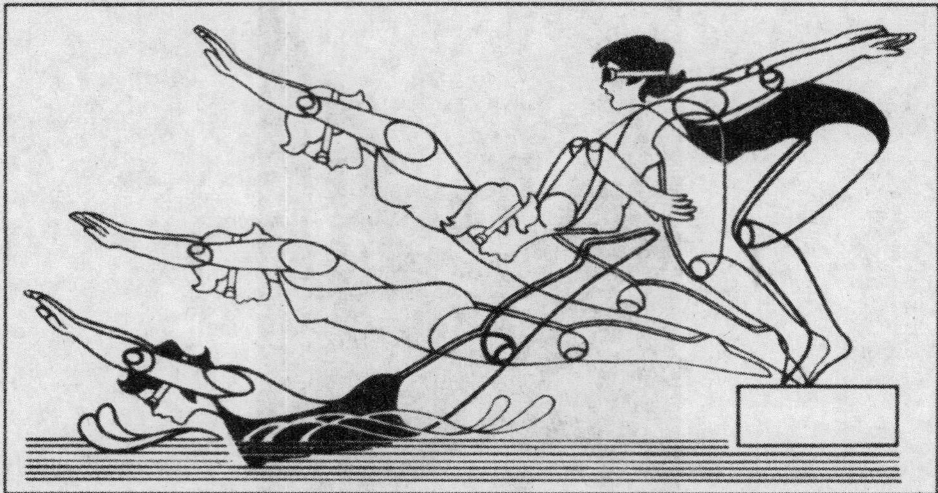

You hear:

[Numéro 1

(Woman) (A) Elle porte toujours un bonnet de bain.

(B) Elle a toujours peur de l'eau.

(C) Le ski nautique lui plaît beaucoup.

(D) Elle est en train de plonger dans l'eau.]

(7 seconds)

Choice (D) is the correct answer to question 1. In this question you see a drawing that shows a slow motion scene of a girl diving into a pool. Choice (D) best reflects what can be seen in the picture. Choices (A), (B), and (C) are incorrect because the girl in the picture is not wearing a cap, does not seem to be afraid of water, and is not shown on water skis.

Part B

Your answer sheet has five answer positions marked A, B, C, D, and E, while the questions throughout this part contain only three choices. Be sure NOT to make any marks in column D or E.

Directions: In this part of the test you will hear several short selections. A tone will announce each new selection. The selections will not be printed in your test booklet. At the end of each selection, you will be asked one or two questions about what was said, each followed by three possible answers, choices (A), (B), and (C). The answers are not printed in your test booklet. You will hear them only *once.* Select the BEST answer and fill in the corresponding circle on the answer sheet. Now listen to the following example, but do not mark the answer on your answer sheet.

You hear:

[(Tone)

(Man B) Papa, ta voiture est chez le garagiste.

(Man A) Mais pourquoi? Elle a toujours bien marché.

(Man B) Euh, en réalité, j'ai eu un accident.

(Man A) Quoi? Tu plaisantes, n'est-ce pas?

(5 seconds)

(Woman A) Qu'est-ce qu'on peut dire de la voiture en question?

(A) Elle est en réparation.

(B) Elle est sur la route.

(C) Elle est chez un ami.]

(7 seconds)

Choice (A) is the correct answer. The best answer to the question, "Qu'est-ce qu'on peut dire de la voiture en question?" is choice (A), "Elle est en réparation" because we heard it got into an accident and that it is at the mechanic.

Questions 2–3

You hear:

[(Tone)

(Man) Votre passeport, madame.

(Woman) Voilà.

(Man) Et qu'est-ce que vous ferez au Canada?

(Woman) Je vais passer les vacances avec ma famille.

(Man) Très bien, madame. Je vous souhaite un bon séjour.]

(5 seconds)

2. [Numéro 2

(Man) Qui parle à cette femme?

(A) Un professeur.
(B) Un douanier.
(C) Un chauffeur.]

(7 seconds)

Choice (B) is the correct answer to question 2, *Un douanier*, because the woman is crossing the border into Canada. In this question, you choose the person who is talking to the woman in the dialogue. *Un professeur* or *un chauffeur* would not ask to see the woman's passport. Therefore, choices (A) and (C) are incorrect.

3. [Numéro 3

(Man) Qu'est-ce que la femme va faire?

(A) Obtenir un passeport.
(B) Chercher sa famille.
(C) Entrer au Canada.]

(7 seconds)

Choice (C) is the correct answer to question 3. This question asks what the woman is about to do. Choice (C) is the only logical answer according to the dialogue. After crossing the border, the woman will enter Canada. Choice (A) is incorrect because she already has a passport, and choice (B) is incorrect because she is vacationing with her family, not looking for them.

Part C

Your answer sheet has five answer positions marked A, B, C, D, and E, while the questions throughout this part contain only four choices. Be sure NOT to make any marks in column E.

Directions: You will now hear some extended dialogues or monologues. You will hear each only once. After each dialogue or monologue, you will be asked several questions about what you have just heard. These questions are also printed in your test book. Select the best answer to each question from among the four choices printed in your test book and fill in the corresponding circle on the answer sheet. There is no sample question for this part.

Questions 4–6

(Man) [Dialogue numéro 1. Marie-Hélène et son amie Maude parlent de cinéma et de littérature.

(Woman A) Tiens, Marie-Hélène, tu as acheté *Danse avec les loups* en anglais?

(Woman B) Oui, j'ai acheté ce livre à Boston. Je me suis dit que c'était, euh, d'abord je n'avais pas vu le film et avant de voir le film j'avais vraiment envie de lire le livre; c'est tout. Et puis, tu sais, Maude, finalement je n'ai pas pu le lire, je n'ai pas eu le temps.

(Woman A) Il faudra te dépêcher de le lire parce que le film est encore sur les écrans mais je ne sais pas combien de temps il va y rester. Il a beaucoup de succès, le film; le livre, je ne le connais pas. Il paraît qu'il est très très bien, le film, mais un peu long; moi, je compte aller le voir la semaine prochaine.]

4. (Man) [Qu'est-ce que Marie-Hélène déclare?]

(12 seconds)

Qu'est-ce que Marie-Hélène déclare?

(A) Avoir vu un film.
(B) Avoir l'intention de lire un livre.
(C) Avoir lu un livre.
(D) Avoir l'intention d'aller à Boston.

Choice (B) is the correct answer to question 4. Marie-Hélène states in the dialogue that she bought the book *Dances with Wolves* in Boston so that she could read it before seeing the movie. She also states *je n'ai pas pu le lire, je n'ai pas eu le temps*, which means that she has not yet read the book. Choice (C) is therefore incorrect. Choices (A) and (D) are incorrect because she did not see the movie (A) and does not mention that she intends to go to Boston (D).

5. (Man) [Qu'est-ce que Maude avoue à son amie?]
(12 seconds)

Qu'est-ce que Maude avoue à son amie?

(A) Elle a lu le livre.

(B) Elle n'a pas encore vu le film.

(C) Elle n'a pas compris la critique.

(D) Elle a écouté la cassette.

Choice (B) is the correct answer to question 5. When Maude answers her friend, she tells her at the end: *Il paraît qu'il est très très bien, le film … je compte aller le voir la semaine prochaine.* Choice (A) is incorrect because Maude states the opposite (*le livre, je ne le connais pas*). According to the dialogue, Maude admits neither choice (C) nor choice (D); both choices are therefore incorrect.

6. (Man) [Dans cette discussion, qu'est-ce qu'on peut dire des deux amies?]
(12 seconds)

Dans cette discussion, qu'est-ce qu'on peut dire des deux amies?

(A) Elles se font des compliments.

(B) Elles s'ignorent.

(C) Elles s'inquiètent.

(D) Elles partagent les mêmes goûts.

Choice (D) is the correct answer to question 6. It can be inferred from the dialogue that the two friends share the same interests, at least with regard to movies. Choices (A), (B), and (C) cannot be said about the two friends. They do not exchange compliments (A), do know each other (B), and do not become anxious or upset (C).

French with Listening Test

Practice Helps

The test that follows is an actual, recently administered SAT Subject Test in French with Listening. To get an idea of what it's like to take this test, practice under conditions that are much like those of an actual test administration.

- Set aside an hour when you can take the test uninterrupted. Make sure you complete the test in one sitting.
- Sit at a desk or table with no other books or papers. Dictionaries, other books, or notes are not allowed in the test room.
- Tear out an answer sheet from the back of this book and fill it in just as you would on the day of the test. One answer sheet can be used for up to three Subject Tests.
- Read the instructions that precede the practice test. During the actual administration, you will be asked to read them before answering test questions.
- Time yourself by placing a clock or kitchen timer in front of you.
- After you finish the practice test, read the sections "How to Score the SAT Subject Test in French with Listening" and "How Did You Do on the Subject Test in French with Listening?"
- The appearance of the answer sheet in this book may differ from the answer sheet you see on test day.

FRENCH TEST WITH LISTENING

The top portion of the section of the answer sheet that you will use in taking the French Test with Listening must be filled in exactly as shown in the illustration below. Note carefully that you have to do all of the following on your answer sheet.

1. Print FRENCH WITH LISTENING on the line under the words "Subject Test (print)."

2. In the shaded box labeled "Test Code" fill in four circles:

   —Fill in circle 5 in the row labeled V.
   —Fill in circle 5 in the row labeled W.
   —Fill in circle 1 in the row labeled X.
   —Fill in circle B in the row labeled Y.

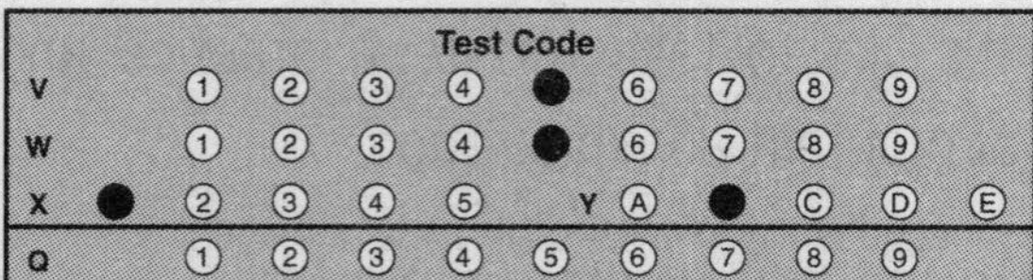

Please answer either Part I or Part II by filling in the specific circle in row Q. You are to fill in ONE and ONLY ONE circle, as described below, to indicate how you obtained your knowledge of French. The information you provide is for statistical purposes only and will not influence your score on the test.

Part I If your knowledge of French does not come primarily from courses taken in grades 9 through 12, fill in circle 9 and leave the remaining circles blank, regardless of how long you studied the subject in school. For example, you are to fill in circle 9 if your knowledge of French comes primarily from any of the following sources: study prior to the ninth grade, courses taken at a college, special study, living in a home in which French is the principal language spoken, or extensive residence abroad that includes significant experience in the French language.

Part II If your knowledge of French does come primarily from courses taken in secondary school, fill in the circle that indicates the level of the French course in which you are currently enrolled. If you are not now enrolled in a French course, fill in the circle that indicates the level of the most advanced course in French that you have completed.

- First year: first or second half —Fill in circle 1.
- Second year: first half —Fill in circle 2.
  second half —Fill in circle 3.
- Third year: first half —Fill in circle 4.
  second half —Fill in circle 5.
- Fourth year: first half —Fill in circle 6.
  second half —Fill in circle 7.
- Advanced Placement course or a course at a level higher than fourth year, second half
  or
  high school course work plus a minimum of four weeks of study abroad —Fill in circle 8.

When the supervisor gives the signal, turn the page and begin the French Test with Listening. There are 100 numbered circles on the answer sheet and 86 questions in the French Test with Listening. Therefore, use only circles 1 to 86 for recording your answers.

FRENCH TEST WITH LISTENING

SECTION I

LISTENING

Approximate time—20 minutes

Questions 1-27

PLEASE NOTE THAT YOUR ANSWER SHEET HAS FIVE ANSWER POSITIONS, MARKED A, B, C, D, AND E, WHILE THE QUESTIONS THROUGHOUT THIS PART CONTAIN ONLY FOUR CHOICES. BE SURE NOT TO MAKE ANY MARKS IN COLUMN E.

Part A

Directions: For each question in this part, you will hear four sentences, designated (A), (B), (C), and (D). They will not be printed in your test booklet. As you listen, look at the picture in your test booklet and select the choice that best reflects what you see in the picture or what someone in the picture might say. Then fill in the corresponding circle on the answer sheet. You will hear the choices only once. Now look at the following example.

You see:

You hear:

Statement (B), "Que c'est agréable de faire du vélo," best reflects what you see in the picture or what someone in the picture might say. Therefore, you should choose answer (B).

3ZLC

GO ON TO THE NEXT PAGE

1.

2.

GO ON TO THE NEXT PAGE

3.

4.

GO ON TO THE NEXT PAGE

5.

6.

GO ON TO THE NEXT PAGE

7.

8.

GO ON TO THE NEXT PAGE

PLEASE NOTE THAT YOUR ANSWER SHEET HAS FIVE ANSWER POSITIONS, MARKED A, B, C, D AND E, WHILE THE QUESTIONS THROUGHOUT PART B CONTAIN ONLY THREE CHOICES. BE SURE NOT TO MAKE ANY MARKS IN COLUMN D OR E.

Part B

Directions: In this part of the test you will hear several short selections. A tone will announce each new selection. The selections will not be printed in your test booklet and will be heard only once. At the end of each selection, you will be asked one or two questions about what was said, each followed by three possible answers, (A), (B), and (C). The answers will not be printed in your test booklet. You will hear them only once. Select the best answer and fill in the corresponding circle on the answer sheet. Now listen to the following example, but do not mark the answer on your answer sheet.

You hear:

The best answer to the question "Qu'est-ce qu'on peut dire de la voiture en question?" is (A), "Elle est en réparation." Therefore, you should choose answer (A).

9. Mark your answer on your answer sheet.
10. Mark your answer on your answer sheet.

11. Mark your answer on your answer sheet.
12. Mark your answer on your answer sheet.

13. Mark your answer on your answer sheet.
14. Mark your answer on your answer sheet.

15. Mark your answer on your answer sheet.
16. Mark your answer on your answer sheet.

GO ON TO THE NEXT PAGE

PLEASE NOTE THAT YOUR ANSWER SHEET HAS FIVE ANSWER POSITIONS, MARKED A, B, C, D, AND E, WHILE THE QUESTIONS THROUGHOUT THIS PART CONTAIN ONLY FOUR CHOICES. BE SURE NOT TO MAKE ANY MARKS IN COLUMN E.

Part C

Directions: You will now hear some extended dialogues or monologues. You will hear each only once. After each dialogue or monologue, you will be asked several questions about what you have just heard. These questions are also printed in your test booklet. Select the best answer to each question from among the four choices printed in your test booklet and fill in the corresponding circle on the answer sheet. There is no sample question for this part.

Dialogue numéro 1

17. Quel genre de film vont-ils voir?

(A) Une histoire de pirates.
(B) Un film d'aventures.
(C) Un film d'espionnage.
(D) Un sujet d'actualité.

18. Qu'est-ce que Bernard et Sophie doivent faire à la fin de leur discussion?

(A) Ils doivent se séparer.
(B) Ils doivent se dépêcher.
(C) Ils doivent rentrer chez eux.
(D) Ils doivent aller dîner.

19. Quelle impression donne le garçon?

(A) Il est conciliant.
(B) Il n'a pas d'opinions.
(C) Il est entêté.
(D) Il est comique.

20. Pourquoi ont-ils choisi ce film?

(A) Parce que la jeune fille n'aime pas rire.
(B) Parce que le garçon en a entendu parler.
(C) Parce que la jeune fille s'intéresse aux problèmes sociaux.
(D) Parce que le garçon a envie de s'amuser ce soir-là.

Dialogue numéro 2

21. Quel est l'un des jours où Philippe va à l'école seulement le matin?

(A) Le samedi.
(B) Le lundi.
(C) Le mardi.
(D) Le jeudi.

22. Que fait Philippe dès qu'il rentre chez lui?

(A) Il prend un goûter.
(B) Il regarde la télé.
(C) Il téléphone à ses amis.
(D) Il lit un roman.

23. A part le tennis, quelle autre activité sportive Philippe préfère-t-il?

(A) Le foot.
(B) La course.
(C) La marche.
(D) Le vélo.

GO ON TO THE NEXT PAGE

Dialogue Numéro 3

24. Qu'est-ce qu'on peut dire du travail de Marie-France?

    (A) Il n'est pas exigeant.
    (B) C'est un emploi temporaire.
    (C) Il oblige Marie-France à se déplacer.
    (D) Il n'intéresse pas Marie-France.

25. Qu'est-ce que Marie-France pense des ordinateurs portatifs?

    (A) Elle les trouve intimidants.
    (B) Elle croit qu'ils déshumanisent la vie.
    (C) Elle trouve qu'ils coûtent trop cher.
    (D) Elle ne s'en occupe pas.

26. Qu'est-ce que Marie-France craint?

    (A) Que ses enfants ne se servent trop de son ordinateur portatif.
    (B) Qu'elle n'efface des lignes importantes dans un dossier.
    (C) Que l'ordinateur portatif ne provoque des disputes.
    (D) Que l'ordinateur portatif n'apporte la vie du travail à la maison.

27. Comment peut-on caractériser l'attitude de Caroline sur l'emploi des ordinateurs portatifs?

    (A) Elle est neutre.
    (B) Elle est désintéressée.
    (C) Elle est sarcastique.
    (D) Elle est encourageante.

END OF SECTION I.
DO NOT GO ON TO SECTION II UNTIL YOU ARE TOLD TO DO SO.

SECTION II

READING

Time—40 minutes

Questions 28-86

WHEN YOU BEGIN THE READING SECTION, BE SURE THAT YOU MARK YOUR ANSWER TO THE FIRST READING QUESTIONS BY FILLING IN ONE OF THE CIRCLES NEXT TO NUMBER 28 ON THE ANSWER SHEET.

Part A

Directions: This part consists of a number of incomplete statements, each having four suggested completions. Select the most appropriate completion and fill in the corresponding circle on the answer sheet.

28. Pour trouver la meilleure route de Paris à Tours, il faut consulter la -------.

(A) ville
(B) plaine
(C) carte
(D) campagne

29. Arrêtez cette radio! Ce ------- me fatigue.

(A) bain
(B) brouillard
(C) bouchon
(D) bruit

30. Les deux candidats voulaient se faire élire, donc chacun a ------- beaucoup d'améliorations au public.

(A) promis
(B) demandé
(C) refusé
(D) repris

31. Il faut attendre le feu vert avant ------- la rue.

(A) de croiser
(B) de traverser
(C) d'éteindre
(D) de réparer

32. Le cinéma ne me passionne pas trop. J'y vais seulement -------.

(A) à tort et à travers
(B) comme-ci, comme-ça
(C) de temps en temps
(D) à plusieurs reprises

33. Yves parle toujours à voix basse; donc personne ne l' -------.

(A) emporte
(B) apprend
(C) entend
(D) attire

34. La soif le tourmentait et il passait sa langue sur ses ------- sèches.

(A) lèvres
(B) joues
(C) mâchoires
(D) paupières

35. Ces murs sont très sales; il faudrait les -------.

(A) retourner
(B) rejoindre
(C) repeindre
(D) remonter

GO ON TO THE NEXT PAGE

36. J'ai tellement mal au ------- que je ne peux pas jouer au tennis.

(A) coude
(B) coup
(C) jambon
(D) droit

37. On voyait son grand âge à ses joues pleines de -------.

(A) lignes
(B) traits
(C) rides
(D) traces

38. Dominique, ferme le robinet! Sinon, tu vas faire ------- la baignoire.

(A) dérober
(B) déborder
(C) dégoûter
(D) dérouter

39. Le bébé a fait ses premiers ------- tout seul et toute la famille a applaudi.

(A) pas
(B) mots
(C) pieds
(D) pleurs

GO ON TO THE NEXT PAGE

Part B

Directions: Each of the following sentences contains a blank. From the four choices given, select the one that can be inserted in the blank to form a grammatically correct sentence and fill in the corresponding circle on the answer sheet. Choice (A) may consist of dashes that indicate that no insertion is required to form a grammatically correct sentence.

40. D'un commun accord, elles se sont toutes -------.

(A) levé
(B) levée
(C) levés
(D) levées

41. L'été prochain je voudrais voyager ------- Mexique.

(A) dans
(B) en
(C) à la
(D) au

42. Les jeunes mariés se sont installés dans leur ------- appartement.

(A) grande
(B) beau
(C) propre
(D) moderne

43. On voudrait bien savoir ------- a volé ces beaux tableaux.

(A) qu'
(B) auquel
(C) qui
(D) quel

44. Fermez la porte, afin que la pièce ------- rester fraîche.

(A) peut
(B) pouvait
(C) pouvez
(D) puisse

45. On partira ------- vous serez prêts.

(A) si
(B) dès que
(C) sans que
(D) avant que

46. Je voudrais y aller avec -------.

(A) elles
(B) tu
(C) leur
(D) ils

47. Croyant qu'Henri serait là, Jeannette ne s'est ------- fait de souci.

(A) souvent
(B) encore
(C) nul
(D) guère

48. Ils ------- à Montréal depuis trois ans et ils s'y plaisent.

(A) seraient
(B) ont été
(C) étaient
(D) sont

49. C'est un événement ------- je me souviendrai toujours.

(A) que
(B) qui
(C) auquel
(D) dont

50. Mon avocat s'occupe bien ------- mes affaires.

(A) des
(B) de
(C) à
(D) en

GO ON TO THE NEXT PAGE

Part C

Directions: The paragraphs below contain blank spaces indicating omissions in the text. For some blanks, it is necessary to choose the completion that is most appropriate to the meaning of the passage; for other blanks, to choose the one completion that forms a grammatically correct sentence. In some instances, choice (A) may consist of dashes that indicate that no insertion is required to form a grammatically correct sentence. In each case, indicate your answer by filling in the corresponding circle on the answer sheet. Be sure to read the paragraph completely before answering the questions related to it.

Hier soir, comme nous n' __(51)__ rien de mieux à faire, nous nous sommes promenés dans le parc pendant deux heures et __(52)__ avant de rentrer nous coucher. Mon copain, __(53)__ rien ne gêne, s'est tout de suite endormi __(54)__ que moi, je n'ai pas pu fermer __(55)__. J'avais toujours devant moi __(56)__ de ce pauvre homme __(57)__ que nous avions vu assis sur __(58)__ près de la porte d'entrée du parc.

51. (A) avons
    (B) avions
    (C) aurions
    (D) ayons

52. (A) midi
    (B) trente
    (C) demie
    (D) le quart

53. (A) que
    (B) quel
    (C) celui
    (D) quelqu'un

54. (A) tandis
    (B) de sorte
    (C) sans
    (D) autant

55. (A) l'oreiller
    (B) le lit
    (C) l'oeil
    (D) la couverture

56. (A) le site
    (B) l'image
    (C) la copie
    (D) le signe

57. (A) filé
    (B) fumé
    (C) enterré
    (D) affamé

58. (A) une banlieue
    (B) un banc
    (C) un banquet
    (D) une banque

GO ON TO THE NEXT PAGE

Hier, nous avons fait une balade en montagne. Nous sommes partis très tôt __(59)__, et c'est mon père __(60)__ a conduit. Il __(61)__ encore très frais, mais le soleil brillait. Et, bien sûr, tout le monde était __(62)__! Quand nous sommes arrivés dans __(63)__ magnifique, nous avons décidé __(64)__ marcher, en nous __(65)__ de temps en temps pour __(66)__ reposer. Vers midi nous avons pique-niqué __(67)__ d'un torrent. Nous avions tous très faim, et les sandwichs ont vite disparu.

59. (A) le matin
    (B) matin
    (C) du matin
    (D) dans le matin

60. (A) ---
    (B) il
    (C) qui
    (D) qu'

61. (A) faisait
    (B) avait
    (C) montait
    (D) était

62. (A) à la rigueur
    (B) de bonne heure
    (C) dans le vent
    (D) de bonne humeur

63. (A) un endroit
    (B) un lac
    (C) une place
    (D) une altitude

64. (A) ---
    (B) pour
    (C) de
    (D) à

65. (A) arrêtons
    (B) arrêter
    (C) arrêtés
    (D) arrêtant

66. (A) ---
    (B) se
    (C) me
    (D) nous

67. (A) au bord
    (B) à bord
    (C) autour
    (D) au fond

GO ON TO THE NEXT PAGE

Part D

Directions: Read the following texts carefully for comprehension. Each is followed by a number of questions or incomplete statements. Select the answer or completion that is best according to the text and fill in the corresponding circle on the answer sheet.

(Ce passage a été écrit en 1856.)

Ligne

Que faites-vous, Gaston? Quand viendrez-vous? Vous aviez pourtant promis de nous rejoindre. Comment avez-vous pu rester dix grands jours sans me voir? Quand nous étions ensemble dans notre cher Arlange, vous ne saviez pas me quitter pour une heure. Dieu! que les heures sont longues à Paris! Maman me parle à chaque instant contre vous, mais à votre nom seul il se fait dans mon coeur un tapage qui m'empêche d'entendre. Elle me dit que vous m'avez abandonnée: vous devinez que je n'en crois rien.

Vous n'êtes pas homme à fermer un si bon livre à la première page. Moi, depuis que je ne vous ai plus, je suis tout hébétée et toute languissante. Imaginez-vous que par moments je crois que je ne suis pas votre femme, et que cette belle cérémonie de l'église, et ce bal où nous étions si heureux, sont un rêve qui a trop tôt fini. Vous n'imaginerez jamais combien vous me manquez. Quand je sors avec maman, je vous cherche dans les rues: tout ce que j'ai vu à Paris jusqu'à présent, c'est que vous n'y êtes pas. Le soir, j'embrouille régulièrement votre nom dans mes prières; le matin, en m'éveillant, je regarde si vous n'êtes point autour de moi. Est-il possible que je pense tant à vous et que vous m'ayez oubliée? Peut-être m'en voulez-vous de vous avoir quitté si brusquement et sans vous dire adieu. Si vous saviez! Ce n'est pas moi qui suis partie; c'est maman qui m'a enlevée.

68. De quoi la narratrice de ce passage se plaint-elle?
    (A) De l'absence de Gaston
    (B) Du bruit de la ville
    (C) De la mère de Gaston
    (D) De sa maladie récente

69. Où la narratrice de ce passage se trouve-t-elle?
    (A) A la campagne
    (B) Près de la mer
    (C) Dans son village natal
    (D) Dans une grande ville

70. Quelle est l'attitude de la mère de la narratrice envers Gaston?
    (A) Elle le trouve assez sympathique.
    (B) Elle éprouve de l'indifférence envers lui.
    (C) Elle montre une certaine hostilité à son égard.
    (D) Elle l'aime presqu'autant que sa fille.

71. A qui la narratrice écrit-elle?
    (A) A son frère
    (B) A son amant
    (C) A son fiancé
    (D) A son mari

72. La phrase, "Vous n'êtes pas homme à fermer un si bon livre à la première page" (lignes 11-12) laisse entendre que
    (A) la narratrice a épousé Gaston récemment
    (B) la narratrice est bibliothécaire
    (C) Gaston se méfie de la narratrice
    (D) Gaston n'aime pas les livres courts

73. D'après le texte, que fait la narratrice quand elle se promène avec sa mère?
    (A) Elle fait des prières pour Gaston.
    (B) Elle achète des cadeaux pour Gaston.
    (C) Elle cherche Gaston partout.
    (D) Elle parle de Gaston à sa mère.

74. Selon la narratrice, quel pourrait être l'état d'esprit de Gaston?
    (A) Il a peur de lui dire adieu.
    (B) Il est triste quand il y a du brouillard.
    (C) Il est plutôt religieux.
    (D) Il est en colère contre elle.

75. La narratrice a quitté Gaston parce qu'elle
    (A) préfère Paris à la campagne
    (B) a été obligée de le faire
    (C) a besoin de soins médicaux
    (D) veut se faire religieuse

GO ON TO THE NEXT PAGE

LA CARTE INTEGRALE
(carte orange annuelle)

La carte Intégrale, c'est :

Un coupon unique, valable toute l'année pour tous vos déplacements en Ile de France.

Un abonnement personnel et permanent, utilisable à volonté sur les RER, Bus, Métros et trains d'Ile de France, en fonction des zones choisies (mêmes zones au choix que la carte orange).

Ses avantages :

"Chaque mois, elle vous simplifie la vie !", une seule démarche lors du premier abonnement.

–Vous n'avez plus de file d'attente en fin de mois.

–Vous n'avez même plus besoin d'y penser.

Vous avez déjà votre coupon.

"Vous choisissez, vous changez d'avis, votre abonnement c'est comme vous en avez envie !"

76. La carte Intégrale vous permettra
    (A) de louer une voiture à tarif réduit
    (B) d'utiliser tous les transports publics
    (C) de régler toutes vos factures mensuelles à la fois
    (D) d'obtenir les hebdomadaires les plus récents

77. Le coupon est valide pendant
    (A) toute la vie
    (B) un mois
    (C) les vacances
    (D) douze mois

GO ON TO THE NEXT PAGE

Oh! ces journées de neige, quelle transformation subite elles opéraient en nous, autour de nous dès les premiers flocons! La lumière se retirait. Tout devenait terne: le plâtre des façades prenait une couleur grise, fanée, les arbres paraissaient plus noirs. Dehors, quand nous levions la tête, c'était presque une ivresse de recevoir sur la figure, sans savoir où elles se poseraient, ces mille petites abeilles blanches dont le froid nous piquait le visage, avec une si furtive, une si délicate précision qu'elles semblaient avoir choisi, tout en tourbillonnant, la place où elles nous atteindraient. Le ciel n'était plus gris; il était roux, opaque. Et peu à peu, les grilles du collège, les branches, les bancs, les toits, devenaient d'autres grilles, d'autres branches, d'autres bancs, d'autres toits.

Mais le vent cessait. Alors elle tombait plus vite et recouvrait tout, uniformément, de sa blancheur duveteuse comme si elle avait profité de ce moment d'inattention pour s'installer, en dominatrice, pour s'infiltrer jusqu'entre les fentes des persiennes, sous les tuiles, et même dans les recoins du grenier en passant par un carreau cassé.

78. Les enfants semblent accueillir la neige avec

(A) plaisir
(B) dégoût
(C) tristesse
(D) crainte

79. Les flocons de neige sont comparés à des

(A) fleurs
(B) pierres
(C) oiseaux
(D) insectes

80. Quel effet la neige a-t-elle pour l'auteur?

(A) Elle détruit le monde qui l'entoure.
(B) Elle crée un nouveau décor.
(C) Elle attriste l'observateur.
(D) Elle enlaidit le paysage.

81. Dans le deuxième paragraphe, la neige envahit

(A) une maison
(B) un jardin
(C) une place
(D) une ville

82. Dans ce passage, la neige est

(A) cultivée
(B) balayée
(C) personnifiée
(D) enlevée

83. L'auteur attribue à la neige un pouvoir

(A) fortifiant
(B) magique
(C) chimique
(D) exotique

GO ON TO THE NEXT PAGE

84. Qu'est-ce que cette publicité veut encourager?

(A) La course à pied
(B) La recherche médicale
(C) Des dons d'argent
(D) Des dons d'organes

85. Qui va participer à l'événement annoncé?

(A) Des médecins
(B) Des malades
(C) Des sportifs
(D) Des chercheurs

86. Qu'est-ce qui doit être amélioré?

(A) L'entraînement des jeunes sportifs
(B) L'éducation des futurs médecins
(C) Les techniques médicales
(D) Les chances de survie

END OF SECTION II

STOP

IF YOU FINISH BEFORE TIME IS CALLED, YOU MAY CHECK YOUR WORK ON SECTION II OF THIS TEST.

DO NOT TURN TO ANY OTHER TEST IN THIS BOOK.

How to Score the SAT Subject Test in French with Listening

When you take an actual SAT Subject Test in French with Listening, you receive an overall composite score as well as two subscores: one for the reading section, one for the listening section.

The reading and listening scores are reported on the College Board's 20–80 scale. However the composite score, which is the most significant of the scores reported to the colleges you specify, is in the form of the College Board's 200–800 scale.

Worksheet 1. Finding Your Raw Listening Subscore

STEP 1: Table A lists the correct answers for all the questions on the Subject Test in French with Listening that is reproduced in this book. It also serves as a worksheet for you to calculate your raw Listening subscore.

- Compare your answers with those given in the table.
- Put a check in the column marked "Right" if your answer is correct.
- Put a check in the column marked "Wrong" if your answer is incorrect.
- Leave both columns blank if you omitted the question.

STEP 2: Count the number of right answers for questions 1–8 and 17–27.

Enter the total here: ________________

STEP 3: Count the number of wrong answers for questions 1–8 and 17–27.

Enter the total here: ________________

STEP 4: Multiply the number of wrong answers by .333.

Enter the product here: ________________

STEP 5: Subtract the result obtained in Step 4 from the total you obtained in Step 2.

Enter the result here: ________________

STEP 6: Count the number of right answers for questions 9–16.

Enter the total here: ________________

STEP 7: Count the number of wrong answers for questions 9–16.

Enter the total here: ________________

STEP 8: Multiply the number of wrong answers for step 7 by .500.

Enter the product here: ________________

STEP 9: Subtract the result obtained in Step 8 from the total you obtained in Step 6.

Enter the result here: ________________

STEP 10: Add the result obtained in Step 5 to the result obtained in Step 9.

Enter the result here: ________________

STEP 11: Round the number obtained in Step 10 to the nearest whole number.

Enter the result here: ________________

The number you obtained in Step 11 is your raw Listening subscore.

Worksheet 2. Finding Your Raw Reading Subscore

STEP 1: Table A lists the correct answers for all the questions on the Subject Test in French with Listening that is reproduced in this book. It also serves as a worksheet for you to calculate your raw Reading subscore.

STEP 2: Count the number of right answers for questions 28–86.

Enter the total here: ________________

STEP 3: Count the number of wrong answers for questions 28–86.

Enter the total here: ________________

STEP 4: Multiply the number of wrong answers by .333.

Enter the product here: ________________

STEP 5: Subtract the result obtained in Step 4 from the total you obtained in Step 2.

Enter the result here: ________________

STEP 6: Round the number obtained in Step 5 to the nearest whole number.

Enter the result here: ________________

The number you obtained in Step 6 is your raw Reading subscore.

Worksheet 3. Finding Your Raw Composite Score

STEP 1: Enter your unrounded raw Reading subscore from Step 5 of Worksheet 2.

Enter the result here: ________________

STEP 2: Enter your unrounded raw Listening subscore from Step 10 of Worksheet 1.

Enter the result here: ________________

STEP 3: Add the result obtained in Step 1 to the result obtained in Step 2.

Enter the result here: ________________

STEP 4: Round the number obtained in Step 3 to the nearest whole number.

Enter the result here: ________________

The number you obtained in Step 4 is your raw composite score.

Table A

Answers to the Subject Test in French with Listening, Form 3ZLC, and Percentage of Students Answering Each Question Correctly									
Question Number	Correct Answer	Right	Wrong	Percentage of Students Answering the Question Correctly*	Question Number	Correct Answer	Right	Wrong	Percentage of Students Answering the Question Correctly*
1	B			94	33	C			87
2	B			56	34	A			63
3	A			90	35	C			76
4	B			70	36	A			43
5	B			36	37	C			26
6	C			49	38	B			33
7	C			75	39	A			38
8	D			55	40	D			97
9	B			94	41	D			59
10	B			82	42	C			37
11	C			51	43	C			88
12	A			82	44	D			45
13	C			95	45	B			44
14	C			62	46	A			55
15	C			30	47	D			22
16	B			27	48	D			35
17	D			92	49	D			36
18	B			69	50	B			60
19	A			51	51	B			72
20	C			84	52	C			85
21	A			55	53	A			38
22	A			61	54	A			45
23	D			73	55	C			73
24	C			55	56	B			93
25	B			26	57	D			42
26	D			50	58	B			44
27	D			75	59	A			26
28	C			92	60	C			87
29	D			86	61	A			69
30	A			90	62	D			77
31	B			87	63	A			55
32	C			92	64	C			60

Table A continued on next page

Table A continued from previous page

Question Number	Correct Answer	Right	Wrong	Percentage of Students Answering the Question Correctly*	Question Number	Correct Answer	Right	Wrong	Percentage of Students Answering the Question Correctly*
65	D			41	76	B			98
66	D			63	77	D			68
67	A			56	78	A			61
68	A			95	79	D			34
69	D			83	80	B			50
70	C			85	81	A			28
71	D			73	82	C			80
72	A			64	83	B			54
73	C			80	84	D			31
74	D			39	85	C			63
75	B			83	86	D			72

* These percentages are based on an analysis of the answer sheets of a representative sample of 1,519 students who took the original form of this test in November 2003, and whose mean composite score was 602. They may be used as an indication of the relative difficulty of a particular question. Each percentage may also be used to predict the likelihood that a typical SAT Subject Test in French with Listening candidate will answer that question correctly on this edition of the test.

Finding Your Scaled Score

When you take SAT Subject Tests, the scores sent to the colleges you specify are reported on the College Board scale, which ranges from 200–800. Subscores are reported on a scale which ranges from 20–80. You can convert your practice test scores to scaled scores by using Tables B, C, and D. To find your scaled score, locate your raw score in the left-hand column of the table; the corresponding score in the right-hand column is your scaled score. For example, a raw score of 47 on this particular edition of the Subject Test in French with Listening corresponds to a scaled composite score of 610.

Raw scores are converted to scaled scores to ensure that a score earned on any one edition of a particular Subject Test is comparable to the same scaled score earned on any other edition of the same Subject Test. Because some editions of the tests may be slightly easier or more difficult than others, College Board scaled scores are adjusted so that they indicate the same level of performance regardless of the edition of the test taken and the ability of the group that takes it. Thus, for example, a score of 400 on one edition of a test taken at a particular administration indicates the same level of achievement as a score of 400 on a different edition of the test taken at a different administration.

When you take the SAT Subject Tests during a national administration, your scores are likely to differ somewhat from the scores you obtain on the tests in this book. People perform at different levels at different times for reasons unrelated to the tests themselves. The precision of any test is also limited because it represents only a sample of all the possible questions that could be asked.

Your scaled composite score from Table B is ____________________ .

Your scaled listening score from Table C is ____________________ .

Your scaled reading score from Table D is ____________________ .

Table B

Scaled Score Conversion Table Subject Test in French with Listening Composite Score (Form 3ZLC)					
Raw Score	Scaled Score	Raw Score	Scaled Score	Raw Score	Scaled Score
86	800	48	620	10	400
85	800	47	610	9	390
84	800	46	600	8	390
83	800	45	600	7	380
82	800	44	590	6	370
81	800	43	590	5	370
80	800	42	580	4	360
79	800	41	580	3	350
78	800	40	570	2	340
77	800	39	560	1	340
76	800	38	560	0	330
75	800	37	550	-1	320
74	790	36	550	-2	320
73	780	35	540	-3	310
72	770	34	540	-4	300
71	770	33	530	-5	290
70	760	32	530	-6	290
69	750	31	520	-7	280
68	750	30	520	-8	280
67	740	29	510	-9	270
66	730	28	510	-10	270
65	730	27	500	-11	260
64	720	26	490	-12	260
63	710	25	490	-13	260
62	710	24	480	-14	260
61	700	23	480	-15	250
60	690	22	470	-16	240
59	690	21	470	-17	230
58	680	20	460	-18	230
57	670	19	460	-19	220
56	670	18	450	-20	220
55	660	17	440	-21	220
54	650	16	440	-22	220
53	650	15	430	-23	210
52	640	14	430	-24	210
51	640	13	420	-25	210
50	630	12	410	-26	210
49	620	11	410	-27	200
				-28	200
				-29	200
				-30	200

Table C

Scaled Score Conversion Table Subject Test in French with Listening Listening Subscore (Form 3ZLC)					
Raw Score	Scaled Score	Raw Score	Scaled Score	Raw Score	Scaled Score
27	80	12	56	-3	30
26	80	11	54	-4	28
25	80	10	53	-5	27
24	79	9	51	-6	26
23	76	8	50	-7	25
22	74	7	48	-8	24
21	72	6	47	-9	23
20	70	5	45	-10	22
19	68	4	43		
18	66	3	42		
17	64	2	40		
16	62	1	38		
15	60	0	36		
14	59	-1	34		
13	57	-2	32		

Table D

Scaled Score Conversion Table Subject Test in French with Listening Reading Subscore (Form 3ZLC)					
Raw Score	Scaled Score	Raw Score	Scaled Score	Raw Score	Scaled Score
59	80	32	61	5	40
58	80	31	60	4	39
57	80	30	59	3	38
56	80	29	59	2	37
55	80	28	58	1	36
54	80	27	57	0	35
53	80	26	56	-1	33
52	79	25	55	-2	32
51	78	24	55	-3	31
50	77	23	54	-4	30
49	76	22	53	-5	29
48	76	21	52	-6	28
47	75	20	52	-7	28
46	74	19	51	-8	27
45	73	18	50	-9	26
44	72	17	49	-10	26
43	71	16	49	-11	25
42	70	15	48	-12	24
41	69	14	47	-13	23
40	68	13	46	-14	22
39	67	12	46	-15	22
38	67	11	45	-16	21
37	66	10	44	-17	21
36	65	9	43	-18	20
35	64	8	42	-19	20
34	63	7	41	-20	20
33	62	6	40		

How Did You Do on the Subject Test in French with Listening?

After you score your test and analyze your performance, think about the following questions:

Did you run out of time before reaching the end of the test?

If so, you may need to pace yourself better. For example, maybe you spent too much time on one or two hard questions. A better approach might be to skip the ones you can't answer right away and try answering all the questions that remain on the test. Then if there's time, go back to the questions you skipped.

Did you take a long time reading the directions?

You will save time when you take the test by learning the directions to the Subject Test in French with Listening ahead of time. Each minute you spend reading directions during the test is a minute that you could use to answer questions.

How did you handle questions you were unsure of?

If you were able to eliminate one or more of the answer choices as wrong and guess from the remaining ones, your approach probably worked to your advantage. On the other hand, making haphazard guesses or omitting questions without trying to eliminate choices could cost you valuable points.

How difficult were the questions for you compared with other students who took the test?

Table A shows you how difficult the multiple-choice questions were for the group of students who took this test during its national administration. The right-hand column gives the percentage of students that answered each question correctly.

A question answered correctly by almost everyone in the group is obviously an easier question. For example, 95 percent of the students answered question 13 correctly. But only 22 percent answered question 47 correctly.

Keep in mind that these percentages are based on just one group of students. They would probably be different with another group of students taking the test.

If you missed several easier questions, go back and try to find out why: Did the questions cover material you haven't yet reviewed? Did you misunderstand the directions?

Chapter 10
German

Purpose

There are two Subject Tests in German: German and German with Listening. The reading-only test measures your ability to understand written German. German with Listening measures your ability to understand spoken and written German.

Format

- The Subject Test in German takes one hour and includes 80 to 85 multiple-choice questions.
- The Subject Test in German with Listening also takes one hour and includes 85 to 90 multiple-choice listening and reading questions. Listening questions require answers to questions based on shorter and longer listening selections.
- Both tests evaluate your reading ability through a variety of questions requiring a wide-ranging knowledge of German.

Content

Both tests comply with the German spelling reform (Rechtschreibreform) as much as possible. They evaluate reading ability in these areas:

Sentence completion and paragraph completion questions test vocabulary and grammar requiring you to know the meaning of words and idiomatic expressions in context and to identify usage that is structurally correct and appropriate. For each omission, you must select the choice that BEST fits each sentence.

Reading comprehension questions test your understanding of the content of various materials taken from sources such as advertisements, timetables, street signs, forms, and tickets. They also examine your ability to read passages representative of various styles and levels of difficulty. Each test edition has several prose passages followed by questions that test your understanding of the passage. The passages, mostly adapted from literary sources and newspapers or magazines, are generally one or two paragraphs in length and test whether you can identify the main idea or comprehend facts or details in the text.

The Subject Test in German with Listening also measures the ability to understand spoken language with two types of listening questions:

Type One contains short dialogues/monologues with one or two multiple-choice questions. Dialogues/monologues, questions, and answer choices are recorded. Questions are also printed in the test book.

Type Two contains longer dialogues and monologues with several multiple-choice questions. Dialogues/monologues and questions are only recorded and not printed in the test book. Answer choices are not recorded; they appear only in the test book.

German	
Skills Measured	Approximate Percentage of Test
Vocabulary in Context and Structure in Context (grammar)	50
Reading Comprehension—(authentic stimulus materials and passages)	50

German with Listening	
Test Sections	Approximate Percentage of Test
Listening Section (20 minutes)	**35**
Short dialogues/monologues Long dialogues/monologues	
Reading Section (40 minutes)	**65**
Vocabulary in Context Structure in Context (grammar) Reading Comprehension—(authentic stimulus materials and passages)	

How to Prepare

Both tests assume differences in language preparation; neither is tied to a specific textbook or method of instruction. The German tests are appropriate for students who have completed two, three, or four years of German language study in high school or the equivalent. Your best preparation for these tests is a gradual development of competence in German over a period of years. Familiarize yourself with directions in advance. The directions in this book are identical to those that appear on the test.

German with Listening

A practice audio CD is included with this book. A practice CD with different sample questions can be obtained, along with a copy of the *SAT Subject Tests Preparation Booklet,* from your school counselor, or you can access the files at www.collegeboard.com. You should also take the practice test included with this book.

CD Players

Using CD Players for Language Tests with Listening

Take an acceptable CD player to the test center. Your CD player must be in good working order, so insert fresh batteries on the day before the test. You may bring additional batteries and a backup player to the test center.

Test center staff won't have batteries, CD players, or earphones for your use, so your CD player must be:

- equipped with earphones
- portable (hand-held)
- battery operated
- for your use only. CD players cannot be shared with other test-takers.

Note

If the volume on your CD player disturbs other test-takers, the test center supervisor may ask you to move to another seat.

What to do if your CD player malfunctions:

- Raise your hand and tell the test supervisor.
- Switch to backup equipment if you have it and continue the test. If you don't have backup equipment, your score on the Subject Test in German with Listening will be canceled. But scores on other Subject Tests you take that day will still be counted.

What if you receive a defective CD on test day? Raise your hand and ask the supervisor for a replacement.

Scores

For both tests, the total score is reported on the 200-to-800 scale. For the listening test, listening and reading subscores are reported on the 20-to-80 scale.

Sample Reading Questions

Your answer sheet has five answer positions marked A, B, C, D, and E, while the questions throughout this test contain only four choices. Be sure NOT to make any marks in column E.

Part A

Directions: This part consists of a number of incomplete statements, each having four suggested completions. Select the most appropriate completion and fill in the corresponding circle on the answer sheet.

1. Ich glaube, er kommt schon.........Mittwoch zurück.
   (A) nächstem
   (B) nächster
   (C) nächstes
   (D) nächsten

Choice (D) is the correct answer to question 1. This question tests your knowledge of the correct weak adjective ending following a presupposed dative-preposition that would answer to the question "when" ("wann"). You need to know that the gender of "Mittwoch" is masculine and that the correct preposition (eliminated here) would be "an." The entire prepositional phrase would be: an dem (am) nächsten Mittwoch; however, "am" or "an dem" is eliminated, an ellipsis very commonly used in temporal phrases. Choices (A), (B), and (C) cannot structurally be preceded by "am" or "an dem."

2. Diesen Sommer konnten die Touristen in Europa gar nicht über das Wetter.........
   (A) sagen
   (B) kennen
   (C) klagen
   (D) denken

Choice (C) is the correct answer to question 2. This question tests your knowledge of verbs in combination with a negation and a preposition. You are asked to choose the verb that fits best. Given the context (tourists could not complain about the weather in Europe this year), "klagen" is the only possible option that not only fits contextually but also structurally.

3. Annie ist die jüngste Tochter der Familie, bei.........wir diesen Sommer gewohnt haben.
   (A) dem
   (B) denen
   (C) der
   (D) die

Choice (C) is the correct answer to question 3. This question asks you to choose the correct form of the relative pronoun "die" following the preposition "bei." You should know that "bei" asks for the dative and that the gender of "Familie," to which the relative pronoun refers, is feminine. Choice (C) is therefore the only possible answer, since "der" is the dative form of "die."

Part B

Directions: In each of the following paragraphs, there are numbered blanks indicating that words or phrases have been omitted. For each numbered blank, four completions are provided. First read through the entire paragraph. Then, for each numbered blank, choose the completion that is most appropriate and fill in the corresponding circle on the answer sheet.

Ich verabschiede mich jetzt, weil ich morgen ______________________

4. (A) gern
   (B) früh
   (C) schon
   (D) langsam

aufstehen muss, um ______________ Berlin zu einer wichtigen

5. (A) auf
   (B) an
   (C) nach
   (D) zu

Konferenz ______________.

6. (A) fährt
   (B) fahren
   (C) gefahren
   (D) zu fahren

Choice (B) is the correct answer to question 4. This question is a vocabulary question that tests your knowledge of adverbs. You are asked to choose the adverb that fits best. Given the context (the person has to go on a business trip), "früh" is the most appropriate of the four choices to complement the verb "aufstehen."

Choice (C) is the correct answer to question 5. In this question, you are asked to choose the correct preposition, which, here is part of an idiomatic expression. You need to know that of the four choices only the preposition "nach" is appropriate in connection with a motion verb (fahren) and the name of a city (Berlin).

Choice (D) is the correct answer to question 6. In this question, you are asked to choose the correct form of the verb "fahren." The infinitive form of "fahren" with "zu" is required because the clause is introduced by "um." The other choices—(A) third person singular present tense, (B) infinitive without "zu," (C) past participle—are therefore not appropriate to form a grammatically correct sentence.

Part C

Directions: Read the following texts carefully for comprehension. Each is followed by a number of questions or incomplete statements. Select the answer or completion that is best according to the text and fill in the corresponding circle on the answer sheet.

Betreten
der Baustelle
verboten
Eltern haften für ihre Kinder!

7. Wo findet man dieses Schild?
   - (A) Auf einem Kinderspielplatz
   - (B) An einem Gefängnis
   - (C) Vor einer Baumschule
   - (D) Auf einem Bauplatz

Choice (D) is the correct answer to question 7. This question asks you where you would see such a sign. This sign tells you that you are not to enter the construction site. It continues that parents are responsible for their children's actions. "Bauplatz" in choice (D) is a synonym for "Baustelle:" both nouns, translated into English, mean construction site. Choice (A) refers to a playground (*Kinderspielplatz*), choice (B) to a prison (*Gefängnis*), and choice (C) to a nursery (*Baumschule*).

Der Frankfurter Sinkkasten ist ein Verein, der von drei jungen Leuten—Aina, Wolfgang und Werner—in einem Kellergewölbe am Main gegründet wurde, nachdem sie sich eines Tages entschlossen hatten, ihren Feierabend nicht weiter in Kneipen zu verbringen.

Der Sinkkasten verlangt einen Mitgliedsbeitrag von drei Euro monatlich, obgleich es ihm gar nicht um Gewinne geht. Hier können aber endlich jeden Abend Jugendliche zusammenkommen und fröhlich sein. Im Sinkkasten treten außerdem viele prominente Musiker und Gruppen auf. Dazu kommen dann noch interessante Theateraufführungen. Oft werden den Gästen auch sehr gute Filme gezeigt. Junge Maler können hier ihre ersten Werke ausstellen, und regelmäßig dürfen die jungen Gäste selbst auch mal Künstler spielen: sie können beim freien Malen ihre bisher verborgenen Talente entdecken. Die schönsten Werke werden anschließend ausgestellt.

Das Programm ersetzt den Jugendlichen Theater, Kino und Kneipe zugleich. Deshalb kommen sie auch in Scharen! Längst hat es sich herumgesprochen, dass man im Sinkkasten ganz nette Leute kennenlernen kann. Die Stadtverwaltung von Frankfurt am Main hat inzwischen den Sinkkasten schätzen gelernt: seit Anfang 1995 wird der Klub vom Kulturamt mit Geld unterstützt.

8. Was können die Gäste in diesem Klub tun?
   (A) Ihre eigenen Schöpfungen ausstellen
   (B) Endlich ihre Kochkunst zeigen
   (C) Ohne monatlichen Beitrag alles mitmachen
   (D) Die täglichen Hausaufgaben erledigen

Choice (A) is the correct answer to question 8. In this question, you are asked what club members and guests can do when visiting the "Sinkkasten." To answer this question, you have to read the second and third paragraphs carefully. Nothing is mentioned with respect to choices (B) "Kochkunst" and (D) "Hausaufgaben." "Monatlicher Beitrag" in choice (C) is mentioned in the second paragraph ("Mitgliedsbeitrag … monatlich"), but it is stated here that each member of the "Sinkkasten" has to contribute 3,-E per month, while choice (C) describes exactly the opposite. Choice (A) *Ihre eigenen Schöpfungen ausstellen* is the only correct answer to the question and is supported by "regelmäßig dürfen die jungen Gäste selbst auch mal Künstler spielen:" … up to … "Die schönsten Werke werden anschließend ausgestellt."

9. Was kann man im allgemeinen über den Klub sagen?
   (A) Er ist das Kulturzentrum der Stadt Frankfurt.
   (B) Er ist finanzieller Mittelpunkt für die Stadtväter.
   (C) Er ist Anziehungspunkt für viele junge Leute.
   (D) Er ist als kultureller Treffpunkt nicht erfolgreich.

Choice (C) is the correct answer to question 9. This question asks what can be said in general about this club ("Der Sinkkasten"). The entire reading passage includes information about how and where young people used to spend their free time and how "der Sinkkasten" has changed their habits and what the club means to them. Choice (C) *Er ist Anziehungspunkt für viele junge Leute*, summarizes in one sentence this passage and is therefore the only correct answer. Choice (A) describes the club as the cultural center ("Kulturzentrum") of the city of Frankfurt, which is obviously never mentioned in the text. Choice (B) refers wrongly to the club as a financial center for representatives of the city government, and choice (D) claims erroneously that the club is unsuccessful as a cultural meeting place.

German Test

Practice Helps

The test that follows is an actual, recently administered SAT Subject Test in German. To get an idea of what it's like to take this test, practice under conditions that are much like those of an actual test administration.

- Set aside an hour when you can take the test uninterrupted. Make sure you complete the test in one sitting.
- Sit at a desk or table with no other books or papers. Dictionaries, other books, or notes are not allowed in the test room.
- Tear out an answer sheet from the back of this book and fill it in just as you would on the day of the test. One answer sheet can be used for up to three Subject Tests.
- Read the instructions that precede the practice test. During the actual administration, you will be asked to read them before answering test questions.
- Time yourself by placing a clock or kitchen timer in front of you.
- After you finish the practice test, read the sections "How to Score the SAT Subject Test in German" and "How Did You Do on the Subject Test in German?"
- The appearance of the answer sheet in this book may differ from the answer sheet you see on test day.

GERMAN TEST

The top portion of the section of the answer sheet that you will use in taking the German Test must be filled in exactly as shown in the illustration below. Note carefully that you have to do all of the following on your answer sheet.

1. Print GERMAN on the line under the words "Subject Test (print)."

2. In the shaded box labeled "Test Code" fill in four circles:

   —Fill in circle 3 in the row labeled V.
   —Fill in circle 4 in the row labeled W.
   —Fill in circle 2 in the row labeled X.
   —Fill in circle D in the row labeled Y.

Test Code											
V		①	②	●	④	⑤	⑥	⑦	⑧	⑨	
W		①	②	③	●	⑤	⑥	⑦	⑧	⑨	
X	①	●	③	④	⑤	Y Ⓐ	Ⓑ	Ⓒ	●	Ⓔ	
Q		①	②	③	④	⑤	⑥	⑦	⑧	⑨	

Subject Test (print)
GERMAN

Please answer either Part I or Part II by filling in the specific circle in row Q. You are to fill in ONE and ONLY ONE circle, as described below, to indicate how you obtained your knowledge of German. <u>The information you provide is for statistical purposes only and will not influence your score on the test.</u>

Part I If your knowledge of German <u>does not</u> come primarily from courses taken in grades 9 through 12, fill in <u>circle 9</u> and leave the remaining circles blank, regardless of how long you studied the subject in school. For example, you are to fill in circle 9 if your knowledge of German comes <u>primarily</u> from any of the following sources: study prior to the ninth grade, courses taken at a college, special study, living in a home in which German is the principal language spoken, or extensive residence abroad that includes significant experience in the German language.

Part II If your knowledge of German <u>does</u> come primarily from courses taken in secondary school or the equivalent, fill in the circle that indicates the level of the German course in which you are currently enrolled. If you are not now enrolled in a German course, fill in the circle that indicates the level of the most advanced course in German that you have completed.

- First year: first or second half —Fill in circle 1.
- Second year: first half —Fill in circle 2.
  second half —Fill in circle 3.
- Third year: first half —Fill in circle 4.
  second half —Fill in circle 5.
- Fourth year: first half —Fill in circle 6.
  second half —Fill in circle 7.
- Advanced Placement course or a course at a level higher than fourth year, second half
  or
  high school course work plus a minimum of four weeks of study abroad —Fill in circle 8.

When the supervisor gives the signal, turn the page and begin the German Test. There are 100 numbered circles on the answer sheet and 85 questions in the German Test. Therefore, use only circles 1 to 85 for recording your answers.

GERMAN TEST

PLEASE NOTE THAT YOUR ANSWER SHEET HAS FIVE ANSWER POSITIONS, MARKED A, B, C, D, E, WHILE THE QUESTIONS THROUGHOUT THIS TEST CONTAIN ONLY FOUR CHOICES. BE SURE NOT TO MAKE ANY MARKS IN COLUMN E.

PART A

Directions: This part consists of a number of incomplete statements, each having four suggested completions. Select the most appropriate completion and fill in the corresponding circle on the answer sheet.

1. ------- ist die neue Schülerin in unserer Klasse.

   (A) Er
   (B) Sie
   (C) Wir
   (D) Ihr

2. Ich möchte mir den Film ansehen. Gehen wir ------- Kino.

   (A) ans
   (B) ins
   (C) aufs
   (D) zum

3. Brigitte, bitte ------- mir nicht böse!

   (A) seien
   (B) sei
   (C) sein
   (D) seist

4. Sie isst viel Gemüse und Obst, ------- es gesund ist.

   (A) weil
   (B) ob
   (C) bevor
   (D) nachdem

5. Ich mache dir eine Skizze, denn mein Haus ist nicht leicht -------.

   (A) zu finden
   (B) finden
   (C) findend
   (D) gefunden

6. Das hier ist doch dein Buch. Siehst du irgendwo -------?

   (A) meine
   (B) meins
   (C) mein
   (D) meinen

7. Warum fragst du mich das schon wieder? Hast du denn nicht -------?

   (A) aufgepasst
   (B) angehört
   (C) wiederholt
   (D) vergessen

8. Deine Bemerkung beim Essen war doch etwas -------.

   (A) richtig
   (B) frühzeitig
   (C) gut
   (D) eigenartig

9. Heike ist arbeitslos. Sie möchte sich bei uns ------- eine Stelle bewerben.

   (A) in
   (B) um
   (C) an
   (D) über

3XAC

GO ON TO THE NEXT PAGE

10. Bei mir zu Hause musste man ------- immer vor dem Essen die Hände waschen.
    (A) wir
    (B) dich
    (C) sie
    (D) sich

11. Es ist ------- sehr spät und ich gehe schlafen.
    (A) fast
    (B) schon
    (C) erst
    (D) schön

12. Wir sind nicht -------, so viel Geld für ein neues Auto auszugeben.
    (A) zufrieden
    (B) fertig
    (C) vollständig
    (D) imstande

13. Franz ist in der Küche und will ------- Hühnchen braten.
    (A) einen
    (B) eine
    (C) ein
    (D) eines

14. Wir sind alle zu ihrem Geburtstag eingeladen -------.
    (A) worden
    (B) wurden
    (C) werden
    (D) geworden

15. Wie spät ist es? Meine ------- ist stehen geblieben.
    (A) Uhr
    (B) Zeit
    (C) Stunde
    (D) Seite

16. Nach ------- Krankheit ist ihr Vater endlich wieder gesund.
    (A) lange
    (B) langer
    (C) langes
    (D) langem

17. Ich sage dir nicht, was dieses Wort -------!
    (A) versteht
    (B) kennt
    (C) kann
    (D) bedeutet

18. Gib mir bitte noch ein Stück -------!
    (A) Brot
    (B) von Brot
    (C) Brote
    (D) dem Brot

GO ON TO THE NEXT PAGE

PART B

Directions: In each of the following paragraphs, there are numbered blanks indicating that words or phrases have been omitted. For each numbered blank, four completions are provided. First read through the entire paragraph. Then, for each numbered blank, choose the completion that is most appropriate and fill in the corresponding circle on the answer sheet.

Mark geht einkaufen

Mark wurde in die Stadt geschickt, um einige Besorgungen __(19)__. Zuerst ging er __(20)__ Markt, wo er Gemüse __(21)__ wollte. Er fand die __(22)__ preiswert und ließ sich ein Kilogramm abwiegen. Dann __(23)__ er auch noch zum Bäcker gehen.

19. (A) machen
    (B) macht
    (C) zu machen
    (D) gemacht

20. (A) zum
    (B) nach
    (C) beim
    (D) im

21. (A) kaufe
    (B) kauft
    (C) kaufen
    (D) kaufst

22. (A) Tasche
    (B) Bohnen
    (C) Blumen
    (D) Torte

23. (A) musst
    (B) müssten
    (C) müsst
    (D) musste

GO ON TO THE NEXT PAGE

Ein Theaterbesuch

Liebe Hilde,

Gestern Abend haben Anne und _(24)_ im Theater die „Dreigroschenoper" gesehen. Du kannst dir nicht _(25)_, wie toll das war. Der Mann, _(26)_ die Hauptrolle gespielt hat, ist nicht nur ein guter Sänger, _(27)_ auch ein großartiger Schauspieler. Als er _(28)_ Tochter von Peachum das Liebeslied sang, wäre ich _(29)_ aufgestanden, um sie vor ihm zu warnen. Die _(30)_ Schauspieler waren aber auch gut. Nächste Woche, wenn du zu uns kommst, solltest du unbedingt die Vorstellung sehen. _(31)_ mir Bescheid, wenn ich dir eine Karte besorgen soll.

Alles Gute,

Gunter

24. (A) er
(B) ich
(C) sie
(D) ihr

25. (A) vorstellen
(B) ansehen
(C) vornehmen
(D) einbilden

26. (A) was
(B) wer
(C) das
(D) der

27. (A) aber
(B) wie
(C) sondern
(D) obwohl

28. (A) die
(B) der
(C) dem
(D) den

29. (A) täglich
(B) morgens
(C) beinahe
(D) immer

30. (A) andere
(B) anderer
(C) anderen
(D) anderes

31. (A) Gib
(B) Gibt
(C) Gebe
(D) Gibst

GO ON TO THE NEXT PAGE

Ein neues Geschäft

Gestern habe ich noch schnell Blumen für meine Freundin __(32)__, denn sie hat heute ihre neue Boutique __(33)__. Auf dieses Geschäft ist sie sehr __(34)__, und ich bin auch begeistert davon. Schließlich war es meine __(35)__ gewesen so etwas anzufangen.

32. (A) gesehen
    (B) bestellt
    (C) besucht
    (D) gewachsen

33. (A) erschöpft
    (B) erwacht
    (C) eröffnet
    (D) erwartet

34. (A) stolz
    (B) steif
    (C) spät
    (D) starr

35. (A) Zeit
    (B) Sorge
    (C) Idee
    (D) Kunst

GO ON TO THE NEXT PAGE

Berufswahl

Sabine kann sehr gut zeichnen. Wegen dieser __(36)__ überlegt sie sich, ob sie sich vielleicht __(37)__ die Werbung interessieren sollte. Dort kann __(38)__ sicher besser verdienen __(39)__ in den anderen Berufen, von __(40)__ sie schon einmal geträumt hat. Sie wird jedenfalls __(41)__ das Abitur machen und sich dann um __(42)__ Studienplatz an einer Fachhochschule __(43)__.

36. (A) Begabung
    (B) Beratung
    (C) Bezeichnung
    (D) Besetzung

37. (A) in
    (B) über
    (C) auf
    (D) für

38. (A) wer
    (B) es
    (C) man
    (D) etwas

39. (A) wie
    (B) als
    (C) so
    (D) dann

40. (A) denen
    (B) dem
    (C) der
    (D) den

41. (A) oft
    (B) neulich
    (C) zuerst
    (D) meistens

42. (A) einen
    (B) einem
    (C) eine
    (D) ein

43. (A) beworben
    (B) bewirbt
    (C) bewerben
    (D) zu bewerben

GO ON TO THE NEXT PAGE

PART C

Directions: Read the following texts carefully for comprehension. Each is followed by a number of questions or incomplete statements. Select the answer or completion that is best according to the text and fill in the corresponding circle on your answer sheet.

DIESE WOCHE

Politik	1–6
Länderspiegel	6
Dossier	7,8
Impressum	9
Wirtschaft	9–12
Feuilleton/Literatur	13–15
Themen der Zeit	16
Zeitläufte	17,18
Politisches Buch	19
Wissenschaft	20
Modernes Leben	21–24

44. Dieses Verzeichnis informiert über den Inhalt
    (A) eines Romans
    (B) einer Zeitung
    (C) eines Pakets
    (D) einer Tasche

GO ON TO THE NEXT PAGE

MARKEN&MOTIVE

Berühmte Frauen porträtiert die Deutsche Bundespost in einer Sondermarken-Dauerserie. Die beiden neuesten Marken sind der Hirnforscherin Cécile Vogt und der Komponistin Fanny Hensel gewidmet. Cécile Vogt (1864–1962), von Geburt Französin, forschte viele Jahrzehnte gemeinsam mit ihrem Mann, dem Neurologen Oskar Vogt. Unter anderem gelang den beiden erstmals eine Zuordnug von Reizeffekten zu architektonisch definierten Feldern der Hirnrinde. Die Komponistin Fanny Hensel (1805–1847) hingegen stammte aus einer berühmten Bankiers- und Philosophenfamilie. Sie aber zog es ebenso wie ihren Bruder, Felix Mendelssohn-Bartholdy, zur Musik; unter dem Namen des Bruders veröffentlichte sie ihre ersten Kunstlieder, später trat sie aber unter ihrem eigenen Namen auf. Zum 750-jährigen Bestehen des Frankfurter Doms und für die wichtige Rolle, die Kinder in der Gesellschaft spielen, haben Professor Ernst Kößlinger und die Berliner Grafikerin Lilo Fromm zwei weitere neue Briefmarken entworfen.

45. Woher stammte die Hirnforscherin Cécile Vogt ursprünglich?
    (A) Aus Berlin
    (B) Aus Frankfurt
    (C) Aus Deutschland
    (D) Aus Frankreich

46. Was war Fanny Hensels Bruder wohl von Beruf?
    (A) Bankier
    (B) Philosoph
    (C) Komponist
    (D) Kunstschmied

47. Weshalb sind Ernst Kößlinger und Lilo Fromm hier genannt?
    (A) Sie haben ein neues Spielzeug erfunden.
    (B) Sie haben den Frankfurter Dom gebaut.
    (C) Sie haben ein neues Kinderzentrum eröffnet.
    (D) Sie haben für die Bundespost Marken gestaltet.

48. Als die Marken herauskamen, bezahlte man am wenigsten für die Briefmarke, die
    (A) den Frankfurter Dom zeigt
    (B) die Hirnforscherin Cécile Vogt darstellt
    (C) ein Porträt der Fanny Hensel abbildet
    (D) den Kindern gewidmet ist

GO ON TO THE NEXT PAGE

Notruf
Klappe hochheben und festhalten! Warten bis Autobahnmeisterei Heimsheim sich meldet!
Notruf
Klappe hochheben und festhalten! Warten bis Autobahnmeisterei Heimsheim sich meldet!

49. Wann würde man diesen Apparat benutzen?

    (A) Bei einem Kinobesuch
    (B) Nur spät abends
    (C) Bei einem Unfall
    (D) Nur früh morgens

GO ON TO THE NEXT PAGE

Der Engel schwieg

Von der Erzählung *Der Zug war pünktlich*, Heinrich Bölls erstem Buch, wurden zunächst etwa 145 Exemplare verkauft. Der noch unbekannte Autor erhielt dafür im Juni 1950 ein Honorar von nur 58 Mark. Obwohl das sehr wenig war, schrieb Böll weiter. Sein erster Roman *Der Engel schwieg* wurde im Jahr 1992, also sieben Jahre nach Bölls Tod, aufgearbeitet und soll Teil einer kritischen Böll-Gesamtausgabe werden. Es ist außerdem bekannt, dass weit über 100 seiner Arbeiten aus den Jahren 1946 bis 1955 noch nicht publiziert sind. Darunter sind Hörspiele, Dramen, Essays und Erzählungen.

Ein Kritiker nennt den Roman *Der Engel schwieg* ein „charakteristisches Exempel der Heimkehrer- und Trümmerliteratur". Der Roman sei ein „literarisches ‚Dokument' über deutsche Zustände und Befindlichkeiten im Mai 1945".

Am Tage der Kapitulation kehrt der Soldat Hans Schnitzler in seine zerbombte Heimatstadt Köln, die auch Bölls Heimatstadt war, zurück. Dieser Roman enthält viel Autobiographisches. Schnitzler hat, wie Böll, Buchhändler gelernt, beide kehren ohne gültige Papiere heim, beide sind sie Moralisten. Eindrucksvoll schildert Böll die Stunde Null, den Hunger, den Gestank, die seelische Verwüstung und natürlich die große Liebe.

50. Was erfahren wir über die Erzählung *Der Zug war pünktlich* ?

(A) Sie war Bölls erster Roman.
(B) Sie wurde schnell und gut verkauft.
(C) Böll bekam nicht viel Geld dafür.
(D) Böll hat sie 1958 geschrieben.

51. Was erfahren wir über Bölls Werke aus den Jahren 1946-1955 ?

(A) Die meisten sind verloren gegangen.
(B) Alle sind im Juni 1950 erschienen.
(C) Sie sind noch nicht interpretiert worden.
(D) Viele sind noch nicht veröffentlicht worden.

52. Die Handlung von Heinrich Bölls Roman *Der Engel schwieg* spielt

(A) während des Ersten Weltkriegs
(B) am Ende des Zweiten Weltkriegs
(C) in den zwanziger Jahren
(D) in den sechziger Jahren

53. Wovon handelt der Roman *Der Engel schwieg* ?

(A) Von einer Zugfahrt
(B) Von einem kranken Kind
(C) Von einem wichtigen Dokument
(D) Von einem Heimkehrer

54. Wie sieht ein Kritiker den Roman *Der Engel schwieg* ?

(A) Als Beschreibung des Lebens in Deutschland unmittelbar nach Kriegsende
(B) Als ein typisches Beispiel der deutschen klassischen Literatur
(C) Als Kapitulation vor den Problemen des Lebens
(D) Als Beschreibung der zerbombten Städte nach dem Krieg

GO ON TO THE NEXT PAGE

Restaurant »Mühlenbach«

Familie W. Marx

Feine und bürgerliche Küche
Wir empfehlen unsere Räume für Familienfeiern, Hochzeiten etc. bis 40 Personen.
Parkplätze vorhanden. Montag Ruhetag.

5166 Kreuzau-Untermaubach • Rurstraße • Telefon 0 24 22 / 41 58

55. Wofür macht das Restaurant besonders Reklame?

(A) Für Parkanlagen
(B) Für günstige Preise
(C) Für die Betriebsstunden
(D) Für Partyräume

GO ON TO THE NEXT PAGE

Der Waldkauz

Hu, Huuu, Huuuuh, seufzt der Waldkauz durch die laue Frühlingsnacht. Er lässt sich von einem Ast fallen, breitet seine ein Meter großen Flügel aus und segelt lautlos über den Waldboden. Es ist stockdunkel, aber der Kauz weicht elegant jedem Hindernis aus, als hätte er eine Infrarot-Brille auf. Hu, Huuu! Wer nachts den Ruf des Waldkauzes hört, denkt an das Jammern schrecklicher Gespenster. Dabei ist sein Ruf nichts anderes als eine Liebeserklärung. Das Huu, Huuu bedeutet: „Hallo, Waldkäuzin, wo bist du? Ich liebe dich."

Warum findet sich der Waldkauz in der Nacht so gut zurecht? Er hat besonders lichtempfindliche Augen und sieht deshalb nachts zehnmal besser als wir Menschen. Er sieht zwar nicht in Farbe, kann aber bei ein bisschen Mondlicht alles erkennen.

Noch viel wichtiger ist sein Gehör. Der Waldkauz hat ein großes Trommelfell, hört im Umkreis von zehn Metern auch das kleinste Geräusch und weiß sofort, ob es nur ein Windhauch oder eine Maus war. Durch sein gutes Gehör kann er zentimetergenau feststellen, wo eine Maus gerade läuft. Lautlos fliegt er über sein Opfer, ergreift es und verspeist es auf einer Lichtung.

Waldkäuze sind Eulen. Sie leben in Wäldern und Parks und werden bis zu 38 cm groß und 10 Jahre alt. Das „Familienleben" des Waldkauzes ist bekannt. Mit seinem Hu-Huuu-Rufen lockt er ein Weibchen in sein bis zu 20 Hektar großes Revier und verjagt damit gleichzeitig andere Männchen. Seiner Partnerin bleibt er ein Leben lang treu und füttert sie auch, während sie die Eier in einer Baumhöhle ausbrütet.

56. Welche Wirkung hat das Rufen des Waldkauzes?

    (A) Es verjagt Gespenster.
    (B) Es erschreckt Rehe.
    (C) Es lockt Weibchen an.
    (D) Es weckt Männchen auf.

57. Was erfahren wir über das Gehör des Waldkauzes?

    (A) Es ist sehr gut entwickelt.
    (B) Es funktioniert nicht bei Dunkelheit.
    (C) Es wird mit zunehmendem Alter besser.
    (D) Es nimmt keine Tierlaute wahr.

58. Warum kann der Waldkauz nachts so gut sehen?

    (A) Seine Augen sind größer als die von Menschen.
    (B) Seine Augen sind sehr dunkel.
    (C) Seine Augen reagieren auf das geringste Licht.
    (D) Seine Augen leuchten in der Nacht auf.

59. Was frisst der Waldkauz wohl?

    (A) Beeren
    (B) Kleintiere
    (C) Vogeleier
    (D) Blätter

60. Was erfahren wir über das Verhältnis des Waldkauzes zu einer Partnerin?

    (A) Er verbringt sein Leben mit nur einer Partnerin.
    (B) Er lebt nur im Sommer mit einer Partnerin.
    (C) Er hat mehrere Partnerinnen gleichzeitig.
    (D) Er teilt eine Partnerin mit anderen Männchen.

GO ON TO THE NEXT PAGE

FÜR DIE GLÜCKWÜNSCHE, BLUMEN UND GESCHENKE ANLÄSSLICH UNSERER HOCHZEIT SAGEN WIR GANZ HERZLICH:

»DANKE SCHÖN«

ROLF UND ANGELIKA NEUMEYER

61. Was lesen wir hier?

    (A) Eine Hochzeitsanzeige
    (B) Eine Danksagung
    (C) Eine Glückwunschkarte
    (D) Eine Einladung

GO ON TO THE NEXT PAGE

62. Was für eine Karte ist das?

    (A) Eine Eintrittskarte
    (B) Eine Platzkarte
    (C) Eine Telefonkarte
    (D) Eine Postkarte

63. Was bedeutet „Freie Platzwahl"?

    (A) Der Eintritt ist frei.
    (B) Die Plätze sind nicht reserviert.
    (C) Man kann umsonst mit dem Bus fahren.
    (D) Man bekommt einen freien Parkplatz.

GO ON TO THE NEXT PAGE

Peter Wiegand aus Tegernsee

So viel ist wohl noch kein Bayer in der Welt herumgekommen: Peter Wiegand aus Tegernsee ist seit 27 Jahren auf allen Meeren unterwegs. Jetzt konnte der Seemann in Sydney (Australien) ein tolles Jubiläum feiern: 30-mal die Welt umrundet, 3 000 000 Kilometer. Es gibt kaum ein Plätzchen dieser Erde, das der 47-Jährige nicht kennt: Ob Alaska oder Grönland, ob die Bora Bora – oder Fidschi-Inseln, ob Leningrad oder New York – er ist mit allen Wassern gewaschen.

Dabei hatte Wiegand eine Bilderbuchkarriere: Als 20-Jähriger begann er als Steward auf dem Luxusschiff Berlin. Damals waren Kreuzfahrten noch weitgehend unbekannt. Seit Jahren ist der „Weltenbummler" Hoteldirektor auf Deutschlands Luxusliner Nummer eins, der MS Europa. Dort ist er nach dem Kapitän der zweite Mann und Chef von 220 Mitarbeitern. Wenn das Schiff – meist morgens – in einen Hafen einläuft, dann ist Wiegand mit dem Proviantmeister auf den Märkten dieser Welt unterwegs, um Frischwaren zu kaufen.

Neun Monate pro Jahr dampft der Seebär durch die Welt, freie Tage gibt's nicht, dafür aber drei Monate durchgehend Urlaub. Den verbringt Wiegand am liebsten im Sommer auf seiner Terrasse mit herrlichem Blick über den Tegernsee. In der Freizeit verreist der „Kilometer-Millionär" kaum, geht höchstens spazieren und steht als Hobbykoch mit „Vorliebe für exotisches Essen" hinter dem Herd.

64. Wiegand war in Australien, weil

(A) er dort seinen Urlaub verbrachte
(B) sein Schiff dort im Hafen lag
(C) er Sydneys 30. Jubiläum feiern wollte
(D) er das Land kennen lernen wollte

65. Warum hat Wiegand den Titel „Hoteldirektor"?

(A) In jeder Hafenstadt muss er Zimmer für die Passagiere finden.
(B) Er bucht nur Zimmer für seine Mitarbeiter.
(C) Ein großes Luxusschiff ist eigentlich wie ein Hotel.
(D) Er wird lieber „Hoteldirektor" als „Weltenbummler" genannt.

66. Auf welchem Schiff arbeitet Wiegand jetzt?

(A) Auf der Berlin
(B) Auf der Sydney
(C) Auf der Tegernsee
(D) Auf der Europa

67. In der Freizeit hat Wiegand keine Lust,

(A) auf der Terrasse seines Hauses zu sitzen
(B) Zeit in der Küche zu verbringen
(C) ausgedehnte Reisen zu machen
(D) den Tegernsee zu besuchen

GO ON TO THE NEXT PAGE

Mosel - Saar - Ruwer
„Ferien nach Herzenslust"

Natur und Gastlichkeit im Landkreis Trier-Saarburg – viele Sehenswürdigkeiten, Burgen, malerische Städte und Dörfer laden ein.

Der neue Ferienkatalog mit vielen interessanten Angeboten wartet auf Ihre Anforderung.

Zu erhalten über: Kreisverwaltung Trier-Saarburg
Mustorstraße 12, 5500 Trier
Telefon (06 51) 71 53 74

197

68. Was will man mit dieser Anzeige?

(A) Ein Urlaubsziel bekannt machen
(B) Zu einer Malklasse einladen
(C) Leute zum Einkaufen anregen
(D) Burgen zum Verkauf anbieten

69. „Ferien nach Herzenslust" bedeutet hier wohl, das zu machen, was

(A) gut für den Kreislauf ist
(B) man anfordern muss
(C) man besonders gerne macht
(D) die Kreisverwaltung vorschlägt

GO ON TO THE NEXT PAGE

Rettung für Halbaffen?

Sie sind so groß wie Katzen, ihre Ohren sehen aus wie die von Fledermäusen, und sie haben Schnauzen wie Ratten. Besonders auffällig ist ihr extrem langer Mittelfinger. Die Fingertiere sind die Primaten, die am ehesten vom Aussterben bedroht sind. Fingertiere gehören zu den 30 Lemurenarten, die noch auf der ostafrikanischen Insel Madagaskar leben.

Im Primatenzentrum der Duke University (US-Staat North Carolina) ist nun vor wenigen Wochen erstmals ein Fingertier, das man auf Madagaskar „Aye-Aye" nennt, in Gefangenschaft geboren worden. Die Primatologen haben bereits insgesamt 400 Tiere aus 15 verschiedenen Lemurenarten in den Wäldern von North Carolina aufgezogen. Sie wollen die ausgewachsenen Halbaffen später einmal in besonderen Reservaten auf Madagaskar aussetzen.

Leider werden die seltenen Lemuren vor allem durch die Zerstörung der tropischen Wälder auf der ostafrikanischen Insel bedroht. Rund 85 Prozent der Bäume sind bereits abgeholzt oder abgebrannt. Außerdem sehen viele, die auf Madagaskar leben, die „Aye-Ayes" als Unglücksbringer; sie verfolgen und töten sie.

70. Warum werden die Lemuren in North Carolina aufgezogen?

(A) Sie sollen vor dem Aussterben gerettet werden.
(B) Sie sollen dort eine neue Heimat finden.
(C) Die Primatologen dürfen in Madagaskar nicht arbeiten.
(D) Es gibt dort keine Unglücksbringer.

71. Welche Gefahr herrscht für die Halbaffen in ihrer ursprünglichen Heimat?

(A) Die Inseln werden bevölkert.
(B) Die Wälder werden zerstört.
(C) Sie werden von Ratten bedroht.
(D) Es gibt dort nicht genug Primatologen.

72. Was haben die US-Wissenschaftler erreicht?

(A) Sie haben den Aberglauben der Leute auf Madagaskar bekämpft.
(B) Sie haben den seltsamen Mittelfinger dieser Tiere entwickelt.
(C) Sie haben die Halbaffen außerhalb ihrer Heimat gezüchtet.
(D) Sie haben den Namen der „Aye-Aye" bekannt gemacht.

73. Was wollen die US-Primatologen eines Tages mit den Halbaffen tun?

(A) Sie nach Madagaskar zurückbringen
(B) Sie den Eingeborenen schenken
(C) Sie in North Carolina aussetzen
(D) Sie in einem Primatenzentrum behalten

74. Wie sehen viele Einwohner Madagaskars die Halbaffen?

(A) Sie halten sie für hässlich.
(B) Sie finden sie uninteressant.
(C) Sie finden sie besonders delikat.
(D) Sie fühlen sich von ihnen bedroht.

GO ON TO THE NEXT PAGE

75. Was kann man mit dieser Karte machen?

(A) In den Zoo gehen
(B) Im Europa-Center arbeiten
(C) Eine Vorstellung besuchen
(D) Eine Berlinrundfahrt buchen

GO ON TO THE NEXT PAGE

76. Worauf macht diese Anzeige den Autofahrer aufmerksam?

    (A) Eine Wetterlage
    (B) Entfernungen
    (C) Eine Umleitung
    (D) Bauarbeiten

77. Weshalb ist diese Anzeige für Autofahrer so wichtig?

    (A) Sie beschreibt Umleitungen.
    (B) Sie gibt Entfernungen an.
    (C) Sie weist auf Tankstellen hin.
    (D) Sie warnt vor schlechter Sicht.

GO ON TO THE NEXT PAGE

Seelendusche

Wäre es nicht wunderbar, wenn man einfach eine Telefonzelle betreten und sich aus einer nervösen, unsicheren Person in einen ruhigen, selbstbewussten Supermenschen verwandeln könnte? Frank Italiane glaubt an diese Möglichkeit. Deswegen hat seine Firma, die Environ Corporation, eine computergelenkte Kabine entworfen, in der der Mensch eine stressfreie Umgebung findet.

Der „Environ" Raum ist dazu gedacht, Menschen bei der Bewältigung von Schmerzen, Stress und verschiedenen psychologischen Problemen zu helfen: und zwar durch gefilterte, ionisierte Luft, wohl riechende Düfte, multidimensionale Klänge und eine Beleuchtung, die ständig ihre Farbe, Form und Intensität wechselt.

Beim Design des „Environ" hat man sich die anthropometrische Technologie der NASA zunutze gemacht. Anthropometrie ist die Erforschung der Größen-, Gestalt- und Bewegungscharakteristika des menschlichen Körpers. Sie hat entscheidende Bedeutung beim Design von Kleidung, Ausrüstung und Arbeitsplätzen in den Flugkörpern der NASA.

Die am Century City Hospital in Los Angeles und im Headache and Pain Center in Beverly Hills getestete Kabine ist 2,30 m hoch, 1,80 m lang und 1,20 m breit. Die erste Generation des „Environ" wird an Krankenhäuser, Stiftungen und andere medizinische Betriebe verkauft werden, aber bis zum Jahre 2010 sollen billigere Modelle für den Hausgebrauch auf dem Markt sein.

78. Wer hat die Zelle entworfen?
   (A) NASA
   (B) Century City Hospital
   (C) Headache and Pain Center
   (D) Environ Corporation

79. Wer oder was steuert die Kabine?
   (A) Ein Psychologe
   (B) Ein Krankenhaus
   (C) Ein Computer
   (D) Ein Supermensch

80. Wie kann in der Kabine Stress abgebaut werden?
   (A) Durch besondere Lichteffekte
   (B) Durch Schocktherapie
   (C) Durch intensives Training
   (D) Durch Schmerzmittel

81. Wer sollte den „Environ" Raum hauptsächlich benutzen?
   (A) Verschiedene Psychologen
   (B) Leidende Menschen
   (C) Supermenschen
   (D) Computerspezialisten

82. Welche Wirkung soll die Kabine haben?
   (A) Sie soll Menschen helfen.
   (B) Sie soll die Welt verändern.
   (C) Sie soll Telekommunikation verbessern.
   (D) Sie soll zur Abrüstung beitragen.

83. Wo sollen diese neuen Kabinen zuerst eingesetzt werden?
   (A) In Privatwohnungen
   (B) In Kasernen
   (C) In Kaufhäusern
   (D) In Krankenhäusern

GO ON TO THE NEXT PAGE

. . . da bleibt noch Zeit für mich
Wenn Sie bei uns als
• Sekretärin
• Sachbearbeiterin
mit EDV-Kenntnissen und Englisch auf Zeit arbeiten.
Den Wunsch nach einer abwechslungsreichen Tätigkeit sollten Sie schon mitbringen.
'TeamWork'
Personal per Sofort
Tel. 089/333041
Leopoldstraße 28a
8000 München 40

84. Wofür ist diese Annonce?

    (A) Eine Arbeitsstelle
    (B) Ein Hotel in den Alpen
    (C) Einen Skiurlaub
    (D) Freizeitkleidung

85. Wenn man bei „TeamWork" angestellt ist,

    (A) bekommt man EDV-Kenntnisse
    (B) lernt man Englisch
    (C) hat man seinen eigenen Telefonanschluss
    (D) hat man ausreichende Freizeit

STOP

IF YOU FINISH BEFORE TIME IS CALLED, YOU MAY CHECK YOUR WORK ON THIS TEST ONLY. DO NOT TURN TO ANY OTHER TEST IN THIS BOOK.

How to Score the SAT Subject Test in German

When you take an actual SAT Subject Test in German, your answer sheet will be "read" by a scanning machine that will record your responses to each question. Then a computer will compare your answers with the correct answers and produce your raw score. You get one point for each correct answer. For each wrong answer, you lose one-third of a point. Questions you omit (and any for which you mark more than one answer) are not counted. This raw score is converted to a scaled score that is reported to you and to the colleges you specify.

Worksheet 1. Finding Your Raw Test Score

STEP 1: Table A lists the correct answers for all the questions on the SAT Subject Test in German that is reproduced in this book. It also serves as a worksheet for you to calculate your raw score.

- Compare your answers with those given in the table.
- Put a check in the column marked "Right" if your answer is correct.
- Put a check in the column marked "Wrong" if your answer is incorrect.
- Leave both columns blank if you omitted the question.

STEP 2: Count the number of right answers.

Enter the total here: ____________________

STEP 3: Count the number of wrong answers.

Enter the total here: ____________________

STEP 4: Multiply the number of wrong answers by .333.

Enter the product here: ________________

STEP 5: Subtract the result obtained in Step 4 from the total you obtained in Step 2.

Enter the result here: ___________________

STEP 6: Round the number obtained in Step 5 to the nearest whole number.

Enter the result here: ___________________

The number you obtained in Step 6 is your raw score.

Table A

Answers to the Subject Test in German, Form 3XAC, and Percentage of Students Answering Each Question Correctly									
Question Number	Correct Answer	Right	Wrong	Percentage of Students Answering the Question Correctly*	Question Number	Correct Answer	Right	Wrong	Percentage of Students Answering the Question Correctly*
1	B			94	33	C			76
2	B			95	34	A			67
3	B			74	35	C			79
4	A			92	36	A			19
5	A			84	37	D			48
6	B			29	38	C			88
7	A			37	39	B			70
8	D			22	40	A			34
9	B			21	41	C			72
10	D			93	42	A			55
11	B			83	43	C			59
12	D			10	44	B			80
13	C			46	45	D			76
14	A			40	46	C			78
15	A			89	47	D			63
16	B			50	48	A			64
17	D			88	49	C			85
18	A			88	50	C			59
19	C			64	51	D			62
20	A			67	52	B			78
21	C			87	53	D			64
22	B			77	54	A			49
23	D			59	55	D			86
24	B			97	56	C			37
25	A			60	57	A			64
26	D			69	58	C			65
27	C			36	59	B			75
28	B			35	60	A			71
29	C			42	61	B			86
30	C			39	62	A			73
31	A			72	63	B			72
32	B			63	64	B			30

Table A continued on next page

Table A continued from previous page

Question Number	Correct Answer	Right	Wrong	Percentage of Students Answering the Question Correctly*	Question Number	Correct Answer	Right	Wrong	Percentage of Students Answering the Question Correctly*
65	C			63	76	A			32
66	D			51	77	D			40
67	C			45	78	D			70
68	A			66	79	C			51
69	C			69	80	A			46
70	A			42	81	B			47
71	B			52	82	A			60
72	C			38	83	D			64
73	A			61	84	A			83
74	D			39	85	D			57
75	C			69					

* These percentages are based on an analysis of the answer sheets of a representative sample of 629 students who took the original form of this test in June 2001, and whose mean score was 543. They may be used as an indication of the relative difficulty of a particular question. Each percentage may also be used to predict the likelihood that a typical SAT Subject Test in German candidate will answer that question correctly on this edition of the test.

Finding Your Scaled Score

When you take SAT Subject Tests, the scores sent to the colleges you specify are reported on the College Board scale, which ranges from 200–800. You can convert your practice test score to a scaled score by using Table B. To find your scaled score, locate your raw score in the left-hand column of Table B; the corresponding score in the right-hand column is your scaled score. For example, a raw score of 37 on this particular edition of the Subject Test in German corresponds to a scaled score of 490.

Raw scores are converted to scaled scores to ensure that a score earned on any one edition of a particular Subject Test is comparable to the same scaled score earned on any other edition of the same Subject Test. Because some editions of the tests may be slightly easier or more difficult than others, College Board scaled scores are adjusted so that they indicate the same level of performance regardless of the edition of the test taken and the ability of the group that takes it. Thus, for example, a score of 400 on one edition of a test taken at a particular administration indicates the same level of achievement as a score of 400 on a different edition of the test taken at a different administration.

When you take the SAT Subject Tests during a national administration, your scores are likely to differ somewhat from the scores you obtain on the tests in this book. People perform at different levels at different times for reasons unrelated to the tests themselves. The precision of any test is also limited because it represents only a sample of all the possible questions that could be asked.

Table B

Scaled Score Conversion Table
Subject Test in German (Form 3XAC)

Raw Score	Scaled Score	Raw Score	Scaled Score	Raw Score	Scaled Score
85	800	47	550	9	350
84	800	46	550	8	350
83	800	45	540	7	340
82	790	44	530	6	340
81	790	43	530	5	330
80	780	42	520	4	330
79	770	41	520	3	320
78	770	40	510	2	320
77	760	39	500	1	310
76	760	38	500	0	310
75	750	37	490	-1	300
74	740	36	490	-2	300
73	740	35	480	-3	300
72	730	34	470	-4	290
71	720	33	470	-5	290
70	720	32	460	-6	280
69	710	31	460	-7	280
68	700	30	450	-8	270
67	690	29	450	-9	270
66	690	28	440	-10	260
65	680	27	440	-11	260
64	670	26	430	-12	250
63	660	25	430	-13	250
62	660	24	420	-14	240
61	650	23	420	-15	240
60	640	22	410	-16	240
59	630	21	410	-17	230
58	630	20	400	-18	230
57	620	19	400	-19	220
56	610	18	390	-20	220
55	610	17	390	-21	210
54	600	16	380	-22	200
53	590	15	380	-23	200
52	580	14	370	-24	200
51	580	13	370	-25	200
50	570	12	360	-26	200
49	560	11	360	-27	200
48	560	10	360	-28	200

How Did You Do on the Subject Test in German?

After you score your test and analyze your performance, think about the following questions:

Did you run out of time before reaching the end of the test?

If so, you may need to pace yourself better. For example, maybe you spent too much time on one or two hard questions. A better approach might be to skip the ones you can't answer right away and try answering all the questions that remain on the test. Then if there's time, go back to the questions you skipped.

Did you take a long time reading the directions?

You will save time when you take the test by learning the directions to the Subject Test in German ahead of time. Each minute you spend reading directions during the test is a minute that you could use to answer questions.

How did you handle questions you were unsure of?

If you were able to eliminate one or more of the answer choices as wrong and guess from the remaining ones, your approach probably worked to your advantage. On the other hand, making haphazard guesses or omitting questions without trying to eliminate choices could cost you valuable points.

How difficult were the questions for you compared with other students who took the test?

Table A shows you how difficult the multiple-choice questions were for the group of students who took this test during its national administration. The right-hand column gives the percentage of students that answered each question correctly.

A question answered correctly by almost everyone in the group is obviously an easier question. For example, 92 percent of the students answered question 4 correctly. But only 19 percent answered question 36 correctly.

Keep in mind that these percentages are based on just one group of students. They would probably be different with another group of students taking the test.

If you missed several easier questions, go back and try to find out why: Did the questions cover material you haven't yet reviewed? Did you misunderstand the directions?

German with Listening

The Subject Test in German with Listening is offered once a year only at designated test centers. To take the test you MUST bring an acceptable CD player with earphones to the test center.

Sample Listening Questions

The text in brackets [ ] is *only* recorded; it will not appear in your test book. The questions in Part A, however, will be recorded and printed in your test book. Please note that the CD does not start here. Begin using the CD when you start the actual practice test on page 504.

Your answer sheet has five answer positions marked A, B, C, D, and E. Because the questions throughout this test contain only three or four choices, do NOT make any marks in column E, and do not make any marks in column D if there are only three choices given.

Part A

Directions: In this part of the test you will hear several selections. They will not be printed in your test book. You will hear them only once. Therefore, you must listen very carefully. In your test book you will read one or two short questions about what was said. Another speaker will read the questions for you. Each question will be followed by four choices marked (A), (B), (C), and (D). The choices are not printed in your test book. You will hear them once. Select the best answer and fill in the corresponding circle on your answer sheet.

(Narrator) [Questions 1 and 2 refer to the following exchange.]

(Woman) [Könnten Sie mir bitte dieses Kleid heute noch reinigen.

(Man) Das ist leider unmöglich. Wir machen in einer Stunde, um neunzehn Uhr, Feierabend.

(Woman) Aber bitte, ich muss dieses Kleid unbedingt heute zum Konzert tragen!]

1. (Man) [Wo findet dieser Dialog wohl statt?]
   Wo findet dieser Dialog wohl statt?

   (Woman) [(A) In einer Reinigung.
   (B) In einem Konzertsaal.
   (C) In einer Boutique.
   (D) Auf einem Ball.]

   (5 seconds)

Choice (A) is the correct answer to question 1. In this question, you are asked to choose from the four answer choices where the short dialogue you just heard takes place. You have to understand the verb “reinigen” and make the connection between “reinigen” mentioned in the dialogue and the noun “Reinigung” in one of the answer choices. Choices (B), (C), and (D) do not apply to “reinigen” and are therefore incorrect.

2. (Man) [Welche Tageszeit ist est?]
   Welche Tageszeit ist est?

   (Woman) [(A) Morgen.
   (B) Mittag.
   (C) Abend.
   (D) Nachtmittag.]

   (5 seconds)

Choice (C) is the correct answer to question 2. In this question, you are asked to select from the four choices at which time of day the dialogue is taking place. The man in the dialogue says that they “machen Feierabend” in an hour, at 7 p.m. Even if the German 24-hour clock is not known, the use of the word “Feierabend” can also lead to the correct answer. Choices (A), (B), and (D) are incorrect because there is no reference to morning, noon, or afternoon in the dialogue.

Part B

Directions: You will now listen to some extended dialogues or monologues. You will hear each only once. After each dialogue or monologue, you will be asked several questions about what you have just heard. These questions are not printed in your test book. From the four printed choices, select the best answer to each question and fill in the corresponding circle on the answer sheet. There is no sample question for this part.

Questions 3–5

(Narrator) [Two students talk about Chris's year abroad.]

(Woman) [Du, Chris, stimmt es? Du wirst das nächste Schuljahr in Amerika verbringen?

(Man) Ja, ich soll bei einer Familie Lazarro in Los Angeles wohnen und mit ihrem Sohn Miguel zur Schule gehen.

(Woman) Welche Fächer wirst du denn da haben?

(Man) Weiß ich noch nicht, aber ich werde mit Miguel die 11. Klasse besuchen.

(Woman) In amerikanischen Highschools wird auch viel Sport getrieben, nicht?

(Man) Ja, Miguel soll sogar ein recht guter Schwimmer sein. Er hat schon einige Medaillen gewonnen.

(Woman) Das ist ja was für dich! Du schwimmst doch auch so gern!

(Man) Ja, aber jetzt muss ich zuerst noch fleißig Englisch üben. Ich will doch so viel wie möglich im Unterricht verstehen und mich natürlich auch mit meiner neuen Familie unterhalten können.

3. (Man) [Was für eine Schule wird Chris in Amerika besuchen?]

(12 seconds)

(A) Eine Kunstakademie.

(B) Eine Universität.

(C) Eine Oberschule.

(D) Eine Sportschule.

Choice (C) is the correct answer to question 3. In this question, you are asked to answer the question about what kind of school Chris will be going to in America. "Oberschule" is the German equivalent to high school mentioned in the dialogue. It is also mentioned that he will be in eleventh grade, thus referring to "Oberschule" but not to the schools in (A), (B), and (D). These choices are therefore incorrect.

4. (Man) [Warum glaubt Chris, dass Miguel ein guter Schwimmer ist?]
   (12 seconds)

   (A) Er besucht die Highschool.
   (B) Er hat Auszeichnungen gewonnen.
   (C) Er wohnt in Kalifornien.
   (D) Er ist im Fernsehen erschienen.

Choice (B) is the correct answer to question 4. This question asks why Chris thinks that Miguel is a good swimmer. Chris states in the dialogue that Miguel has won several medals. The use of "Medaillen" (medals) is a more specific way to describe "Auszeichnungen," which is a more general term. It cannot be inferred from choices (A) and (C) that Miguel is a good swimmer, and choice (D) is not at all mentioned in the dialogue.

5. (Man) [Was will Chris noch vor seiner Reise tun?]
   (12 seconds)

   (A) Studienfächer auswählen.
   (B) Medaillen gewinnen.
   (C) Englisch lernen.
   (D) Viel schwimmen.

Choice (C) is the correct answer to question 5. This question asks what Chris wants to do before he goes on his trip. At the end of the dialogue, Chris says that he needs to practice English in order to understand as much as possible in class and to be able to talk with his new family. Since the activities in the other answer choices are not mentioned as something he wants to do before leaving, choices (A), (B), and (D) are incorrect.

German with Listening Test

Practice Helps

The test that follows is an actual, recently administered SAT Subject Test in German with Listening. To get an idea of what it's like to take this test, practice under conditions that are much like those of an actual test administration.

- Set aside an hour when you can take the test uninterrupted. Make sure you complete the test in one sitting.
- Sit at a desk or table with no other books or papers. Dictionaries, other books, or notes are not allowed in the test room.
- Tear out an answer sheet from the back of this book and fill it in just as you would on the day of the test. One answer sheet can be used for up to three Subject Tests.
- Read the instructions that precede the practice test. During the actual administration, you will be asked to read them before answering test questions.
- Time yourself by placing a clock or kitchen timer in front of you.
- After you finish the practice test, read the sections "How to Score the SAT Subject Test in German with Listening" and "How Did you Do on the Subject Test in German with Listening?"
- The appearance of the answer sheet in this book may differ form the answer sheet you see on test day.

GERMAN TEST WITH LISTENING

The top portion of the section of the answer sheet that you will use in taking the German Test with Listening must be filled in exactly as shown in the illustration below. Note carefully that you have to do all of the following on your answer sheet.

1. Print GERMAN WITH LISTENING on the line under the words "Subject Test (print)."

2. In the shaded box labeled "Test Code" fill in four circles:

—Fill in circle 5 in the row labeled V.
—Fill in circle 4 in the row labeled W.
—Fill in circle 3 in the row labeled X.
—Fill in circle E in the row labeled Y.

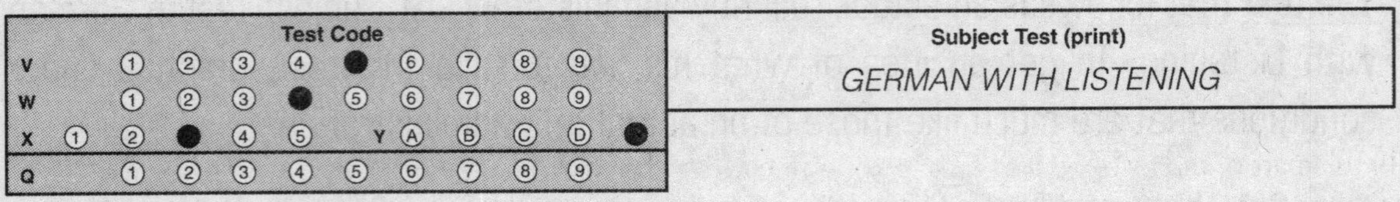

Test Code										Subject Test (print)
V		①	②	③	④	●	⑥	⑦	⑧	⑨
W		①	②	③	●	⑤	⑥	⑦	⑧	⑨
X	①	②	●	④	⑤	Y Ⓐ	Ⓑ	Ⓒ	Ⓓ	●
Q		①	②	③	④	⑤	⑥	⑦	⑧	⑨

Subject Test (print): *GERMAN WITH LISTENING*

Please answer either Part I or Part II by filling in the specific circle in row Q. You are to fill in ONE and ONLY ONE circle, as described below, to indicate how you obtained your knowledge of German. The information you provide is for statistical purposes only and will not influence your score on the test.

Part I If your knowledge of German does not come primarily from courses taken in grades 9 through 12, fill in circle 9 and leave the remaining circles blank, regardless of how long you studied the subject in school. For example, you are to fill in circle 9 if your knowledge of German comes primarily from any of the following sources: study prior to the ninth grade, courses taken at a college, special study, living in a home in which German is the principal language spoken, or extensive residence abroad that includes significant experience in the German language.

Part II If your knowledge of German does come primarily from courses taken in secondary school or the equivalent, fill in the circle that indicates the level of the German course in which you are currently enrolled. If you are not now enrolled in a German course, fill in the circle that indicates the level of the most advanced course in German that you have completed.

- First year: first or second half —Fill in circle 1.
- Second year: first half —Fill in circle 2.
  second half —Fill in circle 3.
- Third year: first half —Fill in circle 4.
  second half —Fill in circle 5.
- Fourth year: first half —Fill in circle 6.
  second half —Fill in circle 7.
- Advanced Placement course or a course at a level higher than fourth year, second half or high school course work plus a minimum of four weeks of study abroad —Fill in circle 8.

When the supervisor gives the signal, turn the page and begin the German Test with Listening. There are 100 numbered circles on the answer sheet and 87 questions in the German Test with Listening. Therefore, use only circles 1 to 87 for recording your answers.

GERMAN TEST WITH LISTENING

PLEASE NOTE THAT YOUR ANSWER SHEET HAS FIVE ANSWER POSITIONS MARKED A, B, C, D, and E, WHILE THE QUESTIONS THROUGHOUT THIS TEST CONTAIN ONLY FOUR CHOICES. BE SURE NOT TO MAKE ANY MARKS IN COLUMN E.

SECTION I

LISTENING

Approximate time—20 minutes

Question 1-27

PART A

Directions: In this part of the test you will hear several selections. They will not be printed in your test book. You will hear them only once. Therefore, you must listen very carefully. In your test book you will read one or two short questions about what was said. Another speaker will read the questions for you. Each question will be followed by four choices marked (A), (B), (C), and (D). The choices are not printed in your test book. You will hear them once. Select the best answer and fill in the corresponding circle on your answer sheet.

Listen to the following example.

You will hear:

You will hear and read: Was schenkt der Mann Lisa zum Geburtstag?

You will hear: Ⓐ ● Ⓒ Ⓓ

The best answer to the question „Was schenkt der Mann Lisa zum Geburtstag?" is (B), „Ein Buch." Therefore you should choose option (B).

Now listen to the first selection.

1. Wie sind Christa und Julia mit Anna verwandt?

   Mark your answer on your answer sheet.

2. Warum gehen die beiden ins Altersheim?

   Mark your answer on your answer sheet.

3. Wo spielt sich diese Szene ab?

   Mark your answer on your answer sheet.

4. Was will die Frau nicht?

   Mark your answer on your answer sheet.

3YLC

GO ON TO THE NEXT PAGE

5. Worüber sprechen die beiden?

   Mark your answer on your answer sheet.

6. Was bemerkt Erich am Anfang?

   Mark your answer on your answer sheet.

---

7. Was macht Tante Mia, als der Telefonanruf kommt?

   Mark your answer on your answer sheet.

8. Warum ruft Sonja ihre Tante an?

   Mark your answer on your answer sheet.

9. Was will dieser Mann?

   Mark your answer on your answer sheet.

10. Warum wird der Mann seinen Zug nicht verpassen?

    Mark your answer on your answer sheet.

---

11. Was hat der Mann nicht verstanden?

    Mark your answer on your answer sheet.

12. Was soll es in der folgenden Woche wieder geben?

    Mark your answer on your answer sheet.

GO ON TO THE NEXT PAGE

PART B

Directions: You will now listen to some extended dialogues or monologues. You will hear each only once. After each dialogue or monologue, you will be asked several questions about what you have just heard. These questions are not printed in your test book. From the four printed choices, select the best answer to each question and fill in the corresponding circle on the answer sheet. There is no sample question for this part.

Selection number 1

13. (A) Handtücher auf dem Boden.
    (B) Handtücher auf der Heizung.
    (C) Handtücher auf dem Regal.
    (D) Handtücher auf dem Halter.

14. (A) Sie beklagen sich über die Aktion.
    (B) Sie kennen die Hausregel nicht.
    (C) Sie boykottieren die Hotelkette.
    (D) Sie befürworten die Aktion.

15. (A) Handtücher zu erneuern.
    (B) Die Hotelkette auszubauen.
    (C) Abfallstoffe zu produzieren.
    (D) Die Umwelt zu schützen.

Selection number 2

16. (A) Am Bau.
    (B) In der Türkei.
    (C) In Frankfurt.
    (D) In Deutschland.

17. (A) Er ist Elektriker.
    (B) Er ist Verkäufer.
    (C) Er ist Baumeister.
    (D) Er ist Hilfsarbeiter.

18. (A) Er hatte kein eigenes Zimmer.
    (B) Er hat bei Fatimas Familie gewohnt.
    (C) Er hatte ein kleines Haus in Kreuzberg.
    (D) Er hatte keine Elektrizität.

19. (A) Sie haben keine Familien.
    (B) Es geht ihnen nicht so gut.
    (C) Sie haben Heimweh.
    (D) Sie arbeiten viel.

GO ON TO THE NEXT PAGE

Selection number 3

20. (A) In England.
    (B) In Paris.
    (C) In Deutschland.
    (D) In Indien.

21. (A) Weil er so schnell verkauft wurde.
    (B) Weil seine Farbe außergewöhnlich ist.
    (C) Weil er nach Indien geschickt wurde.
    (D) Weil er außergewöhnlich groß ist.

22. (A) Er ist weiß.
    (B) Er ist grün.
    (C) Er ist rot.
    (D) Er ist gelb.

23. (A) Er will den Diamanten verkaufen.
    (B) Er will den Diamanten seinem Vater zeigen.
    (C) Er will öfter nach Indien reisen.
    (D) Er will eine englischsprachige Zeitung finden.

Selection number 4

24. (A) Ein Jahr in den USA reisen.
    (B) In England studieren.
    (C) In den USA studieren.
    (D) Englisch unterrichten.

25. (A) Fremdsprachen sind dafür nicht nötig.
    (B) Informatik ist in den USA fortgeschritten.
    (C) Für ihr Fach braucht man Auslandserfahrung.
    (D) Sie will Fernsehansagerin werden.

26. (A) Sie möchte sich persönlich ein Bild vom amerikanischen Leben machen.
    (B) Sie möchte mehr Gelegenheit haben, amerikanisches Fernsehen zu sehen.
    (C) Sie möchte Amerikanern ein anderes Image der Deutschen vermitteln.
    (D) Sie möchte, dass man in Deutschland mehr amerikanische Programme zeigt.

27. (A) Sie weiß, wie gut ihr Image ist.
    (B) Sie hat Reisefieber.
    (C) Sie will einfach von Deutschland weg.
    (D) Sie weiß, was sie will.

END OF SECTION I
DO NOT GO ON TO SECTION II UNTIL YOU ARE TOLD TO DO SO.

SECTION II

READING

Time—40 minutes

Question 28-87

WHEN YOU BEGIN THE READING SECTION, BE SURE THAT YOU MARK YOUR ANSWER TO THE FIRST READING QUESTION BY FILLING IN ONE OF THE CIRCLES NEXT TO NUMBER 28 ON THE ANSWER SHEET.

PART A

Directions: This part consists of a number of incomplete statements, each having four suggested completions. Select the most appropriate completion and fill in the corresponding circle on the answer sheet.

In der Schule

28. Man schreibt mit ------- an die Tafel.

(A) Tusche
(B) Bleistift
(C) Kugelschreiber
(D) Kreide

29. Unsere Lehrerin ------- fünf Fremdsprachen.

(A) kann
(B) weiß
(C) zeigt
(D) bekennt

30. Solche Aufgaben ------- mir keine Schwierigkeiten.

(A) haben
(B) machen
(C) tun
(D) sind

Konversation auf einer Party

31. Ich meine, der Film hat zu lange -------.

(A) gedauert
(B) genommen
(C) geleistet
(D) gesehen

32. Sabine besucht ihre Tante sehr oft, ------- sie wohnt gleich nebenan.

(A) sondern
(B) obwohl
(C) oder
(D) denn

33. ------- ich viel Geld hätte, würde ich eine lange Reise machen.

(A) Ob
(B) Dann
(C) Wenn
(D) Obwohl

34. Was ------- Sie von moderner Musik?

(A) fühlen
(B) betrachten
(C) halten
(D) gefallen

35. Wenn ich das Buch zuerst gelesen hätte, hätte ich den Film sicher besser -------.

(A) verstehen
(B) verstanden
(C) verstände
(D) verstehe

GO ON TO THE NEXT PAGE

Auf der Reise

36. Du bist schon wieder da? Du musst aber schnell gelaufen -------!

(A) sein
(B) gewesen
(C) sei
(D) warst

37. Morgen müssen wir ------- aufstehen, denn wir fahren um 6 Uhr ab.

(A) früh
(B) spät
(C) bald
(D) langsam

Zu Hause

38. Warum sprichst du nicht einmal mit deinem Lehrer -------?

(A) darüber
(B) damit
(C) darin
(D) dafür

39. ------- zwei Wochen wohne ich bei meiner Großmutter.

(A) Vor
(B) Seit
(C) Bis
(D) Um

40. Ich weiß nicht, ------- sie mit uns ins Restaurant kommt.

(A) ob
(B) dass
(C) als
(D) wenn

41. Ich war mit meinen Hausaufgaben heute schnell fertig, denn sie waren sehr -------.

(A) freundlich
(B) einzig
(C) einfach
(D) pünktlich

42. Es ist hier kalt. Ist ------- Heizung an?

(A) der
(B) das
(C) den
(D) die

43. Ich hatte diese politische Lage falsch gesehen und musste meine Meinung -------.

(A) nehmen
(B) umdrehen
(C) ändern
(D) ausprobieren

GO ON TO THE NEXT PAGE

PART B

Directions: In each of the following paragraphs, there are numbered blanks indicating that words or phrases have been omitted. For each numbered blank, four completions are provided. First read through the entire paragraph. Then, for each numbered blank, choose the completion that is most appropriate and fill in the corresponding circle on the answer sheet.

Ein guter Arbeitsplatz

Je länger ich __(44)__ der Firma Meyer bin, __(45)__ besser gefällt es mir dort. Die Firma Meyer ist eine Druckerei, die Einladungen und Glückwunschkarten __(46)__. Ich sitze aber nicht nur im __(47)__, sondern besuche auch Kunden. Meine Kollegen, __(48)__ Arbeit ich weniger interessant finde, sind alle älter als ich. Aber es ist leicht, mit ihnen __(49)__.

44. (A) bei
    (B) vor
    (C) zu
    (D) an

45. (A) denn
    (B) so
    (C) desto
    (D) dann

46. (A) kann
    (B) herstellt
    (C) verbraucht
    (D) legt

47. (A) Auto
    (B) Aufzug
    (C) Büro
    (D) Bahnhof

48. (A) die
    (B) deren
    (C) dessen
    (D) der

49. (A) auszukommen
    (B) auskommen
    (C) ausgekommen
    (D) auskommt

GO ON TO THE NEXT PAGE

Vergessen

Herr Hoffmann wollte gerade das Haus __(50)__, um den Frühzug zu __(51)__, als seine Frau ihm einen __(52)__ in die Hand drückte. „Vergiss bitte nicht, ihn einzuwerfen, __(53)__ du ins Büro gehst, damit __(54)__ Freundin ihn morgen noch bekommt! Er ist sehr wichtig!" Aber __(55)__ Mann vergaß doch, ihn einzuwerfen. __(56)__ er am Abend wieder nach Hause kam, hatte er den Brief immer noch in der Tasche.

50. (A) gehen
    (B) vergehen
    (C) verlassen
    (D) lassen

51. (A) erwerben
    (B) sehen
    (C) hören
    (D) erreichen

52. (A) Schreiben
    (B) Brief
    (C) Telegramm
    (D) Paket

53. (A) bevor
    (B) nachdem
    (C) seitdem
    (D) wonach

54. (A) meiner
    (B) meine
    (C) meines
    (D) mein

55. (A) ihr
    (B) ihre
    (C) ihrer
    (D) ihren

56. (A) Wenn
    (B) Wann
    (C) Als
    (D) Ob

GO ON TO THE NEXT PAGE

Anne-Maries Wunsch

Anne-Marie möchte einen __(57)__ CD-Player, hat aber noch nicht genug __(58)__ dafür gespart. Ihre Eltern sind __(59)__ Meinung, sie solle jobben. Ihr wäre es natürlich lieber, __(60)__ ihr die Eltern einen CD-Player zum Geburtstag __(61)__ würden.

57. (A) neu
    (B) neue
    (C) neuen
    (D) neues

58. (A) Geduld
    (B) Mark
    (C) Zeit
    (D) Geld

59. (A) die
    (B) der
    (C) dem
    (D) das

60. (A) weil
    (B) damit
    (C) nachdem
    (D) wenn

61. (A) belohnen
    (B) schenken
    (C) beibringen
    (D) spielen

GO ON TO THE NEXT PAGE

PART C

Directions: Read the following texts carefully for comprehension. Each is followed by a number of questions or incomplete statements. Select the answer or completion that is best according to the text and fill in the corresponding circle on your answer sheet.

Herzlichen Dank

allen, die uns durch Wort, Schrift, Kranz- und Blumenspenden ihre Anteilnahme an unserer Trauer erwiesen haben.

Im Namen der Angehörigen:
Karl Steinke

Frankfurt am Main, im August 1990

62. Was ist das?

(A) Eine Todesanzeige
(B) Eine Entschuldigung
(C) Eine Hochzeitsanzeige
(D) Eine Danksagung

63. Diese Anzeige ist an Leute gerichtet, die

(A) ihr Beileid ausgedrückt haben
(B) Geschenke verschickt haben
(C) Geld verteilt haben
(D) ihre Angehörigen benachrichtigt haben

GO ON TO THE NEXT PAGE

Pittsburghs Wandlung

Wo man heute in eleganten Boutiquen einkauft und in Feinschmeckerrestaurants speist, rauchten früher die Kamine der Eisen- und Stahlindustrie. Der größte Arbeitgeber in der Stadt ist jetzt die „University of Pittsburgh". Dazu kommen anspruchsvolle Jobs in 170 Forschungsinstitutionen und 700 Hochtechnologiefirmen.

Nach einem kurzen Spaziergang durch Pittsburghs „Downtown", die nach europäischen Maßstäben sauber und sicher ist, erreicht man das William Penn Hotel in der Grant Street. Der Pittsburgher Kohle-König Henry Clay Frick ließ es 1916 bauen, weil er unbedingt das größte und schönste Hotel zwischen Chicago und New York besitzen wollte. Heute gilt das liebevoll restaurierte Haus mit 595 Zimmern als einziges „Grand Hotel" in Pittsburgh. Wenn man die Hotelhalle betritt, fühlt man sich wie in einem Schlosssaal mit hohen Fensterbögen, Stuckdecken, Kristallleuchtern und vielen Zimmerpalmen. Zum „Afternoon-Tea" klimpert ein Klavierspieler heitere Melodien.

Vom „Golden Triangle", der geschäftigen Innenstadt Pittsburghs, lohnt sich ein kleiner Abstecher zum Station Square. Über die Smithfield Street Bridge, die den Monongahela-Fluss überspannt, kommt man zum „Pittsburgh & Lake Erie Railroad"– Bahnhof. Er wurde 1901 fertig gestellt. Ende der sechziger Jahre rollte der letzte Passagierzug aus dem Gebäude. Einige Zeit später baute Charles Muir aus Detroit die unteren Etagen in ein feines Restaurant um: Das Grand Concourse. In der großen Wartehalle richtete er den Speisesaal für 500 Gäste ein.

Doch nicht nur wegen ihrer Sehenswürdigkeiten, sondern auch wegen der Universitäten, des Museumskomplexes und der weltberühmten Krankenhäuser ist die Stadt Pittsburgh für Reisende aus Deutschland interessant; und auf dem Flughafen geht es so schnell und einfach, wie man es sich in den Warteschlangen auf den Airports in New York und Los Angeles immer wünscht.

64. Wofür war Pittsburgh früher bekannt?

(A) Für elegante Boutiquen
(B) Für viele Schulen
(C) Für große Krankenhäuser
(D) Für Schwerindustrie

65. Wo sind die meisten Einwohner von Pittsburgh heute angestellt?

(A) Auf dem Flughafen
(B) An der Universität
(C) Im William Penn Hotel
(D) Im Grand Concourse Restaurant

66. Wer war Henry Clay Frick?

(A) Ein bekannter Architekt
(B) Ein Bürgermeister von Pittsburgh
(C) Ein Industriemagnat
(D) Ein Restaurantbesitzer

67. Wozu wird heute der ehemalige Pittsburgher Bahnhof benutzt?

(A) Als Anschlussbahnhof
(B) Als Lagerhalle für Kohle
(C) Als Kongresshalle
(D) Als gutes Lokal

68. Was war Charles Muir wohl von Beruf?

(A) Lokomotivführer
(B) Museumsdirektor
(C) Baumeister
(D) Reiseführer

69. Warum lohnt es sich, Pittsburgh zu besuchen?

(A) Die Stadt hat viel zu bieten.
(B) Pittsburgh hat ein berühmtes Schloss.
(C) Die Leute sind freundlich.
(D) Die Hotels sind dort sehr billig.

GO ON TO THE NEXT PAGE

Fachbuchhandlung für Geisteswissenschaften

Sämtliche Semesterliteratur haben wir vorrätig, oder wir bemühen uns, diese sofort zu beschaffen. Bestellservice auch telefonisch.

BesTellBuch 8324051

Nahe der Rostlaube, neben der Mensa, Eingang Brümmerstraße, an der U-Bahnlinie zwischen Thielplatz und Dahlem-Dorf. Ein starkes wissenschaftliches Sortiment unterstützt Ihr Studium:

kompetent, freundlich, schnell.

Thielallee 34, Mo. bis Fr. 9-18, Sa. 10-13 Uhr

70. Was für Bücher kauft man bei Tell?

(A) Kinderbücher
(B) Reisebücher
(C) Lehrbücher
(D) Kochbücher

71. Welchen Service bietet die Fachbuchhandlung an?

(A) Bücher können ins Haus geliefert werden.
(B) Bücher können billiger beschafft werden.
(C) Bücher können ausgeliehen werden.
(D) Bücher können telefonisch bestellt werden.

GO ON TO THE NEXT PAGE

Der Kranführer Hans Magnussen sah auf die Uhr: zehn Minuten nach drei. „Bald Feierabend", dachte er. Als Magnussen die Baggerschaufel noch einmal herunterließ, glaubte er, auf etwas Hartes zu stoßen. Er stellte den Bagger* ab und kletterte aus dem Kran, um zu sehen, was es sein könnte. Magnussen holte einen Spaten und begann zu graben. Da fand er eine relativ große Kiste, die – wie sich herausstellte – 23 200 Gold- und Silbermünzen aus dem 14. und 15. Jahrhundert enthielt. Es war der bedeutendste Fund in der Geschichte der deutschen Münzen.

Wem gehörte nun dieser Gold- und Silberschatz? Das Land, auf dem Magnussen die Kiste entdeckt hatte, gehörte dem Land Schleswig-Holstein, und Schleswig-Holstein hatte auch die Demolierung des Gebäudes in der Stadt Lübeck angeordnet, unter dem der Schatz verborgen lag. Nicht nur das Land Schleswig-Holstein, auch die Baggerfirma wollte den ganzen Fund für sich beanspruchen und behauptete, dass ja der Kranführer nur in ihrem Auftrag gehandelt habe.

Das deutsche Gesetz aber bestimmte Folgendes: Wenn etwas entdeckt wird, was schon so lange unter der Erde liegt, dass man den ursprünglichen Eigentümer nicht mehr feststellen kann, dann muss der Fund zwischen dem „Entdecker" und dem Landeigentümer geteilt werden. Und so entschied auch das Bundesgericht. Das Land Schleswig-Holstein will jetzt den kulturell und historisch wertvollen Fund behalten und wird dem Kranführer Magnussen für seinen Anteil 700 000 Mark zahlen.

* *Bagger*: excavator

72. Wann entdeckte der Kranführer Magnussen den Fund?

(A) Kurz vor Arbeitsschluss
(B) Um die Mittagszeit
(C) Am frühen Morgen
(D) Mitten in der Nacht

73. Warum stellte Magnussen den Kran ab?

(A) Er dachte, es sei schon Feierabend.
(B) Der Bagger funktionierte nicht richtig.
(C) Der Schutt war zu schwer für die Schaufel.
(D) Er wollte wissen, was unter der Erde war.

74. Das Land Schleswig-Holstein wollte den ganzen Fund behalten, weil

(A) ihm das Land gehörte
(B) Magnussen in Lübeck wohnte
(C) Magnussen das Gebäude zerstörte
(D) der Eigentümer im Bundesgericht arbeitete

75. Wie alt waren die Münzen?

(A) Fast hundert Jahre
(B) Etwas über tausend Jahre
(C) Genau fünfzig Jahre
(D) Mehrere hundert Jahre

76. Das Bundesgericht entschied, dass

(A) die Baggerfirma die Münzen behalten durfte
(B) Schleswig-Holstein und Magnussen den Fund teilen sollten
(C) der Eigentümer des Fundes gesucht werden sollte
(D) die Demolierungsarbeiten abgebrochen werden sollten

77. Wer bekam am Ende den Schatz?

(A) Die Stadt Lübeck
(B) Die Baggerfirma
(C) Das Land Schleswig-Holstein
(D) Der ursprüngliche Eigentümer

GO ON TO THE NEXT PAGE

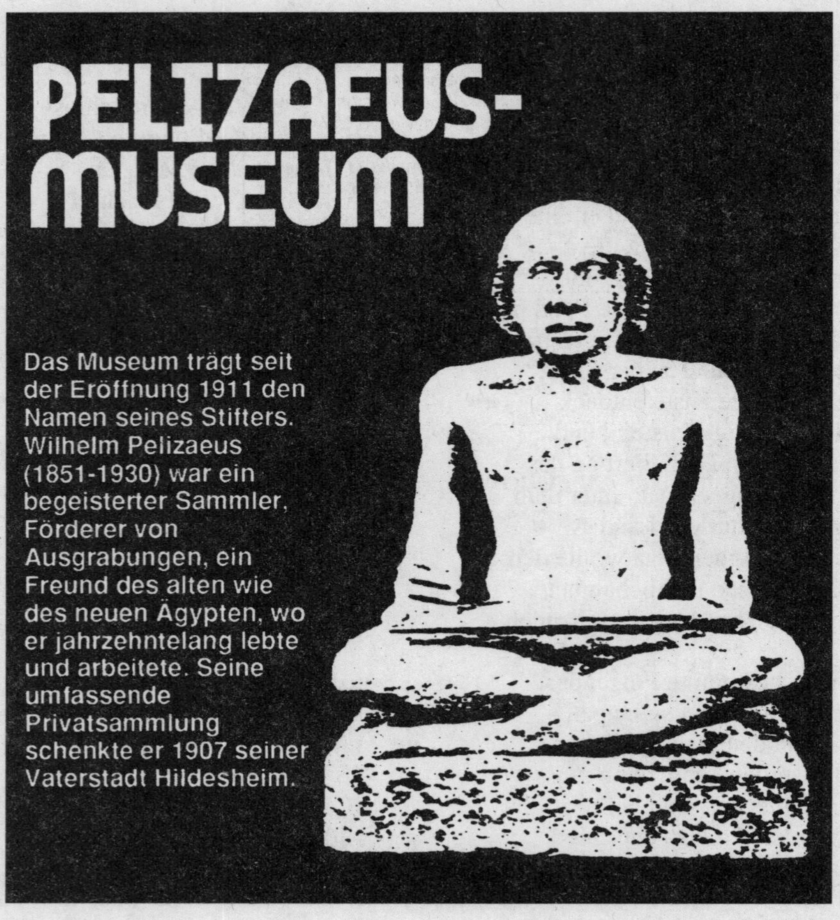

PELIZAEUS-
MUSEUM
Das Museum trägt seit der Eröffnung 1911 den Namen seines Stifters. Wilhelm Pelizaeus (1851-1930) war ein begeisterter Sammler, Förderer von Ausgrabungen, ein Freund des alten wie des neuen Ägypten, wo er jahrzehntelang lebte und arbeitete. Seine umfassende Privatsammlung schenkte er 1907 seiner Vaterstadt Hildesheim.

78. Aus dem Text geht hervor, dass Wilhelm Pelizaeus

(A) 1907 in Ägypten gestorben ist
(B) ein Museum in Ägypten gestiftet hat
(C) 1851 in Hildesheim geboren wurde
(D) Ausgrabungen in Hildesheim gemacht hat

79. Was wird im Pelizaeus-Museum hauptsächlich ausgestellt?

(A) Fotos von Wilhelm Pelizaeus
(B) Bilder einer Vaterstadt
(C) Büsten bekannter Sammler
(D) Funde aus dem alten Ägypten

GO ON TO THE NEXT PAGE

Miami/USA

Aus Altersgründen **zu verkaufen** gut gehendes, solides **Fotogeschäft** für professionelle Fotografen und Öffentlichkeit mit 4 versch. Zweigstellen an günstigen Lokalitäten (total ca. 15 000 sq. feet–1350 m²). International tätig, weiterausbau- und entwicklungsfähig. 40 Mitarbeiter. Erforderliches Kapital: 6 Mio. US-$.
Anfragen unter Chiffre X 240 673 F, NZZ, Inseratenabteilung, Postfach, 8021 Zürich.

VKX240 673F

80. Was will der Besitzer mit dem Geschäft machen?

(A) Er will es vermieten.
(B) Er will es loswerden.
(C) Er will es ausbauen.
(D) Er will es fotografieren.

GO ON TO THE NEXT PAGE

München hat mit dem Englischen Garten ein Rückzugsparadies, in dem man sich auch an den heißesten Sommertagen so wohl fühlt wie sonst nur an den exotischsten Urlaubszielen. Mal ist der Englische Garten ganz spannender Urwald, wo man einsam und allein auf Entdeckungstouren gehen kann, dann wieder die elegante Sonnenterrasse einer ganzen Stadt. Und wer Abkühlung sucht, findet sie im Eisbach und im See.

Wo sich heute Familien, Punks und Hippies sowie Studenten aus der nahen Uni aufhalten, wurden früher Wildschweine und andere Tiere gejagt. Die Idee, aus dem privaten Jagdrevier des Kurfürsten Carl Theodor einen Volksgarten zu machen, stammt eigentlich von Benjamin Thompson aus Massachusetts. Denn der schlug dem Kurfürsten vor, seine Soldaten sollten in ihrer Freizeit die Wildnis in Nutzgärten umwandeln. In den Anfängen des Englischen Gartens waren also Soldaten damit beschäftigt, mit Hacke und Spaten Kartoffeln anzupflanzen, die Thompson aus Amerika mitgebracht hatte. Entsprechend dem neuen Geist der Zeit nach der Französischen Revolution wurde 1792 der neu angelegte Garten den Bürgern übergeben.

Später hat der Landschaftsgärtner Friedrich Ludwig von Skell das grüne Idyll verschönert. Wie in den englischen Landschaftsgärten sollte in dem neuen Park die Natur so gestaltet werden, dass sie „möglichst echt“ aussah. So bekam der See seine drei Inseln, und es wurden neue Bäche, Wasserfälle und harmonisch angeordnete Baumgruppen angelegt. Heute würde man nie ahnen, dass der Englische Garten über 200 Jahre lang eine Großbaustelle war.

81. Welche der folgenden Überschriften passt am besten zu diesem Text?

    (A) Die Entstehung des Englischen Gartens
    (B) Ein exotisches Reiseziel
    (C) Ein Jagdparadies in München
    (D) Das Leben des Kurfürsten Carl Theodor

82. Was haben die Soldaten auf diesem Land gemacht?

    (A) Sie haben es verteidigt.
    (B) Sie haben Gemüsegärten angelegt.
    (C) Sie haben dort exerziert.
    (D) Sie haben Bäume gepflanzt.

83. Benjamin Thompson schlug dem Kurfürsten vor,

    (A) nach Amerika auszuwandern
    (B) eine Universität zu gründen
    (C) das Land anders zu verwenden
    (D) Ludwig von Skell anzustellen

84. Wozu benutzt man heute den Englischen Garten?

    (A) Um neue Kartoffelsorten zu entwickeln
    (B) Um sich weiterzubilden
    (C) Um exotische Tiere anzuschauen
    (D) Um sich zu entspannen

85. Der Kurfürst Carl Theodor benutzte das Land des heutigen Englischen Gartens, um

    (A) darin zu wandern
    (B) einen See anzulegen
    (C) dort zu jagen
    (D) Soldaten auszubilden

GO ON TO THE NEXT PAGE

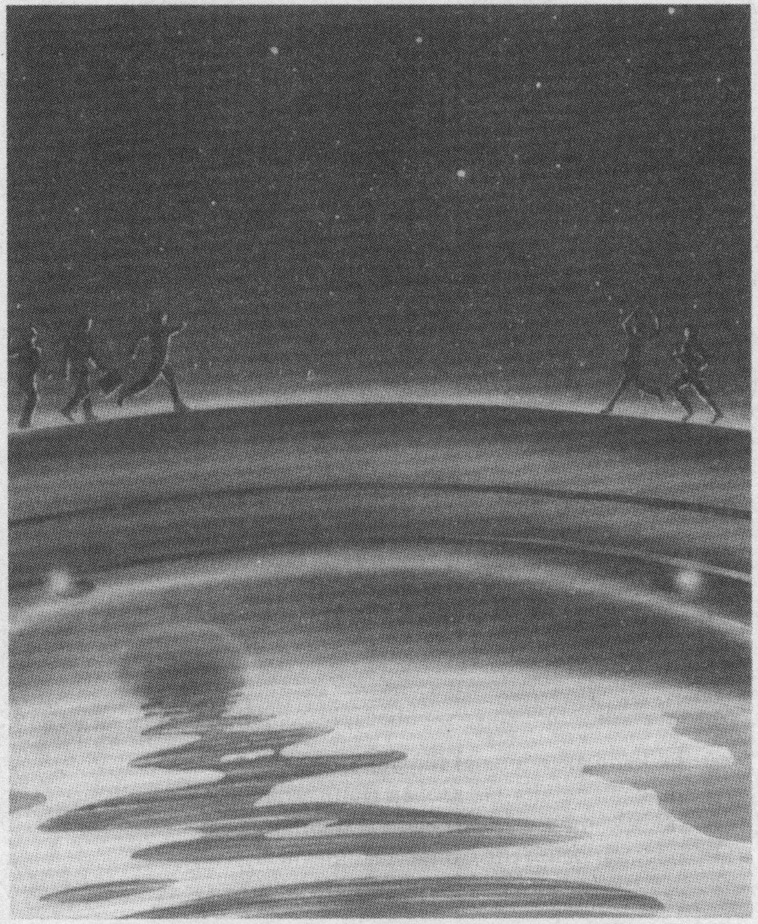

Nordamerika rückt ein Drittel näher :

- Haben Sie Geschäftspartner, Freunde oder Angehörige in Nordamerika?
- Telefonieren Sie oft in die Vereinigten Staaten oder nach Kanada?

Wenn Sie eine dieser Fragen mit ja beantworten können, dann haben Sie einen Grund zur Freude:

Seit 1. Mai telefonieren Sie 37% günstiger von Deutschland in die USA und nach Kanada.

86. Was will man mit dieser Anzeige mitteilen?

(A) Man soll sich Freunde in Amerika suchen.
(B) Deutsche reisen öfter nach Nordamerika.
(C) Man soll viel mehr in der ganzen Welt telefonieren.
(D) Anrufe nach Nordamerika sind jetzt billiger.

GO ON TO THE NEXT PAGE

Menschen '99

"Ich wollte schon immer meinen Weg allein gehen. Ich habe Abitur und danach eine Lehre gemacht. Anschließend habe ich 2 Jahre in einer Galerie in London gearbeitet. Heute weiß ich, was meine Ausbildung wert ist. Sie gibt mir Sicherheit, auch finanziell. Ich verdiene gut und kann sogar für die Zukunft vorsorgen. Wie, das diskutiere ich gerade mit der Deutschen Bank."

87. Warum ist diese Person froh über ihre Ausbildung?

(A) Sie kann ausreichend für sich sorgen.
(B) Sie kann bei der Deutschen Bank arbeiten.
(C) Sie bekommt dadurch viel Prestige.
(D) Sie kann damit ihr Abitur nachmachen.

END OF SECTION II

STOP

IF YOU FINISH BEFORE TIME IS CALLED, YOU MAY CHECK YOUR WORK ON SECTION II OF THIS TEST. DO NO TURN TO ANY OTHER TEST IN THIS BOOK.

How to Score the SAT Subject Test in German with Listening

When you take an actual SAT Subject Test in German with Listening, you receive an overall composite score as well as two subscores: one for the reading section, one for the listening section.

The reading and listening scores are reported on the College Board's 20–80 scale. However the composite score, which is the most significant of the scores reported to the colleges you specify, is in the form of the College Board's 200–800 scale.

Worksheet 1. Finding Your Raw Listening Subscore

STEP 1: Table A lists the correct answers for all the questions on the SAT Subject Test in German with Listening that is reproduced in this book. It also serves as a worksheet for you to calculate your raw Listening subscore.

- Compare your answers with those given in the table.
- Put a check in the column marked "Right" if your answer is correct.
- Put a check in the column marked "Wrong" if your answer is incorrect.
- Leave both columns blank if you omitted the question.

STEP 2: Count the number of right answers for questions 1–27.

Enter the total here: ____________________

STEP 3: Count the number of wrong answers for questions 1–27.

Enter the total here: ____________________

STEP 4: Multiply the number of wrong answers by .333.

Enter the product here: ________________

STEP 5: Subtract the result obtained in Step 4 from the total you obtained in Step 2.

Enter the result here: ___________________

STEP 6: Round the number obtained in Step 5 to the nearest whole number.

Enter the result here: ___________________

The number you obtained in Step 6 is your raw Listening subscore.

Worksheet 2. Finding Your Raw Reading Subscore

STEP 1: Table A lists the correct answers for all the questions on the SAT Subject Test in German with Listening that is reproduced in this book. It also serves as a worksheet for you to calculate your raw Reading subscore.

STEP 2: Count the number of right answers for questions 28–87.

Enter the total here: ____________________

STEP 3: Count the number of wrong answers for questions 28–87.

Enter the total here: ____________________

STEP 4: Multiply the number of wrong answers by .333.

Enter the product here: ________________

STEP 5: Subtract the result obtained in Step 4 from the total you obtained in Step 2.

Enter the result here: ___________________

STEP 6: Round the number obtained in Step 5 to the nearest whole number.

Enter the result here: ___________________

The number you obtained in Step 6 is your raw Reading subscore.

Worksheet 3. Finding Your Raw Composite Score

STEP 1: Enter your unrounded raw Reading subscore from Step 5 of Worksheet 2.

Enter the result here: ________________

STEP 2: Enter your unrounded raw Listening subscore from Step 5 of Worksheet 1.

Enter the result here: ________________

STEP 3: Add the result obtained in Step 1 to the result obtained in Step 2.

Enter the result here: ________________

STEP 4: Round the number obtained in Step 3 to the nearest whole number.

Enter the result here: ________________

The number you obtained in Step 4 is your raw composite score.

Table A

Answers to the Subject Test in German with Listening, Form 3YLC, and Percentage of Students Answering Each Question Correctly

Question Number	Correct Answer	Right	Wrong	Percentage of Students Answering the Question Correctly*	Question Number	Correct Answer	Right	Wrong	Percentage of Students Answering the Question Correctly*
1	A			54	33	C			87
2	D			90	34	C			38
3	A			90	35	B			80
4	B			89	36	A			64
5	C			82	37	A			95
6	A			75	38	A			82
7	B			57	39	B			62
8	D			80	40	A			71
9	A			55	41	C			82
10	B			78	42	D			64
11	B			84	43	C			61
12	D			41	44	A			86
13	A			51	45	C			41
14	D			37	46	B			56
15	D			52	47	C			88
16	D			86	48	B			45
17	A			86	49	A			68
18	A			38	50	C			49
19	B			82	51	D			52
20	D			67	52	B			88
21	B			80	53	A			80
22	C			78	54	B			61
23	A			53	55	A			46
24	C			74	56	C			55
25	B			67	57	C			75
26	A			34	58	D			99
27	D			60	59	B			33
28	D			72	60	D			64
29	A			45	61	B			95
30	B			52	62	D			76
31	A			81	63	A			32
32	D			71	64	D			71

Table A continued on next page

Table A continued from previous page

Question Number	Correct Answer	Right	Wrong	Percentage of Students Answering the Question Correctly*	Question Number	Correct Answer	Right	Wrong	Percentage of Students Answering the Question Correctly*
65	B			66	77	C			67
66	C			50	78	C			54
67	D			46	79	D			73
68	C			73	80	B			27
69	A			90	81	A			66
70	C			85	82	B			56
71	D			85	83	C			54
72	A			47	84	D			52
73	D			55	85	C			31
74	A			57	86	D			87
75	D			68	87	A			50
76	B			59					

* These percentages are based on an analysis of the answer sheets of a representative sample of 483 students who took the original form of this test in November 2002, and whose mean composite score was 589. They may be used as an indication of the relative difficulty of a particular question. Each percentage may also be used to predict the likelihood that a typical SAT Subject Test in German with Listening candidate will answer that question correctly on this edition of the test.

Finding Your Scaled Score

When you take SAT Subject Tests, the scores sent to the colleges you specify are reported on the College Board scale, which ranges from 200–800. Subscores are reported on a scale which ranges from 20–80. You can convert your practice test scores to scaled scores by using Tables B, C, and D. To find your scaled score, locate your raw score in the left-hand column of the table; the corresponding score in the right-hand column is your scaled score. For example, a raw score of 47 on this particular edition of the Subject Test in German with Listening corresponds to a scaled composite score of 570.

Raw scores are converted to scaled scores to ensure that a score earned on any one edition of a particular Subject Test is comparable to the same scaled score earned on any other edition of the same Subject Test. Because some editions of the tests may be slightly easier or more difficult than others, College Board scaled scores are adjusted so that they indicate the same level of performance regardless of the edition of the test taken and the ability of the group that takes it. Thus, for example, a score of 400 on one edition of a test taken at a particular administration indicates the same level of achievement as a score of 400 on a different edition of the test taken at a different administration.

When you take the SAT Subject Tests during a national administration, your scores are likely to differ somewhat from the scores you obtain on the tests in this book. People perform at different levels at different times for reasons unrelated to the tests themselves. The precision of any test is also limited because it represents only a sample of all the possible questions that could be asked.

Your scaled composite score from Table B is ________________ .

Your scaled listening score from Table C is ________________ .

Your scaled reading score from Table D is ________________ .

Table B

Scaled Score Conversion Table Subject Test in German with Listening Composite Score (Form 3YLC)					
Raw Score	Scaled Score	Raw Score	Scaled Score	Raw Score	Scaled Score
87	800	49	580	11	390
86	780	48	580	10	390
85	770	47	570	9	380
84	770	46	570	8	370
83	760	45	570	7	370
82	760	44	560	6	360
81	750	43	560	5	360
80	750	42	550	4	350
79	740	41	550	3	350
78	740	40	540	2	340
77	740	39	540	1	340
76	730	38	540	0	330
75	730	37	530	-1	330
74	720	36	530	-2	330
73	720	35	520	-3	320
72	710	34	520	-4	320
71	710	33	510	-5	320
70	700	32	510	-6	310
69	700	31	500	-7	310
68	690	30	500	-8	310
67	690	29	490	-9	310
66	680	28	490	-10	300
65	680	27	480	-11	300
64	670	26	480	-12	300
63	660	25	470	-13	300
62	660	24	470	-14	300
61	650	23	460	-15	300
60	650	22	460	-16	300
59	640	21	450	-17	300
58	630	20	450	-18	290
57	630	19	440	-19	290
56	620	18	430	-20	290
55	620	17	430	-21	290
54	610	16	420	-22	290
53	600	15	420	-23	290
52	600	14	410	-24	290
51	590	13	400	-25	290
50	590	12	400	-26	290
				-27	280
				-28	280
				-29	270

Table C

Scaled Score Conversion Table Subject Test in German with Listening Listening Subscore (Form 3YLC)					
Raw Score	Scaled Score	Raw Score	Scaled Score	Raw Score	Scaled Score
27	78	13	54	-1	35
26	76	12	53	-2	34
25	74	11	51	-3	33
24	73	10	50	-4	32
23	71	9	49	-5	31
22	69	8	47	-6	31
21	67	7	46	-7	30
20	65	6	45	-8	29
19	63	5	43	-9	28
18	61	4	41		
17	60	3	40		
16	58	2	38		
15	57	1	37		
14	55	0	36		

Table D

Scaled Score Conversion Table Subject Test in German with Listening Reading Subscore (Form 3YLC)					
Raw Score	Scaled Score	Raw Score	Scaled Score	Raw Score	Scaled Score
60	79	33	58	6	39
59	78	32	58	5	38
58	77	31	57	4	37
57	76	30	56	3	37
56	75	29	56	2	36
55	75	28	55	1	35
54	74	27	55	0	34
53	74	26	54	-1	34
52	73	25	53	-2	33
51	72	24	53	-3	33
50	72	23	52	-4	32
49	71	22	51	-5	32
48	70	21	51	-6	31
47	70	20	50	-7	31
46	69	19	49	-8	31
45	68	18	49	-9	30
44	67	17	48	-10	30
43	66	16	47	-11	30
42	66	15	46	-12	30
41	65	14	46	-13	30
40	64	13	45	-14	29
39	63	12	44	-15	29
38	62	11	43	-16	29
37	61	10	42	-17	29
36	60	9	42	-18	29
35	60	8	41	-19	29
34	59	7	40	-20	29

How Did You Do on the Subject Test in German with Listening?

After you score your test and analyze your performance, think about the following questions:

Did you run out of time before reaching the end of the test?

If so, you may need to pace yourself better. For example, maybe you spent too much time on one or two hard questions. A better approach might be to skip the ones you can't answer right away and try answering all the questions that remain on the test. Then if there's time, go back to the questions you skipped.

Did you take a long time reading the directions?

You will save time when you take the test by learning the directions to the Subject Test in German with Listening ahead of time. Each minute you spend reading directions during the test is a minute that you could use to answer questions.

How did you handle questions you were unsure of?

If you were able to eliminate one or more of the answer choices as wrong and guess from the remaining ones, your approach probably worked to your advantage. On the other hand, making haphazard guesses or omitting questions without trying to eliminate choices could cost you valuable points.

How difficult were the questions for you compared with other students who took the test?

Table A shows you how difficult the multiple-choice questions were for the group of students who took this test during its national administration. The right-hand column gives the percentage of students that answered each question correctly.

A question answered correctly by almost everyone in the group is obviously an easier question. For example, 95 percent of the students answered question 37 correctly. But only 27 percent answered question 80 correctly.

Keep in mind that these percentages are based on just one group of students. They would probably be different with another group of students taking the test.

If you missed several easier questions, go back and try to find out why: Did the questions cover material you haven't yet reviewed? Did you misunderstand the directions?

Chapter 11
Italian

Purpose

The Subject Test in Italian measures your ability to understand written Italian. The test allows for variation in language preparation and is independent of particular textbooks or methods of instruction. The test measures reading proficiency based on communicative materials authentic to the Italian culture.

Format

This is a one-hour test with 80 to 85 multiple-choice questions. Test questions are written to reflect current trends in high school curricula and to test reading skills and familiarity with the language structure.

Content

Questions range in difficulty from elementary through advanced, although most questions are at the intermediate level. The test measures reading proficiency through a variety of questions requiring a broad knowledge of the language.

The test covers commonly taught grammatical constructions, and all questions reflect current standard Italian.

The test includes three parts:

Sentence completion questions test your knowledge of high-frequency vocabulary and appropriate idiomatic expressions in the context of paragraphs.

Structure questions test your familiarity with the language structure.

Reading comprehension questions test your understanding of the content of various selections taken from sources such as newspaper and magazine articles, prose fiction, historical works, advertisements, tickets, brochures, forms, and schedules.

Italian	
Skills Measured	**Approximate Percentage of Test**
Vocabulary in Context	30
Structure in Blank	30
Reading Comprehension	40

How to Prepare

The Subject Test in Italian allows for variation in language preparation. You should develop competence in Italian over a period of years by taking two to four years of Italian language study in high school or the equivalent. Familiarize yourself with the directions in advance. The directions in this book are identical to those that appear on the test.

Score

The total score is reported on the 200-to-800 scale.

Sample Questions

Your answer sheet has five answer positions marked A, B, C, D, and E, while the questions throughout this test contain only four choices. Be sure NOT to make any marks in column E.

Part A

Directions: In each of the following passages there are numbered blanks indicating that words or phrases have been omitted. For each numbered blank, four completions are provided. First read through the entire passage. Then, for each numbered blank, choose the completion that is most appropriate given the context of the entire passage and fill in the corresponding circle on the answer sheet.

Un piccolo villaggio siciliano

Baria Dorica è il nome di un piccolo villaggio estivo situato sulla costa siciliana. Tutte le __1__ del villaggio danno sulla piazzetta, dove si trova l'unico locale pubblico: il bar, che fa anche da panineria, pizzeria e panetteria.

La piazzetta è un luogo __2__ riservato solamente ai pedoni e i bambini vi possono correre e giocare liberamente. La sera, i ragazzini formano dei gruppetti sparsi qua e là e __3__ animatamente degli eventi della giornata. Fino a tarda sera tutto è animato e risuona di voci.

1. (A) macchine
   (B) strade
   (C) luci
   (D) corriere

2. (A) silenzioso
   (B) solitario
   (C) sicuro
   (D) privato

3. (A) cantano
   (B) leggono
   (C) parlano
   (D) pensano

Choice (B) is the correct answer to question 1. In this question, you have to choose the appropriate noun from the four answer choices. Only *strade* can be used in connection with *danno sulla piazzetta* to form a meaningful sentence.

Choice (C) is the correct answer to question 2. In this question, you have to choose the adjective that fits best according to the context. The place in question can be considered *un luogo sicuro* since it is *riservato ai pedoni*, which means that there is no car traffic. Choices (A), (B), and (D) are incorrect because they are contradictory to what is said in the passage.

Choice (C) is the correct answer to question 3. In this question, you have to choose the appropriate verb from the four answer choices. The verb *parlare* is the only verb that fits logically. The other choices are not appropriate in this context even if choices (B) and (D) are verbs that could be used in connection with *eventi della giornata*.

Part B

Directions: In each sentence or dialogue below you will find a blank space indicating that a word or phrase has been omitted. Following each sentence are four completions. Of the four choices, select the one that best completes the sentence structurally and logically and fill in the corresponding circle on the answer sheet. In some instances, choice (A) may consist of dashes; by choosing this option, you are indicating that no insertion is required to form a grammatically correct sentence.

4. Molte turiste preferiscono comprare ____________ regali nei negozi del centro.
   (A) il loro
   (B) il suo
   (C) i loro
   (D) i suoi

Choice (C) is the correct answer to question 4. In this question, you are asked to choose the correct possessive adjective from the four answer choices. The possessive adjective *i loro* is used when the subject is third person, plural (*Molte turiste*), and the object is masculine, plural (*regali*). Choice (A) is incorrect because *il* refers to an object in the singular; choice (B) is incorrect because *il suo* refers to a third person, singular subject, and an object in the singular; choice (D) is incorrect because it refers to a third person, singular subject.

5. Dopo ____________ le camicie, il cliente saluta e esce.
   (A) aver comprato
   (B) comprava
   (C) abbia comprato
   (D) comprerà

Choice (A) is the correct answer to question 5. In this question, you have to choose from the four answer choices the form of the verb *comprare* that fits in the sentence grammatically. The verb *comprare* is in a subordinate clause introduced by *Dopo*. You need to know that *dopo* is used with a verb in the past infinitive. The other choices are incorrect because the verb *comprare* is (B) in the imperfect, (C) in the past subjunctive, and (D) in the future tense.

Part C

Directions: Read the following texts carefully for comprehension. Each text is followed by a number of questions or incomplete statements. Select the answer or completion that is best according to the text and fill in the corresponding circle on the answer sheet.

Questions 6–7

QUEL FANTASTICO VENERDI' DI REPUBBLICA.

"Il Venerdì", tutte le settimane con Repubblica, vi porta attualità, grandi reportages, viaggi, inchieste e interviste: centotrentadue pagine a colori tutte per voi. "Il Venerdì" è in edicola ogni venerdì insieme a Repubblica e Affari & Finanza. Il tutto, per solo un euro.

la Repubblica

6. In quest' annuncio, che cos' è "Il Venerdì"?
   (A) Un libro
   (B) Un settimanale
   (C) Un notiziario
   (D) Un' inchiesta

7. Come si ottiene "Il Venerdì"?
   (A) Si deve andare in un negozio.
   (B) Si deve comprare *la Repubblica.*
   (C) Si devono spendere due euro.
   (D) Si deve aspettare la fine del mese.

Choice (B) is the correct answer to question 6. This question asks what *"Il Venerdì"* is. The text mentions *tutte le settimane* and also *"Il Venerdì" è in edicola ogni venerdì.* Choices (A), (C), and (D) are incorrect within the context of the ad.

Choice (B) is the correct answer to question 7. This question asks about how you obtain *"Il Venerdì."* The text mentions *"Il Venerdì"* (...) *con Repubblica,* and also (...) *insieme a Repubblica.* Choices (A), (C), and (D) are incorrect within the context of the ad.

Questions 8–10

È "Ferragosto", festa nazionale, e se ne sono andati tutti. Restano solo alcune auto, abbandonate lo scorso inverno, ancora più solitarie sotto il sole d'agosto.

E incredibile, poter attraversare Milano in un quarto d'ora, da un capo all'altro. E poi fermarsi e parcheggiare dove si vuole. Bellissimo, ma per fare che cosa, se è tutto chiuso da una settimana? ...

Vado all'edicola e la trovo sprangata. Il tabaccaio più vicino adesso si trova a un chilometro di distanza, e non ha più francobolli. Se in questo momento si fulmina una lampadina di casa sono perduto, non saprei dove comprarne una. Fortuna che per cibi e bevande mi ero fatto una scorta. L'assedio durerà fino al giorno 20, e occorre resistere.

Del resto non mi è mai piaciuto lo spettacolo di questo fuggi fuggi, di questo esodo di massa, come se a Milano fosse scoppiata un'epidemia di peste.

8. L'autore del brano si lamenta perchè
   (A) la città è affollata
   (B) è difficile attraversare la città
   (C) gli abitanti se ne vanno
   (D) c'è la peste

9. Secondo il brano durante il "Ferragosto" è probabile che chi ha una macchina possa
   (A) comprare la benzina a buon mercato
   (B) avere difficoltà nel parcheggiare
   (C) muoversi facilmente in auto per la città
   (D) stare in coda per un'ora per arrivare in centro

10. L'autore non morirà di fame perchè
   (A) sua moglie gli ha lasciato cibi e bevande
   (B) suo cognato ha un ristorante
   (C) ha deciso di non fare più la dieta
   (D) ha già comprato provviste sufficienti

Choice (C) is the correct answer to question 8. This question tests literal comprehension and refers to the reason for the author's complaint. The first line of the passage states *…se ne sono andati tutti*, so the correct answer is choice (C) *gli abitanti se ne vanno.* Choices (A), (B), and (D) are incorrect within the context of this passage.

Choice (C) is the correct answer to question 9. This question tests literal comprehension and refers to an important detail mentioned in the text. In the second paragraph, the author states *…È incredibile, poter attraversare Milano in un quarto d'ora,* (…) and also (…) *parcheggiare dove si vuole.* Choices (A), (B), and (D) are incorrect within the context of the passage.

Choice (D) is the correct answer to question 10. This question tests literal comprehension and refers to another important detail mentioned in the text. In the third paragraph, the author states *per cibi e bevande mi ero fatto una scorta,* so the correct answer is choice (D) *ha già comprato provviste sufficienti.* Choices (A), (B), and (C) are incorrect within the context of the passage.

Italian Test

Practice Helps

The test that follows is an actual, recently administered SAT Subject Test in Italian. To get an idea of what it's like to take this test, practice under conditions that are much like those of an actual test administration.

- Set aside an hour when you can take the test uninterrupted. Make sure you complete the test in one sitting.
- Sit at a desk or table with no other books or papers. Dictionaries, other books, or notes are not allowed in the test room.
- Tear out an answer sheet from the back of this book and fill it in just as you would on the day of the test. One answer sheet can be used for up to three Subject Tests.
- Read the instructions that precede the practice test. During the actual administration, you will be asked to read them before answering test questions.
- Time yourself by placing a clock or kitchen timer in front of you.
- After you finish the practice test, read the sections "How to Score the SAT Subject Test in Italian" and "How Did You Do on the Subject Test in Italian?"
- The appearance of the answer sheet in this book may differ from the answer sheet you see on test day.

ITALIAN TEST

The top portion of the section of the answer sheet that you will use in taking the Italian Test must be filled in exactly as shown in the illustration below. Note carefully that you have to do all of the following on your answer sheet.

1. Print ITALIAN on the line under the words "Subject Test (print)."
2. In the shaded box labeled "Test Code" fill in four circles:

   —Fill in circle 1 in the row labeled V.
   —Fill in circle 4 in the row labeled W.
   —Fill in circle 2 in the row labeled X.
   —Fill in circle B in the row labeled Y.

Test Code

V	●	②	③	④	⑤	⑥	⑦	⑧	⑨
W	①	②	③	●	⑤	⑥	⑦	⑧	⑨
X	① ●	③	④	⑤	Y Ⓐ	●	Ⓒ	Ⓓ	Ⓔ
Q	①	②	③	④	⑤	⑥	⑦	⑧	⑨

Subject Test (print)

ITALIAN

Please answer either Part I or Part II by filling in the specific circle in row Q. You are to fill in ONE and ONLY ONE circle, as described below, to indicate how you obtained your knowledge of Italian. The information you provide is for statistical purposes only and will not influence your score on the test.

Part I If your knowledge of Italian does not come primarily from courses taken in grades 9 through 12, fill in circle 9 and leave the remaining circles blank, regardless of how long you studied the subject in school. For example, you are to fill in circle 9 if your knowledge of Italian comes primarily from any of the following sources: study prior to the ninth grade, courses taken at a college, special study, living in a home in which Italian is the principal language spoken, or extensive residence abroad that includes significant experience in the Italian language.

Part II If your knowledge of Italian does come primarily from courses taken in secondary school, fill in the circle that indicates the level of the Italian course in which you are currently enrolled. If you are not now enrolled in an Italian course, fill in the circle that indicates the level of the most advanced course in Italian that you have completed.

- First year: first or second half —Fill in circle 1.
- Second year: first half —Fill in circle 2.
  second half —Fill in circle 3.
- Third year: first half —Fill in circle 4.
  second half —Fill in circle 5.
- Fourth year: first half —Fill in circle 6.
  second half —Fill in circle 7.
- Course at a level higher than fourth year, second half
  or
  high school course work plus a minimum of four weeks of study abroad —Fill in circle 8.

When the supervisor gives the signal, turn the page and begin the Italian Test. There are 100 numbered circles on the answer sheet and 82 questions in the Italian Test. Therefore, use only circles 1 to 82 for recording your answers.

ITALIAN TEST

Part A

Directions: In each of the following passages there are numbered blanks indicating that words or phrases have been omitted. For each numbered blank, four completions are provided. First read through the entire passage. Then, for each numbered blank, choose the completion that is most appropriate given the context of the entire passage and fill in the corresponding circle on the answer sheet.

Vita in un nuovo paese

La situazione degli immigranti che vengono a ___(1)___ in un nuovo paese è qualche volta molto ___(2)___. All'inizio si sentono ___(3)___. Ci sono spesso molte differenze fra la loro vecchia cultura e quella nuova. Sono obbligati ad assumere una nuova identità ed ad imparare una nuova lingua. I bambini ___(4)___ abbastanza velocemente la lingua del paese, ma gli adulti continuano ___(5)___ a parlare il dialetto del loro paese.

1. (A) visitare
   (B) partire
   (C) abitare
   (D) accogliere

2. (A) saggia
   (B) difficile
   (C) disabitata
   (D) irresponsabile

3. (A) svegli
   (B) isolati
   (C) indipendenti
   (D) congeniali

4. (A) vivono
   (B) imparano
   (C) discutono
   (D) consigliano

5. (A) già
   (B) dopo
   (C) molto
   (D) spesso

3VAC

GO ON TO THE NEXT PAGE

Grado

Grado, bella ___(6)___ non lontana da Venezia, Trieste ed Aquileia, fu in origine un villaggio di pescatori. È formata da due isole ed è ___(7)___ alla terraferma da un ponte di sabbia. Ha uno stabilimento balneare, un porto per ___(8)___, e una marina dove approdano candidi yacht. Nella suggestiva basilica si eseguono, soprattutto d'estate, importanti manifestazioni ___(9)___. Le valli intorno alla laguna di Grado sono romantiche e verdi, ordinate e ricche, e vi si ___(10)___ vini sontuosi.

6. (A) società
   (B) spiaggia
   (C) cittadina
   (D) strada

7. (A) unita
   (B) messa
   (C) portata
   (D) sollevata

8. (A) barche da pesca
   (B) cavalli da corsa
   (C) automobili eleganti
   (D) biciclette di marca

9. (A) commerciali
   (B) industriali
   (C) musicali
   (D) sportive

10. (A) mettono
    (B) producono
    (C) compongono
    (D) costruiscono

GO ON TO THE NEXT PAGE

Trasporti

Posti in aereo non se ne trovano più? Volete __(11)__ al minimo la spesa delle vostre vacanze in una capitale europea? Ecco la soluzione ai due __(12)__: viaggiare in autobus.

Da Milano e da Roma, ma anche da Bologna, Firenze e Genova __(13)__ ogni giorno molti pullman granturismo che collegano le principali città d'Europa.

Rispetto all'aereo, il biglietto costa meno __(14)__. Il viaggio dura diverse ore più __(15)__, certo. In ogni caso, gli autobus viaggiano quasi sempre in __(16)__, e il tragitto è diretto, senza __(17)__.

Il biglietto rimane valido per sei mesi. Ogni passeggero può portare con sè una valigia e un bagaglio a __(18)__.

11. (A) includere
(B) dare
(C) ridurre
(D) giungere

12. (A) soggetti
(B) lavori
(C) mezzi
(D) problemi

13. (A) pagano
(B) partono
(C) stendono
(D) toccano

14. (A) dell'energia
(B) dell'economia
(C) della gita
(D) della metà

15. (A) del velo
(B) del volo
(C) della vela
(D) della volta

16. (A) stazione
(B) autostrada
(C) silenzio
(D) compagnia

17. (A) direzione
(B) deviazioni
(C) destinazioni
(D) pazienza

18. (A) mano
(B) piedi
(C) terra
(D) voce

GO ON TO THE NEXT PAGE

L'animatore turistico

Fare l'animatore in un villaggio turistico è il lavoro ___(19)___ per eccellenza e sicuramente anche il più ambito durante l'estate. Significa infatti passare tre o quattro mesi in una ___(20)___ di mare, preferibilmente all'estero, occupandosi di far divertire gli altri, organizzare ___(21)___ e feste per bambini, ___(22)___ tennis, windsurf, yoga o aerobica. L'animatore deve per prima cosa riuscire a trattare con i ___(23)___, e con tutti, anche i più difficili, essere allegro e coinvolgente, senza mai ___(24)___ la vita privata dei turisti.

19. (A) stagionale
(B) mensile
(C) giornaliero
(D) annuale

20. (A) palestra
(B) discoteca
(C) pizzeria
(D) località

21. (A) lavori
(B) giochi
(C) servizi
(D) compiti

22. (A) insegnare
(B) imparare
(C) dare
(D) frequentare

23. (A) pittori
(B) clienti
(C) passeggeri
(D) commercianti

24. (A) cambiare
(B) spiegare
(C) invadere
(D) occupare

GO ON TO THE NEXT PAGE

Part B

Directions: In each sentence or dialogue below you will find a blank space indicating that a word or phrase has been omitted. Following each sentence are four completions. Of the four choices, select the one that best completes the sentence structurally and logically and fill in the corresponding circle on the answer sheet. In some instances, choice (A) consists of dashes; by choosing this option, you are indicating that no insertion is required to form a grammatically correct sentence.

25. Luisa, qui fuori ci sono anche cartoline e giornali -------!

(A) illustrata
(B) illustrati
(C) illustrato
(D) illustrate

26. Buon giorno signora. ------- qualche rivista americana?

(A) È
(B) Ha
(C) Sia
(D) Abbia

27. Posso -------, se vuole.

(A) aiutarmi
(B) aiutarci
(C) aiutarLa
(D) aiutarsi

28. A quest'ora domani ------- già a Venezia.

(A) sia
(B) saremo
(C) eravamo
(D) fossimo

29. Ci sarà anche mio cugino. Sono cinque anni che non ------- vediamo.

(A) si
(B) ne
(C) mi
(D) ci

30. A che ora mi consigli di ------- da casa?

(A) parto
(B) parti
(C) partire
(D) partito

31. La ragazza ha viaggiato in aereo con ------- amici.

(A) dei
(B) nessuno
(C) alcuni
(D) tutti

32. Sei sicura di avere chiuso ------- la porta a chiave?

(A) bene
(B) buona
(C) migliore
(D) buonissima

33. Mi piace il colore ------- tue valigie.

(A) delle
(B) dalle
(C) nelle
(D) sulle

GO ON TO THE NEXT PAGE

34. Il telefono è il mio strumento di lavoro e lo uso ------- tutto il giorno.

(A) ---
(B) da
(C) su
(D) in

35. Cosa ------- fare lui per telefonare all'estero?

(A) dovrai
(B) dovrà
(C) dovrò
(D) dovranno

36. Oggi in Italia lo stress non risparmia -------.

(A) qualcuno
(B) nessuno
(C) chiunque
(D) ognuno

37. Accettò e rispose che avrebbe finito di lavorare entro ------- minuti.

(A) qualche
(B) troppo
(C) pochi
(D) un

38. Quando lui riceverà il mio telegramma, mi ------- subito.

(A) risponde
(B) risponderà
(C) rispondeva
(D) risponderebbe

39. ------- recenti studi delle Nazioni Unite, le donne italiane lavorano moltissimo.

(A) Su
(B) Fra
(C) Sotto
(D) Secondo

40. Gli italiani amano il mare. Molti ------- vanno durante le vacanze estive.

(A) ci
(B) gli
(C) ne
(D) lo

41. Sulla spiaggia è comodo affittare un ombrellone; io voglio ------- verde.

(A) prenderlo
(B) prenderci
(C) prenderne
(D) prendervi

42. Questo è l'albero più alto ------- io abbia mai visto.

(A) quale
(B) chi
(C) che
(D) cui

43. I nostri vicini preferiscono ------- guardare la televisione.

(A) ---
(B) di
(C) a
(D) da

GO ON TO THE NEXT PAGE

44. Vorrei ------- registrazioni di musica popolare moderna.

(A) di
(B) un po'
(C) niente
(D) alcune

45. Scusi, i biglietti per il concerto allo stadio ------- possono comprare qui?

(A) vi
(B) me
(C) si
(D) ti

46. Lo sai Anna, ------- piacciono i complessi italiani che suonano ad alto volume.

(A) mi
(B) me
(C) lo
(D) la

47. Quel pianista è bravissimo. L'ho sentito ------- alla Scala.

(A) suonato
(B) suonava
(C) suonare
(D) suonò

48. Al cinema Rex danno ------- ultimo film con Massimo Troisi.

(A) il
(B) l'
(C) lo
(D) la

49. Laura, ------- piace la pittura moderna?

(A) li
(B) lei
(C) ti
(D) si

50. Nel museo ci sono cataloghi splendidi! Li -------, se non costassero troppo.

(A) comprerei
(B) comprerò
(C) comprai
(D) compro

GO ON TO THE NEXT PAGE

Part C

Directions: Read the following texts carefully for comprehension. Each text is followed by a number of questions or incomplete statements. Select the answer or completion that is best according to the text and fill in the corresponding circle on the answer sheet.

Questions 51-52

Per una gita diversa
lontana dallo stress, in pieno relax
a due passi da voi

CAMPING
CITTÀ DI ANGERA

ristorante tipico con cucina internazionale e piatti tipici locali, ampi saloni per banchetti, piscine, tennis, campi bocce, pallavolo, ping-pong, darsena, pontili d'attracco e spiagge

ANGERA (VA)

Via Bruschera Tel. (0331) 930.736

51. Angera è un luogo adatto per
    - (A) sposarsi
    - (B) riposarsi
    - (C) sciare
    - (D) lavorare

52. Il ristorante offre piatti
    - (A) di ogni paese
    - (B) solamente locali
    - (C) rustici
    - (D) dietetici

GO ON TO THE NEXT PAGE

Questions 53-57

C'era una festa a casa di Rolly Marchi ed io ci andai. Entrai e vidi un quadro ad olio ben illuminato, al centro di una parete del salotto. Riconobbi subito il segno di Guttuso. Ammiravo la sua arte, compravo tutti i disegni che trovavo in giro, ma non ne avevo mai incontrato l'autore. "È un Guttuso, no?", chiesi. "Sì, si chiama I naufraghi", mi rispose il padrone di casa. Il quadro continuava ad affascinarmi. Quando Rolly Marchi, per essere gentile, mi disse delle solite stupidaggini del tipo: "Che cosa posso offrirti?"; io puntai il dito sul Guttuso. "Quello", dissi. Rolly Marchi ci restò malissimo: "Ma come, quello l'ho appena comprato, non posso proprio dartelo". "Ma io te lo ricompro", insistevo io. E lui a dire di no, che semmai me lo avrebbe regalato, un quadro di Guttuso, però non quello. Sentii una voce dietro di me: una voce siciliana, profonda, vellutata. "Daglielo Rolly, te ne farò un altro". Mi girai: "Allora è lei Renato Guttuso? Io sono una sua grande ammiratrice". "Dal prossimo minuto io sarò un suo grande ammiratore", replicò. Tornai a casa felice con il mio quadro, e Renato Guttuso non lo vidi più per molti anni.

53. Chi era Guttuso?

(A) Un pittore
(B) Un attore
(C) Uno scrittore
(D) Uno scultore

54. Come è intitolata l'opera d'arte?

(A) Il padrone
(B) Rolly Marchi
(C) La festa
(D) I naufraghi

55. Che cosa affascinò la signora?

(A) Un dipinto
(B) Un colore
(C) L'accento
(D) La gente

56. Chi aveva una voce vellutata?

(A) Il naufrago
(B) Rolly Marchi
(C) Guttuso
(D) La signora

57. Che cosa ricevette in regalo la signora?

(A) Un'opera d'arte
(B) Un complimento
(C) Una casa
(D) Un ammiratore

GO ON TO THE NEXT PAGE

Questions 58-59

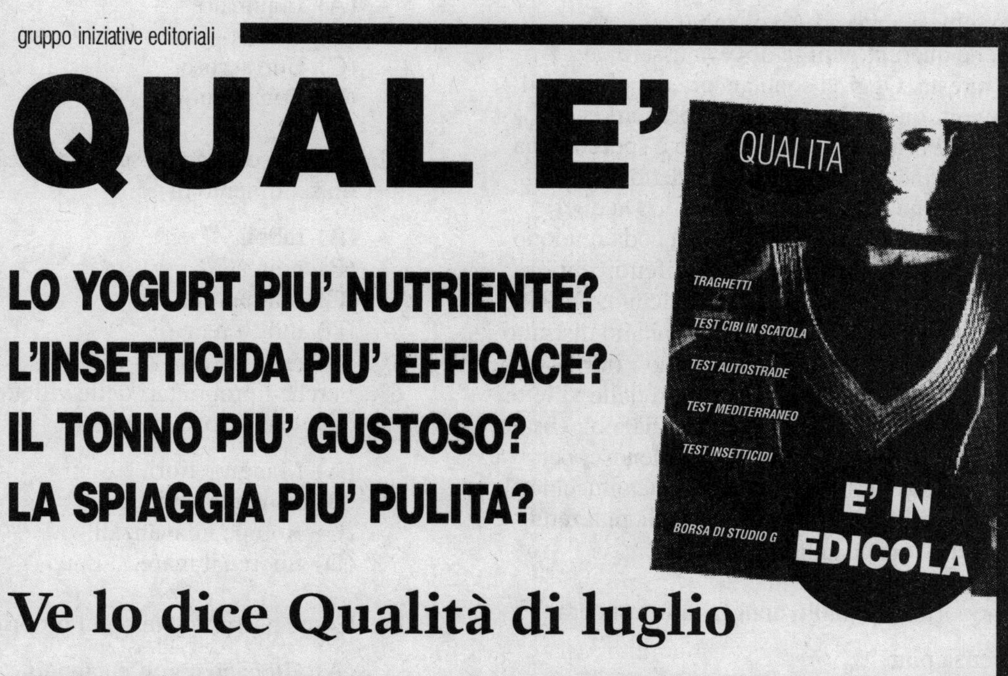

gruppo iniziative editoriali
QUAL E'
LO YOGURT PIU' NUTRIENTE?
L'INSETTICIDA PIU' EFFICACE?
IL TONNO PIU' GUSTOSO?
LA SPIAGGIA PIU' PULITA?
Ve lo dice Qualità di luglio
QUALITA
TRAGHETTI
TEST CIBI IN SCATOLA
TEST AUTOSTRADE
TEST MEDITERRANEO
TEST INSETTICIDI
BORSA DI STUDIO G
E' IN EDICOLA

58. Cosa è *Qualità*?

    (A) Un giornale
    (B) Una rubrica
    (C) Un libro divertente
    (D) Un periodico mensile

59. *Qualità* ci insegna soprattutto quale delle seguenti attività?

    (A) A cucinare all'italiana
    (B) A fare scelte informate
    (C) A superare gli esami
    (D) A nuotare con stile

GO ON TO THE NEXT PAGE

Questions 60-64

Da pochi mesi abito ad Arenzano (Genova), in quella che quarant'anni fa doveva essere una stupenda foresta. Oggi vi sono ancora dei pini, tra il campo da golf, quelli da tennis, il supermarket e la piazzetta tipo Porto Cervo, ma il mare è sporco. Una mattina, dalla finestra della stanza da letto, ho visto uno scoiattolo che sgranocchiava pinoli. Da quel giorno le sue evoluzioni e la sua lunga coda rendono i miei risvegli più sereni. Però ha un difetto: curiosa tra i vasi ed ogni tanto ne rovescia qualcuno; poi, ha fame, proprio come noi uomini che abbiamo distrutto la "sua" pineta, ed allora mangia persino i fiori colorati posti sui davanzali. I proprietari delle villette accanto, travolti dall'ondata ecologica, hanno pensato di cospargere il territorio di trappole velenose, per risolvere l'annoso problema dei fiori smangiucchiati! E poi discutono, seduti sulle panche della piazzetta, sul futuro della foresta amazzonica.

60. Secondo l'autore, molti anni fa la foresta era
    (A) senza pini
    (B) sporca
    (C) piena di scoiattoli
    (D) meravigliosa

61. Com'è il mare?
    (A) Inquinato
    (B) Sereno
    (C) Burrascoso
    (D) Stupendo

62. Quando osserva lo scoiattolo l'autore prova un sentimento di
    (A) rabbia
    (B) noia
    (C) tranquillità
    (D) indifferenza

63. Perchè i proprietari delle villette vogliono avvelenare lo scoiattolo?
    (A) Mangia i fiori.
    (B) Rovina i pini.
    (C) Rompe i davanzali.
    (D) Sporca il mare.

64. Come passano il tempo i proprietari delle villette?
    (A) Giocano a golf e a tennis.
    (B) Preparano trappole velenose.
    (C) Coltivano i fiori.
    (D) Discutono di problemi ecologici.

GO ON TO THE NEXT PAGE

Questions 65-67

L'INFORMATICA A TUA IMMAGINE E SOMIGLIANZA.

Siamo la sola società di servizi informatici che offre una consulenza globale e un servizio completo per ogni problema informatico: dall'istruzione qualificata del personale alla pianificazione dell'ambiente di lavoro.

Siamo in grado di assicurare un servizio qualificato e tempestivo grazie alle nostre trenta filiali, capillarmente operative su tutto il territorio nazionale (indirizzi sulle pagine gialle alla voce "informatica").

65. La Ibimaint non dà solo assistenza tecnica ma offre anche
    (A) corsi di manutenzione
    (B) consulenza e aiuto specifico
    (C) di rendere il computer simile al suo padrone
    (D) consulenza solo nel settore della programmazione

66. Cosa vende la Ibimaint?
    (A) Trenta filiali
    (B) Ambienti di lavoro
    (C) Servizi informatici
    (D) Spazio sulle pagine gialle

67. Secondo la pubblicità, cosa ha la Ibimaint?
    (A) Filiali da trent'anni
    (B) Una filiale solo a Milano
    (C) Filiali solo nell'Italia settentrionale
    (D) Filiali in tutto il paese

GO ON TO THE NEXT PAGE

Questions 68-72

In Italia incombe la paura di gigantesche catastrofi naturali. Acqua, terra e fuoco colpiscono il Belpaese con tragica regolarità e straordinaria forza. La prima minaccia sono i vulcani. Tre sono fra i più pericolosi: Vesuvio, Campi Flegrei e Vulcano.

Il secondo incubo sono i terremoti. In realtà quasi tutte le regioni italiane sono a rischio. Di edifici antisismici, che resistono ai terremoti, però, ne sono stati costruiti davvero pochi.

Un'altra minaccia sono le industrie. In Italia ci sono quattrocento fabbriche a grave rischio ambientale: stabilimenti chimici, farmaceutici, raffinerie rischiano di trasformarsi in bombe tossiche.

Ma non basta. Ogni anno c'è un appuntamento fisso: l'emergenza incendi che ogni estate divora una gran quantità di vegetazione. Negli ultimi quindici anni in Sardegna, in Liguria e in Piemonte intere foreste sono andate in fumo in poche ore.

68. Secondo il brano, gli italiani temono

(A) le esplosioni
(B) l'incubo
(C) i disastri
(D) il fumo

69. Cosa intende l'autore con la parola "Belpaese"?

(A) Una regione
(B) L'Italia
(C) Un vulcano
(D) La campagna

70. Gli edifici antisismici servono a

(A) prevenire i terremoti
(B) proteggere l'ambiente
(C) segnalare il pericolo
(D) ridurre i danni

71. L'articolo sostiene che l'industria italiana

(A) dà l'allarme
(B) costruisce le centrali nucleari
(C) propone un referendum
(D) intossica l'ambiente

72. Secondo l'articolo, gli incendi distruggono

(A) le isole
(B) le spiagge
(C) i boschi
(D) i villaggi

GO ON TO THE NEXT PAGE

Questions 73-74

BASILICA DI SAN MARCO - VENEZIA

in occasione della

VISITA ALLA Pala d'Oro

INTERO DIURNO
ha versato l'offerta di **Lire 3.000**

BIGLIETTI DI CONTROLLO (DA CONSERVARE)

Serie **S** Nº 41828

Offerta per il culto e per il decoro della Basilica. GRAZIE

73. Questo biglietto serve per

(A) pregare nella Basilica
(B) vedere la Pala d'Oro
(C) controllare le offerte
(D) visitare Venezia

74. I soldi pagati per questo biglietto sono usati per

(A) acquistare libri sulla Basilica
(B) conservare i gioielli
(C) decorare la Basilica
(D) ringraziare i turisti

GO ON TO THE NEXT PAGE

Questions 75-78

Dapprincipio non ho fatto caso al rumore. Veniva dal pianerottolo ed era come un lievissimo rosicchiare di topo, mescolato ai tanti cigolii, ronzii, tonfi condominiali, al basso continuo del traffico cinque piani più sotto.

Uno di quei suoni piccoli, insinuanti, mi si è infilato nelle orecchie senza che me ne accorgessi. Quel suono era troppo leggero; per la precisione era furtivo.

Ho messo l'occhio allo spioncino e ho visto il mio illustre ex marito che trafficava attorno alla porta di casa. Ho spalancato; mi è quasi caduto tra le braccia. Teneva in mano un minuscolo cacciavite.

"Riccardo, che fai?" Speravo che gli venisse la faccia del ladro sorpreso a rubare. Niente.

"Oh, ciao," ha detto. "Prendevo la targa."

Aveva già finito di staccare la placca circlee con il nome: Riccardo Prini. Sono rimasta a guardarlo, senza fiatare.

75. Dove si trova la narratrice?

(A) Allo zoo
(B) Al cinema
(C) In strada
(D) In casa

76. Quando si rende conto del rumore?

(A) Quando arriva il marito
(B) A poco a poco
(C) Verso le cinque
(D) Prima di andare a dormire

77. Che stava facendo l'ex marito?

(A) Faceva riparazioni in casa.
(B) Regolava il traffico.
(C) Lucidava la porta.
(D) Toglieva la targa.

78. Come reagisce la narratrice alla situazione?

(A) Tace per la sorpresa.
(B) Chiama immediatamente la polizia.
(C) Finisce il lavoro.
(D) Stacca la placca.

GO ON TO THE NEXT PAGE

Questions 79-81

Tè Star all'Arancia, freddo.
Il segreto della sua bontà è custodito nella sua bustina.
*Per vincere la sete, provate freddo Tè Star all'Arancia. Protetto dalle esclusive **Bustine Salvaroma**, il Tè Star mantiene intatta tutta la sua qualità. Preparatelo utilizzando 3 filtri per ogni litro, zuccheratelo a piacere e, se preferite, per esaltarne il profumo, aggiungete un po' di limone, così potrete assaporare tutta la sua bontà.*
STAR
STAR TEA
tè alla Arancia

79. Secondo la pubblicità, è meglio bere il tè Star

    (A) freddo
    (B) tiepido
    (C) a temperatura ambiente
    (D) con le arancie

80. La parola "Salvaroma" allude a

    (A) una salvaguardia
    (B) un elogio a Roma
    (C) un'esortazione a salvare Roma
    (D) una garanzia di fragranza

81. Secondo la pubblicità, per un maggiore aroma è possibile aggiungere

    (A) ghiaccio
    (B) limone
    (C) latte
    (D) zucchero

GO ON TO THE NEXT PAGE

Question 82

SCUOLA DI LINGUA E CULTURA ITALIANA PER STRANIERI - SIENA

£ 8,000

BUONO MENSA

Primo
Secondo
Contorno
Frutta
Pane

N° 921

AMERICANI. -

CORSO

82. Per quali delle seguenti attività è valido questo biglietto?

(A) Un corso alla scuola per stranieri a Siena
(B) Una gita sul motoscafo "Mensa"
(C) Un viaggio in treno a Siena
(D) Un pasto completo

STOP

IF YOU FINISH BEFORE TIME IS CALLED, YOU MAY CHECK YOUR WORK ON THIS TEST ONLY. DO NOT TURN TO ANY OTHER TEST IN THIS BOOK.

How to Score the SAT Subject Test in Italian

When you take an actual SAT Subject Test in Italian, your answer sheet will be "read" by a scanning machine that will record your responses to each question. Then a computer will compare your answers with the correct answers and produce your raw score. You get one point for each correct answer. For each wrong answer, you lose one-third of a point. Questions you omit (and any for which you mark more than one answer) are not counted. This raw score is converted to a scaled score that is reported to you and to the colleges you specify.

Worksheet 1. Finding Your Raw Test Score

STEP 1: Table A lists the correct answers for all the questions on the Subject Test in Italian that is reproduced in this book. It also serves as a worksheet for you to calculate your raw score.

- Compare your answers with those given in the table.
- Put a check in the column marked "Right" if your answer is correct.
- Put a check in the column marked "Wrong" if your answer is incorrect.
- Leave both columns blank if you omitted the question.

STEP 2: Count the number of right answers.

Enter the total here: ____________________

STEP 3: Count the number of wrong answers.

Enter the total here: ____________________

STEP 4: Multiply the number of wrong answers by .333.

Enter the product here: ________________

STEP 5: Subtract the result obtained in Step 4 from the total you obtained in Step 2.

Enter the result here: __________________

STEP 6: Round the number obtained in Step 5 to the nearest whole number.

Enter the result here: __________________

The number you obtained in Step 6 is your raw score.

Table A

Answers to the Subject Test in Italian, Form 3VAC, and Percentage of Students Answering Each Question Correctly									
Question Number	Correct Answer	Right	Wrong	Percentage of Students Answering the Question Correctly*	Question Number	Correct Answer	Right	Wrong	Percentage of Students Answering the Question Correctly*
1	C			94	33	A			84
2	B			94	34	A			84
3	B			84	35	B			76
4	B			93	36	B			67
5	D			68	37	C			74
6	C			67	38	B			73
7	A			76	39	D			64
8	A			87	40	A			34
9	C			22	41	A			78
10	B			69	42	C			84
11	C			23	43	A			51
12	D			92	44	D			49
13	B			78	45	C			80
14	D			30	46	A			76
15	B			48	47	C			76
16	B			62	48	B			92
17	B			66	49	C			85
18	A			82	50	A			45
19	A			47	51	B			86
20	D			75	52	A			76
21	B			83	53	A			76
22	A			61	54	D			63
23	B			69	55	A			49
24	C			71	56	C			54
25	B			92	57	A			50
26	B			64	58	D			54
27	C			58	59	B			74
28	B			78	60	D			66
29	D			71	61	A			31
30	C			74	62	C			57
31	C			60	63	A			40
32	A			60	64	D			51

Table A continued on next page

Table A continued from previous page

Question Number	Correct Answer	Right	Wrong	Percentage of Students Answering the Question Correctly*	Question Number	Correct Answer	Right	Wrong	Percentage of Students Answering the Question Correctly*
65	B			70	74	C			75
66	C			74	75	D			47
67	D			63	76	B			25
68	C			80	77	D			33
69	B			60	78	A			30
70	D			17	79	A			90
71	D			50	80	D			60
72	C			49	81	B			90
73	B			76	82	D			35

* These percentages are based on an analysis of the answer sheets of a representative sample of 255 students who took the original form of this test in December 1999, and whose mean score was 594. They may be used as an indication of the relative difficulty of a particular question. Each percentage may also be used to predict the likelihood that a typical SAT Subject Test in Italian candidate will answer that question correctly on this edition of the test.

Finding Your Scaled Score

When you take SAT Subject Tests, the scores sent to the colleges you specify are reported on the College Board scale, which ranges from 200–800. You can convert your practice test score to a scaled score by using Table B. To find your scaled score, locate your raw score in the left-hand column of Table B; the corresponding score in the right-hand column is your scaled score. For example, a raw score of 55 on this particular edition of the Subject Test in Italian corresponds to a scaled score of 660.

Raw scores are converted to scaled scores to ensure that a score earned on any one edition of a particular Subject Test is comparable to the same scaled score earned on any other edition of the same Subject Test. Because some editions of the tests may be slightly easier or more difficult than others, College Board scaled scores are adjusted so that they indicate the same level of performance regardless of the edition of the test taken and the ability of the group that takes it. Thus, for example, a score of 400 on one edition of a test taken at a particular administration indicates the same level of achievement as a score of 400 on a different edition of the test taken at a different administration.

When you take the SAT Subject Tests during a national administration, your scores are likely to differ somewhat from the scores you obtain on the tests in this book. People perform at different levels at different times for reasons unrelated to the tests themselves. The precision of any test is also limited because it represents only a sample of all the possible questions that could be asked.

Table B

Scaled Score Conversion Table
Subject Test in Italian (Form 3VAC)

Raw Score	Scaled Score	Raw Score	Scaled Score	Raw Score	Scaled Score
82	800	45	600	8	350
81	800	44	600	7	350
80	800	43	590	6	340
79	800	42	580	5	330
78	800	41	580	4	330
77	790	40	570	3	320
76	780	39	560	2	310
75	770	38	560	1	310
74	760	37	550	0	300
73	760	36	540	-1	290
72	750	35	540	-2	290
71	740	34	530	-3	280
70	740	33	520	-4	270
69	730	32	520	-5	270
68	720	31	510	-6	260
67	720	30	500	-7	250
66	710	29	490	-8	250
65	710	28	490	-9	240
64	700	27	480	-10	230
63	690	26	470	-11	230
62	690	25	460	-12	220
61	680	24	460	-13	220
60	680	23	450	-14	210
59	670	22	440	-15	210
58	670	21	440	-16	200
57	660	20	430	-17	200
56	660	19	430	-18	200
55	660	18	420	-19	200
54	650	17	410	-20	200
53	640	16	410	-21	200
52	640	15	400	-22	200
51	630	14	390	-23	200
50	630	13	390	-24	200
49	620	12	380	-25	200
48	620	11	370	-26	200
47	610	10	370	-27	200
46	610	9	360		

How Did You Do on the Subject Test in Italian?

After you score your test and analyze your performance, think about the following questions:

Did you run out of time before reaching the end of the test?

If so, you may need to pace yourself better. For example, maybe you spent too much time on one or two hard questions. A better approach might be to skip the ones you can't answer right away and try answering all the questions that remain on the test. Then if there's time, go back to the questions you skipped.

Did you take a long time reading the directions?

You will save time when you take the test by learning the directions to the Subject Test in Italian ahead of time. Each minute you spend reading directions during the test is a minute that you could use to answer questions.

How did you handle questions you were unsure of?

If you were able to eliminate one or more of the answer choices as wrong and guess from the remaining ones, your approach probably worked to your advantage. On the other hand, making haphazard guesses or omitting questions without trying to eliminate choices could cost you valuable points.

How difficult were the questions for you compared with other students who took the test?

Table A shows you how difficult the multiple-choice questions were for the group of students who took this test during its national administration. The right-hand column gives the percentage of students that answered each question correctly.

A question answered correctly by almost everyone in the group is obviously an easier question. For example, 94 percent of the students answered question 2 correctly. But only 17 percent answered question 70 correctly.

Keep in mind that these percentages are based on just one group of students. They would probably be different with another group of students taking the test.

If you missed several easier questions, go back and try to find out why: Did the questions cover material you haven't yet reviewed? Did you misunderstand the directions?

Chapter 12
Japanese with Listening

Purpose

The SAT Subject Test in Japanese with Listening measures your ability to communicate in Japanese in a culturally appropriate way.

Format

This is a one-hour test with about 20 minutes of listening and 40 minutes of usage and reading. There are 80 to 85 multiple-choice listening, reading, and usage questions written with high school curricula in mind. Questions represent situations you might readily encounter and reflect realistic and commonplace communication. Questions range in difficulty from elementary through advanced, although most are in the intermediate level.

Content

The test has a variety of questions requiring a wide-ranging knowledge of the Japanese language.

Listening comprehension is based on short, spoken dialogues and narratives primarily about everyday topics. A brief explanation about each selection and the question(s) are given in English. Explanations are also printed in your test book.

Usage questions require you to complete Japanese sentences in a way that is appropriate in terms of structure (grammar), vocabulary, and context. Usage questions are printed in three different ways of representing Japanese. In the center column, the Japanese is presented in standard Japanese script and all *kanji* are supplied with *furigana*. In the other two columns, the Japanese is written in the two most common types of romanization (*rōmaji*). To the left, a modified Hepburn system is used. In that system, the Japanese word for "bicycle" is written as *jitensha*. In the right-hand column, a modified *kunrei-shiki* is used. In that system, the same Japanese word for "bicycle" is written as *ziten̄sya*. You should choose the writing system you are familiar with and read only from that column on the test.

Reading comprehension questions are in English and test your understanding of such points as main and supporting ideas. The selections in this section are taken from materials you might encounter in everyday situations, such as notes, menus, newspaper articles, advertisements, and letters. The text is written in *katakana*, *hiragana*, and *kanji* without *furigana*.

Japanese with Listening	
Skills Measured	Approximate Percentage of Test
Listening Comprehension	35
Usage	30
Reading Comprehension	35

How to Prepare

The best preparation is gradual development of competence in Japanese over a period of years. The test is appropriate for students who have studied Japanese as a second or foreign language for two, three, or four years in high school or the equivalent. You are more likely to perform successfully if you have completed at least two full years of Japanese language study. A practice audio CD is included with this book. A practice CD with different sample questions can be obtained, along with a copy of the *SAT Subject Tests Preparation Booklet*, from your school counselor, or you can access the listening files at www.collegeboard.com. You should also take the practice test included with this book. Familiarize yourself with the test directions in advance. The directions in this book are identical to those that appear on the test.

CD Players

Using CD Players for Language Tests with Listening

Take an acceptable CD player to the test center. Your CD player must be in good working order, so insert fresh batteries on the day before the test. You may bring additional batteries and a backup player to the test center.

Test center staff won't have batteries, CD players, or earphones for your use, so your CD player must be:

- equipped with earphones
- portable (hand-held)
- battery operated
- for your use only. CD players cannot be shared with other test-takers.

Note

If the volume on your CD player disturbs other test-takers, the test center supervisor may ask you to move to another seat.

What to do if your CD player malfunctions:

- Raise your hand and tell the test supervisor.
- Switch to backup equipment if you have it and continue the test. If you don't have backup equipment, your score on the Japanese with Listening Test will be canceled. But scores on other Subject Tests you take that day will still be counted.

What if you receive a defective CD on test day? Raise your hand and ask the supervisor for a replacement.

Note

The Subject Test in Japanese with Listening is offered once a year only at designated tests centers. To take the test you MUST bring an acceptable CD player with earphones to the test center.

Scores

The total score is reported on the 200-to-800 scale. Listening, usage, and reading subscores are reported on the 20-to-80 scale.

Sample Questions

Your answer sheet has five answer positions marked A, B, C, D, and E, while the questions throughout this test contain only four choices. Be sure NOT to make any marks in column E.

Sample Listening Question

The text in brackets [ ] is *only* recorded; it is not printed in your test booklet. Please note that the CD does not start here. Begin using the CD when you start the actual practice test on page 573.

Directions: In this section of the test you will hear short dialogues and monologues. You will hear them <u>only once</u>, and they are not printed in your test booklet. At the end of each selection, you will be asked questions about what was said. Now listen to the following example.

(Narrator) [Listen to the following conversation in an office.

(Man) 明日(あした)家(うち)に電話してくださいませんか。

(Woman) ええ、いいですよ。　電話番号は？

(Man) あ、書きましょう。

(Narrator) Question 1. What does the man ask the woman to do?]

(16 seconds)

1. (A) Tell him her phone number.
   (B) Call him at home.
   (C) Check with him tomorrow at work.
   (D) Write down her phone number.

Choice (B) is the correct answer to question 1. This question tests students' knowledge of request forms. Choice (B) is the correct answer because this indicates the man's request. Choices (A), (C), and (D) are incorrect because they are not stated by the man.

Sample Usage Question

Directions: This section consists of a number of incomplete statements, each of which has four suggested completions. In some instances, choice (A) may consist of dashes that indicate that no insertion is required to form a correct sentence. Select the choice that best completes the sentence structurally and logically and fill in the corresponding circle on the answer sheet.

This section of the test is presented in three columns that provide identical information. Look at the example below and choose the one column of writing with which you are most familiar in order to answer this question. **DO NOT WASTE TIME BY SWITCHING FROM COLUMN TO COLUMN IN THIS SECTION.**

2. Sore wa totemo kirei ----- hana desu ne.

(A) -----

(B) no

(C) ni

(D) na

2. それはとてもきれい----- 花(はな)ですねえ。

(A) -----

(B) の

(C) に

(D) な

2. Sore wa totemo kiree ----- hana desu nee.

(A) -----

(B) no

(C) ni

(D) na

Choice (D) is the correct answer to question 2. This question tests the proper usage of *kirei*. Choice (D) is the correct answer because *na* is always used to connect *kirei* with the noun that it modifies (in this case *hana*). Choices (A), (B), and (C) are incorrect because they do not follow this rule.

Sample Reading Question

Directions: Read the following texts carefully for comprehension. Each text is followed by one or more questions or incomplete statements based on its content. Select the answer or completion that is best according to the text and fill in the corresponding circle on the answer sheet.

This is a note to Akio from his mother.

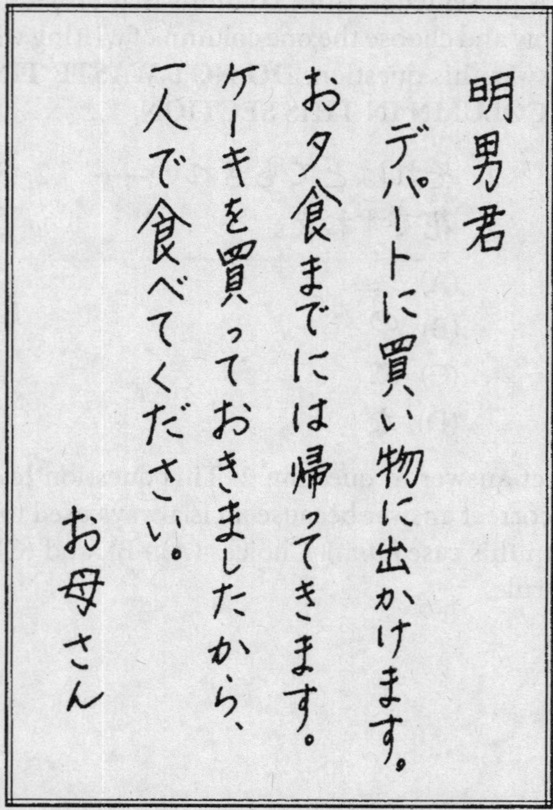
明男君
デパートに買い物に出かけます。
お夕食までには帰ってきます。
ケーキを買っておきましたから、
一人で食べてください。
お母さん

3. What does Akio's mother tell him to do?
   (A) Come home by dinner time
   (B) Eat the cake she bought
   (C) Buy some cake
   (D) Have dinner by himself

Choice (B) is the correct answer to question 3. To answer this question, students must know the content of the request, including the identity of the object about which the request is made. This is a request to eat the cake the writer bought. Choice (B) is the correct answer because it explicitly reflects the content of the written request. Choices (A), (C), and (D) are all incorrect because the note does not request Akio to come home by dinner time, buy cake, or have dinner by himself.

Japanese with Listening Test

Practice Helps

The test that follows is an actual, recently administered SAT Subject Test in Japanese with Listening. To get an idea of what it's like to take this test, practice under conditions that are much like those of an actual test administration.

- Set aside an hour when you can take the test uninterrupted. Make sure you complete the test in one sitting.
- Sit at a desk or table with no other books or papers. Dictionaries, other books, or notes are not allowed in the test room.
- Tear out an answer sheet from the back of this book and fill it in just as you would on the day of the test. One answer sheet can be used for up to three Subject Tests.
- Read the instructions that precede the practice test. During the actual administration, you will be asked to read them before answering test questions.
- Time yourself by placing a clock or kitchen timer in front of you.
- After you finish the practice test, read the sections "How to Score the SAT Subject Test in Japanese with Listening" and "How Did You Do on the Subject Test in Japanese with Listening?"
- The appearance of the answer sheet in this book may differ from the answer sheet you see on test day.

JAPANESE TEST WITH LISTENING

The top portion of the section of the answer sheet that you will use in taking the Japanese Test with Listening must be filled in exactly as shown in the illustration below. Note carefully that you have to do all of the following on your answer sheet.

1. Print JAPANESE WITH LISTENING on the line under the words "Subject Test (print)."

2. In the shaded box labeled "Test Code" fill in four circles:

   —Fill in circle 2 in the row labeled V.
   —Fill in circle 4 in the row labeled W.
   —Fill in circle 1 in the row labeled X.
   —Fill in circle C in the row labeled Y.

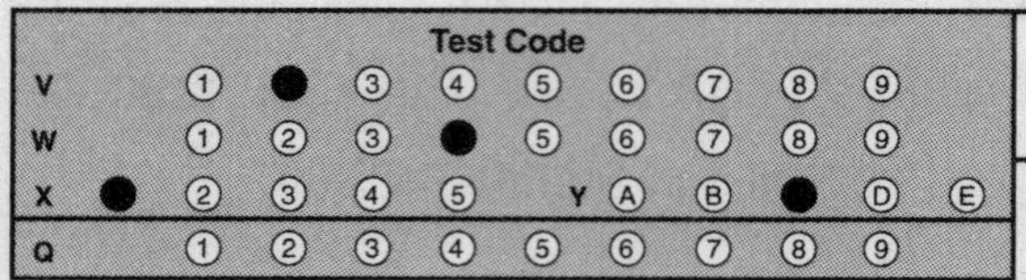

Please answer the questions below by filling in the specific circles in row Q. Please respond to only <u>one</u> question from I through IV. Then proceed to questions V **OR** VI. <u>The information you provide is for statistical purposes only and will not affect your score on the test.</u> Fill in only the circles that apply.

I If your knowledge of Japanese comes <u>primarily</u> from extensive residence in Japan after age ten, from courses taken in college, or from living in a home where Japanese is the principal language spoken, fill in <u>circle 9</u> and then answer questions V **OR** VI.

II If your knowledge of Japanese comes <u>primarily</u> from courses taken in grades nine through twelve, fill in the circle that represents the total number of years you have studied Japanese.

- Less than 2 years —Fill in circle 1.
- 2 to 3 years —Fill in circle 2.
- 4 years —Fill in circle 3.

III If you have studied Japanese in a *nihongo gakkō* (supplementary program) <u>and</u> for less than two years beyond the eighth grade,
—Fill in circle 4.

IV If you have studied Japanese in a *nihongo gakkō* (supplementary program) <u>and</u> for two or more years beyond the eighth grade,
—Fill in circle 5.

V If you use the following romanization: Ōkii jisho o tsukaimashita. Fill in circle 6.
If you use the following romanization: Ookii zisyo o tukaimasita. Fill in circle 7.

VI If you feel comfortable using <u>ONLY</u> Japanese script in a test-taking situation, Fill in circle 8.

When the supervisor gives the signal, turn the page and begin the Japanese Test with Listening. There are 100 numbered circles on the answer sheet and 80 questions in the Japanese Test with Listening. Therefore, use only circles 1 to 80 for recording your answers.

JAPANESE TEST WITH LISTENING

PLEASE NOTE THAT YOUR ANSWER SHEET HAS FIVE ANSWER POSITIONS MARKED A, B, C, D, AND E, WHILE THE QUESTIONS THROUGHOUT THIS TEST CONTAIN ONLY FOUR CHOICES. BE SURE NOT TO MAKE ANY MARKS IN COLUMN E.

Directions: In this section of the test you will hear short dialogues and monologues. You will hear them only once, and they are not printed in your test booklet. At the end of each selection, you will be asked questions about what was said. Now listen to the following example, but do not mark the answer on your answer sheet.

You will hear:

Listen to this short conversation between two acquaintances.

How did the woman travel today?

(A) By bus.
(B) By car.
(C) By train.
(D) On foot.

The best answer to the question is (A), "By bus." Therefore, you would select choice (A) and fill in the corresponding circle on the answer sheet. Now listen to the first selection.

Listen to a conversation between two friends.

1. How does the man describe his weekend?

   (A) Tiring.
   (B) Restful.
   (C) Boring.
   (D) Fun.

Listen to a conversation during a flight to the United States.

2. What is the purpose of the man's trip?

   (A) Sightseeing.
   (B) Study.
   (C) Business.
   (D) Visiting friends.

3. How long does the man plan to stay in the United States?

   (A) One month.
   (B) Two months.
   (C) Three months.
   (D) Four months.

Listen to Kenta's mother talking to him.

4. What did Kenta do to upset his mother?

   (A) He forgot to do his homework.
   (B) He kept bothering Aki.
   (C) He failed to clean his room.
   (D) He came home late.

5. Why is Kenta's mother worried?

   (A) Because Kenta's teacher called.
   (B) Because Kenta's grandmother is coming.
   (C) Because Aki complained.
   (D) Because Aki is waiting.

3ZLC

GO ON TO THE NEXT PAGE

Listen to André introduce himself.

6. André is a citizen of what country?

(A) France.
(B) United States.
(C) Russia.
(D) Japan.

7. What does André say about Tokyo?

(A) He was born there.
(B) His parents live there.
(C) He studied Japanese there.
(D) He is visiting there for the first time.

Listen to this conversation in a classroom.

8. How is the window best described?

(A) It is tinted.
(B) It is closed.
(C) It is broken.
(D) It is covered.

9. What is the woman worried about?

(A) Noise.
(B) Heat.
(C) Drafts.
(D) Sunlight.

Two friends are talking on the street.

10. What type of place is under discussion?

(A) A restaurant.
(B) A ticket counter.
(C) A hotel lobby.
(D) A convenience store.

11. On what basis do the two friends make their decision?

(A) Price.
(B) Cleanliness.
(C) Quality of service.
(D) Number of customers.

Listen to the following exchange between a couple.

12. When was the baby born to the Yamashitas?

(A) On the second of last month.
(B) On the twentieth of last month.
(C) On the second of this month.
(D) On the twentieth of this month.

13. What does the man say about the baby?

(A) That he has already heard about the baby.
(B) That the baby's name sounds like a girl's.
(C) That the Yamashitas wanted a girl this time.
(D) That he wants to see the baby.

This is an announcement in a department store.

14. Why is the customer being paged?

(A) They located her lost child.
(B) She had an emergency telephone call.
(C) She left something behind in the store.
(D) The person she was to meet is looking for her.

Listen to this short conversation about the weather.

15. What was yesterday's weather probably like?

(A) Rainy.
(B) Cloudy.
(C) Clear.
(D) Snowy.

16. What will tomorrow's weather probably be like?

(A) Rainy.
(B) Cloudy.
(C) Clear.
(D) Snowy.

GO ON TO THE NEXT PAGE

Listen to the following conversation in a post office.

17. What is the woman trying to send?

(A) A postcard.
(B) A certified letter.
(C) A money order.
(D) A small package.

18. How long will the delivery take?

(A) One day.
(B) A few days.
(C) One week.
(D) Two weeks.

Listen to a man shouting.

19. What is the man shouting not to do?

(A) Stand in the doorway.
(B) Close the door.
(C) Knock on the door.
(D) Go in through the door.

This is a conversation between Kayoko and Satoshi at a party.

20. Why is Kayoko impressed?

(A) All the pizza was eaten.
(B) The pizza is easy to make.
(C) Satoshi taught cooking.
(D) Satoshi made pizza.

21. What is planned for Saturday?

(A) Satoshi will visit Kayoko.
(B) Kayoko will visit Satoshi.
(C) Satoshi and Kayoko will have pizza at Kayoko's house.
(D) Satoshi and Kayoko will go out for pizza.

Listen to a conversation at a hospital.

22. Who is Yuko's visitor?

(A) Her classmate.
(B) Her colleague.
(C) Her teacher.
(D) Her father.

23. Where is Yuko's hospital room located?

(A) By a nurses' station.
(B) On the eighth floor.
(C) Near a gift shop.
(D) Across from the elevator.

Listen to the following call to a radio station.

24. What does the caller want?

(A) To voice his opinion.
(B) To give away a puppy.
(C) To order an item.
(D) To get advice.

25. What does the woman in the studio learn about the caller?

(A) He is moving to another city.
(B) He does not like his college.
(C) He cannot sleep well.
(D) He is planning a party.

26. What does the caller say about the dog he mentions?

(A) It is annoying.
(B) It is cute.
(C) It is housebroken.
(D) It is too big.

GO ON TO THE NEXT PAGE

Listen to the following exchange between a customer and a bookstore clerk.

27. What does the customer learn about the book?

(A) It is not yet available in bookstores.
(B) It is coming in that afternoon.
(C) It is sold out.
(D) It is out of print.

28. What does the customer decide to do?

(A) Go to another store.
(B) Place a special order.
(C) Call the publisher.
(D) Come back in a few days.

Listen to a conversation at the entrance to a house.

29. Why has Mr. Tanaka stopped at the woman's house?

(A) To lend her something.
(B) To get out of the rain.
(C) To borrow something.
(D) To return something.

Listen to Mr. Yoshida and his daughter talking.

30. What does Mr. Yoshida urge his daughter to do?

(A) Leave soon.
(B) Come home early.
(C) Eat her breakfast.
(D) Call home.

END OF SECTION I.
DO NOT GO ON TO SECTION II UNTIL YOU ARE TOLD TO DO SO.

TIME FOR SECTIONS II AND III - 40 minutes

SECTION II

Usage

WHEN YOU BEGIN SECTION II, BE SURE THAT YOU MARK YOUR ANSWER TO THE FIRST USAGE QUESTION BY FILLING IN ONE OF THE CIRCLES NEXT TO NUMBER 31 ON THE ANSWER SHEET.

Directions: This section consists of a number of incomplete statements, each of which has four suggested completions. In some instances, choice (A) may consist of dashes that indicate that no insertion is required to form a correct sentence. Select the choice that best completes the sentence structurally and logically and fill in the corresponding circle on the answer sheet.

THIS SECTION OF THE TEST IS PRESENTED IN THREE COLUMNS THAT PROVIDE IDENTICAL INFORMATION. LOOK AT THE EXAMPLE BELOW AND CHOOSE THE ONE COLUMN OF WRITING WITH WHICH YOU ARE MOST FAMILIAR IN ORDER TO ANSWER THE QUESTION. DO NOT WASTE TIME BY SWITCHING FROM COLUMN TO COLUMN IN THIS SECTION.

Example:

Tōkyō wa -----	東京(とうきょう)は -----	Tookyoo wa -----
arimasu.	あります。	arimasu.
(A) Doitsu de	(A) ドイツで	(A) Doitu de
(B) Mekishiko o	(B) メキシコを	(B) Mekisiko o
(C) Furansu e	(C) フランスへ	(C) Hurañsu e
(D) Nihon ni	(D) 日本(にほん)に	(D) Nihoñ ni

The best completion is choice (D). Therefore, you would select choice (D) and fill in the corresponding circle on the answer sheet.

GO ON TO THE NEXT PAGE

31. Gakkō e -----.

(A) benkyō-shimashita

(B) ikimashita

(C) mimashita

(D) yasumimashita

31. 学校(がっこう)へ ----- 。

(A) 勉強(べんきょう)しました

(B) 行(い)きました

(C) 見(み)ました

(D) 休(やす)みました

31. Gakkoo e -----.

(A) be n̄kyoo-simasita

(B) ikimasita

(C) mimasita

(D) yasumimasita

32. Kirei ----- heya desu ne.

(A) -----

(B) ni

(C) da

(D) na

32. きれい ----- 部屋(へや)ですね。

(A) -----

(B) に

(C) だ

(D) な

32. Kiree ----- heya desu ne.

(A) -----

(B) ni

(C) da

(D) na

33. Kyō wa asa kara ban ----- terebi o mite imashita.

(A) ni mo

(B) ni wa

(C) made

(D) e mo

33. 今日(きょう)は朝(あさ)から晩(ばん) ----- テレビを見(み)ていました。

(A) にも

(B) には

(C) まで

(D) へも

33. Kyoo wa asa kara ban̄ ----- terebi o mite imasita.

(A) ni mo

(B) ni wa

(C) made

(D) e mo

GO ON TO THE NEXT PAGE

34. Yūmei ----- desu ne.

    (A) -----

    (B) na

    (C) da

    (D) ni

34. 有名(ゆうめい) ----- ですね。

    (A) -----

    (B) な

    (C) だ

    (D) に

34. Yuumee ----- desu ne.

    (A) -----

    (B) na

    (C) da

    (D) ni

35. Hayaku genki ----- natte kudasai.

    (A) -----

    (B) na

    (C) ni

    (D) no

35. 早(はや)く元気(げんき) ----- なってください。

    (A) -----

    (B) な

    (C) に

    (D) の

35. Hayaku geñki ----- natte kudasai.

    (A) -----

    (B) na

    (C) ni

    (D) no

36. Nōto o -----.

    (A) mimashita

    (B) arimashita

    (C) dekimashita

    (D) wakarimashita

36. ノートを ----- 。

    (A) 見(み)ました

    (B) ありました

    (C) できました

    (D) わかりました

36. Nooto o -----.

    (A) mimasita

    (B) arimasita

    (C) dekimasita

    (D) wakarimasita

GO ON TO THE NEXT PAGE

37. Kodomo ga hitori ----- imasu.

(A) -----

(B) ga

(C) mo

(D) ni

37. 子供が一人----- います。

(A) -----

(B) が

(C) も

(D) に

37. Kodomo ga hitori ----- imasu.

(A) -----

(B) ga

(C) mo

(D) ni

38. Ashita wa ame ga furu -----.

(A) deshō

(B) desu

(C) deshita

(D) omoimasu

38. あしたは雨が降る ----- 。

(A) でしょう

(B) です

(C) でした

(D) 思います

38. Asita wa ame ga huru -----.

(A) desyoo

(B) desu

(C) desita

(D) omoimasu

39. Taihen ----- ga kakarimasu ne.

(A) jikan

(B) go-jikan

(C) en

(D) go man-en

39. 大変 ----- がかかりますね。

(A) 時間

(B) 五時間

(C) 円

(D) 五万円

39. Taihen̄ ----- ga kakarimasu ne.

(A) zikan̄

(B) go-zikan̄

(C) en̄

(D) go man̄-en̄

GO ON TO THE NEXT PAGE

40. Atama ga itai ----- kaerimasu.

(A) de

(B) no de

(C) na no de

(D) da kara

40. 頭(あたま)が痛(いた)い ----- 帰(かえ)ります。

(A) で

(B) ので

(C) なので

(D) だから

40. Atama ga itai ----- kaerimasu.

(A) de

(B) no de

(C) na no de

(D) da kara

41. Ichi-ban ----- wa dore?

(A) omoshiroi

(B) omoshiroku

(C) omoshirokute

(D) omoshiroi no

41. 一番(いちばん) ----- はどれ？

(A) おもしろい

(B) おもしろく

(C) おもしろくて

(D) おもしろいの

41. Iti-bañ ----- wa dore?

(A) omosiroi

(B) omosiroku

(C) omosirokute

(D) omosiroi no

42. Motto ----- dekimasen ka.

(A) sukunaku

(B) sukunai

(C) sukoshi

(D) shōshō

42. もっと -----できませんか。

(A) 少(すく)なく

(B) 少(すく)ない

(C) 少(すこ)し

(D) 少々(しょうしょう)

42. Motto ----- dekimaseñ ka.

(A) sukunaku

(B) sukunai

(C) sukosi

(D) syoosyoo

GO ON TO THE NEXT PAGE

43. Chichi wa haha ----- jōzu desu.

(A) kara

(B) hodo

(C) made

(D) yori

43. 父(ちち)は母(はは) ----- 上手(じょうず)です。

(A) から

(B) ほど

(C) まで

(D) より

43. Titi wa haha ----- zyoozu desu.

(A) kara

(B) hodo

(C) made

(D) yori

44. Ato ----- futatsu kudasai.

(A) shika

(B) dake

(C) yori

(D) mō

44. あと ----- 二(ふた)つください。

(A) しか

(B) だけ

(C) より

(D) もう

44. Ato ----- hutatu kudasai.

(A) sika

(B) dake

(C) yori

(D) moo

45. Osoku ----- dōmo sumimasen.

(A) naru

(B) natte

(C) natta

(D) natta kara

45. 遅(おそ)く ----- どうも すみません。

(A) なる

(B) なって

(C) なった

(D) なったから

45. Osoku ----- doomo sumimasen̄.

(A) naru

(B) natte

(C) natta

(D) natta kara

GO ON TO THE NEXT PAGE

46. ----- ni kite kudasai.

    (A) Ashita

    (B) Kayōbi

    (C) Mata

    (D) Kesa

46. ----- に来(き)てください。

    (A) 明日(あした)

    (B) 火曜日(かようび)

    (C) また

    (D) 今朝(けさ)

46. ----- ni kite kudasai.

    (A) Asita

    (B) Kayoobi

    (C) Mata

    (D) Kesa

47. ----- kedo wakarimasen.

    (A) Mimashō

    (B) Mimashita

    (C) Mite

    (D) Mitara

47. ----- けどわかりません。

    (A) 見(み)ましょう

    (B) 見(み)ました

    (C) 見(み)て

    (D) 見(み)たら

47. ----- kedo wakarimasen̄.

    (A) Mimasyoo

    (B) Mimasita

    (C) Mite

    (D) Mitara

48. Ashita iku -----
    kyō wa ie ni imasu

    (A) to

    (B) kara

    (C) demo

    (D) desu ga

48. あした行(い)く -----
    今日(きょう)は家(いえ)にいます。

    (A) と

    (B) から

    (C) でも

    (D) ですが

48. Asita iku -----
    kyoo wa ie ni imasu.

    (A) to

    (B) kara

    (C) demo

    (D) desu ga

GO ON TO THE NEXT PAGE

49. ----- ikenai.

(A) Tsukau

(B) Tsukatta

(C) Tsukawanaku

(D) Tsukatte wa

49. ----- いけない。

(A) 使(つか)う

(B) 使(つか)った

(C) 使(つか)わなく

(D) 使(つか)っては

49. ----- ikenai.

(A) Tukau

(B) Tukatta

(C) Tukawanaku

(D) Tukatte wa

50. Iya ----- omotte yamemashita.

(A) -----

(B) da to

(C) ni natte

(D) de

50. いや ----- 思(おも)って やめました。

(A) -----

(B) だと

(C) になって

(D) で

50. Iya ----- omotte yamemasita.

(A) -----

(B) da to

(C) ni natte

(D) de

51. Chotto ----- shite kudasai.

(A) yasuku

(B) benri na

(C) chiisai

(D) shizuka

51. ちょっと ----- してください。

(A) 安(やす)く

(B) 便利(べんり)な

(C) 小(ちい)さい

(D) 静(しず)か

51. Tyotto ----- site kudasai.

(A) yasuku

(B) ben̄ri na

(C) tiisai

(D) sizuka

GO ON TO THE NEXT PAGE

52. ----- ga shimashō.

(A) Watashi

(B) Anata

(C) Ano hito

(D) Imōto

52. ----- がしましょう。

(A) 私（わたし）

(B) あなた

(C) あの人（ひと）

(D) 妹（いもうと）

52. ----- ga simasyoo.

(A) Watasi

(B) Anata

(C) Ano hito

(D) Imooto

53. Gakusei ----- no?

(A) na

(B) da

(C) darō

(D) ni

53. 学生（がくせい） ----- の？

(A) な

(B) だ

(C) だろう

(D) に

53. Gakusee ----- no?

(A) na

(B) da

(C) daroo

(D) ni

END OF SECTION II.
GO ON TO SECTION III.

SECTION III

Reading

Directions: Read the following texts carefully for comprehension. Each text is followed by one or more questions or incomplete statements based on its content. Select the answer or completion that is best according to the text and fill in the corresponding circle on the answer sheet. There is no example for this section.

This is a message Lisa received.

リサさん
高木さんから電話がありました。
山下さんが二時十五分に駅に着くから、
迎えに行ってくださいとのことです。
川村

54. This message relays
    (A) an apology
    (B) a complaint
    (C) an invitation
    (D) a request

55. What is Lisa expected to do after reading the note?
    (A) Contact Takagi
    (B) Call Kawamura
    (C) Wait for Takagi
    (D) Meet Yamashita

GO ON TO THE NEXT PAGE

Yuri sent the following e-mail message to Saori.

> さおり
>
> あさってうちでバーベキューするんだけど来ない？
> こうすけもよしも来るって！
> それからわるいけど、クッキー持って来てくれる？
> 来られるかどうか今日中に教えてね。
>
> ゆり

56. What is the reader expected to bring to the barbecue?

(A) Cookies
(B) A cake
(C) A fruit salad
(D) Barbecue sauce

57. Who will host a barbecue?

(A) Saori
(B) Kosuke
(C) Yoshi
(D) Yuri

GO ON TO THE NEXT PAGE

This is part of a restaurant menu.

きょうのスペシャル

（サラダ又はスープ付き）

バーベキュー・リブ ¥1,700
（やわらかいリブを特製マリネにつけ込んでグリル）

シーフード・ミックスグリル ¥1,800
（新鮮な海の幸をバターソースでさっとグリル）

ベジタリアン・ミックスグリル ¥1,500
（ボリュームいっぱい。でも低カロリーのヘルシーチョイス）

58. The most expensive item uses

(A) a mixture of spices
(B) butter sauce
(C) imported ingredients
(D) fresh fruit

59. The least expensive dish is described as having

(A) few calories
(B) low cholesterol
(C) a small volume
(D) a special sauce

GO ON TO THE NEXT PAGE

The following is part of Mrs. Iwata's calendar for the coming week.

日	1:00 けんた 水泳大会（スイミングクラブ）
月	9:30 エアロビクス　2:00 メガネをとりにいく
火	7:00 マリ ピアノ
水	
木	マリのバースデーケーキ　4:00 パーティー（6人）
金	2:00 けんたの父母会
土	5:00 お父さん ゴルフ

60. Mrs. Iwata will pick up her eyeglasses on
    - (A) Sunday
    - (B) Monday
    - (C) Tuesday
    - (D) Saturday

61. Mrs. Iwata's activities this week include
    - (A) visiting Kenta's school
    - (B) competing in a swim meet
    - (C) playing golf with friends
    - (D) taking a piano lesson

62. Mrs. Iwata will host a birthday party for
    - (A) herself
    - (B) her husband
    - (C) her daughter
    - (D) her son

GO ON TO THE NEXT PAGE

This advertisement was placed in a newspaper.

大川駅前通りに新しくオープン！

カフェアルプス

モーニングサービスは７００円！
今週のスペシャルはフレンチトースト

忙しいあなたの朝に便利です！

63. The advertisement is for a
    (A) take-out shop
    (B) coffee shop
    (C) French bakery
    (D) natural food store

64. What does the advertisement say about the special?
    (A) It is organic.
    (B) It is tasty.
    (C) It is featured for a week.
    (D) It is available only in the afternoon.

65. What does the advertisement say about the establishment?
    (A) It is located near the station.
    (B) It provides friendly service.
    (C) It offers numerous discounts.
    (D) It will open next week.

GO ON TO THE NEXT PAGE

This is an excerpt from a newspaper column.

ボディーランゲージ

「若いカップルが手をつないで歩いている」というのはもう古いそうである。ではこのごろの若いカップルはどうしてカップルだとわかるのだろうか。町に出て見てみた。腕を組んだり、肩を組んだり、ちょっと新しいのはシャツのそでを結んでいる二人。

66. What is the topic of this passage?
(A) Body language
(B) New fashions
(C) Health issues
(D) Travel information

67. Why did the writer go into town?
(A) To do some window-shopping
(B) To make some observations
(C) To interview some couples
(D) To collect some new products

GO ON TO THE NEXT PAGE

This is a comment a math teacher wrote on Mamoru's homework paper.

二番だけもう一度考えてごらん。
それ以外はよくできたね。
次の問題に進んでよろしい。

68. How can the teacher's comment be characterized?

(A) Apologetic
(B) Humorous
(C) Ambiguous
(D) Encouraging

69. What does the teacher say about Mamoru's answer to the second problem?

(A) He should rethink it.
(B) He should rewrite it.
(C) He should compare it to the correct answer.
(D) He should share the solution with others.

GO ON TO THE NEXT PAGE

This is the beginning of a letter from Mr. Takamatsu to Ms. Sekine.

　お手紙ありがとう。先月久しぶりに会えて、とっても楽しかったです。先週からのかぜでまだ声がよく出ません。９月のリサイタルまでに直るかどうか心配です。
　送ってもらったテープ、さっそく聞いてみました。コロンビアのギター音楽は、ベネズエラのとゼンゼン違うんですね。いただいたのは軽くて明るいと思いました。

70. The last time Mr. Takamatsu saw Ms. Sekine was

(A) the previous day
(B) the previous month
(C) nine weeks before
(D) nine months before

71. What does Mr. Takamatsu plan to do soon?

(A) See Ms. Sekine.
(B) Give a recital.
(C) Send Ms. Sekine a ticket.
(D) Buy a guitar.

72. What does Mr. Takamatsu say about the cassette tape he just received?

(A) It is different from Colombian music.
(B) It is the same cassette tape he already owns.
(C) It is a collection of Venezuelan guitar music.
(D) It is light and cheerful.

GO ON TO THE NEXT PAGE

This is an e-mail message from Ms. Hayashi.

> 先日お話しした洋画友の会を九月十日にすることになりました。私も当日は出席しますので、よろしかったら、ご一緒にいかがでしょうか。若い人中心の楽しい会です。
>
> 林　由紀子

73. What does Ms. Hayashi say about the meeting?

(A) It attracts young people.
(B) Her friend organized it.
(C) There will be fun games.
(D) It is a good place to make friends.

GO ON TO THE NEXT PAGE

The following is a set of guidelines for foreign students in a homestay program in Japan.

(1) なるべく日本語でホストファミリーと話しましょう。分からない時は、辞書を調べながら話しましょう。

(2) 決められた時間には帰るようにしてください。ホストファミリーの人が心配しますから、遅くなる時は、電話をしてください。

(3) ホストファミリーの電話はなるべく使わないようにしてください。

(4) できるだけそうじや食事の手伝いをするようにしましょう。

(5) エネルギーをむだ使いしないようにしましょう。

74. What are the students encouraged to do?

(A) Return home by midnight
(B) Help with meals
(C) Ask questions about Japanese culture
(D) Do their own laundry

75. Students are asked not to

(A) let friends stay over at the house
(B) waste electricity and gas
(C) stay in their rooms all the time
(D) take food without asking

GO ON TO THE NEXT PAGE

Ms. Smith found the following note from her friend Akira Nishimura.

> スミスさん
>
> 約束の時間にビデオを取りに来たのですが、いらっしゃらないので、お借りしていきます。明日の英語のクラスの前にお返しします。
>
> 西村晃

76. Akira went to Ms. Smith's room because he wanted to

 (A) borrow something from Ms. Smith
 (B) make some plans with Ms. Smith
 (C) return something to Ms. Smith
 (D) give Ms. Smith a gift

77. What does Akira say he will do the next day?

 (A) Record a video.
 (B) Rent a video.
 (C) Show a video.
 (D) Return a video.

GO ON TO THE NEXT PAGE

This is a part of an advertisement.

スポーツの夏がやって来ました！

ショート・ヘアーはスポーツのあとのお手入れも簡単。
コンピューター・シミュレーションでいろいろなスタイルを見て、お選びいただけます。

78. What is being advertised?

(A) Sporting goods
(B) Computer classes
(C) A hair salon
(D) A driving school

GO ON TO THE NEXT PAGE

This message is printed on an envelope from a local bank.

あなたのひまわり銀行

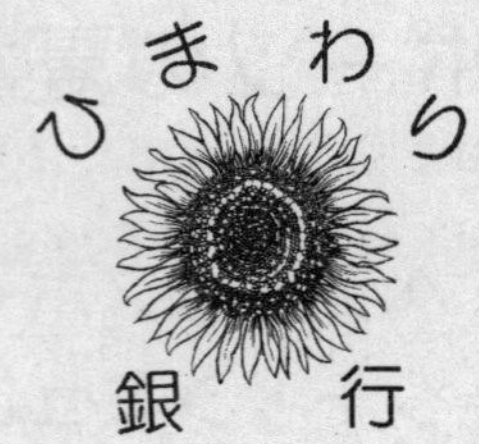

ニューイヤーギフト

1月中にひまわりの住宅ローン「フューチャー」に申し込んで、
ゲームソフトをもらおう！！

79. As an incentive to customers, the bank offers
    (A) additional ATM locations
    (B) reduced service fees
    (C) financial counseling
    (D) attractive gifts

80. The purpose of this message is for the bank to promote
    (A) computerized banking
    (B) extended business hours
    (C) mortgage loans
    (D) new investment opportunities

STOP

IF YOU FINISH BEFORE TIME IS CALLED, YOU MAY CHECK YOUR WORK ON THIS TEST ONLY. DO NOT TURN TO ANY OTHER TEST IN THIS BOOK.

How to Score the SAT Subject Test in Japanese with Listening

When you take an actual SAT Subject Test in Japanese with Listening, you receive an overall composite score as well as three subscores: one for the reading section, one for the listening section, and one for the usage section.

The reading, listening, and usage scores are reported on the College Board's 20–80 scale. However the composite score, which is the most significant of the scores reported to the colleges you specify, is in the form of the College Board's 200–800 scale.

Worksheet 1. Finding Your Raw Listening Subscore

STEP 1: Table A lists the correct answers for all the questions on the Subject Test in Japanese with Listening that is reproduced in this book. It also serves as a worksheet for you to calculate your raw Listening subscore.

- Compare your answers with those given in the table.
- Put a check in the column marked "Right" if your answer is correct.
- Put a check in the column marked "Wrong" if your answer is incorrect.
- Leave both columns blank if you omitted the question.

STEP 2: Count the number of right answers for questions 1–30.

Enter the total here: ____________________

STEP 3: Count the number of wrong answers for questions 1–30.

Enter the total here: ____________________

STEP 4: Multiply the number of wrong answers from Step 3 by .333.

Enter the product here: ________________

STEP 5: Subtract the result obtained in Step 4 from the total you obtained in Step 2.

Enter the result here: ___________________

STEP 6: Round the number obtained in Step 5 to the nearest whole number.

Enter the result here: ___________________

The number you obtained in Step 6 is your raw Listening subscore.

Worksheet 2. Finding Your Raw Reading Subscore

STEP 1: Table A lists the correct answers for all the questions on the Subject Test in Japanese with Listening that is reproduced in this book. It also serves as a worksheet for you to calculate your raw Reading subscore.

STEP 2: Count the number of right answers for questions 54-80.

Enter the total here: ____________________

STEP 3: Count the number of wrong answers for questions 54-80.

Enter the total here: ____________________

STEP 4: Multiply the number of wrong answers by .333.

Enter the product here: ________________

STEP 5: Subtract the result obtained in Step 4 from the total you obtained in Step 2.

Enter the result here: __________________

STEP 6: Round the number obtained in Step 5 to the nearest whole number.

Enter the result here: __________________

The number you obtained in Step 6 is your raw Reading subscore.

Worksheet 3. Finding Your Raw Usage Subscore

STEP 1: Table A lists the correct answers for all the questions on the Subject Test in Japanese with Listening that is reproduced in this book. It also serves as a worksheet for you to calculate your raw Usage subscore.

STEP 2: Count the number of right answers for questions 31–53.

Enter the total here: ____________________

STEP 3: Count the number of wrong answers for questions 31–53.

Enter the total here: ____________________

STEP 4: Multiply the number of wrong answers by .333.

Enter the product here: ________________

STEP 5: Subtract the result obtained in Step 4 from the total you obtained in Step 2.

Enter the result here: __________________

STEP 6: Round the number obtained in Step 5 to the nearest whole number.

Enter the result here: __________________

The number you obtained in Step 6 is your raw Usage subscore.

Worksheet 4. Finding Your Raw Composite Score

STEP 1: Enter your unrounded raw Reading subscore from Step 5 of Worksheet 2.

Enter the result here: ________________

STEP 2: Enter your unrounded raw Listening subscore from Step 5 of Worksheet 1.

Enter the result here: ________________

STEP 3: Enter your unrounded raw Usage subscore from Step 5 of Worksheet 3.

Enter the result here: ________________

STEP 4: Add the results obtained in Steps 1, 2 and 3.

Enter the sum here: ________________

STEP 5: Round the number obtained in Step 4 to the nearest whole number.

Enter the result here: ________________

The number you obtained in Step 5 is your raw composite score.

Table A

Answers to the Subject Test in Japanese with Listening, Form 3ZLC, and Percentage of Students Answering Each Question Correctly									
Question Number	Correct Answer	Right	Wrong	Percentage of Students Answering the Question Correctly*	Question Number	Correct Answer	Right	Wrong	Percentage of Students Answering the Question Correctly*
1	D			96	33	C			90
2	B			82	34	A			78
3	C			88	35	C			88
4	C			96	36	A			83
5	B			92	37	A			59
6	B			92	38	A			75
7	D			73	39	A			55
8	B			79	40	B			51
9	A			91	41	D			59
10	A			89	42	A			29
11	D			43	43	D			83
12	B			65	44	D			60
13	B			55	45	B			52
14	C			62	46	B			72
15	A			86	47	B			61
16	C			86	48	B			44
17	D			39	49	D			75
18	B			70	50	B			64
19	D			81	51	A			49
20	D			84	52	A			40
21	B			49	53	A			46
22	D			55	54	D			74
23	B			69	55	D			83
24	D			47	56	A			87
25	C			67	57	D			89
26	A			72	58	B			87
27	C			63	59	A			85
28	A			50	60	B			96
29	D			61	61	A			55
30	A			50	62	C			87
31	B			90	63	B			59
32	D			92	64	C			83

Table A continued on next page

Table A continued from previous page

Question Number	Correct Answer	Right	Wrong	Percentage of Students Answering the Question Correctly*	Question Number	Correct Answer	Right	Wrong	Percentage of Students Answering the Question Correctly*
65	A			71	73	A			41
66	A			88	74	B			55
67	B			59	75	B			75
68	D			87	76	A			67
69	A			61	77	D			64
70	B			81	78	C			48
71	B			71	79	D			84
72	D			44	80	C			69

* These percentages are based on an analysis of the answer sheets of a representative sample of 371 students who took the original form of this test in November 2003, and whose mean composite score was 566. They may be used as an indication of the relative difficulty of a particular question. Each percentage may also be used to predict the likelihood that a typical SAT Subject Test in Japanese with Listening candidate will answer that question correctly on this edition of the test.

Finding Your Scaled Score

When you take SAT Subject Tests, the scores sent to the colleges you specify are reported on the College Board scale, which ranges from 200–800. Subscores are reported on a scale which ranges from 20–80. You can convert your practice test scores to scaled scores by using Tables B, C, D and E. To find your scaled score, locate your raw score in the left-hand column of the table; the corresponding score in the right-hand column is your scaled score. For example, a raw score of 59 on this particular edition of the Subject Test in Japanese with Listening corresponds to a scaled composite score of 640.

Raw scores are converted to scaled scores to ensure that a score earned on any one edition of a particular Subject Test is comparable to the same scaled score earned on any other edition of the same Subject Test. Because some editions of the tests may be slightly easier or more difficult than others, College Board scaled scores are adjusted so that they indicate the same level of performance regardless of the edition of the test taken and the ability of the group that takes it. Thus, for example, a score of 400 on one edition of a test taken at a particular administration indicates the same level of achievement as a score of 400 on a different edition of the test taken at a different administration.

When you take the SAT Subject Tests during a national administration, your scores are likely to differ somewhat from the scores you obtain on the tests in this book. People perform at different levels at different times for reasons unrelated to the tests themselves. The precision of any test is also limited because it represents only a sample of all the possible questions that could be asked.

Your scaled composite score from Table B is ________________ .

Your scaled listening score from Table C is ________________ .

Your scaled reading score from Table D is ________________ .

Your scaled usage score from Table E is ________________ .

Table B

Scaled Score Conversion Table
Subject Test in Japanese with Listening
Composite Score (Form 3ZLC)

Raw Score	Scaled Score	Raw Score	Scaled Score	Raw Score	Scaled Score
80	800	44	520	8	290
79	800	43	510	7	290
78	800	42	510	6	280
77	790	41	500	5	270
76	780	40	490	4	270
75	770	39	490	3	260
74	770	38	480	2	250
73	760	37	480	1	250
72	750	36	470	0	240
71	740	35	460	-1	230
70	730	34	460	-2	230
69	720	33	450	-3	220
68	710	32	440	-4	220
67	710	31	440	-5	210
66	700	30	430	-6	200
65	690	29	430	-7	200
64	680	28	420	-8	200
63	670	27	410	-9	200
62	660	26	410	-10	200
61	650	25	400	-11	200
60	640	24	390	-12	200
59	640	23	390	-13	200
58	630	22	380	-14	200
57	620	21	370	-15	200
56	610	20	370	-16	200
55	600	19	360	-17	200
54	590	18	360	-18	200
53	580	17	350	-19	200
52	580	16	340	-20	200
51	570	15	340	-21	200
50	560	14	330	-22	200
49	550	13	320	-23	200
48	550	12	320	-24	200
47	540	11	310	-25	200
46	530	10	300	-26	200
45	530	9	300	-27	200

Table C

Scaled Score Conversion Table Subject Test in Japanese with Listening Listening Subscore (Form 3ZLC)					
Raw Score	Scaled Score	Raw Score	Scaled Score	Raw Score	Scaled Score
30	80	16	50	2	29
29	77	15	48	1	27
28	75	14	47	0	26
27	72	13	45	-1	25
26	70	12	44	-2	23
25	68	11	42	-3	22
24	66	10	40	-4	21
23	64	9	39	-5	20
22	62	8	37	-6	20
21	59	7	36	-7	20
20	57	6	34	-8	20
19	55	5	33	-9	20
18	54	4	32	-10	20
17	52	3	30		

Table D

Scaled Score Conversion Table Subject Test in Japanese with Listening Reading Subscore (Form 3ZLC)					
Raw Score	Scaled Score	Raw Score	Scaled Score	Raw Score	Scaled Score
27	80	15	51	3	32
26	77	14	49	2	30
25	74	13	47	1	29
24	71	12	45	0	28
23	69	11	44	-1	27
22	67	10	42	-2	26
21	64	9	40	-3	24
20	62	8	39	-4	23
19	60	7	37	-5	22
18	57	6	36	-6	21
17	55	5	34	-7	20
16	53	4	33	-8	20
				-9	20

Table E

Scaled Score Conversion Table Subject Test in Japanese with Listening Usage Subscore (Form 3ZLC)					
Raw Score	Scaled Score	Raw Score	Scaled Score	Raw Score	Scaled Score
23	80	12	54	1	33
22	78	11	52	0	32
21	75	10	50	-1	30
20	73	9	48	-2	28
19	70	8	46	-3	26
18	68	7	44	-4	24
17	65	6	43	-5	22
16	63	5	41	-6	21
15	60	4	39	-7	20
14	58	3	37	-8	20
13	56	2	35		

How Did You Do on the Subject Test in Japanese with Listening?

After you score your test and analyze your performance, think about the following questions:

Did you run out of time before reaching the end of the test?

If so, you may need to pace yourself better. For example, maybe you spent too much time on one or two hard questions. A better approach might be to skip the ones you can't answer right away and try answering all the questions that remain on the test. Then if there's time, go back to the questions you skipped.

Did you take a long time reading the directions?

You will save time when you take the test by learning the directions to the Subject Test in Japanese with Listening ahead of time. Each minute you spend reading directions during the test is a minute that you could use to answer questions.

How did you handle questions you were unsure of?

If you were able to eliminate one or more of the answer choices as wrong and guess from the remaining ones, your approach probably worked to your advantage. On the other hand, making haphazard guesses or omitting questions without trying to eliminate choices could cost you valuable points.

How difficult were the questions for you compared with other students who took the test?

Table A shows you how difficult the multiple-choice questions were for the group of students who took this test during its national administration. The right-hand column gives the percentage of students that answered each question correctly.

A question answered correctly by almost everyone in the group is obviously an easier question. For example, 96 percent of the students answered question 4 correctly. But only 29 percent answered question 42 correctly.

Keep in mind that these percentages are based on just one group of students. They would probably be different with another group of students taking the test.

If you missed several easier questions, go back and try to find out why: Did the questions cover material you haven't yet reviewed? Did you misunderstand the directions?

Chapter 13

Korean with Listening

Purpose

The Subject Test in Korean with Listening measures your understanding of Korean and your ability to engage in purposeful communication in the context of contemporary Korean culture.

Format

This is a one-hour test with about 20 minutes of listening and 40 minutes of usage and reading. There are 80 to 85 multiple-choice questions.

Content

Listening comprehension questions test your ability to understand the spoken language. They are based on short, spoken Korean dialogues and narratives primarily about everyday topics. All listening questions and possible answers are in English. The questions will be spoken on a CD. They will also be printed in the test book.

Usage questions are written entirely in *Hangŭl* and require you to complete Korean sentences or phrases so that they are structurally and logically correct. Areas covered include vocabulary, honorifics, and various aspects of structure.

Reading comprehension questions test your understanding of such points as main and supporting ideas. All the passages in this section are written in *Hangŭl* and all the questions are in English. Most questions deal with understanding literal meaning, although some inference questions may be included. The Korean selections are drawn from authentic materials, such as notes, diaries, menus, newspaper articles, advertisements, letters, and literary texts.

Korean with Listening	
Skills Measured	Approximate Percentage of Test
Listening Comprehension	35
Usage	30
Reading Comprehension	35

How to Prepare

This test is appropriate for students who have studied Korean as a second or foreign language for two to four years in high school, or the equivalent.

The best preparation is gradual development of competence in Korean over a period of years. A practice audio CD is included with this book. A practice CD with different sample questions can be obtained, along with a copy of the *SAT Subject Tests Preparation Booklet*, from your school counselor, or you can access the listening files at www.collegeboard.com. You should also take the practice test included with this book. Familiarize yourself with the directions in advance. The directions in this book are identical to those that appear on the test.

CD Players

Using CD Players for Language Tests with Listening

Take an acceptable CD player to the test center. Your CD player must be in good working order, so insert fresh batteries on the day before the test. You may bring additional batteries and a backup player to the test center.

Test center staff won't have batteries, CD players, or earphones for your use, so your CD player must be:

- equipped with earphones
- portable (hand-held)
- battery operated
- for your use only. CD players cannot be shared with other test-takers.

Note

If the volume on your CD player disturbs other test-takers, the test center supervisor may ask you to move to another seat.

What to do if your CD player malfunctions:

- Raise your hand and tell the test supervisor.

- Switch to backup equipment if you have it and continue the test. If you don't have backup equipment, your score on the Korean with Listening Test will be canceled. But scores on other Subject Tests you take that day will not be canceled.

What if you receive a defective CD on test day? Raise your hand and ask the supervisor for a replacement.

Note

The Subject Test in Korean with Listening is offered only once a year at designated test centers. Check the current year *SAT Registration Booklet* for dates. To take the test, you MUST bring an acceptable CD player with earphones to the test center.

Scores

The total score is reported on the 200-to-800 scale. Listening, usage, and reading subscores are reported on the 20-to-80 scale.

Sample Listening Questions

The text in brackets [ ] is *only* recorded; it is not printed in your test book. Please note that the CD does not start here. Begin using the CD when you start the actual practice test on page 617.

Please note that your answer sheet has five answer positions marked A, B, C, D, and E, while the questions throughout this test contain only four choices. Be sure not to make any marks in column E.

Directions: In this part of the test you will hear several spoken selections. They will not be printed in your test book. You will hear them only once. After each selection you will be asked one or more questions about what you have just heard. These questions, with four possible answers, are printed in your test book. Select the best answer to each question from among the four choices printed and fill in the corresponding circle on your answer sheet. Now listen to the first selection.

(Narrator) [Listen to this short exchange between friends. Then answer Question 1.

(Man) 이번 방학에 뭐 해요?

(Woman) 방학에요? 일하려고 해요.

(Man) 그럼 일자리는 구했어요?

(Woman) 지금 찾는 중이에요.
일자리 있으면 소개해 주세요.

(Man) 요새는 일자리 구하기가
어려운데.

(Narrator) Question 1. What is the woman doing now?] (16 seconds)

1. (A) Looking for work.
   (B) Looking for an apartment.
   (C) Writing a paper.
   (D) Preparing for summer school.

Choice (A) is the correct answer to question 1. This question requires the students' knowledge of vocabulary and expressions such as "-는 중이다," which conveys an action currently taking place.

Sample Usage Questions

Directions: This section consists of a number of incomplete statements, each of which has four suggested completions. Select the word or words that best complete the sentence structurally and logically and fill in the corresponding circle on the answer sheet.

2. 영수: 철수 일어났어요?
   철수 누나: 아니오.
   _____ 안 일어났어요.

   (A) 방금
   (B) 금방
   (C) 아직
   (D) 먼저

Choice (C) is the correct answer to question 2. To answer this question, students need to understand the usage of the adverb "아직," which best completes the sentence in the given context.

Sample Reading Questions

Directions: Read the following selections carefully for comprehension. Each selection is followed by one or more questions or incomplete statements based on its content. Choose the answer or completion that is best according to the selection and fill in the corresponding circle on the answer sheet.

Questions 3–4

행사 : 수미의 첫돌 잔치
장소 : 서울시 종로구 신영동
신영 아파트 234호
날짜 : 오월 삼십일 토요일
시간 : 저녁 여섯시 반

3. What is the occasion?
   (A) Baby shower
   (B) Baby's one hundredth day
   (C) Baby's first birthday
   (D) Nursery school graduation

4. The event will start at
   (A) 5:00 P.M.
   (B) 5:30 P.M.
   (C) 6:00 P.M.
   (D) 6:30 P.M.

Choice (C) is the correct answer to question 3. Choice (D) is the correct answer to question 4. The questions test the students' comprehension of vocabulary and time-related expressions.

Korean with Listening Test

Practice Helps

The test that follows is an actual, recently administered SAT Subject Test in Korean with Listening. To get an idea of what it's like to take this test, practice under conditions that are much like those of an actual test administration.

- Set aside 60 minutes when you can take the test uninterrupted. Make sure you complete the test in one sitting.
- Sit at a desk or table with no other books or papers. Dictionaries, other books, or notes are not allowed in the test room.
- Tear out an answer sheet from the back of this book and fill it in just as you would on the day of the test. One answer sheet can be used for up to three Subject Tests.
- Read the instructions that precede the practice test. During the actual administration, you will be asked to read them before answering test questions.
- Time yourself by placing a clock or kitchen timer in front of you.
- After you finish the practice test, read the sections "How to Score the SAT Subject Test in Korean with Listening" and "How Did You Do on the SAT Subject Test in Korean with Listening?"
- The appearance of the answer sheet in this book may differ from the answer sheet you see on test day.

KOREAN TEST WITH LISTENING

The top portion of the section of the answer sheet that you will use in taking the Korean Test with Listening must be filled in exactly as shown in the illustration below. Note carefully that you have to do all of the following on your answer sheet.

1. Print KOREAN WITH LISTENING on the line under the words "Subject Test (print)."

2. In the shaded box labeled "Test Code" fill in four circles:

—Fill in circle 1 in the row labeled V.
—Fill in circle 8 in the row labeled W.
—Fill in circle 4 in the row labeled X.
—Fill in circle A in the row labeled Y.

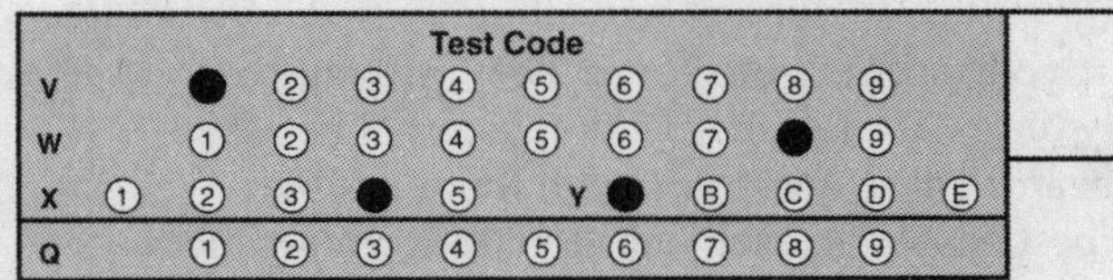

Please answer all questions that apply by filling in the specific circles in the row Q.
<u>The information you provide is for statistical purposes only and will not affect your score on the test.</u>

I. Where have you learned Korean? (Fill in ALL circles that apply.)

- If you have learned Korean at home, —Fill in circle 1.
- If you have studied Korean in a US high school, —Fill in circle 2.
- If you have studied Korean in a Korean Language School while attending grades K-8, —Fill in circle 3.
- If you have studied Korean in a Korean Language School while attending grades 9-12, —Fill in circle 4.
- If you have lived in Korea longer than one year after age ten, —Fill in circle 5.

II. How long did you study Korean while in grades 9-12 ? (Fill in the ONE circle that applies.)

- Less than 2 years —Fill in circle 6.
- 2 to 2-1/2 years —Fill in circle 7.
- 3 to 3-1/2 years —Fill in circle 8.
- More than 3-1/2 years —Fill in circle 9.

When the supervisor gives the signal, turn the page and begin the Korean Test with Listening. There are 100 numbered circles on the answer sheet and 80 questions in the Korean Test with Listening. Therefore, use only circles 1 to 80 for recording your answers.

KOREAN TEST WITH LISTENING

PLEASE NOTE THAT YOUR ANSWER SHEET HAS FIVE ANSWER POSITIONS MARKED A, B, C, D, AND E, WHILE THE QUESTIONS THROUGHOUT THIS TEST CONTAIN ONLY FOUR CHOICES. BE SURE NOT TO MAKE ANY MARKS IN COLUMN E.

SECTION I

LISTENING

Approximate time — 20 minutes

Questions 1-28

Directions: In this part of the test you will hear several spoken selections. They will not be printed in your test book. You will hear them only once. After each selection you will be asked one or more questions about what you have just heard. These questions, with four possible answers, are printed in your test book. Select the best answer to each question from among the four choices printed and fill in the corresponding circle on your answer sheet.

Now listen to the following example, but do not mark the answer on your answer sheet.

You will hear:

You will hear and see: What is the woman going to do during the vacation?

Sample Answer: Ⓐ ● Ⓒ Ⓓ

You will see:
(A) Stay home.
(B) Go to Korea.
(C) Go to school.
(D) Study Korean.

The best answer to the question is (B) "Go to Korea." Therefore, you should select choice (B) and fill in the corresponding circle on the answer sheet. Now listen to the first selection.

1. What is the father looking for?

(A) A letter from his daughter's school.
(B) A letter from the bank.
(C) His new checkbook.
(D) A receipt for a new desk.

2. Where is the item the father is looking for?

(A) Inside his briefcase.
(B) On the bookshelf.
(C) In the desk drawer.
(D) On the dining table.

3XLC

GO ON TO THE NEXT PAGE

3. Why does the student have to reschedule the lesson?
   (A) His teacher's schedule has changed.
   (B) His concert is scheduled on the same day.
   (C) His teacher is going out of town.
   (D) His orchestra rehearsal was canceled.

4. What does the teacher suggest to him?
   (A) Move the lesson to Sunday.
   (B) Skip this week's lesson.
   (C) Change the lesson to a different time of the day.
   (D) Reschedule the lesson for the day after tomorrow.

---

5. What does the student want to know?
   (A) The school orientation date.
   (B) The after-school sports schedule.
   (C) His grade from last semester.
   (D) His upcoming class schedule.

6. What level did the student take last semester?
   (A) Beginning.
   (B) Intermediate.
   (C) Advanced.
   (D) Honors.

---

7. What does the woman ask the man to do?
   (A) Help her move tomorrow.
   (B) Look for a roommate.
   (C) Play basketball with her.
   (D) Help her with her homework.

8. What does the man say?
   (A) He will play basketball with the woman.
   (B) He will introduce his friends to the woman.
   (C) He will find someone to help the woman.
   (D) He will call the woman back with an answer.

9. What problem did the man have?
   (A) He fell ill.
   (B) He overslept.
   (C) He missed the train.
   (D) He lost his briefcase.

10. Why does the man feel fortunate?
    (A) He barely made it on time.
    (B) His proposal was accepted.
    (C) The meeting was postponed.
    (D) The woman attended in his place.

---

11. Why did the woman intend to call the man?
    (A) To ask for help.
    (B) To borrow some printer paper.
    (C) To invite him over.
    (D) To say hello.

12. What seems to be the man's reaction?
    (A) Disturbed.
    (B) Impressed.
    (C) Hesitant.
    (D) Enthusiastic.

GO ON TO THE NEXT PAGE

13. Where is the man trying to go?

    (A) The American embassy.
    (B) A gas station.
    (C) A glass shop.
    (D) The foreign exchange bank.

14. To reach his destination, where should the man turn left after crossing the street?

    (A) At the bank.
    (B) At the glass shop.
    (C) At the gas station.
    (D) At the embassy.

15. How is the building described?

    (A) New and made of brick.
    (B) New and made of glass.
    (C) Tall and made of glass.
    (D) Tall and made of brick.

---

16. Why is the woman interested in Dr. Oh?

    (A) She wants to choose him as her doctor.
    (B) She wants to take his class at her college.
    (C) She plans to review his book.
    (D) She plans to write an article about him.

17. What does Mr. Kim say about Dr. Oh?

    (A) He is a lung specialist.
    (B) He lectures at universities.
    (C) He does a lot of charity work.
    (D) He writes articles for the newspapers.

18. What is the recording?

    (A) Information on an area code change.
    (B) Information on a company's telephone menu.
    (C) Introduction of a new long-distance system.
    (D) Instructions on how to record a message.

---

19. Where is this conversation most likely taking place?

    (A) A park.
    (B) A plant nursery.
    (C) Sumi's backyard.
    (D) Sangjin's office.

20. What is Sangjin most likely going to do?

    (A) Visit his friend.
    (B) Go to Sumi's housewarming party.
    (C) Look for a bigger office.
    (D) Plant a tree.

21. What has Sangjin heard about Sumi?

    (A) Sumi has a flower garden.
    (B) Sumi has moved.
    (C) Sumi found a new job.
    (D) Sumi likes him.

GO ON TO THE NEXT PAGE

22. What kind of party is this?

    (A) A birthday party.
    (B) A wedding reception.
    (C) A wedding anniversary.
    (D) A family reunion.

23. Who is the speaker?

    (A) A professional singer.
    (B) One of the children.
    (C) A minister from the church.
    (D) An honoree of the celebration.

---

24. Who made the reservation?

    (A) The man himself.
    (B) The man's wife.
    (C) The man's secretary.
    (D) A travel agent.

25. What does the man claim?

    (A) He has a confirmation number.
    (B) He always gets a corporate discount rate.
    (C) The room was guaranteed with a credit card.
    (D) The reservation was made a week ago.

26. What is the son's plan for the summer?

    (A) To attend summer school.
    (B) To get a job.
    (C) To volunteer at a senior home.
    (D) To study abroad.

27. What does the mother request that the son do?

    (A) Visit home soon.
    (B) Call home often.
    (C) Help his father with his business.
    (D) Write to the grandparents.

28. What would the grandparents like to do for the grandson?

    (A) Take him out to dinner.
    (B) Find him a job.
    (C) Pay for the airfare.
    (D) Pay for his tuition.

END OF SECTION I.
DO NOT GO ON TO SECTION II UNTIL YOU ARE TOLD TO DO SO.

SECTION II
USAGE

Time — 40 minutes for Sections II and III

Questions 29-51

WHEN YOU BEGIN THE USAGE SECTION, BE SURE THAT YOU MARK YOUR ANSWER TO THE FIRST USAGE QUESTION BY FILLING IN ONE OF THE CIRCLES NEXT TO NUMBER 29 ON THE ANSWER SHEET.

Part A

Directions: This section consists of a number of incomplete statements, each of which has four suggested completions. Select the word or words that best complete the sentence structurally and logically and fill in the corresponding circle on the answer sheet.

29. 너무나 음식을 많이 만들어서 _____ 남았어요.

(A) 음식이
(B) 음식을
(C) 음식에
(D) 음식과

30. 영선: 지난여름 휴가에는 캐나다에 갔었어요.
승진: 그 때 거기 날씨가 _____?

(A) 어떨까요
(B) 어떤지요
(C) 어땠어요
(D) 어떻게요

31. 어제 우리 집에 누가 밤늦게 전화를 해서 받았는데, 전화를 받자마자 그 쪽에서 딱 끊어 _____.

(A) 두었다
(B) 말았다
(C) 놓았다
(D) 버렸다

32. 한 시간 전에 _____ 지금쯤은 틀림없이 도착했을 텐데요.

(A) 떠났으니까
(B) 떠날 테니까
(C) 떠나려니까
(D) 떠난다니까

GO ON TO THE NEXT PAGE

33. 우리 언니는 _____ 2년 됐어요.

    (A) 결혼했던지
    (B) 결혼하는지
    (C) 결혼할지
    (D) 결혼한 지

34. 할머니_____ 낮잠을 _____.

    (A) 께.....주무십니다
    (B) 께서.....주무십니다
    (C) 께는.....잡니다
    (D) 께로.....잡니다

35. 제가 어제 무슨 일이 생겨서
    집에 늦게 _____
    모두 기다리고 있었어요.

    (A) 들어가다가
    (B) 들어가더니
    (C) 들어갔더니
    (D) 들어갔다가

36. 머리가 _____ 여자가 제
    여동생이에요.

    (A) 길
    (B) 긴
    (C) 기른
    (D) 기는

37. 내가 아기를 보는 동안 아기가
    웬일인지 자꾸 _____.
    그러니까 어머니는 나한테
    왜 아기를 _____고 꾸중을 하셨다.

    (A) 울렸다.....울리느냐
    (B) 울었다.....울리느냐
    (C) 울었다.....우느냐
    (D) 울렸다.....우느냐

38. 현승: 주말에 보통 뭐 하세요?
    민정: 영화 보_____ 운동해요.

    (A) 기도
    (B) 기만
    (C) 거든
    (D) 거나

39. 어제 우리 언니는
    저희 할머님을 _____
    시골집에 다녀왔습니다.

    (A) 데리고
    (B) 모시고
    (C) 지니고
    (D) 가지고

GO ON TO THE NEXT PAGE

40. 장미꽃 다섯 _____를 주세요.

    (A) 켤레
    (B) 자루
    (C) 마리
    (D) 송이

41. 제발 내가 늘 가는 서점에 이런 책이 _____ 바란다.

    (A) 있다고
    (B) 있기를
    (C) 있으니
    (D) 있을까

42. 같이 있었을 때 동생을 좀 더 잘 도와 _____ 이제 와서 내가 뉘우치지 않을걸.

    (A) 줬더라면
    (B) 주느라고
    (C) 줬는데
    (D) 줬으니

43. 오늘은 저녁을 하지 않고 중국 음식을 _____ 먹었습니다.

    (A) 샀다가
    (B) 사다가
    (C) 샀고
    (D) 사고

44. 경석: 하와이에 갔다 왔다면서요?
    승진: 네, 간 _____에 관광도 많이 하고 수영도 많이 했어요.

    (A) 김
    (B) 일
    (C) 중
    (D) 새

45. 일이 너무 많이 _____ 내일까지 해주세요.

    (A) 해야 하니까
    (B) 밀렸으니까
    (C) 만드니까
    (D) 보니까

46. 할아버지께 언제 _____ 여쭤 보아라.

    (A) 오시느냐고
    (B) 오시느라고
    (C) 오신다고
    (D) 오시려고

GO ON TO THE NEXT PAGE

Part B

Directions: In each of the following paragraphs there are numbered blanks indicating that words or phrases have been omitted. For each numbered blank, four completions are provided. First read through the entire paragraph. Then, for each numbered blank, choose the completion that is most appropriate and fill in the corresponding circle on the answer sheet.

어느 날 공중전화에서 집 __47__ 전화를 거는데, 동전 10전짜리 두 개와 5전짜리를 넣는 대로 __48__ 도로 나왔다. 그래서 나는 전화통이 고장이 났나 해서 몇 번이고 다시 해 __49__ 다른 전화통에도 가서 해 보았지만 __50__ 마찬가지로 전화는 안 되고 동전이 도로 나왔다. 나는 왜 전화통마다 이 모양인가 하면서 투덜댔지만 아무 소용이 없었다. 나중에 알고 보니 공중 전화요금이 __51__ 35전이 됐다는 것이었다.

47. (A) 을
    (B) 은
    (C) 에다
    (D) 에서

48. (A) 방글방글
    (B) 주르르
    (C) 반짝반짝
    (D) 따르릉

49. (A) 보면
    (B) 봐도
    (C) 보다가
    (D) 보니까

50. (A) 역시
    (B) 절대
    (C) 겨우
    (D) 별로

51. (A) 올라서
    (B) 몰라서
    (C) 걸어서
    (D) 나와서

END OF SECTION II.
GO ON TO SECTION III.

SECTION III

READING COMPREHENSION

Questions 52-80

Directions: Read the following selections carefully for comprehension. Each selection is followed by one or more questions or incomplete statements based on its content. Choose the answer or completion that is best according to the selection and fill in the corresponding circle on the answer sheet.

Questions 52-53

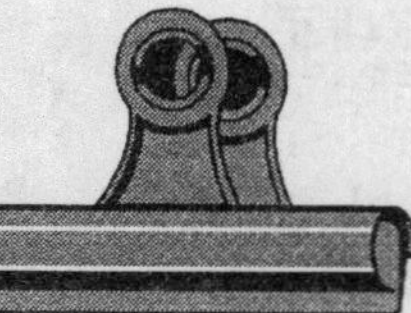

엄마,

오늘 늦으시네요. 엄마 오시면 뵙고 나가려고
했는데요, 오늘 꼭 부쳐야 하는 소포가 있어서
우체국에 다녀와야겠어요. 5시면 문을 닫잖아요?
참! 좀 전에 아빠가 전화하셨는데 오늘 회의가
있어서 늦으신대요. 우리끼리 그냥 저녁 먹으라고
하셨어요.
그럼 저 금방 다녀올게요.

제인

52. The main purpose of the note is to tell the mother that Jane

(A) will be home late
(B) is going to her father's office
(C) has to go mail a package
(D) is having dinner with her friend

53. What was the message from Jane's father?

(A) He is bringing home a guest.
(B) He wants Jane to pick him up.
(C) He will be attending a meeting.
(D) He wants to take the family out to dinner.

GO ON TO THE NEXT PAGE

Questions 54-55

제일 정비소

정비부: 나사 하나라도 소홀히 하지 않습니다.
오일 교환부터 엔진 수리까지
완벽을 추구합니다.

바디부: 99.99% 원형 복구를 추구합니다.
무료 토잉과 무료 견적 서비스합니다.

예약 필요 없습니다. 즉석에서 해 드립니다.
(510)123-4567

54. What is the ad about?
    (A) An automobile dealership
    (B) An automobile repair shop
    (C) A gasoline station
    (D) An auto parts store

55. The ad promises
    (A) free window washing
    (B) free air pumps
    (C) no need for appointment
    (D) no need for advance payment

GO ON TO THE NEXT PAGE

Questions 56-57

세계 운송 회사

이삿짐 전문 업체

* 무료 상담
* 약속한 날짜에 도착 책임짐
* 안전한 포장
* 선박 또는 항공 2주 특별 서비스
* 학생 반액 할인

이삿짐 문의: 1-800-123-2424

56. What is advertised?

(A) Express mail
(B) A travel agency
(C) Office supplies
(D) A moving company

57. What is offered?

(A) A student discount
(B) Free delivery
(C) Free assembly
(D) Flight insurance

GO ON TO THE NEXT PAGE

Question 58

안내 광고 게재 신청서

신청자 이름 __________ 전화 ________
주소 ______________________________
게재란 __________ 게재 기간 ________
광고비 금액 ________
광고 내용
____

58. What is the form above?

(A) A form for advertisement
(B) A form for registered mail
(C) A library card application
(D) A job application

GO ON TO THE NEXT PAGE

Questions 59-60

옛날에 한 가난한 농부가 살았다. 이 농부는 가난했지만 열심히 일해서 좋은 포도밭을 가지게 되었다. 이 농부가 병이 나서 더 이상 일을 할 수 없게 되었다. 농부의 아들들은 게을러서 일을 하지 않았다. 그래서 밭에는 풀이 나고 포도는 열리지 않았다. 농부는 죽으면서 아들들에게 말했다. "포도밭을 파면 보물이 나올 것이다." 아들들은 포도밭으로 달려가서 포도밭을 파헤쳐 보았지만 아무것도 나오지 않았다. 그 해에 탐스러운 포도가 다시 주렁주렁 달렸다. 아들들은 그 때서야 아버지의 보물이 무엇인지 깨달았다.

59. Why did the sons dig in the field?

(A) To find a treasure
(B) To kill weeds
(C) To have more fruit
(D) To help their father

60. Which sentence best describes the story?

(A) The farmer sold his treasure.
(B) The farmer's sons were very diligent.
(C) The farmer died in an accident.
(D) The farmer was a wise, hardworking man.

GO ON TO THE NEXT PAGE

Question 61

저울질할 수 없는 당신의 건강!
어떻게 관리하고 계십니까?
여러분의 소중한 건강을 위하여
성실하고 세심한 의료 서비스를 제공하는
한미 종합병원

61. What is being advertised?

(A) A nursing home
(B) A fitness center
(C) A pharmacy
(D) A medical center

GO ON TO THE NEXT PAGE

Question 62

독방 세 놓음
쾌적하고 조용한 지역
가족적인 분위기
학생 환영
(216) 310-4421

62. What is the purpose of this notice?

(A) To find a tutor.
(B) To lease a house.
(C) To rent a room.
(D) To get a roommate.

GO ON TO THE NEXT PAGE

Questions 63-64

3월 7일 흐렸다가 맑아짐

오늘은 아주 바쁜 날이다. 일 주일만 있으면 봄 방학이 시작되기 때문에 그 전에 마쳐야 할 일이 많다. 방학을 기다리기가 아주 힘들다. 방학이 되면 친구들이랑 보스턴으로 놀러 가기로 했다. 이 방학이 내가 대학을 졸업하기 전에 있는 마지막 방학이다. 그래서 친구끼리 놀러 가기로 했다. 다섯 명이서 갈까 했는데 한 명은 무슨 일이 생겨서 못 간다고 했다. 거기 가면 배도 타고 말도 타고 하면서 실컷 놀 계획이다.

63. The writer is a

(A) freshman
(B) sophomore
(C) junior
(D) senior

64. How many people are going on vacation together?

(A) Three
(B) Four
(C) Five
(D) Six

GO ON TO THE NEXT PAGE

Questions 65-66

독자 여러분의 원고를 모읍니다.
여러분의 경험담, 체험담, 감상문, 그리고
일터에서의 보람 등 흥미있는 이야기가 있으면
보내 주십시오.
보낼 곳은 서울 중앙 사서함 201호 편집부입니다.
채택된 원고에 대해선 기념품을 드리며
원고는 돌려 드리지 않습니다.
주소, 성명, 나이, 성별, 전화 번호를 명기하십시오.

65. What is the most appropriate form of writing requested here?

    (A) Essays
    (B) Poems
    (C) Novels
    (D) Dramas

66. What does the announcement say?

    (A) Manuscripts will not be returned.
    (B) Stories written by children will not be considered.
    (C) Cash prizes will be awarded.
    (D) Full-length novels will be considered.

GO ON TO THE NEXT PAGE

Questions 67-69

할머님께

그 동안 안녕하셨어요? 요즘 서울은 날씨가 어때요? 할머니께서 다녀가신 후 여기는 갑자기 태풍이 와서 온 동네가 물바다가 된 곳도 있고, 전기가 다 끊어진 곳도 많고 하지만 많은 사람들이 자기 집을 떠나 다른 곳으로 피신해서 다친 사람은 없습니다. 그런데 집, 가게, 빌딩들은 물이 들어와서 많이 버렸어요. 저희 집은 뒷마당에 있는 조그만 나무 하나가 쓰러졌지만 그것은 아무것도 아니지요.

할머니, 할머니께서 떠나신 지 열흘밖에 안 됐지만 아주 오래된 것 같아요. 겨울 방학 하면 할머니 뵈러 갈게요. 큰이모부랑 큰이모도 안녕하시지요? 안부 전해 주세요.
그럼 다시 뵐 때까지 안녕히 계십시오.

용진 올림

67. Yongjin tells his grandmother about

(A) the monsoon in Seoul
(B) a hurricane in his town
(C) an earthquake in his town
(D) an extended heat wave in Seoul

68. What information is given in Yongjin's letter?

(A) Most people did not leave town.
(B) Buildings were not damaged.
(C) People did not lose electricity.
(D) People were not injured.

69. What is Yongjin's plan?

(A) To plant more trees
(B) To buy additional insurance
(C) To visit his grandmother
(D) To help clean up the neighborhood

GO ON TO THE NEXT PAGE

Questions 70-71

국립 민속박물관은 1998년에 새로 문을 열었다. 대중 교육을 통하여 방문객에게 역사 지식을 넣어 주고 우리 문화에 대한 친밀감을 키우는 데에 목적을 두고 교육 활동을 하고 있다.

대중 교육 활동 내용

* 할머니 - 손녀 공예 교실
* 청소년 민속 강좌
* 외국인을 위한 민속 교실
* 각종 공연 및 학술 발표회

70. What institution is offering the service?

(A) The local school district
(B) The local public library
(C) The National Folk Museum
(D) The Ministry of Education

71. What is the stated objective of this institution?

(A) To introduce Korean history and culture
(B) To teach the Korean language to adults
(C) To demonstrate Korean song and dance
(D) To disseminate literature on Korea

GO ON TO THE NEXT PAGE

Questions 72-74

요즘에는 사람들이 무엇이든지 겉모양을 더 중요하게 생각하고 그 안에 든 내용물은 무시하는 것 같다. 그러다 보니 사람을 평가할 때에도 인격을 알기 전에 용모에 따라 판단해 버린다. 얼마 전, 가까운 친구들과 이에 관련된 이야기를 나눌 기회가 있었는데 우리가 얻은 결론은 사람의 겉모습이 인생에서 가장 중요한 것이 될 수 없다는 것이었다. 물론 부드러운 첫인상이 도움이 될 수도 있고 또, 누구나 텔레비전이나 잡지에서 예쁜 얼굴을 보기 원하는 것은 사실이지만, 시간이 흐르면 사람의 겉모습은 변하게 마련이다. 그러므로 먼저 훌륭한 인격을 갖추도록 노력하는 것이 더욱 중요한 일일 것이다.

72. According to the passage, people put too much emphasis on

(A) money
(B) career
(C) maturity
(D) looks

73. How did the writer arrive at the conclusion?

(A) By watching television
(B) By reading magazine articles
(C) By talking to friends
(D) By interviewing experts

74. What does the writer recommend?

(A) Developing good character
(B) Pursuing higher education
(C) Having a goal in life
(D) Exercising regularly

GO ON TO THE NEXT PAGE

Questions 75-76

사람은 누구도 이 세상을 혼자서 살아갈 수는 없다. 우리는 수많은 사람들과 만나고 관계를 맺으며 살아간다. 이처럼 여러 사람들이 공동체를 이루고 살아나가는 데는 반드시 지켜야 할 예절이 있게 마련이다. 예절은 인간만이 가지고 있는 아름다운 삶의 모습이다. 사람들끼리 만나서 인사를 주고받으며 친절한 말씨를 쓸 때, 우리가 사는 세상은 따뜻하고 사랑스러운 곳이 될 것이다.

75. What is the writer's main point?

(A) People should plan ahead.
(B) Smiling is a universal language.
(C) People tend to be more assertive nowadays.
(D) Every society has etiquette to observe.

76. The writer suggests that people should be

(A) patient
(B) polite
(C) diligent
(D) organized

GO ON TO THE NEXT PAGE

Questions 77-80

대학 졸업반이라 바쁘다고 하며 여기저기 뛰어 다니던 상호의 모습을 본 지가 엊그제 같은데, 상호가 벌써 애를 둘이나 둔 아버지가 되었다. 상호는 매년 여름 휴가 때면 식구들과 같이 2주일 동안 놀러 간다. 때로는 캠핑을 하면서 낚시질도 하고 뱃놀이도 한다. 좀 먼 곳이라도 상호는 가능하면 비행기를 안 타고 자동차로 여행하고 호텔에는 묵지 않는다. 그 이유는 비행기 여행은 요금이 많이 들고 또 호텔에 묵으면 식사로 비용이 거의 다 나가기 때문이다. 최소의 금액으로 최대의 효과를 내자는 것이다. 휴가는 건강에도 좋고 정신적으로도 마음의 안정을 주는 큰 힘과 약이 된다는 것을 휴가를 갈 때마다 상호는 절실히 느낀다고 한다.

77. What is still vivid in the writer's memory?

(A) Sangho's graduation
(B) Sangho's wedding
(C) Sangho's senior year
(D) Sangho's childhood

78. What does Sangho do for family vacations?

(A) He usually stays in hotels.
(B) He usually travels off-season.
(C) He avoids traveling by car as much as possible.
(D) He avoids traveling by airplane as much as possible.

79. Which word best characterizes Sangho's attitude toward money?

(A) Generous
(B) Frugal
(C) Greedy
(D) Careless

80. What does Sangho think about vacations?

(A) They are difficult to plan.
(B) They are over before you know it.
(C) They bring tranquility.
(D) They require lots of energy.

END OF SECTION III.

STOP

IF YOU FINISH BEFORE TIME IS CALLED, YOU MAY CHECK YOUR WORK ON THIS TEST ONLY. DO NOT TURN TO ANY OTHER TEST IN THIS BOOK.

How to Score the SAT Subject Test in Korean with Listening

When you take an actual SAT Subject Test in Korean with Listening, you receive an overall composite score as well as three subscores: one for the reading section, one for the listening section, and one for the usage section.

The reading, listening, and usage scores are reported on the College Board's 20–80 scale. However the composite score, which is the most significant of the scores reported to the colleges you specify, is in the form of the College Board's 200–800 scale.

Worksheet 1. Finding Your Raw Listening Subscore

STEP 1: Table A lists the correct answers for all the questions on the Subject Test in Korean with Listening that is reproduced in this book. It also serves as a worksheet for you to calculate your raw Listening subscore.

- Compare your answers with those given in the table.
- Put a check in the column marked "Right" if your answer is correct.
- Put a check in the column marked "Wrong" if your answer is incorrect.
- Leave both columns blank if you omitted the question.

STEP 2: Count the number of right answers for questions 1–28.

Enter the total here: ____________________

STEP 3: Count the number of wrong answers for questions 1–28.

Enter the total here: ____________________

STEP 4: Multiply the number of wrong answers from Step 3 by .333.

Enter the product here: ________________

STEP 5: Subtract the result obtained in Step 4 from the total you obtained in Step 2.

Enter the result here: __________________

STEP 6: Round the number obtained in Step 5 to the nearest whole number.

Enter the result here: __________________

The number you obtained in Step 6 is your raw Listening subscore.

Worksheet 2. Finding Your Raw Reading Subscore

STEP 1: Table A lists the correct answers for all the questions on the Subject Test in Korean with Listening that is reproduced in this book. It also serves as a worksheet for you to calculate your raw Reading subscore.

STEP 2: Count the number of right answers for questions 52–80.

Enter the total here: ____________________

STEP 3: Count the number of wrong answers for questions 52–80.

Enter the total here: ____________________

STEP 4: Multiply the number of wrong answers by .333.

Enter the product here: ________________

STEP 5: Subtract the result obtained in Step 4 from the total you obtained in Step 2.

Enter the result here: __________________

STEP 6: Round the number obtained in Step 5 to the nearest whole number.

Enter the result here: __________________

The number you obtained in Step 6 is your raw Reading subscore.

Worksheet 3. Finding Your Raw Usage Subscore

STEP 1: Table A lists the correct answers for all the questions on the Subject Test in Korean with Listening that is reproduced in this book. It also serves as a worksheet for you to calculate your raw Usage subscore.

STEP 2: Count the number of right answers for questions 29–51.

Enter the total here: ____________________

STEP 3: Count the number of wrong answers for questions 29–51.

Enter the total here: ____________________

STEP 4: Multiply the number of wrong answers by .333.

Enter the product here: ________________

STEP 5: Subtract the result obtained in Step 4 from the total you obtained in Step 2.

Enter the result here: ___________________

STEP 6: Round the number obtained in Step 5 to the nearest whole number.

Enter the result here: ___________________

The number you obtained in Step 6 is your raw Usage subscore.

Worksheet 4. Finding Your Raw Composite Score

STEP 1: Enter your unrounded raw Reading subscore from Step 5 of Worksheet 2.

Enter the result here: ________________

STEP 2: Enter your unrounded raw Listening subscore from Step 5 of Worksheet 1.

Enter the result here: ________________

STEP 3: Enter your unrounded raw Usage subscore from Step 5 of Worksheet 3.

Enter the result here: ________________

STEP 4: Add the results obtained in Steps 1, 2 and 3.

Enter the sum here: ________________

STEP 5: Round the number obtained in Step 4 to the nearest whole number.

Enter the result here: ________________

The number you obtained in Step 5 is your raw composite score.

Table A

Answers to the Subject Test in Korean with Listening, Form 3XLC, and Percentage of Students Answering Each Question Correctly

Question Number	Correct Answer	Right	Wrong	Percentage of Students Answering the Question Correctly*	Question Number	Correct Answer	Right	Wrong	Percentage of Students Answering the Question Correctly*
1	B			99	33	D			90
2	C			98	34	B			83
3	B			96	35	C			86
4	A			80	36	B			77
5	D			83	37	B			81
6	B			53	38	D			85
7	A			100	39	B			93
8	D			97	40	D			83
9	B			100	41	B			82
10	C			98	42	A			74
11	A			93	43	B			63
12	D			89	44	A			62
13	D			99	45	B			77
14	C			59	46	A			68
15	B			95	47	C			80
16	D			90	48	B			69
17	B			81	49	C			75
18	B			81	50	A			58
19	B			93	51	A			87
20	A			85	52	C			89
21	B			84	53	C			97
22	A			80	54	B			87
23	B			90	55	C			88
24	C			52	56	D			77
25	C			61	57	A			87
26	B			82	58	A			70
27	A			94	59	A			86
28	C			95	60	D			88
29	A			94	61	D			83
30	C			97	62	C			56
31	D			85	63	D			80
32	A			89	64	B			76

Table A continued on next page

Table A continued from previous page

Question Number	Correct Answer	Right	Wrong	Percentage of Students Answering the Question Correctly*	Question Number	Correct Answer	Right	Wrong	Percentage of Students Answering the Question Correctly*
65	A			51	73	C			81
66	A			80	74	A			82
67	B			76	75	D			56
68	D			85	76	B			89
69	C			93	77	C			54
70	C			65	78	D			84
71	A			79	79	B			81
72	D			92	80	C			84

* These percentages are based on an analysis of the answer sheets of a representative sample of 952 students who took the original form of this test in November 2001, and whose mean composite score was 691. They may be used as an indication of the relative difficulty of a particular question. Each percentage may also be used to predict the likelihood that a typical SAT Subject Test in Korean with Listening candidate will answer that question correctly on this edition of the test.

Finding Your Scaled Score

When you take SAT Subject Tests, the scores sent to the colleges you specify are reported on the College Board scale, which ranges from 200–800. Subscores are reported on a scale which ranges from 20–80. You can convert your practice test scores to scaled scores by using Tables B, C, D and E. To find your scaled score, locate your raw score in the left-hand column of the table; the corresponding score in the right-hand column is your scaled score. For example, a raw score of 59 on this particular edition of the Subject Test in Korean with Listening corresponds to a scaled composite score of 680.

Raw scores are converted to scaled scores to ensure that a score earned on any one edition of a particular Subject Test is comparable to the same scaled score earned on any other edition of the same Subject Test. Because some editions of the tests may be slightly easier or more difficult than others, College Board scaled scores are adjusted so that they indicate the same level of performance regardless of the edition of the test taken and the ability of the group that takes it. Thus, for example, a score of 400 on one edition of a test taken at a particular administration indicates the same level of achievement as a score of 400 on a different edition of the test taken at a different administration.

When you take the SAT Subject Tests during a national administration, your scores are likely to differ somewhat from the scores you obtain on the tests in this book. People perform at different levels at different times for reasons unrelated to the tests themselves. The precision of any test is also limited because it represents only a sample of all the possible questions that could be asked.

Your scaled composite score from Table B is ________________ .

Your scaled listening score from Table C is ________________ .

Your scaled reading score from Table D is ________________ .

Your scaled usage score from Table E is ________________ .

Table B

Scaled Score Conversion Table Subject Test in Korean with Listening Composite Score (Form 3XLC)					
Raw Score	Scaled Score	Raw Score	Scaled Score	Raw Score	Scaled Score
80	800	44	590	8	370
79	800	43	590	7	370
78	800	42	580	6	360
77	790	41	570	5	350
76	790	40	570	4	350
75	780	39	560	3	340
74	780	38	560	2	340
73	770	37	550	1	330
72	760	36	540	0	320
71	760	35	540	-1	320
70	750	34	530	-2	310
69	750	33	520	-3	300
68	740	32	520	-4	300
67	730	31	510	-5	290
66	730	30	510	-6	290
65	720	29	500	-7	280
64	710	28	490	-8	270
63	710	27	490	-9	270
62	700	26	480	-10	260
61	700	25	480	-11	260
60	690	24	470	-12	250
59	680	23	460	-13	240
58	680	22	460	-14	240
57	670	21	450	-15	230
56	670	20	450	-16	220
55	660	19	440	-17	220
54	650	18	430	-18	210
53	650	17	430	-19	210
52	640	16	420	-20	200
51	640	15	410	-21	200
50	630	14	410	-22	200
49	620	13	400	-23	200
48	620	12	400	-24	200
47	610	11	390	-25	200
46	600	10	380	-26	200
45	600	9	380	-27	200

Table C

Scaled Score Conversion Table Subject Test in Korean with Listening Listening Subscore (Form 3XLC)					
Raw Score	Scaled Score	Raw Score	Scaled Score	Raw Score	Scaled Score
28	80	15	52	2	37
27	79	14	50	1	36
26	77	13	48	0	35
25	75	12	47	-1	34
24	73	11	46	-2	33
23	70	10	45	-3	33
22	67	9	43	-4	32
21	64	8	42	-5	31
20	62	7	41	-6	30
19	59	6	40	-7	29
18	57	5	39	-8	28
17	55	4	38	-9	26
16	53	3	38		

Table D

Scaled Score Conversion Table Subject Test in Korean with Listening Reading Subscore (Form 3XLC)					
Raw Score	Scaled Score	Raw Score	Scaled Score	Raw Score	Scaled Score
29	80	16	63	3	47
28	79	15	62	2	45
27	78	14	61	1	44
26	76	13	60	0	43
25	75	12	58	-1	41
24	74	11	57	-2	40
23	73	10	56	-3	39
22	71	9	54	-4	38
21	70	8	53	-5	36
20	69	7	52	-6	35
19	67	6	51	-7	34
18	66	5	49	-8	32
17	65	4	48	-9	31
				-10	30

Table E

Scaled Score Conversion Table Subject Test in Korean with Listening Usage Subscore (Form 3XLC)					
Raw Score	Scaled Score	Raw Score	Scaled Score	Raw Score	Scaled Score
23	79	12	61	1	44
22	77	11	60	0	43
21	75	10	58	-1	41
20	74	9	57	-2	40
19	72	8	55	-3	38
18	71	7	54	-4	37
17	69	6	52	-5	35
16	68	5	51	-6	33
15	66	4	49	-7	32
14	65	3	47	-8	30
13	63	2	46		

How Did You Do on the Subject Test in Korean with Listening?

After you score your test and analyze your performance, think about the following questions:

Did you run out of time before reaching the end of the test?

If so, you may need to pace yourself better. For example, maybe you spent too much time on one or two hard questions. A better approach might be to skip the ones you can't answer right away and try answering all the questions that remain on the test. Then if there's time, go back to the questions you skipped.

Did you take a long time reading the directions?

You will save time when you take the test by learning the directions to the Subject Test in Korean with Listening ahead of time. Each minute you spend reading directions during the test is a minute that you could use to answer questions.

How did you handle questions you were unsure of?

If you were able to eliminate one or more of the answer choices as wrong and guess from the remaining ones, your approach probably worked to your advantage. On the other hand, making haphazard guesses or omitting questions without trying to eliminate choices could cost you valuable points.

How difficult were the questions for you compared with other students who took the test?

Table A shows you how difficult the multiple-choice questions were for the group of students who took this test during its national administration. The right-hand column gives the percentage of students that answered each question correctly.

A question answered correctly by almost everyone in the group is obviously an easier question. For example, 96 percent of the students answered question 3 correctly. But only 54 percent answered question 77 correctly.

Keep in mind that these percentages are based on just one group of students. They would probably be different with another group of students taking the test.

If you missed several easier questions, go back and try to find out why: Did the questions cover material you haven't yet reviewed? Did you misunderstand the directions?

Chapter 14
Latin

Purpose

The Subject Test in Latin measures a wide-ranging knowledge of Latin. It is written to reflect general trends in high school curricula and is independent of particular textbooks or methods of instruction.

Format

This one-hour test includes 70 to 75 multiple-choice questions.

Content

The reading comprehension part has 30 to 37 questions based on three to five reading passages and one or two poetry passages. A set of questions following a poetry passage always includes one question requiring you to scan the first four feet of a line of dactylic hexameter verse or to determine the number of elisions in a line.

- **Forms**—select appropriate grammatical forms of Latin words
- **Derivatives**—choose Latin words from which English words are derived
- **Translation**—translate from Latin to English
- **Sentence completion**—complete Latin sentences
- **Substitution**—choose alternate ways of expressing the same thought in Latin
- **Reading comprehension**—answer a variety of questions based on short passages of prose or poetry

Latin	
Skills Measured	Approximate Percentage of Test
Grammar and Syntax	30
Derivatives	5
Translation and Reading Comprehension	65

How to Prepare

The test is intended for students who have studied Latin for two to four years in high school (the equivalent of two to four semesters in college). The best way to prepare is by gradually developing competence in sight-reading Latin over a period of years. You may also prepare for the Subject Test in Latin as you would for any comprehensive test that requires knowledge of facts and concepts and the ability to apply them, thereby acquiring the equivalent of two to four years of classroom preparation. Familiarize yourself with the directions in advance. The directions in this book are identical to those that appear on the test.

Score

The total score is reported on the 200-to-800 scale.

Sample Questions

Please note: Your answer sheet has five circles marked A, B, C, D, and E, while the questions throughout this test contain only four choices. Be sure not to make any marks in column E.

Forms

This type of question asks you to select a specific grammatical form of a Latin word. Any form of a noun, pronoun, adjective, adverb, or verb can be asked for.

Directions: In the statement below, you are asked to give a specific form of the underlined word. Select the correct form from the choices given. Then fill in the corresponding circle on the answer sheet.

1. The future indicative of <u>potest</u> is

   (A) <u>potuerat</u>

   (B) <u>poterat</u>

   (C) <u>potuerit</u>

   (D) <u>poterit</u>

Choice (D) is the correct answer to question 1. In this question, you are asked to identify the future indicative of a very common irregular verb. Choice (A) is the pluperfect tense, choice (B) the imperfect, and choice (C) the future perfect.

Derivatives

In this type of question, you are given an English sentence with one word underlined. You must choose the Latin word from which the underlined English word is derived.

Directions: The English sentence below contains a word that is underlined. From among the choices, select the Latin word to which the underlined word is related by derivation. Then fill in the corresponding circle on the answer sheet.

2. The goalkeeper was out of position.
   (A) populus
   (B) pons
   (C) possum
   (D) pōnō

Choice (D) is the correct answer to question 2. The English word "position" is derived from *positus*, the past participle of the Latin verb *pōnō*, "to put or place." *Position* is not derived from the nouns *populus* and *pons*, which mean "people" and "bridge," nor from the verb *possum*, which means "to be able." Note that you will need to know the various forms of different Latin verbs to answer these questions.

Translation

You must choose the correct translation of the underlined Latin word or words. This type of question is more complex than the previous types, as it is based on the syntax of a complete Latin sentence.

Directions: In this section, part or all of the sentence is underlined. From among the choices, select the best translation for the underlined word or words. Then fill in the corresponding circle on the answer sheet.

3. Dux dīxit sē mīlitēs laudātūrum esse.
   (A) that they would praise the soldiers
   (B) that the soldiers had praised him
   (C) that he would praise the soldiers
   (D) that the soldiers should be praised

Choice (C) is the correct answer to question 3. To answer this question correctly, you must know that the underlined part of the sentence is testing an indirect statement that depends on the verb *dīxit*. The singular form of the future participle, *laudātūrum*, tells you that *sē* (he) is the subject of the indirect statement; therefore *mīlitēs* must be the direct object. The past tense of *dīxit* tells you that "would praise" is the correct translation of *laudātūrum esse*. None of the incorrect choices (A), (B), and (D) have both the correct subject of the indirect statement and the correct translation of the verb.

Sentence Completion

This type of question contains a Latin sentence in which a word or phrase has been omitted. You must select the Latin word or phrase that best fits grammatically into the sentence.

Directions: The sentence below contains a blank space indicating that a word or phrase has been omitted. For each blank, four completions are provided. Choose the word or phrase that best completes the sentence and fill in the corresponding circle on the answer sheet.

4. Ē castrīs ... nōluit.
   (A) ēgressus est
   (B) ēgredere
   (C) ut ēgrediātur
   (D) ēgredī

Choice (D) is the correct answer to question 4. To answer this question correctly, you must be able to translate the words *Ē castrīs ... nōluit* ("He did not wish ... from the camp") and then select the only choice that can be added to these two words to make a complete, grammatical Latin sentence. Here the correct answer is choice (D) *ēgredī*, the infinitive, since *nōlō* takes the infinitive. Choice (A) is incorrect because it is the present perfect form, choice (B) because it is the imperative, and choice (C) because *nōlō* does not take *ut* and the subjunctive. Note that *ēgredior* is a deponent verb.

Substitution

This type of question contains a complete Latin sentence, part or all of which is underlined. You are asked to select the substitution that is closest in meaning to the underlined words.

Directions: In the sentence below, part or all of the sentence is underlined. Select from the choices the expression that, when substituted for the underlined portion of the sentence, changes the meaning of the sentence LEAST. Then fill in the corresponding circle on the answer sheet.

5. Vēnit Rōmam ad mātrem videndam.
   (A) cum mātrem vīdisset
   (B) mātre vīsā
   (C) qui mātrem vīdit
   (D) mātris videndae causā

Choice (D) is the correct answer to question 5. In this example, the underlined portion is translated: "to see his/her mother." You must select the answer choice whose translation is closest in meaning to this underlined part: choice (D), *mātris videndae causā*, which also expresses purpose or intention. None of the other choices does so.

Reading Comprehension

This type of question presents you with a series of short passages of prose or poetry followed by several questions. These questions test either grammatical points (9 below), translation of a phrase or clause, grammatical reference (6), or summary/comprehension (7, 8, and 10). In addition, poetry passages always have one question on the scansion of the first four feet of a line of dactylic hexameter verse.

Note: The passages have titles, include definitions of uncommon words that appear in the text, and are adapted from Latin authors. There are approximately three to five passages with a total of 32 to 37 questions on the test. At least one (and no more than two) poetry passage appears on the test.

Directions: Read the following text carefully for comprehension. The text is followed by a number of questions or incomplete statements. Select the answer or completion that is best according to the text and fill in the corresponding circle on the answer sheet.

An enemy attack

Sabīnī multī, ut ad moenia Rōmae venīrent, illōs in agrīs vīventēs oppugnābant. Agrī dēlēbantur; terror urbī iniectus (injectus) est. Tum plēbs benignē arma cēpit ad Sabīnōs repellendōs. Recūsantibus[1] frūstrā senātōribus, duo tamen exercitūs magnī cōnscriptī sunt.

[1] recūsō, recūsāre: oppose

6. The word vīventēs (line 1) refers to
   - (A) Sabīnī (line 1)
   - (B) moenia (line 1)
   - (C) illōs (line 1)
   - (D) agrīs (line 1)

Choice (C) is the correct answer to question 6. The word *vīventēs* refers to *illōs*. Choice (B) cannot be the correct answer because *moenia* is neuter plural, and choice (D) *agrīs* is incorrect because the fields cannot be living somewhere. The sense of the sentence tells you that choice (A) *Sabīnī* is incorrect and that the words *illōs in agrīs vīventēs* belong together.

7. The sentence Sabīnī … oppugnābant (line 1) tells us that the
   - (A) Sabines wanted to get to the city walls
   - (B) Sabines were the people living in the fields
   - (C) Romans wanted to go nearer to the city walls
   - (D) Romans wanted to attack the people living in the fields

Choice (A) is the correct answer to question 7. To answer this question correctly, you must know that *Sabīnī* is the subject of the sentence and that *illōs in agrīs vīventēs* is the object. You must also understand the purpose clause *ut ad moenia Rōmae venīrent* in line 1. The Sabines are therefore not the people living in the fields (B), nor is it the Romans who want to get nearer to the city walls (C) or to attack the people living in the fields (D).

8. The sentence Agrī … iniectus (injectus) est (lines 1–2) tells us that the
   (A) Sabines were destroyed in the fields
   (B) Sabines were frightened of the city
   (C) fearful city was destroyed
   (D) city was filled with fear

Choice (D) is the correct answer to question 8. The sentence tells us that the fields were destroyed and that fear was "thrown into" the city.

9. The subject of cēpit (line 2) is
   (A) terror (line 2)
   (B) plēbs (line 2)
   (C) arma (line 2)
   (D) he (understood)

Choice (B) is the correct answer to question 9 because *plēbs* is in the nominative case and the subject of the sentence. Choice (A) *terror* is the subject of the previous clause and choice (C) *arma* is the object of *cēpit*. Choice (D) "he (understood)" is not the subject of this sentence, since there is an expressed subject.

10. The sentence Recūsantibus … cōnscriptī sunt (lines 3–4) tells us that
   (A) armies were raised for the senators
   (B) armies were raised in vain
   (C) the senators prevented the raising of armies
   (D) the senators did not want armies to be raised

Choice (D) is the correct answer to question 10. The ablative absolute *Recūsantibus frūstrā senātōribus* tells us that the armies were raised with the senators resisting in vain.

Latin Test

Practice Helps

The test that follows is an actual, recently administered SAT Subject Test in Latin. To get an idea of what it's like to take this test, practice under conditions that are much like those of an actual test administration.

- Set aside an hour when you can take the test uninterrupted. Make sure you complete the test in one sitting.
- Sit at a desk or table with no other books or papers. Dictionaries, other books, or notes are not allowed in the test room.
- Tear out an answer sheet from the back of this book and fill it in just as you would on the day of the test. One answer sheet can be used for up to three Subject Tests.
- Read the instructions that precede the practice test. During the actual administration, you will be asked to read them before answering test questions.
- Time yourself by placing a clock or kitchen timer in front of you.
- After you finish the practice test, read the sections "How to Score the SAT Subject Test in Latin" and "How Did You Do on the Subject Test in Latin?"
- The appearance of the answer sheet in this book may differ from the answer sheet you see on test day.

LATIN TEST

The top portion of the section of the answer sheet that you will use in taking the Latin Test must be filled in exactly as shown in the illustration below. Note carefully that you have to do all of the following on your answer sheet.

1. Print LATIN on the line under the words "Subject Test (print)."

2. In the shaded box labeled "Test Code" fill in four circles:

   —Fill in circle 4 in the row labeled V.
   —Fill in circle 2 in the row labeled W.
   —Fill in circle 2 in the row labeled X.
   —Fill in circle C in the row labeled Y.

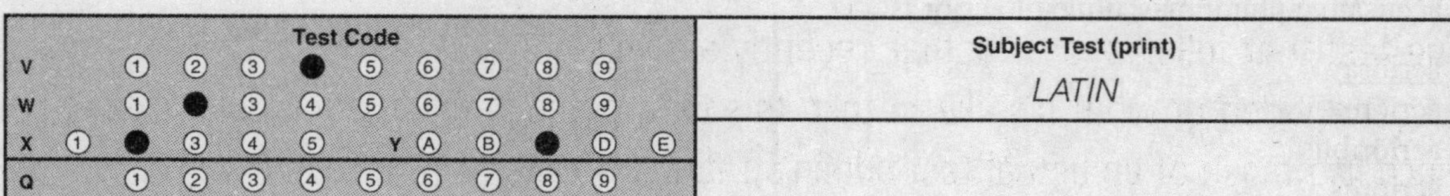

In the group of nine circles labeled Q, you are to fill in ONE and ONLY ONE circle, as described below, to indicate how you obtained your knowledge of Latin. The information you provide is for statistical purposes only and will not influence your score on the test.

Part I — If your knowledge of Latin does not come primarily from courses taken in grades 9 through 12, fill in circle 9 and leave the remaining circles blank, regardless of how long you studied the subject in school. For example, you are to fill in circle 9 if your knowledge of Latin comes primarily from any of the following sources: study prior to the ninth grade, courses taken at a college, or special study.

Part II — If your knowledge of Latin does come primarily from courses taken in grades 9 through 12, fill in the circle that indicates the level of the Latin course in which you are currently enrolled. If you are not now enrolled in a Latin course, fill in the circle that indicates the level of the most advanced course in Latin that you have completed.

- First level: first or second half —Fill in circle 1.
- Second level: first half —Fill in circle 2.
  second half —Fill in circle 3.
- Third level: first half —Fill in circle 4.
  second half —Fill in circle 5.
- Fourth level: first half —Fill in circle 6.
  second half —Fill in circle 7.
- Advanced Placement course or a course beyond fourth level, second half —Fill in circle 8.

When the supervisor gives the signal, turn the page and begin the Latin Test. There are 100 numbered circles on the answer sheet and 74 questions in the Latin Test. Therefore, use only circles 1 to 74 for recording your answers.

LATIN TEST

PLEASE NOTE: Your answer sheet has five circles, marked A, B, C, D and E, while the questions throughout this test have only four choices. Be sure not to make any marks in column E.

Note: In some questions in this test, variations of Latin terms will appear in parentheses.

Part A

Directions: In each statement below, you are asked to give a specific form of the underlined word. Select the correct form from the choices given. Then fill in the corresponding circle on the answer sheet.

1. The accusative plural masculine of ācrior is
   (A) ācriōra
   (B) ācriōre
   (C) ācriōribus
   (D) ācriōrēs

2. The genitive singular of is is
   (A) eum
   (B) eius (ejus)
   (C) eī
   (D) eō

3. The present imperative plural of ferō is
   (A) ferātis
   (B) ferte
   (C) ferēs
   (D) fer

4. The imperfect indicative of dūcunt is
   (A) dūxērunt
   (B) dūcerent
   (C) dūxerint
   (D) dūcēbant

5. The accusative plural of hoc is
   (A) hōs
   (B) hās
   (C) hīs
   (D) haec

6. The perfect passive infinitive of dīligō is
   (A) dīligī
   (B) dīlectum esse
   (C) dīlexī
   (D) dīlexisse

7. The future of sequitur is
   (A) sequētur
   (B) sequātur
   (C) sequerētur
   (D) sequēbātur

8. The subjunctive of amāvī is
   (A) amārem
   (B) amāvissem
   (C) amāverim
   (D) amāverō

3WAC

GO ON TO THE NEXT PAGE

Part B

Directions: Each of the following English sentences contains a word that is underlined. From among the choices, select the Latin word to which the underlined word is related by derivation. Then fill in the corresponding circle on the answer sheet.

9. Claudia showed great fortitude in her troubles.

(A) forum
(B) fore
(C) fortūna
(D) fortis

10. The volcano erupted violently.

(A) ēripiō
(B) errō
(C) ērumpō
(D) ērigō

11. He committed suicide.

(A) cadō
(B) caedō
(C) cēdō
(D) censeō

12. The congressional caucus intrigued the visiting reporters.

(A) conqueror
(B) congredior
(C) congruō
(D) congerō

GO ON TO THE NEXT PAGE

Part C

Directions: In each of the sentences below, part or all of the sentence is underlined. From among the choices, select the best translation for the underlined word or words. Then fill in the corresponding circle on the answer sheet.

13. Ubi eōs in cīvitātem adduxerō, concordia inter cīvēs omnēs erit.

(A) When I will draw them against the state
(B) When I might have induced them into the state
(C) When I will have led them into the state
(D) When I will have prompted them in the state

14. Trēs annōs rex aequē rexit.

(A) For the third year
(B) In the third year
(C) In three years
(D) For three years

15. Timeō nē amīcās meās nōn videam hodiē.

(A) that I may see my friends
(B) that I may not see my friends
(C) not to see my friends
(D) that my friends will not see

16. Quod dōnum Claudiae ā suīs amīcīs datum est?

(A) Because
(B) Since
(C) Who
(D) Which

17. Ab omnibus cīvibus īdem dux laudātus est.

(A) this
(B) himself
(C) a certain
(D) the same

18. Sī hoc dīcat, eum laudēmus.

(A) says
(B) should say
(C) has said
(D) will say

19. Lēgēs omnibus cīvibus defendendae sunt.

(A) from all citizens
(B) of all citizens
(C) to all citizens
(D) by all citizens

20. Amīcīs vīsīs, Anna ad oppidum currēbat.

(A) As her friends watched
(B) After her friends had been seen
(C) With the friends she had seen
(D) Since she was going to see her friends

21. Mercātor māne Rōmā profectus est.

(A) in Rome
(B) to Rome
(C) from Rome
(D) near Rome

22. Litterās coniugis (conjugis) legens, sibi putāvit: "Utinam nunc adessēs!"

(A) "So that you might be here now!"
(B) "As you are here now!"
(C) "Indeed you are here now!"
(D) "Would that you were here now!"

GO ON TO THE NEXT PAGE

23. Māter rēgis fīliō suō verba gravia locūtūra est.
    (A) will speak
    (B) is spoken
    (C) was spoken
    (D) has been spoken

24. Num hoc templum vīdistī?
    (A) Have you never seen this temple?
    (B) Did you see this temple?
    (C) You haven't seen this temple, have you?
    (D) You did see this temple, didn't you?

25. Anna līberōs ad hortum mīsit quī fructūs carperent.
    (A) who picked fruit
    (B) to pick fruit
    (C) who had picked fruit
    (D) who will pick fruit

26. Parvus puer clāmantem timet.
    (A) The little boy shouting is frightened.
    (B) The little boy is afraid of the person shouting.
    (C) The little boy fears the shouting.
    (D) The little boy is afraid to shout.

GO ON TO THE NEXT PAGE

Part D

Directions: Each of the sentences below contains a blank space indicating that a word or phrase has been omitted. For each blank, four completions are provided. Choose the option that best completes the sentence and fill in the corresponding circle on the answer sheet.

27. Peditēs in Galliam cum equitibus . . . imperātor.

(A) eīs
(B) ā Caesare
(C) mīsit
(D) et

28. . . . signum dedit.

(A) Ā tubā
(B) Tubam
(C) Tubās
(D) Tubā

29. Iūlia (Jūlia) dīxit . . . ad oppidum ventūram esse.

(A) eum
(B) illa
(C) suās
(D) sē

30. Marcus multa dōna . . . fīliae dedit.

(A) suō
(B) suae
(C) sē
(D) suus

31. Rēgīna, fēmina . . ., multa sacrificia fēcit.

(A) ad magnam pietātem
(B) magnae pietātis
(C) magnā cum pietāte
(D) magnam pietātem

32. Poēta . . . nocuit.

(A) eī
(B) eum
(C) eō
(D) eae

33. Crās . . . ab omnibus cīvibus.

(A) audiēminī
(B) audītis
(C) audīminī
(D) audiēbāminī

GO ON TO THE NEXT PAGE

Part E

Directions: In each of the sentences below, part or all of the sentence is underlined. Select from the choices the expression that, when substituted for the underlined portion of the sentence, changes the meaning of the sentence LEAST. Then fill in the corresponding circle on the answer sheet.

34. Est mihi canis bonus et magnus.

(A) Canem bonum et magnum habeō.
(B) Canem bonum habeō ut magnus sim.
(C) Canis, quī erat magnus, erat bonus.
(D) Canem, quī bonus et magnus erat, habēbam.

35. Sī Marcus imperātor erit, Rōma servābitur.

(A) Sī Marcus imperātor esset
(B) Marcō imperātōre
(C) Sī Marcus imperātor fuisset
(D) Marcum imperātōrem

36. Hae lēgēs magis idōneae quam illae sunt.

(A) illīs
(B) illī
(C) illae
(D) illā

37. Marcus nuntium mīsit ut ducem monēret.

(A) dum
(B) quī
(C) quae
(D) quod

38. Historia mihi legenda est.

(A) Mea historia lecta est.
(B) Placet mihi historiam legī.
(C) Ego historiam lēgī.
(D) Dēbeō historiam legere.

GO ON TO THE NEXT PAGE

Part F

Directions: Read the following texts carefully for comprehension. Each is followed by a number of questions or incomplete statements. Select the answer or completion that is best according to the text and fill in the corresponding circle on the answer sheet.

Rome then and now

Simplicitās rudis[1] ante fuit: nunc aurea Rōma est.
Et domitī[2] magnās possidet orbis opēs.
Aspice[3] quae nunc sunt Capitōlia, quaeque fuērunt:
alterius dīcēs illa fuisse Iovis (Jovis).
Prīsca[4] iuvent (juvent) aliōs:[5] ego mē nunc dēnique nātum
grātulor: haec aetās mōribus apta meīs.

[1] rudis, rude, adj.: plain
[2] domitī = victī
[3] Aspice = Spectā
[4] Prīsca = antīqua
[5] iuvent (juvent) aliōs = placeant aliīs

39. The case and number of aurea (line 1) are

(A) nominative singular
(B) nominative plural
(C) accusative plural
(D) ablative singular

40. How many elisions occur in line 1 ?

(A) One
(B) Two
(C) Three
(D) Four

41. In line 2, magnās modifies

(A) Simplicitās (line 1)
(B) rudis (line 1)
(C) orbis (line 2)
(D) opēs (line 2)

42. The understood subject of possidet (line 2) refers to

(A) Simplicitās (line 1)
(B) Rōma (line 1)
(C) orbis (line 2)
(D) opēs (line 2)

43. The words domitī . . . opēs (line 2) are translated

(A) the conquerors possess great wealth
(B) it possesses the great wealth of the conquered world
(C) great wealth conquers the possessors
(D) the world possesses great resources

44. Aspice (line 3) is translated

(A) to look at
(B) they look at
(C) look at
(D) he looks at

GO ON TO THE NEXT PAGE

45. The case and number of Capitōlia (line 3) are

    (A) nominative singular
    (B) nominative plural
    (C) accusative singular
    (D) ablative singular

46. The case and number of illa (line 4) are

    (A) nominative singular
    (B) nominative plural
    (C) accusative plural
    (D) ablative singular

47. In line 4, fuisse is translated

    (A) are
    (B) were
    (C) will be
    (D) will have been

48. Which of the following is the most accurate translation of the words Prīsca iuvent (juvent) (line 5) ?

    (A) Let ancient times please
    (B) If ancient times pleased
    (C) Ancient times please
    (D) Ancient times will please

49. The case and number of mōribus (line 6) are

    (A) genitive plural
    (B) dative plural
    (C) accusative plural
    (D) ablative plural

50. In line 6, the words haec . . . meīs are translated

    (A) these ways are suitable to me
    (B) my age makes me inclined to delay
    (C) this age is fitting for my ways
    (D) this time delays me

51. In the passage, the poet praises the

    (A) former leaders of Rome
    (B) wealth and power of Rome
    (C) simplicity of Roman life
    (D) good old ways

GO ON TO THE NEXT PAGE

A Roman dictator opposes Hannibal.

Dictātōrem populus creāvit et huic negōtium ab senātū datum, ut mūrōs turrēsque urbis firmāret, et pontēs flūminis dēlēret. Prō urbe ac penātibus[1] eī pugnandum erat, cum Italia dēfendī nōn posset.

Hannibal[2] rectō itinere vēnit. Vastātō agrō, urbem oppugnāre incēpit. Repulsus magnā caede suōrum, in agrum iter āvertit.

[1]penātēs, penātium, m.: Penates, household gods
[2]Hannibal, Hannibālis, m.: Hannibal, a Carthaginian general

52. The words huic negōtium ab senātū datum (lines 1-2) are translated

(A) he assigned this task to the senate
(B) the task was given to him by the senate
(C) this task was dedicated to the senate
(D) the senate handed over this task

53. The subject of firmāret (line 2) is

(A) dictātor (understood)
(B) Hannibal (understood)
(C) populus (line 1)
(D) negōtium (line 1)

54. The case of the word pontēs (line 3) is

(A) nominative
(B) genitive
(C) dative
(D) accusative

55. The words eī pugnandum erat (lines 3-4) are translated

(A) it is fought for him
(B) it should be fought for him
(C) he had to fight
(D) they had to fight

56. The word cum (line 4) is translated

(A) with
(B) so that
(C) therefore
(D) since

57. We learn in the first paragraph that one task of the dictator is to

(A) build bridges
(B) strengthen the city's walls
(C) negotiate for the senate
(D) conquer Italy

GO ON TO THE NEXT PAGE

58. Repulsus (line 6) modifies

    (A) Hannibal (understood)
    (B) caede (line 6)
    (C) agrum (line 7)
    (D) iter (line 7)

59. The words in agrum (lines 6-7) are translated

    (A) in the countryside
    (B) through the countryside
    (C) into the countryside
    (D) around the countryside

60. In the second paragraph, we learn which of the following about Hannibal's attack on the city?

    (A) He attacked after destroying the countryside.
    (B) He attacked before the city could be fortified.
    (C) He intended to complete his conquest of Italy.
    (D) He intended to slaughter the entire population.

GO ON TO THE NEXT PAGE

A multilingual monarch

Quintus Ennius tria corda habēre sēsē dīcēbat, quod loquī Graecē et Oscē et Latīnē scīret. Mithridātēs autem, Pontī atque Bīthȳniae rex clārus, quī ā Pompēiō bellō superātus est, quinque et vīgintī gentium quās sub diciōne[1] habuit linguās scīvit eārumque omnium gentium virīs numquam per interpretem conlocūtus est. Sed ut quisque ā rēge appellātus est, statim linguā et ōrātiōne ipsīus nōn minus scītē[2] quam sī gentīlis[3] eius (ejus) esset locūtus est.

[1] diciō, diciōnis, f.: power, sovereignty
[2] scītē: skillfully
[3] gentīlis, gentīlis, m.: fellow countryman

61. The case and number of corda (line 1) are
    (A) nominative singular
    (B) accusative plural
    (C) ablative singular
    (D) nominative plural

62. In line 1, habēre is translated
    (A) have
    (B) had
    (C) having
    (D) has

63. In line 1, sēsē is translated
    (A) it
    (B) they
    (C) he
    (D) his

64. Graecē, Oscē, and Latīnē in line 2 are
    (A) adjectives
    (B) nouns
    (C) pronouns
    (D) adverbs

65. The first sentence (lines 1-2) tells us that Quintus Ennius
    (A) wanted to learn the Oscan language
    (B) was able to speak several languages
    (C) knew the Greek, Oscan, and Latin peoples
    (D) had only the Latin language in his heart

66. In line 3, quī refers to
    (A) Mithridates
    (B) Pontus
    (C) Ennius
    (D) Bithynia

67. In line 4, bellō is translated
    (A) war
    (B) for war
    (C) from war
    (D) in war

68. The subject of habuit (line 5) is
    (A) Ennius (line 1)
    (B) Mithridātēs (line 2)
    (C) Bīthȳniae (line 3)
    (D) Pompēiō (line 3)

GO ON TO THE NEXT PAGE

LATIN TEST—*Continued*

69. In lines 4-5, quinque et . . . scīvit tells us that Mithridates knew

    (A) 20 people who spoke 5 languages
    (B) 25 people who spoke regional languages
    (C) many nations where 25 languages were spoken
    (D) the languages of 25 peoples in his realm

70. In line 7, ut is translated

    (A) in order that
    (B) as
    (C) because
    (D) lest

71. The word rēge (line 7) refers to

    (A) Ennius (line 1)
    (B) Mithridātēs (line 2)
    (C) Pontī (line 3)
    (D) Pompēiō (line 3)

72. In line 8, quam is translated

    (A) which
    (B) whom
    (C) than
    (D) who

73. In line 9, esset is translated

    (A) he were
    (B) he had been
    (C) he would be
    (D) he will be

74. In lines 7-9, statim linguā . . . locūtus est tells us that

    (A) he spoke the language as well as a native of that country
    (B) his language was as impressive as his oration
    (C) his countrymen appreciated his skillful attempt
    (D) he had never spoken the language of his countrymen

STOP

IF YOU FINISH BEFORE TIME IS CALLED, YOU MAY CHECK YOUR WORK ON THIS TEST ONLY. DO NOT TURN TO ANY OTHER TEST IN THIS BOOK.

How to Score the SAT Subject Test in Latin

When you take an actual SAT Subject Test in Latin, your answer sheet will be "read" by a scanning machine that will record your responses to each question. Then a computer will compare your answers with the correct answers and produce your raw score. You get one point for each correct answer. For each wrong answer, you lose one-third of a point. Questions you omit (and any for which you mark more than one answer) are not counted. This raw score is converted to a scaled score that is reported to you and to the colleges you specify.

Worksheet 1. Finding Your Raw Test Score

STEP 1: Table A lists the correct answers for all the questions on the Subject Test in Latin that is reproduced in this book. It also serves as a worksheet for you to calculate your raw score.

- Compare your answers with those given in the table.
- Put a check in the column marked "Right" if your answer is correct.
- Put a check in the column marked "Wrong" if your answer is incorrect.
- Leave both columns blank if you omitted the question.

STEP 2: Count the number of right answers.

Enter the total here: ________________

STEP 3: Count the number of wrong answers.

Enter the total here: ________________

STEP 4: Multiply the number of wrong answers by .333.

Enter the product here: ________________

STEP 5: Subtract the result obtained in Step 4 from the total you obtained in Step 2.

Enter the result here: ________________

STEP 6: Round the number obtained in Step 5 to the nearest whole number.

Enter the result here: ________________

The number you obtained in Step 6 is your raw score.

Table A

Answers to the Subject Test in Latin, Form 3WAC, and Percentage of Students Answering Each Question Correctly									
Question Number	Correct Answer	Right	Wrong	Percentage of Students Answering the Question Correctly*	Question Number	Correct Answer	Right	Wrong	Percentage of Students Answering the Question Correctly*
1	D			91	33	A			56
2	B			74	34	A			80
3	B			72	35	B			35
4	D			88	36	A			34
5	D			51	37	B			44
6	B			71	38	D			30
7	A			70	39	A			81
8	C			43	40	A			63
9	D			94	41	D			87
10	C			48	42	B			83
11	B			53	43	B			80
12	B			65	44	C			86
13	C			86	45	B			45
14	D			88	46	C			28
15	B			83	47	B			50
16	D			79	48	A			53
17	D			55	49	B			61
18	B			52	50	C			63
19	D			74	51	B			55
20	B			57	52	B			83
21	C			39	53	A			70
22	D			43	54	D			77
23	A			53	55	C			54
24	C			38	56	D			75
25	B			31	57	B			74
26	B			16	58	A			74
27	C			70	59	C			77
28	D			58	60	A			68
29	D			54	61	B			70
30	B			68	62	B			34
31	B			49	63	C			56
32	A			22	64	D			11

Table A continued on next page

Table A continued from previous page

Question Number	Correct Answer	Right	Wrong	Percentage of Students Answering the Question Correctly*	Question Number	Correct Answer	Right	Wrong	Percentage of Students Answering the Question Correctly*
65	B			85	70	B			36
66	A			70	71	B			48
67	D			70	72	C			67
68	B			67	73	A			35
69	D			68	74	A			74

* These percentages are based on an analysis of the answer sheets of a representative sample of 802 students who took the original form of this test in December 2000, and whose mean score was 593. They may be used as an indication of the relative difficulty of a particular question. Each percentage may also be used to predict the likelihood that a typical SAT Subject Test in Latin candidate will answer that question correctly on this edition of the test.

Finding Your Scaled Score

When you take SAT Subject Tests, the scores sent to the colleges you specify are reported on the College Board scale, which ranges from 200–800. You can convert your practice test score to a scaled score by using Table B. To find your scaled score, locate your raw score in the left-hand column of Table B; the corresponding score in the right-hand column is your scaled score. For example, a raw score of 36 on this particular edition of the Subject Test in Latin corresponds to a scaled score of 580.

Raw scores are converted to scaled scores to ensure that a score earned on any one edition of a particular Subject Test is comparable to the same scaled score earned on any other edition of the same Subject Test. Because some editions of the tests may be slightly easier or more difficult than others, College Board scaled scores are adjusted so that they indicate the same level of performance regardless of the edition of the test taken and the ability of the group that takes it. Thus, for example, a score of 400 on one edition of a test taken at a particular administration indicates the same level of achievement as a score of 400 on a different edition of the test taken at a different administration.

When you take the SAT Subject Tests during a national administration, your scores are likely to differ somewhat from the scores you obtain on the tests in this book. People perform at different levels at different times for reasons unrelated to the tests themselves. The precision of any test is also limited because it represents only a sample of all the possible questions that could be asked.

Table B

Scaled Score Conversion Table
Subject Test in Latin (Form 3WAC)

Raw Score	Scaled Score	Raw Score	Scaled Score	Raw Score	Scaled Score
74	800	40	610	6	410
73	800	39	600	5	410
72	800	38	600	4	400
71	800	37	590	3	400
70	800	36	580	2	400
69	800	35	580	1	390
68	800	34	570	0	390
67	800	33	560	-1	380
66	800	32	560	-2	380
65	790	31	550	-3	370
64	780	30	540	-4	370
63	770	29	540	-5	360
62	770	28	530	-6	360
61	760	27	520	-7	350
60	750	26	520	-8	350
59	740	25	510	-9	340
58	740	24	510	-10	340
57	730	23	500	-11	330
56	720	22	490	-12	330
55	720	21	490	-13	320
54	710	20	480	-14	320
53	700	19	480	-15	320
52	700	18	470	-16	310
51	690	17	470	-17	310
50	680	16	460	-18	300
49	670	15	460	-19	300
48	670	14	450	-20	290
47	660	13	450	-21	290
46	650	12	440	-22	290
45	650	11	440	-23	280
44	640	10	430	-24	280
43	630	9	430	-25	270
42	620	8	420		
41	620	7	420		

How Did You Do on the Subject Test in Latin?

After you score your test and analyze your performance, think about the following questions:

Did you run out of time before reaching the end of the test?

If so, you may need to pace yourself better. For example, maybe you spent too much time on one or two hard questions. A better approach might be to skip the ones you can't answer right away and try answering all the questions that remain on the test. Then if there's time, go back to the questions you skipped.

Did you take a long time reading the directions?

You will save time when you take the test by learning the directions to the Subject Test in Latin ahead of time. Each minute you spend reading directions during the test is a minute that you could use to answer questions.

How did you handle questions you were unsure of?

If you were able to eliminate one or more of the answer choices as wrong and guess from the remaining ones, your approach probably worked to your advantage. On the other hand, making haphazard guesses or omitting questions without trying to eliminate choices could cost you valuable points.

How difficult were the questions for you compared with other students who took the test?

Table A shows you how difficult the multiple-choice questions were for the group of students who took this test during its national administration. The right-hand column gives the percentage of students that answered each question correctly.

A question answered correctly by almost everyone in the group is obviously an easier question. For example, 88 percent of the students answered question 4 correctly. But only 16 percent answered question 26 correctly.

Keep in mind that these percentages are based on just one group of students. They would probably be different with another group of students taking the test.

If you missed several easier questions, go back and try to find out why: Did the questions cover material you haven't yet reviewed? Did you misunderstand the directions?

Chapter 15

Modern Hebrew

Purpose

The Subject Test in Modern Hebrew measures competence in Modern Hebrew and allows for variation in language preparation.

Format

This one-hour test consists of 85 multiple-choice questions. The test evaluates your mastery of vocabulary, structure, and reading comprehension through questions that require a wide-ranging knowledge of the language.

Content

The test evaluates reading ability in three areas:

Vocabulary questions test knowledge of words representing different parts of speech and some basic idioms within culturally authentic contexts.

Structure questions test grammar, including parts of speech as well as your ability to recognize appropriate language patterns.

Reading comprehension questions test your understanding of passages of varying levels of difficulty. These passages, most of which are vocalized, are generally adapted from literary sources and newspaper or magazine articles. Authentic material such as advertisements have been added to the test. (A sample advertisement appears in the Sample Questions below.) While some passages have biblical references, no material in the test is written in biblical Hebrew.

Modern Hebrew	
Skills Measured	Approximate Percentage of Test
Vocabulary in Context	30
Structure in Context (grammar)	30
Reading Comprehension	40

How to Prepare

The Subject Test in Modern Hebrew allows for variation in language preparation. It does not depend on any particular textbooks or methods of instruction. You should develop competence in Modern Hebrew over a period of years by taking two to four years of Modern Hebrew language study in high school or the equivalent. Familiarize yourself with the directions in advance. The directions in this book are identical to those that appear on the test.

Score

The total score is reported on the 200-to-800 scale.

Sample Questions

The three types of multiple-choice questions used in the test are:

- sentence completion questions
- paragraph completion questions
- questions based on a series of passages that test your understanding of those passages

Please note that your answer sheet has five answer positions, marked A, B, C, D, and E, while the questions throughout this test contain only four choices. Be sure not to make any marks in column E.

Part A—Sentence Completion

This type of question tests vocabulary mastery and requires the student to know the meaning of words and idiomatic expressions in context. Other sentence completion questions test mastery of structure and require students to identify usage that is structurally correct.

Directions: This part consists of a number of incomplete statements, each having four suggested completions. Select the most appropriate completion and fill in the corresponding circle on the answer sheet.

1. הוּא בָּא מֵאֵירוֹפָּה וְקָשֶׁה לוֹ ______ לַחֹם בְּיִשְׂרָאֵל.

   (A) לְהִתְרַגֵּל

   (B) לְהִתְבַּיֵּשׁ

   (C) לְהִשְׁתַּזֵּף

   (D) לְהִתְיַבֵּשׁ

2. הַמִּשְׁפָּחָה שֶׁלָּנוּ ______ בִּכְפָר קָטָן.

   (A) גָּרִים

   (B) גָּרוֹת

   (C) גָּרָה

   (D) לָגוּר

Choice (A) is correct answer to question 1. This question tests how well you have mastered vocabulary. All four choices are verbs, but choice (A) is the only one which expresses idiomatically that it is difficult for the person to *get used* to the hot weather in Israel. The other choices are inappropriate verbs in this particular context.

Choice (C) is the correct answer to question 2. This question tests command of structure. To answer correctly you need to recognize correct noun-verb agreement. The noun *family* is feminine singular, and choice (C) is the feminine singular verb. The other options are verbs of the same root but do not agree with the noun.

Part B—Paragraph Completion

In paragraph completion questions, you are presented with a paragraph(s) from which words have been omitted. You must select the option that is most appropriate to the context. The main difference between sentence completion and paragraph completion is that the paragraph enables you to answer correctly based on the content of the entire passage rather than a single sentence.

Directions: In each of the following paragraphs there are numbered blanks indicating that words or phrases have been omitted. For each numbered blank, four completions are provided; only one is correct. First read through the entire passage. Then for each numbered blank, choose the completion that is most appropriate and fill in the corresponding circle on the answer sheet.

בְּלֵיל הַסֵּדֶר יָשַׁב סַבָּא בְּרֹאשׁ הַשֻּׁלְחָן
(3) _________כָּל בְּנֵי הַמִּשְׁפָּחָה.
אֲנַחְנוּ, הַנְּכָדִים הַצְּעִירִים, יָשַׁבְנוּ קָרוֹב
(4) _________, וְכָל אֶחָד מֵאִתָּנוּ
(5) _________ בְּיָדוֹ הַגָּדָה מְצֻיֶּרֶת.
כְּשֶׁסַּבָּא (6) _________ שֶׁכָּל אֶחָד
מֵהַיְלָדִים יִקְרָא שׁוּרוֹת (7) _________
מִן הַהַגָּדָה, (8) _________ לִפְתֹּחַ אֶת
הַסֵּפֶר שֶׁלִּי, וְקָרָאתִי בּוֹ בְּשֶׁקֶט לְעַצְמִי,
כְּדֵי שֶׁלֹּא (9) _________ כְּשֶׁיַּגִּיעַ תּוֹרִי.

3. (A) כְּשֶׁסְּבִיבוֹ
(B) כְּשֶׁעָלָיו
(C) כְּשֶׁבְּתוֹכוֹ
(D) כְּשֶׁבִּשְׁבִילוֹ

4. (A) מִמֶּנּוּ
(B) אֵלָיו
(C) שֶׁלּוֹ
(D) אוֹתוֹ

5. (A) הִשְׁמִיעַ
(B) הִבִּיט
(C) הִקְשִׁיב
(D) הֶחְזִיק

6. (A) כִּבֵּד
(B) דִּבֵּר
(C) בִּקֵּשׁ
(D) סִפֵּר

7. (A) מְעַט
(B) אֲחָדוֹת
(C) קְצָת
(D) עֲשָׂרוֹת

8. (A) הִפְסַקְתִּי
(B) שָׁכַחְתִּי
(C) הִשְׁאַרְתִּי
(D) מִהַרְתִּי

9. (A) אֶטְעֶה
(B) טוֹעֶה
(C) יִטְעֶה
(D) טָעִיתִי

Choice (A) is the correct answer to question 3. You must find the correct preposition among the four prepositions that appear with the masculine singular. Choice (A), meaning *around him,* is the only choice that fits in this context.

Choice (B) is the correct answer to question 4. This question tests another preposition. The children sat close to *him*.

Choice (D) is the answer to question 5. This is a vocabulary question, and you are to choose the answer that means *held.*

Choice (C) is the correct answer to question 6. It is the only verb that fits idiomatically in the sentence, "Grandfather *asked.*"

Choice (B) is the correct answer to question 7. In this question, you are to choose the correct adjective to describe the noun *lines,* which is feminine plural. Choice (B) meaning *several or a few* is the correct answer.

Choice (D) is the correct answer to question 8. This question tests vocabulary. You are to find the appropriate verb. The verb *I hurried* is the only option that can be used correctly in this context.

Choice (A) is the correct answer to question 9. In this question, you are to choose the right tense of the verb *to make a mistake, to err.* Choice (A) is future tense for first person singular.

Part C—Reading Comprehension

This part examines your ability to read passages representative of various styles and levels of difficulty. Each SAT Subject Test in Modern Hebrew has several prose passages followed by questions that test understanding. Some are short newspaper items and/or ads; some are textual passages, one of which is unvocalized. The passages are generally adapted from literary sources. Most of the questions focus on main and supporting ideas. These questions test whether you comprehend the main idea and some facts and details contained in the text. The ad and the passage that follow are samples of the material that appears in the test.

Directions: Read the following passages carefully for comprehension. Each is followed by a number of questions or incomplete statements. Select the completion or answer that is best according to the passage and fill in the corresponding circle on the answer sheet.

דרושים מורים למתמטיקה ולמדע לכיתות ה-ו,
לחצי משרה או למשרה מלאה.
דרישות: תואר ראשון בתחום מתאים,
ותעודת הוראה.
בית ספר תומר, רח׳ בן יהודה.
טלפון: 556677.

10. הַפִּרְסוֹמֶת מוֹדִיעָה עַל
(A) מוֹרִים שֶׁמְּחַפְּשִׂים עֲבוֹדָה
(B) מְקוֹמוֹת עֲבוֹדָה לְמוֹרִים
(C) סִפְרֵי לִמּוּד לְמָתֵמָטִיקָה וּמַדָּע
(D) תְּעוּדוֹת לְמוֹרִים

11. לְפִי הַפִּרְסוֹמֶת דְּרוּשִׁים
(A) מוֹרִים בְּאַרְצוֹת-הַבְּרִית
(B) כִּתּוֹת גְּדוֹלוֹת
(C) סִפְרֵי לִמּוּד
(D) בַּעֲלֵי תּוֹאַר רִאשׁוֹן

12. 556677 הוּא מִסְפַּר הַטֶּלֶפוֹן שֶׁל
(A) הַמּוֹרָה
(B) בֵּית סֵפֶר תּוֹמֶר
(C) בֶּן יְהוּדָה
(D) הַכִּתָּה

Questions 10–12 ask details about the advertisement.

Choice (B) is the correct answer to question 10. To answer this question, you need to know what is advertised in the ad. The correct answer is the school is looking for teachers.

Choice (D) is the correct answer to question 11. This question asks what are the requirements. Teachers holding a B.A. in Hebrew, their first academic degree, is correctly expressed in choice (D).

Choice (B) is the correct answer to question 12. This question checks if the reader understood whose phone number is given.

לָאַחֲרוֹנָה, הִתְחִילָה הַטֶּלֶוִויזְיָה הַיִּשְׂרְאֵלִית לְשַׁדֵּר כָּל יוֹם חֲדָשׁוֹת בַּשָּׂפָה הָאַנְגְּלִית. הַתָּכְנִית מְשֻׁדֶּרֶת בְּשָׁעָה שְׁמוֹנֶה בָּעֶרֶב וְהִיא נִמְשֶׁכֶת חֲמֵשׁ-עֶשְׂרֵה דַּקּוֹת. תָּכְנִית הַחֲדָשׁוֹת בְּאַנְגְּלִית זָכְתָה לְהַצְלָחָה גְּדוֹלָה מִשּׁוּם שֶׁהִיא מְשַׁדֶּרֶת אֶת הַחֲדָשׁוֹת בְּסִגְנוֹן אֲמֶרִיקָנִי וְיֵשׁ בָּהּ לְפָחוֹת עֲשָׂרָה נוֹשְׂאִים שׁוֹנִים.

קַרְיָנֵי-הַחֲדָשׁוֹת הֵם אֲנָשִׁים נְעִימִים עִם חִיּוּךְ עַל הַפָּנִים. בִּמְיֻחָד מָצְאָה-חֵן בְּעֵינֵי הַיִּשְׂרְאֵלִים הַקַּרְיָנִית סוּזַאן, יְלִידַת בּוֹסְטוֹן, בִּגְלַל סִגְנוֹנָהּ הַמְּיוּחָד. סוּזַאן שֶׁלָּמְדָה עִבְרִית בְּאַרְצוֹת-הַבְּרִית, בָּאָה לְיִשְׂרָאֵל לִשְׁנַת לִמּוּדִים וְהֶחְלִיטָה לְהִשָּׁאֵר. לְאַחַר שֶׁעָלְתָה לָאָרֶץ הִיא לָמְדָה תִּקְשֹׁרֶת בָּאוּנִיבֶרְסִיטָה הָעִבְרִית בִּירוּשָׁלַיִם.

13. אֵיךְ קִבְּלוּ הַיִּשְׂרְאֵלִים אֶת הַתָּכְנִית?

(A) הֵם הִתְנַגְּדוּ לִשְׂפַת-הַחֲדָשׁוֹת

(B) הֵם הִתְפַּלְאוּ עַל שְׁעַת-הַחֲדָשׁוֹת

(C) הֵם בִּטְּלוּ אֶת הַתָּכְנִית

(D) הֵם קִבְּלוּ אוֹתָהּ בְּהִתְלַהֲבוּת

14. הַתָּכְנִית הִצְלִיחָה כִּי

(A) הָיְתָה עֲשִׁירָה וּמְעַנְיֶנֶת

(B) שֻׁדְּרָה פַּעֲמַיִם בַּיּוֹם

(C) נֶעֶרְכָה עַל-יְדֵי הָאוּנִיבֶרְסִיטָה

(D) הַתִּקְשֹׁרֶת הָיְתָה טוֹבָה

15. מַדּוּעַ הִצְלִיחָה סוּזָאן כְּקַרְיָנִית?

(A) כִּי הִיא לָמְדָה עִבְרִית בְּאַרְצוֹת-הַבְּרִית

(B) כִּי הִיא הֶחְלִיטָה לַעֲלוֹת לְיִשְׂרָאֵל

(C) כִּי הִיא נוֹלְדָה בְּבּוֹסְטוֹן

(D) כִּי הִגִּישָׁה יְדִיעוֹת בְּאֹפֶן מְעַנְיֵן

Questions 13–15 refer to the passage on the Israeli television's recently initiated news broadcast.

Choice (D) is the correct answer to question 13. This question asks how the Israelis accepted the new program. The passage describes the new program as having *gained much success*, thus choice (D) *they received it with enthusiasm* is the correct answer. The remaining three choices do not answer the question correctly.

Choice (A) is the correct answer to question 14. This question asks the reason for its success. *It was rich and interesting.* The passage describes the reason as: *It deals with at least ten different topics.* The other three choices are not the reasons for the program's success.

Choice (D) is the correct answer to question 15. This question asks the reason for the success of the broadcast's announcer. The correct answer is *She delivered the news in an interesting manner.* The passage talks about *her special style.* The other choices give additional details about her but are not the reason for her success.

Modern Hebrew Test

Practice Helps

The test that follows is an actual, recently administered SAT Subject Test in Modern Hebrew. To get an idea of what it's like to take this test, practice under conditions that are much like those of an actual test administration.

- Set aside an hour when you can take the test uninterrupted. Make sure you complete the test in one sitting.
- Sit at a desk or table with no other books or papers. Dictionaries, other books, or notes are not allowed in the test room.
- Tear out an answer sheet from the back of this book and fill it in just as you would on the day of the test. One answer sheet can be used for up to three Subject Tests.
- Read the instructions that precede the practice test. During the actual administration, you will be asked to read them before answering test questions.
- Time yourself by placing a clock or kitchen timer in front of you.
- After you finish the practice test, read the sections "How to Score the SAT Subject Test in Modern Hebrew" and "How Did You Do on the Subject Test in Modern Hebrew?"
- The appearance of the answer sheet in this book may differ from the answer sheet you see on test day.

MODERN HEBREW TEST

The top portion of the section of the answer sheet that you will use in taking the Modern Hebrew Test must be filled in exactly as shown in the illustration below. Note carefully that you have to do all of the following on your answer sheet.

1. Print MODERN HEBREW on the line under the words "Subject Test (print)."

2. In the shaded box labeled "Test Code" fill in four circles:

   —Fill in circle 1 in the row labeled V.
   —Fill in circle 3 in the row labeled W.
   —Fill in circle 4 in the row labeled X.
   —Fill in circle C in the row labeled Y.

Test Code												
V		●	2	3	4	5	6	7	8	9		
W		1	2	●	4	5	6	7	8	9		
X	1	2	3	●	5	Y	A	B	●	D	E	
Q		1	2	3	4	5	6	7	8	9		

Subject Test (print)
MODERN HEBREW

Please answer either Part I or Part II by filling in the specific circle in row Q. The information you provide is for statistical purposes only and will not influence your score on the test.

Part I If your knowledge of Hebrew comes primarily from extensive residence in Israel after age 10, courses taken in college, or from living in a home where Hebrew is the principal language spoken, fill in circle 9 and skip the remaining questions on this page.

Part II If your knowledge of Hebrew comes primarily from courses taken in grades 9 through 12, fill in the circle that represents the total number of years you have studied Hebrew. Fill in only one of circles 1-7. (Leave circle 8 blank).

- Less than 2 years —Fill in circle 4.
- 2 to 2-1/2 years —Fill in circle 5.
- 3 to 3-1/2 years —Fill in circle 6.
- 4 years —Fill in circle 7.
- If you have studied Hebrew in a Jewish/Hebrew Day School up to the 8th grade only, —Fill in circle 1.
- If you have studied Hebrew in a Jewish/Hebrew Day School and less than 2 years in high school, —Fill in circle 2.
- If you have studied Hebrew in a Jewish/Hebrew Day School and 2 or more years of study beyond 8th grade, —Fill in circle 3.

When the supervisor gives the signal, turn the page and begin the Modern Hebrew Test. There are 100 numbered circles on the answer sheet and 85 questions in the Modern Hebrew Test. Therefore, use only circles 1 to 85 for recording your answers.

MODERN HEBREW TEST

PLEASE NOTE THAT YOUR ANSWER SHEET HAS FIVE ANSWER POSITIONS, MARKED A, B, C, D, AND E, WHILE THE QUESTIONS THROUGHOUT THIS TEST CONTAIN ONLY FOUR CHOICES. BE SURE NOT TO MAKE ANY MARKS IN COLUMN E.

Be sure to note that the questions are numbered on the RIGHT side of each column and begin on the RIGHT side of the page.

Part A

Directions: This part consists of a number of incomplete statements, each having four suggested completions. Select the most appropriate completion and fill in the corresponding circle on the answer sheet.

1. כַּאֲשֶׁר מְטַיְּלִים בִּירוּשָׁלַיִם ______ לְבַקֵּר גַּם בַּכְּנֶסֶת.

(A) יָכוֹל
(B) כְּדֵי
(C) כְּדַאי
(D) רוֹצֶה

2. חֲבֶרְתִּי הָאַרְכֵאוֹלוֹגִית ______ תַּפְקִיד חָשׁוּב בְּמַחְלֶקֶת הָעַתִּיקוֹת.

(A) הִתְקַבְּלָה
(B) מִתְקַבֶּלֶת
(C) קִבְּלָה
(D) מְקַבֶּלֶת

3. כַּאֲשֶׁר נוֹסְעִים בְּאוֹטוֹבּוּס מִתֵּל-אָבִיב לִירוּשָׁלַיִם, ______ בָּעִיר רַמְלָה.

(A) אוֹסְפִים
(B) עוֹבְרִים
(C) בּוֹדְקִים
(D) שׁוֹמְרִים

4. כָּל הַסְּפָרִים עַל הַנּוֹשֵׂא הַזֶּה ______ מֵהַסִּפְרִיָּה.

(A) נֶעֶלְמוּ
(B) נִכְנְסוּ
(C) נִקְרְעוּ
(D) נִרְשְׁמוּ

5. כַּאֲשֶׁר הִסְתַּיְּמָה הַמִּלְחָמָה, חָתְמוּ שְׁתֵּי הַמְּדִינוֹת עַל ______ שָׁלוֹם.

(A) עִתּוֹן
(B) הֶסְכֵּם
(C) הֶסְבֵּר
(D) סִפּוּר

6. אִם אַף אֶחָד לֹא רוֹצֶה לִקְרֹא אֶת הַסֵּפֶר הַזֶּה, אֲנִי ______ אוֹתוֹ לַסִּפְרִיָּה.

(A) הֶחְזַרְתִּי
(B) חוֹזֵר
(C) אֶחְזוֹר
(D) אַחְזִיר

3YAC

GO ON TO THE NEXT PAGE

7. דִּינָה וְדַלְיָה הֶחְלִיטוּ ______ בְּכָל יוֹם שֵׁנִי.

(A) לִפְגֹּשׁ
(B) לְהִפָּגֵשׁ
(C) נִפְגְּשׁוּ
(D) פָּגְשׁוּ

8. אֲנָשִׁים רַבִּים חוֹשְׁבִים שֶׁלַּמֶּמְשָׁלָה אֵין זְכוּת ______ בְּעִנְיְנֵי הַפְּרָט.

(A) לְהִתְעָרֵב
(B) לְהִתְפַּלֵּא
(C) לְהִתְקַשֵּׁר
(D) לְהִתְעַשֵּׁר

9. הָרַעַשׁ בַּחוּץ הִפְרִיעַ לָנוּ ______ בַּלִּמּוּדִים.

(A) לִלְמֹד
(B) לִקְרֹא
(C) לְהִתְרַכֵּז
(D) לְהִתְגַּבֵּר

10. אֲנִי אֲנַסֶּה לְהַגִּיעַ לַמּוּזֵאוֹן מֻקְדָּם כְּדֵי לִקְנוֹת כַּרְטִיסֵי ______.

(A) שְׁמִירָה
(B) כְּנִיסָה
(C) סְגִירָה
(D) בְּחִירָה

11. נְשִׂיא מְדִינַת יִשְׂרָאֵל יְקַבֵּל בְּבֵיתוֹ ______ מִכָּל עֵדָה בְּיִשְׂרָאֵל לִכְבוֹד הַשָּׁנָה הַחֲדָשָׁה.

(A) נָצִיג
(B) נָבִיא
(C) שׁוֹפֵט
(D) שַׁלִּיט

12. הַאִם יֵשׁ ______ שֶׁתָּבוֹאִי לַמְּסִבָּה הָעֶרֶב?

(A) שִׁנּוּי
(B) סִכּוּי
(C) חֵשֶׁק
(D) נִסָּיוֹן

13. דָּן נִרְאֶה הַיּוֹם בְּדִיּוּק כְּמוֹ שֶׁהָיָה נִרְאֶה לִפְנֵי עֶשְׂרִים שָׁנָה. הוּא בִּכְלָל לֹא ______.

(A) יִשְׁתַּנֶּה
(B) מְשַׁנֶּה
(C) שִׁנָּה
(D) הִשְׁתַּנָּה

14. בִּזְמַן חוּפְשַׁת הַקַּיִץ מַגִּיעִים לְנְיוּ-יוֹרְק תַּיָּרִים מֵאֲרָצוֹת ______.

(A) אַחֲרוֹנוֹת
(B) קוֹדְמוֹת
(C) רִאשׁוֹנוֹת
(D) שׁוֹנוֹת

GO ON TO THE NEXT PAGE

15. בְּכָל יוֹם הַמַּדְעָנִים _____ מֵידָע חָדָשׁ בַּמֶּחְקָרִים שֶׁלָּהֶם.
    (A) מְצַוִּים
    (B) מְצַפִּים
    (C) מְקַיְּמִים
    (D) מְגַלִּים

16. יְרוּשָׁלַיִם הִיא עִיר מְפוּרְסֶמֶת בַּמְּקוֹמוֹת _____ שֶׁבָּהּ.
    (A) הַקְּדוֹשׁוֹת
    (B) קְדוֹשׁוֹת
    (C) קְדוֹשִׁים
    (D) הַקְּדוֹשִׁים

17. דִּינָה קָנְתָה אֶת הַסֵּפֶר, כִּי הִיא שָׁמְעָה _____הַרְבֵּה דְּבָרִים טוֹבִים.
    (A) מִמֶּנּוּ
    (B) אֵלָיו
    (C) אוֹתוֹ
    (D) עָלָיו

18. בַּזְּמַן הָאַחֲרוֹן_____ הַמַּחְשֵׁב לִכְלִי חָשׁוּב וְשִׁמּוּשִׁי.
    (A) לַהֲפוֹךְ
    (B) הָפַךְ
    (C) מִתְהַפֵּךְ
    (D) יִתְהַפֵּךְ

19. הָעִיר_____ מְאֹד כִּי בָּאוּ לְשָׁם הַרְבֵּה תּוֹשָׁבִים חֲדָשִׁים.
    (A) פִּתְּחָה
    (B) הִתְפַּתְּחָה
    (C) נִפְתְּחָה
    (D) פָּתְחָה

20. הִיא הוֹדִיעָה לוֹ שֶׁאֵין לָהּ_____ לָצֵאת אִתּוֹ.
    (A) תְּנַאי
    (B) פְּנַאי
    (C) עִתִּים
    (D) זְמַנִּים

21. הָאוּנִיבֶרְסִיטָה הָעִבְרִית בִּירוּשָׁלַיִם_____ בִּשְׁנַת 1925 .
    (A) נוֹלְדָה
    (B) נוֹסְדָה
    (C) נוֹסְפָה
    (D) נוֹעֲדָה

22. _____שֶׁיָּרְדוּ גְּשָׁמִים רַבִּים בַּשָּׁבוּעוֹת הָאַחֲרוֹנִים, עֲדַיִן קַיָּם מַחְסוֹר חָמוּר בְּמַיִם בְּרֹב חֶלְקֵי הָאָרֶץ.
    (A) בִּגְלַל
    (B) מִפְּנֵי
    (C) לְעֻמַּת
    (D) אַף-עַל-פִּי

GO ON TO THE NEXT PAGE

23. שָׂרָה ______ בְּסַבּוֹן מְיֻחָד, כִּי עוֹרָהּ רָגִישׁ.

(A) שִׁמְשָׁה

(B) לְהִשְׁתַּמֵּשׁ

(C) מִשְׁתַּמֶּשֶׁת

(D) מְשַׁמֶּשֶׁת

24. יוֹפִי הָאָרֶץ ______ אֵלֶיהָ מְבַקְּרִים רַבִּים.

(A) מוֹשֵׁךְ

(B) מַמְשִׁיךְ

(C) מוֹשֶׁכֶת

(D) מַמְשִׁיכָה

25. בַּבְּחִירוֹת הִצְבַּעְתִּי ______ הַנָּשִׂיא הֶחָדָשׁ.

(A) עַל

(B) אֶל

(C) בִּגְלַל

(D) בְּעַד

GO ON TO THE NEXT PAGE

Part B

Directions: In each of the following passages, there are numbered blanks indicating that words or phrases have been omitted. For each numbered blank, four completions are provided, of which only one is correct. First read through the entire passage. Then for each numbered blank, choose the completion that is most appropriate and fill in the corresponding circle on the answer sheet.

שְׁלוֹשָׁה אַחִים, רְאוּבֵן שִׁמְעוֹן וְדָנִי, בָּאוּ לְנְיוּ-יוֹרְק (26)_____ בָּעִיר הַגְּדוֹלָה. הֵם שָׂכְרוּ חֶדֶר בַּקּוֹמָה הַשִּׁשִּׁים שֶׁל (27)_____ גָּדוֹל. רְאוּבֵן נָתַן אֶת הַמַּפְתֵּחַ לְדָנִי וְאָמַר לוֹ (28) _____ הֵיטֵב עַל הַמַּפְתֵּחַ. אַחֲרֵי כֵן הֵם יָרְדוּ בַּמַּעֲלִית וְיָצְאוּ לְטַיֵּל בָּעִיר. הֵם טִיְּלוּ כָּל הַיּוֹם, וּכְשֶׁחָזְרוּ רָאוּ שֶׁהַמַּעֲלִית לֹא (29)_____. הֵם הִתְחִילוּ לַעֲלוֹת בָּרֶגֶל לַקּוֹמָה הַשִּׁשִּׁים. רְאוּבֵן אָמַר: ״יֵשׁ לִי (30)_____ טוֹב. עַד הַקּוֹמָה הָעֶשְׂרִים אֲנִי אָשִׁיר שִׁירִים יָפִים. עַד הַקּוֹמָה הָאַרְבָּעִים שִׁמְעוֹן יְסַפֵּר (31) _____ מַצְחִיקִים, וְעַד הַקּוֹמָה הַשִּׁשִּׁים דָּנִי יְתָאֵר מִקְרִים עֲצוּבִים״, וְכֻלָּם הִסְכִּימוּ. אֲבָל כְּשֶׁהִגִּיעַ תּוֹרוֹ שֶׁל דָּנִי הוּא אָמַר: ״רַק דָּבָר עָצוּב אֶחָד קָרָה, (32) _____ אֶת הַמַּפְתֵּחַ לְמַטָּה״.

26. (A) לְבַקֵּר
(B) לִרְאוֹת
(C) לְחַפֵּשׂ
(D) לְהִסְתַּכֵּל

27. (A) מָלוֹן
(B) מָכוֹן
(C) בִּנְיָן
(D) מָדוֹר

28. (A) לִשְׁבֹּר
(B) לִזְרֹק
(C) לִכְתֹּב
(D) לִשְׁמֹר

29. (A) פּוֹעֶלֶת
(B) עוֹמֶדֶת
(C) נִקְשֶׁרֶת
(D) נִכְנֶסֶת

30. (A) הִגָּיוֹן
(B) חֲלוֹם
(C) רַעְיוֹן
(D) חֶשְׁבּוֹן

31. (A) חִבּוּרִים
(B) שִׁעוּרִים
(C) לִמּוּדִים
(D) סִפּוּרִים

32. (A) סָגַרְתִּי
(B) שָׁכַחְתִּי
(C) חָזַרְתִּי
(D) גָּמַרְתִּי

GO ON TO THE NEXT PAGE

בְּאֵיזוֹ שָׂפָה יְדַבְּרוּ?

לִפְנֵי שָׁנָה טַנְיָה (33) ______לָאָרֶץ מֵרוּסְיָה וְאָלֶכְּס בָּא מֵאַנְגְּלִיָּה. הֵם (34) ______ בְּיִשְׂרָאֵל וְהִתְחַתְּנוּ, וְעַכְשָׁו (35)______ לָהֶם בַּת נֶחְמָדָה. בְּאֵיזוֹ שָׂפָה יְדַבְּרוּ אֶל הַתִּינֹקֶת? דּוֹדָה אַחַת אוֹמֶרֶת שֶׁיְּדַבְּרוּ בְּאַנְגְּלִית כִּי זֹאת שָׂפָה חֲשׁוּבָה בָּעוֹלָם. דּוֹדָה אַחֶרֶת אוֹמֶרֶת שֶׁיְּדַבְּרוּ בְּרוּסִית, הֲרֵי (36) ______מְאֹד שֶׁאִמָּא תְּדַבֵּר אֶל הַיַּלְדָּה בַּשָּׂפָה שֶׁלָּהּ. הִיא צְרִיכָה לָשִׁיר לָהּ שִׁירִים (37)______ אוֹתָהּ אֶת הַמִּלִּים הָרִאשׁוֹנוֹת. הַדֶּרֶךְ הַטּוֹבָה בְּיוֹתֵר הִיא בַּשָּׂפָה הַטִּבְעִית שֶׁל הָאֵם. אֲבָל הֵם הֶחְלִיטוּ לֹא לְדַבֵּר בְּרוּסִית וְלֹא לְדַבֵּר בְּאַנְגְּלִית. הֵם עַכְשָׁו בְּיִשְׂרָאֵל וְהַיַּלְדָּה צְרִיכָה לִשְׁמֹעַ עִבְרִית מִן הַיּוֹם הָרִאשׁוֹן.

33. (A) עוֹלָה
(B) עָלְתָה
(C) עֲלִיָּה
(D) תַּעֲלֶה

34. (A) פָּגְשׁוּ
(B) יִפְגְּשׁוּ
(C) נִפְגְּשׁוּ
(D) יִפָּגְשׁוּ

35. (A) יָלְדָה
(B) הוֹלִידָה
(C) נוֹלֶדֶת
(D) נוֹלְדָה

36. (A) חָשׁוּב
(B) חָשְׁבוּ
(C) נֶחְשָׁב
(D) חֲשׁוּבָה

37. (A) וּלְלַמֵּד
(B) וְלִלְמֹד
(C) וְלִמְדָה
(D) וְלִמֵּד

GO ON TO THE NEXT PAGE

דִּינָה הִיא רַק בַּת עֶשֶׂר וְהִיא כְּבָר (38) ______ בָּאוּנִיבֶרְסִיטָה. בִּגְלַל גִּילָהּ הַצָּעִיר הִיא (39) ______ לַלִּמּוּדִים כָּל יוֹם כְּשֶׁאִמָּהּ (40)______ אוֹתָהּ. לֹא כָּל הַסְּטוּדֶנְטִים הַמְּבֻגָּרִים (41)______ מִכָּךְ שֶׁיַּלְדָּה כָּל כָּךְ (42) ______לוֹמֶדֶת בְּאוֹתָהּ כִּתָּה אִתָּם. "אִם הִיא (43) ______ צִיּוּנִים יוֹתֵר טוֹבִים מִמֶּנִּי אֲנִי עוֹזֶבֶת אֶת הָאוּנִיבֶרְסִיטָה", אָמְרָה אַחַת הַסְּטוּדֶנְטִיּוֹת. "קָשֶׁה לִי (44)______ שֶׁיַּלְדָּה בַּת עֶשֶׂר לוֹמֶדֶת אִתִּי בְּאוֹתָהּ כִּתָּה וַאֲנִי בַּת עֶשְׂרִים", הִיא הוֹסִיפָה.

וְדִינָה אוֹמֶרֶת: "אֲנִי רוֹצָה (45)______ אֵלַי כְּמוֹ אֶל סְטוּדֶנְטִית רְגִילָה".

38. (A) לוֹמֶדֶת
    (B) חוֹשֶׁבֶת
    (C) לַמְדָנִית
    (D) יַדְעָנִית

39. (A) מַצִּיעָה
    (B) מַגִּיעָה
    (C) מַבִּיעָה
    (D) מוֹדִיעָה

40. (A) מְבִיאָה
    (B) מַגִּישָׁה
    (C) מַשְׁפִּיעָה
    (D) מַחְלִיפָה

41. (A) רוֹצִים
    (B) מְרוּצִים
    (C) יִרְצוּ
    (D) רָצוּ

42. (A) עֲשִׁירָה
    (B) מְהִירָה
    (C) צְעִירָה
    (D) בְּהִירָה

43. (A) תְּקַבֵּל
    (B) תְּסַפֵּר
    (C) תְּחַבֵּר
    (D) תְּתָאֵר

44. (A) לְהַחְלִיט
    (B) לְהַזְמִין
    (C) לְהַאֲמִין
    (D) לְהַגְבִּיר

45. (A) שֶׁיִּשְׁמְעוּ
    (B) שֶׁיִּתְיַחֲסוּ
    (C) שֶׁיִּשְׁאֲלוּ
    (D) שֶׁיִּתְבַּקְּשׁוּ

GO ON TO THE NEXT PAGE

הָעִיר רוֹמָא הָיְתָה (46) ______ בַּחֲכָמֶיהָ. אֶחָד מֵהֶם בָּא לִירוּשָׁלַיִם וְרָצָה לִבְחֹן אֶת חָכְמָתָם (47) ______ יַלְדֵי יְרוּשָׁלַיִם. הָלַךְ הָאִישׁ וּפָגַשׁ (48)______ יֶלֶד קָטָן. נָתַן לוֹ שְׁקָלִים אֲחָדִים וּבִקֵּשׁ (49)______ לִקְנוֹת בֵּיצִים וּגְבִינוֹת. קָנָה הַיֶּלֶד גְּבִינוֹת (50) ______ בֵּיצִים וְנָתַן לָאִישׁ. שָׁאַל אוֹתוֹ הָאִישׁ: "הֲתוּכַל לְהַכִּיר אֵיזוֹ גְּבִינָה הִיא מֵעֵז לְבָנָה וְאֵיזוֹ מֵעֵז שְׁחוֹרָה?" עָנָה לוֹ הַיֶּלֶד: "אַתָּה (51)______ מִמֶּנִּי בְּשָׁנִים וּבְחָכְמָה; הַרְאֵה נָא לִי (52) ______ אֵיזוֹ בֵּיצָה הִיא שֶׁל תַּרְנְגֹלֶת לְבָנָה וְאֵיזוֹ שֶׁל שְׁחוֹרָה".

46. (A) מְפַרְנֶסֶת
(B) מְפוּזֶּרֶת
(C) מְפַרְסֶמֶת
(D) מְפוּרְסֶמֶת

47. (A) שֶׁל
(B) עִם
(C) אֵצֶל
(D) אֶל

48. (A) בְּמַקְלוֹ
(B) בְּדַלְתּוֹ
(C) בִּדְבָרוֹ
(D) בְּדַרְכּוֹ

49. (A) לוֹ
(B) מִמֶּנּוּ
(C) אֵלָיו
(D) אֶצְלוֹ

50. (A) וּשְׁנֵי
(B) וּשְׁנַיִם
(C) וּשְׁתַּיִם
(D) וּשְׁתֵּי

51. (A) גָּדוֹל
(B) אָרֹךְ
(C) יָשָׁן
(D) עַתִּיק

52. (A) אֵיפֹה
(B) קוֹדֶם
(C) אֵיךְ
(D) לִפְנֵי

GO ON TO THE NEXT PAGE

אֲנַחְנוּ כָּל כָּךְ (53) ______ לִשְׁמוֹת הֶחֳדָשִׁים
בַּלּוּחַ הָעִבְרִי --תִּשְׁרֵי, חֶשְׁוָן, כִּסְלֵו, עַד שֶׁלִּפְעָמִים
אָנוּ (54) ______ שֶׁאֵלֶּה אֵינָם שֵׁמוֹת עִבְרִיִּים
(55)______ שֵׁמוֹת בַּבְלִיִּים (56) ______
לַלּוּחַ הָעִבְרִי בִּזְמַן שֶׁהָעָם יָשַׁב בַּגָּלוּת. בַּתַּנַ"ךְ
(57)______ שֵׁמוֹת אֲחֵרִים כְּמוֹ "יֶרַח זִיו" אוֹ
"הַחֹדֶשׁ הַשְּׁבִיעִי". נִשְׁאֶלֶת הַשְּׁאֵלָה אִם הָיָה
קַיָּם לוּחַ שָׁנָה קָדוּם.

בַּחֲפִירוֹת הָעִיר גֶּזֶר שֶׁבְּהָרֵי יְהוּדָה נִתְגַּלְּתָה
בִּשְׁנַת 1908 אֶבֶן (58) ______ חֲרוּטִים שֵׁמוֹת
שֶׁל שְׁמוֹנָה חֳדָשִׁים, וְזֶהוּ כַּנִּרְאֶה לוּחַ שָׁנָה עַתִּיק.
הַלּוּחַ הוּא מִתְּקוּפַת דָּוִד וּשְׁלֹמֹה. הַכְּתָב שֶׁבּוֹ
הִשְׁתַּמְּשׁוּ אָז בְּאֶרֶץ-יִשְׂרָאֵל הָיָה (59)______
לָעִבְרִים, לַכְּנַעֲנִים, לַמּוֹאָבִים וְלָאֱדוֹמִים.
הַלּוּחַ נִמְצָא כַּיּוֹם בְּמוּזֵאוֹן בְּטוּרְקִיָּה.

53. (A) רְגִילִים
(B) מְרֻגָּלִים
(C) מַרְגִּילִים
(D) מִתְרַגְּלִים

54. (A) שׁוֹמְרִים
(B) שׁוֹכְחִים
(C) שׁוֹפְטִים
(D) שׁוֹאֲלִים

55. (A) אֵלֶּה
(B) אִלּוּ
(C) אֶל
(D) אֶלָּא

56. (A) שֶׁהִתְכַּנְּסוּ
(B) שֶׁנִּכְנְסוּ
(C) שֶׁכִּנְּסוּ
(D) שֶׁנִּכְנָסִים

57. (A) נִזְכָּרִים
(B) נִזְכָּרוֹת
(C) מַזְכִּירוֹת
(D) זוֹכְרִים

58. (A) שֶׁאֵלֶיהָ
(B) שֶׁאֶצְלָהּ
(C) שֶׁעָלֶיהָ
(D) שֶׁבִּגְלָלָהּ

59. (A) מִשְׁתַּתֵּף
(B) שׁוּתָף
(C) מְשֻׁתָּף
(D) הִשְׁתַּתֵּף

GO ON TO THE NEXT PAGE

Part C

Directions: Read the following passages carefully for comprehension. Each passage is followed by a number of questions or incomplete statements. Select the answer or completion that is best according to the passage and fill in the corresponding circle on the answer sheet.

הַמַּשְׁקֶה הָאֲמֶרִיקָאִי קוֹקָה-קוֹלָה מוּכָּר בְּכָל הָעוֹלָם, מוּכָּר כִּמְעַט יוֹתֵר מֵאֲמֶרִיקָה עַצְמָהּ. אֲבָל לֹא יָדוּעַ שֶׁהֵכִינוּ וּמָכְרוּ אֶת הַכּוֹס הָרִאשׁוֹנָה שֶׁל קוֹקָה-קוֹלָה בְּבֵית הַמִּרְקַחַת שֶׁל יְהוּדִי אֲמֶרִיקָאִי בְּשֵׁם יוֹסֵף גֵ׳ייקוֹבְּס (Jacobs). אֶת הַמַּשְׁקֶה הִמְצִיא רוֹקֵחַ בְּשֵׁם פֶּמְבֶּרְטוֹן (Pemberton), אֲבָל לֹא הָיָה לוֹ כֶּסֶף אוֹ מָקוֹם לְיַצֵּר אוֹתוֹ. גֵ׳ייקוֹבְּס הִצְטָרֵף אֵלָיו וְהֵם הִתְחִילוּ לְיַצֵּר קוֹקָה-קוֹלָה בַּמַּרְתֵּף שֶׁל בֵּית הַמִּרְקַחַת שֶׁל גֵ׳ייקוֹבְּס.

כְּדַאי לְצַיֵּן שֶׁבַּיָּמִים הָהֵם נָהֲגוּ לִמְכֹּר בְּבָתֵּי מִרְקַחַת לֹא רַק תְּרוּפוֹת אֶלָּא גַּם אוֹכֶל קַל וּשְׁתִיָּה. בְּהַתְחָלָה הַטַּעַם שֶׁל הַמַּשְׁקֶה הָיָה מַר וְלֹא צִפּוּ לְהַצְלָחָתוֹ. לָכֵן מָכַר מַר גֵ׳ייקוֹבְּס אֶת חֶלְקוֹ בָּעֵסֶק. לְעֻמַּת זאת מַר פֶּמְבֶּרְטוֹן הִמְשִׁיךְ לְפַתֵּחַ אֶת הָעֵסֶק. הוּא הוֹסִיף סֻכָּר וְאָרַז אֶת הַמַּשְׁקֶה בְּבַקְבּוּק מְיֻחָד, וְעַד מְהֵרָה כָּבְשָׁה הַקּוֹקָה-קוֹלָה אֶת הָעוֹלָם וְהִיא נִמְכֶּרֶת בְּהַצְלָחָה רַבָּה עַד הַיּוֹם הַזֶּה.

60. לְפִי הַקֶּטַע, בְּבֵית מִרְקַחַת אֲמֶרִיקָאִי אִי אֶפְשָׁר הָיָה לִקְנוֹת

(A) תְּרוּפוֹת

(B) דִּבְרֵי אוֹכֶל

(C) מַשְׁקָאוֹת קַלִּים

(D) צַעֲצוּעִים

61. מַדּוּעַ לֹא זָכָה הַמַּשְׁקֶה לְהַצְלָחָה בַּהַתְחָלָה ?

(A) לֹא הָיְתָה פִּרְסֹמֶת טוֹבָה

(B) הָיָה מָתוֹק מִדַּי

(C) הוּא לֹא הָיָה טָעִים

(D) הוּא נִמְכַּר בְּבֵית מִרְקַחַת

62. יוֹסֵף גֵ׳ייקוֹבְּס הִפְסִיד אֶת הַהִזְדַּמְּנוּת

(A) לְהַצְלִיחַ בַּעֲסָקִים

(B) לְטַיֵּל בָּעוֹלָם

(C) לַעֲבֹד בְּבֵית מִרְקַחַת

(D) לִמְכֹּר מַשְׁקָאוֹת

GO ON TO THE NEXT PAGE

מַרְטִין לוּתֶר קִינְג הַשְּׁלִישִׁי, בְּנוֹ שֶׁל הַמַּנְהִיג הַשָּׁחוֹר הַמְּפֻרְסָם, בִּקֵּר לָאַחֲרוֹנָה בְּיִשְׂרָאֵל, כְּדֵי לְהַכִּיר אֶת הַמַּצָּב בָּאָרֶץ. הַבִּקּוּר נֶעֱרַךְ בְּהַזְמָנַת אִרְגּוּן "בְּנֵי בְּרִית".

הוּא טִיֵּל בָּאָרֶץ בְּמֶשֶׁךְ שְׁמוֹנָה יָמִים וְנִפְגַּשׁ עִם שָׁמִיר, פֶּרֶס וּפְעִילִים לְמַעַן זְכֻיּוֹת הָאֶזְרָח שֶׁל יְהוּדֵי רוּסְיָה. הוּא נָטַע עֵץ בְּיַעַר הַנּוֹשֵׂא אֶת שֵׁם אָבִיו, בְּאֵזוֹר הַגָּלִיל.

"עֵץ זֶה", אָמַר הַבֵּן, "מְסַמֵּל אֶת הֶמְשֵׁךְ מִפְעָלוֹ שֶׁל אָבִי".

63. לְפִי הַקֶּטַע, מַרְטִין לוּתֶר קִינְג הַשְּׁלִישִׁי בָּא לְיִשְׂרָאֵל כְּדֵי

(A) לְקַיֵּם אֶת הַבְטָחָתוֹ לְאָבִיו

(B) לְבַקֵּר בְּהָרֵי הַגָּלִיל

(C) לִפְגֹּשׁ מַנְהִיגִים יִשְׂרְאֵלִיִּים

(D) לִלְמֹד עַל הַחַיִּים בְּיִשְׂרָאֵל

64. הוּא נָטַע עֵץ בְּיַעַר

(A) "מִפְעַל הַגָּלִיל"

(B) "מַרְטִין לוּתֶר קִינְג"

(C) "בְּנֵי בְּרִית"

(D) "יַהֲדוּת רוּסְיָה

65. מַה מְּסַמֵּל הָעֵץ שֶׁהוּא נָטַע ?

(A) אֶת מְדִינַת יִשְׂרָאֵל

(B) אֶת חֲלוֹמוֹ שֶׁל אָבִיו

(C) אֶת יְהוּדֵי אַרְצוֹת הַבְּרִית

(D) אֶת עֲבוֹדַת "בְּנֵי בְּרִית"

GO ON TO THE NEXT PAGE

משה ושרה כהן
מודיעים בשמחה על הולדת התאומים
אחים לרחל
הברית תתקיים ביום ג׳, 12 בספטמבר 1995
בשעה 10 לפנה״צ בביתנו
ברחוב קפלן 5, קרית שמונה
נשמח לראותכם

66. על מה המודעה ?

(A) על חגיגת יום הולדת
(B) על הולדת שני בנים
(C) על חגיגת אירוסין
(D) על חגיגה לרחל

67. לאן מוזמנים האורחים ?

(A) לבית משפחת כהן
(B) לבית משפחת קפלן
(C) לבית החולים
(D) לבית של רחל

GO ON TO THE NEXT PAGE

TA TEL-AVIV

שרות מוניות תל-אביב

הראשון, הגדול והפעיל ביותר בניו-יורק

מחפש נהגים מקצועיים, זהירים ומנומסים,
בעלי רכב חדיש.

* שעות עבודה - **24** שעות ביממה
* קהל לקוחות גדול
* הנהלה בעלת נסיון וידע מקצועי
* הכנסה גבוהה

בדבר פרטים נא לפנות ישירות לכתובתנו:

139 1st Ave (bet. 8-9 St)

לבקש את יונתן או חגית.

68. מי מתבקש לענות למודעה ?
(A) שירות מוניות
(B) נוסעים לתל-אביב
(C) נהגים
(D) לקוחות

69. מה מבטיחה המודעה ?
(A) משכורת טובה
(B) מכוניות חדשות
(C) נסיון מעניין
(D) עבודה קלה

GO ON TO THE NEXT PAGE

האם המחשב שלך דובר עברית?

עכשיו יוכלו ילדיך ללמוד עברית בקלות ובכיף

אליעזר בן יהודה (הנכבד) מלמד
בעזרת המחשב כיצד לדבר,
לקרוא ולכתוב עברית.
התוכנה צבעונית ומעניינת
ומתאימה את עצמה לקצב
האישי של התלמיד.

אין צורך בקלטות, ספרים או וידיאו. המחשב עושה הכל עבור $99.95

אפשר לרכוש דיסק ללימוד לבר-מצווה

התקשר 1-800-555-4242

24 שעות ביממה

(24 Hours)

70. מה מציעה המודעה?

(A) קלטות בעברית

(B) וידיאו בעברית

(C) תוכנה שמלמדת עברית

(D) מחשב שמלמד לבר-מצוה

71. לפי המודעה, כדי להשתמש בתוכנה צריך

(A) לקרוא ספרים

(B) מכשיר וידיאו

(C) רק מחשב

(D) להכיר את בן יהודה

GO ON TO THE NEXT PAGE

זְקֵנָה אַחַת, מִזְּקֵנוֹת הָעִיר צְפַת, נִפְטְרָה לִפְנֵי כַּמָּה יָמִים. הִיא בִּקְּשָׁה לְהִקָּבֵר בְּבֵית-הַקְּבָרוֹת הַיָּשָׁן שֶׁל צְפַת, לְיַד קֶבֶר בִּתָּהּ, שֶׁמֵּתָה לִפְנֵי שְׁלוֹשִׁים וָשֵׁשׁ שָׁנִים.

אַנְשֵׁי "חֶבְרָה קַדִּישָׁא" לֹא הִסְכִּימוּ לִקְבֹּר שָׁם אֶת הָאִשָּׁה, מִפְּנֵי שֶׁלֹּא קוֹבְרִים יוֹתֵר בְּבֵית-הַקְּבָרוֹת הַיָּשָׁן.

בְּנֵי מִשְׁפַּחְתָּהּ שֶׁל הַזְּקֵנָה אָמְרוּ, שֶׁהִיא קָנְתָה אֶת חֶלְקַת הַקֶּבֶר לִפְנֵי שְׁלוֹשִׁים שָׁנָה, וּבִקְּשָׁה מֵהֶם לִקְבֹּר אוֹתָהּ רַק שָׁם. לֹא הָיוּ לָהֶם הוֹכָחוֹת בִּכְתָב, אַךְ הָיְתָה לָהֶם הוֹכָחָה אַחֶרֶת: כַּאֲשֶׁר קָנְתָה הָאִשָּׁה אֶת הַקֶּבֶר, הִיא הֶחְבִּיאָה בְּתוֹכוֹ בַּקְבּוּק שֶׁמֶן כְּסִימָן שֶׁזֶּה הַקֶּבֶר שֶׁקָּנְתָה.

אַנְשֵׁי "חֶבְרָה קַדִּישָׁא" שָׁמְעוּ אֶת הַדְּבָרִים וְאָמְרוּ שֶׁיְּחַפְּשׂוּ אֶת הַבַּקְבּוּק. אִם הֵם יִמְצְאוּ אֶת הַבַּקְבּוּק בַּקֶּבֶר יִהְיֶה זֶה סִימָן שֶׁהַקֶּבֶר שַׁיָּךְ לַזְּקֵנָה וְהִיא תִּקָּבֵר בְּחֶלְקָהּ. לְאַחַר חִפּוּשִׂים הֵם מָצְאוּ אֶת הַבַּקְבּוּק. הָאִשָּׁה נִקְבְּרָה כְּפִי שֶׁבִּקְּשָׁה, לְיַד קֶבֶר בִּתָּהּ, וּבְנֵי הַמִּשְׁפָּחָה לָקְחוּ אִתָּם אֶת בַּקְבּוּק הַשֶּׁמֶן כִּסְגוּלָּה לְרִפּוּי מַחֲלוֹת.

72. מַדּוּעַ רָצְתָה הַזְּקֵנָה לְהִקָּבֵר דַּוְקָא בְּאוֹתוֹ מָקוֹם ?

(A) כִּי בַּעֲלָהּ נִקְבַּר בְּבֵית הַקְּבָרוֹת הַיָּשָׁן
(B) בִּגְלַל הַקִּרְבָה לְקֶבֶר אֶחָד מִיְּלָדֶיהָ
(C) בִּגְלַל הַקִּרְבָה לְבֵיתָהּ בִּצְפַת
(D) כִּי הִיא אָהֲבָה אֶת בֵּית הַקְּבָרוֹת הַיָּשָׁן

73. מַדּוּעַ הָיוּ לַמִּשְׁפָּחָה קְשָׁיִים ?

(A) כִּי עַכְשָׁו קוֹבְרִים בְּבֵית הַקְּבָרוֹת הֶחָדָשׁ
(B) כִּי לֹא הָיָה לָהֶם כֶּסֶף לִקְבוּרָה
(C) כִּי בַּקְבּוּק הַשֶּׁמֶן אָבַד
(D) כִּי לֹא מָצְאוּ אֶת קִבְרָהּ שֶׁל הַבַּת

74. מֶה עָשְׂתָה הַזְּקֵנָה בְּבַקְבּוּק הַשֶּׁמֶן ?

(A) הִיא הִשְׁתַּמְּשָׁה בּוֹ כְּדֵי לְרַפֵּא אֶת בִּתָּהּ.
(B) הִיא שָׁמְרָה אוֹתוֹ כְּדֵי שֶׁיִּקְבְּרוּ אוֹתוֹ.
(C) הִיא קָבְרָה אוֹתוֹ בֶּחָצֵר בֵּיתָהּ.
(D) הִיא שָׂמָה אוֹתוֹ בְּתוֹךְ הַקֶּבֶר.

75. הַשֵּׁם הַמַּתְאִים בְּיוֹתֵר לַסִּפּוּר הוּא

(A) הַהִיסְטוֹרְיָה שֶׁל צְפַת
(B) בִּקּוּר קְרוֹבֵי הַמִּשְׁפָּחָה
(C) תְּמוּנַת בַּקְבּוּק הַשֶּׁמֶן
(D) הַסִּימָן שֶׁעָזַר

GO ON TO THE NEXT PAGE

הַזַּמֶּרֶת שׁוּלִי נָתָן

שְׁמָהּ הָיָה פַּעַם שׁוּלָה בָּאוּרְפְרוֹיְנְד. כְּשֶׁהָיְתָה לְזַמֶּרֶת בִּקְּשׁוּ מִמֶּנָּה לְהַחְלִיף אֶת שְׁמָהּ לְשֵׁם עִבְרִי פָּשׁוּט, וְאָז הִיא בָּחֲרָה בַּשֵּׁם נָתָן, שֶׁהוּא שֵׁם הַמִּשְׁפָּחָה שֶׁל אִמָּהּ, חַוָּה נָתָן.

הַשִּׁיר שֶׁבִּזְכוּתוֹ הָפְכָה שׁוּלִי נָתָן לְזַמֶּרֶת מְפֻרְסֶמֶת אַחֲרֵי מִלְחֶמֶת שֵׁשֶׁת הַיָּמִים, הוּא "יְרוּשָׁלַיִם שֶׁל זָהָב", אוּלַי הַשִּׁיר הַמְּפֻרְסָם בְּיוֹתֵר אַחֲרֵי "הַתִּקְוָה". הָיוּ אֲפִילוּ כָּאֵלֶּה שֶׁהִצִּיעוּ לַהֲפֹךְ אוֹתוֹ לַהִמְנוֹן הַלְּאֻמִּי בִּמְקוֹם "הַתִּקְוָה".

בַּשָּׁנִים הָאַחֲרוֹנוֹת לֹא שָׁמַעְנוּ מִמֶּנָּה שִׁירִים חֲדָשִׁים. אֲבָל לָאַחֲרוֹנָה הִיא הִתְחִילָה שׁוּב לְהוֹפִיעַ עַל בָּמוֹת קְטַנּוֹת וְגַם קִבְּלָה הַזְמָנוֹת לְהוֹפִיעַ בְּחוּץ לָאָרֶץ. הִיא הוֹצִיאָה לֹא מִזְּמַן שְׁתֵּי קַלָּטוֹת וּבָהֶן שִׁירִים חֲדָשִׁים וּמְחֻדָּשִׁים.

שׁוּלִי חַיָּה עִם בַּעֲלָהּ וַחֲמֵשֶׁת יַלְדֵיהֶם. שׁוּלִי מַסְבִּירָה: "בְּמֶשֶׁךְ שְׁמוֹנֶה שָׁנִים גִּדַּלְתִּי אֶת יְלָדַי וְהָיִיתִי כָּל כָּךְ מְאֻשֶּׁרֶת שֶׁהַשִּׁירָה וְהַהוֹפָעוֹת כְּאִלּוּ נִשְׁכְּחוּ מִמֶּנִּי. אֲבָל לִפְנֵי שְׁנָתַיִם, בַּיּוֹם שֶׁלָּקַחְתִּי אֶת בְּנִי בֶּן הַשְּׁנָתַיִם לְגַן הַיְּלָדִים, חָזַרְתִּי הַבַּיְתָה וּבְלִי לְהַרְגִּישׁ הוֹצֵאתִי אֶת הַגִּיטָרָה מֵחֲדַר הַשֵּׁנָה וְהִתְחַלְתִּי לָשִׁיר".

מַה דַּעְתָּהּ שֶׁל שׁוּלִי עַל הַצְלָחַת הַשִּׁיר "יְרוּשָׁלַיִם שֶׁל זָהָב"? תְּשׁוּבָתָהּ: "עַד הַיּוֹם לֹא נוֹתְנִים לִי לָרֶדֶת מִשּׁוּם בָּמָה, בָּאָרֶץ אוֹ בְּחוּץ לָאָרֶץ, בְּלִי לָשִׁיר גַּם אֶת "יְרוּשָׁלַיִם שֶׁל זָהָב". זֶה לִפְעָמִים מַפְרִיעַ לִי, וַאֲנִי רוֹצָה לוֹמַר לָאֲנָשִׁים: - יֵשׁ לִי עוֹד שִׁירִים - עִם זֹאת כָּל כָּךְ הַרְבֵּה דְּלָתוֹת נִפְתְּחוּ בְּפָנַי הוֹדוֹת לַשִּׁיר הַזֶּה, שֶׁאֲנִי מַרְגִּישָׁה אֶת עַצְמִי מְבֹרֶכֶת".

"הַאִם אַתְּ מְחַכָּה לְעוֹד אֵיזֶה "יְרוּשָׁלַיִם שֶׁל זָהָב"?

"בִּכְלָל לֹא" עוֹנָה שׁוּלִי.

76. לָמָּה שׁוּלִי שִׁנְּתָה אֶת שֵׁם מִשְׁפַּחְתָּהּ?

(A) כִּי הוּא הָיָה שֵׁם נְעוּרִים
(B) כִּי הִיא לֹא אָהֲבָה אוֹתוֹ
(C) כִּי אִמָּהּ בִּקְּשָׁה מִמֶּנָּה לְשַׁנּוֹת אוֹתוֹ
(D) כִּי שֵׁם קַל וְקָצָר חָשׁוּב לְפִרְסוּם

77. הַשִּׁיר "יְרוּשָׁלַיִם שֶׁל זָהָב" הָפַךְ

(A) לַהִמְנוֹן שֶׁל מְדִינַת יִשְׂרָאֵל
(B) לְשִׁיר יוֹתֵר מְפֻרְסָם מֵ"הַתִּקְוָה"
(C) לְשִׁיר מְפֻרְסָם כִּמְעַט כְּמוֹ "הַתִּקְוָה"
(D) לְשִׁיר מְפֻרְסָם רַק בְּחוּץ לָאָרֶץ

78. שׁוּלִי הִפְסִיקָה לָשִׁיר בְּמֶשֶׁךְ מִסְפַּר שָׁנִים כִּי

(A) הָיְתָה עֲסוּקָה בְּטִפּוּל בִּילָדֶיהָ
(B) הָיְתָה בְּחוּץ לָאָרֶץ וְלֹא הָיָה לָהּ זְמַן
(C) כֻּלָּם הִכִּירוּ אֶת הַשִּׁיר "יְרוּשָׁלַיִם שֶׁל זָהָב"
(D) הַקָּהָל לֹא אָהַב אֶת הַשִּׁירִים שֶׁלָּהּ

79. מָתַי חָזְרָה שׁוּלִי לָשִׁיר?

(A) אַחֲרֵי שֶׁהָיוּ לָהּ שְׁנֵי יְלָדִים
(B) אַחֲרֵי שֶׁשִּׁנְּתָה אֶת שְׁמָהּ
(C) כְּשֶׁבַּעֲלָהּ בִּקֵּשׁ מִמֶּנָּה
(D) כְּשֶׁבְּנָהּ הַצָּעִיר הָלַךְ לְגַן יְלָדִים

80. אֵיךְ הִשְׁפִּיעַ הַשִּׁיר "יְרוּשָׁלַיִם שֶׁל זָהָב" עַל שׁוּלִי?

(A) עָזַר לָהּ לְהִתְפַּרְסֵם
(B) גָּרַם לָהּ לְהַפְסִיק לָשִׁיר
(C) גָּרַם לָהּ לְחַכּוֹת לְשִׁירִים דּוֹמִים
(D) עָזַר לָהּ בְּגִדּוּל יְלָדֶיהָ

GO ON TO THE NEXT PAGE

אורן ואילן היו חברים טובים. הם למדו יחד ועזרו זה לזה בהכנת השיעורים. הם גם שיחקו ביחד בשכונה. בגלל החברות שביניהם גם ההורים התיידדו ובילו ביחד בחגים ובשמחות. יום אחד אורן ואילן רבו, וכשהלכו הביתה סיפרו להוריהם על הריב שהיה ביניהם. גם ההורים הצטרפו למריבה ולא דיברו ביניהם.

עבר זמן, הילדים השלימו והמשיכו להיות חברים טובים, אך ההורים היו עדיין ברוגז. השכנים התפלאו שההורים עדיין כעסו גם אחרי שהילדים השלימו ביניהם. כל משפחה חיכתה שהשנייה תעשה את הצעד הראשון להשלים.

לפני ראש השנה, כשכל אדם עושה את חשבון הנפש שלו, חשבו ההורים על הריב שהיה ביניהם וחיפשו דרך לחדש את יחסי החברות. בערב יום הכיפורים, בדיוק באותו זמן, יצאו ההורים מביתם לכיוון בית חבריהם. באמצע הדרך ניפגשו שתי המשפחות, התחבקו בשמחה ואיחלו זו לזו שנה טובה, שנת אושר ושלום. הילדים שהיו בדרכם לבית הכנסת, שמעו את הברכות וענו "אמן".

81. איך נוצר הקשר בין המשפחות ?
(A) האימהות היו אחיות
(B) הן גרו באותה עיר
(C) היו להן אותם שכנים
(D) הבנים היו ידידים

82. שתי המשפחות
(A) עבדו באותו בית
(B) חגגו ביחד
(C) נסעו יחד לחופשה
(D) רבו בזמן החג

83. המשפחות רבו ביניהן כי
(A) כל אחת רצתה אותו תפקיד
(B) שני הבנים רצו את המתנה
(C) היה ריב בין שני הבנים
(D) השכנים כעסו על הבנים

84. מדוע לא השלימו שתי המשפחות ביניהן ?
(A) אף אחת לא רצתה לוותר
(B) אף אחת לא רצתה בשלום
(C) כי הבנים עדיין כעסו
(D) כי זה לא היה חשוב

85. מה אפשר ללמוד מהסיפור הזה ?
(A) שצריך להתערב בחיי הילדים
(B) שלא צריך לוותר לשכנים
(C) שצריך להיות עקשן
(D) שצריך לסלוח זה לזה

STOP

IF YOU FINISH BEFORE TIME IS CALLED, YOU MAY CHECK YOUR WORK ON THIS TEST ONLY. DO NOT TURN TO ANY OTHER TEST IN THIS BOOK.

How to Score the SAT Subject Test in Modern Hebrew

When you take an actual SAT Subject Test in Modern Hebrew, your answer sheet will be "read" by a scanning machine that will record your responses to each question. Then a computer will compare your answers with the correct answers and produce your raw score. You get one point for each correct answer. For each wrong answer, you lose one-third of a point. Questions you omit (and any for which you mark more than one answer) are not counted. This raw score is converted to a scaled score that is reported to you and to the colleges you specify.

Worksheet 1. Finding Your Raw Test Score

STEP 1: Table A lists the correct answers for all the questions on the Subject Test in Modern Hebrew that is reproduced in this book. It also serves as a worksheet for you to calculate your raw score.

- Compare your answers with those given in the table.
- Put a check in the column marked "Right" if your answer is correct.
- Put a check in the column marked "Wrong" if your answer is incorrect.
- Leave both columns blank if you omitted the question.

STEP 2: Count the number of right answers.

Enter the total here: ____________________

STEP 3: Count the number of wrong answers.

Enter the total here: ____________________

STEP 4: Multiply the number of wrong answers by .333.

Enter the product here: ________________

STEP 5: Subtract the result obtained in Step 4 from the total you obtained in Step 2.

Enter the result here: __________________

STEP 6: Round the number obtained in Step 5 to the nearest whole number.

Enter the result here: __________________

The number you obtained in Step 6 is your raw score.

Table A

Answers to the Subject Test in Modern Hebrew, Form 3YAC, and Percentage of Students Answering Each Question Correctly									
Question Number	Correct Answer	Right	Wrong	Percentage of Students Answering the Question Correctly*	Question Number	Correct Answer	Right	Wrong	Percentage of Students Answering the Question Correctly*
1	C			72	33	B			91
2	C			89	34	C			27
3	B			90	35	D			71
4	A			73	36	A			74
5	B			93	37	A			85
6	D			57	38	A			97
7	B			38	39	B			82
8	A			55	40	A			85
9	C			52	41	B			41
10	B			91	42	C			97
11	A			50	43	A			98
12	B			48	44	C			95
13	D			52	45	B			83
14	D			85	46	D			83
15	D			46	47	A			71
16	D			60	48	D			94
17	D			90	49	B			78
18	B			81	50	D			70
19	B			38	51	A			82
20	B			33	52	B			82
21	B			39	53	A			59
22	D			72	54	B			84
23	C			90	55	D			72
24	A			23	56	B			63
25	D			57	57	A			66
26	A			82	58	C			83
27	A			74	59	C			76
28	D			97	60	D			71
29	A			84	61	C			82
30	C			98	62	A			69
31	D			96	63	D			73
32	B			97	64	B			65

Table A continued on next page

Table A continued from previous page

Question Number	Correct Answer	Right	Wrong	Percentage of Students Answering the Question Correctly*	Question Number	Correct Answer	Right	Wrong	Percentage of Students Answering the Question Correctly*
65	B			89	76	D			89
66	B			92	77	C			80
67	A			93	78	A			84
68	C			86	79	D			91
69	A			52	80	A			79
70	C			90	81	D			92
71	C			95	82	B			90
72	B			84	83	C			98
73	A			87	84	A			88
74	D			90	85	D			97
75	D			82					

* These percentages are based on an analysis of the answer sheets of a representative sample of 564 students who took the original form of this test in June 2002 (Sunday), and whose mean score was 573. They may be used as an indication of the relative difficulty of a particular question. Each percentage may also be used to predict the likelihood that a typical SAT Subject Test in Modern Hebrew candidate will answer that question correctly on this edition of the test.

Finding Your Scaled Score

When you take SAT Subject Tests, the scores sent to the colleges you specify are reported on the College Board scale, which ranges from 200–800. You can convert your practice test score to a scaled score by using Table B. To find your scaled score, locate your raw score in the left-hand column of Table B; the corresponding score in the right-hand column is your scaled score. For example, a raw score of 55 on this particular edition of the Subject Test in Modern Hebrew corresponds to a scaled score of 530.

Raw scores are converted to scaled scores to ensure that a score earned on any one edition of a particular Subject Test is comparable to the same scaled score earned on any other edition of the same Subject Test. Because some editions of the tests may be slightly easier or more difficult than others, College Board scaled scores are adjusted so that they indicate the same level of performance regardless of the edition of the test taken and the ability of the group that takes it. Thus, for example, a score of 400 on one edition of a test taken at a particular administration indicates the same level of achievement as a score of 400 on a different edition of the test taken at a different administration.

When you take the SAT Subject Tests during a national administration, your scores are likely to differ somewhat from the scores you obtain on the tests in this book. People perform at different levels at different times for reasons unrelated to the tests themselves. The precision of any test is also limited because it represents only a sample of all the possible questions that could be asked.

Table B

Scaled Score Conversion Table Subject Test in Modern Hebrew (Form 3YAC)					
Raw Score	Scaled Score	Raw Score	Scaled Score	Raw Score	Scaled Score
85	800	47	490	9	340
84	800	46	480	8	340
83	800	45	480	7	330
82	800	44	470	6	330
81	800	43	470	5	320
80	770	42	460	4	320
79	750	41	460	3	310
78	740	40	460	2	310
77	720	39	450	1	300
76	710	38	450	0	290
75	700	37	440	-1	290
74	680	36	440	-2	280
73	670	35	440	-3	280
72	660	34	430	-4	270
71	650	33	430	-5	260
70	640	32	430	-6	250
69	630	31	420	-7	250
68	620	30	420	-8	240
67	610	29	420	-9	230
66	610	28	410	-10	220
65	600	27	410	-11	210
64	590	26	410	-12	200
63	580	25	400	-13	200
62	580	24	400	-14	200
61	570	23	400	-15	200
60	560	22	390	-16	200
59	550	21	390	-17	200
58	550	20	390	-18	200
57	540	19	380	-19	200
56	530	18	380	-20	200
55	530	17	380	-21	200
54	520	16	370	-22	200
53	520	15	370	-23	200
52	510	14	360	-24	200
51	510	13	360	-25	200
50	500	12	360	-26	200
49	500	11	350	-27	200
48	490	10	350	-28	200

How Did You Do on the Subject Test in Modern Hebrew?

After you score your test and analyze your performance, think about the following questions:

Did you run out of time before reaching the end of the test?

If so, you may need to pace yourself better. For example, maybe you spent too much time on one or two hard questions. A better approach might be to skip the ones you can't answer right away and try answering all the questions that remain on the test. Then if there's time, go back to the questions you skipped.

Did you take a long time reading the directions?

You will save time when you take the test by learning the directions to the Subject Test in Modern Hebrew ahead of time. Each minute you spend reading directions during the test is a minute that you could use to answer questions.

How did you handle questions you were unsure of?

If you were able to eliminate one or more of the answer choices as wrong and guess from the remaining ones, your approach probably worked to your advantage. On the other hand, making haphazard guesses or omitting questions without trying to eliminate choices could cost you valuable points.

How difficult were the questions for you compared with other students who took the test?

Table A shows you how difficult the multiple-choice questions were for the group of students who took this test during its national administration. The right-hand column gives the percentage of students that answered each question correctly.

A question answered correctly by almost everyone in the group is obviously an easier question. For example, 93 percent of the students answered question 5 correctly. But only 23 percent answered question 24 correctly.

Keep in mind that these percentages are based on just one group of students. They would probably be different with another group of students taking the test.

If you missed several easier questions, go back and try to find out why: Did the questions cover material you haven't yet reviewed? Did you misunderstand the directions?

Chapter 16
Spanish

Purpose

There are two Subject Tests in Spanish: Spanish and Spanish with Listening. The reading-only test measures your ability to understand written Spanish. The Subject Test in Spanish with Listening measures your ability to understand spoken and written Spanish.

Format

- The Subject Test in Spanish takes one hour and includes 85 multiple-choice questions.
- The Subject Test in Spanish with Listening also takes one hour, with about 20 minutes for listening questions and 40 minutes for the reading section; it includes 85 multiple-choice listening and reading questions.
- Both tests evaluate your reading skills through precision of vocabulary, structure use, and comprehension of a variety of texts.

Content

In the reading section, the questions implicitly test vocabulary throughout the test, but some questions specifically test word meaning in the context of a sentence that reflects spoken or written language. Understanding of various parts of speech (nouns, verbs, adjectives, adverbs, etc.) and idiomatic expressions is tested. The reading section also asks structure and reading questions.

Structure questions ask you to identify usage that is both structurally correct and contextually appropriate. Other reading questions test vocabulary and grammatical usage in longer paragraphs.

Reading questions are based on selections from prose fiction, historical works, newspaper and magazine articles, as well as advertisements, flyers, and letters. They test points such as main and supporting ideas, themes, style, tone, and the spatial and temporal settings of a passage.

In addition to the reading questions, the Subject Test in Spanish with Listening also measures your ability to understand the spoken language with three parts of listening questions:

Part A asks you to identify the sentence that most accurately describes what is presented in a photograph or what someone in the photograph might say.

Part B questions test your ability to identify a plausible continuation of a short conversation.

Part C requires that you answer comprehension questions based on more extensive listening selections.

Spanish	
Skills Measured	Approximate Percentage of Test
Vocabulary and Structure	33
Paragraph Completion	33
Reading Comprehension	33

Spanish with Listening	
Types of Questions	Approximate Percentage of Test
Listening Section (about 20 minutes) (about 30 questions)	40
Pictures Rejoinders Selections	
Reading Section (40 minutes) (about 55 questions)	60
Vocabulary and Structure Paragraph Completion Reading Comprehension	

How to Prepare

Both tests are written to reflect general trends in high school curricula and are independent of particular textbooks or methods of instruction. The Spanish tests are appropriate for you if you have studied the language for three to four years in high school or the equivalent; however, if you have two years of strong preparation in Spanish, you are also encouraged to take the tests. Your best preparation for the tests is a gradual development of competence in Spanish over a period of years. Familiarize yourself with the directions in advance. The directions in this book are identical to those that appear on the test.

Spanish with Listening

A practice audio CD is included with this book. A practice CD with different sample questions can be obtained, along with a copy of the *SAT Subject Tests Preparation Booklet*, from your school counselor, or you can access the listening files at www.collegeboard.com. You should also take the practice test included with this book.

CD Players

Using CD Players for Language Tests with Listening

Take an acceptable CD player to the test center. Your CD player must be in good working order, so insert fresh batteries on the day before the test. You may bring additional batteries and a backup player to the test center.

Test center staff won't have batteries, CD players, or earphones for your use, so your CD player must be:

- equipped with earphones
- portable (hand-held)
- battery operated
- for your use only. CD players cannot be shared with other test-takers.

Note

If the volume on your CD player disturbs other test-takers, the test center supervisor may ask you to move to another seat.

What to do if your CD player malfunctions:

- Raise your hand and tell the test supervisor.
- Switch to backup equipment if you have it and continue the test. If you don't have backup equipment, your score on the Spanish with Listening Test will be canceled. But scores on other Subject Tests you take that day will still be counted.

What if you receive a defective CD on test day? Raise your hand and ask the supervisor for a replacement.

Scores

For both tests, the total score is reported on the 200-to-800 scale. For the listening test, listening and reading subscores are reported on the 20-to-80 scale.

Sample Reading Questions

Your answer sheet has five answer positions marked A, B, C, D, and E, while the questions throughout this test contain only four choices. Be sure NOT to make any marks in column E.

Part A

Directions: This part consists of a number of incomplete statements, each having four suggested completions. Select the most appropriate completion and fill in the corresponding circle on the answer sheet.

1. Juan Pablo tuvo que esperar unos minutos antes de tomar la sopa porque estaba demasiado ____________.
   (A) caliente
   (B) calurosa
   (C) mojada
   (D) perfumada

2. Me gustó tanto la novela de Isabel Allende que ____________ voy a recomendar a mis amigos.
   (A) le
   (B) lo
   (C) me la
   (D) se la

Choice (A) is the correct answer to question 1. This question tests how well you have mastered vocabulary. To answer correctly, you need to know that the only adjective that fits the context of the sentence is (A) *caliente*. The wrong choices, (B), (C), and (D), are inappropriate adjectives for describing soup in this context.

Choice (D) is the correct answer to question 2. This question tests command of structure. To answer correctly, you need to know the correct object pronoun usage and choose an indirect object with a singular, feminine direct object pronoun in the correct sequence. Choices (A), (B), and (C) have either an indirect object pronoun that would not agree with the plural indirect object, *mis amigos*, or a direct object pronoun that would not agree with the singular, feminine direct object, *la novela*.

Part B

Directions: In each of the following paragraphs, there are numbered blanks indicating that words or phrases have been omitted. For each numbered blank, four completions are provided. First, read through the entire paragraph. Then, for each numbered blank, choose the completion that is most appropriate given the context of the entire paragraph and fill in the corresponding circle on the answer sheet.

> El mural más polémico del siempre volcánico Diego Rivera, *Sueño de una tarde dominical en la Alameda Central*, ya está por fin __3__ de todos. Considerada una de las __4__ más logradas de la corriente nacionalista mexicana, este mural __5__ encendidas controversias desde su creación en 1948.

3. (A) en vez
   (B) al lado
   (C) a la vista
   (D) a mediados

4. (A) manifestaciones
   (B) cuadras
   (C) artes
   (D) paredes

5. (A) despertó
   (B) despertará
   (C) despertando
   (D) despierte

Choice (C) is the correct answer to question 3. This question tests how well you have mastered vocabulary. To answer correctly, you need to know that the only phrase that fits the context of the passage is choice (C) *a la vista*. Choices (A), (B), and (D) are inappropriate for describing the state of the mural in this context.

Choice (A) is the correct answer to question 4. This question tests how well you have mastered vocabulary. To answer correctly, you need to know that the only noun that fits the context of the passage is choice (A) *manifestaciones*. The wrong choices, (B), (C), and (D), are inappropriate in this phrase describing the mural's significance as they do not apply to a mural.

Choice (A) is the correct answer to question 5. This question tests command of structure. To answer correctly, you need to know the correct preterite verb tense. The wrong choices, (B) *despertará*, (C) *despertando*, and (D) *despierte*, are different forms of the verb despertar that do not fit the syntax and context of the passage.

Part C

Directions: Read the following texts carefully for comprehension. Each is followed by a number of questions or incomplete statements. Select the answer or completion that is best according to the text and fill in the corresponding circle on the answer sheet.

Question 6

Complete su
Enciclopedia Universal
El Periódico

Para conseguir los tomos que le falten de la ***Enciclopedia Universal El Periódico****, sólo tiene que rellenar el cupón de pedido—adjuntando 75. euro cents en sellos por cada tomo que solicite, más 45. euro cents en sellos por gastos de envío—y remitirlo a la siguiente dirección:*

El Periódico de Catalunya
Departamento de Distribución
C/. Comte d'Urgell, n.º 100
08011 Barcelona

6. ¿Para qué hay que mandar 45 euro cents?
   (A) Para pagar el costo de correos
   (B) Para recibir cupones de pedido
   (C) Para comprar un periódico catalán
   (D) Para pagar un anuncio ilustrado

Choice (A) is the correct answer to question 6. This question asks about a specific detail mentioned in the ad: the reason for sending 45 euro cents. In the text, *más 45 euro cents en sellos por gastos de envío* refers to shipping charges, so the correct answer is choice (A). Choices (B), (C), and (D) are incorrect within the context of the ad.

Questions 7–9

Un aire marino, pesado y fresco, entró en mis pulmones con la primera sensación confusa de la ciudad; una masa de casas dormidas; de establecimientos cerrados, de faroles como centinelas borrachos de soledad. Una respiración grande, dificultosa, venía con el cuchicheo de la madrugada. Muy cerca, a mi espalda, enfrente de las callejuelas misteriosas que conducen al Borne, sobre mi corazón excitado, estaba el mar.

El olor especial, el gran rumor de la gente, las luces siempre tristes de la estación de tren, tenían para mí un gran encanto, ya que envolvían todas mis impresiones en la maravilla de haber llegado por fin a una ciudad grande, adorada en mis ensueños por desconocida.

7. ¿Cómo se siente la narradora al llegar a la ciudad?
   (A) Perdida
   (B) Encantada
   (C) Cansada
   (D) Tranquila

8. ¿Qué efecto producen en la narradora las luces de la estación?
   (A) Le agradan mucho.
   (B) Le dan vergüenza.
   (C) La desorientan.
   (D) La adormecen.

9. ¿Dónde está la ciudad a la que llega la narradora?
    (A) En la costa
    (B) En una cordillera
    (C) Al lado de un río
    (D) Cerca de un lago

Choice (B) is the correct answer to question 7. This question tests literal comprehension, and refers to how the protagonist feels upon her arrival in the city. In the second paragraph, she describes her impressions of the city using words such as *especial*, *encanto*, and *maravilla*. Later in the same paragraph, she also refers to *haber llegado por fin a una ciudad grande, adorada en mis ensueños* (…), so the correct answer is choice (B) *Encantada*. Choices (A), (C), and (D) are incorrect within the context of the passage.

Choice (A) is the correct answer to question 8. This question tests literal comprehension and refers to the effect that the lights of the station have on the protagonist. In the second paragraph, she specifically mentions them, saying *tenían un gran encanto*. Thus, the correct answer is choice (A) *Le agradan mucho*. Choices (B), (C), and (D) are incorrect within the context of the passage.

Choice (A) is the correct answer to question 9. This question tests literal comprehension and asks about the setting of the narrative. In the first paragraph, both the first line, *Un aire marino* (…) and the last sentence, *Muy cerca (…) estaba el mar*, refer to being close to the sea. The correct answer is choice (A) *En la costa*. Choices (B), (C), and (D) are incorrect within the context of the passage.

Spanish Test

Practice Helps

The test that follows is an actual, recently administered SAT Subject Test in Spanish. To get an idea of what it's like to take this test, practice under conditions that are much like those of an actual test administration.

- Set aside an hour when you can take the test uninterrupted. Make sure you complete the test in one sitting.
- Sit at a desk or table with no other books or papers. Dictionaries, other books, or notes are not allowed in the test room.
- Tear out an answer sheet from the back of this book and fill it in just as you would on the day of the test. One answer sheet can be used for up to three Subject Tests.
- Read the instructions that precede the practice test. During the actual administration, you will be asked to read them before answering the test questions.
- Time yourself by placing a clock or kitchen timer in front of you.
- After you finish the practice test, read the sections "How to Score the SAT Subject Test in Spanish" and "How Did You Do on the Subject Test in Spanish?"
- The appearance of the answer sheet in this book may differ from the answer sheet you see on test day.

SPANISH TEST

The top portion of the section of the answer sheet that you will use in taking the Spanish Test must be filled in exactly as shown in the illustration below. Note carefully that you have to do all of the following on your answer sheet.

1. Print SPANISH on the line under the words "Subject Test (print)."

2. In the shaded box labeled "Test Code" fill in four circles:

   —Fill in circle 4 in the row labeled V.
   —Fill in circle 1 in the row labeled W.
   —Fill in circle 3 in the row labeled X.
   —Fill in circle B in the row labeled Y.

Test Code

V ① ② ③ ● ⑤ ⑥ ⑦ ⑧ ⑨
W ● ② ③ ④ ⑤ ⑥ ⑦ ⑧ ⑨
X ① ② ● ④ ⑤ Y Ⓐ ● Ⓒ Ⓓ Ⓔ
Q ① ② ③ ④ ⑤ ⑥ ⑦ ⑧ ⑨

Subject Test (print)

SPANISH

Please answer either Part I or Part II by filling in the specific circle in row Q. You are to fill in ONE and ONLY ONE circle, as described below, to indicate how you obtained your knowledge of Spanish. The information you provide is for statistical purposes only and will not influence your score on the test.

Part I If your knowledge of Spanish does not come primarily from courses taken in grades 9 through 12, fill in circle 9 and leave the remaining circles blank, regardless of how long you studied the subject in school. For example, you are to fill in circle 9 if your knowledge of Spanish comes primarily from any of the following sources: study prior to the ninth grade, courses taken at a college, special study, living in a home in which Spanish is the principal language spoken, or extensive residence abroad that includes significant experience in the Spanish language.

Part II If your knowledge of Spanish does come primarily from courses taken in secondary school, fill in the circle that indicates the level of the Spanish course in which you are currently enrolled. If you are not now enrolled in a Spanish course, fill in the circle that indicates the level of the most advanced course in Spanish that you have completed.

- First year: first or second half —Fill in circle 1.
- Second year: first half —Fill in circle 2.
  second half —Fill in circle 3.
- Third year: first half —Fill in circle 4.
  second half —Fill in circle 5.
- Fourth year: first half —Fill in circle 6.
  second half —Fill in circle 7.
- Advanced Placement course or a course at a level higher than fourth year, second half
  or
  high school course work plus a minimum of four weeks of study abroad —Fill in circle 8.

When the supervisor gives the signal, turn the page and begin the Spanish Test. There are 100 numbered circles on the answer sheet and 85 questions in the Spanish Test. Therefore, use only circles 1 to 85 for recording your answers.

SPANISH TEST

PLEASE NOTE THAT YOUR ANSWER SHEET HAS FIVE ANSWER POSITIONS, MARKED A, B, C, D, E, WHILE THE QUESTIONS THROUGHOUT THIS TEST CONTAIN ONLY FOUR CHOICES. BE SURE NOT TO MAKE ANY MARKS IN COLUMN E.

Part A

Directions: This part consists of a number of incomplete statements, each having four suggested completions. Select the most appropriate completion and fill in the corresponding circle on the answer sheet.

1. Si quieren mandar hoy esta carta a Lucía, ------- un buzón en la esquina.

(A) haya
(B) han
(C) hay
(D) ha

2. ¡Elena, ya son las ocho! ¿Estás ------- para salir?

(A) lista
(B) lenta
(C) ligera
(D) larga

3. Mi ------- favorito es el pastel de manzana.

(A) camino
(B) comedor
(C) helado
(D) postre

4. Pepe es el mejor alumno ------- la clase.

(A) a
(B) de
(C) desde
(D) hasta

5. La casa de techo rojo es -------.

(A) el mío
(B) la nuestra
(C) el tuyo
(D) las suyas

6. Hacía un mes que queríamos ver esa película de Raúl Juliá y por fin ------- vimos la semana pasada.

(A) le
(B) lo
(C) la
(D) se

7. Cuando yo era pequeña, todos los años ------- el mes de agosto en la Playa de Luquillo.

(A) pasamos
(B) pasábamos
(C) hemos pasado
(D) pasaremos

8. Se me olvidó el bolígrafo. ¿Puedes ------- el tuyo?

(A) recordarme
(B) devolverme
(C) prestarme
(D) enseñarme

9. Me dijo que tenía muchas ganas de ------- a su pueblo en Paraguay.

(A) volver
(B) volviendo
(C) volverá
(D) volvería

10. Cuando va al supermercado, Roberto ------- demasiado dinero.

(A) extiende
(B) gasta
(C) busca
(D) cuesta

3YAC2

GO ON TO THE NEXT PAGE

11. Lola, ¿qué ------- te dieron en la clase de química?

(A) señal
(B) nota
(C) tierra
(D) saco

12. Los incas eran los ------- progresistas políticamente de todas las culturas indígenas.

(A) mucho
(B) muy
(C) muchos
(D) más

13. ------- gente se acercó para oír la discusión.

(A) Este
(B) El
(C) La
(D) Toda

14. El enorme tamaño de los murales mexicanos es ------- me gusta más.

(A) los que
(B) el que
(C) lo que
(D) las que

15. Me visitaron de -------; no los esperaba hasta el sábado.

(A) orgullo
(B) sospecha
(C) pereza
(D) sorpresa

16. Como ------- me fastidia, hago gimnasia para mantenerme en forma.

(A) corro
(B) él corre
(C) corriendo
(D) el correr

17. Quiero coser este botón; dame el ------- blanco y una aguja.

(A) hielo
(B) nivel
(C) nido
(D) hilo

18. Como Angela nunca lleva reloj, siempre me pregunta -------.

(A) el tiempo
(B) la hora
(C) la vez
(D) el lugar

19. ------- la una de la tarde.

(A) Está
(B) Es
(C) Están
(D) Son

20. Como la clase ya había empezado, entró ------- para que no lo viera el profesor.

(A) alegremente
(B) amargamente
(C) disimuladamente
(D) superficialmente

21. Después de hacer tanto ejercicio, los niños ------- muy cansados.

(A) estaban
(B) eran
(C) tenían
(D) hacían

22. Fernando siempre cumple ------- haber prometido algo.

(A) sin que
(B) después de
(C) cuando
(D) sobre

23. Mi hermana Cristina es aficionada a los ------- históricos de la Edad Media.

(A) materias
(B) temas
(C) obras
(D) ideas

24. Carlos, si quieres llegar al aeropuerto antes de las cinco, ------- ahora mismo para evitar el tráfico.

(A) sale
(B) salga
(C) salgas
(D) sal

GO ON TO THE NEXT PAGE

25. La abogada renunció a su ------- porque decidió jubilarse.

    (A) dimensión
    (B) pereza
    (C) artículo
    (D) puesto

26. Los turistas dijeron que ------- habían visto nada tan impresionante como los murales de Diego Rivera.

    (A) todavía
    (B) también
    (C) nunca
    (D) además

27. El lago Titicaca es tan profundo que no se puede ver -------.

    (A) el fondo
    (B) el inferior
    (C) la base
    (D) la orilla

GO ON TO THE NEXT PAGE

Part B

Directions: In each of the following paragraphs, there are numbered blanks indicating that words or phrases have been omitted. For each numbered blank, four completions are provided. First read through the entire paragraph. Then, for each numbered blank, choose the completion that is most appropriate given the context of the entire paragraph and fill in the corresponding circle on the answer sheet.

Soy oriunda de Bolivia, residente en Ottawa __(28)__ 1982, y me __(29)__ vuelto una lectora asidua de su __(30)__, que es una de las pocas publicaciones en idioma español que __(31)__ a Canadá. He leído con __(32)__ interés los artículos que publican, especialmente el dedicado a la "Historia Viva" de los carnavales, en __(33)__ mencionaban los de Venecia, Santiago de Cuba, Río de Janeiro . . . y en el cual se omite el carnaval de Oruro que __(34)__ en Bolivia todos los años y es único en su __(35)__: es el único carnaval folclórico en el cual participan miles y miles de danzarines y en donde el __(36)__ favorito es la Diablada de Oruro.

28. (A) donde
(B) desde
(C) hacia
(D) entre

29. (A) hubiera
(B) habré
(C) haya
(D) he

30. (A) revista
(B) lectura
(C) noticiero
(D) anuncio

31. (A) lleguen
(B) llegan
(C) llegaran
(D) llegarían

32. (A) mucha
(B) muchas
(C) mucho
(D) muchos

33. (A) quien
(B) lo cual
(C) el que
(D) cuyo

34. (A) se lleva a cabo
(B) viene a ser
(C) al parecer
(D) se da cuenta

35. (A) geranio
(B) género
(C) cansancio
(D) cariño

36. (A) conjunto
(B) camino
(C) freno
(D) monte

GO ON TO THE NEXT PAGE

María Fernández y su hijo Ángel son los únicos habitantes, ___(37)___ más de quince años, de Foncebadón, una localidad de la provincia de León, que ___(38)___ parte del Camino de Santiago. Madre e hijo se dedican a la ganadería. En sus establos, ___(39)___ casas de otros vecinos, duermen ahora ovejas, cabras y vacas. Y ___(40)___ más fieles compañeros son una gran multitud de perros que dormitan ___(41)___ por todo el pueblo.

María es una mujer con una fortaleza de carácter ___(42)___. Cuando se quedó sola en Foncebadón, su hijo ___(43)___ tenía doce años. Y desde entonces, siempre ha luchado con ___(44)___ por conservar lo poco que queda en pie de su pueblo y ___(45)___ ello hace lo imposible.

37. (A) sin embargo
 (B) supuesto
 (C) desde hace
 (D) a pesar de

38. (A) hace
 (B) debe
 (C) sueña
 (D) forma

39. (A) antiguo
 (B) antigüedad
 (C) antiquísimo
 (D) antiguamente

40. (A) su
 (B) sus
 (C) suyo
 (D) suyos

41. (A) perezosos
 (B) frenéticos
 (C) despegados
 (D) entusiasmados

42. (A) por lo general
 (B) fuera de lo común
 (C) a fin de cuentas
 (D) de buenas a primeras

43. (A) poco
 (B) nunca
 (C) apenas
 (D) aunque

44. (A) jabón y toalla
 (B) pan y vino
 (C) cuchara y tenedor
 (D) uñas y dientes

45. (A) para
 (B) sin
 (C) como
 (D) aun

GO ON TO THE NEXT PAGE

Investigaciones recientes realizadas sobre __(46)__ la vida en la especie humana parecen demostrar que el hombre está programado __(47)__ vivir 200 años, pero las circunstancias que lo rodean __(48)__ esa posibilidad. Al menos eso es __(49)__ asegura un profesor de la Universidad Complutense de Madrid.

El ocio y los vicios acortan la vida. Las personas __(50)__ trabajo requiere actividad física al aire libre y llevan una vida sencilla, tienen más posibilidades __(51)__ a viejos.

Un hecho que se ha observado repetidamente es que en __(52)__ la gente vive mucho __(53)__ en el continente. La dieta __(54)__ parece influir y así se ha visto que casi todas las personas que sobrepasan los __(55)__ años se han alimentado a base de vegetales, leche, yogur, quesos sin grasa, pan, carnes y frutas.

46. (A) el éxito en
(B) la duración de
(C) la dieta en
(D) el auxilio de

47. (A) para
(B) por
(C) de
(D) en

48. (A) ayudan
(B) representan
(C) realizan
(D) disminuyen

49. (A) lo que
(B) que
(C) como
(D) cual

50. (A) cuyas
(B) cuyo
(C) de quien
(D) de quienes

51. (A) para matar
(B) de morir
(C) de llegar
(D) a pasar

52. (A) las islas
(B) los hospitales
(C) las nubes
(D) los hogares

53. (A) no más que
(B) más de que
(C) más de
(D) más que

54. (A) ninguna
(B) nunca
(C) también
(D) tal vez

55. (A) cien
(B) ciento
(C) cientos
(D) centenares

GO ON TO THE NEXT PAGE

Part C

Directions: Read the following texts carefully for comprehension. Each text is followed by a number of questions or incomplete statements. Select the answer or completion that is best according to the text and fill in the corresponding circle on the answer sheet.

La América del Sur

La característica más notable del continente suramericano es la variedad de sus bellezas geográficas naturales, y la enorme extensión de los territorios donde éstas se encuentran. El sur de la Argentina, conocido como Tierra del Fuego, es una zona fría y desértica, que contrasta con las selvas amazónicas del Perú, el Ecuador y el Brasil. Las montañas que atraviesan el continente de norte a sur, y que conocemos como la cordillera de los Andes, recorren el oeste de las inmensas pampas argentinas —terrenos llanos de gran riqueza agrícola y ganadera—y llegan a los no menos extensos llanos de Venezuela, ricos también en ganadería. Las hermosas playas del Uruguay y del Brasil, bañadas por el Atlántico, o las de Colombia, que se extienden por los océanos Atlántico y Pacífico, contrastan con la aridez del desierto de Atacama, en Chile, rico en minas de hierro y cobre, pero donde pasan años sin que caiga una gota de lluvia. Las cataratas del Iguazú, frontera entre el Brasil y la Argentina, son 21 metros más altas que las cataratas del Niágara, en América del Norte, y su volumen de agua es muchas veces mayor. No obstante, una bellísima catarata en Venezuela, conocida como el Salto del Ángel, es la más alta del mundo; sus aguas caen desde más de 900 metros de altura.

56. Este texto probablemente se podría leer en
    (A) una leyenda infantil
    (B) un editorial político
    (C) una revista deportiva
    (D) un folleto turístico

57. Según el artículo, el sur de la Argentina es conocido por
    (A) tener un clima cálido
    (B) ser un área fría
    (C) sus playas
    (D) sus cataratas

GO ON TO THE NEXT PAGE

58. Las pampas son una zona geográfica muy

(A) fértil
(B) montañosa
(C) desértica
(D) poblada

59. Según el pasaje, hay minas de hierro y cobre en

(A) las playas de Colombia
(B) los llanos de Venezuela
(C) el desierto de Chile
(D) las selvas del Brasil

60. ¿Porqué se distingue la catarata del Salto del Ángel?

(A) Por su altura
(B) Por el color del agua
(C) Por sus plantas hidroeléctricas
(D) Por ser la única catarata del continente

61. Según el artículo, se puede concluir que lo más destacado de la geografía suramericana es la

(A) diversidad de sus paisajes
(B) variedad de animales y plantas
(C) selva amazónica
(D) riqueza agrícola

Un fascinante viaje a través de 15.000 años para descubrir las obras de arte más bellas creadas por la humanidad.

Ahora el Club Internacional del Libro ha editado la colección *Tesoros Artísticos del Mundo*, en colaboración con los más prestigiosos Catedráticos y Profesores universitarios y especialistas en la historia del arte. Todo ello en 10 espectaculares volúmenes con más de 1.500 páginas ilustradas a todo color.

Realice la reserva de la colección antes de 15 días y consiga

GRATIS

Una colección de 10 vídeos de Grandes Épocas del Arte.

GO ON TO THE NEXT PAGE

62. ¿Cuántos años de arte incluye la colección de *Tesoros artísticos del mundo* ?

(A) Quince mil
(B) Quinientos
(C) Mil quinientos
(D) Quince

63. Según el anuncio, ¿quiénes han trabajado en esta colección?

(A) Artistas famosos
(B) Expertos en arte
(C) Estudiantes universitarios
(D) Los socios de un club

64. Para obtener esta colección con el regalo, es necesario

(A) hacer un viaje fascinante
(B) asistir a una universidad
(C) hacer una reserva lo antes posible
(D) llamar al museo de arte

65. Según el anuncio, ¿cómo se puede pagar por esta colección?

(A) A vuelta de correo
(B) Con tarjeta de crédito
(C) En efectivo
(D) A plazos mensuales

GO ON TO THE NEXT PAGE

Mi caballo, Cachito

Cuando era jovencita, me encantaba montar a caballo y siempre competía con las demás amazonas para atraer la atención de nuestra instructora, la Sra. Gómez. Yo creía ser una de las mejores amazonas puesto que nunca tenía miedo de saltar obstáculos por altos que fueran. Desafortunadamente mi caballo Cachito no tenía las mismas aspiraciones que yo.

A Cachito le encantaba comer y, al pasar de los años, había engordado a tal punto que se le dificultaban los obstáculos altos y empezó a rehusarlos. Esto tuvo un gran efecto en nuestra participación en las competencias. Después de una mala temporada de concursos, la Sra. Gómez puso a dieta a Cachito para que pudiera recuperar su habilidad en la pista. Esto no le gustó nada a Cachito, quien empezó a glotonear en cuanto se le presentaba la oportunidad. Cachito desarrolló varias nuevas costumbres, una de las cuales le disgustaba mucho a su cuidador, Manuel. Cachito lograba escapar de Manuel y, al soltarse, corría dos kilómetros al extremo del club hípico y comía pasto. Cachito permitía que Manuel se le acercara lo suficiente para tocarlo, pero en cuanto trataba de agarrar su cuerda corría al otro extremo del club donde repetía sus acciones. Al fracasar el plan de poner en forma a Cachito, la Sra. Gómez me dio un nuevo caballo, el Macadú, con el que volví a ganar competencias. Empezaron a usar a Cachito para enseñar a los novatos del club. Como éstos sólo saltaban obstáculos bajos, este trabajo no le disgustaba a Cachito.

66. ¿Cuál era uno de los placeres de Cachito?

(A) Dormir en el campo
(B) Pasear con Manuel
(C) Comer cuanto pudiera
(D) Volver al establo

67. ¿Por qué pensaba la narradora que montaba bien a caballo?

(A) Porque siempre ganaba
(B) Porque era muy rápida en las carreras
(C) Porque no le temía a los obstáculos difíciles
(D) Porque montaba sin silla

68. ¿Qué afectó negativamente la habilidad de Cachito?

(A) La tierra
(B) El peso
(C) La estatura
(D) El clima

69. ¿Por qué se enojaba el cuidador con Cachito?

(A) Porque se peleaba con otros caballos
(B) Porque no le permitía bañarlo
(C) Porque lo pateaba y mordía
(D) Porque se le escapaba constantemente

70. ¿Qué le ocurrió a la narradora como resultado de los problemas de Cachito?

(A) Dejó de montar.
(B) Nunca llegó a ganar una competencia.
(C) Recibió otro caballo.
(D) Cambió de club.

71. ¿Qué hicieron con el Cachito?

(A) Lo usaron para entrenar.
(B) Lo mandaron a otro rancho.
(C) Lo vendieron a una familia.
(D) Lo usaron para la agricultura.

72. Esta narración probablemente proviene de

(A) una autobiografía
(B) una novela de aventuras
(C) un artículo científico
(D) una enciclopedia

GO ON TO THE NEXT PAGE

De Miami a Nueva York
$49*
Todos los asientos se convierten en camas
Sale de Miami: martes • jueves • sábado
*Mes de enero
"Duerma en primera clase mientras viaja"
888-555-0022
"EL BUS CÓMODO"

73. Según este anuncio, una de las ventajas de este servicio es que

    (A) los conductores son de primera clase
    (B) se puede descansar durante el viaje
    (C) se sirven bebidas durante el viaje
    (D) el viaje dura tres días

GO ON TO THE NEXT PAGE

Ahora mi mamá me observa. He pasado anoche un susto terrible. Mis hermanos jugaban después de comer, corriendo en el patio, y yo los miraba desde el corredor, pensando en Angélica, cuando oí que mi mamá le decía a mi abuela: —¿Estará enfermo?—Y entonces me imaginé que estaban hablando de mí. No me atreví a mirarlas, pero sentía que ellas me miraban a mí. Y así era, de mí hablaban, porque mi mamá volvió a decir: —Hace muchas noches que no juega—. Y mi abuela le dijo que me dejara, que yo era así, apagado y tristón y no vivo como mis hermanos; pero mi mamá me llamó. Yo estaba como una estatua; ni voz tenía del susto . . . La pura verdad, yo creo que me estoy enfermando de amor, porque ya es mucho lo nervioso que me he puesto pensando en Angélica . . . —¿Por qué no corres tú también un poco?—me preguntó mi mamá, y yo le contesté que tenía sueño, y ella me tocaba la frente, creyendo que estaría con fiebre; pero yo le aseguré que no tenía nada, y me puse a reír, a la fuerza, eso sí, y porque sólo de pensar que, me creyeran enfermo, temblé. Mi abuela me encontró la frente fresca. Mi abuela opina siempre antes de examinar; así es que antes de haberme tocado ya tenía resuelto hallarme fresco. Algo bueno había de tener, la pobre. Si mi mamá tuviera ese carácter, yo sería muy independiente y más feliz. Pero me cuida demasiado. Porque me quiere será . . . y a mí me gusta que me quiera . . . pero es fastidioso que se fijen tanto en uno . . . y no le dejen vivir su vida privada y sus fantasías.

74. Se puede deducir del cuento que el narrador no participaba en los juegos de sus hermanos porque

(A) tenía un poco de fiebre
(B) su madre no se lo permitía
(C) estaba terriblemente asustado
(D) pensaba en una chica

75. Lo que el narrador del cuento desea es que

(A) su familia lo deje tranquilo
(B) sus hermanos lo traten bien
(C) su abuela lo quiera más
(D) Angélica piense en él

76. La madre estaba preocupada porque creía que el niño

(A) tenía problemas de salud
(B) estaba muy nervioso
(C) era demasiado travieso
(D) era un poco descuidado

77. Según el narrador, su abuela se caracteriza por

(A) su personalidad dominante
(B) su carácter analítico
(C) sus decisiones prematuras
(D) su naturaleza delicada

78. ¿Cómo reacciona el narrador ante las preguntas de su madre?

(A) Le confiesa sus preocupaciones.
(B) Se niega a contestarlas.
(C) Trata de engañarla.
(D) Se pone a llorar.

79. La abuela opina que el narrador es de temperamento

(A) melancólico
(B) hostil
(C) inestable
(D) vivo

80. ¿Qué le molesta al narrador?

(A) No poder entender a su mamá.
(B) Que no le den suficiente independencia.
(C) Que sus hermanos se rían de él.
(D) Sentir la soledad de la noche.

GO ON TO THE NEXT PAGE

SI VIENE A CONOCER ESPAÑA, NO PUEDE IRSE SIN VISITAR EL CORTE INGLÉS.

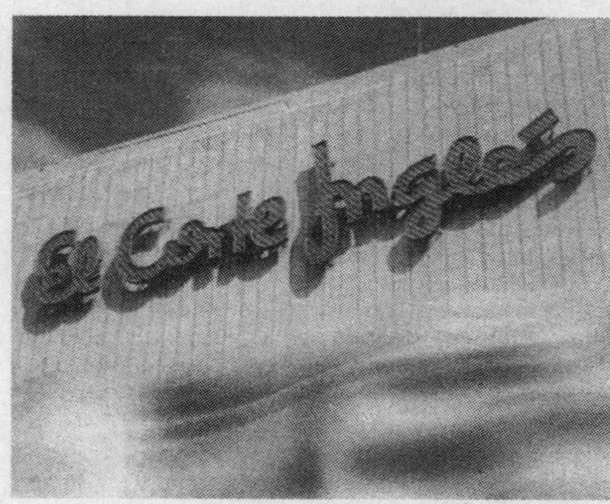

EN ESTE VIAJE, DESCUBRA LA PRIMERA CADENA EUROPEA DE GRANDES ALMACENES. UN NÚMERO UNO EN MODA, HOGAR, REGALOS, PRIMERAS MARCAS, EXCLUSIVIDAD Y EN OFRECER GARANTÍA Y SERVICIO.

ADEMÁS, PODRÁ HABLAR EN SU IDIOMA, COMPRAR UN RECUERDO, ALMORZAR CÓMODAMENTE EN EL RESTAURANTE, DARSE UN CORTE DE PELO, LLAMAR POR TELÉFONO A SU PAÍS, REVELAR LAS FOTOS EN UNA HORA, ENVIAR PAQUETES A CUALQUIER PARTE DEL MUNDO.

EN ESTE VIAJE A ESPAÑA, DESCUBRA LA PRIMERA CADENA EUROPEA DE GRANDES ALMACENES.

GRANDES ALMACENES

UN LUGAR PARA COMPRAR. UN LUGAR PARA SOÑAR.

81. Según el anuncio, ¿qué se puede encontrar en El Corte Inglés?
   (A) Un banco
   (B) Una agencia de viajes
   (C) Un hotel de lujo
   (D) Una peluquería

82. Según el anuncio, El Corte Inglés ofrece el servicio de
   (A) envíos a otros países
   (B) enseñanza de idiomas
   (C) fotocopiado gratis
   (D) cuidado de niños

83. ¿A quién se dirige este anuncio principalmente?
   (A) Turistas extranjeros
   (B) Españoles que viajan fuera del país
   (C) Profesores españoles
   (D) Estudiantes de la escuela primaria

GO ON TO THE NEXT PAGE

¡PARTICIPA Y GANA!

¡PARTICIPA EN EL SORTEO DE 3 VIAJES A EURODISNEY!

Pensando en ti, sorteamos 3 fantásticos viajes a Eurodisney en París para 4 personas cada uno. Para que disfrutes, con tu familia y amigos, del maravilloso reino de Disney donde creatividad y magia se mezclan en un sueño que nunca olvidarás.
Y para que la estancia sea totalmente feliz, cada ganador recibirá además, una "bolsa de viaje" de 1.000 euros, como agradable complemento para todos sus gastos.

Por cualquier compra que realices de productos de catálogo YVES ROCHER, entrarás en el sorteo. Uno de estos viajes puede ser tuyo.

El sorteo se realizará ante notario el día 25 de enero.

84. ¿Qué se puede ganar en este sorteo?
    - (A) Un papel en una película
    - (B) Un viaje a París y dinero
    - (C) Un producto de un catálogo
    - (D) Un curso de magia

85. ¿Cómo se puede participar en este sorteo?
    - (A) Viajando frecuentemente
    - (B) Comprando billetes de lotería
    - (C) Adquiriendo un producto
    - (D) Siendo creativo

STOP

IF YOU FINISH BEFORE TIME IS CALLED, YOU MAY CHECK YOUR WORK ON THIS TEST ONLY.

DO NOT TURN TO ANY OTHER TEST IN THIS BOOK.

How to Score the SAT Subject Test in Spanish

When you take an actual SAT Subject Test in Spanish, your answer sheet will be "read" by a scanning machine that will record your responses to each question. Then a computer will compare your answers with the correct answers and produce your raw score. You get one point for each correct answer. For each wrong answer, you lose one-third of a point. Questions you omit (and any for which you mark more than one answer) are not counted. This raw score is converted to a scaled score that is reported to you and to the colleges you specify.

Worksheet 1. Finding Your Raw Test Score

STEP 1: Table A lists the correct answers for all the questions on the Subject Test in Spanish that is reproduced in this book. It also serves as a worksheet for you to calculate your raw score.

- Compare your answers with those given in the table.
- Put a check in the column marked "Right" if your answer is correct.
- Put a check in the column marked "Wrong" if your answer is incorrect.
- Leave both columns blank if you omitted the question.

STEP 2: Count the number of right answers.

Enter the total here: ________________

STEP 3: Count the number of wrong answers.

Enter the total here: ________________

STEP 4: Multiply the number of wrong answers by .333.

Enter the product here: ______________

STEP 5: Subtract the result obtained in Step 4 from the total you obtained in Step 2.

Enter the result here: _______________

STEP 6: Round the number obtained in Step 5 to the nearest whole number.

Enter the result here: _______________

The number you obtained in Step 6 is your raw score.

Table A

Answers to the Subject Test in Spanish, Form 3YAC2, and Percentage of Students Answering Each Question Correctly

Question Number	Correct Answer	Right	Wrong	Percentage of Students Answering the Question Correctly*	Question Number	Correct Answer	Right	Wrong	Percentage of Students Answering the Question Correctly*
1	C			77	33	C			33
2	A			92	34	A			34
3	D			88	35	B			51
4	B			98	36	A			27
5	B			66	37	C			68
6	C			75	38	D			80
7	B			83	39	D			28
8	C			75	40	B			80
9	A			76	41	A			36
10	B			72	42	B			41
11	B			92	43	C			48
12	D			87	44	D			40
13	C			85	45	A			39
14	C			80	46	B			82
15	D			77	47	A			78
16	D			29	48	D			67
17	D			41	49	A			62
18	B			75	50	B			20
19	B			87	51	C			43
20	C			47	52	A			79
21	A			83	53	D			61
22	B			47	54	C			76
23	B			45	55	A			55
24	D			46	56	D			93
25	D			41	57	B			85
26	C			82	58	A			72
27	A			41	59	C			89
28	B			83	60	A			90
29	D			63	61	A			84
30	A			69	62	A			83
31	B			63	63	B			79
32	C			60	64	C			94

Table A continued on next page

Table A continued from previous page

Question Number	Correct Answer	Right	Wrong	Percentage of Students Answering the Question Correctly*	Question Number	Correct Answer	Right	Wrong	Percentage of Students Answering the Question Correctly*
65	D			51	76	A			74
66	C			79	77	C			33
67	C			72	78	C			33
68	B			55	79	A			46
69	D			79	80	B			61
70	C			76	81	D			49
71	A			80	82	A			67
72	A			76	83	A			84
73	B			81	84	B			89
74	D			68	85	C			87
75	A			40					

* These percentages are based on an analysis of the answer sheets of a representative sample of 3,750 students who took the original form of this test in December 2002, and whose mean score was 566. They may be used as an indication of the relative difficulty of a particular question. Each percentage may also be used to predict the likelihood that a typical SAT Subject Test in Spanish candidate will answer that question correctly on this edition of the test.

Finding Your Scaled Score

When you take SAT Subject Tests, the scores sent to the colleges you specify are reported on the College Board scale, which ranges from 200–800. You can convert your practice test score to a scaled score by using Table B. To find your scaled score, locate your raw score in the left-hand column of Table B; the corresponding score in the right-hand column is your scaled score. For example, a raw score of 37 on this particular edition of the Subject Test in Spanish corresponds to a scaled score of 480.

Raw scores are converted to scaled scores to ensure that a score earned on any one edition of a particular Subject Test is comparable to the same scaled score earned on any other edition of the same Subject Test. Because some editions of the tests may be slightly easier or more difficult than others, College Board scaled scores are adjusted so that they indicate the same level of performance regardless of the edition of the test taken and the ability of the group that takes it. Thus, for example, a score of 400 on one edition of a test taken at a particular administration indicates the same level of achievement as a score of 400 on a different edition of the test taken at a different administration.

When you take the SAT Subject Tests during a national administration, your scores are likely to differ somewhat from the scores you obtain on the tests in this book. People perform at different levels at different times for reasons unrelated to the tests themselves. The precision of any test is also limited because it represents only a sample of all the possible questions that could be asked.

Table B

Scaled Score Conversion Table
Subject Test in Spanish (Form 3YAC2)

Raw Score	Scaled Score	Raw Score	Scaled Score	Raw Score	Scaled Score
85	800	47	540	9	350
84	800	46	540	8	350
83	800	45	530	7	340
82	790	44	520	6	340
81	790	43	520	5	340
80	780	42	510	4	330
79	780	41	510	3	330
78	770	40	500	2	320
77	760	39	500	1	320
76	760	38	490	0	310
75	750	37	480	-1	310
74	750	36	480	-2	300
73	740	35	470	-3	300
72	740	34	470	-4	290
71	730	33	460	-5	290
70	720	32	460	-6	280
69	710	31	450	-7	280
68	700	30	450	-8	270
67	700	29	440	-9	270
66	690	28	440	-10	260
65	680	27	430	-11	250
64	670	26	430	-12	250
63	660	25	420	-13	240
62	650	24	420	-14	230
61	640	23	420	-15	230
60	640	22	410	-16	230
59	630	21	410	-17	220
58	620	20	400	-18	220
57	610	19	400	-19	210
56	610	18	390	-20	210
55	600	17	390	-21	200
54	590	16	380	-22	200
53	580	15	380	-23	200
52	570	14	380	-24	200
51	570	13	370	-25	200
50	560	12	370	-26	200
49	550	11	360	-27	200
48	550	10	360	-28	200

How Did You Do on the Subject Test in Spanish?

After you score your test and analyze your performance, think about the following questions:

Did you run out of time before reaching the end of the test?

If so, you may need to pace yourself better. For example, maybe you spent too much time on one or two hard questions. A better approach might be to skip the ones you can't answer right away and try answering all the questions that remain on the test. Then if there's time, go back to the questions you skipped.

Did you take a long time reading the directions?

You will save time when you take the test by learning the directions to the Subject Test in Spanish ahead of time. Each minute you spend reading directions during the test is a minute that you could use to answer questions.

How did you handle questions you were unsure of?

If you were able to eliminate one or more of the answer choices as wrong and guess from the remaining ones, your approach probably worked to your advantage. On the other hand, making haphazard guesses or omitting questions without trying to eliminate choices could cost you valuable points.

How difficult were the questions for you compared with other students who took the test?

Table A shows you how difficult the multiple-choice questions were for the group of students who took this test during its national administration. The right-hand column gives the percentage of students that answered each question correctly.

A question answered correctly by almost everyone in the group is obviously an easier question. For example, 87 percent of the students answered question 12 correctly. But only 27 percent answered question 36 correctly.

Keep in mind that these percentages are based on just one group of students. They would probably be different with another group of students taking the test.

If you missed several easier questions, go back and try to find out why: Did the questions cover material you haven't yet reviewed? Did you misunderstand the directions?

Spanish with Listening

The SAT Subject Test in Spanish with Listening is offered once a year only at designated test centers. To take the test you MUST bring an acceptable CD player with earphones to the test center.

Sample Listening Questions

The text in brackets [ ] is *only* recorded; it is not printed in your test book. Please note that the CD does not start here. Begin using the CD when you start the actual practice test on page 750 .

Please note your answer sheet has five answer positions marked A, B, C, D, and E, while the questions throughout this test contain only four choices. Be sure not to make any marks in column E.

Part A

Directions: For each question in this part, you will hear four sentences, designated (A), (B), (C), and (D). They will not be printed in your test booklet. As you listen, look at the picture in your test booklet and select the choice that best reflects what you see in the picture or what someone in the picture might say. Then fill in the corresponding circle on the answer sheet. You will hear the choices only once. Now look at the following example.

You see:

You hear:

(Woman) [(A) Siento darles tan mala noticia.

(B) Tiene quince días para pagar la multa.

(C) Y aquí les mando la foto más reciente.

(D) Es preciso que se presente ante el juez.]

(7 seconds)

Choice (C) is the correct answer. *Y aquí les mando la foto más reciente* best reflects what you see in the picture or what someone in the picture might say.

Now we will begin. Look at the first picture and listen to the four choices.

1. (Narrator) [Número 1]

   (Man) [(A) ¡Otro micrófono, por favor!

   (B) La guitarra no tiene cuerdas.

   (C) Adiós, ya estoy aburrido.

   (D) ¡Cantemos todos juntos!]

   (7 seconds)

Choice (D) is the correct answer to question 1. This question tests listening comprehension. To answer correctly, you need to recognize that (D) best reflects what the person in the photograph might say. The wrong choices, (A), (B), and (C), do not reflect what the singer might say in this instance.

Part B

Directions: In this part of the test you will hear several short conversations, or parts of conversations, followed by four choices designated (A), (B), (C), and (D). After you hear the four choices, choose the one that most logically continues or completes the conversation and mark your answer on your answer sheet. What you see in brackets ([ ]) will not be printed in your test booklet. Now listen to the following example.

You will hear:

(Man) [Yo creo que leer es muy importante.]

You will also hear:

(Woman) [(A) Pues no leas tanto.
(B) Estoy totalmente de acuerdo.
(C) No te acuerdas de nada.
(D) No me importan esas leyes.]

(7 seconds)

Choice (B) is the correct answer. It is the choice that most logically continues the conversation.

Now listen to the first conversation.

2. (Narrator) [Número 2]
(Woman) [Llegaste tarde; ¡ya no quedan entradas para esa obra!]
(Man) [(A) ¡Qué entradas tan caras!
(B) Hay otra puerta por aquí.
(C) Perdona, se atrasó el autobús.
(D) A la izquierda está la entrada.]

(7 seconds)

Choice (C) is the correct answer to question 2. This question tests listening comprehension. Choice (C) *Perdona, se atrasó el autobús* is the correct choice. To answer correctly, you need to recognize that choice (C) is the most appropriate response to the woman's statement. The wrong choices, (A), (B), and (D), are inappropriate responses to the woman's statement that there are no tickets left for the performance.

Part C

Directions: You will now hear a series of selections. For each selection, you will see printed in your test booklet one or more questions with four possible answers. They will not be spoken. Select the best answer to each question from among the four choices and fill in the corresponding circle on your answer sheet. You will have 12 seconds to answer each question. There will be no example for this part. Now listen to the first selection.

(Narrator) [Selección Número 1. Escuchen esta conversación en la recepción del Hotel California.]

(Man) [Hola, buenas tardes, señorita. ¿Tiene Ud. una reservación a nombre de Escalante?

(Woman) Déjeme ver. Mmm. . . No la veo, señor. ¿La hizo directamente con nosotros?

(Man) Sí, con ustedes. Aquí tengo la confirmación

(Woman) Pues, señor, el problema es que el hotel está lleno y no quedan habitaciones

(Man) Pero, ¿qué hago yo? He pagado un depósito.

(Woman) Un momento, por favor. Llamaré al gerente para solucionar el problema.]

(Narrator) [Ahora contesten las preguntas 3 y 4.]

(24 seconds)

3. ¿Qué problema tiene el Sr. Escalante?
   (A) Perdió su confirmación.
   (B) No quiere alojarse en el Hotel California.
   (C) El hotel no tiene su reservación.
   (D) Olvidó pagar el depósito.

4. ¿Cómo trata la recepcionista al Sr. Escalante?
   (A) Bruscamente
   (B) Respetuosamente
   (C) Insolentemente
   (D) Alegremente

Choice (C) *El hotel no tiene su reservación* is the correct answer to question 3. This question tests listening comprehension. To answer correctly, you need to recognize that Sr. Escalante's problem is that the hotel does not have his reservation. He made a reservation, paid a deposit, and received a confirmation from the hotel; therefore choices (A), (B), and (D) are incorrect.

Choice (B) *Respetuosamente* is the correct answer to question 4. This question tests listening comprehension. To answer correctly, you need to recognize that the receptionist treats Sr. Escalante respectfully in trying to help him. The wrong choices, (A), (C), and (D), do not accurately describe her manner towards him during the conversation.

Spanish with Listening Test

Practice Helps

The test that follows is an actual, recently administered SAT Subject Test in Spanish with Listening. To get an idea of what it's like to take this test, practice under conditions that are much like those of an actual test administration.

- Set aside an hour when you can take the test uninterrupted. Make sure you complete the test in one sitting.
- Sit at a desk or table with no other books or papers. Dictionaries, other books, or notes are not allowed in the test room.
- Tear out an answer sheet from the back of this book and fill it in just as you would on the day of the test. One answer sheet can be used for up to three Subject Tests.
- Read the instructions that precede the practice test. During the actual administration, you will be asked to read them before answering test questions.
- Time yourself by placing a clock or kitchen timer in front of you.
- After you finish the practice test, read the sections "How to Score the SAT Subject Test in Spanish with Listening" and "How Did You Do on the Subject Test in Spanish with Listening?"
- The appearance of the answer sheet in this book may differ from the answer sheet you see on test day.

SPANISH TEST WITH LISTENING

The top portion of the section of the answer sheet that you will use in taking the Spanish Test with Listening must be filled in exactly as shown in the illustration below. Note carefully that you have to do all of the following on your answer sheet.

1. Print SPANISH WITH LISTENING on the line under the words "Subject Test (print)."
2. In the shaded box labeled "Test Code" fill in four circles:

—Fill in circle 5 in the row labeled V.

—Fill in circle 1 in the row labeled W.

—Fill in circle 4 in the row labeled X.

—Fill in circle B in the row labeled Y.

Test Code											Subject Test (print)
V		1	2	3	4	●	6	7	8	9	*SPANISH WITH LISTENING*
W		●	2	3	4	5	6	7	8	9	
X	1	2	3	●	5	Y A	●	C	D	E	
Q		1	2	3	4	5	6	7	8	9	

Please answer either Part I or Part II by filling in the specific circle in row Q. You are to fill in ONE and ONLY ONE circle, as described below, to indicate how you obtained your knowledge of Spanish. The information you provide is for statistical purposes only and will not influence your score on the test.

Part I If your knowledge of Spanish does not come primarily from courses taken in grades 9 through 12, fill in circle 9 and leave the remaining circles blank, regardless of how long you studied the subject in school. For example, you are to fill in circle 9 if your knowledge of Spanish comes primarily from any of the following sources: study prior to the ninth grade, courses taken at a college, special study, living in a home in which Spanish is the principal language spoken, or extensive residence abroad that includes significant experience in the Spanish language.

Part II If your knowledge of Spanish does come primarily from courses taken in secondary school, fill in the circle that indicates the level of the Spanish course in which you are currently enrolled. If you are not now enrolled in a Spanish course, fill in the circle that indicates the level of the most advanced course in Spanish that you have completed.

- First year: first or second half —Fill in circle 1.
- Second year: first half —Fill in circle 2.
  second half —Fill in circle 3.
- Third year: first half —Fill in circle 4.
  second half —Fill in circle 5.
- Fourth year: first half —Fill in circle 6.
  second half —Fill in circle 7.
- Advanced Placement course
  or a course at a level higher
  than fourth year, second half
  or
  high school course work plus
  a minimum of four weeks of
  study abroad. —Fill in circle 8.

When the supervisor gives the signal, turn the page and begin the Spanish Test with Listening. There are 100 numbered circles on the answer sheet and 85 questions in the Spanish Test with Listening. Therefore, use only circles 1 to 85 for recording your answers.

SPANISH TEST WITH LISTENING

PLEASE NOTE THAT YOUR ANSWER SHEET HAS FIVE ANSWER POSITIONS, MARKED A, B, C, D, AND E, WHILE THE QUESTIONS THROUGHOUT THIS TEST CONTAIN ONLY FOUR CHOICES. BE SURE NOT TO MAKE ANY MARKS IN COLUMN E.

SECTION I

LISTENING

Approximate time—20 minutes

Questions 1-30

Part A

Directions: For each question in this part, you will hear four sentences, designated (A), (B), (C), and (D). They will not be printed in your test booklet. As you listen, look at the picture in your test booklet and select the choice that best reflects what you see in the picture or what someone in the picture might say. Then fill in the corresponding circle on the answer sheet. You will hear the choices only once. Now look at the following example.

You see:

You hear:

Statement (C), "Y aquí les mando la foto más reciente," best reflects what you see in the picture or what someone in the picture might say. Therefore, you would choose answer (C). Now we will begin. Look at the first picture and listen to the four choices.

3XLC

GO ON TO THE NEXT PAGE

1.

2.

GO ON TO THE NEXT PAGE

3.

4.

GO ON TO THE NEXT PAGE

5.

©Elyse Lewin / The Image Bank

6.

UPI/Bettmann

GO ON TO THE NEXT PAGE

7.

8.

GO ON TO THE NEXT PAGE

9.

GO ON TO THE NEXT PAGE

Part B

Directions: In this part of the test you will hear several short conversations or parts of conversations, followed by four choices, designated (A), (B), (C), and (D). After you hear the four choices, choose the one that most logically continues or completes the conversation and mark your answer on your answer sheet. Neither the conversations nor the choices will be printed in your test booklet. Now listen to the following example.

You will hear:

You will also hear:

The choice that most logically continues the conversation is (B), "Estoy totalmente de acuerdo." Therefore, you should choose answer (B). Now listen to the first conversation.

10. Mark your answer on your answer sheet.

11. Mark your answer on your answer sheet.

12. Mark your answer on your answer sheet.

13. Mark your answer on your answer sheet.

14. Mark your answer on your answer sheet.

15. Mark your answer on your answer sheet.

16. Mark your answer on your answer sheet.

17. Mark your answer on your answer sheet.

GO ON TO THE NEXT PAGE

Part C

Directions: You will now hear a series of selections. For each selection, you will see printed in your test booklet one or more questions with four possible answers. They will not be spoken. Select the best answer to each question from among the four choices printed and fill in the corresponding circle on your answer sheet. You will have twelve seconds to answer each question. There will be no example for this part. Now listen to the first selection.

Selección número 1

18. ¿Qué sugiere hacer el joven para entender mejor la película?

(A) Verla otra vez.
(B) Discutirla con ella.
(C) Ir de compras.
(D) Tomar un helado.

19. ¿Qué deciden hacer con respecto a la película?

(A) Tratar de recordarla.
(B) Entenderla del todo.
(C) No pensar más en ella.
(D) Comprar un video.

Selección número 2

20. ¿Dónde reina la tranquilidad para la narradora?

(A) En la plaza mayor.
(B) En el patio de su casa.
(C) En un parque cercano.
(D) En las calles céntricas.

21. ¿Qué se puede apreciar en este ambiente?

(A) Los coches que van y vienen.
(B) Los pájaros que cantan.
(C) El ruido de los niños.
(D) Las relaciones familiares.

22. ¿De qué hablan los ancianos?

(A) De los árboles del parque.
(B) De las frescas fuentes.
(C) De asuntos del pasado.
(D) Del ambiente sofocante.

Selección número 3

23. ¿Por qué es excepcional este parque zoológico?

(A) Porque tiene animales exóticos.
(B) Porque siempre está abierto.
(C) Porque tiene animales de la región.
(D) Porque tiene todo tipo de peces.

24. ¿Qué se dice en el anuncio de la entrada a este zoológico?

(A) Cuesta cinco dólares.
(B) Cuesta nueve dólares.
(C) Es gratis.
(D) Es libre.

25. ¿Cuándo está abierto el zoológico?

(A) De lunes a domingo.
(B) Todos los días.
(C) De martes a domingo.
(D) Todos los lunes.

GO ON TO THE NEXT PAGE

Selección número 4

26. ¿De qué hablan estas personas?

(A) De una clase.
(B) Del tiempo.
(C) De un horario.
(D) Del día.

27. ¿Qué expresa el joven?

(A) Indiferencia.
(B) Molestia.
(C) Sorpresa.
(D) Alivio.

28. ¿Cómo reacciona Rosaura al final?

(A) Con buen humor.
(B) Con mucha compasión.
(C) Con entusiasmo.
(D) Con admiración.

Selección número 5

29. ¿Qué tiene que hacer Paula?

(A) Llamar a Mariluz.
(B) Salir a la discoteca.
(C) Ayudar a su mamá.
(D) Terminar su tarea.

30. ¿De qué se preocupa la mamá de Paula?

(A) De las vacaciones.
(B) Del trabajo escolar.
(C) De la amiga Mariluz.
(D) De las clases aeróbicas.

END OF SECTION I.
DO NOT GO ON TO SECTION II UNTIL YOU ARE TOLD TO DO SO.

SECTION II

READING

Suggested Time—40 minutes

Questions 31-85

WHEN YOU BEGIN THE READING SECTION, BE SURE THAT YOU MARK YOUR ANSWER TO THE FIRST READING QUESTION BY FILLING IN ONE OF THE CIRCLES NEXT TO NUMBER 31 ON THE ANSWER SHEET.

Part A

Directions: This part consists of a number of incomplete statements, each having four suggested completions. Select the most appropriate completion and fill in the corresponding circle on the answer sheet.

31. Siempre voy al mercado temprano para comprar carne y vegetales -------.

(A) fresco
(B) fresca
(C) frescos
(D) frescas

32. Adopté este sistema de programación porque me pareció ------- al otro.

(A) superior
(B) venturoso
(C) creador
(D) talentoso

33. Si quieres que te ayude, tienes que ------- lo que necesitas.

(A) decirme
(B) escogerme
(C) consultarme
(D) esconderme

34. Como Bárbara no podía ver bien, se ------- al escenario.

(A) amarró
(B) acercó
(C) abrazó
(D) arregló

35. Uno de los ------- más usados en la comida hispanoamericana es el cilantro.

(A) concursos
(B) utensilios
(C) condimentos
(D) colores

36. Francisco me invitó a ver el Ballet Folklórico de Cuba; ¡qué lástima que yo no haya podido ir -------!

(A) consigo
(B) con nosotros
(C) conmigo
(D) con él

37. Hay que ------- los documentos a la embajada hoy o mañana.

(A) lleva
(B) lleve
(C) llevar
(D) llevara

38. Los guerreros españoles fueron ------- valientes como los árabes.

(A) tan
(B) tanto
(C) tantos
(D) todo

GO ON TO THE NEXT PAGE

39. Era invierno y los árboles no tenían -------.

    (A) ramas
    (B) raíces
    (C) grasa
    (D) hojas

40. ¿Has sacado muchas fotos de tu viaje a Guatemala? ¿Cuándo vas a -------?

    (A) enseñárnoslas
    (B) enseñárnoslos
    (C) enseñárnoslo
    (D) enseñárnosla

41. La velocidad de ese corredor es -------.

    (A) indivisible
    (B) asombrosa
    (C) escéptica
    (D) sabrosa

GO ON TO THE NEXT PAGE

Part B

Directions: In each of the following paragraphs, there are numbered blanks indicating that words or phrases have been omitted. For each numbered blank, four completions are provided. First read through the entire paragraph. Then, for each numbered blank, choose the completion that is most appropriate given the context of the entire paragraph and fill in the corresponding circle on the answer sheet.

Aquella ciudad era muy grande. Las casas alineadas __(42)__ la repetición de una sola: ventanas iguales, puertas iguales. Había muchos coches, que no hacían __(43)__ y se alineaban frente a las casas. No existían muchos peatones como Gloria, pero __(44)__ había guardaban el más absoluto silencio. Esta ciudad daba la impresión de __(45)__ sumamente ordenada.

42. (A) parecían
    (B) parecer
    (C) parecidas
    (D) parecieran

43. (A) siesta
    (B) soledad
    (C) rueda
    (D) ruido

44. (A) los que
    (B) los cuales
    (C) lo que
    (D) lo cual

45. (A) mirar
    (B) ser
    (C) haber
    (D) hacer

GO ON TO THE NEXT PAGE

Desde que era muy pequeña a Isabel le __(46)__ las flores y para su octavo cumpleaños pidió un jardín. Su padre decidió que, __(47)__ vivían en un pequeño apartamento en el centro de la Ciudad de México, __(48)__ conseguirle un jardín a su hijita. Él fue en busca de macetas que fueran lo suficientemente grandes para __(49)__ rosas de varios tipos. Al final pudo encontrar una maceta que __(50)__ poner en su pequeño balcón.

46. (A) intentaban
    (B) encantaban
    (C) ocasionaban
    (D) merecían

47. (A) aunque
    (B) ni
    (C) para que
    (D) sin

48. (A) trataría de
    (B) trataría con
    (C) trataría a
    (D) trataría

49. (A) ahorrar
    (B) mejorar
    (C) esperar
    (D) cultivar

50. (A) pudiendo
    (B) podido
    (C) podría
    (D) pueda

GO ON TO THE NEXT PAGE

Hoy en día, nuestro planeta se encuentra __(51)__ un serio dilema. __(52)__, el alarmante crecimiento de la población mundial; por otro lado, la continua destrucción de los recursos naturales y de la herencia natural. A __(53)__ ritmo, nuestro mundo avanza hacia un desastre ecológico. Ésta es la razón por __(54)__ el equilibrio del medio ambiente se ha convertido en una prioridad __(55)__ para la humanidad. Como toda __(56)__ causa, este desafío planetario tiene sus líderes. Presidentes, príncipes y científicos no han dudado en usar su __(57)__, su fama o sus conocimientos, para que nuestro mundo __(58)__ a tomar decisiones urgentes y necesarias.

51. (A) en vez de
    (B) en medio de
    (C) con tal de
    (D) a eso de

52. (A) Por eso
    (B) Por fin
    (C) Por un lado
    (D) Por lo menos

53. (A) este
    (B) el
    (C) cual
    (D) eso

54. (A) la cual
    (B) el cual
    (C) lo cual
    (D) cual

55. (A) residual
    (B) decidida
    (C) esencial
    (D) preliminar

56. (A) bien
    (B) buen
    (C) bueno
    (D) buena

57. (A) poder
    (B) conferencia
    (C) planeta
    (D) retrato

58. (A) empiece
    (B) empezara
    (C) empezará
    (D) empezaría

GO ON TO THE NEXT PAGE

En la oficina nadie hablaba de fútbol. Todo el mundo pasaba su tiempo con la __(59)__ baja atendiendo a su tarea hasta la hora de __(60)__. Por la tarde no se trabajaba, lo cual alegró mucho a Fernando, __(61)__ cada vez más ante la idea de tener tan poco que hacer.

59. (A) calabaza
    (B) pelota
    (C) cabeza
    (D) paleta

60. (A) cierran
    (B) cerrar
    (C) cerrado
    (D) cerrando

61. (A) animándose
    (B) despreciándose
    (C) vistiéndose
    (D) escuchándose

GO ON TO THE NEXT PAGE

Part C

Directions: Read the following texts carefully for comprehension. Each text is followed by a number of questions or incomplete statements. Select the answer or completion that is best according to the text and fill in the corresponding circle on the answer sheet.

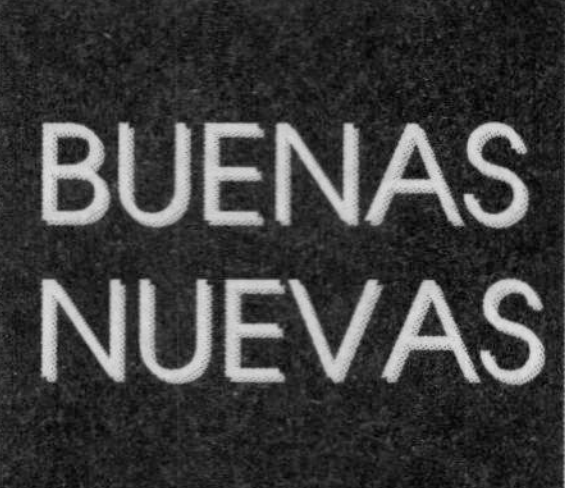

Un nuevo bombero

Ayer, a las cinco de la mañana pasaba una pareja por el cuartel del Cuerpo de Bomberos de Guadalajara rumbo al hospital, y se debieron quedar ahí. Sonia Imelda Santos tuvo a su hijo en el cuartel, con la ayuda de un bombero paramédico. "Hay un nuevo bombero en nuestras filas", dijo el paramédico.

62. El cuartel de bomberos anuncia que hay un nuevo bombero porque

(A) ha asistido en el nacimiento de un niño
(B) la Señora Santos se ha unido al cuartel
(C) se ha incorporado un nuevo miembro
(D) una pareja decidió vivir allí

GO ON TO THE NEXT PAGE

Tres cosas me intrigaban de Pedro Camacho: lo que decía, la austeridad de su vida enteramente consagrada a una obsesión, y su capacidad de trabajo. Esto último, sobre todo. En una biografía sobre Napoleón había leído cómo el emperador seguía dictando mientras sus secretarios se derrumbaban. Yo solía imaginarme al Emperador de los Franceses con la cara nariguda de Camacho y durante algún tiempo lo llamé el Napoleón del Altiplano. Por curiosidad, llegué a establecer su horario de trabajo y, pese a que lo verifiqué muchas veces, siempre me pareció imposible.

Empezó con cuatro radioteatros al día, pero, en vista del éxito, fueron aumentando hasta diez, que se radiaban de lunes a sábado, con una duración de media hora cada capítulo (en realidad, 23 minutos, pues la publicidad acaparaba siete). Como los dirigía e interpretaba todos, debía permanecer en el estudio unas siete horas diarias, calculando que el ensayo y grabación de cada programa durasen cuarenta minutos (entre diez y quince para su arenga y las repeticiones). Escribía los radioteatros a medida que se iban radiando; comprobé que cada capítulo le tomaba apenas el doble de tiempo que su interpretación, una hora. Lo cual significaba, de todos modos, unas diez horas en la máquina de escribir. Esto disminuía algo gracias a los domingos, su día libre, que él, por supuesto, pasaba en su cubículo, adelantando el trabajo de la semana. Su horario era, pues, entre quince y dieciséis horas de lunes a sábado y de ocho a diez los domingos. Todas ellas prácticamente productivas, de rendimiento "artístico" sonante.

Llegaba a Radio Central a las ocho de la mañana y partía cerca de medianoche; sus únicas salidas a la calle las hacía conmigo, al Café Bransa, para tomar las infusiones de té. Almorzaba en su cubículo, un sandwich y un refresco que le iban a comprar. Jamás aceptaba una invitación, jamás le oí decir que había estado en un cine, un teatro, un partido de fútbol o en una fiesta. Jamás lo vi leer un libro, una revista o un periódico, fuera del enorme cuaderno de apuntes y de esos planos que eran sus "instrumentos de trabajo". Aunque miento, un día le descubrí un Boletín de Socios del Club Nacional.

63. El narrador llama a Pedro Camacho el Napoleón del Altiplano por su

(A) dedicación al trabajo
(B) nariz aguileña
(C) vida austera
(D) manera de hablar

64. ¿Cuál es una de las actividades profesionales de Pedro Camacho?

(A) Productor de anuncios comerciales
(B) Escritor de programas de radio
(C) Compositor de canciones populares
(D) Locutor de noticieros regionales

65. ¿Cómo pasaba Pedro los domingos?

(A) Asistiendo a fiestas
(B) Radiando interpretaciones originales
(C) Trabajando en su oficina
(D) Leyendo periódicos

66. ¿Qué usaba a veces Pedro en su trabajo?

(A) Una colección de anotaciones
(B) Artículos periodísticos
(C) Obras de teatro
(D) Biografías

67. ¿Cómo se puede caracterizar la vida de Pedro?

(A) Disciplinada
(B) Divertida
(C) Romántica
(D) Corrupta

68. Se puede concluir que la actitud del narrador hacia Pedro es de

(A) desprecio
(B) indiferencia
(C) envidia
(D) curiosidad

GO ON TO THE NEXT PAGE

OFERTA DE INVIERNO

¡50% MENOS!

Sólo $27^{50}

una habitación, una noche
una a cuatro personas

A sólo una milla del
parque principal de atracciones

Este cupón ofrece un descuento de 50% sobre la tarifa habitual, desde el 3 de enero hasta el 11 de febrero. Tenemos disponibles 40 habitaciones que dan al jardín. También hay otras tarifas. Limitado a disponibilidad. Válido sólo con reservas hechas por adelantado.

Llame al 1-800-555-0887 en la Florida.

MAINGATE
7571 W. Irlo Bronson Memorial Hwy.
(US 192 W)
Kissimmee, FL 34747

69. ¿Cuándo se ofrece este precio especial?
    (A) Llegando antes del mediodía
    (B) La primera semana de cada mes
    (C) Solamente los fines de semana
    (D) Durante unas cuantas semanas

70. Para disfrutar de esta oferta hay que
    (A) tener cuatro personas en la familia
    (B) hacer reservación antes de llegar
    (C) pagar en efectivo al llegar
    (D) alquilar también un coche

71. Según el anuncio, una gran ventaja de quedarse en este hotel es
    (A) que no cobra las llamadas locales
    (B) que diariamente ofrece desayuno gratis
    (C) su accesibilidad al parque de diversiones
    (D) su jardín con juegos para niños

72. ¿A quienes se dirige este anuncio principalmente?
    (A) A los vecinos de la zona
    (B) A todos los jardineros del parque
    (C) A turistas que planean vacaciones
    (D) A participantes en convenciones

GO ON TO THE NEXT PAGE

Los mundos de Chile

Puede que haya otros mundos, pero seguro que están en Chile. Y es que, según cuentan sus habitantes, cuando se creó la Tierra, con los restos que sobraron de aquí y de allá, se hizo su país. ¿Dónde si no es posible encontrar semejante contraste de paisajes y gentes? Un desierto como el de Atacama, en el que no cae una gota desde hace medio siglo, pero, también, una de las zonas más lluviosas del planeta, Puerto Montt. Playas paradisíacas a hora y media de cumbres andinas, con nieve perpetua, en las que esquiar todo el año. Enormes y despobladas llanuras verdes en la Patagonia, junto a los impresionantes glaciares de Punta Arenas, en plena Tierra del Fuego, a un paso de la Antártida. Y, por si fuera poco, la Isla de Pascua, perdida en el Pacífico, testigo misterioso del paso de civilizaciones.

73. ¿Cómo se dice que se creó Chile?

(A) Con habitantes de otros mundos
(B) Con partes de varios lugares
(C) Con gentes de la Tierra
(D) Con desiertos inhabitados

74. ¿Qué dice el artículo sobre la zona de Atacama?

(A) Tiene una gran riqueza vegetal.
(B) Ha sido modernizada en las últimas décadas.
(C) Es un lugar lleno de volcanes.
(D) No llueve allí desde hace muchos años.

75. El artículo indica que en los Andes chilenos se puede

(A) disfrutar de la nieve permanentemente
(B) ver un paisaje parecido al de otro planeta
(C) nadar en piscinas termales
(D) conocer civilizaciones misteriosas

76. Según el artículo, ¿cómo es el clima de Chile?

(A) Hace un calor semejante al fuego.
(B) Es principalmente frío y seco.
(C) Exhibe una gran variedad.
(D) Tiene tendencia a la lluvia.

77. Este artículo probablemente proviene de

(A) una novela de aventuras
(B) la introducción de un informe gubernamental
(C) la sección de turismo de un periódico
(D) un anuncio de seguros

GO ON TO THE NEXT PAGE

Reciba Noticias del Mundo
de lunes a sábado,
en su casa*
Por sólo
25¢
al día
Póngase al día en lo que sucede en su comunidad, en su país y en el mundo, con Noticias del Mundo.
Todos nuestros periodistas son hispanos y saben lo que a usted le interesa.
En Noticias del Mundo, usted encontrará: deportes, noticias locales, nacionales e internacionales, entretenimiento, y una extensa sección de clasificados. Además, secciones especiales acerca del mundo de los negocios, la salud, religión y más, mucho más.
PARA SOLICITARLO POR TELÉFONO LLAME GRATIS AL:
1.800.555.6997 EXT. 5
NOTICIAS del MUNDO
*ENTREGA SOLAMENTE DISPONIBLE EN ÁREAS EXCLUSIVAS DE QUEENS.

78. ¿Cuándo aparece el periódico *Noticias del Mundo* ?

(A) Los siete días de la semana
(B) Sólo los lunes y los sábados
(C) A diario excepto los domingos
(D) Sólo los fines de semana

79. En este anuncio se menciona que una ventaja de recibir *Noticias del Mundo* es que

(A) hay ediciones por la mañana y por la tarde
(B) los periodistas son exclusivamente hispanos
(C) tiene una sección especial sobre viajes
(D) contiene muchos anuncios comerciales

GO ON TO THE NEXT PAGE

Cristóbal Colón partió de España en busca de metales preciosos y especias, sin imaginarse que nunca los encontraría. Lo que sí encontró fue un Nuevo Mundo lleno de frutas y verduras, como el tomate y la papa, que en ese entonces eran exóticas para los europeos.

En sus viajes, Colón equipó sus naves con carne salada, sardinas, anchoas, ajos y cebollas para que sirvieran de alimento a su tripulación. Si hubiera sabido las maravillas culinarias que le esperaban, habría llevado harina, arroz y azúcar, y en vez de marineros recién salidos de las cárceles se habría embarcado con algunos buenos cocineros de la corte real española.

Así, el Nuevo y el Viejo Mundo habrían disfrutado mucho antes platos hoy conocidos por todos nosotros: la carne con papas fritas, las tortas de chocolate, las pastas con salsa de tomate, la pizza. Tal vez Colón en vez de llegar a ser almirante de la mar ahora sería mencionado en los libros de historia como "embajador gastronómico". Y esa misma historia hablaría del humo proveniente no de la pólvora de las armas, sino de los hornos donde se cocinaban tantas delicias.

A la larga, del encuentro de estos dos mundos que no se conocían surgió una fabulosa revolución en el área alimenticia, aunque los chocolates dulces no nos deben permitir olvidar que tantas culturas de las Américas fueron víctimas de amargos sufrimientos.

80. ¿De qué trata este artículo?

(A) De una revolución indígena
(B) Del segundo viaje de Cristóbal Colón
(C) De la grasa en la dieta actual
(D) Del encuentro alimenticio entre dos culturas

81. Según el pasaje, ¿qué encontró Colón en el Nuevo Mundo?

(A) Los condimentos que buscaba
(B) Frutos que no existían en España
(C) Joyas preciosas
(D) Armas para sus marineros

82. Los que acompañaron a Colón eran

(A) navegantes de mala fama
(B) cocineros destacados
(C) embajadores para las Américas
(D) almirantes famosos

83. Un producto que Colón llevó en sus barcos a América era

(A) pescado
(B) oro
(C) hornos
(D) plata

84. Colón no pudo exigir el título de embajador gastronómico porque

(A) a sus marineros sólo les gustaba la comida española
(B) desconocía la comida típica de las Américas
(C) le faltaban expertos en la preparación de la comida
(D) prefería comer pastas con tomates

GO ON TO THE NEXT PAGE

ÉSTA ES SU VIDA
EL PAIS AGENDA ANUAL
EL PAIS AGENDA ANUAL
EL PAIS AGENDA ANUAL
Ya están a la venta las agendas anuales El País. Elija el modelo que más se adapte a sus necesidades: de Sobremesa, de Bolsillo o Mini. Rellene hoy mismo este cupón.
Para más información llamar al teléfono (91) 555 83 90.

AGENDA **EL PAIS**

Solicítela enviando este cupón a
DIARIO EL PAÍS, S.A.
APARTADO F.D. 797. 28080 MADRID

	Cantidad
❒ Agenda de Sobremesa	______
❒ Agenda de Bolsillo	______
❒ Agenda de Bolsillo Mini	______

FORMAS DE PAGO:

❒ Cheque ❒ Tarjeta de crédito

Nombre y Apellidos ______________________

Dirección ______________________

C.P. ________ Localidad ____________ Provincia ____________

FIRMA:

85. Para obtener una de estas agendas es necesario

    (A) llamar por teléfono
    (B) mandar el cupón adjunto
    (C) comprar el diario *El País*
    (D) ir a la oficina

END OF SECTION II

S T O P

IF YOU FINISH BEFORE TIME IS CALLED, YOU MAY CHECK YOUR WORK ON SECTION II OF THIS TEST.

DO NOT TURN TO ANY OTHER TEST IN THIS BOOK.

NO TEST MATERIAL ON THIS PAGE

How to Score the SAT Subject Test in Spanish with Listening

When you take an actual SAT Subject Test in Spanish with Listening, you receive an overall composite score as well as two subscores: one for the reading section, one for the listening section.

The reading and listening scores are reported on the College Board's 20–80 scale. However, the composite score, which is the most significant of the scores reported to the colleges you specify, is in the form of the College Board's 200–800 scale.

Worksheet 1. Finding Your Raw Listening Subscore

STEP 1: Table A lists the correct answers for all the questions on the Subject Test in Spanish with Listening that is reproduced in this book. It also serves as a worksheet for you to calculate your raw Listening subscore.

- Compare your answers with those given in the table.
- Put a check in the column marked "Right" if your answer is correct.
- Put a check in the column marked "Wrong" if your answer is incorrect.
- Leave both columns blank if you omitted the question.

STEP 2: Count the number of right answers for questions 1–30.

Enter the total here: ____________________

STEP 3: Count the number of wrong answers for questions 1–30.

Enter the total here: ____________________

STEP 4: Multiply the number of wrong answers by .333.

Enter the product here: ________________

STEP 5: Subtract the result obtained in Step 4 from the total you obtained in Step 2.

Enter the result here: __________________

STEP 6: Round the number obtained in Step 5 to the nearest whole number.

Enter the result here: __________________

The number you obtained in Step 6 is your raw Listening subscore.

Worksheet 2. Finding Your Raw Reading Subscore

STEP 1: Table A lists the correct answers for all the questions on the Subject Test in Spanish with Listening that is reproduced in this book. It also serves as a worksheet for you to calculate your raw Reading subscore.

STEP 2: Count the number of right answers for questions 31–85.

Enter the total here: ____________________

STEP 3: Count the number of wrong answers for questions 31–85.

Enter the total here: ____________________

STEP 4: Multiply the number of wrong answers by .333.

Enter the product here: ________________

STEP 5: Subtract the result obtained in Step 4 from the total you obtained in Step 2.

Enter the result here: __________________

STEP 6: Round the number obtained in Step 5 to the nearest whole number.

Enter the result here: __________________

The number you obtained in Step 6 is your raw Reading subscore.

Worksheet 3. Finding Your Raw Composite Score

STEP 1: Enter your unrounded raw Reading subscore from Step 5 of Worksheet 2.

Enter the result here: ________________

STEP 2: Enter your unrounded raw Listening subscore from Step 5 of Worksheet 1.

Enter the result here: ________________

STEP 3: Add the result obtained in Step 1 to the result obtained in Step 2.

Enter the result here: ________________

STEP 4: Round the number obtained in Step 3 to the nearest whole number.

Enter the result here: ________________

The number you obtained in Step 4 is your raw composite score.

Table A

Answers to the Subject Test in Spanish with Listening, Form 3XLC, and Percentage of Students Answering Each Question Correctly									
Question Number	Correct Answer	Right	Wrong	Percentage of Students Answering the Question Correctly*	Question Number	Correct Answer	Right	Wrong	Percentage of Students Answering the Question Correctly*
1	B			96	33	A			90
2	C			96	34	B			54
3	A			93	35	C			88
4	A			81	36	D			79
5	A			75	37	C			65
6	B			65	38	A			64
7	C			83	39	D			71
8	D			80	40	A			70
9	B			86	41	B			30
10	B			78	42	A			86
11	B			91	43	D			71
12	C			73	44	A			58
13	B			67	45	B			77
14	D			47	46	B			84
15	A			84	47	A			82
16	B			87	48	A			45
17	D			35	49	D			95
18	A			46	50	C			77
19	C			67	51	B			70
20	C			87	52	C			62
21	B			83	53	A			82
22	C			54	54	A			14
23	A			77	55	C			78
24	C			71	56	D			79
25	C			72	57	A			56
26	C			68	58	A			40
27	B			77	59	C			60
28	A			62	60	B			56
29	D			87	61	A			47
30	B			88	62	A			72
31	C			73	63	A			71
32	A			88	64	B			87

Table A continued on next page

Table A continued from previous page

Question Number	Correct Answer	Right	Wrong	Percentage of Students Answering the Question Correctly*	Question Number	Correct Answer	Right	Wrong	Percentage of Students Answering the Question Correctly*
65	C			81	76	C			81
66	A			25	77	C			81
67	A			84	78	C			78
68	D			44	79	B			84
69	D			90	80	D			63
70	B			88	81	B			83
71	C			74	82	A			35
72	C			92	83	A			47
73	B			46	84	C			28
74	D			78	85	B			90
75	A			58					

* These percentages are based on an analysis of the answer sheets of a representative sample of 2,800 students who took the original form of this test in November 2001, and whose mean composite score was 584. They may be used as an indication of the relative difficulty of a particular question. Each percentage may also be used to predict the likelihood that a typical SAT Subject Test in Spanish with Listening candidate will answer that question correctly on this edition of the test.

Finding Your Scaled Score

When you take SAT Subject Tests, the scores sent to the colleges you specify are reported on the College Board scale, which ranges from 200–800. Subscores are reported on a scale which ranges from 20–80. You can convert your practice test scores to scaled scores by using Tables B, C, and D. To find your scaled score, locate your raw score in the left-hand column of the table; the corresponding score in the right-hand column is your scaled score. For example, a raw score of 59 on this particular edition of the Subject Test in Spanish with Listening corresponds to a scaled score of 610.

Raw scores are converted to scaled scores to ensure that a score earned on any one edition of a particular Subject Test is comparable to the same scaled score earned on any other edition of the same Subject Test. Because some editions of the tests may be slightly easier or more difficult than others, College Board scaled scores are adjusted so that they indicate the same level of performance regardless of the edition of the test taken and the ability of the group that takes it. Thus, for example, a score of 400 on one edition of a test taken at a particular administration indicates the same level of achievement as a score of 400 on a different edition of the test taken at a different administration.

When you take the SAT Subject Tests during a national administration, your scores are likely to differ somewhat from the scores you obtain on the tests in this book. People perform at different levels at different times for reasons unrelated to the tests themselves. The precision of any test is also limited because it represents only a sample of all the possible questions that could be asked.

Your scaled composite score from Table B is _______________.

Your scaled listening score from Table C is _______________.

Your scaled reading score from Table D is _______________.

Table B

Scaled Score Conversion Table
Subject Test in Spanish with Listening
Composite Score (Form 3XLC)

Raw Score	Scaled Score	Raw Score	Scaled Score	Raw Score	Scaled Score
85	800	47	540	9	330
84	800	46	530	8	330
83	800	45	530	7	320
82	800	44	520	6	320
81	790	43	510	5	310
80	780	42	510	4	310
79	780	41	500	3	300
78	770	40	500	2	290
77	760	39	490	1	290
76	750	38	490	0	280
75	740	37	480	-1	280
74	730	36	470	-2	270
73	730	35	470	-3	260
72	720	34	460	-4	250
71	710	33	460	-5	250
70	700	32	450	-6	240
69	690	31	450	-7	240
68	680	30	440	-8	230
67	670	29	430	-9	230
66	660	28	430	-10	220
65	650	27	420	-11	220
64	650	26	420	-12	220
63	640	25	410	-13	210
62	630	24	410	-14	210
61	630	23	400	-15	200
60	620	22	400	-16	200
59	610	21	390	-17	200
58	610	20	390	-18	200
57	600	19	380	-19	200
56	590	18	380	-20	200
55	590	17	370	-21	200
54	580	16	370	-22	200
53	570	15	360	-23	200
52	570	14	360	-24	200
51	560	13	350	-25	200
50	550	12	350	-26	200
49	550	11	340	-27	200
48	540	10	340	-28	200

Table C

Scaled Score Conversion Table Subject Test in Spanish with Listening Listening Subscore (Form 3XLC)					
Raw Score	Scaled Score	Raw Score	Scaled Score	Raw Score	Scaled Score
30	79	16	50	2	32
29	75	15	49	1	30
28	73	14	48	0	29
27	70	13	46	-1	27
26	67	12	45	-2	25
25	65	11	44	-3	24
24	63	10	42	-4	23
23	61	9	41	-5	22
22	59	8	40	-6	21
21	58	7	39	-7	20
20	56	6	37	-8	20
19	54	5	36	-9	20
18	53	4	35	-10	20
17	52	3	33		

Table D

Scaled Score Conversion Table Subject Test in Spanish with Listening Reading Subscore (Form 3XLC)					
Raw Score	Scaled Score	Raw Score	Scaled Score	Raw Score	Scaled Score
55	80	30	55	5	35
54	80	29	54	4	34
53	80	28	53	3	33
52	79	27	52	2	32
51	78	26	51	1	31
50	77	25	51	0	30
49	76	24	50	-1	30
48	75	23	49	-2	28
47	74	22	48	-3	27
46	73	21	47	-4	26
45	71	20	46	-5	25
44	70	19	45	-6	24
43	69	18	45	-7	23
42	67	17	44	-8	22
41	66	16	43	-9	21
40	65	15	42	-10	20
39	64	14	41	-11	20
38	63	13	41	-12	20
37	62	12	40	-13	20
36	61	11	39	-14	20
35	60	10	38	-15	20
34	59	9	38	-16	20
33	58	8	37	-17	20
32	57	7	36	-18	20
31	56	6	35		

How Did You Do on the Subject Test in Spanish with Listening?

After you score your test and analyze your performance, think about the following questions:

Did you run out of time before reaching the end of the test?

If so, you may need to pace yourself better. For example, maybe you spent too much time on one or two hard questions. A better approach might be to skip the ones you can't answer right away and try answering all the questions that remain on the test. Then if there's time, go back to the questions you skipped.

Did you take a long time reading the directions?

You will save time when you take the test by learning the directions to the Subject Test in Spanish with Listening ahead of time. Each minute you spend reading directions during the test is a minute that you could use to answer questions.

How did you handle questions you were unsure of?

If you were able to eliminate one or more of the answer choices as wrong and guess from the remaining ones, your approach probably worked to your advantage. On the other hand, making haphazard guesses or omitting questions without trying to eliminate choices could cost you valuable points.

How difficult were the questions for you compared with other students who took the test?

Table A shows you how difficult the multiple-choice questions were for the group of students who took this test during its national administration. The right-hand column gives the percentage of students that answered each question correctly.

A question answered correctly by almost everyone in the group is obviously an easier question. For example, 96 percent of the students answered question 1 correctly. But only 14 percent answered question 54 correctly.

Keep in mind that these percentages are based on just one group of students. They would probably be different with another group of students taking the test.

If you missed several easier questions, go back and try to find out why: Did the questions cover material you haven't yet reviewed? Did you misunderstand the directions?

SAT Subject Tests™

DO NOT USE A MECHANICAL PENCIL

COMPLETE MARK ● EXAMPLES OF INCOMPLETE MARKS

You must use a No. 2 pencil. It is very important that you fill in the entire circle darkly and completely. If you change your response, erase as completely as possible. Incomplete marks or erasures may affect your score. It is very important that you follow these instructions when filling out your answer sheet.

1 Your Name: (Print)

Last First M.I.

I agree to the conditions on the back of the SAT Subject Tests™ booklet. I also agree to use only a No. 2 pencil to complete my answer sheet.

Signature: **Date:** / /

Home Address:

Number and Street City State Zip Code

Home Phone: ( ) **Center:** (Print) City State/Country

2 YOUR NAME

Last Name (First 6 Letters) | First Name (First 4 Letters) | Mid. Init.

– ' A B C D E F G H I J K L M N O P Q R S T U V W X Y Z

3 DATE OF BIRTH

MONTH | DAY | YEAR

Jan Feb Mar Apr May Jun Jul Aug Sep Oct Nov Dec

0 1 2 3 4 5 6 7 8 9

4 ZIP CODE

0 1 2 3 4 5 6 7 8 9

5 SEX

Female Male

6 REGISTRATION NUMBER

(Copy from Admission Ticket.)

0 1 2 3 4 5 6 7 8 9

I turned in my registration form today.

7 SOCIAL SECURITY NUMBER

0 1 2 3 4 5 6 7 8 9

8 BOOK CODE

(Copy and grid as on back of test book.)

0 1 2 3 4 5 6 7 8 9

A B C D E F G H I J K L M N O P Q R S T U V W X Y Z

9 BOOK ID

(Copy from back of test book.)

10 BOOK SERIAL NUMBER

(Copy from front of test book.)

0 1 2 3 4 5 6 7 8 9

11 TEST CENTER

(Supplied by Test Center Supervisor.)

0 1 2 3 4 5 6 7 8 9

FOR OFFICIAL USE ONLY

0 1 2 3 4 5 6

172624-001:654321 ISD5959

00272-36392 • NS85E950 • Printed in U.S.A.

732653

PLEASE DO NOT WRITE IN THIS AREA

SERIAL #

COMPLETE MARK ● EXAMPLES OF INCOMPLETE MARKS

You must use a No. 2 pencil. Do not use a mechanical pencil. It is very important that you fill in the entire circle darkly and completely. If you change your response, erase as completely as possible. Incomplete marks or erasures may affect your score.

If there are more answer spaces than you need, leave them blank.

Test Code

V ① ② ③ ④ ⑤ ⑥ ⑦ ⑧ ⑨

W ① ② ③ ④ ⑤ ⑥ ⑦ ⑧ ⑨

X ① ② ③ ④ ⑤

Y Ⓐ Ⓑ Ⓒ Ⓓ Ⓔ

Q ① ② ③ ④ ⑤ ⑥ ⑦ ⑧ ⑨

Print Subject Test Name:

If you are taking a Language Test select: ○ Reading Only ○ Reading and Listening

1–100 Ⓐ Ⓑ Ⓒ Ⓓ Ⓔ

8 BOOK CODE (Copy and grid as on back of test book.)

9 BOOK ID (Copy from back of test book.)

10 BOOK SERIAL NUMBER (Copy from front of test book.)

Quality Assurance Mark

Chemistry *Fill in circle CE only if II is correct explanation of I.

	I	II	CE*		I	II	CE*
101	Ⓣ Ⓕ	Ⓣ Ⓕ	○	109	Ⓣ Ⓕ	Ⓣ Ⓕ	○
102	Ⓣ Ⓕ	Ⓣ Ⓕ	○	110	Ⓣ Ⓕ	Ⓣ Ⓕ	○
103	Ⓣ Ⓕ	Ⓣ Ⓕ	○	111	Ⓣ Ⓕ	Ⓣ Ⓕ	○
104	Ⓣ Ⓕ	Ⓣ Ⓕ	○	112	Ⓣ Ⓕ	Ⓣ Ⓕ	○
105	Ⓣ Ⓕ	Ⓣ Ⓕ	○	113	Ⓣ Ⓕ	Ⓣ Ⓕ	○
106	Ⓣ Ⓕ	Ⓣ Ⓕ	○	114	Ⓣ Ⓕ	Ⓣ Ⓕ	○
107	Ⓣ Ⓕ	Ⓣ Ⓕ	○	115	Ⓣ Ⓕ	Ⓣ Ⓕ	○
108	Ⓣ Ⓕ	Ⓣ Ⓕ	○				

FOR OFFICIAL USE ONLY

R/C	W/S1	FS/S2	CS/S3	WS

CERTIFICATION STATEMENT

Copy the statement below (do not print) and sign your name as you would an official document.

I hereby agree to the conditions set forth online at www.collegeboard.com and/or in the SAT Registration Booklet and certify that I am the person whose name and address appear on this answer sheet.

By signing below, I agree not to share any specific test questions with anyone after I test by any form of communication, including, but not limited to: email, text messages, or use of the Internet.

Signature ______________________ Date ______________

COMPLETE MARK ● EXAMPLES OF INCOMPLETE MARKS

You must use a No. 2 pencil. Do not use a mechanical pencil. *It is very important that you fill in the entire circle darkly and completely. If you change your response, erase as completely as possible. Incomplete marks or erasures may affect your score.*

If there are more answer spaces than you need, leave them blank.

Test Code

V	1 2 3 4 5 6 7 8 9
W	1 2 3 4 5 6 7 8 9
X	1 2 3 4 5
Y	A B C D E
Q	1 2 3 4 5 6 7 8 9

Print Subject Test Name:

If you are taking a Language Test select: ○ Reading Only ○ Reading and Listening

1	A B C D E	26	A B C D E	51	A B C D E	76	A B C D E
2	A B C D E	27	A B C D E	52	A B C D E	77	A B C D E
3	A B C D E	28	A B C D E	53	A B C D E	78	A B C D E
4	A B C D E	29	A B C D E	54	A B C D E	79	A B C D E
5	A B C D E	30	A B C D E	55	A B C D E	80	A B C D E
6	A B C D E	31	A B C D E	56	A B C D E	81	A B C D E
7	A B C D E	32	A B C D E	57	A B C D E	82	A B C D E
8	A B C D E	33	A B C D E	58	A B C D E	83	A B C D E
9	A B C D E	34	A B C D E	59	A B C D E	84	A B C D E
10	A B C D E	35	A B C D E	60	A B C D E	85	A B C D E
11	A B C D E	36	A B C D E	61	A B C D E	86	A B C D E
12	A B C D E	37	A B C D E	62	A B C D E	87	A B C D E
13	A B C D E	38	A B C D E	63	A B C D E	88	A B C D E
14	A B C D E	39	A B C D E	64	A B C D E	89	A B C D E
15	A B C D E	40	A B C D E	65	A B C D E	90	A B C D E
16	A B C D E	41	A B C D E	66	A B C D E	91	A B C D E
17	A B C D E	42	A B C D E	67	A B C D E	92	A B C D E
18	A B C D E	43	A B C D E	68	A B C D E	93	A B C D E
19	A B C D E	44	A B C D E	69	A B C D E	94	A B C D E
20	A B C D E	45	A B C D E	70	A B C D E	95	A B C D E
21	A B C D E	46	A B C D E	71	A B C D E	96	A B C D E
22	A B C D E	47	A B C D E	72	A B C D E	97	A B C D E
23	A B C D E	48	A B C D E	73	A B C D E	98	A B C D E
24	A B C D E	49	A B C D E	74	A B C D E	99	A B C D E
25	A B C D E	50	A B C D E	75	A B C D E	100	A B C D E

Quality Assurance Mark

8 BOOK CODE (Copy and grid as on back of test book.)

0–9 | A–Z | 0–9

9 BOOK ID (Copy from back of test book.)

10 BOOK SERIAL NUMBER (Copy from front of test book.)

0 1 2 3 4 5 6 7 8 9 (six columns)

Chemistry *Fill in circle CE only if II is correct explanation of I.

	I	II	CE*		I	II	CE*
101	T F	T F	○	109	T F	T F	○
102	T F	T F	○	110	T F	T F	○
103	T F	T F	○	111	T F	T F	○
104	T F	T F	○	112	T F	T F	○
105	T F	T F	○	113	T F	T F	○
106	T F	T F	○	114	T F	T F	○
107	T F	T F	○	115	T F	T F	○
108	T F	T F	○				

FOR OFFICIAL USE ONLY

R/C	W/S1	FS/S2	CS/S3	WS

COMPLETE MARK ● EXAMPLES OF INCOMPLETE MARKS

You must use a No. 2 pencil. Do not use a mechanical pencil. It is very important that you fill in the entire circle darkly and completely. If you change your response, erase as completely as possible. Incomplete marks or erasures may affect your score.

If there are more answer spaces than you need, leave them blank.

Test Code

V	① ② ③ ④ ⑤ ⑥ ⑦ ⑧ ⑨
W	① ② ③ ④ ⑤ ⑥ ⑦ ⑧ ⑨
X	① ② ③ ④ ⑤
Y	Ⓐ Ⓑ Ⓒ Ⓓ Ⓔ
Q	① ② ③ ④ ⑤ ⑥ ⑦ ⑧ ⑨

Print Subject Test Name:

If you are taking a Language Test select: ○ Reading Only ○ Reading and Listening

1 Ⓐ Ⓑ Ⓒ Ⓓ Ⓔ	26 Ⓐ Ⓑ Ⓒ Ⓓ Ⓔ	51 Ⓐ Ⓑ Ⓒ Ⓓ Ⓔ	76 Ⓐ Ⓑ Ⓒ Ⓓ Ⓔ
2 Ⓐ Ⓑ Ⓒ Ⓓ Ⓔ	27 Ⓐ Ⓑ Ⓒ Ⓓ Ⓔ	52 Ⓐ Ⓑ Ⓒ Ⓓ Ⓔ	77 Ⓐ Ⓑ Ⓒ Ⓓ Ⓔ
3 Ⓐ Ⓑ Ⓒ Ⓓ Ⓔ	28 Ⓐ Ⓑ Ⓒ Ⓓ Ⓔ	53 Ⓐ Ⓑ Ⓒ Ⓓ Ⓔ	78 Ⓐ Ⓑ Ⓒ Ⓓ Ⓔ
4 Ⓐ Ⓑ Ⓒ Ⓓ Ⓔ	29 Ⓐ Ⓑ Ⓒ Ⓓ Ⓔ	54 Ⓐ Ⓑ Ⓒ Ⓓ Ⓔ	79 Ⓐ Ⓑ Ⓒ Ⓓ Ⓔ
5 Ⓐ Ⓑ Ⓒ Ⓓ Ⓔ	30 Ⓐ Ⓑ Ⓒ Ⓓ Ⓔ	55 Ⓐ Ⓑ Ⓒ Ⓓ Ⓔ	80 Ⓐ Ⓑ Ⓒ Ⓓ Ⓔ
6 Ⓐ Ⓑ Ⓒ Ⓓ Ⓔ	31 Ⓐ Ⓑ Ⓒ Ⓓ Ⓔ	56 Ⓐ Ⓑ Ⓒ Ⓓ Ⓔ	81 Ⓐ Ⓑ Ⓒ Ⓓ Ⓔ
7 Ⓐ Ⓑ Ⓒ Ⓓ Ⓔ	32 Ⓐ Ⓑ Ⓒ Ⓓ Ⓔ	57 Ⓐ Ⓑ Ⓒ Ⓓ Ⓔ	82 Ⓐ Ⓑ Ⓒ Ⓓ Ⓔ
8 Ⓐ Ⓑ Ⓒ Ⓓ Ⓔ	33 Ⓐ Ⓑ Ⓒ Ⓓ Ⓔ	58 Ⓐ Ⓑ Ⓒ Ⓓ Ⓔ	83 Ⓐ Ⓑ Ⓒ Ⓓ Ⓔ
9 Ⓐ Ⓑ Ⓒ Ⓓ Ⓔ	34 Ⓐ Ⓑ Ⓒ Ⓓ Ⓔ	59 Ⓐ Ⓑ Ⓒ Ⓓ Ⓔ	84 Ⓐ Ⓑ Ⓒ Ⓓ Ⓔ
10 Ⓐ Ⓑ Ⓒ Ⓓ Ⓔ	35 Ⓐ Ⓑ Ⓒ Ⓓ Ⓔ	60 Ⓐ Ⓑ Ⓒ Ⓓ Ⓔ	85 Ⓐ Ⓑ Ⓒ Ⓓ Ⓔ
11 Ⓐ Ⓑ Ⓒ Ⓓ Ⓔ	36 Ⓐ Ⓑ Ⓒ Ⓓ Ⓔ	61 Ⓐ Ⓑ Ⓒ Ⓓ Ⓔ	86 Ⓐ Ⓑ Ⓒ Ⓓ Ⓔ
12 Ⓐ Ⓑ Ⓒ Ⓓ Ⓔ	37 Ⓐ Ⓑ Ⓒ Ⓓ Ⓔ	62 Ⓐ Ⓑ Ⓒ Ⓓ Ⓔ	87 Ⓐ Ⓑ Ⓒ Ⓓ Ⓔ
13 Ⓐ Ⓑ Ⓒ Ⓓ Ⓔ	38 Ⓐ Ⓑ Ⓒ Ⓓ Ⓔ	63 Ⓐ Ⓑ Ⓒ Ⓓ Ⓔ	88 Ⓐ Ⓑ Ⓒ Ⓓ Ⓔ
14 Ⓐ Ⓑ Ⓒ Ⓓ Ⓔ	39 Ⓐ Ⓑ Ⓒ Ⓓ Ⓔ	64 Ⓐ Ⓑ Ⓒ Ⓓ Ⓔ	89 Ⓐ Ⓑ Ⓒ Ⓓ Ⓔ
15 Ⓐ Ⓑ Ⓒ Ⓓ Ⓔ	40 Ⓐ Ⓑ Ⓒ Ⓓ Ⓔ	65 Ⓐ Ⓑ Ⓒ Ⓓ Ⓔ	90 Ⓐ Ⓑ Ⓒ Ⓓ Ⓔ
16 Ⓐ Ⓑ Ⓒ Ⓓ Ⓔ	41 Ⓐ Ⓑ Ⓒ Ⓓ Ⓔ	66 Ⓐ Ⓑ Ⓒ Ⓓ Ⓔ	91 Ⓐ Ⓑ Ⓒ Ⓓ Ⓔ
17 Ⓐ Ⓑ Ⓒ Ⓓ Ⓔ	42 Ⓐ Ⓑ Ⓒ Ⓓ Ⓔ	67 Ⓐ Ⓑ Ⓒ Ⓓ Ⓔ	92 Ⓐ Ⓑ Ⓒ Ⓓ Ⓔ
18 Ⓐ Ⓑ Ⓒ Ⓓ Ⓔ	43 Ⓐ Ⓑ Ⓒ Ⓓ Ⓔ	68 Ⓐ Ⓑ Ⓒ Ⓓ Ⓔ	93 Ⓐ Ⓑ Ⓒ Ⓓ Ⓔ
19 Ⓐ Ⓑ Ⓒ Ⓓ Ⓔ	44 Ⓐ Ⓑ Ⓒ Ⓓ Ⓔ	69 Ⓐ Ⓑ Ⓒ Ⓓ Ⓔ	94 Ⓐ Ⓑ Ⓒ Ⓓ Ⓔ
20 Ⓐ Ⓑ Ⓒ Ⓓ Ⓔ	45 Ⓐ Ⓑ Ⓒ Ⓓ Ⓔ	70 Ⓐ Ⓑ Ⓒ Ⓓ Ⓔ	95 Ⓐ Ⓑ Ⓒ Ⓓ Ⓔ
21 Ⓐ Ⓑ Ⓒ Ⓓ Ⓔ	46 Ⓐ Ⓑ Ⓒ Ⓓ Ⓔ	71 Ⓐ Ⓑ Ⓒ Ⓓ Ⓔ	96 Ⓐ Ⓑ Ⓒ Ⓓ Ⓔ
22 Ⓐ Ⓑ Ⓒ Ⓓ Ⓔ	47 Ⓐ Ⓑ Ⓒ Ⓓ Ⓔ	72 Ⓐ Ⓑ Ⓒ Ⓓ Ⓔ	97 Ⓐ Ⓑ Ⓒ Ⓓ Ⓔ
23 Ⓐ Ⓑ Ⓒ Ⓓ Ⓔ	48 Ⓐ Ⓑ Ⓒ Ⓓ Ⓔ	73 Ⓐ Ⓑ Ⓒ Ⓓ Ⓔ	98 Ⓐ Ⓑ Ⓒ Ⓓ Ⓔ
24 Ⓐ Ⓑ Ⓒ Ⓓ Ⓔ	49 Ⓐ Ⓑ Ⓒ Ⓓ Ⓔ	74 Ⓐ Ⓑ Ⓒ Ⓓ Ⓔ	99 Ⓐ Ⓑ Ⓒ Ⓓ Ⓔ
25 Ⓐ Ⓑ Ⓒ Ⓓ Ⓔ	50 Ⓐ Ⓑ Ⓒ Ⓓ Ⓔ	75 Ⓐ Ⓑ Ⓒ Ⓓ Ⓔ	100 Ⓐ Ⓑ Ⓒ Ⓓ Ⓔ

Chemistry *Fill in circle CE only if II is correct explanation of I.

	I	II	CE*		I	II	CE*
101	Ⓣ Ⓕ	Ⓣ Ⓕ	○	109	Ⓣ Ⓕ	Ⓣ Ⓕ	○
102	Ⓣ Ⓕ	Ⓣ Ⓕ	○	110	Ⓣ Ⓕ	Ⓣ Ⓕ	○
103	Ⓣ Ⓕ	Ⓣ Ⓕ	○	111	Ⓣ Ⓕ	Ⓣ Ⓕ	○
104	Ⓣ Ⓕ	Ⓣ Ⓕ	○	112	Ⓣ Ⓕ	Ⓣ Ⓕ	○
105	Ⓣ Ⓕ	Ⓣ Ⓕ	○	113	Ⓣ Ⓕ	Ⓣ Ⓕ	○
106	Ⓣ Ⓕ	Ⓣ Ⓕ	○	114	Ⓣ Ⓕ	Ⓣ Ⓕ	○
107	Ⓣ Ⓕ	Ⓣ Ⓕ	○	115	Ⓣ Ⓕ	Ⓣ Ⓕ	○
108	Ⓣ Ⓕ	Ⓣ Ⓕ	○				

8 BOOK CODE

(Copy and grid as on back of test book.)

⓪	Ⓐ	⓪
①	Ⓑ	①
②	Ⓒ	②
③	Ⓓ	③
④	Ⓔ	④
⑤	Ⓕ	⑤
⑥	Ⓖ	⑥
⑦	Ⓗ	⑦
⑧	Ⓘ	⑧
⑨	Ⓙ	⑨
	Ⓚ	
	Ⓛ	
	Ⓜ	
	Ⓝ	
	Ⓞ	
	Ⓟ	
	Ⓠ	
	Ⓡ	
	Ⓢ	
	Ⓣ	
	Ⓤ	
	Ⓥ	
	Ⓦ	
	Ⓧ	
	Ⓨ	
	Ⓩ	

9 BOOK ID (Copy from back of test book.)

10 BOOK SERIAL NUMBER (Copy from front of test book.)

⓪	⓪	⓪	⓪	⓪	⓪
①	①	①	①	①	①
②	②	②	②	②	②
③	③	③	③	③	③
④	④	④	④	④	④
⑤	⑤	⑤	⑤	⑤	⑤
⑥	⑥	⑥	⑥	⑥	⑥
⑦	⑦	⑦	⑦	⑦	⑦
⑧	⑧	⑧	⑧	⑧	⑧
⑨	⑨	⑨	⑨	⑨	⑨

Quality Assurance Mark

FOR OFFICIAL USE ONLY

R/C	W/S1	FS/S2	CS/S3	WS

PLEASE DO NOT WRITE IN THIS AREA

SERIAL #

SAT Subject Tests™

DO NOT USE A MECHANICAL PENCIL

COMPLETE MARK ● EXAMPLES OF INCOMPLETE MARKS

You must use a No. 2 pencil. *It is very important that you fill in the entire circle darkly and completely. If you change your response, erase as completely as possible. Incomplete marks or erasures may affect your score. It is very important that you follow these instructions when filling out your answer sheet.*

1 **Your Name:** (Print) Last First M.I.

I agree to the conditions on the back of the SAT Subject Tests™ booklet. I also agree to use only a No. 2 pencil to complete my answer sheet.

Signature: **Date:** / /

Home Address: Number and Street City State Zip Code

Home Phone: ( ) **Center:** (Print) City State/Country

2 YOUR NAME

Last Name (First 6 Letters) | First Name (First 4 Letters) | Mid. Init.

– ' A B C D E F G H I J K L M N O P Q R S T U V W X Y Z

3 DATE OF BIRTH

MONTH | DAY | YEAR

Jan, Feb, Mar, Apr, May, Jun, Jul, Aug, Sep, Oct, Nov, Dec

0 1 2 3 4 5 6 7 8 9

4 ZIP CODE

0 1 2 3 4 5 6 7 8 9

5 SEX

○ Female ○ Male

6 REGISTRATION NUMBER

(Copy from Admission Ticket.)

0 1 2 3 4 5 6 7 8 9

○ I turned in my registration form today.

7 SOCIAL SECURITY NUMBER

0 1 2 3 4 5 6 7 8 9

8 BOOK CODE

(Copy and grid as on back of test book.)

0 1 2 3 4 5 6 7 8 9 | A B C D E F G H I J K L M N O P Q R S T U V W X Y Z | 0 1 2 3 4 5 6 7 8 9

9 BOOK ID

(Copy from back of test book.)

10 BOOK SERIAL NUMBER

(Copy from front of test book.)

0 1 2 3 4 5 6 7 8 9

11 TEST CENTER

(Supplied by Test Center Supervisor.)

0 1 2 3 4 5 6 7 8 9

FOR OFFICIAL USE ONLY

0 1 2 3 4 5 6

0 1 2 3 4 5 6

0 1 2 3 4 5 6

172624-001:654321 ISD5959

00272-36392 • NS85E950 • Printed in U.S.A.

732653

PLEASE DO NOT WRITE IN THIS AREA

SERIAL #

COMPLETE MARK ● EXAMPLES OF INCOMPLETE MARKS

You must use a No. 2 pencil. Do not use a mechanical pencil. *It is very important that you fill in the entire circle darkly and completely. If you change your response, erase as completely as possible. Incomplete marks or erasures may affect your score.*

If there are more answer spaces than you need, leave them blank.

Test Code	
V	1 2 3 4 5 6 7 8 9
W	1 2 3 4 5 6 7 8 9
X	1 2 3 4 5
Y	A B C D E
Q	1 2 3 4 5 6 7 8 9

Print Subject Test Name:

If you are taking a Language Test select: ○ Reading Only ○ Reading and Listening

1 A B C D E	26 A B C D E	51 A B C D E	76 A B C D E
2 A B C D E	27 A B C D E	52 A B C D E	77 A B C D E
3 A B C D E	28 A B C D E	53 A B C D E	78 A B C D E
4 A B C D E	29 A B C D E	54 A B C D E	79 A B C D E
5 A B C D E	30 A B C D E	55 A B C D E	80 A B C D E
6 A B C D E	31 A B C D E	56 A B C D E	81 A B C D E
7 A B C D E	32 A B C D E	57 A B C D E	82 A B C D E
8 A B C D E	33 A B C D E	58 A B C D E	83 A B C D E
9 A B C D E	34 A B C D E	59 A B C D E	84 A B C D E
10 A B C D E	35 A B C D E	60 A B C D E	85 A B C D E
11 A B C D E	36 A B C D E	61 A B C D E	86 A B C D E
12 A B C D E	37 A B C D E	62 A B C D E	87 A B C D E
13 A B C D E	38 A B C D E	63 A B C D E	88 A B C D E
14 A B C D E	39 A B C D E	64 A B C D E	89 A B C D E
15 A B C D E	40 A B C D E	65 A B C D E	90 A B C D E
16 A B C D E	41 A B C D E	66 A B C D E	91 A B C D E
17 A B C D E	42 A B C D E	67 A B C D E	92 A B C D E
18 A B C D E	43 A B C D E	68 A B C D E	93 A B C D E
19 A B C D E	44 A B C D E	69 A B C D E	94 A B C D E
20 A B C D E	45 A B C D E	70 A B C D E	95 A B C D E
21 A B C D E	46 A B C D E	71 A B C D E	96 A B C D E
22 A B C D E	47 A B C D E	72 A B C D E	97 A B C D E
23 A B C D E	48 A B C D E	73 A B C D E	98 A B C D E
24 A B C D E	49 A B C D E	74 A B C D E	99 A B C D E
25 A B C D E	50 A B C D E	75 A B C D E	100 A B C D E

8 BOOK CODE (Copy and grid as on back of test book.)

0 1 2 3 4 5 6 7 8 9 / A B C D E F G H I J K L M N O P Q R S T U V W X Y Z / 0 1 2 3 4 5 6 7 8 9

9 BOOK ID (Copy from back of test book.)

10 BOOK SERIAL NUMBER (Copy from front of test book.)

0 1 2 3 4 5 6 7 8 9

Quality Assurance Mark

Chemistry *Fill in circle CE only if II is correct explanation of I.

	I	II	CE*		I	II	CE*
101	T F	T F	○	109	T F	T F	○
102	T F	T F	○	110	T F	T F	○
103	T F	T F	○	111	T F	T F	○
104	T F	T F	○	112	T F	T F	○
105	T F	T F	○	113	T F	T F	○
106	T F	T F	○	114	T F	T F	○
107	T F	T F	○	115	T F	T F	○
108	T F	T F	○				

FOR OFFICIAL USE ONLY

R/C	W/S1	FS/S2	CS/S3	WS

CERTIFICATION STATEMENT

Copy the statement below (do not print) and sign your name as you would an official document.

I hereby agree to the conditions set forth online at www.collegeboard.com and/or in the SAT Registration Booklet and certify that I am the person whose name and address appear on this answer sheet.

By signing below, I agree not to share any specific test questions with anyone after I test by any form of communication, including, but not limited to: email, text messages, or use of the Internet.

Signature ______________________ Date ______________________

COMPLETE MARK ● EXAMPLES OF INCOMPLETE MARKS

You must use a No. 2 pencil. Do not use a mechanical pencil. It is very important that you fill in the entire circle darkly and completely. If you change your response, erase as completely as possible. Incomplete marks or erasures may affect your score.

If there are more answer spaces than you need, leave them blank.

Test Code

V ① ② ③ ④ ⑤ ⑥ ⑦ ⑧ ⑨
W ① ② ③ ④ ⑤ ⑥ ⑦ ⑧ ⑨
X ① ② ③ ④ ⑤
Y Ⓐ Ⓑ Ⓒ Ⓓ Ⓔ
Q ① ② ③ ④ ⑤ ⑥ ⑦ ⑧ ⑨

Print Subject Test Name:

If you are taking a Language Test select: ◯ Reading Only ◯ Reading and Listening

1 Ⓐ Ⓑ Ⓒ Ⓓ Ⓔ	26 Ⓐ Ⓑ Ⓒ Ⓓ Ⓔ	51 Ⓐ Ⓑ Ⓒ Ⓓ Ⓔ	76 Ⓐ Ⓑ Ⓒ Ⓓ Ⓔ
2 Ⓐ Ⓑ Ⓒ Ⓓ Ⓔ	27 Ⓐ Ⓑ Ⓒ Ⓓ Ⓔ	52 Ⓐ Ⓑ Ⓒ Ⓓ Ⓔ	77 Ⓐ Ⓑ Ⓒ Ⓓ Ⓔ
3 Ⓐ Ⓑ Ⓒ Ⓓ Ⓔ	28 Ⓐ Ⓑ Ⓒ Ⓓ Ⓔ	53 Ⓐ Ⓑ Ⓒ Ⓓ Ⓔ	78 Ⓐ Ⓑ Ⓒ Ⓓ Ⓔ
4 Ⓐ Ⓑ Ⓒ Ⓓ Ⓔ	29 Ⓐ Ⓑ Ⓒ Ⓓ Ⓔ	54 Ⓐ Ⓑ Ⓒ Ⓓ Ⓔ	79 Ⓐ Ⓑ Ⓒ Ⓓ Ⓔ
5 Ⓐ Ⓑ Ⓒ Ⓓ Ⓔ	30 Ⓐ Ⓑ Ⓒ Ⓓ Ⓔ	55 Ⓐ Ⓑ Ⓒ Ⓓ Ⓔ	80 Ⓐ Ⓑ Ⓒ Ⓓ Ⓔ
6 Ⓐ Ⓑ Ⓒ Ⓓ Ⓔ	31 Ⓐ Ⓑ Ⓒ Ⓓ Ⓔ	56 Ⓐ Ⓑ Ⓒ Ⓓ Ⓔ	81 Ⓐ Ⓑ Ⓒ Ⓓ Ⓔ
7 Ⓐ Ⓑ Ⓒ Ⓓ Ⓔ	32 Ⓐ Ⓑ Ⓒ Ⓓ Ⓔ	57 Ⓐ Ⓑ Ⓒ Ⓓ Ⓔ	82 Ⓐ Ⓑ Ⓒ Ⓓ Ⓔ
8 Ⓐ Ⓑ Ⓒ Ⓓ Ⓔ	33 Ⓐ Ⓑ Ⓒ Ⓓ Ⓔ	58 Ⓐ Ⓑ Ⓒ Ⓓ Ⓔ	83 Ⓐ Ⓑ Ⓒ Ⓓ Ⓔ
9 Ⓐ Ⓑ Ⓒ Ⓓ Ⓔ	34 Ⓐ Ⓑ Ⓒ Ⓓ Ⓔ	59 Ⓐ Ⓑ Ⓒ Ⓓ Ⓔ	84 Ⓐ Ⓑ Ⓒ Ⓓ Ⓔ
10 Ⓐ Ⓑ Ⓒ Ⓓ Ⓔ	35 Ⓐ Ⓑ Ⓒ Ⓓ Ⓔ	60 Ⓐ Ⓑ Ⓒ Ⓓ Ⓔ	85 Ⓐ Ⓑ Ⓒ Ⓓ Ⓔ
11 Ⓐ Ⓑ Ⓒ Ⓓ Ⓔ	36 Ⓐ Ⓑ Ⓒ Ⓓ Ⓔ	61 Ⓐ Ⓑ Ⓒ Ⓓ Ⓔ	86 Ⓐ Ⓑ Ⓒ Ⓓ Ⓔ
12 Ⓐ Ⓑ Ⓒ Ⓓ Ⓔ	37 Ⓐ Ⓑ Ⓒ Ⓓ Ⓔ	62 Ⓐ Ⓑ Ⓒ Ⓓ Ⓔ	87 Ⓐ Ⓑ Ⓒ Ⓓ Ⓔ
13 Ⓐ Ⓑ Ⓒ Ⓓ Ⓔ	38 Ⓐ Ⓑ Ⓒ Ⓓ Ⓔ	63 Ⓐ Ⓑ Ⓒ Ⓓ Ⓔ	88 Ⓐ Ⓑ Ⓒ Ⓓ Ⓔ
14 Ⓐ Ⓑ Ⓒ Ⓓ Ⓔ	39 Ⓐ Ⓑ Ⓒ Ⓓ Ⓔ	64 Ⓐ Ⓑ Ⓒ Ⓓ Ⓔ	89 Ⓐ Ⓑ Ⓒ Ⓓ Ⓔ
15 Ⓐ Ⓑ Ⓒ Ⓓ Ⓔ	40 Ⓐ Ⓑ Ⓒ Ⓓ Ⓔ	65 Ⓐ Ⓑ Ⓒ Ⓓ Ⓔ	90 Ⓐ Ⓑ Ⓒ Ⓓ Ⓔ
16 Ⓐ Ⓑ Ⓒ Ⓓ Ⓔ	41 Ⓐ Ⓑ Ⓒ Ⓓ Ⓔ	66 Ⓐ Ⓑ Ⓒ Ⓓ Ⓔ	91 Ⓐ Ⓑ Ⓒ Ⓓ Ⓔ
17 Ⓐ Ⓑ Ⓒ Ⓓ Ⓔ	42 Ⓐ Ⓑ Ⓒ Ⓓ Ⓔ	67 Ⓐ Ⓑ Ⓒ Ⓓ Ⓔ	92 Ⓐ Ⓑ Ⓒ Ⓓ Ⓔ
18 Ⓐ Ⓑ Ⓒ Ⓓ Ⓔ	43 Ⓐ Ⓑ Ⓒ Ⓓ Ⓔ	68 Ⓐ Ⓑ Ⓒ Ⓓ Ⓔ	93 Ⓐ Ⓑ Ⓒ Ⓓ Ⓔ
19 Ⓐ Ⓑ Ⓒ Ⓓ Ⓔ	44 Ⓐ Ⓑ Ⓒ Ⓓ Ⓔ	69 Ⓐ Ⓑ Ⓒ Ⓓ Ⓔ	94 Ⓐ Ⓑ Ⓒ Ⓓ Ⓔ
20 Ⓐ Ⓑ Ⓒ Ⓓ Ⓔ	45 Ⓐ Ⓑ Ⓒ Ⓓ Ⓔ	70 Ⓐ Ⓑ Ⓒ Ⓓ Ⓔ	95 Ⓐ Ⓑ Ⓒ Ⓓ Ⓔ
21 Ⓐ Ⓑ Ⓒ Ⓓ Ⓔ	46 Ⓐ Ⓑ Ⓒ Ⓓ Ⓔ	71 Ⓐ Ⓑ Ⓒ Ⓓ Ⓔ	96 Ⓐ Ⓑ Ⓒ Ⓓ Ⓔ
22 Ⓐ Ⓑ Ⓒ Ⓓ Ⓔ	47 Ⓐ Ⓑ Ⓒ Ⓓ Ⓔ	72 Ⓐ Ⓑ Ⓒ Ⓓ Ⓔ	97 Ⓐ Ⓑ Ⓒ Ⓓ Ⓔ
23 Ⓐ Ⓑ Ⓒ Ⓓ Ⓔ	48 Ⓐ Ⓑ Ⓒ Ⓓ Ⓔ	73 Ⓐ Ⓑ Ⓒ Ⓓ Ⓔ	98 Ⓐ Ⓑ Ⓒ Ⓓ Ⓔ
24 Ⓐ Ⓑ Ⓒ Ⓓ Ⓔ	49 Ⓐ Ⓑ Ⓒ Ⓓ Ⓔ	74 Ⓐ Ⓑ Ⓒ Ⓓ Ⓔ	99 Ⓐ Ⓑ Ⓒ Ⓓ Ⓔ
25 Ⓐ Ⓑ Ⓒ Ⓓ Ⓔ	50 Ⓐ Ⓑ Ⓒ Ⓓ Ⓔ	75 Ⓐ Ⓑ Ⓒ Ⓓ Ⓔ	100 Ⓐ Ⓑ Ⓒ Ⓓ Ⓔ

Quality Assurance Mark

8 BOOK CODE

(Copy and grid as on back of test book.)

⓪	Ⓐ	⓪
①	Ⓑ	①
②	Ⓒ	②
③	Ⓓ	③
④	Ⓔ	④
⑤	Ⓕ	⑤
⑥	Ⓖ	⑥
⑦	Ⓗ	⑦
⑧	Ⓘ	⑧
⑨	Ⓙ	⑨
	Ⓚ	
	Ⓛ	
	Ⓜ	
	Ⓝ	
	Ⓞ	
	Ⓟ	
	Ⓠ	
	Ⓡ	
	Ⓢ	
	Ⓣ	
	Ⓤ	
	Ⓥ	
	Ⓦ	
	Ⓧ	
	Ⓨ	
	Ⓩ	

9 BOOK ID

(Copy from back of test book.)

10 BOOK SERIAL NUMBER

(Copy from front of test book.)

⓪	⓪	⓪	⓪	⓪	⓪
①	①	①	①	①	①
②	②	②	②	②	②
③	③	③	③	③	③
④	④	④	④	④	④
⑤	⑤	⑤	⑤	⑤	⑤
⑥	⑥	⑥	⑥	⑥	⑥
⑦	⑦	⑦	⑦	⑦	⑦
⑧	⑧	⑧	⑧	⑧	⑧
⑨	⑨	⑨	⑨	⑨	⑨

Chemistry *Fill in circle CE only if II is correct explanation of I.

	I	II	CE*		I	II	CE*
101	Ⓣ Ⓕ	Ⓣ Ⓕ	◯	109	Ⓣ Ⓕ	Ⓣ Ⓕ	◯
102	Ⓣ Ⓕ	Ⓣ Ⓕ	◯	110	Ⓣ Ⓕ	Ⓣ Ⓕ	◯
103	Ⓣ Ⓕ	Ⓣ Ⓕ	◯	111	Ⓣ Ⓕ	Ⓣ Ⓕ	◯
104	Ⓣ Ⓕ	Ⓣ Ⓕ	◯	112	Ⓣ Ⓕ	Ⓣ Ⓕ	◯
105	Ⓣ Ⓕ	Ⓣ Ⓕ	◯	113	Ⓣ Ⓕ	Ⓣ Ⓕ	◯
106	Ⓣ Ⓕ	Ⓣ Ⓕ	◯	114	Ⓣ Ⓕ	Ⓣ Ⓕ	◯
107	Ⓣ Ⓕ	Ⓣ Ⓕ	◯	115	Ⓣ Ⓕ	Ⓣ Ⓕ	◯
108	Ⓣ Ⓕ	Ⓣ Ⓕ	◯				

FOR OFFICIAL USE ONLY

R/C	W/S1	FS/S2	CS/S3	WS

COMPLETE MARK ● EXAMPLES OF INCOMPLETE MARKS

You must use a No. 2 pencil. Do not use a mechanical pencil. *It is very important that you fill in the entire circle darkly and completely. If you change your response, erase as completely as possible. Incomplete marks or erasures may affect your score.*

If there are more answer spaces than you need, leave them blank.

Test Code	
V	① ② ③ ④ ⑤ ⑥ ⑦ ⑧ ⑨
W	① ② ③ ④ ⑤ ⑥ ⑦ ⑧ ⑨
X	① ② ③ ④ ⑤
Y	Ⓐ Ⓑ Ⓒ Ⓓ Ⓔ
Q	① ② ③ ④ ⑤ ⑥ ⑦ ⑧ ⑨

Print Subject Test Name:

If you are taking a Language Test select: ○ Reading Only ○ Reading and Listening

8 BOOK CODE (Copy and grid as on back of test book.)

9 BOOK ID (Copy from back of test book.)

10 BOOK SERIAL NUMBER (Copy from front of test book.)

1 Ⓐ Ⓑ Ⓒ Ⓓ Ⓔ	26 Ⓐ Ⓑ Ⓒ Ⓓ Ⓔ	51 Ⓐ Ⓑ Ⓒ Ⓓ Ⓔ	76 Ⓐ Ⓑ Ⓒ Ⓓ Ⓔ
2 Ⓐ Ⓑ Ⓒ Ⓓ Ⓔ	27 Ⓐ Ⓑ Ⓒ Ⓓ Ⓔ	52 Ⓐ Ⓑ Ⓒ Ⓓ Ⓔ	77 Ⓐ Ⓑ Ⓒ Ⓓ Ⓔ
3 Ⓐ Ⓑ Ⓒ Ⓓ Ⓔ	28 Ⓐ Ⓑ Ⓒ Ⓓ Ⓔ	53 Ⓐ Ⓑ Ⓒ Ⓓ Ⓔ	78 Ⓐ Ⓑ Ⓒ Ⓓ Ⓔ
4 Ⓐ Ⓑ Ⓒ Ⓓ Ⓔ	29 Ⓐ Ⓑ Ⓒ Ⓓ Ⓔ	54 Ⓐ Ⓑ Ⓒ Ⓓ Ⓔ	79 Ⓐ Ⓑ Ⓒ Ⓓ Ⓔ
5 Ⓐ Ⓑ Ⓒ Ⓓ Ⓔ	30 Ⓐ Ⓑ Ⓒ Ⓓ Ⓔ	55 Ⓐ Ⓑ Ⓒ Ⓓ Ⓔ	80 Ⓐ Ⓑ Ⓒ Ⓓ Ⓔ
6 Ⓐ Ⓑ Ⓒ Ⓓ Ⓔ	31 Ⓐ Ⓑ Ⓒ Ⓓ Ⓔ	56 Ⓐ Ⓑ Ⓒ Ⓓ Ⓔ	81 Ⓐ Ⓑ Ⓒ Ⓓ Ⓔ
7 Ⓐ Ⓑ Ⓒ Ⓓ Ⓔ	32 Ⓐ Ⓑ Ⓒ Ⓓ Ⓔ	57 Ⓐ Ⓑ Ⓒ Ⓓ Ⓔ	82 Ⓐ Ⓑ Ⓒ Ⓓ Ⓔ
8 Ⓐ Ⓑ Ⓒ Ⓓ Ⓔ	33 Ⓐ Ⓑ Ⓒ Ⓓ Ⓔ	58 Ⓐ Ⓑ Ⓒ Ⓓ Ⓔ	83 Ⓐ Ⓑ Ⓒ Ⓓ Ⓔ
9 Ⓐ Ⓑ Ⓒ Ⓓ Ⓔ	34 Ⓐ Ⓑ Ⓒ Ⓓ Ⓔ	59 Ⓐ Ⓑ Ⓒ Ⓓ Ⓔ	84 Ⓐ Ⓑ Ⓒ Ⓓ Ⓔ
10 Ⓐ Ⓑ Ⓒ Ⓓ Ⓔ	35 Ⓐ Ⓑ Ⓒ Ⓓ Ⓔ	60 Ⓐ Ⓑ Ⓒ Ⓓ Ⓔ	85 Ⓐ Ⓑ Ⓒ Ⓓ Ⓔ
11 Ⓐ Ⓑ Ⓒ Ⓓ Ⓔ	36 Ⓐ Ⓑ Ⓒ Ⓓ Ⓔ	61 Ⓐ Ⓑ Ⓒ Ⓓ Ⓔ	86 Ⓐ Ⓑ Ⓒ Ⓓ Ⓔ
12 Ⓐ Ⓑ Ⓒ Ⓓ Ⓔ	37 Ⓐ Ⓑ Ⓒ Ⓓ Ⓔ	62 Ⓐ Ⓑ Ⓒ Ⓓ Ⓔ	87 Ⓐ Ⓑ Ⓒ Ⓓ Ⓔ
13 Ⓐ Ⓑ Ⓒ Ⓓ Ⓔ	38 Ⓐ Ⓑ Ⓒ Ⓓ Ⓔ	63 Ⓐ Ⓑ Ⓒ Ⓓ Ⓔ	88 Ⓐ Ⓑ Ⓒ Ⓓ Ⓔ
14 Ⓐ Ⓑ Ⓒ Ⓓ Ⓔ	39 Ⓐ Ⓑ Ⓒ Ⓓ Ⓔ	64 Ⓐ Ⓑ Ⓒ Ⓓ Ⓔ	89 Ⓐ Ⓑ Ⓒ Ⓓ Ⓔ
15 Ⓐ Ⓑ Ⓒ Ⓓ Ⓔ	40 Ⓐ Ⓑ Ⓒ Ⓓ Ⓔ	65 Ⓐ Ⓑ Ⓒ Ⓓ Ⓔ	90 Ⓐ Ⓑ Ⓒ Ⓓ Ⓔ
16 Ⓐ Ⓑ Ⓒ Ⓓ Ⓔ	41 Ⓐ Ⓑ Ⓒ Ⓓ Ⓔ	66 Ⓐ Ⓑ Ⓒ Ⓓ Ⓔ	91 Ⓐ Ⓑ Ⓒ Ⓓ Ⓔ
17 Ⓐ Ⓑ Ⓒ Ⓓ Ⓔ	42 Ⓐ Ⓑ Ⓒ Ⓓ Ⓔ	67 Ⓐ Ⓑ Ⓒ Ⓓ Ⓔ	92 Ⓐ Ⓑ Ⓒ Ⓓ Ⓔ
18 Ⓐ Ⓑ Ⓒ Ⓓ Ⓔ	43 Ⓐ Ⓑ Ⓒ Ⓓ Ⓔ	68 Ⓐ Ⓑ Ⓒ Ⓓ Ⓔ	93 Ⓐ Ⓑ Ⓒ Ⓓ Ⓔ
19 Ⓐ Ⓑ Ⓒ Ⓓ Ⓔ	44 Ⓐ Ⓑ Ⓒ Ⓓ Ⓔ	69 Ⓐ Ⓑ Ⓒ Ⓓ Ⓔ	94 Ⓐ Ⓑ Ⓒ Ⓓ Ⓔ
20 Ⓐ Ⓑ Ⓒ Ⓓ Ⓔ	45 Ⓐ Ⓑ Ⓒ Ⓓ Ⓔ	70 Ⓐ Ⓑ Ⓒ Ⓓ Ⓔ	95 Ⓐ Ⓑ Ⓒ Ⓓ Ⓔ
21 Ⓐ Ⓑ Ⓒ Ⓓ Ⓔ	46 Ⓐ Ⓑ Ⓒ Ⓓ Ⓔ	71 Ⓐ Ⓑ Ⓒ Ⓓ Ⓔ	96 Ⓐ Ⓑ Ⓒ Ⓓ Ⓔ
22 Ⓐ Ⓑ Ⓒ Ⓓ Ⓔ	47 Ⓐ Ⓑ Ⓒ Ⓓ Ⓔ	72 Ⓐ Ⓑ Ⓒ Ⓓ Ⓔ	97 Ⓐ Ⓑ Ⓒ Ⓓ Ⓔ
23 Ⓐ Ⓑ Ⓒ Ⓓ Ⓔ	48 Ⓐ Ⓑ Ⓒ Ⓓ Ⓔ	73 Ⓐ Ⓑ Ⓒ Ⓓ Ⓔ	98 Ⓐ Ⓑ Ⓒ Ⓓ Ⓔ
24 Ⓐ Ⓑ Ⓒ Ⓓ Ⓔ	49 Ⓐ Ⓑ Ⓒ Ⓓ Ⓔ	74 Ⓐ Ⓑ Ⓒ Ⓓ Ⓔ	99 Ⓐ Ⓑ Ⓒ Ⓓ Ⓔ
25 Ⓐ Ⓑ Ⓒ Ⓓ Ⓔ	50 Ⓐ Ⓑ Ⓒ Ⓓ Ⓔ	75 Ⓐ Ⓑ Ⓒ Ⓓ Ⓔ	100 Ⓐ Ⓑ Ⓒ Ⓓ Ⓔ

Chemistry *Fill in circle CE only if II is correct explanation of I.

	I	II	CE*		I	II	CE*
101	Ⓣ Ⓕ	Ⓣ Ⓕ	○	109	Ⓣ Ⓕ	Ⓣ Ⓕ	○
102	Ⓣ Ⓕ	Ⓣ Ⓕ	○	110	Ⓣ Ⓕ	Ⓣ Ⓕ	○
103	Ⓣ Ⓕ	Ⓣ Ⓕ	○	111	Ⓣ Ⓕ	Ⓣ Ⓕ	○
104	Ⓣ Ⓕ	Ⓣ Ⓕ	○	112	Ⓣ Ⓕ	Ⓣ Ⓕ	○
105	Ⓣ Ⓕ	Ⓣ Ⓕ	○	113	Ⓣ Ⓕ	Ⓣ Ⓕ	○
106	Ⓣ Ⓕ	Ⓣ Ⓕ	○	114	Ⓣ Ⓕ	Ⓣ Ⓕ	○
107	Ⓣ Ⓕ	Ⓣ Ⓕ	○	115	Ⓣ Ⓕ	Ⓣ Ⓕ	○
108	Ⓣ Ⓕ	Ⓣ Ⓕ	○				

FOR OFFICIAL USE ONLY

R/C	W/S1	FS/S2	CS/S3	WS

Quality Assurance Mark

PLEASE DO NOT WRITE IN THIS AREA

SERIAL #

SAT Subject Tests™

DO NOT USE A MECHANICAL PENCIL

COMPLETE MARK ● EXAMPLES OF INCOMPLETE MARKS

You must use a No. 2 pencil. *It is very important that you fill in the entire circle darkly and completely. If you change your response, erase as completely as possible. Incomplete marks or erasures may affect your score. It is very important that you follow these instructions when filling out your answer sheet.*

1 **Your Name:** (Print) ______ Last ______ First ______ M.I.

I agree to the conditions on the back of the SAT Subject Tests™ booklet. I also agree to use only a No. 2 pencil to complete my answer sheet.

Signature: ______ **Date:** __/__/__

Home Address: ______ Number and Street ______ City ______ State ______ Zip Code

Home Phone: ( ) ______ **Center:** (Print) ______ City ______ State/Country

2 YOUR NAME

Last Name (First 6 Letters) | First Name (First 4 Letters) | Mid. Init.

3 DATE OF BIRTH

MONTH | DAY | YEAR

Jan, Feb, Mar, Apr, May, Jun, Jul, Aug, Sep, Oct, Nov, Dec

4 ZIP CODE

5 SEX

Female Male

6 REGISTRATION NUMBER

(Copy from Admission Ticket.)

I turned in my registration form today.

7 SOCIAL SECURITY NUMBER

8 BOOK CODE

(Copy and grid as on back of test book.)

9 BOOK ID

(Copy from back of test book.)

10 BOOK SERIAL NUMBER

(Copy from front of test book.)

11 TEST CENTER

(Supplied by Test Center Supervisor.)

FOR OFFICIAL USE ONLY

172624-001:654321 ISD5959

00272-36392 • NS85E950 • Printed in U.S.A.

732653

PLEASE DO NOT WRITE IN THIS AREA

SERIAL #

COMPLETE MARK ● EXAMPLES OF INCOMPLETE MARKS

You must use a No. 2 pencil. Do not use a mechanical pencil. It is very important that you fill in the entire circle darkly and completely. If you change your response, erase as completely as possible. Incomplete marks or erasures may affect your score.

If there are more answer spaces than you need, leave them blank.

Test Code

V	1 2 3 4 5 6 7 8 9
W	1 2 3 4 5 6 7 8 9
X	1 2 3 4 5
Y	A B C D E
Q	1 2 3 4 5 6 7 8 9

Print Subject Test Name:

If you are taking a Language Test select: ○ Reading Only ○ Reading and Listening

1–100 A B C D E

8 BOOK CODE (Copy and grid as on back of test book.)

9 BOOK ID (Copy from back of test book.)

10 BOOK SERIAL NUMBER (Copy from front of test book.)

Quality Assurance Mark

Chemistry *Fill in circle CE only if II is correct explanation of I.

	I	II	CE*		I	II	CE*
101	T F	T F	○	109	T F	T F	○
102	T F	T F	○	110	T F	T F	○
103	T F	T F	○	111	T F	T F	○
104	T F	T F	○	112	T F	T F	○
105	T F	T F	○	113	T F	T F	○
106	T F	T F	○	114	T F	T F	○
107	T F	T F	○	115	T F	T F	○
108	T F	T F	○				

FOR OFFICIAL USE ONLY

R/C	W/S1	FS/S2	CS/S3	WS

CERTIFICATION STATEMENT

Copy the statement below (do not print) and sign your name as you would an official document.

I hereby agree to the conditions set forth online at www.collegeboard.com and/or in the SAT Registration Booklet and certify that I am the person whose name and address appear on this answer sheet.

By signing below, I agree not to share any specific test questions with anyone after I test by any form of communication, including, but not limited to: email, text messages, or use of the Internet.

Signature ______________________ Date ______________

COMPLETE MARK ● EXAMPLES OF INCOMPLETE MARKS

You must use a No. 2 pencil. Do not use a mechanical pencil. *It is very important that you fill in the entire circle darkly and completely. If you change your response, erase as completely as possible. Incomplete marks or erasures may affect your score.*

If there are more answer spaces than you need, leave them blank.

	Test Code
V	1 2 3 4 5 6 7 8 9
W	1 2 3 4 5 6 7 8 9
X	1 2 3 4 5
Y	A B C D E
Q	1 2 3 4 5 6 7 8 9

Print Subject Test Name:

If you are taking a Language Test select: ○ Reading Only ○ Reading and Listening

1 A B C D E	26 A B C D E	51 A B C D E	76 A B C D E
2 A B C D E	27 A B C D E	52 A B C D E	77 A B C D E
3 A B C D E	28 A B C D E	53 A B C D E	78 A B C D E
4 A B C D E	29 A B C D E	54 A B C D E	79 A B C D E
5 A B C D E	30 A B C D E	55 A B C D E	80 A B C D E
6 A B C D E	31 A B C D E	56 A B C D E	81 A B C D E
7 A B C D E	32 A B C D E	57 A B C D E	82 A B C D E
8 A B C D E	33 A B C D E	58 A B C D E	83 A B C D E
9 A B C D E	34 A B C D E	59 A B C D E	84 A B C D E
10 A B C D E	35 A B C D E	60 A B C D E	85 A B C D E
11 A B C D E	36 A B C D E	61 A B C D E	86 A B C D E
12 A B C D E	37 A B C D E	62 A B C D E	87 A B C D E
13 A B C D E	38 A B C D E	63 A B C D E	88 A B C D E
14 A B C D E	39 A B C D E	64 A B C D E	89 A B C D E
15 A B C D E	40 A B C D E	65 A B C D E	90 A B C D E
16 A B C D E	41 A B C D E	66 A B C D E	91 A B C D E
17 A B C D E	42 A B C D E	67 A B C D E	92 A B C D E
18 A B C D E	43 A B C D E	68 A B C D E	93 A B C D E
19 A B C D E	44 A B C D E	69 A B C D E	94 A B C D E
20 A B C D E	45 A B C D E	70 A B C D E	95 A B C D E
21 A B C D E	46 A B C D E	71 A B C D E	96 A B C D E
22 A B C D E	47 A B C D E	72 A B C D E	97 A B C D E
23 A B C D E	48 A B C D E	73 A B C D E	98 A B C D E
24 A B C D E	49 A B C D E	74 A B C D E	99 A B C D E
25 A B C D E	50 A B C D E	75 A B C D E	100 A B C D E

Quality ● Assurance Mark

8 BOOK CODE (Copy and grid as on back of test book.)

0	A	0
1	B	1
2	C	2
3	D	3
4	E	4
5	F	5
6	G	6
7	H	7
8	I	8
9	J	9
	K	
	L	
	M	
	N	
	O	
	P	
	Q	
	R	
	S	
	T	
	U	
	V	
	W	
	X	
	Y	
	Z	

9 BOOK ID (Copy from back of test book.)

10 BOOK SERIAL NUMBER (Copy from front of test book.)

0	0	0	0	0	0
1	1	1	1	1	1
2	2	2	2	2	2
3	3	3	3	3	3
4	4	4	4	4	4
5	5	5	5	5	5
6	6	6	6	6	6
7	7	7	7	7	7
8	8	8	8	8	8
9	9	9	9	9	9

Chemistry *Fill in circle CE only if II is correct explanation of I.

	I	II	CE*		I	II	CE*
101	T F	T F	○	109	T F	T F	○
102	T F	T F	○	110	T F	T F	○
103	T F	T F	○	111	T F	T F	○
104	T F	T F	○	112	T F	T F	○
105	T F	T F	○	113	T F	T F	○
106	T F	T F	○	114	T F	T F	○
107	T F	T F	○	115	T F	T F	○
108	T F	T F	○				

FOR OFFICIAL USE ONLY

R/C	W/S1	FS/S2	CS/S3	WS

COMPLETE MARK ● EXAMPLES OF INCOMPLETE MARKS

You must use a No. 2 pencil. Do not use a mechanical pencil. It is very important that you fill in the entire circle darkly and completely. If you change your response, erase as completely as possible. Incomplete marks or erasures may affect your score.

If there are more answer spaces than you need, leave them blank.

Test Code	
V	① ② ③ ④ ⑤ ⑥ ⑦ ⑧ ⑨
W	① ② ③ ④ ⑤ ⑥ ⑦ ⑧ ⑨
X	① ② ③ ④ ⑤
Y	Ⓐ Ⓑ Ⓒ Ⓓ Ⓔ
Q	① ② ③ ④ ⑤ ⑥ ⑦ ⑧ ⑨

Print Subject Test Name:

If you are taking a Language Test select: ○ Reading Only ○ Reading and Listening

1 Ⓐ Ⓑ Ⓒ Ⓓ Ⓔ	26 Ⓐ Ⓑ Ⓒ Ⓓ Ⓔ	51 Ⓐ Ⓑ Ⓒ Ⓓ Ⓔ	76 Ⓐ Ⓑ Ⓒ Ⓓ Ⓔ
2 Ⓐ Ⓑ Ⓒ Ⓓ Ⓔ	27 Ⓐ Ⓑ Ⓒ Ⓓ Ⓔ	52 Ⓐ Ⓑ Ⓒ Ⓓ Ⓔ	77 Ⓐ Ⓑ Ⓒ Ⓓ Ⓔ
3 Ⓐ Ⓑ Ⓒ Ⓓ Ⓔ	28 Ⓐ Ⓑ Ⓒ Ⓓ Ⓔ	53 Ⓐ Ⓑ Ⓒ Ⓓ Ⓔ	78 Ⓐ Ⓑ Ⓒ Ⓓ Ⓔ
4 Ⓐ Ⓑ Ⓒ Ⓓ Ⓔ	29 Ⓐ Ⓑ Ⓒ Ⓓ Ⓔ	54 Ⓐ Ⓑ Ⓒ Ⓓ Ⓔ	79 Ⓐ Ⓑ Ⓒ Ⓓ Ⓔ
5 Ⓐ Ⓑ Ⓒ Ⓓ Ⓔ	30 Ⓐ Ⓑ Ⓒ Ⓓ Ⓔ	55 Ⓐ Ⓑ Ⓒ Ⓓ Ⓔ	80 Ⓐ Ⓑ Ⓒ Ⓓ Ⓔ
6 Ⓐ Ⓑ Ⓒ Ⓓ Ⓔ	31 Ⓐ Ⓑ Ⓒ Ⓓ Ⓔ	56 Ⓐ Ⓑ Ⓒ Ⓓ Ⓔ	81 Ⓐ Ⓑ Ⓒ Ⓓ Ⓔ
7 Ⓐ Ⓑ Ⓒ Ⓓ Ⓔ	32 Ⓐ Ⓑ Ⓒ Ⓓ Ⓔ	57 Ⓐ Ⓑ Ⓒ Ⓓ Ⓔ	82 Ⓐ Ⓑ Ⓒ Ⓓ Ⓔ
8 Ⓐ Ⓑ Ⓒ Ⓓ Ⓔ	33 Ⓐ Ⓑ Ⓒ Ⓓ Ⓔ	58 Ⓐ Ⓑ Ⓒ Ⓓ Ⓔ	83 Ⓐ Ⓑ Ⓒ Ⓓ Ⓔ
9 Ⓐ Ⓑ Ⓒ Ⓓ Ⓔ	34 Ⓐ Ⓑ Ⓒ Ⓓ Ⓔ	59 Ⓐ Ⓑ Ⓒ Ⓓ Ⓔ	84 Ⓐ Ⓑ Ⓒ Ⓓ Ⓔ
10 Ⓐ Ⓑ Ⓒ Ⓓ Ⓔ	35 Ⓐ Ⓑ Ⓒ Ⓓ Ⓔ	60 Ⓐ Ⓑ Ⓒ Ⓓ Ⓔ	85 Ⓐ Ⓑ Ⓒ Ⓓ Ⓔ
11 Ⓐ Ⓑ Ⓒ Ⓓ Ⓔ	36 Ⓐ Ⓑ Ⓒ Ⓓ Ⓔ	61 Ⓐ Ⓑ Ⓒ Ⓓ Ⓔ	86 Ⓐ Ⓑ Ⓒ Ⓓ Ⓔ
12 Ⓐ Ⓑ Ⓒ Ⓓ Ⓔ	37 Ⓐ Ⓑ Ⓒ Ⓓ Ⓔ	62 Ⓐ Ⓑ Ⓒ Ⓓ Ⓔ	87 Ⓐ Ⓑ Ⓒ Ⓓ Ⓔ
13 Ⓐ Ⓑ Ⓒ Ⓓ Ⓔ	38 Ⓐ Ⓑ Ⓒ Ⓓ Ⓔ	63 Ⓐ Ⓑ Ⓒ Ⓓ Ⓔ	88 Ⓐ Ⓑ Ⓒ Ⓓ Ⓔ
14 Ⓐ Ⓑ Ⓒ Ⓓ Ⓔ	39 Ⓐ Ⓑ Ⓒ Ⓓ Ⓔ	64 Ⓐ Ⓑ Ⓒ Ⓓ Ⓔ	89 Ⓐ Ⓑ Ⓒ Ⓓ Ⓔ
15 Ⓐ Ⓑ Ⓒ Ⓓ Ⓔ	40 Ⓐ Ⓑ Ⓒ Ⓓ Ⓔ	65 Ⓐ Ⓑ Ⓒ Ⓓ Ⓔ	90 Ⓐ Ⓑ Ⓒ Ⓓ Ⓔ
16 Ⓐ Ⓑ Ⓒ Ⓓ Ⓔ	41 Ⓐ Ⓑ Ⓒ Ⓓ Ⓔ	66 Ⓐ Ⓑ Ⓒ Ⓓ Ⓔ	91 Ⓐ Ⓑ Ⓒ Ⓓ Ⓔ
17 Ⓐ Ⓑ Ⓒ Ⓓ Ⓔ	42 Ⓐ Ⓑ Ⓒ Ⓓ Ⓔ	67 Ⓐ Ⓑ Ⓒ Ⓓ Ⓔ	92 Ⓐ Ⓑ Ⓒ Ⓓ Ⓔ
18 Ⓐ Ⓑ Ⓒ Ⓓ Ⓔ	43 Ⓐ Ⓑ Ⓒ Ⓓ Ⓔ	68 Ⓐ Ⓑ Ⓒ Ⓓ Ⓔ	93 Ⓐ Ⓑ Ⓒ Ⓓ Ⓔ
19 Ⓐ Ⓑ Ⓒ Ⓓ Ⓔ	44 Ⓐ Ⓑ Ⓒ Ⓓ Ⓔ	69 Ⓐ Ⓑ Ⓒ Ⓓ Ⓔ	94 Ⓐ Ⓑ Ⓒ Ⓓ Ⓔ
20 Ⓐ Ⓑ Ⓒ Ⓓ Ⓔ	45 Ⓐ Ⓑ Ⓒ Ⓓ Ⓔ	70 Ⓐ Ⓑ Ⓒ Ⓓ Ⓔ	95 Ⓐ Ⓑ Ⓒ Ⓓ Ⓔ
21 Ⓐ Ⓑ Ⓒ Ⓓ Ⓔ	46 Ⓐ Ⓑ Ⓒ Ⓓ Ⓔ	71 Ⓐ Ⓑ Ⓒ Ⓓ Ⓔ	96 Ⓐ Ⓑ Ⓒ Ⓓ Ⓔ
22 Ⓐ Ⓑ Ⓒ Ⓓ Ⓔ	47 Ⓐ Ⓑ Ⓒ Ⓓ Ⓔ	72 Ⓐ Ⓑ Ⓒ Ⓓ Ⓔ	97 Ⓐ Ⓑ Ⓒ Ⓓ Ⓔ
23 Ⓐ Ⓑ Ⓒ Ⓓ Ⓔ	48 Ⓐ Ⓑ Ⓒ Ⓓ Ⓔ	73 Ⓐ Ⓑ Ⓒ Ⓓ Ⓔ	98 Ⓐ Ⓑ Ⓒ Ⓓ Ⓔ
24 Ⓐ Ⓑ Ⓒ Ⓓ Ⓔ	49 Ⓐ Ⓑ Ⓒ Ⓓ Ⓔ	74 Ⓐ Ⓑ Ⓒ Ⓓ Ⓔ	99 Ⓐ Ⓑ Ⓒ Ⓓ Ⓔ
25 Ⓐ Ⓑ Ⓒ Ⓓ Ⓔ	50 Ⓐ Ⓑ Ⓒ Ⓓ Ⓔ	75 Ⓐ Ⓑ Ⓒ Ⓓ Ⓔ	100 Ⓐ Ⓑ Ⓒ Ⓓ Ⓔ

Chemistry *Fill in circle CE only if II is correct explanation of I.

	I	II	CE*		I	II	CE*
101	Ⓣ Ⓕ	Ⓣ Ⓕ	○	109	Ⓣ Ⓕ	Ⓣ Ⓕ	○
102	Ⓣ Ⓕ	Ⓣ Ⓕ	○	110	Ⓣ Ⓕ	Ⓣ Ⓕ	○
103	Ⓣ Ⓕ	Ⓣ Ⓕ	○	111	Ⓣ Ⓕ	Ⓣ Ⓕ	○
104	Ⓣ Ⓕ	Ⓣ Ⓕ	○	112	Ⓣ Ⓕ	Ⓣ Ⓕ	○
105	Ⓣ Ⓕ	Ⓣ Ⓕ	○	113	Ⓣ Ⓕ	Ⓣ Ⓕ	○
106	Ⓣ Ⓕ	Ⓣ Ⓕ	○	114	Ⓣ Ⓕ	Ⓣ Ⓕ	○
107	Ⓣ Ⓕ	Ⓣ Ⓕ	○	115	Ⓣ Ⓕ	Ⓣ Ⓕ	○
108	Ⓣ Ⓕ	Ⓣ Ⓕ	○				

8 BOOK CODE (Copy and grid as on back of test book.)

0	A	0
1	B	1
2	C	2
3	D	3
4	E	4
5	F	5
6	G	6
7	H	7
8	I	8
9	J	9
	K	
	L	
	M	
	N	
	O	
	P	
	Q	
	R	
	S	
	T	
	U	
	V	
	W	
	X	
	Y	
	Z	

9 BOOK ID (Copy from back of test book.)

10 BOOK SERIAL NUMBER (Copy from front of test book.)

0	0	0	0	0	0
1	1	1	1	1	1
2	2	2	2	2	2
3	3	3	3	3	3
4	4	4	4	4	4
5	5	5	5	5	5
6	6	6	6	6	6
7	7	7	7	7	7
8	8	8	8	8	8
9	9	9	9	9	9

Quality Assurance Mark

FOR OFFICIAL USE ONLY

R/C	W/S1	FS/S2	CS/S3	WS

PLEASE DO NOT WRITE IN THIS AREA

SERIAL #

SAT Subject Tests™

DO NOT USE A MECHANICAL PENCIL

COMPLETE MARK ● EXAMPLES OF INCOMPLETE MARKS

***You must use a No. 2 pencil.** It is very important that you fill in the entire circle darkly and completely. If you change your response, erase as completely as possible. Incomplete marks or erasures may affect your score. It is very important that you follow these instructions when filling out your answer sheet.*

1 **Your Name:** (Print) Last First M.I.

I agree to the conditions on the back of the SAT Subject Tests™ booklet. I also agree to use only a No. 2 pencil to complete my answer sheet.

Signature: **Date:** / /

Home Address: Number and Street City State Zip Code

Home Phone: ( ) **Center:** (Print) City State/Country

2 YOUR NAME

Last Name (First 6 Letters) | First Name (First 4 Letters) | Mid. Init.

– ' A B C D E F G H I J K L M N O P Q R S T U V W X Y Z

3 DATE OF BIRTH

MONTH | DAY | YEAR

Jan Feb Mar Apr May Jun Jul Aug Sep Oct Nov Dec

4 ZIP CODE

0 1 2 3 4 5 6 7 8 9

5 SEX

Female Male

6 REGISTRATION NUMBER

(Copy from Admission Ticket.)

0 1 2 3 4 5 6 7 8 9

I turned in my registration form today.

7 SOCIAL SECURITY NUMBER

0 1 2 3 4 5 6 7 8 9

8 BOOK CODE

(Copy and grid as on back of test book.)

0 1 2 3 4 5 6 7 8 9 | A B C D E F G H I J K L M N O P Q R S T U V W X Y Z

9 BOOK ID

(Copy from back of test book.)

10 BOOK SERIAL NUMBER

(Copy from front of test book.)

0 1 2 3 4 5 6 7 8 9

11 TEST CENTER

(Supplied by Test Center Supervisor.)

0 1 2 3 4 5 6 7 8 9

FOR OFFICIAL USE ONLY

0 1 2 3 4 5 6

0 1 2 3 4 5 6

0 1 2 3 4 5 6

172624-001:654321 ISD5959

00272-36392 • NS85E950 • Printed in U.S.A.

732653

PLEASE DO NOT WRITE IN THIS AREA

SERIAL #

COMPLETE MARK ● EXAMPLES OF INCOMPLETE MARKS

You must use a No. 2 pencil. Do not use a mechanical pencil. *It is very important that you fill in the entire circle darkly and completely. If you change your response, erase as completely as possible. Incomplete marks or erasures may affect your score.*

If there are more answer spaces than you need, leave them blank.

Test Code

V ① ② ③ ④ ⑤ ⑥ ⑦ ⑧ ⑨
W ① ② ③ ④ ⑤ ⑥ ⑦ ⑧ ⑨
X ① ② ③ ④ ⑤
Y Ⓐ Ⓑ Ⓒ Ⓓ Ⓔ
Q ① ② ③ ④ ⑤ ⑥ ⑦ ⑧ ⑨

Print Subject Test Name:

If you are taking a Language Test select: ○ Reading Only ○ Reading and Listening

1–100 Ⓐ Ⓑ Ⓒ Ⓓ Ⓔ

8 BOOK CODE (Copy and grid as on back of test book.)

9 BOOK ID (Copy from back of test book.)

10 BOOK SERIAL NUMBER (Copy from front of test book.)

Quality Assurance Mark

Chemistry *Fill in circle CE only if II is correct explanation of I.

	I	II	CE*		I	II	CE*
101	Ⓣ Ⓕ	Ⓣ Ⓕ	○	109	Ⓣ Ⓕ	Ⓣ Ⓕ	○
102	Ⓣ Ⓕ	Ⓣ Ⓕ	○	110	Ⓣ Ⓕ	Ⓣ Ⓕ	○
103	Ⓣ Ⓕ	Ⓣ Ⓕ	○	111	Ⓣ Ⓕ	Ⓣ Ⓕ	○
104	Ⓣ Ⓕ	Ⓣ Ⓕ	○	112	Ⓣ Ⓕ	Ⓣ Ⓕ	○
105	Ⓣ Ⓕ	Ⓣ Ⓕ	○	113	Ⓣ Ⓕ	Ⓣ Ⓕ	○
106	Ⓣ Ⓕ	Ⓣ Ⓕ	○	114	Ⓣ Ⓕ	Ⓣ Ⓕ	○
107	Ⓣ Ⓕ	Ⓣ Ⓕ	○	115	Ⓣ Ⓕ	Ⓣ Ⓕ	○
108	Ⓣ Ⓕ	Ⓣ Ⓕ	○				

FOR OFFICIAL USE ONLY

R/C	W/S1	FS/S2	CS/S3	WS

CERTIFICATION STATEMENT

Copy the statement below (do not print) and sign your name as you would an official document.

I hereby agree to the conditions set forth online at www.collegeboard.com and/or in the SAT Registration Booklet and certify that I am the person whose name and address appear on this answer sheet.

By signing below, I agree not to share any specific test questions with anyone after I test by any form of communication, including, but not limited to: email, text messages, or use of the Internet.

Signature ____________________ Date ____________________

COMPLETE MARK ● EXAMPLES OF INCOMPLETE MARKS

You must use a No. 2 pencil. Do not use a mechanical pencil. It is very important that you fill in the entire circle darkly and completely. If you change your response, erase as completely as possible. Incomplete marks or erasures may affect your score.

If there are more answer spaces than you need, leave them blank.

Test Code	
V	1 2 3 4 5 6 7 8 9
W	1 2 3 4 5 6 7 8 9
X	1 2 3 4 5
Y	A B C D E
Q	1 2 3 4 5 6 7 8 9

Print Subject Test Name:

If you are taking a Language Test select: ○ Reading Only ○ Reading and Listening

1 A B C D E	26 A B C D E	51 A B C D E	76 A B C D E
2 A B C D E	27 A B C D E	52 A B C D E	77 A B C D E
3 A B C D E	28 A B C D E	53 A B C D E	78 A B C D E
4 A B C D E	29 A B C D E	54 A B C D E	79 A B C D E
5 A B C D E	30 A B C D E	55 A B C D E	80 A B C D E
6 A B C D E	31 A B C D E	56 A B C D E	81 A B C D E
7 A B C D E	32 A B C D E	57 A B C D E	82 A B C D E
8 A B C D E	33 A B C D E	58 A B C D E	83 A B C D E
9 A B C D E	34 A B C D E	59 A B C D E	84 A B C D E
10 A B C D E	35 A B C D E	60 A B C D E	85 A B C D E
11 A B C D E	36 A B C D E	61 A B C D E	86 A B C D E
12 A B C D E	37 A B C D E	62 A B C D E	87 A B C D E
13 A B C D E	38 A B C D E	63 A B C D E	88 A B C D E
14 A B C D E	39 A B C D E	64 A B C D E	89 A B C D E
15 A B C D E	40 A B C D E	65 A B C D E	90 A B C D E
16 A B C D E	41 A B C D E	66 A B C D E	91 A B C D E
17 A B C D E	42 A B C D E	67 A B C D E	92 A B C D E
18 A B C D E	43 A B C D E	68 A B C D E	93 A B C D E
19 A B C D E	44 A B C D E	69 A B C D E	94 A B C D E
20 A B C D E	45 A B C D E	70 A B C D E	95 A B C D E
21 A B C D E	46 A B C D E	71 A B C D E	96 A B C D E
22 A B C D E	47 A B C D E	72 A B C D E	97 A B C D E
23 A B C D E	48 A B C D E	73 A B C D E	98 A B C D E
24 A B C D E	49 A B C D E	74 A B C D E	99 A B C D E
25 A B C D E	50 A B C D E	75 A B C D E	100 A B C D E

Quality Assurance Mark

8 BOOK CODE (Copy and grid as on back of test book.)

0–9 | A–Z | 0–9

9 BOOK ID (Copy from back of test book.)

10 BOOK SERIAL NUMBER (Copy from front of test book.)

0–9 (six columns)

Chemistry *Fill in circle CE only if II is correct explanation of I.

	I	II	CE*		I	II	CE*
101	T F	T F	○	109	T F	T F	○
102	T F	T F	○	110	T F	T F	○
103	T F	T F	○	111	T F	T F	○
104	T F	T F	○	112	T F	T F	○
105	T F	T F	○	113	T F	T F	○
106	T F	T F	○	114	T F	T F	○
107	T F	T F	○	115	T F	T F	○
108	T F	T F	○				

FOR OFFICIAL USE ONLY				
R/C	W/S1	FS/S2	CS/S3	WS

COMPLETE MARK ● EXAMPLES OF INCOMPLETE MARKS

You must use a No. 2 pencil. Do not use a mechanical pencil. *It is very important that you fill in the entire circle darkly and completely. If you change your response, erase as completely as possible. Incomplete marks or erasures may affect your score.*

If there are more answer spaces than you need, leave them blank.

Test Code

V ① ② ③ ④ ⑤ ⑥ ⑦ ⑧ ⑨

W ① ② ③ ④ ⑤ ⑥ ⑦ ⑧ ⑨

X ① ② ③ ④ ⑤

Y Ⓐ Ⓑ Ⓒ Ⓓ Ⓔ

Q ① ② ③ ④ ⑤ ⑥ ⑦ ⑧ ⑨

Print Subject Test Name:

If you are taking a Language Test select: ○ Reading Only ○ Reading and Listening

1–100 Ⓐ Ⓑ Ⓒ Ⓓ Ⓔ

8 BOOK CODE (Copy and grid as on back of test book.)

9 BOOK ID (Copy from back of test book.)

10 BOOK SERIAL NUMBER (Copy from front of test book.)

Quality Assurance Mark

Chemistry *Fill in circle CE only if II is correct explanation of I.

	I	II	CE*		I	II	CE*
101	Ⓣ Ⓕ	Ⓣ Ⓕ	○	109	Ⓣ Ⓕ	Ⓣ Ⓕ	○
102	Ⓣ Ⓕ	Ⓣ Ⓕ	○	110	Ⓣ Ⓕ	Ⓣ Ⓕ	○
103	Ⓣ Ⓕ	Ⓣ Ⓕ	○	111	Ⓣ Ⓕ	Ⓣ Ⓕ	○
104	Ⓣ Ⓕ	Ⓣ Ⓕ	○	112	Ⓣ Ⓕ	Ⓣ Ⓕ	○
105	Ⓣ Ⓕ	Ⓣ Ⓕ	○	113	Ⓣ Ⓕ	Ⓣ Ⓕ	○
106	Ⓣ Ⓕ	Ⓣ Ⓕ	○	114	Ⓣ Ⓕ	Ⓣ Ⓕ	○
107	Ⓣ Ⓕ	Ⓣ Ⓕ	○	115	Ⓣ Ⓕ	Ⓣ Ⓕ	○
108	Ⓣ Ⓕ	Ⓣ Ⓕ	○				

FOR OFFICIAL USE ONLY

R/C	W/S1	FS/S2	CS/S3	WS

PLEASE DO NOT WRITE IN THIS AREA

SERIAL #

SAT Subject Tests™

DO NOT USE A MECHANICAL PENCIL

COMPLETE MARK ● EXAMPLES OF INCOMPLETE MARKS

You must use a No. 2 pencil. *It is very important that you fill in the entire circle darkly and completely. If you change your response, erase as completely as possible. Incomplete marks or erasures may affect your score. It is very important that you follow these instructions when filling out your answer sheet.*

1 Your Name: (Print) Last ______ First ______ M.I. ______

I agree to the conditions on the back of the SAT Subject Tests™ booklet. I also agree to use only a No. 2 pencil to complete my answer sheet.

Signature: ______ Date: __/__/__

Home Address: ______ Number and Street ______ City ______ State ______ Zip Code

Home Phone: ( ) ______ Center: (Print) ______ City ______ State/Country

2 YOUR NAME

Last Name (First 6 Letters) | First Name (First 4 Letters) | Mid. Init.

3 DATE OF BIRTH

MONTH | DAY | YEAR

Jan, Feb, Mar, Apr, May, Jun, Jul, Aug, Sep, Oct, Nov, Dec

4 ZIP CODE

5 SEX

Female Male

6 REGISTRATION NUMBER

(Copy from Admission Ticket.)

I turned in my registration form today.

7 SOCIAL SECURITY NUMBER

8 BOOK CODE

(Copy and grid as on back of test book.)

9 BOOK ID

(Copy from back of test book.)

10 BOOK SERIAL NUMBER

(Copy from front of test book.)

11 TEST CENTER

(Supplied by Test Center Supervisor.)

FOR OFFICIAL USE ONLY

172624-001:654321 ISD5959

00272-36392 • NS85E950 • Printed in U.S.A.

732653

PLEASE DO NOT WRITE IN THIS AREA

SERIAL #

COMPLETE MARK ● EXAMPLES OF INCOMPLETE MARKS

You must use a No. 2 pencil. Do not use a mechanical pencil. It is very important that you fill in the entire circle darkly and completely. If you change your response, erase as completely as possible. Incomplete marks or erasures may affect your score.

If there are more answer spaces than you need, leave them blank.

Test Code	
V	1 2 3 4 5 6 7 8 9
W	1 2 3 4 5 6 7 8 9
X	1 2 3 4 5
Y	A B C D E
Q	1 2 3 4 5 6 7 8 9

Print Subject Test Name:

If you are taking a Language Test select: ○ Reading Only ○ Reading and Listening

1–100 Ⓐ Ⓑ Ⓒ Ⓓ Ⓔ

8 BOOK CODE (Copy and grid as on back of test book.)

9 BOOK ID (Copy from back of test book.)

10 BOOK SERIAL NUMBER (Copy from front of test book.)

Quality Assurance Mark

Chemistry *Fill in circle CE only if II is correct explanation of I.

	I	II	CE*		I	II	CE*
101	T F	T F	○	109	T F	T F	○
102	T F	T F	○	110	T F	T F	○
103	T F	T F	○	111	T F	T F	○
104	T F	T F	○	112	T F	T F	○
105	T F	T F	○	113	T F	T F	○
106	T F	T F	○	114	T F	T F	○
107	T F	T F	○	115	T F	T F	○
108	T F	T F	○				

FOR OFFICIAL USE ONLY

R/C	W/S1	FS/S2	CS/S3	WS

CERTIFICATION STATEMENT

Copy the statement below (do not print) and sign your name as you would an official document.

I hereby agree to the conditions set forth online at www.collegeboard.com and/or in the SAT Registration Booklet and certify that I am the person whose name and address appear on this answer sheet.

By signing below, I agree not to share any specific test questions with anyone after I test by any form of communication, including, but not limited to: email, text messages, or use of the Internet.

Signature ____________________ Date ____________________

COMPLETE MARK ● EXAMPLES OF INCOMPLETE MARKS

You must use a No. 2 pencil. Do not use a mechanical pencil. It is very important that you fill in the entire circle darkly and completely. If you change your response, erase as completely as possible. Incomplete marks or erasures may affect your score.

If there are more answer spaces than you need, leave them blank.

	Test Code
V	1 2 3 4 5 6 7 8 9
W	1 2 3 4 5 6 7 8 9
X	1 2 3 4 5
Y	A B C D E
Q	1 2 3 4 5 6 7 8 9

Print Subject Test Name:

If you are taking a Language Test select: ○ Reading Only ○ Reading and Listening

1 Ⓐ Ⓑ Ⓒ Ⓓ Ⓔ	26 Ⓐ Ⓑ Ⓒ Ⓓ Ⓔ	51 Ⓐ Ⓑ Ⓒ Ⓓ Ⓔ	76 Ⓐ Ⓑ Ⓒ Ⓓ Ⓔ
2 Ⓐ Ⓑ Ⓒ Ⓓ Ⓔ	27 Ⓐ Ⓑ Ⓒ Ⓓ Ⓔ	52 Ⓐ Ⓑ Ⓒ Ⓓ Ⓔ	77 Ⓐ Ⓑ Ⓒ Ⓓ Ⓔ
3 Ⓐ Ⓑ Ⓒ Ⓓ Ⓔ	28 Ⓐ Ⓑ Ⓒ Ⓓ Ⓔ	53 Ⓐ Ⓑ Ⓒ Ⓓ Ⓔ	78 Ⓐ Ⓑ Ⓒ Ⓓ Ⓔ
4 Ⓐ Ⓑ Ⓒ Ⓓ Ⓔ	29 Ⓐ Ⓑ Ⓒ Ⓓ Ⓔ	54 Ⓐ Ⓑ Ⓒ Ⓓ Ⓔ	79 Ⓐ Ⓑ Ⓒ Ⓓ Ⓔ
5 Ⓐ Ⓑ Ⓒ Ⓓ Ⓔ	30 Ⓐ Ⓑ Ⓒ Ⓓ Ⓔ	55 Ⓐ Ⓑ Ⓒ Ⓓ Ⓔ	80 Ⓐ Ⓑ Ⓒ Ⓓ Ⓔ
6 Ⓐ Ⓑ Ⓒ Ⓓ Ⓔ	31 Ⓐ Ⓑ Ⓒ Ⓓ Ⓔ	56 Ⓐ Ⓑ Ⓒ Ⓓ Ⓔ	81 Ⓐ Ⓑ Ⓒ Ⓓ Ⓔ
7 Ⓐ Ⓑ Ⓒ Ⓓ Ⓔ	32 Ⓐ Ⓑ Ⓒ Ⓓ Ⓔ	57 Ⓐ Ⓑ Ⓒ Ⓓ Ⓔ	82 Ⓐ Ⓑ Ⓒ Ⓓ Ⓔ
8 Ⓐ Ⓑ Ⓒ Ⓓ Ⓔ	33 Ⓐ Ⓑ Ⓒ Ⓓ Ⓔ	58 Ⓐ Ⓑ Ⓒ Ⓓ Ⓔ	83 Ⓐ Ⓑ Ⓒ Ⓓ Ⓔ
9 Ⓐ Ⓑ Ⓒ Ⓓ Ⓔ	34 Ⓐ Ⓑ Ⓒ Ⓓ Ⓔ	59 Ⓐ Ⓑ Ⓒ Ⓓ Ⓔ	84 Ⓐ Ⓑ Ⓒ Ⓓ Ⓔ
10 Ⓐ Ⓑ Ⓒ Ⓓ Ⓔ	35 Ⓐ Ⓑ Ⓒ Ⓓ Ⓔ	60 Ⓐ Ⓑ Ⓒ Ⓓ Ⓔ	85 Ⓐ Ⓑ Ⓒ Ⓓ Ⓔ
11 Ⓐ Ⓑ Ⓒ Ⓓ Ⓔ	36 Ⓐ Ⓑ Ⓒ Ⓓ Ⓔ	61 Ⓐ Ⓑ Ⓒ Ⓓ Ⓔ	86 Ⓐ Ⓑ Ⓒ Ⓓ Ⓔ
12 Ⓐ Ⓑ Ⓒ Ⓓ Ⓔ	37 Ⓐ Ⓑ Ⓒ Ⓓ Ⓔ	62 Ⓐ Ⓑ Ⓒ Ⓓ Ⓔ	87 Ⓐ Ⓑ Ⓒ Ⓓ Ⓔ
13 Ⓐ Ⓑ Ⓒ Ⓓ Ⓔ	38 Ⓐ Ⓑ Ⓒ Ⓓ Ⓔ	63 Ⓐ Ⓑ Ⓒ Ⓓ Ⓔ	88 Ⓐ Ⓑ Ⓒ Ⓓ Ⓔ
14 Ⓐ Ⓑ Ⓒ Ⓓ Ⓔ	39 Ⓐ Ⓑ Ⓒ Ⓓ Ⓔ	64 Ⓐ Ⓑ Ⓒ Ⓓ Ⓔ	89 Ⓐ Ⓑ Ⓒ Ⓓ Ⓔ
15 Ⓐ Ⓑ Ⓒ Ⓓ Ⓔ	40 Ⓐ Ⓑ Ⓒ Ⓓ Ⓔ	65 Ⓐ Ⓑ Ⓒ Ⓓ Ⓔ	90 Ⓐ Ⓑ Ⓒ Ⓓ Ⓔ
16 Ⓐ Ⓑ Ⓒ Ⓓ Ⓔ	41 Ⓐ Ⓑ Ⓒ Ⓓ Ⓔ	66 Ⓐ Ⓑ Ⓒ Ⓓ Ⓔ	91 Ⓐ Ⓑ Ⓒ Ⓓ Ⓔ
17 Ⓐ Ⓑ Ⓒ Ⓓ Ⓔ	42 Ⓐ Ⓑ Ⓒ Ⓓ Ⓔ	67 Ⓐ Ⓑ Ⓒ Ⓓ Ⓔ	92 Ⓐ Ⓑ Ⓒ Ⓓ Ⓔ
18 Ⓐ Ⓑ Ⓒ Ⓓ Ⓔ	43 Ⓐ Ⓑ Ⓒ Ⓓ Ⓔ	68 Ⓐ Ⓑ Ⓒ Ⓓ Ⓔ	93 Ⓐ Ⓑ Ⓒ Ⓓ Ⓔ
19 Ⓐ Ⓑ Ⓒ Ⓓ Ⓔ	44 Ⓐ Ⓑ Ⓒ Ⓓ Ⓔ	69 Ⓐ Ⓑ Ⓒ Ⓓ Ⓔ	94 Ⓐ Ⓑ Ⓒ Ⓓ Ⓔ
20 Ⓐ Ⓑ Ⓒ Ⓓ Ⓔ	45 Ⓐ Ⓑ Ⓒ Ⓓ Ⓔ	70 Ⓐ Ⓑ Ⓒ Ⓓ Ⓔ	95 Ⓐ Ⓑ Ⓒ Ⓓ Ⓔ
21 Ⓐ Ⓑ Ⓒ Ⓓ Ⓔ	46 Ⓐ Ⓑ Ⓒ Ⓓ Ⓔ	71 Ⓐ Ⓑ Ⓒ Ⓓ Ⓔ	96 Ⓐ Ⓑ Ⓒ Ⓓ Ⓔ
22 Ⓐ Ⓑ Ⓒ Ⓓ Ⓔ	47 Ⓐ Ⓑ Ⓒ Ⓓ Ⓔ	72 Ⓐ Ⓑ Ⓒ Ⓓ Ⓔ	97 Ⓐ Ⓑ Ⓒ Ⓓ Ⓔ
23 Ⓐ Ⓑ Ⓒ Ⓓ Ⓔ	48 Ⓐ Ⓑ Ⓒ Ⓓ Ⓔ	73 Ⓐ Ⓑ Ⓒ Ⓓ Ⓔ	98 Ⓐ Ⓑ Ⓒ Ⓓ Ⓔ
24 Ⓐ Ⓑ Ⓒ Ⓓ Ⓔ	49 Ⓐ Ⓑ Ⓒ Ⓓ Ⓔ	74 Ⓐ Ⓑ Ⓒ Ⓓ Ⓔ	99 Ⓐ Ⓑ Ⓒ Ⓓ Ⓔ
25 Ⓐ Ⓑ Ⓒ Ⓓ Ⓔ	50 Ⓐ Ⓑ Ⓒ Ⓓ Ⓔ	75 Ⓐ Ⓑ Ⓒ Ⓓ Ⓔ	100 Ⓐ Ⓑ Ⓒ Ⓓ Ⓔ

Quality Assurance Mark

8 BOOK CODE (Copy and grid as on back of test book.)

0–9 | A–Z | 0–9

9 BOOK ID (Copy from back of test book.)

10 BOOK SERIAL NUMBER (Copy from front of test book.)

0 1 2 3 4 5 6 7 8 9 (six columns)

Chemistry *Fill in circle CE only if II is correct explanation of I.

	I	II	CE*		I	II	CE*
101	Ⓣ Ⓕ	Ⓣ Ⓕ	○	109	Ⓣ Ⓕ	Ⓣ Ⓕ	○
102	Ⓣ Ⓕ	Ⓣ Ⓕ	○	110	Ⓣ Ⓕ	Ⓣ Ⓕ	○
103	Ⓣ Ⓕ	Ⓣ Ⓕ	○	111	Ⓣ Ⓕ	Ⓣ Ⓕ	○
104	Ⓣ Ⓕ	Ⓣ Ⓕ	○	112	Ⓣ Ⓕ	Ⓣ Ⓕ	○
105	Ⓣ Ⓕ	Ⓣ Ⓕ	○	113	Ⓣ Ⓕ	Ⓣ Ⓕ	○
106	Ⓣ Ⓕ	Ⓣ Ⓕ	○	114	Ⓣ Ⓕ	Ⓣ Ⓕ	○
107	Ⓣ Ⓕ	Ⓣ Ⓕ	○	115	Ⓣ Ⓕ	Ⓣ Ⓕ	○
108	Ⓣ Ⓕ	Ⓣ Ⓕ	○				

FOR OFFICIAL USE ONLY				
R/C	W/S1	FS/S2	CS/S3	WS

COMPLETE MARK ● EXAMPLES OF INCOMPLETE MARKS

You must use a No. 2 pencil. Do not use a mechanical pencil. *It is very important that you fill in the entire circle darkly and completely. If you change your response, erase as completely as possible. Incomplete marks or erasures may affect your score.*

If there are more answer spaces than you need, leave them blank.

Test Code	
V	① ② ③ ④ ⑤ ⑥ ⑦ ⑧ ⑨
W	① ② ③ ④ ⑤ ⑥ ⑦ ⑧ ⑨
X	① ② ③ ④ ⑤
Y	Ⓐ Ⓑ Ⓒ Ⓓ Ⓔ
Q	① ② ③ ④ ⑤ ⑥ ⑦ ⑧ ⑨

Print Subject Test Name:

If you are taking a Language Test select: ○ Reading Only ○ Reading and Listening

1 Ⓐ Ⓑ Ⓒ Ⓓ Ⓔ	26 Ⓐ Ⓑ Ⓒ Ⓓ Ⓔ	51 Ⓐ Ⓑ Ⓒ Ⓓ Ⓔ	76 Ⓐ Ⓑ Ⓒ Ⓓ Ⓔ
2 Ⓐ Ⓑ Ⓒ Ⓓ Ⓔ	27 Ⓐ Ⓑ Ⓒ Ⓓ Ⓔ	52 Ⓐ Ⓑ Ⓒ Ⓓ Ⓔ	77 Ⓐ Ⓑ Ⓒ Ⓓ Ⓔ
3 Ⓐ Ⓑ Ⓒ Ⓓ Ⓔ	28 Ⓐ Ⓑ Ⓒ Ⓓ Ⓔ	53 Ⓐ Ⓑ Ⓒ Ⓓ Ⓔ	78 Ⓐ Ⓑ Ⓒ Ⓓ Ⓔ
4 Ⓐ Ⓑ Ⓒ Ⓓ Ⓔ	29 Ⓐ Ⓑ Ⓒ Ⓓ Ⓔ	54 Ⓐ Ⓑ Ⓒ Ⓓ Ⓔ	79 Ⓐ Ⓑ Ⓒ Ⓓ Ⓔ
5 Ⓐ Ⓑ Ⓒ Ⓓ Ⓔ	30 Ⓐ Ⓑ Ⓒ Ⓓ Ⓔ	55 Ⓐ Ⓑ Ⓒ Ⓓ Ⓔ	80 Ⓐ Ⓑ Ⓒ Ⓓ Ⓔ
6 Ⓐ Ⓑ Ⓒ Ⓓ Ⓔ	31 Ⓐ Ⓑ Ⓒ Ⓓ Ⓔ	56 Ⓐ Ⓑ Ⓒ Ⓓ Ⓔ	81 Ⓐ Ⓑ Ⓒ Ⓓ Ⓔ
7 Ⓐ Ⓑ Ⓒ Ⓓ Ⓔ	32 Ⓐ Ⓑ Ⓒ Ⓓ Ⓔ	57 Ⓐ Ⓑ Ⓒ Ⓓ Ⓔ	82 Ⓐ Ⓑ Ⓒ Ⓓ Ⓔ
8 Ⓐ Ⓑ Ⓒ Ⓓ Ⓔ	33 Ⓐ Ⓑ Ⓒ Ⓓ Ⓔ	58 Ⓐ Ⓑ Ⓒ Ⓓ Ⓔ	83 Ⓐ Ⓑ Ⓒ Ⓓ Ⓔ
9 Ⓐ Ⓑ Ⓒ Ⓓ Ⓔ	34 Ⓐ Ⓑ Ⓒ Ⓓ Ⓔ	59 Ⓐ Ⓑ Ⓒ Ⓓ Ⓔ	84 Ⓐ Ⓑ Ⓒ Ⓓ Ⓔ
10 Ⓐ Ⓑ Ⓒ Ⓓ Ⓔ	35 Ⓐ Ⓑ Ⓒ Ⓓ Ⓔ	60 Ⓐ Ⓑ Ⓒ Ⓓ Ⓔ	85 Ⓐ Ⓑ Ⓒ Ⓓ Ⓔ
11 Ⓐ Ⓑ Ⓒ Ⓓ Ⓔ	36 Ⓐ Ⓑ Ⓒ Ⓓ Ⓔ	61 Ⓐ Ⓑ Ⓒ Ⓓ Ⓔ	86 Ⓐ Ⓑ Ⓒ Ⓓ Ⓔ
12 Ⓐ Ⓑ Ⓒ Ⓓ Ⓔ	37 Ⓐ Ⓑ Ⓒ Ⓓ Ⓔ	62 Ⓐ Ⓑ Ⓒ Ⓓ Ⓔ	87 Ⓐ Ⓑ Ⓒ Ⓓ Ⓔ
13 Ⓐ Ⓑ Ⓒ Ⓓ Ⓔ	38 Ⓐ Ⓑ Ⓒ Ⓓ Ⓔ	63 Ⓐ Ⓑ Ⓒ Ⓓ Ⓔ	88 Ⓐ Ⓑ Ⓒ Ⓓ Ⓔ
14 Ⓐ Ⓑ Ⓒ Ⓓ Ⓔ	39 Ⓐ Ⓑ Ⓒ Ⓓ Ⓔ	64 Ⓐ Ⓑ Ⓒ Ⓓ Ⓔ	89 Ⓐ Ⓑ Ⓒ Ⓓ Ⓔ
15 Ⓐ Ⓑ Ⓒ Ⓓ Ⓔ	40 Ⓐ Ⓑ Ⓒ Ⓓ Ⓔ	65 Ⓐ Ⓑ Ⓒ Ⓓ Ⓔ	90 Ⓐ Ⓑ Ⓒ Ⓓ Ⓔ
16 Ⓐ Ⓑ Ⓒ Ⓓ Ⓔ	41 Ⓐ Ⓑ Ⓒ Ⓓ Ⓔ	66 Ⓐ Ⓑ Ⓒ Ⓓ Ⓔ	91 Ⓐ Ⓑ Ⓒ Ⓓ Ⓔ
17 Ⓐ Ⓑ Ⓒ Ⓓ Ⓔ	42 Ⓐ Ⓑ Ⓒ Ⓓ Ⓔ	67 Ⓐ Ⓑ Ⓒ Ⓓ Ⓔ	92 Ⓐ Ⓑ Ⓒ Ⓓ Ⓔ
18 Ⓐ Ⓑ Ⓒ Ⓓ Ⓔ	43 Ⓐ Ⓑ Ⓒ Ⓓ Ⓔ	68 Ⓐ Ⓑ Ⓒ Ⓓ Ⓔ	93 Ⓐ Ⓑ Ⓒ Ⓓ Ⓔ
19 Ⓐ Ⓑ Ⓒ Ⓓ Ⓔ	44 Ⓐ Ⓑ Ⓒ Ⓓ Ⓔ	69 Ⓐ Ⓑ Ⓒ Ⓓ Ⓔ	94 Ⓐ Ⓑ Ⓒ Ⓓ Ⓔ
20 Ⓐ Ⓑ Ⓒ Ⓓ Ⓔ	45 Ⓐ Ⓑ Ⓒ Ⓓ Ⓔ	70 Ⓐ Ⓑ Ⓒ Ⓓ Ⓔ	95 Ⓐ Ⓑ Ⓒ Ⓓ Ⓔ
21 Ⓐ Ⓑ Ⓒ Ⓓ Ⓔ	46 Ⓐ Ⓑ Ⓒ Ⓓ Ⓔ	71 Ⓐ Ⓑ Ⓒ Ⓓ Ⓔ	96 Ⓐ Ⓑ Ⓒ Ⓓ Ⓔ
22 Ⓐ Ⓑ Ⓒ Ⓓ Ⓔ	47 Ⓐ Ⓑ Ⓒ Ⓓ Ⓔ	72 Ⓐ Ⓑ Ⓒ Ⓓ Ⓔ	97 Ⓐ Ⓑ Ⓒ Ⓓ Ⓔ
23 Ⓐ Ⓑ Ⓒ Ⓓ Ⓔ	48 Ⓐ Ⓑ Ⓒ Ⓓ Ⓔ	73 Ⓐ Ⓑ Ⓒ Ⓓ Ⓔ	98 Ⓐ Ⓑ Ⓒ Ⓓ Ⓔ
24 Ⓐ Ⓑ Ⓒ Ⓓ Ⓔ	49 Ⓐ Ⓑ Ⓒ Ⓓ Ⓔ	74 Ⓐ Ⓑ Ⓒ Ⓓ Ⓔ	99 Ⓐ Ⓑ Ⓒ Ⓓ Ⓔ
25 Ⓐ Ⓑ Ⓒ Ⓓ Ⓔ	50 Ⓐ Ⓑ Ⓒ Ⓓ Ⓔ	75 Ⓐ Ⓑ Ⓒ Ⓓ Ⓔ	100 Ⓐ Ⓑ Ⓒ Ⓓ Ⓔ

Chemistry *Fill in circle CE only if II is correct explanation of I.

	I	II	CE*		I	II	CE*
101	Ⓣ Ⓕ	Ⓣ Ⓕ	○	109	Ⓣ Ⓕ	Ⓣ Ⓕ	○
102	Ⓣ Ⓕ	Ⓣ Ⓕ	○	110	Ⓣ Ⓕ	Ⓣ Ⓕ	○
103	Ⓣ Ⓕ	Ⓣ Ⓕ	○	111	Ⓣ Ⓕ	Ⓣ Ⓕ	○
104	Ⓣ Ⓕ	Ⓣ Ⓕ	○	112	Ⓣ Ⓕ	Ⓣ Ⓕ	○
105	Ⓣ Ⓕ	Ⓣ Ⓕ	○	113	Ⓣ Ⓕ	Ⓣ Ⓕ	○
106	Ⓣ Ⓕ	Ⓣ Ⓕ	○	114	Ⓣ Ⓕ	Ⓣ Ⓕ	○
107	Ⓣ Ⓕ	Ⓣ Ⓕ	○	115	Ⓣ Ⓕ	Ⓣ Ⓕ	○
108	Ⓣ Ⓕ	Ⓣ Ⓕ	○				

8 BOOK CODE (Copy and grid as on back of test book.)

0	A	0
1	B	1
2	C	2
3	D	3
4	E	4
5	F	5
6	G	6
7	H	7
8	I	8
9	J	9
	K	
	L	
	M	
	N	
	O	
	P	
	Q	
	R	
	S	
	T	
	U	
	V	
	W	
	X	
	Y	
	Z	

9 BOOK ID (Copy from back of test book.)

10 BOOK SERIAL NUMBER (Copy from front of test book.)

0	0	0	0	0	0
1	1	1	1	1	1
2	2	2	2	2	2
3	3	3	3	3	3
4	4	4	4	4	4
5	5	5	5	5	5
6	6	6	6	6	6
7	7	7	7	7	7
8	8	8	8	8	8
9	9	9	9	9	9

Quality Assurance Mark

FOR OFFICIAL USE ONLY

R/C	W/S1	FS/S2	CS/S3	WS

PLEASE DO NOT WRITE IN THIS AREA

SERIAL #

Also Available from the College Board

The College Board College Handbook 2007

Get instant access to crucial information on every accredited college in the United States. Completely updated and verified for 2007, this handbook contains detailed descriptions of 3,800 colleges, universities, and technical schools.

2,100 pages, paperbound
ISBN 0-87447-764-6
$28.95

The College Board Book of Majors, 2nd Edition

What's the major for you? Where can you study it? In this book, 180 college professors describe the majors they teach: what you'll study, careers the major can lead to, and how to prepare for the major in high school. Includes listings showing which colleges offer each of 900 majors, and at what degree level.

1,250 pages, paperbound
ISBN 0-87447-765-4
$24.95

The College Board Guide to Getting Financial Aid 2007

This step-by-step guide tells you how to get aid, when to apply, and what kinds of aid to expect from colleges. Includes a planning calendar, tips from college financial aid officers, and indexes showing which colleges offer merit scholarships for your interests.

1,000 pages, paperbound
ISBN 0-87447-766-2
$19.95

The College Board Scholarship Handbook 2007

This no-nonsense guide speeds you straight to scholarships targeted to who you are, where you live, and what you want to study. Includes detailed profiles of more than 2,100 scholarship, internship, and loan programs.

600 pages, paperbound
ISBN 0-87447-767-0
$27.95

The College Application Essay, Revised Edition

by Sarah Myers McGinty

Trying to find a topic for your application essay? Former admissions dean Sarah Myers McGinty shares strategies that will help you stand out from the crowd. Includes critiqued sample essays written by real students, jump starts for writer's block, and a chapter for your parents that explains their role in the process.

160 pages, paperbound
ISBN 0-87447-711-5
$15.95

Campus Visits & College Interviews, 2nd Edition

by Zola Dincin Schneider

Visiting campuses and talking to admissions deans is a great way to learn more about which colleges are right for you. Experienced school counselor Zola Dincin Schneider shows you how to make the most of your visits and make a good impression during interviews. Includes interview tips for the shy.

140 pages, paperbound
ISBN 0-87447-675-5
$12.95

Available wherever books are sold.
Distributed by Holtzbrinck Publishers, Inc.

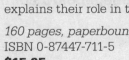